The Age of Elizabeth

Social and Economic History of England

Edited by Asa Briggs

* Already published

Social and economic history of England

The Age of Elizabeth: England under the later Tudors 1547–1603

D. M. Palliser
Senior Lecturer in Economic and Social History,
University of Birmingham

Longman
London and New York

Longman Group Limited
Longman House, Burnt Mill, Harlow
Essex CM20 2JE, England
Associated companies throughout the world

*Published in the United States of America
by Longman Inc., New York*

First published 1983

British Library Cataloguing in Publication Data

Palliser, D. M.
   The age of Elizabeth: England under the later
   Tudors 1547–1603. – (Social and economic history
   of England)
   1. Great Britain – History – Tudors, 1485–1603
   I. Title   II. Series
   942.05'5   DA355

   ISBN 0-582-48580-0
   ISBN 0-582-48579-7 Pbk

Library of Congress Cataloging in Publication Data

Palliser, D. M. (David Michael), 1939–
   The Age of Elizabeth.

   (Social and economic history of England)
   Bibliography: p.
   Includes index.
   1. Great Britain – Economic conditions – 16th
century. 2. Great Britain – Social conditions – 16th
century. I. Title. II. Series.
HC254.4.P34   330.942'05   82-117
ISBN 0-582-48580-0 (cased)   AACR2
ISBN 0-582-48579-7 (pbk.)

Set in 10/12 Linotron 202 Times New Roman.
Printed in Singapore by
Kyodo Shing Loong Printing Industries Pte Ltd.

For Mary

Indeed he [Sir Thomas Pope] lived in an age which one may call the harvest of wealth, wherein any that would work might get good wages, at the dissolution of abbeys.

(Thomas Fuller, *The Worthies of England* (ed. J. Freeman), Allen & Unwin, 1952, p. 362)

Contents

List of figures

List of tables

Introductory note

This is the latest volume in an established series which sets out to relate economic history to social history. Interest in economic history has grown enormously in recent years. In part, the interest is a by-product of twentieth-century preoccupation with economic issues and problems. In part, it is a facet of the revolution in the study of history. The scope of the subject has been immensely enlarged, and with the enlargement has come increasing specialization. There has also been a change in the approach to it as a result of the collection of a wider range of data and the development of new quantitative techniques. New research is being completed each year both in history and economics departments, and there are now enough varieties of approach to make for frequent controversy, enough excitement in the controversy to stimulate new writing. Interest in social history has boomed even more than interest in economic history since the first volume in this series was published, and debates continue both about its scope and its methods. It remains the purpose of this series, however, to bracket together the two adjectives economic and social. There is no need for two different sets of historians to carry out their work in separate workshops. Most of the problems with which they are concerned demand cooperative effort. However refined the analysis of the problems may be or may become, however precise the statistics, something more than accuracy and discipline is needed in the study of social and economic history. Many of the most lively economic historians of this century have been singularly undisciplined, and their hunches and insights have often proved invaluable. Behind the abstractions of economist or sociologist is the experience of real people, who demand sympathetic understanding as well as searching analysis. One of the dangers of economic history is that it can be written far too easily in impersonal terms: real people seem to play little part in it. One of the dangers of social history is that it concentrates on categories rather than on flesh and blood human beings. This series is designed to avoid both dangers, at least as·far as they can be avoided in the light of available evidence. Quantitative evidence is used where it is available, but it is not the only kind of evidence which is taken into the reckoning.

Within this framework each author has complete freedom to describe the period covered by his volume along lines of his own choice. No attempt has been made to secure general uniformity of style or treatment. The volumes will necessarily overlap. Social and economic history seldom moves within generally accepted periods, and each author has had the freedom to decide where the limits of his chosen period are set. It has been for him to decide of what the 'unity' of his period consists.

It has also been his task to decide how far it is necessary in his volume to take into account the experience of other countries as well as England in order to understand English economic and social history. The term 'England' itself has been employed generally in relation to the series as a whole, not because Scotland, Wales or Ireland are thought to be less important or less interesting than England, but because their historical experience at various times was separate from or diverged from that of England: where problems and endeavours were common or where issues arose when the different societies confronted each other, these problems, endeavours and issues find a place in this series. In certain periods Europe, America, Asia, Africa and Australia must find a place also. One of the last volumes in the series will be called 'Britain and the World Economy'.

The variety of approaches to the different periods will be determined, of course, not only by the values, background or special interests of the authors but by the nature of the surviving sources and the extent to which economic and social factors can be separated out from other factors in the past. For many of the periods described in this series it is extremely difficult to disentangle law or religion from economic and social structure and change. Facts about 'economic and social aspects' of life must be supplemented by accounts of how successive generations thought about 'economy and society'. The very terms themselves must be dated. Above all, there must be an attempt to relate society to culture, visual and verbal, separating out elements of continuity and discontinuity.

Where the facts are missing or the thoughts impossible to recover, it is the duty of the historian to say so. Many of the crucial problems in English social and economic history remain mysterious or only partially explored. This series must point, therefore, to what is not known as well as what is known, to what is a matter of argument as well as what is agreed upon. At the same time, it is one of the particular excitements of the economic and social historian to be able, as G. M. Trevelyan has written, 'to know more in some respects than the dweller in the past himself knew about the conditions that enveloped and controlled his life'.

ASA BRIGGS

Preface

Many books have been published in the last thirty years on government, politics and ecclesiastical affairs in Tudor England and Wales, but general surveys of social and economic history have been remarkably few. For the economy, Peter Ramsey's excellent, but brief and selective, *Tudor Economic Problems* (1963) stands almost alone, while for a survey of society there is still nothing to supersede A. L. Rowse's brilliant, if inevitably dated, *The England of Elizabeth* (1950), although Penry Williams's *Life in Tudor England* (1964) and A. H. Dodd's *Life in Elizabethan England* (1961) have much valuable information. Articles and specialised monographs abound, but the student has no ready guide to them. It is hoped that this volume will, to some extent, meet that need.

Economic and social change tends to be uneven, and – at least before the industrial revolution – very gradual: the conventional periods adopted by political historians are not usually appropriate divisions. The terminal dates of this volume were dictated by the preceding and following volumes in the series, and although they have some long-term significance outside the political sphere (notably the establishment of Protestantism in 1547–48 and the union of the crowns in 1603) they do not make the most appropriate termini. Part of the problem in writing about later sixteenth-century changes is that so many recent debates have hinged on alleged changes between 1540 and 1640 that it is often difficult to separate out those parts of the changes that may have happened between 1547 and 1603.

Social and economic history has changed enormously over the last generation. Scholars have become much more interested in the population as a whole rather than merely the 'political nation' or ruling élite, and they have been using or compiling statistical sources as never before. Such new approaches demand techniques of sampling. It is possible for one man to read almost all the national archives relating to politics, or to overseas commerce, over a short period; it is certainly not possible to read all the relevant local archives – wills, inventories, legal records, borough minutes, manor court rolls and so on – over a similar period. Documentation for early modern England is so rich that the mere assembly and indexing of all relevant documents for 'a moderately small parish' would, it has been suggested, take twenty man-years.[1]

Fortunately the Cambridge Group for the History of Population and Social Structure have had the resources to analyse one crucial source, the parish registers, through a very large sample which is likely to be typical of the whole country; but many scholars have had to confine their detailed researches to a single county or even a single parish, and even then to select their documents rigorously. Much of the best recent work has been written at the local level, but there is a danger that areas with especially rich archives, or which happen to have been much studied, are assumed to have been typical of England as a whole. There are now nearly a dozen books on Tudor and Stuart Essex, which has superb county archives but which, with its exceptionally high turnover of population, active Puritanism, proximity to the capital and high incidence of witchcraft prosecutions, was manifestly not typical in all respects.[2]

Since total objectivity in a historical work is impossible (and probably undesirable), it may avoid misunderstanding if I admit at the outset to being sceptical of any linear or inevitable progress in history, and of all simplistic monocausal theories of change. I am also conscious that for some major problems of sixteenth-century history satisfactory explanations are not now, and perhaps never will be, available. That is partly a matter of the limitations imposed by the sources. It is the earliest period of English history for which statistics became a recognised part of government briefs and economic tracts, and it is tempting to put more weight on those figures than they can properly bear. Wherever I could give an argument more precision by the use of statistics I have done so; but it is unwise to be too quantitative in approach, for the available figures are often partial, ambiguous, or downright unreliable. Too heavy a reliance on those aspects of society and economy which are quantifiable can involve the subtle suggestion that they were more fundamental than those which are not; whereas, as Stone has pointed out, 'there is an extraordinarily complex two-way flow of interactions between facts of population, food supply, climate, bullion supply, prices, on the one hand, and values, ideas and customs on the other'. Furthermore, 'there are more, and often more potent, motors of individual and group behaviour than those which can be demonstrated in a statistical table'.[3]

A survey of this kind is not an appropriate vehicle for extensive footnotes. I have therefore confined the references largely to quotations, manuscript sources, and important statistics, but the extended bibliography indicates most of the principal sources of information as well as providing a guide to further reading. Quotations are given, where possible, in original spelling but with modernised capitals and punctuation: for that reason, some older editions with original spelling (notably Furnivall's Harrison and Lamond's *Discourse*) are cited in preference to the latest, modernised editions. I should add that I accept Miss Dewar's argument that the *Discourse* was written by Smith, and for the sake of simplicity I refer to it as Smith's throughout: the evidence is discussed in Appendix II. Quotations from Shakespeare are drawn from the First Folio of 1623.

Both the units of currency and the geographical counties of Elizabethan England endured until the early 1970s; I have not thought it necessary to change them, but a map of the historic counties is included. Foreign place-names are given in either their current native forms or in their English versions.

Elizabethans, despite celebrating 1 January as New Year's Day, usually dated their years from 25 March. To avoid double dating, or the ugly use of 'O.S.' and 'N.S.', I have corrected dates to New Style, involving an occasional alteration to standard dating. No historian now dates the death of Elizabeth I to 1602, but the 1598 statutes on poor relief, enclosures and vagabonds are still often given as 1597, the second edition of Harrison's *Description* (1587) as 1586, and Wilson's *State of England* (1601) as 1600. Where possible, the earliest version of a text is cited. It is remarkable how often, for example, Harrison's considerably expanded second edition is cited as if it were the first,[4] and Furnivall's practice of carefully distinguishing the alterations is an additional justification for citing his edition. Where a point hinges on the date of a reference in Harrison, I have indicated which edition first included it.

I have incurred many debts to friends, colleagues and students. I owe much to Dr A. L. Rowse for the inspiration of his publications, to Professor W. G. Hoskins for many years of encouragement, example and friendship, and to the late Dr A. B. Appleby, whose untimely death is such a loss to studies of diet, disease and famine. The University of Birmingham kindly granted me two terms of study leave which were of great assistance. Dr R. A. P. Finlay, Dr C. J. Harrison, Dr P. A. Slack and Dr Margaret Spufford allowed me to read and make use of their unpublished theses. Mr P. Laxton, Dr R. B. Outhwaite, Mr J. Schofield, Dr B. Stapleton and Dr D. M. Woodward lent me papers in advance of publication, and

Professor E. A. Wrigley and Dr R. S. Schofield very generously allowed me to consult the proofs of their *Population History of England and Wales 1541–1871*, a generosity of crucial importance since their book was not published until this book was going to press. Dr G. W. Bernard, Dr J. Binns, Dr Peter Clark, Dr C. S. L. Davies, Dr A. D. Dyer, Dr Eric Hopkins, Mr R. W. Hoyle, Dr E. W. Ives, Dr R. M. Smith and Dr Ian Sutherland kindly supplied useful references. I am most grateful to the late Dr Appleby and to Dr C. E. Challis, Professor D. C. Coleman, Mr Richard Cust, Dr C. C. Dyer, Dr F. M. Heal, Dr Schofield, Dr Slack, Dr Joan Thirsk and Dr P. H. Williams, who read drafts of part of the text and helped very materially to improve it. I would also like to thank Miss S. P. Swann and Miss S. E. Kennedy for typing successive drafts and for coping so effectively with my handwriting. Finally, I am deeply indebted to the general editor, Lord Briggs who read the entire text in successive drafts and made many useful comments. Any remaining errors of fact or interpretation are, of course, entirely my own responsibility. I would value any corrections which readers may care to send me, which will be considered for incorporation in any future edition.

Birmingham, December 1981   D. M. P.

Acknowledgements

We are grateful to the following for permission to reproduce copyright material:

George Allen & Unwin Ltd for our Table 4.3; Edward Arnold Ltd and Harvard University Press for our Tables 2.1(b) and 2.2; Associated Book Publishers Ltd for our Fig 2 from Fig 17.18 p 464 by H. H. Lamb in *Climate, Present, Past and Future* Vol 11 (1977); Dr J. Blanchard for our Table 8.3; Cambridge University Press for our Figs 9, 10 and 15, our Tables 5.3 and 5.4 and the short Table on page 104 from p 328 by Heal in *Of Prelates and Princes* (1980); Granada Publishing for our Table 4.1; Harvard University Press for our Table 9.3; Professor W. G. Hoskins for our Fig 13 from Fig 1 pp 29–50 in *Agricultural History Review* xii (1964); London School of Economics and Political Science for our Fig 6 from Fig 1 by E. H. Phelps Brown & S. V. Hopkins in *Economica* (November 1956); Lutterworth Press Ltd and the author, M. W. Beresford for our Fig 12; Macmillan London & Basingstoke for our Figs 11(a) and 11(b) and our Tables 9.2 and 9.4; Manchester University Press for our Fig 7 and our Tables 5.1 and 9.5; Oxford University Press for our Table 10.1; Past & Present Society and the author, D. Cressy, for our Table 12.2; Princeton University Press for our Table 12.1; Dr John Sheail for our Fig 5 from *Trans. Inst. Brit. Geogr.* No 55 (1972).

Fig. 1 Sixteenth-century England.

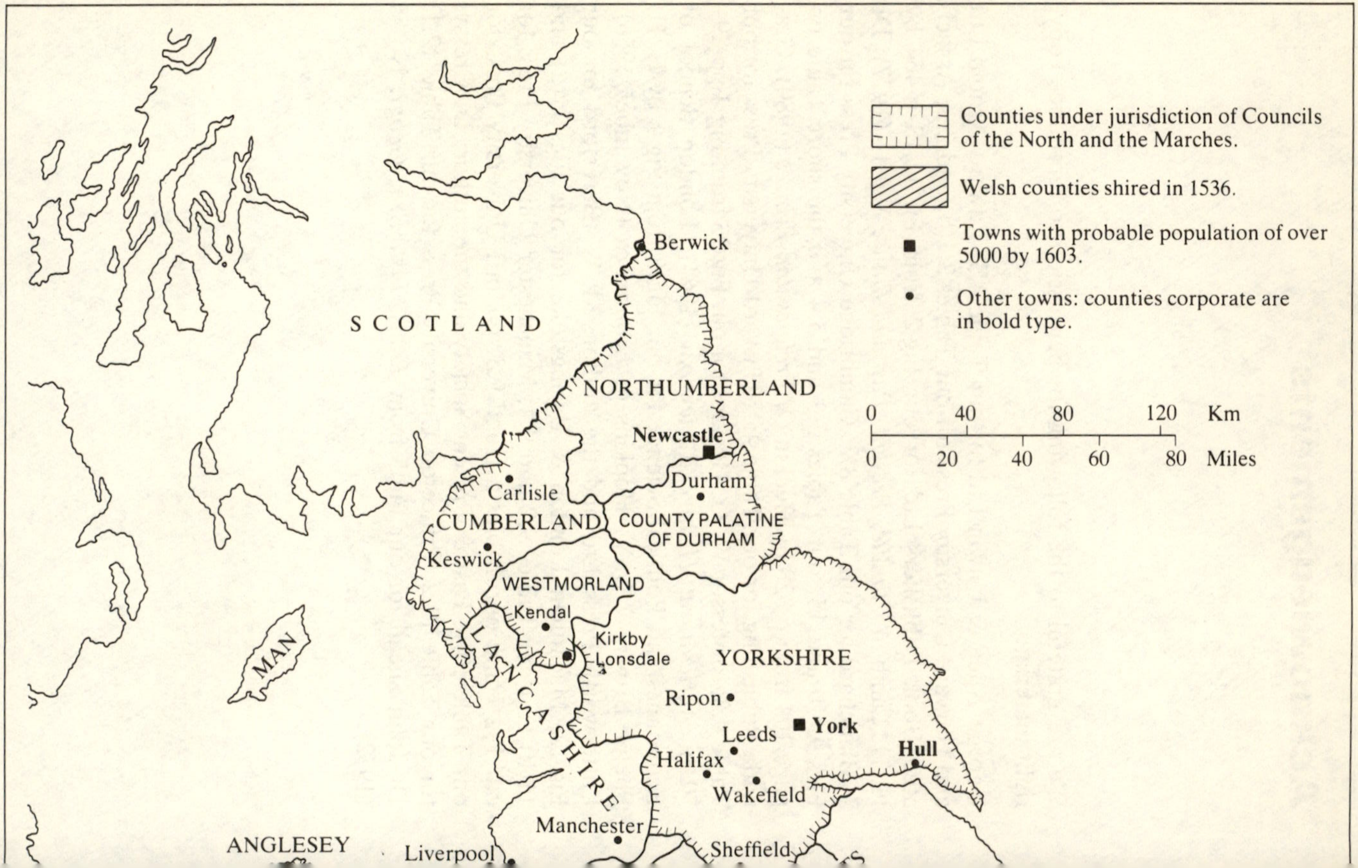

Counties under jurisdiction of Councils of the North and the Marches.
Welsh counties shired in 1536.
Towns with probable population of over 5000 by 1603.
Other towns: counties corporate are in bold type.
0
40
80
120
Km
0
20
40
60
80
Miles
SCOTLAND
Berwick
NORTHUMBERLAND
Newcastle
Durham
COUNTY PALATINE OF DURHAM
Carlisle
CUMBERLAND
Keswick
WESTMORLAND
Kendal
Kirkby Lonsdale
MAN
LANCASHIRE
YORKSHIRE
Ripon
York
Leeds
Hull
Halifax
Wakefield
Manchester
Sheffield
ANGLESEY
Liverpool

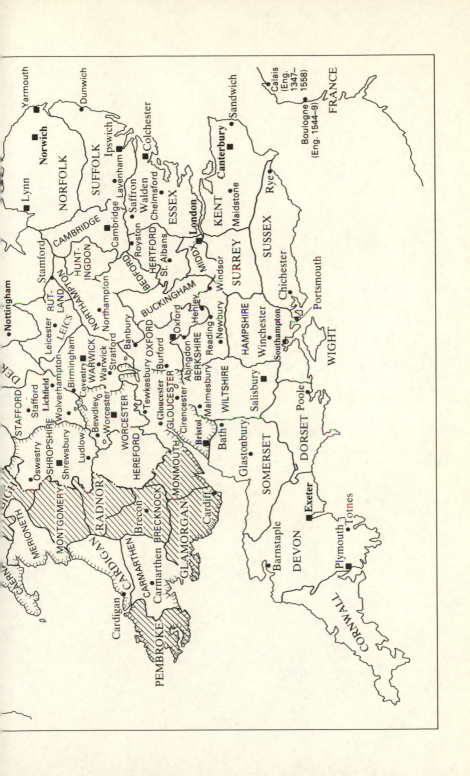

'The greatest Isle'

. . . the Commonwealth of England, a corner of the world,
O Lord, which thou hast singled out for the magnifieng
of thy majestie . . .

    prayer by 'A. F.', *c.* 1587[1]

. . . O Goddesse heavenly bright,
Mirrour of grace and Majestie divine,
Great Lady of the greatest Isle, whose light
Like Phoebus' lampe throughout the world doth shine . . .

    Edmund Spenser, *The Faerie Queene*, bk I (1590)

1

England in 1547 was a second-rank European power with considerable potential economic resources but thinly populated, beset by social and economic problems, at odds over religion, and increasingly isolated from its traditional allies and trading partners. The religious revolutions since 1534 had sharply divided opinion at home, and had provoked the hostility of Francis I of France and the Emperor Charles V, the most powerful monarchs in western Europe. Only bitter mutual rivalry had prevented them from combining to invade England, as had seemed likely in 1538–39. In the event England remained at peace with the emperor, and free to continue the vital export of English cloth to his Burgundian (Netherlands) provinces. But she inherited from Henry VIII a futile war with France and Scotland which almost bankrupted the Crown and nearly provoked a French invasion (troops actually landed on the Isle of Wight in 1545). It was largely to meet the cost of the war that the Crown embarked on a disastrous debasement of the coinage between 1544 and 1551, and which in turn led, after a short-lived boom, to a temporary collapse of England's vital cloth exports. Politics, society and the economy were closely interrelated, as they have always been; and a brief account of political institutions and change may make the economic and social changes more comprehensible. First, however, a broad view will be taken of the land over which the third Tudor generation ruled between 1547 and 1603.

With unlimited space an account of Tudor England might begin, like Braudel's masterpiece on the contemporary Mediterranean world, with a lengthy excursus on 'man in his relationship to the environment, a history in which all change is slow', before shortening the perspective to long-term trends and then to short-term events. For the danger to an English reader of studying Tudor history is that so much is familiar in its geography, settlements and administrative divisions that the cumulative differences produced over four centuries are neglected. (This would be far from true to a French, Italian or German reader considering the sixteenth-century history of his own land.) Naturally, the physical matrix of mountains, plains and coasts which dictated the pattern of settlements, communications and agriculture was broadly what it is today, but their constraints operated differently. Water transport was much more important relative to overland transport then than now, so that ports and river crossings were crucial to the economy. In particular England's indented coastline, which is longer in proportion to its area than that of any other European country except Norway, served in effect as a vital boundary river. No place lay more than 50 miles from the coast or navigable water, and most large and prosperous towns were seaports or river ports.

Despite the efforts of many generations, there were still large areas of waste land, marsh and fen awaiting cultivation or reclamation after abandonment during the late medieval population decline. The yet more uncultivated landscape of earlier times was still a lively memory. Shakespeare's speech put into the mouth of the dying Henry IV reflected real awareness of the thin crust of agrarian civilisation:

O my poore kingdome (sicke, with civill blowes) . . .
What wilt thou do, when ryot is thy care?
O, thou wilt be a wildernesse againe,
Peopled with wolves, thy old inhabitants.

Nor was it only man's relationship with the land that was slowly changing, but the shape of the land itself. The silting up of the Dee estuary was undermining the importance of Chester, which in the following century gave place to Liverpool as the major north-western port. Dunwich in Suffolk still paid more tax to Henry VIII's government than Birmingham, but it was being eroded by the sea, notably by a great incursion in 1570. The opposite process was destroying the prosperity of the Cinque Ports. 'Within the memorie of manie yet lyving', noted Norden about 1600, 'ther have anchored above 400 sayles of the talleste ships of all nations in a place called the Camber, nere Rye, where nowe sheepe and cattle feede.'[2]

Another slow but very significant change may have been a deterioration in the climate. Lamb, Ladurie and others have postulated colder winters and cooler, wetter summers setting in from around the 1540s, in the onset of a 'little ice age' which reached its peak between about 1550 and 1700. There is some supporting evidence in that records of severe weather increase at that time (the Thames, for instance, freezing over in 1537, 1565, 1595 and 1608) and that bad harvests were commoner, and good harvests less frequent, between 1550 and 1620 than in the preceding seventy years. Certainly there were periods of terrible weather throughout western Europe, notably in the mid-1590s (Fig. 2). However, historians of climate are still divided over the chronology and even the concept of a 'little ice age',

Fig. 2   Weather pattern in western Europe, July 1596

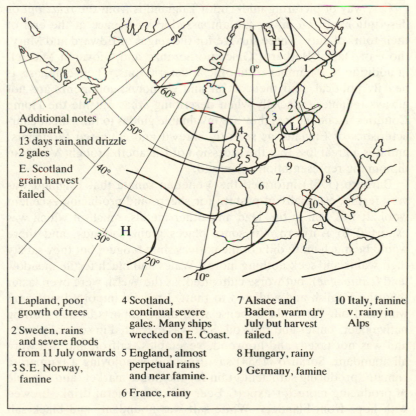

Additional notes
Denmark
13 days rain and drizzle
2 gales

E. Scotland
grain harvest
failed

1 Lapland, poor growth of trees	4 Scotland, continual severe gales. Many ships wrecked on E. Coast.	7 Alsace and Baden, warm dry July but harvest failed.	10 Italy, famine v. rainy in Alps
2 Sweden, rains and severe floods from 11 July onwards	5 England, almost perpetual rains and near famine.	8 Hungary, rainy	
3 S.E. Norway, famine	6 France, rainy	9 Germany, famine	

and the acute contemporary Camden was sceptical, attributing the disappearance of English vineyards rather to the laziness of the cultivators than to climatic deterioration.

England and Wales probably contained about 3 million people in 1547, rising slowly and erratically to 4.3 million in 1603 – a total of the order of modern Denmark or Norway. Yet the land contained some 9,400 separate parishes, and almost as many villages and hamlets as there are today, so that the size of the average settlement was naturally small. The average population of twenty-three Norfolk parishes in 1557 was only 216; and at the end of the period, after considerable population growth, the large Middlesex village of Ealing contained only 404 souls. The largest provincial towns, Norwich, York and Bristol, had between 10,000 and 20,000 inhabitants, and only London, with perhaps 200,000 in 1603, was a large city by European standards. Laslett has fairly characterised Tudor and Stuart England as 'a large rural hinterland attached to a vast metropolis through a network of insignificant local centres'.[3]

One way of picturing mid-Tudor England is from the *relazioni* or descriptions drawn up by the ambassadors of Venice at the end of their tours of duty. Three survive for the reigns of Edward and Mary, those of Daniel Barbaro, Giacomo Soranzo and Giovanni Michiel, in addition to a number of unofficial descriptions. Their emphasis is heavily political, and their social and economic comments are not always reliable, especially when describing areas outside the Home Counties. None the less they are invaluable guides to the salient characteristics of England as seen by shrewd and educated foreigners, and it is a great loss that the accession of Elizabeth brought Venetian diplomatic representation to an end.

Barbaro (1551) informed the Venetian senate that England was very fertile, especially in pasture for sheep, and producing excellent wool. It was rich in tin, lead and other metals, much of which was exported to Antwerp. 'In some places grain abounds, and there would be much more did not the natives shun fatigue; but they satisfy their wants and seek nothing more.' Wales had much fertile meadow land (*campagne*), but worse cultivated, as the Welsh were even lazier than the English and addicted to theft. England imported sufficient wine and oil, but could dispense with these imports by substituting native beer, butter and rape oil. Salt was extracted in several places, and was not taxed; and firewood, vegetables, saffron and fish were all abundant. Soranzo (1554) saw England as enjoying a temperate climate, producing sufficient grain for the home market, and capable of producing more for export. Beer was the general drink, brewed with hops from Flanders. White salt was abundant, and black salt was imported from Normandy. A little olive oil was imported, but generally English butter was used for food and imported rape oil for cloth-working. A huge number of sheep provided the wool to manufacture 300,000 pieces of cloth annually, as well as 2,000 tons of unwrought wool for export. There were lead and tin mines in Cornwall, iron mines in Derbyshire, and coal mines 'in the north towards Scotland'. Michiel (1557) likewise stressed England's fertility and temperate climate, its diverse exports and imports and its many harbours. In consequence, 'England is frequented by all the nations of Europe, from Poland onward, and lately even by Muscovy and Russia, . . . by Brazil, and by the Guinea coast; so it is considered commodious, delightful and wealthy above all other islands in the world'. He ended, however, on a more sombre note, reporting 'the great scarcity which has prevailed in England during the last three years'.[4]

England was gradually moving from local and regional economies towards an integrated national economy, a transition which had been in progress for centuries and which was not completed until the nineteenth century. It is important not to fall into the opposite errors of exaggerating the isolation and self-sufficiency of Tudor communities or of anticipating their fusion into a national market. Macfarlane has argued vigorously that England was as capitalist in 1250 as in 1550 or 1750, with individual ownership of property, profit motive, a market economy, and geographical and social mobility permanent features from the thirteenth century onwards. Nevertheless, the degree to which farmers and craftsmen produced for profit, and the areas over which they traded, were greater under Elizabeth than they had been under Henry VIII, and were to be greater still under the Stuarts.

It would be generally true to say that England was more unified and homogeneous in 1603 than in 1547; that the period under review saw considerable economic, social and political integration. Again, however, it would be wrong to exaggerate the trend or to forget the still-powerful localism and diversity of England in a quest for the supposedly progressive unifying forces. 'The consciousness and power of the [local] community is perhaps the most difficult aspect of early modern England for the twentieth-century historian to grasp'.[5] For example, farming regions and markets were becoming increasingly specialised, producing and dealing in those goods to which they were best suited, selling much of their surplus for cash or credit, and buying other products in exchange. The rapid growth of the capital accelerated this process, as Londoners traded their goods and services further afield in exchange for the foodstuffs they needed. Yet this commercial activity, though it had beneficial effects throughout the economy, was patchy in its incidence, affecting the South and East more than the North, the West, or the landlocked Midlands, and the large farmers more than the smallholders. Furthermore, London was the only really large city, and the only one growing rapidly.

The effect of increasing trade and commercial farming was reflected in a richer diet for the well-to-do. They enjoyed plentiful meat, fish, dairy produce, wheaten bread, beer and wine. It may have been a diet too rich in animal fats, but by the end of the century fruits and vegetables were also abundant. The German copper miners at Keswick could in 1569 afford to import artichokes and oranges from London by way of Newcastle. By 1587, noted Harrison, parsnips, carrots, cabbages, turnips 'and all kinds of salad herbes' had become staple fare not only among the 'poore commons' but even 'at the tables of delicate merchants, gentlemen and the nobilitie'. But what was extra variety to the rich was a necessity to the poor, whose diet may well have worsened in Elizabeth's reign. Harrison had earlier observed (1577) that the poor relied on 'white meats' (dairy produce) instead of flesh, and on bread of barley or rye instead of wheat, while the price of grain had lately risen so much 'that the artificer and poore laboring man is not able to reach unto it, but is driven to content himselfe with horssecorne, I meane, beanes, peason, otes, tares and lintels'.[6] And when the harvest failed, as it did in 1555 and 1556, it produced the mass starvation recorded by the Venetian ambassador.

What was true of the economy was true also of society. Although geographical mobility was widespread, many middling and humbler folk remained in their native parish or moved only within a range of 5 or 10 miles, and their world was geographically very limited. Men of Littlebourne in Kent were in 1554 using the term 'countrymen' only for fellow-villagers. Gentlemen had a less parochial outlook, but even the greater among them tended to be primarily concerned with one county, or 'country' as they significantly called it. Hence differences of custom and speech were wide between well-born as well as humble. Among Elizabeth's courtiers, Hatton habitually wrote – and probably said – 'axe' for 'ask'; Leicester wrote 'hit' for 'it'; and Raleigh, Aubrey was told, 'spake broad Devonshire to his dyeing day', notwithstanding 'his conversation with the learnedst and politest persons'. William Thomas observed that although there was between different regions of Italy 'great diversitee of speeche, as with us betwene a Londoner and a Yorkeshyreman', Italian gentlemen all spoke the 'courtisane' tongue and had no regional accents – an implied contrast with England.[7]

However, travel and education were slowly reducing local differences. The gentry were coming to speak a standardised English by the end of the century – Aubrey's anecdote about Raleigh has a defensive ring – and the gaps between the dialects of commoners seem to have been reduced as printing popularised a common norm. The Cornish language, still generally in use in 1549, was by the early seventeenth century, according to Norden, largely confined to the west. Even there, he said, most Cornish were bilingual, 'unless it be some obscure people, that seldome conferr with the better sorte'. Welsh, of course, was more deeply rooted, and many Welshmen spoke no English. As a Welsh Catholic priest put it in belittling the missionary efforts of English priests in the mountains, 'what should English men do there which have not the languadge?'[8] Henry VIII's government attempted in the 1530s and 1540s to solve the problem by persuading or compelling all Welshmen to learn English, but a more humane attitude prevailed under Elizabeth, and Welsh became the official language of the Church if not of the lawcourts.

The role of language in later Tudor England deserves altogether more study from historians. Men's use of language affects their perception of the world as well as vice versa, but there is a deep gulf between Tudor historians and students of Renaissance literature which deters all but the hardiest. It is recognised that everyday speech was a less heightened form of the English of Shakespeare and the Authorised Version, but complicated by the existence of a wide range of accents and dialects. What is less often appreciated is that polite society was multilingual and not, as today, monolingual.

Education was still dominated by the international language of scholarship. Most instruction in grammar schools and universities was in Latin; Henry VIII and Elizabeth I were familiar enough with it to write letters and talk to ambassadors in that medium. Scholars and senior clergy habitually wrote, and probably composed, in it. Influential works of literature and history first published in Latin included Polydore Vergil's *Anglica Historia* (1534), Foxe's *Rerum in Ecclesia Gestarum . . . Narratio* (1559) – the so-called *Book of Martyrs* – and Camden's *Britannia* (1586) and *Annales* (1615). The only near-contemporary narrative of Kett's rebellion to be published at the time was Neville's *De Furoribus Norfolciensium Ketto Duce* (1575). It is true that spoken Latin was in decline, and that some works, like Foxe's, were quickly translated for the benefit of the growing number who were literate only in English; but the number of printed works available solely in Latin was considerable.

The decline of colloquial Latin left diplomacy without a universal language, and most international dealings were conducted in French,

Italian or Spanish. Ottaviano Maggi (1556) thought that a good ambassador should understand these three languages, together with German and even Turkish – but not English. 'Nobody in the sixteenth century except an Englishman was expected to speak English.' Again, educated Englishmen and women were equal to the challenge. Elizabeth, Leicester and Burghley were fluent in Italian and French; Burghley 'never read any books or praiers, but in Lattin, French, or Italian: very seldome in Englishe'.[9] Knowledge of Italian was spread by William Thomas's *Principal Rules of the Italian Grammar* (1550), which Sir Walter Mildmay arranged to have published as 'a necessary book' for the public. Many influential scholars, diplomats and writers spent time in Venice or Padua absorbing Italian culture and literature, including Sir Thomas Hoby, who translated Castiglione's *Courtier*, and Sir Philip Sidney. Above all, Spenser, though he did not visit Italy, was inspired to write his great work, *The Faerie Queene*, in imitation of the Italian romances of Ariosto and Tasso. Gradually the demand for instruction in foreign languages was met professionally, especially by immigrant refugees. The most notable, Claude de Sainliens, settled in London as a schoolmaster about 1565, and anglicised his name to Claudius Hollyband. Under this name he published very successful manuals, in the form of dialogues: *The Frenche Schoolemaister* (1573), *The Italian Schoole-Maister* (1575), and *Campo di Fior: the Flourie Field of Foure Languages* (1583).

Bishop Gibson scarcely exaggerated when he wrote that in the 1530s and 1540s 'the counties of England were then more strangers to the affairs of their neighbours, than the nations of Europe have since been to one another'. He was arguing for a great change between the 1530s and 1540s, when Leland was compiling his *Itinerary*, and 'when travelling was not much in fashion', and Camden's compilation of his *Britannia* in the 1570s and 1580s; and he was certainly right. Increased travel and geographical awareness went hand in hand with the publications of the first English maps, plans and guidebooks, in what Rowse has happily called 'the Elizabethan discovery of England'. Laurence Nowell produced manuscript maps in the 1560s, and Christopher Saxton published a complete set of county maps between 1574 and 1579. By 1603 Saxton's maps were 'usual with all noblemen and gentlemen, and daily perused by them'. Burghley, who patronised both Nowell and Saxton, was well aware of the value of county maps, and kept a framed set hanging in his house. 'What province, countie, cittie or notable place in England could he not describe?', it was said of him. If anyone applied to the Privy Council for licence to travel abroad, Burghley 'would first examine him of England. And, if he found him ignorant, would bid him stay at home, and know his own country first.'[10] Descriptions and local histories went hand in hand with improved cartography. The first county survey, Lambarde's *Perambulation of Kent*, was begun in 1570 and published in 1576, an example followed by Carew for Cornwall, Erdeswicke for Staffordshire, Owen for Pembrokeshire, Smith for Cheshire, and Norden for seven or eight other counties, though not all were published at the time. Camden, encouraged by the Dutch geographer Ortelius, published *Britannia* in 1586, an account of the whole realm, and brought out revised editions in 1587, 1590, 1594 and 1600.

The realm was becoming more integrated politically as well as economically and socially. It was, of course, already by the early Tudor period a relatively centralised state with a long, stable and unified tradition, in marked contrast to France, Spain, Italy and the Empire. English noblemen, for example, 'had fewer privileges and less regional authority than their contemporaries in mainland Europe', though they 'made up for this by exercising greater influence at the centre, upon the court'.[11] The few lingering exceptions to a uniform government from the centre had been mostly swept away by Henry VIII. In 1536 the King's writ was made to run in the palatinate of Durham, and in other liberties and franchises; in 1536 and 1543 Welsh local government was reorganised on the English model; and in 1543 Wales, Monmouthshire and Cheshire were given parliamentary representation. Only County Durham was thereafter unrepresented in parliament.

At the same time, the end of England's possessions on the Continent saved a great drain on her resources. Boulogne, taken and held at great cost by Henry VIII, fell in 1549, and the ancient possession of Calais was lost in 1558, while the temporary occupation of Le Havre (1562–63) was no substitute. Only the Channel Islands remained of England's continental connections. Meanwhile Henry VIII also strengthened the powers of the Council in the North, with its jurisdiction over five northern counties, and the Council in the Marches, which governed Wales and five English border counties. Both councils played an important part for the rest of the century in integrating the more distant parts of the realm with the South and the Midlands. It is true that Elizabeth's reign could be viewed as reversing these centralising trends, for on the one hand the queen delegated more and more responsibility to the county officials – lords-lieutenant, sheriffs and justices of the peace – while on the other, local gentry were more often taking concerted political action at the county level. Yet in neither case was there any threat to the unity of the realm;

political devolution to the nobility and gentry went hand in hand in partnership with the Crown, and not in opposition to it. Indeed, Elizabeth strengthened the judicial powers of the three counties palatine (Chester, Durham and Lancaster) precisely because they no longer represented devolved royal authority to private persons but integral parts of a national system.

One sign of the growing stability and integration of the realm was that the sovereigns could afford to remain in the Thames valley for more of the time. Henry VII and Henry VIII had inherited, built or acquired most of the favourite Tudor palaces – Whitehall, St James's, Windsor, Greenwich, Richmond, Nonsuch, Hampton, Oatlands – but they had still had to travel extensively on occasion to avert or suppress revolts and to show their power. Edward VI travelled widely in 1552, but his sisters were less mobile. Elizabeth, in particular, spent most of her long reign in and around London and Windsor. It is true that she also combined business with pleasure by extensive and almost annual summer 'progresses' through the shires, but she never travelled further north or west than Stafford, Shrewsbury and Bristol. She was able to rely on her lords president in Wales and the North to control those outlying regions – devoted servants like Sir Henry Sidney at Ludlow (1559–86) and Henry, earl of Huntingdon at York (1572–95).

The monarch ruled by hereditary right, though the exact order of succession was not undisputed in the absence of a legitimate son of the sovereign. Henry VIII was followed by his son Edward VI, but as Edward died young and unmarried, the succession passed in turn to his two sisters Mary I and Elizabeth I. The succession of a queen regnant was unprecedented except for the scarcely encouraging case of Matilda in the twelfth century, that of two was completely without precedent; and many politicians doubted the wisdom of allowing it, preferring the contemporary French practice which barred women from the throne. The monarch, after the abolition of papal supremacy in 1534, was head of the Church in England as well as the state. He or she had very extensive powers by royal prerogative, including the decisions to make war and peace, to coin money of any weight, value and quantity, and to appoint to all important offices in Church and state. He or she was assisted by a Council on all important decisions, and increasingly from the 1530s by a small inner ring which became known as the Privy Council; but the Council could only advise the sovereign, who might or might not accept that advice. Indeed, Conrad Russell has suggested that 'Tudor England was for practical purposes a one-party state'.[12]

Yet there was a balance of powers within the national community rather than a royal despotism, and the constraints on the monarch's powers in practice were considerable. Law and custom required government to be carried on in accordance with rules which the personal act of the sovereign was supposed not to transcend. And a king or queen who tried to ignore such feelings ran up against more tangible difficulties. It was difficult to pursue any unpopular policy in the absence of a standing army, and without losing the goodwill of the political nation – the nobles, the gentry, and the leading lawyers, churchmen and merchants.

Henry VIII may possibly have intended to rule despotically without parliaments; this once-discredited accusation has been recently revived, though it remains unproven. Yet whatever his intentions, the effects of his actions were to make it far more difficult for any of his successors to attempt despotic rule. The vast quantities of Church land and plate which he confiscated, and which might have financed authoritarian rule, were mostly sold to pay for extravagant and futile wars. The lands passed into the hands of his wealthier subjects, so strengthening them at the expense of the Crown in an age when land was the chief measure of wealth, prestige and political influence. And Henry's religious revolution was carried out through parliament, a parliament which sat at intervals for the unprecedented duration of seven years (1529–36). The members of that parliament developed a sense of continuity and political importance which was never forgotten.

Admittedly, parliaments were called generally for short periods and only at the will of the sovereign; they sat, for example, for a total of under three years during the forty-four-year reign of Elizabeth. Nevertheless, their influence and powers could not be ignored. The House of Lords included all peers and bishops, and the Commons a rising proportion of the more important gentlemen, lawyers and merchants. Its membership was steadily increased from 341 at the accession of Edward to 462 at the death of Elizabeth, making it the largest representative assembly in Europe, not only proportionately to population but absolutely. It was already accepted constitutional practice that no new sources of royal revenue could be exploited without the assent of the House of Commons. No Tudor parliament voted money to maintain a standing army beyond the needs of wartime, in contrast to France, where the States General had in 1439 granted the Crown the permanent resources to maintain one.

Money, indeed, was at the heart of the differences between the English monarchy and some of its neighbours. The Crown was expected to rely for ordinary revenue on the income from Crown lands, on customs, on the profits of justice and certain feudal incidents, and after the 1530s on first fruits and tenths from Church benefices. These sources barely sufficed in peacetime, and only with stringent economy. War demanded extraordinary revenue in the form of parliamentary taxation, which was not usually intended for the ordinary charges of peacetime government before the seventeenth century. Parliamentary taxation was in any case relatively low, and Bacon had some justification for boasting that 'the Englishman is most master of his own valuation and the least bitten in purse of any nation in Europe'. It also affected only a minority. When the parliamentary subsidy was introduced in 1512–15 it was levied on some 60 per cent of the adult male population, but the level was not maintained; and by the second half of the century, in one Leicestershire village at least, only one household in every dozen paid any direct taxation at all. Furthermore, there was no equivalent to the internal tolls and purchase taxes levied in many other states. Some exports and imports were liable to customs duties, and goods sold in urban markets to tolls, but the great bulk of buying, selling and transporting of goods was free of all imposts.

One final element of strength in the position of England in the mid-sixteenth century, though it would not have seemed so to contemporaries, was that lack of foreign possessions already noted. The Tudor monarchs, with the disastrous exception of Henry VIII, were not tempted to try to emulate the exploits of Edward III and Henry V on the Continent, a wise forbearance in view of the changed continental balance of power. More sensible was the dream of a union with Scotland which attracted politicians from the 1540s onwards and which finally came to pass in 1603; but the brutal policy of Henry VIII and Somerset delayed it by half a century. As it was, the spectacle of a divided Britain added to the dangers of mid-century politics, as Charles V and later Philip II dreamed of using England to encircle France, and France of using her ally Scotland to encircle England. In 1559 the French were said to be hoping 'to make Yorke the bounds of England'.[13] If, however, the English were fortunate to be able to stand apart from continental entanglements, they came gradually to believe that extra-European trade and colonisation was a different matter. Spain and Portugal had, with the pope's blessing, divided the undiscovered parts of the globe between them in 1493–94. This Iberian monopoly could expect respect from the northern European maritime powers only as long as they were both weak at sea and obedient to the pope; English Protestants, like their brothers in France and the Netherlands, were to show it scant respect.

2

Henry VIII (1509–47) was an outstandingly forceful monarch, making himself head of the Church in place of the pope, dissolving the monastic houses, suppressing a major rebellion, executing potential claimants to the throne, and indulging in costly wars which brought little return. His religious revolutions imposed between 1534 and 1540 were achieved at the cost of limited executions but a great deal of informing and threats. H. A. L. Fisher long ago characterised those years as 'a period of terror', and although Elton has defended the king and his ministers against the charge of tyranny, it was certainly not a revolution made with rose-water. His wars with Scotland (from 1542) and France (1543 –46) cost over £2 million, and to cover the costs Henry exacted unprecedented sums in taxes and forced loans. He also sold vast amounts of Crown land, mainly ex-monastic possessions, debased the coinage, and contracted large loans in Antwerp at high interest. The cost of war was high in manpower as well as money: 37,000 men were sent abroad in 1544, almost certainly the largest English army ever sent overseas before the reign of William III. When Henry died on 28 January 1547 he left an unwelcome legacy; as Elton rightly says, 'in order to pursue his futile and ill-conducted wars, the king destroyed the financial independence of the crown and undermined the prosperity of his country'.[14]

That all his matrimonial ventures to secure a male heir had resulted in only one legitimate son, and he a boy of nine, only added to the disaster. His other two surviving children, Mary and Elizabeth, born to different queens, were legally bastards at the time of his death because the marriages of their mothers had been annulled. Those who governed during Edward's minority have been fairly characterised in the previous volume in this series as an 'unprincipled gang of political adventurers and predators', but without mitigating their greed and lack of principle it needs to be remembered that all governments from 1547 to about 1570 struggled with an unhappy legacy. They inherited the economic disasters and religious divisions born of Henry VIII's policies, and they had to deal with the external threat of foreign domination and the internal weaknesses produced by three changes of sovereign, each with policies different from his or her predecessor but all vulnerable for lack of male heirs.

Elizabeth's official biographer characterised England on the death of Henry VIII as a land 'groaning to see its wealth exhausted, its money debased with copper, its abbeys demolished . . . and the land embroiled in a war with Scotland'. That war was, indeed, the worst of the legacy. Edward VI's short reign – he died in 1553 before reaching his majority – saw the Tudor system of government under severe strain as the Privy Council broke up into warring factions. That is not to say that, as is sometimes suggested, 'faction' was necessarily a sign of misgovernment. Tudor politics often polarised around groups of ministers and courtiers with rival aims, and a strong monarch like Henry VIII or Elizabeth I turned them to advantage. Elizabeth was said to have 'ruled much by faction and parties, which she herselfe both made, upheld and weakned, as her owne great judgement advised'.[15] The tragedy of Edward's reign was that faction was unrestrained and turned to greed, shortsightedness and bloodshed.

The Council was uneasily dominated in turn by Edward, duke of Somerset (1547–49) as lord protector, and then by his rival John, duke of Northumberland (1550–53). Somerset adopted a policy of social and economic reforms, but it would be wrong to see the 'good duke' of later tradition as an egalitarian or an enlightened economist. His government, Bush argues, 'acted neither to ensure economic growth nor a regulated economy, but to maintain the security and stability of the realm'. In any case, the continuing war with Scotland, which was one of Somerset's major preoccupations, made economic affairs worse by provoking him to a further debasement of the coinage. In two years' war Somerset spent nearly double what Henry VIII had incurred in five, and the financial position was desperate. His abortive scheme for a tax on sheep and cloth in 1549 was largely intended to raise money for the war, and when it helped to provoke rebellion in Devon the protector told the rebels in some irritation that 'ye do not consyder what infinite charge it is to keepe such warres as hathe ben . . . now contynued almost these eight yeres'.[16]

The only major domestic policies which Somerset carried through were the dissolutions of chantries, colleges and hospitals in 1547–48 and the introduction of a Protestant Church settlement in 1548–49. In 1548 he attempted to attack depopulating enclosures by instituting local inquiries by commission, notably in the Midlands; but strong opposition from landlords, coupled with the pressures of war, prevented him from achieving results, while storing up unpopularity for him among the political nation. In 1549 his troubles came home to roost. A Protestant Prayer book was enacted to be the sole legal form of worship from Whit Sunday, 9 June. Its introduction triggered off a serious rebellion in Devon and Cornwall, a conservative religious protest mixed with agrarian grievances. On 8 July, while the government was preoccupied with the western rising and hoping not to distract its forces from the Scottish border, anti-enclosure riots began in Norfolk which quickly sparked off a second regional revolt. Lesser revolts broke out in July in many other counties with a mixture of religious and economic motives. To make matters worse, the French, who had been aiding the Scots already, declared war on England on 8 August. The government, with the aid of foreign mercenaries, were able to suppress all the provincial revolts by 27 August, but Somerset was held by his colleagues largely to blame for the chaotic situation, and he was overthrown in a *coup d'état* in October.

The remainder of Edward's reign was dominated by Northumberland, who maintained himself in power by the trust of the boy-king and by a series of shifting alliances with different factions on the Council. He was ambitious and unscrupulous but also the best military commander of the day, and in many ways a better domestic minister than Somerset. He made peace with France and Scotland, ended the disastrous debasement of the coinage and initiated a reform of the Crown's finances, though he was hampered in his efforts by the effects of the bad harvests of 1550 and 1551 and by a commercial crisis in 1551–52 which dealt a severe blow to the crucial cloth trade with Antwerp. In 1552 he laid the foundations of a more even-handed trade with northern Europe by rescinding the privileges of the Hanseatic merchants, and he patronised the first English voyages to Morocco, the Gold Coast and Muscovy. At the same time he pressed on with a more radical religious settlement at home, with a second Prayer Book in 1552 which was much more thoroughly Protestant than the first of 1549.

Northumberland's tough and successful rule depended, however, on the king's life, for the next heir in blood was Edward's Catholic half-sister Mary. When Edward was clearly dying in the summer of 1553, Northumberland persuaded him to bequeath the Crown instead to Jane Grey, a granddaughter of Henry VIII's sister Mary, and more important a zealous Protestant and Northumberland's own daughter-in-law. On 6 July Edward died, and Jane was proclaimed queen by the Council in London; but Mary proclaimed herself queen in East Anglia, and within a fortnight had secured recognition throughout the realm and a complete collapse of Northumberland's regime. This dramatic turn of events is often regarded as inevitable with the advantage of hindsight; but Jane, puppet or no, had been lawfully proclaimed by the Council, while her rival was declared disinherited and illegitimate. Mary's easy success should be seen not as that of the sole legitimate claimant over a usurper, but as the only successful Tudor rebellion. It demonstrated the deep and widespread feeling in favour of the nearest heir in blood, regardless of religious divisions or of legal technicalities about legitimacy.

Mary herself, however, believed that she had a divine duty to restore the realm to Catholicism, and saw her easy triumph as a demonstration of support for her religion as well as her title. She rapidly restored Catholic worship; in November 1554 the realm was formally reconciled to the see of Rome; and in the following January parliament repealed all the anti-papal and anti-ecclesiastical laws passed since 1529. The process was delayed because of fears that the holders of Church lands might lose their new possessions; in the event, the queen reluctantly left them undisturbed, and contented herself with refounding a handful of religious houses. There was considerable resistance to her religious settlement, as there had been to the previous Edwardian settlements; opinion was deeply divided in the nation. Both Protestant and nationalist sentiments were further inflamed when she decided to marry the Catholic Prince Philip, heir to Spain and the Netherlands. Plots were fomented by the French ambassador, anxious to prevent an Anglo-Spanish alliance, and one of them resulted in a formidable rising in Kent in January 1554. The rebels were crushed after coming close to capturing London, but Mary was undeterred.

In July 1554 Philip married Mary in Winchester Cathedral; in October 1555 he inherited the Netherlands, and in January 1556 Spain, Spanish Italy and Spanish America, so making him the richest ruler in western Europe. He was also styled king of England while Mary lived, but she could not obtain his coronation or his right of succession to the throne after her. She proved a loyal wife, and in 1557 declared war on France to assist Spain. The war was expensive and generally unsuccessful (Calais was lost to the French in January 1558), although it was more popular with the ruling class than has often been allowed by historians. There was also an economic war with the Hanseatic League from 1557, after Mary had first reinstated and then revoked their privileges in England. Mary was grief-stricken by the loss of Calais, by the neglect of Philip, by their failure to produce an heir, and by the lack of enthusiasm for her religious policies.

Nearly 300 Protestants, mainly humble folk, were burned for heresy between 1555 and 1558, and some 800 others, largely gentlemen, clergy or merchants, fled into exile on the Continent; yet discontent was not stilled. On 17 November 1558 Mary died a disappointed woman, not least because her next heir was her Protestant half-sister Elizabeth, and she foresaw the ruin of all her plans.

It is not surprising that Pollard should have concluded, in a famous dictum, that 'sterility was the conclusive note of Mary's reign'.[17] But not all was negative. Had she lived longer, many more of her plans might have succeeded. As it was, she had much to her credit in the financial field, largely with the aid of William Paulet, first marquess of Winchester, who retained his post as lord treasurer from

1550 to 1572. He was one of a group of efficient officials retained in office throughout all the political and religious revolutions of the mid-Tudor period, and whose careers help to explain the underlying stability and strength of the regime. Financial reforms were carried through in 1554; in 1555 the Muscovy Company, prototype of a new trading organisation, was founded; the navy was rebuilt and the militia reorganised; and in 1558 a new book of rates substantially increased the Crown's revenue from customs. War with France prevented Mary from liquidating the Crown debts, but she continued to be able to borrow money in Antwerp at normal rates (12–13 %) because of her good credit, while the French and Spanish crowns went bankrupt in 1557. In that year Mary was nearly persuaded to revalue the coinage, and although the reform was deferred, Elizabeth's government could never have tackled the problem so swiftly had the ground not been prepared.

Above all, simply by establishing her own claim to the throne and then successfully maintaining it, Mary re-established the legitimacy of the Tudor succession and put Elizabeth in her debt. She bequeathed to her sister a stable throne and manageable finances. Even the impact of the burnings of Protestants may have been exaggerated through Foxe's enormously influential account of the persecutions (1559 and many later editions). Clark has soberly pointed out that 'only one Kentish gentleman expressed regret at the time of the burnings', and that probably more poor were hanged for petty crime every year in the mid-1590s than were burned altogether in the 1550s.[18]

Mary's real tragedy was to be overwhelmed by catastrophe, demographic and agrarian as well as political, and not to live long enough to ride out the short-term difficulties. Heavy rain produced disastrous harvests in 1555 and 1556, leading to severe famine in England (and over most of northern and western Europe). Hard on its heels came the worst epidemic of the century, ravaging most of the country in 1557 and 1558, and possibly killing the queen herself.

Elizabeth, a woman of twenty-five, succeeded peacefully to the throne in 1558. The unpopularity of her sister's rule made a Protestant Church settlement (1559) easier. The harvest of 1558 was good, and the mysterious epidemic died away in 1559; furthermore, the harvests continued generally average to good for the first thirty years of her reign. England was able to join in peace settlements in 1559 with France and Spain, though she was unable to recover Calais; and in 1559–60 a short-lived military intervention in Scotland ended with the Treaty of Edinburgh and a Protestant and Anglophile government in power north of the border. Thereafter England was officially at peace with her ancient enemy for the rest of the queen's long reign, although the tradition of border feuding died hard. Peace with the other old enemy, France, took a little longer. In 1562 Elizabeth intervened on the Protestant side in the first of France's religious civil wars, taking le Havre as security for the return of Calais, but in the following year the town was recovered by the French, and in 1564 the fruitless war was ended by the Treaty of Troyes. England was at peace for the next twenty-one years and Elizabeth wisely used the opportunity to initiate a diplomatic revolution, forging understandings with France and Scotland as Spain came to seem more and more inimical to England's interests.

If, however, 1558 is seen as a dividing line in English history, that is because Elizabeth survived so long, and her political and religious settlements endured. 'The "Elizabethan age", as we think of it, belongs to the second half of the reign, and in 1558 another mid-Tudor ruler was trying to make another mid-Tudor settlement with the aid of the same body of mid-Tudor councillors.' The reports of English councillors and ambassadors in 1559 were full of fears that England was ripe for invasion and conquest, with French troops in Scotland and Calais, and with the realm weak, poor, unfortified, and divided in religion. England could easily become 'a Piedmont' or 'another Milane', a state disputed or divided between French and Spanish. Philip's minister Granvelle shrewdly asked the English ambassador:

What present store either of expert capitens or good menne of warre ye have? what treasure? what other furniture for defence? Is there oon fortresse or hold in all Inglande, that is hable oon daye to endure the breath of a canon?[19]

That the fears in the event proved groundless did not make them unjustified. Elizabeth did secure peace, and a breathing-space to build up England's armed strength (from 1561 Cecil, her chief minister, was consciously encouraging a native armaments industry to make England independent of imports), but she showed no serious intention of marrying, and her nearest heir in blood was the Catholic Queen Mary of Scotland, who was anathema to the English Protestants. There was a note of desperation in the way that councillors and parliaments throughout the 1560s urged her to marry and beget an heir. The precarious situation was underlined in 1562, when the queen nearly died of smallpox, and the Council was rumoured to be split between the rival claims of Catherine Grey and Henry, earl of Huntingdon, two Protestant candidates for the succession. Civil war seemed very near until Elizabeth recovered. Her Council and court, as was usual, was divided into factions, a source of strength for an able ruler, but a threat to stability if any one became too powerful. For the first thirty years of her reign, the chief factions coalesced loosely round Sir William Cecil, her chief minister, and Robert Dudley, earl of Leicester, her favourite courtier.

Economically and socially, 'the opening years of Elizabeth were a period of conservative reconstruction'.[20] Building on the groundwork of her sister and Lord Winchester, Elizabeth was able to increase the customs revenue and, in 1560–61, to revalue the coinage. The parliament of 1563 passed a series of important statutes including a Poor Law, a tillage act, an act for the maintenance of the navy and another prohibiting manufactured imports. Most important of all was the Statute of Artificers which attempted to regulate labour, wage-rates and apprenticeship. An anonymous programme submitted to the previous parliament had foreshadowed most of these acts and argued for others which failed to be enacted, including the enslavement of vagabonds, the restriction of land purchases to the gentry and greater merchants, and confining the legal profession to the nobility and gentry. This conservative, not to say reactionary, programme provides a valuable clue to early Elizabethan thinking. The government aimed not at change but at social and economic stability after a period of flux and uncertainty. The chief aim of Elizabeth and Cecil was to avoid a repetition of the tensions, discontents and upheavals of the 1540s and 1550s by a pragmatic conservatism and an avoidance of the heavy cost of war and of unpopular devices of revenue-raising like debasement. The Statute of Artificers, because it remained partially in force until 1814, tends to be seen as a new departure with long-term consequences. In reality it was probably, like much Tudor legislation, a short-term measure to meet immediate needs. If somewhere between 5 and 20 per cent of the population had died in the recent epidemic, then the attempt to freeze wages and prevent mobility of labour is an understandable short-term reaction, parallel to the 1349–50 legislation following the Great Pestilence. By the 1570s the pretext for it vanished as the population recovered; but the statute was not repealed and was even spasmodically enforced.

In terms of overseas trade and foreign relations, the 1560s were years of consolidation and cautious expansion. The Hanseatic League, which had enjoyed privileged trade with England since 1474, was compelled to accept an agreement in 1560 by which its special position was almost completely abrogated (though the final abolition of their privileges was delayed until 1598). England now enjoyed freer access to the Baltic and its vital supplies of naval materials. Sir

Thomas Gresham, the queen's agent at Antwerp, succeeded in keeping down the level of foreign borrowing despite the heavy cost of rearmament and the Scots war. And Elizabeth, unlike Mary, quietly sanctioned English trade with West Africa in defiance of the Portuguese monopoly. Cecil was reported to have told the Spanish ambassador in 1561 'that the pope had no right to partition the world and to give and take kingdoms to whomever he pleased'.[21] On the other hand, the English government was careful not to antagonise its own Catholic subjects during the 1560s, and in some areas, especially the North, the 1559 settlement was scarcely enforced.

The year 1570 marks as good a point as any at which to divide the later Tudor period, certainly a better point than 1558. The years of political and religious uncertainty inaugurated by Henry VIII's revolution were coming to an end, and a settled policy was being created which endured until the late 1630s. The Elizabethan regime faced and overcame its greatest challenge, starting with the unwelcome arrival in the realm of Mary Queen of Scots (1568). This triggered off an aristocratic plot to bring down Cecil, marry Mary to the duke of Norfolk and declare her heir to the throne, and to enlist Spanish or French support if necessary. Prompt action by Elizabeth and Cecil nipped the plot in the bud, and the only results were a northern rising under the earls of Northumberland and Westmorland, which was harshly suppressed (1569), an abortive Catholic plot in 1571, and the consequent execution of Norfolk for treason (1572). The bull of Pope Pius V declaring Elizabeth deposed and excommunicated (1570) made matters worse, as English Catholics were forced to choose between their pope and their queen, and religious persecution, virtually suspended in the 1560s, begun again in 1571. Mary also, a prisoner rather than a guest in exile, was an inevitable focus for Catholic plots for twenty years.

The events of 1568–71, therefore, marked a watershed: the government was forced into becoming more hostile to papal pretensions and more anxious to support fellow Protestants abroad. Meanwhile in 1568 William Allen founded an English College at Douai to train priests for the reconversion of England, and in 1579 Pope Gregory XIII founded a second English college at Rome. Missionary priests began arriving in England from 1574, and Jesuits from 1580: Catholic survivalism gave way to Catholic revivalism of the Counter Reformation. A series of plots threatened Elizabeth's life: Ridolfi's in 1571, Throckmorton's in 1583 and Babington's in 1586. The government, spurred on by violent Protestant feelings in parliament, was driven to harsh measures. The first Catholic priest was executed in 1577, and by the end of the reign some 200 priests, laymen and women had suffered death. The climate of insecurity is illuminated by a casual remark of Richard Hakluyt in assessing the value of Frobisher's North American discoveries in the late 1570s: the new lands might not only furnish trade but also a sanctuary 'if change of religion or civil warres should happen in this realme'.[22]

The government had to face opposition to its ecclesiastical policy not only from Catholics but from zealous Protestants. By the late 1560s there existed a loose coalition of pressure groups aiming to transform the Church into a more thorough-going Protestant institution than the 1559 settlement had envisaged. Its adherents, the so-called Puritans, were a minority of the population, but a well-educated, influential and vocal minority. They were especially strong among the gentry (including many MPs), university graduates, the yeomanry, and the richer urban merchants and craftsmen – those whom Slingsby Bethel was later to categorise as 'the industrious sort of people'. In the 1560s and 1570s they made use of 'prophesyings', meeting of local clergy and laymen, to improve preaching standards and to subvert the 1559 settlement from within, until in 1577 the queen suppressed the prophesyings and suspended Archbishop Grindal for refusing to co-operate with her. In the 1570s and 1580s the Puritans also campaigned vigorously in successive parliaments for fundamental ecclesiastical changes, and in the 1580s some of them established a 'classical' system to presbyterianise the Church from within. However, Archbishop Whitgift (1583–1604), with Elizabeth's wholehearted support, vigorously imposed conformity, and by 1590 the threat to the established Church was, for the time being, defeated.

But despite this growth of religious division, the realm was more peaceful and prosperous between 1570 and 1585 than it had been for half a century; only Ireland, with endemic disorder in the 1560s and 1570s, formed an exception. It was simply a fortunate accident for the Crown that population was rising again and making up the losses of the 1550s, so that the fears of 1559–63 were seen to have been groundless. But the queen and Council can take some credit for other changes. Netherlands refugees flocked to England in large numbers from the mid-1560s, many of them skilled craftsmen who boosted new industries; and the Council protected them from the inevitable xenophobia. A native armaments industry was fostered to make England independent of imported supplies, and other new industries were encouraged with the help of immigrant skills, such as paper-making and glass-making. Statutes of 1572 and 1576 made the treatment of the poor more effective and more humane, while in 1573 the militia system was reorganised to make the defence of the realm more effective. Much of the credit for domestic policy belongs to William Cecil (created Lord Burghley in 1571), who provided powerful continuity as the queen's chief minister for the first forty years of her reign, first as principal secretary (1558–72) and then, in succession to Winchester, as lord treasurer (1572–98).

Burghley had, of course, the advantage of peace, which he was anxious to maintain. One of his favourite sayings was that 'a realm gaineth more by one year's peace then ten years' warr', and a proclamation he drafted in 1580 boasted of the twenty years' peaceful reign, unequalled 'for these thousand years'. It was a rhetorical flourish but perhaps none the less true; certainly the period between 1559 and 1585 was the longest period of official peace England had enjoyed since the reign of Henry III. But Burghley had a poor grasp of foreign affairs, and some of his colleagues were well aware that the continuing peace owed less to England's strength than to the distractions of her potential enemies, the French with their religious civil wars and the Spaniards with threats from the Turks and revolt in the Netherlands. Thomas Wilson shrewdly noted in 1577 that

yf wee thynke that by our own political wisdome in Englande we have hetherto had quietnes, wee deceave ourselfes greatelie: it is the weakenes of our neighboures who, being hetherto trowbled, cowld never have power to deale agaynst us, although they never wanted wil and cowrage.[23]

The international situation was darkening, and it proved more and more difficult for England to remain neutral. In 1563–64 trade between England and the Netherlands was interrupted and from 1565 Philip's repressive regime in those provinces provoked resistance, and the flight of many refugees to England. Growing invasions of the Spanish Americas by English ships culminated in a violent response by the Spaniards against Hawkins and Drake at San Juan de Ulua in September 1568, while in December of the same year Elizabeth confiscated Spanish bullion intended for the army in the Netherlands. This led to a trade war between England and Spain in 1569 and another interruption to Anglo-Netherlandish trade. In 1572 English Protestants were put on their guard by an open revolt against Spain in the Netherlands for religious and political liberty, followed a few months later by the St Bartholomew's Day Massacre, one of the bloodiest incidents in the continuing religious civil wars in France. In 1574 Spain and England, neither willing to risk war, patched up their trading disputes in the Treaty of Bristol, but real friendship was not restored.

Increasingly a war party in the Privy Council regarded conflict with the Catholic powers as inevitable, and looked to the Protestants of

Scotland, France, Germany and the Netherlands as allies; while Elizabeth and Burghley tried hard to maintain peace and to foster the old-established special trading relationship with the Netherlands. In an early version of the balance of power theory, they had no wish to see either France or Spain grow too strong at the expense of the other, 'and so prove a more daingerous neighbeure to us of England'. Elizabeth, striving for a compromise settlement between Philip and the Dutch rebels, pointed out that England had, next to Spain, the greatest interest in those provinces 'with which our progenitors here had so auncient and straight alliances, and so longe have lived in peace with them and they with our progenitors and our nation, as hathe not been the like in Christendom between twoe contries joyned so together'.[24] Nevertheless, queen and Council were aware that – as Philip had said when king of England – 'the kingdom of England is and must always remain strong at sea'. In 1578 Elizabeth appointed Sir John Hawkins treasurer of the royal navy, and he did wonders in building up an effective fighting force at a modest cost.

While peace lasted, the government continued to encourage trading into new areas to diversify and to reduce England's dangerous dependence on one main overseas cloth market. The temporary interruptions of the Merchant Adventurers' trade with Antwerp after 1563, permanently after 1585, led to the opening up of alternative outlets in the northern Netherlands and Germany. Trade with Russia, admittedly on a small scale, increased after the foundation of the Muscovy Company (1555), while the much more important Baltic trade was regulated by the creation of an Eastland Company (1579). Trade with Spain continued until war came, and was organised under a Spanish Company (1577), while growing trade with the Levant, Morocco and West Africa was marked by the creation of a Turkey Company (1581), a Barbary Company (1585) and a Guinea Company (1588). Trade and piracy in the New World throve despite Spanish hostility, and Francis Drake obtained his revenge for San Juan de Ulua by a successful and lucrative plundering raid in Spanish America that turned almost accidentally into a voyage round the world, the first circumnavigation of the globe by English ships (1577–80). There were projects to establish English colonies in those parts of North America not settled by Spain, and in 1585–87 abortive attempts were made to found colonies in what was called, in honour of Elizabeth, Virginia. Meanwhile, other Englishmen, notably John Davis, made strenuous but abortive efforts to discover a 'North-West Passage' by which to outflank Spain and to enter the Pacific via the Arctic.

Between 1574 and 1585, when England and Spain were drifting

Fig. 3   Europe in 1580

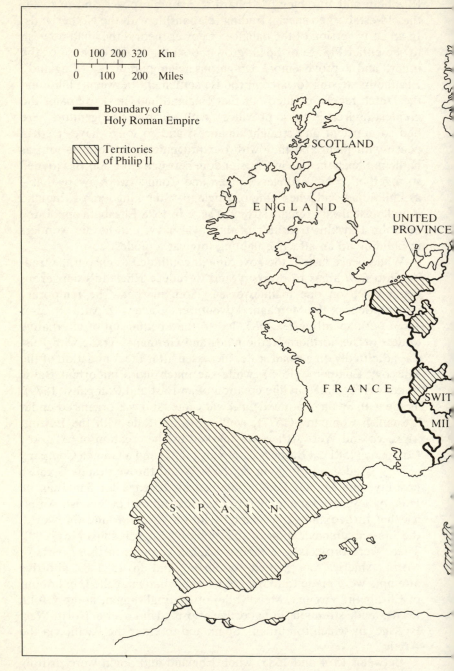

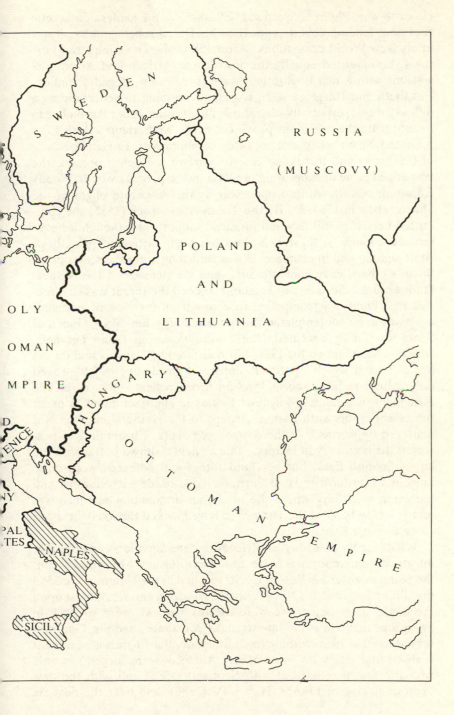

closer to war, Philip of Spain saw Elizabeth as the leader of a heretic coalition, lending covert support to his Dutch rebels and to pirates in his New World possessions. After 1580, when he conquered Portugal, he inherited equally the Portuguese African and Asian possessions with which Englishmen were (in his view illegally) trading. Elizabeth and Burghley were reluctantly coming to see Philip as a military threat, especially when his brilliant commander Parma began to subjugate the rebellious provinces in the Netherlands. Both sides hesitated, Spain because of her other commitments, England because of the heavy and increasing cost of warfare, and each because the two-edged game of supporting rebels could be played by both. Finally Elizabeth was drawn into open war by the desperate plight of the Dutch rebels in 1584–85. By the Treaty of Nonsuch (1585) she committed herself to military and financial support, and though it never seemed enough to the rebels, and has been castigated recently as short-sighted and inadequate, it was sufficient to tip the scales given Spain's other heavy commitments, and the defence of the Netherlands ensured the safety of England. Indeed the threat was so effective that Philip was compelled to consider an invasion of England, an invasion he contemplated the more readily when Mary Queen of Scots was finally executed (1587) after declaring Philip her heir. Invasion was planned for 1587, but frustrated by Drake's raid on the Spanish coast which destroyed ships and naval supplies. It proved only a brief respite, and in 1588 an invasion fleet – the 'invincible Armada' – was launched against England. The fleet failed to make the essential link with Parma's troops in the Netherlands, and was scattered by storms, but the danger was acute. Elizabeth now possessed the best navy in Europe, able to fight a drawn battle with the larger Spanish fleet, but her land forces and defences were quite inadequate to have resisted Parma's battle-hardened veterans; and the camp at Tilbury where she made her dramatic appearance was on the wrong bank of the Thames to have blocked the likely invasion route through Kent.

Whatever the later myths of English determination and strength, informed contemporaries were under no illusions. Burghley's son, the rising minister Sir Robert Cecil, recalled in the Commons in 1593 that Philip had sent 'his Navy termed *Invincible*, and was almost upon the banks of us before we were aware. Yea, we were so slack in provision, that it was too late to make resistance, had not God preserved us.' Far from wishing to stand alone, the English government realised that safety lay in numbers. Alliances were forged not only with the Dutch rebels but with Scotland (1586) and with the new Protestant king of France, Henry IV (1589), and over the next six years five separate expeditionary forces were sent to fight for Henry against his Catholic rebels. The diplomatic revolution was complete, as Burghley acknowleged to Shrewsbury:

My Lord, the state of the world is marveloosly changed, whan we trew Englishmen have cause for our own quietnes to wish good succes to a French Kyng, and a Kyng of Scotts.[25]

If England could encourage Dutch and French Protestants against the power of Spain, there was always the danger that Spain might retaliate in Ireland. In 1580 Spanish troops had landed at Smerwick to assist a papal-inspired revolt, though they were disowned by Philip and were quickly captured and put to death. In 1585 MPs prophetically quoted the proverb, 'Look to Ireland, if we will rest quiet in England', and from the early 1590s a major revolt against the English began in Ulster and, encouraged by Philip, spread throughout the island by 1598. Spain was, however, too preoccupied to send assistance until 1601, when a small force landed at Kinsale, too late to affect the revival of English power; and the rebel earls finally surrendered as Elizabeth lay dying. But the cost for England, at war on several fronts, was heavy. Land forces had to be maintained in France, Ireland and the Netherlands, and in addition naval expeditions were mounted in 1589, 1591, 1595 and 1597. The reconquest of Ireland in the last four years of her reign was thought to have cost the queen over £1,255,000 against a total royal income of only £932,000. England's resources were pitifully inadequate in comparison with those of Spain: the money sent by Elizabeth to the Netherlands between 1585 and 1603 was said to have been £1,486,000 or 14.86 million florins, whereas Spain was sending some 9 million florins there every year.[26]

To add to the strains of rebellion and foreign war, England suffered in the 1590s from famine, discontent, faction and social dislocation. There had been two disastrous harvests in 1586 and 1587, but after that adequate harvests had resumed, and in 1593 parliament had felt secure enough to repeal the anti-enclosure legislation which had been in force for most of the reign. However, the four harvests from 1594 to 1597 were terrible, the worst consecutive run of the century. Conversions of arable to pasture which followed the 1593 repeal only made matters worse, and Baltic grain had to be imported on a large scale. Even so, grain prices reached their highest level of the century in 1596, and rural discontent erupted into an attempted revolt in Oxfordshire which badly frightened the Privy Council. The wages of labourers, at least judging by the Phelps Brown and Hopkins index, reached their lowest level in 1596–97, measured against purchasing power and inflated prices. The cost of government soared as the Irish revolt grew and the naval war with Spain became less successful. One rich carrack was captured in 1592, but Philip steadily built up his naval forces; Drake and Hawkins died on an abortive West Indian raid in 1595–96; and despite a daring English raid on Cadiz, a second Spanish Armada put to sea in 1596, and was dispersed by storms and not by the enemy. It has become fashionable to write of 'the crisis of the 1590s', and without doubt England suffered severely from warfare, poverty, inflation and famine. Yet actual disorder, when measured by records of crime rather than the hysterical statements of contemporaries, was remarkably slight in comparison with other areas of Europe or with England's own experience fifty years before, and 'more remarkable than the tensions and eruptions of those years was the success and stability of Tudor rule'.[27]

Some contemporaries towards the end of the queen's reign certainly viewed the national situation in a jaundiced way. Frustrated religious radicals turned to separatism – a complete rejection of the idea of a comprehensive state Church – and two of their leaders were executed in 1593. The parliaments of 1593, 1597–98 and 1601 displayed friction over the increased financial demands of the Crown – even though many MPs acknowledged that the increasing underassessment of taxpayers was as much to blame as the escalating cost of warfare – and over the queen's prerogatives, especially her sanction of unpopular patents and monopolies. The sense of gloom was intensified by the death of Burghley in 1598 after holding the post of first minister for forty years, by the subsequent faction-fighting between Robert Cecil and the earl of Essex, and by the attempted rebellion and death of the defeated but popular Essex in 1600–1.

Yet it would be wrong to end a brief survey of the later sixteenth century by giving too much weight to contemporary pessimism. The international situation was lightening by the end of the queen's reign in 1603. In France Henry IV, partly with English help, had won control of his country against the pro-Spanish Guise faction. The independence of the northern Netherlands was almost secure. The war between England and Spain diminished in intensity after the death of Philip II, though peace was not signed until 1604; and the great Irish rebellion was crushed in 1603. At home, better harvests followed the dearth of 1596–98, and the parliament of 1597–98 reintroduced safeguards against the conversion of arable to pasture, while in 1598 and 1601 the poor laws were amplified and made more humane. Even before peace was restored, there continued to be wealth available for building and luxury goods for the more fortunate: for the impact of war taxation in real terms was less in the 1590s than it had been in the 1540s, and Englishmen were less burdened by taxes than Spaniards and Frenchmen. While Philip II may have taken 10 per cent of Castile's national income to pay for his wars, it is doubtful whether Elizabeth took more than 3 per cent of England's total.[28]

Above all, the last twenty years of the queen's reign witnessed a surge of interest in colonisation and in new trading opportunities, witnessed by the appearance of the massive tomes of Richard Hakluyt's *Principall Navigations, Voyages and Discoveries of the English Nation* (1589; 1598–1600) and by the royal charter creating an East India Company on 31 December 1600. Optimism and national pride joined in the exultant prose of Hakluyt, whose dedication of his first edition to Walsingham averred that Elizabeth's subjects 'in searching the most opposite corners and quarters of the world, and . . . in compassing the vaste globe of the earth more then once, have excelled all the nations and peoples of the earth'. His 1599 dedication to Robert Cecil was more soberly phrased, but still optimistic. Should 'a good and godly peace' be obtained, he hoped that God would stir the queen to colonise North America, much as Columbus had been encouraged by the queen of Castile 'upon the ceasing of the warres of Granada'. The trade with Turkey was flourishing, and the Portuguese colonies ripe for conquest. Many Englishmen, like Hakluyt, looked forward to the seventeenth century with confidence rather than foreboding, a confidence that was to be justified by the event.

Penry Williams has recently demonstrated, convincingly and at length, that the Elizabethan regime was largely successful despite a cumbersome and inefficient machinery of administration and enforcement. A summary of its achievements makes impressive reading.

England did become Protestant, the attack on the Church was a success, law and order improved, the food supply was controlled, the problem of vagrancy tackled, a start made with an effective Poor Law. There was a genuine response to the overriding and urgent problems of the age: those of violence, religious disunity, dearth, population growth, and inflation.[29]

How great an achievement that was will be clearer when the growth of population, the problem of poverty, and the scale of price inflation have been passed under review.

Chapter 2

Population

Birth, and copulation, and death.
That's all the facts when you come to brass tacks:
Birth, and copulation, and death.
    T. S. Eliot, *Sweeney Agonistes*

1

The demographic structure of a pre-industrial society is arguably more crucial than its social or economic structure, yet until recently most historians of Tudor England gave the topic very cursory treatment. Among their reasons seem to have been an understandable reluctance to venture into another discipline, and their assumption that population has historically been a 'dependent variable'. In other words, demographic fluctuations were conceived as dependent on changes in society, law, the economy or other spheres, and it was thought that once the fundamental characteristics were accounted for, then the demographic fluctuations could be easily explained.

One version of this argument still prevalent may be termed neo-Malthusian: the periods of population growth are explained as natural responses to spare agricultural capacity, and the checks which followed as the nemesis that inevitably overtakes those who outbreed their resources. Yet another line of argument had been that, whether population was 'dependent' or no, its history before 1801 could only be speculative in the absence of adequate sources. Some Sussex jurors frankly confessed in 1549 that they were 'not able to express' the numbers of inhabitants of their towns and villages. This view finds some support from foreign visitors, who were accustomed to European population statistics and estimates, but who despaired of finding English equivalents. Jakob Rathgreb commented in 1592 that 'it is impossible to give a correct estimate of the population of this kingdom'.[1]

Yet such caution is less excusable than it was even twenty years ago. Historians and demographers, led by Louis Henry in France, and in England by the Cambridge Group for the History of Population and Social Structure, have applied refined demographic techniques to the data available for the sixteenth and seventeenth centuries. J. D. Chambers and others have challenged the assumption that population was always a 'dependent variable', and have argued that major demographic changes could be caused by reasons unconnected with human behaviour, such as climatic changes and fluctuations in the virulence of disease. The scepticism over sources has been even more convincingly refuted. Thomas Cromwell ordered parish priests in 1538 to keep registers of baptisms, marriages and burials, and these long-known records have been systematically exploited with great success. It is true that some scholars remain sceptical, and Hill has stated flatly that 'wherever parish records can be checked against other sources, they turn out to be hopelessly inaccurate'.[2] Yet many historians (including the present writer) consider this unnecessarily pessimistic. All qualifications made for imperfect data, the broad trends established by recent research on the registers are consistent both internally and with other available sources.

In a technical field like historical demography the scope and trustworthiness of the sources cannot easily be separated from presentation of their evidence, and the characteristics and limitations of the main types of source should therefore be briefly considered. Firstly, the more reliable parish registers can be exploited by aggregative analysis, in other words the simple addition of all vital events. These can be plotted on graphs to yield a pattern of annual or monthly variations, or (by using a moving average) of long-term trends which smooth out the short-term fluctuations. One objection frequently raised to aggregation is that registers record baptisms and not births. If the interval between the two events was significant, many infants would be unrecorded if they died before baptism, and any calculations of 'conception' rates nine months before baptismal entries would be invalidated. Too much has perhaps been made of this, for where both dates are known, baptism was nearly always within a week of birth, as indeed the Church insisted, to avoid the risk of the child's dying unbaptised. A York merchant avouched that when a child was born to him in 1540, 'the same day at or aftre nowne [he] prepared to have it crystened at his parish church'.[3] A more important objection is that a single parish is too small a unit in isolation, since it assumes a closed population, and discounts migration as a factor. Better results are obtainable by considering a bloc of adjacent parishes to reduce the likelihood of error through this and other reasons. Best of all, the Cambridge Group have now calculated the grand totals of vital events for 404 English parishes (Fig. 4), a suffi-

Fig. 4   Totals of births and deaths in England, 1539–1610

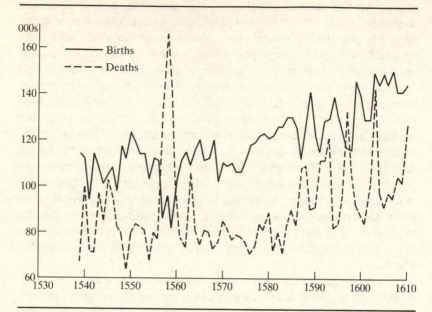

ciently large and varied sample to be typical of the country as a whole and one from which national estimates of births and deaths can be derived with some confidence (Fig. 4).

In addition, a technique known as family reconstitution has been developed by which selected families are analysed in detail. The method yields refined calculations for the small populations concerned, though there is no certainty that these 'stay-at-homes' had the same demographic structure as the more mobile families which are by definition unable to be fully reconstituted. Moreover, both methods involve distortion by omitting some vagrants and mobile poor, who are unlikely ever to have been adequately registered. Furthermore, the Cambridge Group have recently developed a technique called 'aggregative back projection' by which, given assumptions about the level of migration, plausible national population estimates can be extrapolated backwards in time from data of the last two centuries.

Well-known sources which list part of the population can also be exploited, such as taxation records and totals of households or communicants. Assumptions about the ratio of taxpayers or communicants to those excluded can be applied to yield rough estimates of the total population. The one comment that need be made here, in view of the use of communicant statistics below, is that actual ages of confirmation and first communion (not necessarily the same) are surprisingly obscure for the sixteenth century. Russell assumed that communicants in 1545–48 represented the population aged 14 and over, but 7 appears to have been the normal age before the Reformation and even, in conservative areas, in Edward VI's reign. The age was certainly raised by the Protestant bishops, and 14 or 16 is commonly taken as the standard age for first communion after the Reformation. It may have been even higher, as Wilson in 1601 suggested that 18 was the normal age.

Finally, and for some purposes best of all, are censuses or community listings. There was, of course, no national census before 1801, but local enumerations of the sixteenth to eighteenth centuries have been coming to light in large numbers in recent years, the earliest of which are for Coventry in 1523, Poole in 1574 and Ealing in 1599. They can be used to calculate average household size, and the best, such as the Ealing list, specify occupations, ages and family relationships, and can yield data far beyond the strictly demographic.

2

Historians have been in agreement for some time on the general trend of early modern population change. The great increase in English population between the Norman Conquest and the Great Pestilence, traced by Miller and Hatcher in an earlier volume, had been followed by a severe late medieval decline, but at the end of the Middle Ages renewed growth began which continued until the mid-seventeenth century. Since there are no useful sources at a national level between 1377 and the 1520s, disagreement continues on whether the renewed growth began in the later fifteenth or early sixteenth centuries. Hatcher believes that population was recovering from its lowest point by the 1460s or 1470s, and Hollingsworth dates the main period of population recovery between 1475 and 1556. Hoskins, however, points to evidence from Cambridgeshire and elsewhere of little population growth between 1524 and 1563, and argues that 'the population explosion came generally in England in the last quarter of the sixteenth century'.[4] It suffices here to say that growth was under way by 1547, that it continued on a considerable scale for the rest of the century, despite a savage cutback in 1557–59, and that it was still in progress after 1603. The later Tudor age undoubtedly fell within one of at least three long-term periods of substantial population growth since the Norman Conquest, the others being between about 1100 and 1300 and since about 1750.

Table 2.1 sets out estimates of population totals for 1545–48, 1563 and 1603, the only dates for which sources with a national coverage survive. Alternative totals are given to show the results of differing assumptions about multipliers, the ratios required to convert partial

Table 2.1   Some population estimates, 1541–1611

(a) Ecclesiastical returns (England and Wales)		Total (millions)		
		England	Wales	E. & W.
1545–48 chantry certificates, listing 'houslings' (communicants)	J. C. Russell's estimate	3.22	0.26	3.48
	R. S. Schofield's estimate	3.0	—	—
	J. Cornwall's estimate	2.8	0.25	3.05
1563 ecclesiastical 'census' listing households (families)	Estimate by D. M. Palliser and L. J. Jones	2.6	0.2	2.8
1603 ecclesiastical 'census', listing communicants, non-communicants and recusants	T. H. Hollingsworth's estimate	—	—	4.0
	J. Cornwall's estimate	3.75	—	—
	R. M. Smith's alternative estimates	3.4	—	—
		3.1	—	—

(b) By aggregative back-projection (England only)			
Date	Total (thousands)	Percentage increase since last total	Compound annual growth rate since last total
1541	2,774	—	—
1546	2,854	2.88	0.56
1551	3,011	5.51	1.08
1556	3,159	4.90	0.96
1561	2,985	−5.51	−1.13
1566	3,128	4.81	0.94
1571	3,271	4.56	0.90
1576	3,413	4.34	0.85
1581	3,598	5.42	1.06
1586	3,806	5.79	1.13
1591	3,899	2.45	0.49
1596	4,012	2.88	0.57
1601	4,110	2.45	0.49
1606	4,253	3.49	0.69
1611	4,416	3.83	0.76

Sources: (a) J. C. Russell, *British Medieval Population*, University of New Mexico Press, Albuquerque, 1948, pp. 270–81; J. Cornwall, 'English population in the early 16th century', *Econ. H.R.*[2], xxiii (1970), 32–44; T. H. Hollingsworth, *Historical Demography*, Sources of History Ltd. (in association with Hodder & Stoughton) 1969, pp. 79–88; R. M. Smith, in *An Historical Geography of England and Wales*, eds. R. A. Dodgshon & R. A. Butlin, Academic Press 1978, pp. 200f.; unpublished 1563 calculations from B. L., MS Harley, 594–5 and 618. (b) E. A. Wrigley & R. S. Schofield, *The Population History of England 1541–1871*, Arnold 1981, p. 208.

to total populations. Alongside them are set quinquennial estimates derived by the Cambridge Group from back projection: this complex method has been sufficiently thoroughly explored, and its findings are consistent enough with other sources, to suggest that these are now the best estimates available.

The most widely quoted estimates are those of Cornwall, who suggests an English population of 2.3 million in 1522–25, rising to 2.8 million by 1545. Some other recent estimates are slightly higher – Hoskins suggests 2.36 million in 1522–25 (2.6 m. including Wales), and Hatcher suggests 2.25–2.75 – though the Cambridge Group's 2.85 for 1546 is remarkably close to Cornwall's figure. Measured against a peak of perhaps 5 or 6 million before the Great Pestilence, all these are extremely low figures, and it is not surprising that acute observers in mid-Tudor England were well aware of 'depopulation'. Thomas Starkey asserted about 1535 that 'in tyme past . . . the cuntrey hath byn more populos, then hyt ys now', John Hales in 1548 that 'the people of this realm . . . is greatly decayed', and John Coke in 1549 that much of England was 'waste, desert, and salvaige grounde, not inhabyted'.[5]

Even as they wrote, however, the population recovery was under way. The earliest parish registers indicate a healthy surplus of baptisms over burials already in full swing by the late 1530s, and the Cambridge Group's sample of 404 registers suggests such a surplus throughout the 1540s and the early 1550s. An analysis of six Worcester parishes concludes that population growth was rapid before 1555, more rapid than it was to be under Elizabeth, and the Cambridge back-projection suggests that national population was growing between 1546 and 1556 by about 1 per cent per annum. Indeed, the evidence for growth is so strong that contemporaries can scarcely have been unaware of the rising trend. Either they were still so concerned at the low base from which it was occurring, and mesmerised by the memory of the medieval peak, or they were thinking in terms of quality rather than quantity. Smith, at least, in 1549, was in no doubt of the fact of 'the people still encreasing'.[6]

It was once believed that the population rise continued without a break, though at varying tempo, from the early sixteenth century to the mid-seventeenth, but in 1965 F. J. Fisher, in a brilliant note, postulated two periods of growth separated by two decades of stagnation. Taking up contemporary records of severe mortality in the last two years of Mary's reign, he discerned a nationwide epidemic on the heels of bad harvests, followed by stagnation until the 1570s. Paradoxically, the epidemic was so severe that many parish registers ceased to be kept, so that at a cursory glance there was no exceptional mortality. Fisher therefore turned to the numbers of wills proved, which averaged 1,772 a year in 7 dioceses in the quinquennium 1551–55 and 1,721 in 1561–65, but 4,543 in the intervening 5 years, about 150 per cent above normal. However, the shaky basis of probate figures, which reflect a small and variable minority of the population, can be corroborated by parish registers, not all of which were defective. Registers for Worcester city and nearby rural parishes all show peak mortality in the late 1550s, and the Cambridge 404-parish sample reveals a similar pattern, while at Colyton 1558 was the worst year of the century.

Fisher himself suggested that the population might have been reduced by almost 20 per cent, and Dyer has used Gloucestershire and Somerset data to suggest a fall of over 20 per cent between 1548–51 and 1563. Such estimates would have made 1557–59 the most severe demographic catastrophe since the Great Pestilence of 1348–50, and they receive some support from an ecclesiastical 'census' of 1563, listing the numbers of households in 11 dioceses out of 26. It has not received the same attention as the figures for 1545–48 and 1603, but a very rough calculation, based on a household size of 5.05 (as recorded for part of Norfolk in 1557), would allow only 2.6 million people in England and 0.2 in Wales. The Cambridge Group's estimates, on the other hand, suggest a population decline of only 5.5 per cent between 1556 and 1561. If so, the effect of the epidemic was little more than to wipe out the population growth of the previous five years, although it was still the worst population crisis of the century.

After 1559, although harvest crises and epidemics were by no means a thing of the past, none cut back national population on any scale. Hoskins's harvest classification reveals no dearth (prices of wheat 50% above average) between 1556 and 1596; and the worst epidemics struck urban areas only. Bubonic plague in 1563, for example, killed perhaps one in five Londoners, but there was then no comparable plague for forty years, and although it was followed by outbreaks elsewhere it was not universal even in the towns. The 404-parish sample indicates that baptismal totals were generally rising from 1560 to 1586, and were well ahead of burial rates nationally, especially as, by general consent, baptismal registers understate births more than burial registers under-record deaths.

Alderman Box told Burghley about 1576 that 'the tyme is alterid' and 'the people are increassid'; while to William Harrison in 1587 'the great increase of people in these daies' was unarguable. Sir Humphrey Gilbert was in no doubt that 'England is pestered with people', and in 1584 Hakluyt asserted that 'throughe our longe peace and seldome sicknes . . . wee are growen more populous than ever heretofore'. By 1594 Lambarde was worried by what he saw as a connection between overpopulation and poverty. 'We have not . . . been touched with any extreme mortality, either by sword or sickness, that might abate the overgrown number of us.' This, together with younger marriages, had multiplied the numbers of paupers. Hakluyt himself, however, was careful to argue that the problem was one of underemployment and not of overpopulation, scorning the 'fooles' who 'for the swarminge of beggars alleage that the realme is toto populous'.[7] Certainly the findings of the Cambridge Group support his assertion of population growth: they calculate that between 1576 and 1586 national population growth was over 1 per cent per annum.

Population growth slackened after 1586, dropping to about 0.5 per cent per annum for the rest of the reign. Burials in the 404-parish sample drew level with baptisms in 1587, 1591 and 1592, and rose well ahead of them in 1597, though in most other years there was a comfortable surplus of baptisms. A bad harvest produced widespread famine over the winter and spring of 1586–87, while in Cumbria excess mortality continued over 1587–88 as well. The mortality of 1591–92 remains unexplained, though the harvest of 1590 was deficient, but that of 1596–98 is explicable as a widespread famine. Four successive bad harvests between 1594 and 1597 triggered off a doubling of mortality rates in many regions, and even heavier rates at the peak of the crisis in the winter of 1597–98. Yet although mortality was high in some pastoral and upland areas, it was not, apparently, in the South and East, and nationally death-rates were lower than in 1557–59.

By the end of Elizabeth's reign the population of England may have been as much as 35 per cent higher than it was at the start. In 1603, the Privy Council demanded returns of communicants and non-communicants for every parish: as in 1563 not all the returns survive, but in this case contemporary totals exist for the whole country, giving in all 2.27 million men and women of communicant age. Comparison with some surviving returns shows that they err on the low side, and Hollingsworth suggests a revised figure of 2.3 million, which, assuming that they represent those aged over sixteen, would yield a total English and Welsh population of some 4 million. This is reasonably close to the Cambridge Group estimate of 4.15 million for England alone in 1603, especially if the normal age of confirmation was eighteen rather than sixteen.

It is possible to be confident, therefore, that population was rising fairly sharply from about 1510 at latest until the mid-1550s, and then again, after the nationwide epidemic, from 1570 to 1630. Contemporaries were, at any rate, certain that population had grown considerably by the early seventeenth century. 'We are grown to be a great people', wrote one observer in 1609, 'so that one lot is not sufficient for us', while another in 1612 wrote of 'so great a body of many millions which yearly do increase amongst us'.[8] The national totals suggested for certain years are, however, highly speculative, and should be taken as no more than orders of magnitude with wide margins of error. Fortunately, the subject need not be left there. Detailed analysis of registers and listings allows a great deal to be learned about fertility, nuptiality, mortality, family structure and migration, at least at the local level, and evidence of this kind is more important than the quest for unattainable national totals.

3

Part of the myth of 'the world we have lost' is a belief in the prevalence of large households in Tudor and Stuart times. The typical household is thought to have included both a large nuclear family – parents and children – and other relatives, forming an 'extended' family, but it is now clear that such large households were not the norm. Some community listings were compiled by household, allowing mean household size (MHS) to be precisely calculated, and although most such listings are of the seventeenth century and later, the evidence of the few Tudor examples is entirely consistent with them. The Cambridge Group have evolved a careful series of distinctions between families (or households) and housefuls, and between different measurements of their size and composition, which is not possible to discuss fully here. Attention will be confined to figures for MHS, which has become widely used for comparisons over space and time, and the terms 'household' and 'family' will be treated as interchangeable, as they were by the compilers of the 1563 returns. Mean household size was 3.82 at Coventry in 1523, 5.28 at Poole in 1574, 4.5 in Duffield Frith in 1587, and 4.75 at Ealing in 1599. Better still, a census survives for the entire hundred of Clackclose in southwest Norfolk in 1557: its 23 parishes comprised 4,979 persons living in 985 households, giving a MHS of 5.05.[9]

The normal household was modest in size because it was a simple nuclear family. The censuses for Coventry and Ealing leave no doubt as to its prevalence, which Laslett has identified as one of the features of a 'Western family pattern'. It does not seem to have been new in 1523, although Coventry during a severe depression can scarcely count as a typical Tudor community; Chambers, Smith and Macfarlane suggest that the nuclear family was already the norm in the later Middle Ages. Be that as it may, the Ealing evidence for 1599 is clear and unambiguous: its 404 inhabitants were grouped into 85 families; only 6 per cent of the households were 'extended' families, with resident kin other than parents and children, and only 2 per cent were 'multiple' families containing two or more conjugal units. Not a single household contained a grandchild, or a child living at home after marriage. Admittedly, the known mortality rates suggest that few grandparents survived to see their grandchildren, but enough cases are known of surviving grandparents living alone to suggest that they, or their children, preferred it so. Berkner has ingeniously argued that one type of extended family, the 'stem' family, may have been widespread in England but been masked by the nature of the sources, but recent research has cast serious doubt on his claims. The normality of the nuclear family is undeniable, with all its consequences for attitudes and childhood influences as well as for demographic structure.

There are also important economic implications, for the family group was the basic unit of production both in town and country. Indeed, it is likely that late marriage was a conscious or unconscious response to economic conditions, as the community sought to regulate the creation of new economic units, which is what marriage implied. Wrigley has suggested that marriages in a farming community like Colyton were allowed only when there was a vacant holding to be occupied, thus preventing the population from exceeding its means of subsistence. Obviously such a control would be weaker in large towns, where young immigrants often lived away from parental control, but even there marriage could be forcibly delayed, at least among those who aspired to being masters. In 1556 the Common Council of London, disturbed by poverty produced by 'over-hasty marriages and over-soon setting up of households by the youth', ordered no one to be granted the freedom of the city before the age of twenty-four. This 'effective marriage bar', as Stone calls it, was made general by the Statute of Artificers (1563), which laid down as a minimum age for completing an apprenticeship twenty-four for corporate towns and twenty-one for agricultural labour.

One qualification to the nuclear family norm is that many households, middling as well as wealthy, contained living-in servants. Of the 404 inhabitants of Ealing in 1599, 109 (25.5%) were servants, living in 34 per cent of all households. It is clear that many were not in service for life, but as youngsters before setting up their own homes. The commonest age to be in service was between twenty and twenty-four, when 78 per cent of all males and 58 per cent of females were servants. Stone, summarising much work on this and other lists, suggests that 'from just before puberty until they married some ten years later, about two out of every three boys and three out of every four girls were living away from home' in service.[10]

Servants were naturally most numerous in the wealthiest families, and the largest household in Ealing (discounting a private school) was that of a resident JP and government official, who had a wife, no children at home, four clerks, and no fewer than fifteen other in-servants. However, servants were kept also by men of modest means: several Ealing husbandmen had a servant or two, as did the village smith. The large number of child and teenage servants were 'an offering, so to speak, of the children of the poor to those above them'.[11] Consequently, the size of household correlated approximately with the wealth and social status of its head, partly perhaps because he had more surviving children, but certainly because of an influx of the children of others.

Furthermore, the implications of the nuclear family norm are not quite so straightforward as they might appear. At the level of statistical interpretation it would be easy to be misled by what has been dubbed 'the meaningless mean'. Real people lived in a very varied pattern of family units which averages can conceal: Laslett's demonstration that MHS between 1574 and 1821 was 4.75 is often cited, but he also showed that a majority of individuals lived in households numbering 6 or more. Quite apart from that, some critics of the Cambridge Group maintain that the figures are misleading. Berkner and Stone have postulated that families expanded and contracted over time, and that the proportion which were extended *at some stage* was larger than a community listing at one point in time would reveal. And Chaytor has argued that, although nuclear families were the norm, family composition was very fluid because of frequent deaths and remarriages of husbands and wives. In one Durham parish high mortality rates and the effects of poverty bound kinsfolk closely together even when they lived in different households.

4

Marriage rates and age at marriage should be the first demographic variables to consider, since they are so crucial a determinant of population growth. Contrary to popular belief, youthful marriage was not the norm, and child marriage was normally confined to aristocratic property transactions, and was rare even in that circle. Burghley himself, flattered that one of his daughters was asked in marriage for an earl's son, nevertheless argued that 'she shold not, with my lykyng, be marryed before she war neare xviii, or xx'.[12] Furnivall in 1897 provided records of thirty child couples in a single diocese over a six-year period, but this apparently impressive figure represents only 0.3 per cent of all marriages. The aristocratic norm was for marriages in the late teens or early twenties, while commoners' marriages took place later still. A family reconstitution sample of ten widely scattered parishes shows a mean age at first marriage for women of almost 25 years in the period 1550–99, rising to 26 in the following half-century.

As Laslett comments, 'it is not true to say that . . . people, either ordinary or privileged, married much younger than we marry now. In fact they were very much older in relation to their expectation of life.' He has been accused of unnecessary pleading in demonstrating that *Romeo and Juliet* (*c.* 1595) need have borne no relationship to the facts of Tudor age at marriage. Since, however, a specialist in Tudor literature could recently declare that 'sixteen or later' was the usual age of marriage for girls, the myths based on literature still need refuting.[13] It is true that in certain times and places the commonest age at marriage could fall almost to 20, and oddly enough the Stratford of Shakespeare's youth was one such place. The mean age of Stratford brides in the 1580s was 20.6 years, and Shakespeare himself married at 18. Londoners also married young, judging from a family reconstitution sample of four parishes, two rich and two poor (1580–1650). The mean age of brides ranged between 21.3 and 24.7.

Later Tudor England falls neatly into the 'European' (or strictly north-west European) marriage pattern identified by J. Hajnal. He argues that at some time between the fourteenth and eighteenth centuries the region adopted a demographic regime with a late age at marriage and a high minority of celibates, a regime which may have laid the groundwork for 'the uniquely European "take-off" into modern economic growth'. There is still some disagreement over the dating of the transition, inevitable in the light of the inadequate sources before 1538. Hollingsworth sees no clear evidence of the 'European' pattern before about 1560, whereas R. M. Smith details hints of it as early as 1377. Unquestionably a relatively late age at marriage was normal by Elizabeth's reign, and so apparently was a high minority of celibates. One-quarter of the women aged between forty and seventy at Ealing in 1599 were still single, and Hakluyt evidently regarded celibacy as a widespread choice. 'When people knowe howe to lyve, and howe to maynetayne and feede their wyves and children', he wrote in 1584, 'they will not abstaine from marriage as nowe they doe'.[14] His words have been strikingly corroborated by recent research by the Cambridge Group, which shows that the crude marriage rate fell throughout Elizabeth's reign, following the decline in real wages after a short time-lag.

Equally contrary to folk-belief are the known rates for illegitimacy and pre-nuptial conception. The proportion of live births recorded as illegitimate in a sample of 98 parishes was 2.8 per cent in the 1580s and 3.1 in the 1590s, and for a carefully checked and more reliable sample of 23 parishes, 3.7 and 4.6 respectively. The authors of this study rightly warn that they are minimal figures, far from representing all illegitimate conceptions. They also draw attention to an unexplained peak in recorded illegitimacy about 1600. Nevertheless, all their figures are much below similar rates for the last two centuries. Naturally sexual behaviour, like everything else in Tudor England, varied significantly from region to region: at Prestbury in Cheshire, the rate in the 1570s was at least 14 per cent, and it was Cheshire women who were described by a contemporary as 'frutefull in bearing of children after they be maried, and sometymes beffore'.[15] The same is true of pre-nuptial conception. In seven parishes analysed by family reconstitution for the period 1550–99, nearly one-third of all first children born to married couples arrived within nine months, and again the rates varied significantly by region. The main point, however, is that illegitimacy was apparently low, and even the pre-nuptial conception figures may represent only the prevalent practice of commencing sexual relations after the nuptials rather than the church marriage. The customary views of what constituted a binding marriage, and at what point the couple could start to cohabit, apparently varied considerably.

It seems clear that late marriage in Tudor England did not cause a high level of extra- and pre-marital conceptions, or rather not a high level that resulted in recorded live births, for information on infanticide, abortifacients and contraception is naturally almost entirely absent. Occasional cryptic accusations, as against a Cheshire vicar in 1590 for being 'an instructor of yoong folkes how to comyt the syn of adultrie or fornication and not to beget . . . children',[16] simply arouse curiosity to know more, for the contraceptive practices discussed by contemporary theologians were confined largely to coitus interruptus, potions and magical practices. Spenser's *Faerie Queene* does, however, list herbs with allegedly contraceptive properties, and Schnucker has collected contemporary references to pessaries and oral contraceptives.

It would, therefore, be rash to conclude that the illegitimacy figures indicate a high level of chastity. Hill argues for the existence among the poor of widespread 'radical sexual practices', and Emmison's evidence suggests that 1 per cent of the sexually mature population of Essex was accused of sexual offences every year. In one Essex parish, Terling, illegitimacy reached a sharp peak between 1598 and 1605, largely among the labouring poor. And London was proverbially a city of refuge for pregnant and abandoned women. Certainly the numbers of foundlings in London, and of Londoners' 'nurse children' recorded widely in the Home Counties, suggest a considerable abandonment and concealment of bastard children, although some were prosperous citizens' children being suckled in the healthier air of the country. Altogether the pressures and opportunities of life in the capital probably worked against family stability. The London Church courts in the mid-sixteenth century heard many more cases involving marital breakdown than other diocesan courts.

Given a relatively high age at marriage, a considerable minority not marrying at all, and an apparently low level of illegitimacy, a population rise rarely as high as 1 per cent per annum becomes explicable. The birth-rate was apparently of the order of 35 per 1,000, whereas some underdeveloped countries have or recently had birth-rates of 40–45 per 1,000. Hakluyt was convinced that 'wee are growen more populous than ever heretofore', yet he also held that England could support a fivefold increase in population.[17] Furthermore, married couples were not so fecund as is widely believed. Rough calculations can be made on entire populations by averaging baptisms per marriage, and the Cambridge Group have calculated baptism/marriage ratios for the entire 404-parish sample. The result allows only 3.37 for the decade 1560–69, 3.41 for 1570–79, 3.46 for 1580–89 and 3.54 for 1590–99.

Family reconstitution studies are better in providing profiles of 'completed' families, those which remained in the same parish from their marriage until they ceased to bear children. Such a sample for Colyton reveals an average 7.3 children for women marrying under the age of 25, and 5.7 for those marrying in their late twenties. Such families, of course, may not have been typical – footloose families might well have had a different demographic profile – and they were certainly atypically large, since many families were ruptured by the death of one or other partner before the end of the childbearing period. In three Forest of Arden parishes in the last quarter of the century, mean completed family size was 4.5, whereas the 'closed' family size (counting couples where either partner's burial is recorded, irrespective of the length of the union) was only 3.5. Even these modest-sized families represented an increase over previous generations. Phythian-Adams has pointed out that Coventry's mean household size of 3.8 in 1523 was very much in line with those of other late medieval cities, and that the rise to 4.75 as a mean size by the late sixteenth century represented a considerable increase in fertility.

Part of the reason for such modest family sizes was the relatively late age of marriage, when couples had passed their fertility peak. The mean interval between births (taking intervals between the first four children only) was 27.5 months at Colyton (1560–1646) and 31.9 in the Arden parishes (1575–99). An additional reason for these figures may well have been the general practice of prolonged suckling, which is known to reduce the mother's fertility. This can safely be assumed from family reconstitution studies, which show markedly shorter birth intervals when the first baby died very young than when it survived; and it can be confirmed from the few literary references to suckling. Elizabeth I herself, for example, was weaned at 25 months.

It may be significant that one of the lowest mean intervals discovered so far is 23 months for two wealthy London parishes, either because of a lower age of marriage, or the employment of wet nurses, or both. Certainly some of the most fertile women were well-to-do wives among whom wet nurses were the fashion. Thomas Godfrey noted in 1627 of his thirteenth child by his second wife: 'This child my wife nursed, being the first that ever shee gave suck unto.' Regular breast-feeding among the gentry was rare enough to be remarked on as a mark of maternal devotion. Benjamin Brand proudly recorded on his tomb (1636) that his wife bore him twelve children 'all nursed with her unborrowed milk'.[18]

Even with a late age at marriage and relatively few births per couple, the population could still have risen rapidly but for heavy mortality. Infant mortality in eight parishes averaged 134 per 1,000 live births (1550–99), and in another sixteen parishes (1580s only) it averaged 149. These figures could easily be exceeded in overcrowded or unhealthy districts. Nine parishes in York in the 1590s – not the very poorest – had rates ranging from 160 to 280. The Lincolnshire marsh parish of Wrangle (1597–1642) had a rate of about 240, while the exceptional sample of foundlings admitted to Christ's Hospital in London (1563–83) suffered a rate as high as 450–500. On the other hand, the rates in two wealthy London parishes (1580–1650) were as low as 95 and 114. Child mortality, if not quite so appalling, remained high. The eight parishes with mean infant mortality rates of 134 also had mortality rates of 72 and 68 for male and female children aged between 1 and 4, and 32 and 28 for children between 5 and 9. It must have been with pride and thankfulness that the parents of Archbishop Abbot, who lived into their eighties, could record on their epitaph that they 'had six sonnes all whome they left alive'.

It is misleading to speak of sixteenth-century mortality rates in general, for they varied much more than birth-rates. Heavy mortality gave place to less heavy child mortality and to even lighter adult mortality, but superimposed on the 'normal' mortality pattern were the irregular demographic crises which require separate consideration. The Cambridge 404-parish sample shows aggregate burials in most years well below baptisms. Expectation of life, from eight family reconstitution studies, was 47.5 at birth in the second half of the sixteenth century, but was still 29 at age 30; in other words, a man or woman surviving his or her first 30 years could hope on average to live another 30. However, crowded urban areas could be much less healthy. Expectation of life at birth in some wealthy central London parishes was about 30–35 years, and in the poorer parishes only 20–25.

The infant and child mortality rates prevented many from ever reaching maturity, as is clear from the Ealing census of 1599. Of the villagers, 49.4 per cent were aged under 20, a ratio intermediate between those of modern developing and industrialised societies, while only 26 per cent were aged between 20 and 40, 24.5 per cent over 50, and 7 per cent over 60. Furthermore, the Cambridge Group have estimated the national age-structure at five-year intervals back to 1541, although they warn that the earliest figures become progressively more conjectural (Table 2.2). In short, over half the population was under the age of 25 throughout the period. Table 2.2 also demonstrates strikingly the results of the 1557–59 crisis, with a smaller than usual cohort of infants in 1561, of older children in 1571 and of youths and young adults in 1581. However, it would be wrong to overstress mortality and early death, for in comparison with many

Table 2.2 Estimated national age-structure, 1551–1601

	Percentage of population aged:				
	0–4	5–14	15–24	25–59	60+
1551	14.7	21.5	17.9	37.5	8.4
1561	10.2	23.6	19.6	39.3	7.3
1571	13.3	19.5	19.8	40.1	7.3
1581	13.5	21.1	16.4	41.4	7.6
1591	12.4	22.3	17.9	39.5	7.9
1601	12.3	20.6	19.3	39.5	8.3

Source: E. A. Wrigley & R. S. Schofield, *The Population History of England and Wales, 1541–1871*, Arnold 1981, p. 528.

traditional societies Elizabethan England was fortunate. Back-projection suggests that expectation of life at birth was exceptionally high between 1566 and 1621, never falling below 37.4 years (1591) and reaching a peak of 43.7 years in 1581: these were high levels by the general standards of early modern Europe. The best years lay between 1566 and 1586, when mortality was lower than it was again to be until after 1815.

The medical causes of most mortality are likely to remain uncertain. Parish clerks seldom noted causes of death, except for striking and untypical cases or during epidemics. The London bills of mortality list total burials and 'plague' deaths but do not distinguish other fatal diseases before 1629. Poor diet, lack of hygiene, injuries from accidents or assaults, primitive medicine, scarcity of medical services, and perhaps a deteriorating climate, must all have increased susceptibility to a wide range of diseases and ailments, many of which have been eliminated from Britain or have ceased to be fatal. Diseases known to have been prevalent in Tudor England, or plausibly suggested to explain cryptic contemporary references, include bubonic plague, influenza, typhus, dysentery, scurvy, smallpox, measles, syphilis and even malaria. Admittedly, some had a high morbidity but a low mortality rate, though they probably debilitated men and weakened their resistance to other diseases. For example, a 'new straunge sicknes', probably influenza, was widespread throughout northern Europe in 1580. In London it was reported to 'greeve men in the head, and with a stitche over the stomacke: fewe doe dye therof, and yet many are infected'.[19]

High mortality inevitably broke up many families by removing one parent or other while their children were still minors. The existence of the Court of Wards for the children of royal tenants-in-chief is a well-known testimony to the fact, and the courts of orphans operated by many towns were set up for the same reason. Exactly a quarter of the children dwelling at home in Ealing in 1599 had lost one or both parents. Stepparents were inevitably common, as remarriages were frequent, though the only data compiled so far on the extent of remarriage come from the seventeenth century.

5

Helleiner has argued that the most significant difference that the modern demographic transition made to west European rates was the ending of mortality crises rather than a general decline in normal mortality: 'it was the peaks rather than the plateau that were lowered'.[20] It was the existence of these 'peaks' that most differentiated patterns of English mortality before and after the seventeenth century. Local studies of Tudor population reveal frequent short bursts of high mortality punctuating the normal oscillation of burial figures; and national indices, such as the Cambridge Group's series, reveal occasional crises on such a scale that, for a year or more, burials nationally exceeded baptisms. Intensive recent researches into such 'peaks' have made them more puzzling than before; old certainties have dissolved as a complex pattern has been unveiled. Most crises of mortality were at one time attributed to 'plague', meaning bubonic plague. It is a word blurred by ambiguity, since its Tudor usage embraced many killing diseases, although it appears that by the later sixteenth century attempts were being made to confine its use to bubonic plague. There is now an appreciation of a wide range of epidemic diseases prevalent in the Tudor period, although it would be vain to hope that all epidemics can ever be medically identified with certainty. Most are recorded only by concentrations of burial entries, without accompanying descriptions, and seasonal incidence is not a conclusive guide to identification. Furthermore, it is possible that some diseases have changed their nature since the development of medical science.

The study of crises is also clouded by uncertainty about the relationship between malnutrition and disease. A common neo-Malthusian view among historians is that plague and other diseases were endemic, and flared into major epidemics only when conditions were right. A growing population pressed on the means of subsistence; there was widespread malnutrition, intensifying to starvation when a bad harvest occurred; and the weakened population became susceptible to an epidemic. It was a view held also at the time: 'Experience teacheth us', wrote Sir John Cheke in 1549, 'that after a great dearth commeth a great death', and, more specifically, 'that vehemencie of plague . . . naturallie followeth the dint of hunger'.[21] However, recent research has called this into question. Of the major pandemics of urban plague in and after 1535, 1563, 1592 and 1603, only the first two followed bad harvests. Conversely, the widespread subsistence crisis of 1596–98 was unaccompanied by any serious epidemic disease.

Furthermore, some recent medical research doubts the common-sense correlation between malnutrition and a lowered resistance to infectious diseases. Appleby's study of London epidemics and bread prices suggests that 'largely independent of environmental factors, the course of disease may have to be treated as an autonomous influence on population growth', while a study of subsistence crises in Cumbria implies the complementary view 'that starvation, unassisted by disease, could determine population change'.[22] Famines and epidemics, therefore, merit separate consideration, although the two cannot be completely dissociated, and Slack has pointed out that some epidemics were linked with malnutrition in 'mixed crises'. Whether or not malnutrition lowered resistance to disease, a famine was certainly likely to spread epidemics because starving people would take to the road in search of food, and spread those diseases which were active.

A famine is identified by a combination of scarcity of grain, as measured by high prices, and a high mortality in the 'harvest year' following, a year arbitrarily taken to begin on 1 August. French historians speak of such episodes as *crises de subsistance*, defined as periods when the annual death-rate doubled and the number of conceptions resulting in live births fell by at least a third. Perhaps the term 'crises of subsistence' should be avoided in English studies, since although bad harvests were sometimes followed by higher mortality and lower fertility the mortality rarely exceeded twice the average. There are also difficulties in measuring harvest qualities. The whole period 1547–1603 is covered by the harvest classifications of Hoskins and Harrison (Appendix I), the former based on wheat prices and the latter on wheat, barley and oats; differences between the wheat index and the average of all grains are sometimes considerable. Both classifications inevitably rely on the few satisfactory price series, which cover London, Exeter, Norwich, Lincoln and other places, but do not adequately reflect the north-western half of England. In an age of regional agrarian economies, that is a serious limitation. In December 1578 the bishop of Carlisle referred to 'the great darth that we susteyned in this countrie' in 'the last yere', although the 1577 harvest was 'average' for all grains, suggesting that Cumbria had its own harvest economy. The Hoskins index may be the more reliable of the two as a guide to crises, and there is evidence that the prices of all grains tended to move together, at least in times of dearth. In the spring of 1561 there was 'such a scarcity of wheate and other graine' in London and 'the countries neare adioyning' that the corporation had to buy wheat and rye in bulk from overseas.[23] The Hoskins index rates the wheat harvest of 1560 as bad, whereas the three-grain aggregate emerges as average.

Both indexes rate 1555 and 1556 as successive years of dearth, and the nationwide epidemics of 1557–59 seem to provide the best Tudor example of 'first dearth and then plague'. Strype, summarising contemporary chronicles, say that 'hot burning fevers, and other strange diseases, began in the great dearth 1556, and increased more and more the two following years'. The crisis is poorly recorded, and it is not possible to assess the relative effect of malnutrition and disease; but plainly the former had a share in the mortality, even in the capital. In March 1557 the Privy Council spoke of some Englishmen as 'pinched with famine'. The causes of death are recorded against burials at St Margaret's, Westminster, between May and November 1557: 15 out of 269 were attributed to 'famine', but at least 51 others can be interpreted as resulting from starvation or from diseases consequent on malnutrition. After that, however, England was spared widespread starvation for a generation. The harvests of the 1560s, 1570s and early 1580s were mostly average to good, though it needed only one exception to endanger the poor. Thus the harvest of 1562 was characterised by Hoskins as 'bad', and in July 1563 Archbishop Parker wrote of Canterbury as 'molested . . . by famyn'. As a contemporary had remarked, whenever the corn failed 'a great nombre of the people shalbe in dainger of famyne'.[24]

There were three widespread dearths in 1586–88, 1596–98 and 1622–23. A bad harvest in 1586 was followed by widespread mortality over the next two harvest years. There is evidence for high mortality in Essex, Devon, Staffordshire, Lancashire, Yorkshire and Cumbria, and no doubt elsewhere, often rising to two or three times the annual average. Howson attributed the severe mortality in the North-west to 'plague', but Appleby has shown that the seasonal mortality, reaching a peak between December and February, was inconsistent with bubonic plague, and that there was a drop in conceptions in some parishes, consistent with amenorrhoea triggered by malnutrition. He suggests that the cause of the mortality was typhus, aggravated by famine. In parts of the North famine may have been the killer without the assistance of disease. One of Burghley's correspondents told him that 'dyvers in thes partes [the West Riding] have peryshid this year by famyn', and in the fields outside York a poor man was 'found deade . . . by famishment'.

Certainly there is clear evidence for such a pattern in 1596–98. Hoskins's figures give bad harvests for 1594 and 1595, worsening to dearth in 1596 and 1597, and the effect was catastrophic. In December 1596 George Abbot preached:

Behold what a famine (God) hath brought into our land . . . One yeare there hath been hunger; the second year there was a dearth, and a third, which is this yeare, there is great cleannesse of teeth . . . our yeares are turned upside downe; our sommers are no sommers; our harvests are no harvests; our seed-times are no seed-times . . . [25]

His words find an echo in *A Midsummer Night's Dream* (*c.* 1597), where Titania complains that

The oxe hath therefore stretch'd his yoake in vaine,
The ploughman lost his sweat, and the greene corne
Hath rotted, ere his youth attain'd a beard.

Cumbrian registers reveal clear evidence of high mortality in 1596–98, apparently from starvation except for a plague epidemic at the end of the period. The Barony of Gilsland was described in 1597 as decayed by the 'great dearth and famyn wherwith the country hath been punished extreamelie theis [?] three hard yeares bypast'. New-castle corporation, in September and October 1597, paid for the burial of twenty-five 'poore folkes who died for want in the streets'. At Chester 1596–97 was 'a deare yeare . . . manye people perished in this dearth in manye partes of Wales and other places, but not one in this Cittye'. Other cities may not have been so fortunate. Salisbury, Reading and York suffered high mortality in 1597, apparently from famine without the aid of plague, though not on the same scale as a major epidemic. In Cheshire itself 'greate syckness by famyne ensued and many poore dyed thereoff' during 'the greatt darthe', and there was also widespread mortality in Staffordshire, Herefordshire and Devon.[26]

The Tamworth parish register leaves no doubt about the cause. 'Dyvers died of the blouddie flixe', the clerk noted at the end of the peak mortality (March 1598), 'at which tyme the darth of corne somwhat abated by reason of deathe and Danske rye.' The 'bloody flux' was probably not an infectious disease but a symptom of terminal starvation. Similarly, the register for Minehead (Somerset) records exceptional mortality in 1597, when 'the blouddye flux raged'.[27] Even in London there is some evidence of increased mortality from starvation. Altogether, the evidence for 1596–98 is of very widespread famine, perhaps the last in English history, although its impact seems to have been more severe in the North and West than in the South and East; in Kent, for example, there is almost no evidence of deaths from starvation. The Cambridge Group's evidence is that between May 1596 and June 1598 84 out of 301 parishes in observation were seriously affected, and that only a few regions, notably East Anglia and the North-west Midlands, escaped lightly.

Yet if starvation could still kill independently of disease, epidemic diseases were much more feared. The most notorious was bubonic plague, a bacterial disease caused by the micro-organism *Pasteurella pestis*. The disease obsessed contemporaries and fascinates historians, but despite having been discussed more than any other early modern disease, it remains puzzling. There is general agreement that it was, by the later sixteenth century, a largely urban disease, and that severe epidemics usually occurred in the summer. Shrewsbury's maxim that a crisis level of mortality in which more than two-thirds of burials occurred between July and September is almost certainly indicative of bubonic plague is a safe guide, though dysentery also has a pattern of summer peaks. Unfortunately, his denial that winter epidemics can ever be attributed to bubonic plague, or to the more virulent pneumonic form, is to say the least controversial. Part of the difficulty stems from deductions based on twentieth-century plagues, despite evidence that the aetiology of plague may not historically have been uniform. The accepted view is that plague was almost entirely spread by one of the rat fleas, the human mortality being so to speak an accidental by-product of a plague among rats. Biraben's argument that bubonic plague may largely have been spread by human fleas and lice has left most historians of plague unconvinced. Rat fleas as vectors would best explain the urban concentration of the disease, since the black rat (the prevalent species until the 1720s) concentrated in the towns.

What is undeniable is that the incidence of the disease gradually changed during the pandemic of 1348–1671. At first it had been a nationwide killer on a large scale, and Hatcher sees repeated visitations of epidemics, especially plague, as the chief cause of late medieval population decline and stagnation. By the later sixteenth century this can no longer have been so, for plague was largely confined to the towns, and the national population balance was sufficiently favourable to allow urban and rural populations to increase. In other words, if as seems likely larger towns generally suffered a surplus of deaths over births, the rural surplus was sufficient both to increase the numbers who stayed on the land, and also to more than make up the losses in the towns by migration.

London itself suffered plague years in 1563, 1578–79, 1582, 1592–93 and 1603, defining them as years in which total burials were at least double the normal plague-free level. The plague of 1563, possibly the worst, may have killed 23 per cent of the population, and that of 1603 20 per cent. Norwich was struck in 1554–55, 1579–80, 1584–85, 1589–92 and 1603–4, and suffered even heavier losses than the capital: mortality was at least 30 per cent in 1579–80 and nearly 25 per cent in 1603–4. Bristol experienced serious plagues in 1551–52, 1565, 1575 and 1603–4, each of the last three accounting for perhaps 16–18 per cent of the population. York suffered severely from plague and 'sweat' in 1550–52 and from the 'new ague' in 1558–59, but then enjoyed forty-five years' immunity from epidemics, an unprecedented stroke of fortune for a large Tudor city. However, when plague did return, in 1604, it carried off some 30 per cent of the population, perhaps because any immunity acquired from previous exposure to the disease was lacking. The catalogue need not be extended; but it is clear that many provincial outbreaks followed plague in London, which in turn was often triggered by plague in the Netherlands. It may well have been endemic in London and a few other large cities, but it was serious continental epidemics in 1563, 1589 and 1603 that spread along the trade routes and produced the worst mortality.

Plague was unpredictable in its chronology, incidence and severity. For example, the Hollingsworths have analysed one especially informative London register for 1603 to construct mortality rates. They show that children were much more at risk than adults, and they confirm the contemporary belief that male mortality was higher than female. Yet Slack shows that, though this was normal in large towns, smaller towns suffered a heavier female mortality; and Finlay has found that in other London epidemics both sexes were equally at risk. Plague was also socially and geographically selective. It did not cull an urban population evenly, but wiped out whole families while sparing neighbouring families altogether. It also struck the poor much more than the rich, especially after the middle of the sixteenth century. A detailed study of one Bristol parish has shown that mortality was much more severe in a poor back alley than in the main commercial streets; and in October 1565 Gloucester corporation certified that 'though God's blessed hand, in dyverse places of the suburbs and backe lanes, hathe been felt', yet there had been no plague deaths 'nere to the place of greatest traffic, or the houses of the greatest occupiers'.[28] Middling and smaller towns generally suffered less than the cities, and villages less still; but there was no consistent relationship between population size and severity of plague.

By no means all epidemics were of bubonic plague. Those affecting town and country equally are likely not to have been plague, and certainly not if they broke out simultaneously in many scattered localities, since plague even in a crowded city usually took weeks to spread from parish to parish. Contemporary descriptions are usually inadequate to allow firm identification, but among the epidemic diseases were the sweating sickness, the 'new ague', smallpox and typhus. The sweating sickness or 'sweat' was a mysterious infection which had caused widespread mortality from 1485, the fifth and final epidemic breaking out at Shrewsbury in March or April 1551 and spreading rapidly to London, Devon and elswhere. It seems to have appalled contemporaries more by its suddenness, its high morbidity and its fatality among the social élite (who often escaped plague) than by its mortality rate. London produced some 900 victims in only a fortnight, but after that the disease ceased, and the total was far below that of any major epidemic of plague. Slack considers the mortality of 1551 generally modest compared to the ravages of plague, and it was recorded in only 11 parishes out of 67 under observation in the Cambridge Group's sample. However, severe mortality in north Staffordshire that year was explicitly ascribed by the registers to 'the greate sweate', and although equally heavy summer mortality in York was apparently from plague, it continued into the autumn, when it was 'now perceyved to be a kynd of plague and swyttyng'.[29] When contemporaries were so confused, the historian can be pardoned for copying them.

If mortality from the sweat was exaggerated, no such doubt need be felt about the equally mysterious 'new ague' of 1557–59, which Fisher suggests was a form of influenza. The broad picture of high mortality for the late 1550s, which Fisher established, can be corroborated from other studies. Thus the annual totals of wills proved before the Prerogative Court of Canterbury, which averaged 350 in 1549–56, rose to 630 in 1557, 935 in 1558 and 1,090 in 1559. Total probates for the city of York, which averaged 11 in the healthy 1560s, were 56 in 1558, the worst year of the century by this measurement. Probate figures are of course socially selective, and it has been suggested by Slack that, in the towns at least, the 'new ague' did not cause mortality comparable to the worst plagues. However, there is evidence that some parish registers were seriously defective during the height of the epidemic, and even so 1558 was easily the commonest year of crisis mortality (double or more the usual number of burials) for *any* year from the start of registration to 1809. The high and prolonged mortality seems to have been the result of a 'mixed' crisis of famine, famine-associated diseases and a virus epidemic, which unlike plague was equally lethal to townsmen and countryfolk.

Other epidemic diseases seem to have been less virulent than plague, and often socially selective in an opposite direction. Thus the smallpox epidemic of 1562, which nearly killed Elizabeth and changed the course of history, was fatal to the countess of Bedford and other well-born victims, but parish registers reveal no major rise in burials. Indeed, an esquire who died the year before confessed on his deathbed that he had never expected to die 'by this dessease, consyderinge it is but the small pockes'.[30] The name was coined to differentiate it from the great or French pox (syphilis), which can be documented in England from 1503, and which was the subject of a treatise by William Clowes in 1579. He asserted that he and his colleagues had cured over 1,000 victims of it at St Bartholomew's hospital within five years, and that three out of four patients admitted to the hospital 'have the pocks'. However, although syphilis was a major killer in the late fifteenth century, it is not clear whether it was still lethal a century later.

There is less doubt about the lethal nature of 'gaol fever', endemic in Tudor prisons. Periodically, lawyers and gentry were shocked by a 'black assizes', when justices and jurors caught a disease transmitted by the prisoners; there were outbreaks at Oxford in 1577, Exeter in 1586 and Lincoln in 1590. At Oxford the two judges, the sheriff, eight JPs, almost all the jurors and 100 scholars are said to have died from contact with prisoners, and only those present at the assizes caught the fever, though at Exeter it was said by Hooker to have spread throughout Devon after killing the judge, eight justices and eleven jurors. Almost certainly it was typhus which was endemic in the appalling gaol conditions, and which aroused little comment until it flared up in this way.

The Merton College register, which gives the best contemporary account of the Oxford Black Assizes, notes casually that it was suspected to have arisen from the pestilent air of thieves brought from the prison, 'of whom two or three died in chains a few days before'. Certainly typhus and dysentery were both widespread killers among soldiers and sailors, together with scurvy among sailors. The armed forces were indeed more vulnerable to disease than to firearms; it was plague which forced the English to surrender Le Havre in 1563, and it was the subject of special gratitude to God in 1596 for preserving the queen's forces 'all this sommer time from all contagion and mortalitie by sword or sicknesse'.[31]

6

Discussion has so far centred on 'natural' population change, but account must also be taken of migration. If much of the population was geographically mobile, then the conclusions that can be drawn from individual parish registers about whole populations are limited, and national or regional studies are needed. Contemporary writers, followed by most later historians, concentrated on social rather than spatial mobility, but the role of migration is now attracting increasing attention, and its scale is accepted as considerable. This still occasions some surprise, but it is fully consistent with some basic characteristics of Tudor society: the rarity of basic economic units composed of extended families; the movement of adolescents to other homes as resident servants; the dominance of production for the market; the normality of individual inheritance of property; and much individual choice of marriage partners, often from other communities. Population mobility, together with the prevalence of nuclear families and the 'European' marriage pattern, may have played a key role in economic development.

The chance survival of two tax lists for Towcester hundred in 1524 and 1525 shows that 15 per cent of the taxpayers had migrated within a single year. It may have been an area of unusual mobility; but Rich's work on Elizabethan muster rolls, whatever their defects, suggests a high rate of population turnover in many counties. And in the Hampshire parish of Odiham, only one-third of those baptised between 1540 and 1600 can be traced in the burial register, suggesting that most of the rest had migrated elsewhere. For London there is the testimony of the minister John Greenwood, writing in the 1580s, that every twelve years or so 'the most part of the parish changeth, as I by experience know, some goinge and some comminge'.[32] In Nottinghamshire, only some 10 or 20 per cent of the surnames recorded in tax assessments of 1544 were still in the same parishes in 1641. In general, recent studies of rural communities suggest that the prosperous yeomen and husbandmen were more likely to stay, as one might expect, and the poor, the landless and the youths more likely to migrate.

Early modern migration studies are still, however, at the stage of gathering and evaluating data, rather than of explaining the underlying patterns with any conviction. Clark, relying on deposition books relating to three Kentish towns, has proposed a broad division between betterment migration, largely short-range and rural–urban, and subsistence migration, longer-range and more often more inter-urban, but Patten feels that there is yet insufficient evidence to justify such correlations. He himself proposes a different scheme, distinguishing between frequent short-distance movements of up to 5 or 10 miles – 'mere local, undynamic mobility' – and dynamic longer-range migration. He suggests that each large town would have an 'apprenticeshed' of 20 or 30 miles around, on which would be superimposed 'substantial and often localized streams of longer-distance migration'.[33]

It can already be suggested that short-distance spatial mobility was common enough, both within towns and between villages, but that longer-distance migration was less so. A welter of individual instances of movement, and a few large statistical samples, suggest that men and women moved residence in large numbers – whether middling or well-to-do folk finding homes, jobs and marriage partners, or paupers and vagabonds simply moving to stay alive. For instance, the great majority of men appear to have married women from another parish, who then moved to their husbands' home. Souden's work on female mobility suggests that only a quarter or a third of women married between 1590 and 1640 came from the same parish as their partners.

Two broad though not universal trends were a drift of surplus population from north-west to south and east, and a considerable rural–urban migration, increasing in scale in proportion to the size and economic importance of the town concerned. Both can be seen in studies of very different social groups: the relatively prosperous recruits to apprenticeship and franchise in London, Norwich, York and Bristol, and the vagrants apprehended in Colchester, Salisbury and Warwick. In nearly every case a marked drift to the south-east can be discerned, especially from what Patten identifies as 'counties of difficulty' in the North and the Welsh Marches. This does not necessarily mean numerous cases of long-distance movement, but often of 'stepwise' migration as those moving south were replaced by others from still further north and west.

Large towns, with their often unfavourable demographic balance, had to attract immigrants just to remain the same size. Since most towns increased their size in the second half of the century, rural–urban migration was substantial, and since the larger the town the greater the natural surplus of burials, the greater was the degree of immigration also. The doubling of Worcester's population between 1563 and 1645 is attributed by Dyer half to natural increase and half to immigration: this human tribute of country to town was possible because the rural population was increasing twice as fast as the urban. Similarly, at least half of the Gloucester witnesses who appeared before the Church courts in the early seventeenth century were first-generation immigrants.

Judging from the few cases available for comparison, the larger the town the smaller the proportion of native-born residents. Eighty per cent of Sheffield apprentices (at a rather later period) were natives, but a mere 30 per cent of Cambridge freemen, and 28 per cent of York freemen and of Bristol apprentices; while among apprentices to one London Livery Company the proportion was only 18 per cent. All towns drew the majority of their recruits from their own hinterlands, but all drew also a significant minority from further afield, a proportion that grew with the size and attraction of the urban magnet. A large Canterbury sample includes 28.5 per cent of males born outside Kent; and a different sample of 276 men and women in three Kentish towns includes 40 (14.5 %) from the six northern counties. York attracted 20 per cent of its immigrant freemen from outside Yorkshire, half of them from Cumbria alone; while even in the London apprentices' sample 11 per cent came from the northern and western counties. Other examples could be multiplied: thus, of 342 Oxford apprentices admitted between 1538 and 1557, 16 (5 %) came from Yorkshire alone; while of 104 East London witnesses between 1580 and 1639, only 26 per cent were born in the Home Counties, 10 per cent came from the North, and 5 per cent from Wales, Ireland and the Continent.

Foreign immigrants were a permanent element of considerable economic and cultural importance, especially in London and in towns on or near the south-east coast. Skilled aliens had long been encouraged to settle in England, but their numbers were greatly swollen by religious as well as economic motives after the Reformation. Many continental Protestants came over during Edward's reign, mostly to leave again at the accession of Mary; but a larger and more permanent influx came over from the 1560s onwards, fleeing persecution in the Netherlands, France and Germany, and even Spain and Italy. The French ambassador reckoned that in 1553 there were 15,000 French, Flemish and German Protestants in London alone; and in 1560 Philip's ambassador put the number of Flemish Protestants in England at 2,000 families or 10,000 people.

More reliable statistics for London are available from 1563, as the Privy Council wished for accurate and detailed figures on the growing minority. In 1563 the lord mayor certified a total of 4,534 'strangers' dwelling in London, Westminster, Southwark and the suburbs. In 1567 the bishop submitted figures totalling 4,851 for the same area but without Southwark, while in the following year the total had increased to 6,704, whom only 880 were denizens.[34] This would suggest that by 1568 immigrants numbered some 7–8 per cent of the total population of the metropolis. The great majority in that year were Netherlanders (5,225) and French (1,119).

The second largest immigrant community was in Norwich, where it formed a much higher proportion of the total population. The Privy Council authorised thirty families of 'strangers' to settle there in 1565, but their number had risen to some 3,000 persons in 1569, 4,000 in 1571, and 6,000 in 1579, about one-third of the city's population, and proportionately a much greater influx of alien immigrants than any other known example in English history. Their numbers were cut back by at least 45 per cent by the epidemic of 1579, yet by 1583 their community had recovered to 4,679. Other towns were licensed by the Privy Council to receive smaller communities, but it is not possible to give a total of immigrants for the country as a whole.

These 'strangers' were to play a vital part in England's social and economic development, and they formed a striking example of that mobility which was so general a feature of the Tudor population.

7

Population deserves pride of place among the features of later Tudor England because it helps to explain so much else. Certainly it was affected by other social and economic changes, but they in turn were certainly affected by it, and especially by the sustained growth of population. Indeed it would be possible to make that growth the single major cause of much that happened to Elizabethan England.

For those who care for the overmastering pattern, the elements are evidently there for a heroically simplified version of English history before the nineteenth century in which the long-term movements in prices, in income distribution, in investment, in real wages, and in migration are dominated by changes in the growth of population. Rising population: rising prices, rising agricultural profits, low real incomes for the mass of the population, unfavourable terms of trade for industry . . . this might stand for a description of the thirteenth century, the sixteenth century and the early seventeenth, and the period 1750–1815. Falling or stationary population with depressed agricultural profits but higher mass incomes might be said to be characteristic of the intervening periods.[35]

Yet, as Habakkuk observed after sketching this interpretation, 'there are dangers as well as fascinations in an explanatory influence of such power'. A model of Tudor history in which population was the fundamental variable would be as oversimplified as a Marxian model giving that role to the distribution of wealth. Without question, if numbers increase more rapidly than food production in a pre-industrial society, then (unless other production is increased sufficiently to pay for food imports) the amount of food per capita will fall. But such a 'Malthusian' tautology is not helpful. Population might well grow, but grow more slowly than the available resources would warrant; and if the country enjoyed a wide margin over subsistence, the number of mouths might increase for some time without seriously endangering prosperity. In such a country 'there was some chance that an initial increase in population would set in motion favourable reactions on the side of resources, and since the living standards would stand a good deal of compression, there was time for these favourable reactions to occur'.[36]

It could reasonably be argued that such was the case in later Tudor England. A crude 'Malthusian' model would demand a continuous series of population surges, each brutally cut back by the positive checks of war, famine and disease. Yet in fact it was a century or so after the Great Pestilence before population began a sustained rise; and that rise, when it came, remained modest in scale. For the period between 1541 and 1656 as a whole, average growth was only 0.52 per cent per annum, in contrast to the 1.3 per cent maximum reached in England in the early nineteenth century, or the 2–3 per cent attained in some underdeveloped countries in the twentieth century. Even in a parish like Terling (Essex),where population pressure was acute, the annual growth-rate between 1550 and 1624 averaged only 0.86 per cent. 'Early modern England', say Wrigley and Schofield, 'was a land in which both fertility and mortality were low by the standards of many traditional societies.'[37] Despite all the evidence of land hunger, inflation of food prices and very real hardship for much of the population, Englishmen appear to have had a greater margin over subsistence than many other Europeans. After all, they lived in a country which even by 1603 was supporting perhaps only three-quarters of the population it had sustained before the Great Pestilence in 1348.

There is much to be said for the view that the relationship between Elizabethan population growth and economic growth was generally positive, and not negative as it is in so many pre-industrial countries today; and the belief that the English population was teetering on the brink of a so-called Malthusian crisis in the late sixteenth and early seventeenth centuries remains unproven. England's experience of subsistence crises was relatively mild in comparison to those in France and Scotland. Wrightson and Levine, in their impressive family reconstitution study of the parish of Terling, found that fertility and nuptiality were much more important than mortality as a brake on population growth: villagers married relatively late, and had fewer children than might be expected. Such controls allowed the English population to grow sufficiently to stimulate the economy, but not so fast as to create mass poverty and starvation.

Chapter 3

Society and social change

Plenti and grase bi in this plase;
Whyle everi man is plesed in his degre
There is both pease and uniti;
Salaman saith there is none acorde
When everi man would be a lorde.

Inscription at Grafton Manor, Worcs., 1567[1]

Well, I say, it was never merrie world in England,
since gentlemen came up.

Shakespeare, *Henry VI*, Part II, IV. ii.

1

Tudor society is often described as a ladder of ranks or classes
descending from Crown and nobles to paupers, vagrants and bondmen. It is a traditional form of description which was widely current
at the time: Harrison and Smith, for instance, both divided the population into six: queen, nobility, gentry, citizens, yeomen, and artificers or labourers. Such a scheme is oversimplified, for the lines of
social demarcation were often blurred, and there were men and
women who did not easily fit into such a ladder or pyramid model.
It is, however, useful shorthand for very real differences which per-
meated all aspects of life, and makes a good starting-point for a
detailed analysis. It might, however, mislead a reader attuned to
modern concepts of social class, by implying that society was an
agglomeration of individuals. It was not: it was composed of households, and only the heads of those households constituted the 'commonwealth' or political nation. The rest of the population was subsumed (to adopt an ugly but necessary term) under those heads.

Sir Thomas Smith said much the same in the language of his day.
The commonwealth did not consist simply 'of a multitude of houses
and families which make stretes and villages', but was confined to
free men. For bondmen

be taken but as instruments and the goods and possessions of others. In
which consideration also we do reject women, as those whom nature hath

made to keepe home and to nourish their familie and children, and not to medle with matters abroade, nor to beare office in a citie or common wealth no more than children and infantes.[2]

Servants he would have excluded also, and he probably considered them as 'bondmen'. There is nothing surprising in this; almost all political thinkers until the late seventeenth century excluded women, servants and apprentices, as well as children, from the political nation.

The basic unit of society, then, was the household or family. The terms were used interchangeably, for all living-in members, including servants, were considered part of the family. Statutes, proclamations and by-laws all laid injunctions on 'householders' with the firm understanding that they could speak for their dependants. The few surviving lists of entire populations are categorised by households, and in 1563 the Privy Council asked the bishops for the numbers of households, not individuals, in every parish. Youths and young adults remained under the authority of parents or masters until they married and set up families of their own. The mature adult who was unmarried and his own master was a rarity. A Kentish gentleman in 1523, almost certainly a life-long bachelor, demonstrated the strength of such norms by asking his executors to 'provide a faire stone with the pictures of a man and of a woman and of children . . . upon my grave'. Marriage was a test of adult status: Sir Thomas Smith said that no one was styled yeoman until he was married and had children, and one Gloucestershire parish decided couples' precedence in church by the dates of their weddings.[3]

It has been shown that the mean Tudor household was relatively small, and that it was typically a nuclear family of husband, wife and children, with or without servants. The large family of many children, like the extended family, was as rare in reality as it is common in folk-belief.[4] Admittedly the contrast between image and reality should not be exaggerated. At the upper end of the social scale large households were indeed common, both from the presence of living-in servants and kin, and because more children were born and survived. Stone has argued for the prevalence of an 'open lineage family' of many kinsfolk among the nobles and greater gentry in the sixteenth century; and although nuclear families were normal among lesser folk, servant-keeping was practised well down the social scale, and it is almost impossible to establish how many servants were also relations.

Average household sizes conceal a wide range from rich to poor. The houses of gentlemen, yeomen, merchants and the more prosperous husbandmen and craftsmen were places of business as well as homes. The children would be more likely to live at home to help with the estate, farm or family business, while children and youths from other families would live in as servants or apprentices. The mean size of Coventry households in 1523 ranged from 2.6 among the poorest tenants to 9.2 among the richest. Among 100 English communities between 1574 and 1821 analysed by the Cambridge Group, the average gentleman's household had 6 or 7 members, the yeoman's nearly 6, the husbandman's 5, the labourer's 4.5 and the pauper's under 4. The palaces and 'prodigy houses' of the great were intended to house really large numbers of permanent residents as well as hordes of temporary visitors. Bess of Hardwick kept about 30 resident servants on her payroll, and at nearby Wollaton the resident household in 1598 totalled 46. The earl of Derby had a staff of 118 at Knowsley Hall in 1587, while Archbishop Parker described his own household as 'having not many under a hundred uprising and down-lying therein'.

Many other dependants – servants, labourers and journeymen in the towns – would eat, and spend most of their waking hours, in their masters' houses.

There was thus a fundamental division, not often commented upon by historians, between . . . those whose dwellings were deserted daily by the menfolk, and probably any others of their families who were old enough to go out to work; and . . . those homes where the inmates both lived and worked together with, in some cases, daily outside additions. This division was recognised by contemporaries who drew a distinction between householders and cottagers. . . . The living and working areas of houses in fact had to be larger to accommodate more people.[5]

It was that division which made possible the existence of many one-roomed hovels for labourers, and that cramped accommodation which in turn drove many menfolk out of doors even when they were not working. Coventry (1547) and York (1587) both tried to legislate against the preference of 'the pooreste sorte' to 'sytte all daye in the halehouse' drinking and gambling away the resources that should have maintained their wives and children.

Yet in Tudor England 'the inequality which affected the largest number of people was not a social, but a sexual, one'. A woman was subordinated first to parents (or guardians) and later to husband, and in law it was only as a widow that she could hope to enjoy equality in disposing of her person or property. (A married woman could bequeath no land by testament, though with her husband's consent she might bequeath goods and chattels.) The biological accidents that gave England sixty years of rule by two able queens regnant made little difference towards women's political rights. A husband was held liable for his wife's conduct; and when a mayor of York was haled before the Northern Ecclesiastical Commission to answer for his wife's absence from church, the archbishop told him roundly 'that he is unmete to governe a cittie that can not governe his owne howsehold'. Married women wore hats both indoors and out, while the unmarried (other than daughters of nobles and gentry) went bareheaded to set them apart. As late as Charles I's reign, even the proudest daughter of a Lancashire yeoman 'durst not have offered to weare an hood, or a scarfe . . . noe, nor soe much as a gowne, till her wedding day'.[6]

That wedding would be arranged by the bride's parents, at least among the well-to-do, with blood, money and property in mind, and the bargaining over settlements and dowries in *The Taming of the Shrew* represented a common reality. The conservative ideal was that children should be married to those of equal rank, although alliances of blue blood and money were often preferred in practice. Between 1485 and 1569 over half the peers and male heirs of peers married within the peerage, but between 1570 and 1599 the proportion fell to a third. About 1591 Lord Stafford asked Burghley to put pressure on 'a riche citizen for his only dowghter and heire to be maryed unto my sonne', and in 1592 Lord Howard of Bindon did marry a daughter to the son of a London alderman. Burghley certainly opposed the latter match on the ground of social incompatibility, yet he advised his own son Robert in choosing a wife, 'Let her not be poore, how generous soever. For a man can buy nothing in the market with gentility.'[7]

What was certainly rare among the aristocracy was marriage which ensured neither equality of rank nor wealth. Edward, third earl of Rutland, insisted in 1573 on making a love match with the daughter of a Cheshire gentleman, and he was said to be willing to marry her even without a marriage portion, to the general disapproval of his peers. At the social level of arranged marriages it was becoming commoner for fathers to take their daughters' feelings into account; but a northern squire, William Shaftoe, could curtly order by his will 'To my daughter Margerie. LX shepe, and I bestowe hir in mariage upon Edward son of Reynolde Shaftoe.' Less is known of the marriages of the poor, and it may well be that more of their children could choose their own partners. Equally, however, they had less financial protection. Nearly one in ten of all women in their thirties, receiving poor relief at Norwich in 1570, were deserted wives; and there are hints that the practice of wife sales, certainly common in the eighteenth century, was in use in the sixteenth. The Ecclesiastical Commission was attacked by MPs in 1610 for granting alimony to separated wives 'to the great encouragement of wives to be disobedient and contemptuous against their husbands'.[8]

Yet it would be wrong to depict all women as in practice unfree; and Protestantism seems to have helped to free some women, at least, from a subordinate role. Van Meteren (d. 1612), a Dutch consul in London, noted that unmarried English girls 'are kept much more rigorously and strictly than in the Low Countries', but that wives 'have the free management of the house or housekeeping, after the fashion of those of the Netherlands'. It was thought a special sign of humility in Margaret Clitherow, the York butcher's wife, that 'she would not disdain, as many do . . . to make the fire, to sweep the house, to wash the dishes, and more gross matters also, choosing rather to do them herself, and to set her maids about sweeter business'.[9] Even local office was not entirely barred to women, *pace* Smith; a number of them served as churchwardens and manorial officials. Municipal custom was more favourable to women than the common law, and many freemen's widows, and even a few single women, were able to trade in their own right.

Children were subject to parents as were wives to husbands. In accordance with the prevalent theory of correspondences, a king was the father of his people, and a father the king of a little commonwealth. Parents had almost despotic powers over children living at home, and often even after they had grown up and moved away. Grown men were expected to kneel to ask a father's blessing, and, as Aubrey recalled, 'to stand like mutes and fools bareheaded before their parents'. Yet the subordination of children, as of women, had limits in practice. They had some legal rights over the age of majority (21 at common law) and often younger than that. By northern custom a dying parent could nominate a guardian for a son aged under fourteen or a daughter under twelve; but above those ages the orphans could 'chuse their owne curators'.

And if many contemporaries can be cited urging total obedience by children and the power of the rod, humane voices can be cited on the opposite side. The idea for Roger Ascham's *Scholemaister* (1570) originated in an after-dinner conversation at Cecil's table at court in 1563, over some Eton boys who had run away for fear of beating. Some Privy Councillors present were in favour of beating, but Cecil, Wotton and Sackville supported Ascham's plea for gentler education. Naturally, as in all periods, the conservatives were worried about the sapping of strict discipline. Cecil himself lived to muse that 'the unthriftie loosenes of yewthe in this age, was the parents' fault', and the epitaph on one York alderman (1599) stated flatly that his children were 'not bad as children are now, but all good' (*non mali ut liberi nunc sunt, omnes forsitan bonos*).[10]

Society was gerontocratic, and age was equated with privilege and respect. Between 1542 and 1642 the median age of Privy Councillors was never less than fifty-one. That was so partly because of the patriarchal ideal, and the popular belief that men's souls grew with their bodies, and partly because oral memory was treasured as a source of knowledge and authority. One landowner at the end of Elizabeth's reign resolved 'to walck the bounds justly of Nonington parishe whilest owld men be yet lyving'; and even parliaments could prefer oral to written testimony. In a dispute between the two houses in 1597 the peers placed most reliance on the evidence of their oldest colleagues, and especially on Burghley, 'the most antient parliament-man of any that are at this present'.[11]

There was indeed some sign of a conflict of generations over the Reformation. Feria wrote to Philip II a month after Elizabeth's accession that 'the kingdom is entirely in the hands of young folks, heretics and traitors', while the Elizabethan minister Henry Smith declared that 'if there were any good to be done in these days it is the young men that must do it, for the old men are out of date'.[12] There are signs by the end of the century, especially in the more fluid urban societies, of conflicts between young and old: at Coventry, for instance, 'young men' and 'ancients' clashed within the craft companies, and junior and senior officers within the corporation. Perhaps the frustrations of greater longevity were to blame, in making the young and ambitious wait longer for dead men's shoes.

The crucial mechanisms for transfer of wealth and power between the generations were of course inheritance customs. Primogeniture, in the sense that the bulk of an estate descended to the eldest son and heir, was already the norm among nobles and greater gentry. Some lesser gentry divided their lands more equally, but during the century strict primogeniture spread downwards, and Thomas Wilson could complain bitterly that a younger son's portion was 'that which the catt left on the malt heape, perhaps some smale annuytye . . .'.[13] He had legitimate grounds for complaint, because primogeniture among the landed families of Spain, France and the Empire seems to have allowed for a more generous treatment of younger sons, while the Danish nobility still practised partible inheritance. Among English yeomen, husbandmen and smallholders, however, inheritance customs varied widely. Primogeniture was apparently usual in areas of open-field cultivation and of strong manorial control, and partible inheritance more common in old-enclosed areas, uplands, woodland, forest and fen. In other words, it prevailed where land sufficed for all the sons (areas of rich soil or of low population) or where farmland was less important as a source of livelihood than fishing, fowling or rural industries.

Stone, in an impressively documented analysis of the early modern family, has detected a gradual shift from an extended family with stress on kin solidarity and limited affection for children, to the modern nuclear family based on deep affection within a narrow circle. The 'open lineage family', prevalent from about 1450 to 1630, was superseded in turn by 'the restricted patriarchal nuclear family' (*c.* 1550–1700) and by 'the closed domesticated nuclear family' (after 1640). The pattern is similar to that of Ariès, who has used mainly French evidence to suggest that modern attitudes to childhood and family affection developed in the seventeenth century. Both models are, however, based largely on literary evidence, and Stone's thesis partly on the high level of infant and child mortality. 'The omnipresence of death coloured affective relations at all levels of society, by reducing the amount of emotional capital available for prudent investment in any single individual, especially in such ephemeral creatures as infants.'[14]

Yet the Cambridge Group have found that children born between 1566 and 1586 had a higher expectation of life than any other cohorts before the nineteenth century. Already in Elizabeth's reign, therefore, one may hope to find 'affective individualism', and so one can. The paintings of Lord Cobham (1567) and Lord Windsor (1568) with their families already set the note of domesticity and affection for children that recurs in many more portraits of the Elizabethan and early Stuart periods, while a gentleman's household in County Durham provided a separate nursery as early as 1567. Such Tudor diaries and family letters as survive – those of the Lisles in the 1530s, for instance, or the Newdigates at the end of the century – reveal warm mutual relationships between husbands and wives, parents and children, and a close emphasis on the immediate family rather than on more distant kin. There may be a sense in which the aristocracy were gradually moving away from 'open lineage' to 'closed domesticated families', but as far back as the evidence goes there is evidence of 'modern' domestic attitudes.

It is true that the children of noblemen and gentlemen were often sent at an early age to the households of others for service and education. To a disapproving Venetian in 1497, it had demonstrated 'the want of affection in the English . . . towards their children' but the conclusion was no more reasonable than if the same point were made today about boarding schools, which make quite a good analogy. The households of Elizabethan nobles such as Burghley and

Huntingdon were popular finishing schools for many well-born children, and Edward, earl of Derby (d. 1572) was remembered for having 'bredd up many youths of noblemen, knights, and esquires' sonns . . . in his house'. There is much evidence of mutual affection between guardians and wards, and little of harsh or callous treatment. Admittedly, ordinary servants and apprentices could be treated much more rigorously.

What was certainly different from a 'modern' attitude to the family was that all subordinates living in a household, whether children, apprentices or servants, were considered members of that 'family', and were all equally subject to the authority of master and mistress. The prayer books insisted that 'all fathers, mothers, maisters, and dames, shall cause theyr children, servauntes, and prentises' to attend church to learn the catechism; masters and dames were surrogate parents which is not surprising since most apprentices and many servants were teenagers. Many urban merchants and craftsmen had living-in apprentices, while servant-keeping was very widespread, and not only among the wealthy; 34 per cent of the households at Ealing in 1599 had at least one servant and about 40 per cent at Coventry in 1523. On the other hand, living-in servants should be thought of not as a permanent class but as a constantly renewed supply of children, youths and young adults, for whom service was a phase in their life-cycle.

2

The Elizabethans were the first Englishmen to anatomise their society, just as they were the earliest to explore and map their country systematically. William Harrison, writing in or by the 1560s, was the first to analyse clearly the orders of society: his account was copied and revised by Sir Thomas Smith in *De Republica Anglorum*, and Smith in turn was drawn on by Harrison when he finally revised his own work for publication in the 1570s.[15] These two mutually dependent writers, who have caused a great deal of historiographical confusion, provide an excellent starting-point for a discussion of Tudor social structure.

'We in England', wrote Harrison,

divide our people commonlie into foure sorts, as gentlemen, citizens or burgesses, yeomen, and artificers, or laborers. Of gentlemen the first and cheefe (next the king) be the prince, dukes, marquesses, earls, viscounts, and barons: and these are called the nobilitie; they are also named lordes and noble men; and next to them be knights and esquires, and simple gentlemen . . . Citizens and burgesses have next place to gentlemen, who be those that are free within the cities, and are of some substance to beare office in the same . . . Our yeomen are those, which by our lawyers are called *Legales homines*, free men borne English, and may dispend of their owne free land in yearelie revenue, to the summe of fortie shillings sterling. . . . The fourth and last sort of people in England are daie labourers, poore husbandmen, and some retailers . . ., copie holders, and all artificers . . .[16]

The monarch formed a separate 'estate' by himself; this was a recognition that the wearer of the Crown possessed so much authority and power as to be in a class of his or her own. Smith listed among the monarch's powers the sole right to make war and peace, to choose the Privy Council, to make decisions on foreign affairs, to invoke martial law, to fix and alter the currency, to grant pardons and dispensations from the laws, and to fill all the chief offices of Church and state; 'to be short, the prince is the life, the head, and the authoritie of all thinges that be doone in the realme of England'.[17] For this reason parliaments were conceived as comprising three estates of the realm, monarch, lords and commons, and no statute could be passed without the consent of all three.

Next came the lay peers, those 'brave halfe paces between a throne and a people' in Fulke Greville's phrase.[18] They numbered only 48 in 1547, 56 in 1553, 57 in 1558 and 55 in 1603. These few men were unique in English society because admission to their ranks was controlled entirely by the sovereign, and their continuance was secured by hereditary succession. Henry VIII had created many new titles, but Elizabeth created or recognised only eighteen peerages in all her long reign, a number almost exactly balanced by attainders and extinctions. Even of those eighteen, all but two (Burghley and Compton) were restorations or grants to old aristocratic families or to royal cousins. The consequence was that a raw new peerage was given time to acquire the patina of age. When she came to the throne, almost half (46%) of the peers were first or second generation; when she died, the proportion had fallen to less than one-fifth (18%). She also prevented too wide a disparity in dignity among the peerage. The overweening ambition of Somerset and Northumberland in Edward's reign made Mary and Elizabeth unwilling to advance any other subjects to a dukedom; and when the Norfolk title was put into abeyance after the execution of the fourth duke in 1572, there were no more dukes in England until 1623.

Next to the peers ranked the gentry, but to distinguish nobles from gentry is to imply a sharp line between two quite distinct groups, as there was in France or the Empire, but not in England. Harrison made it quite clear that peers were also gentlemen ('gentlemen of the greater sort' as he glossed them in his revision of 1587), if superior to knights, esquires, and 'they that are simplie called gentlemen'. Smith concurred, speaking of the peerage as 'the first part of gentlemen of Englande called *nobilitas maior*' and of the rest as 'the second sort of gentlemen which may be called *nobilitas minor*'.[19] Nobles had a superior legal and social status to other gentlemen, and that was all. Since only the eldest son and heir of a peer succeeded to his title, all his other sons were untitled gentlemen, again in contrast to much of the Continent. It is true that peers sat apart in parliament, but their younger brothers and sons often sat in the Commons, and there was no sharp social divide between the two Houses. The fundamental unity of the order of gentry must be stressed, since much of the recent debate about social mobility has hinged on an alleged distinction and even class hostility between nobles and gentry.

Precedence among the gentry belonged to the knights, whose military origin was fading. They could still be dubbed by commanders in the field as well as by the sovereign, but they were now created, as Harrison admitted, 'most commonlie according to their yearelie revenues or substance and riches'. Elizabeth was generally sparing in her grants of knighthood, and she (or her generals and lords deputy) created only 878 knights in all. The total numbers at any one time have been estimated by Stone at 600 in 1558, 300 around 1580, and 550 in 1603, figures which may well be much too high. Cooper suggests only 300–350 at the beginning and end of the reign.[20] The last figure was, in any case, inflated by the lavish dubbings of knights by Essex, which more than anything else turned the queen against him. On his Irish expedition he created 81 knights without even the excuse of a military victory.

Esquires and 'simple' gentlemen were less sharply separated. Esquires, explained Wilson in 1601, 'are gentlemen whose ancestors are or have bin knights, or else they are the heyres and eldest of their houses and of some competent quantity of revenue fitt to be called to office and authority in their country'.[21] Furthermore all sheriffs, JPs and other officials could call themselves esquires while in office. All other men entitled to a coat of arms were simply gentlemen. The old informal ways by which landowners were recognised as *generosi* had given way to an organised system by which claims were recognised or created by the College of Arms. About once a generation a herald made a visitation of each county, formally acknowledging the arms and pedigrees of recognised gentry and publicly 'disclaiming' those who had assumed the title without sufficient warrant. The heralds' intention was to regulate movement into the gentry, not to prevent it. As Harrison put it frankly in a famous passage,

Who soever studieth the lawes of the realme, who so studieth in the
universitie or professeth physicke and the liberall sciences, or beside his
service in the roome of a capteine in the warres, can live ydlely and
without manuell labour, and thereto is able and will beare the port,
charge, and countenance of a gentleman, he shall be called master, which
is the title that men give to esquiers and gentlemen, and reputed for a
gentleman. Which is so much the lesse to be disalowed of, as that the
prince dooth loose nothing by it, the gentleman being so much subject to
taxes and publike paiments as is the yeoman or husbandman . . .

It was, as he added in 1587, a case of gentility for sale, gentlemen
'being made so good cheape', or as Burghley put it more bluntly,
'gentility is nothing else but antient riches'.[22]

The heralds could register anyone of free birth with £10 a year in
land or £300 in movable goods, and they made nearly 4,000 grants
of arms between 1560 and 1640. By the end of Elizabeth's reign the
number of recognised gentry must have been enormous; Wilson's
figure of 16,000 in 1601, if applied to all gentlemen and not merely
esquires as he said, may not have been far out. There were at least
424 gentry in Norfolk around 1580, 641 in Yorkshire in 1603, and
perhaps 1,000 in Kent at the same period. Exact figures are impossible, partly because despite the heralds' best efforts some uncertainty remained over who were gentry and who not. Cliffe, for
instance, kept to heralds' visitations as his criterion of Yorkshire gentility, and admitted that his figures would be increased by more than
half had he included all self-styled gentry. Probably the best method
in studying the gentry of any county is to include all those consistently
called gentlemen by their contemporaries.

Gentility was a concept in search of a role in society. Medieval
barons, knights and bachelors had held land in return for military
and other obligations, but most of those services were now obsolete.
The problem faced by sixteenth-century humanists was whether to
abolish redundant titles of status or to invest them with new mean-
ings, and they chose the latter. Their preferred conception was
adapted from Aristotle's definition of a citizen, as one with sufficient
wealth and leisure to govern the community instead of working for
a living, and with the independence as well as wealth that he derived
from freehold land. Gentility came to mean the virtue, education,
and capacity necessary to govern. The greater gentry provided county
governors – sheriffs, justices, officers of the militia – while the lesser
gentry acted as manorial lords and high constables.

Despite some uncertainty over who were gentry and who were
not, the line between them and 'commons' was crucial. Indeed, it

was precisely because the title of gentleman mattered so much that some prospering commoners were desperately keen to assume it. As Laslett puts it,

The term gentleman marked the exact point at which the traditional social system divided up the population into two extremely unequal sections. About a twenty-fifth, at most a twentieth, of all the people alive in the England of the Tudors . . . belonged to the gentry and to those above them in the social hierarchy. This tiny minority owned most of the wealth, wielded the power and made all the decisions, political, economic and social for the national whole.[23]

There is some overstatement here. The number of real gentry was probably more like 1 or 2 per cent than 4 or 5; and there were important groups outside the gentry who were not without wealth, power and influence. Of the 102 families which provided JPs for Essex in Elizabeth's reign, for instance, 37 were non-gentry. But as a bold simplification it is correct, and was indeed a commonplace of the time.

Richard Mulcaster merely reflected conventional wisdom in 1581 when he wrote that 'all the people . . . in our contrie be either gentlemen or of the commonalty'. It was manifested daily in terms of address. All members of the nobility and gentry had titles which were employed on formal occasions; those 'mere' gentry with no other title were still called 'master', and their wives 'mistress'. Even yeomen, as Harrison noted (1587), 'be not called master as gentlemen are, or sir as to knights apperteineth, but onelie John and Thomas, etc.'. Stubbes's assertion that 'now a daies every . . . husbandman . . . artificer and other . . . of the vilest sorte of men . . . muste bee called by the vaine name of maisters' is certainly a gross exaggeration.[24]

In the countryside, yeomen or franklins ranked next to the gentry. Legally a yeoman was a freeman who held land worth 40*s* (£2) a year, the same status of 'forty-shilling freeholder' that was the qualification for a parliamentary vote. In practice, he was a substantial farmer (whether freeholder or tenant), separated off from the gentleman by working his holding himself, and from the husbandman by his acreage and local standing. 'Yeomen', said Harrison, 'have a certeine preheminence, and more estimation than labourers and artificers, and commonlie live wealthilie, keepe good houses, and travell [work] to get riches.' Some were not inferior in wealth to many gentry: John Lyon, the 'Yeoman John' who founded and endowed Harrow School, was granted a royal charter for it under the name of yeoman, and was so styled on his memorial brass. And in areas like the Weald of Kent and Sussex, where armigerous gentry were scarce, the lead in society was taken by substantial farmers on the status borderline, whom Celia Fiennes called 'yeomanly gentry' when she visited the area a century later.[25]

Below the yeomen came the husbandmen, the ruck of the tenant farmers, and below them in turn the cottagers (or smallholders) and day labourers. They formed the overwhelming majority of the rural population in which gentry and yeomen were heavily outnumbered. Gregory King in 1688 estimated that England contained 17,000 families of gentry, 310,000 of freeholders and farmers (yeomen and husbandmen), 364,000 of labourers and servants, and 400,000 of cottagers and paupers. The nearest Elizabethan equivalent is Thomas Wilson, who reckoned 16,000 gentry, 10,000 'yeomen of the richest sort', 80,000 'yeomen of meaner ability', and copyholders and cottagers of whom 'the number . . . is uncertaine'.[26] He gave his statistics an air of accuracy by claiming the authority of state papers and sheriffs' books, but it is difficult to know how reliable they are. At Myddle (Shropshire) in the last thirty years of the sixteenth century, the parish register records among the adult males 10 gentry, 17 yeomen, 52 (40%) husbandmen, 17 craftsmen and 30 labourers. At Ealing in 1599, the male heads of households included 7 gentlemen, 8 yeomen, 41 husbandmen, 9 craftsmen and 1 labourer.

Miserable as was the state of many cottagers and labourers, at least almost all Englishmen were free. Slavery in the classic sense did not exist in Tudor England, although Englishmen were beginning to sell Africans into slavery in America. There still existed bondmen or villeins, tied to their masters' lands, but their numbers were fast diminishing. On the manor of Forncett (Norfolk) the last three bond families were enfranchised in 1556, although two or three serfs paid chevage yearly until 1575. A fair number of bond tenants were enfranchised by royal licence in Elizabeth's reign, and the last case of villeinage was heard before the royal courts in 1618. Furthermore, the vagrancy acts of 1547 and 1598 prescribed slavery as a punishment for vagabondage, though it is not known how often, if at all, this savage penalty was ever invoked.

Harrison's ladder of rural status is a highly simplified model, in which the powerful and wealthy few are distinguished carefully and the many are lumped together at the end as 'the fourth and last sort of people'. In practice, local and regional variations were considerable. Some villages were dominated by a resident nobleman or gentleman, while others like Wigston Magna had no resident lord and were ruled by a group of rich yeomen. Extensive common rights might encourage a large population of smallholders or landless cottagers, as in the Lincolnshire Fens or the Forest of Arden, whereas the Lincolnshire marshland was populated mainly by prosperous yeomen and husbandmen. And there were still areas with very different social systems altogether, like North Tynedale and Redesdale in Northumberland. There, until the 1580s, men still grouped themselves into a clan or 'surname' system which gave them mutual protection in a violent area, but which was feared by the neighbouring lowlanders – the Merchants Adventurers of Newcastle totally refused to accept young men from those dales as apprentices. Tynedale and Redesdale were unusual even within a Border context: but there were large parts of the four northern counties where tenants were valued as armed retainers and not merely as rent-payers, and the system only slowly decayed as the Borders became quieter after 1586.

Urban merchants are another reminder of the omissions from Harrison's useful but already old-fashioned analysis of society. It was a traditional scheme suited to a rural society, and although Tudor England was largely rural and its concepts of social status based on land, there was a growing complexity of society which makes analogies like ladders or pyramids inadequate. Lawrence Stone has suggested that English society around 1500 can be usefully regarded as a single status ladder based on landownership, though 'a tall skyscraper erected on top of a vast low podium' would be a more accurate model than the conventional stepped pyramid. During the sixteenth and seventeenth centuries, however, it becomes a totally inadequate model, because Church, law, commerce and government office gradually became separate hierarchies from that based on land. Instead, he postulates 'the San Gimignano model', a series of separate towers or hierarchies rising from a hill representing 'the amorphous mass of the poor and the humble'.[27]

Elizabethans, though denied the blessings of historical sociology, were well aware that the traditional picture of society needed modification. Harrison incorporated urban society into his model by inserting citizens, burgesses and merchants between gentlemen and yeomen, and some retailers and all artificers among the 'fourth and last sort'. He also noted that merchants were to be included among his second class of citizens. In other words, he was uneasily aware that trade and handicrafts could not easily be fitted into a hierarchy based on landownership; but his solution was to assimilate urban society to the traditional model. In this he was typical of his age. Middling townsmen like butchers and bakers often described themselves formally as yeomen; city councillors expected to be addressed as 'master' by Elizabeth's reign, in other words to be considered gentlemen. The city oligarchs and greater merchants aimed higher still. The aldermen of London and York styled themselves esquires, and every lord mayor of London who survived to the end of his year of office was knighted by the sovereign as a matter of course.

Towndwellers included not only most merchants and many craftsmen but also most of what would now be called the professions except for the clergy. Barristers, solicitors and attorneys proliferated in London, as did doctors, surgeons and apothecaries, while the provincial capitals and larger towns possessed smaller numbers. The court and royal administration in the London area already employed a miniature civil service, and larger local authorities such as the counties and the corporation of London needed numerous clerks, secretaries and messengers. There were also over 9,000 clergy and an unknown but large number of schoolmasters. None fitted easily into the conventional ladder of status except, perhaps, for the bishops, but all were acutely conscious of their professional role and anxious to establish and maintain a recognised social position. However, it cannot be said that there were any distinct status ladders not based on land before 1603 other than the clergy.

The clergy are a somewhat surprising omission from Harrison's model, since he was himself a parish priest. They were headed by two archbishops and twenty-four English and Welsh bishops, all of whom ranked as spiritual peers and sat in the House of Lords; indeed, the archbishop of Canterbury took precedence over all the lay peers. Admittedly, they lost prestige as well as wealth after the Reformation – Harrison bemoaned the 'general contempt of the ministerie' – and more of them were drawn from humble backgrounds. Whereas at least twelve out of the twenty-six bishops in 1545 came from gentle and propertied families, only a small minority of Elizabeth's bishops were gentlemen born. But the office made the man, as so often in Tudor England, and at least a third of the sons of Elizabethan bishops established themselves among the landed gentry.

The bishops ruled over a hierarchy of priests, or ministers to use the newer Protestant terminology, the bulk of whom were the 8,000 or so rectors, vicars and curates each in charge of a parish. These too lost some prestige at the Reformation, but during the second half of the sixteenth century the Reformed Church made a vigorous effort to recruit and train an able, educated clergy. It is generally maintained that the clerical profession attracted a wide range of recruits, from gentry downwards, before the Reformation and again after the 1580s, but that during the dislocations of the Reformation well-born applicants were deterred. Archbishops Parker and Whitgift both complained that 'artificers' and 'the basest sort' were the chief recruits, but there is as yet no detailed study of the social origins of the clergy. There are some indications that recruitment was broader in mid-century than later: the clergy of two archdeaconries in the Lincoln diocese in the early 1560s included five ex-serving men and three ex-husbandmen, whereas by the beginning of the seventeenth century considerable numbers of gentlemen's sons and clergymen's sons were being recruited.

The lawyers represented a clear example of growing 'profession-alisation' in this period. Harrison complained (1577) that 'of late years . . . the number of lawyers and attorneys has . . . exceedingly increased', and that growth continued. Calls to the bar rose by 40 per cent between the 1590s and 1630s, while the humbler attorneys and solicitors multiplied even more rapidly. The attorneys of a single central court (Common Pleas at Westminster) rose from 313 in 1578 to 1,383 by 1633. Many were poor and struggling, but there were glittering prizes for the successful. Sir Edmund Anderson, CJ, of a minor Lincolnshire family, made a fortune, married the dowager countess of Derby, and entertained Queen Elizabeth at Harefield Place, one of his two country mansions. Sir Edward Coke, CJ – another Elizabethan, though he lived on to be better-known under the Stuarts – rose even more spectacularly. Only son of a Norfolk manorial lord, he married first a rich heiress, and later Burghley's granddaughter Lady Hatton. This second match was 'to the great admiration of all men, that after so many large and likely offers she shold decline to a man of his qualitie'.[28] But what he lacked in blue blood he more than compensated for in wealth, and he died the lord of fifty-eight manors, including his two great mansions of Holkham and Stoke Poges.

Another growing profession was that of medicine. During the six-teenth century its practitioners were organised into a tripartite system of physicians, the academics of the profession, surgeons, who dealt with a wide range of advice and treatment, and apothecaries, who dispensed medicines. Total numbers of practitioners grew consider-ably: at least 250, excluding midwives, are known to have practised in Norfolk and Suffolk alone in the second half of the century, and Pelling and Webster estimate that by the last two decades there was at least one to every 400 inhabitants in London, Ipswich and Lynn, and one to 250 in Norwich. Such numbers are minima, because many were unlicensed – even John Dee, who was consulted about the queen's health, had no formal medical qualifications.

It was until recently fashionable to incorporate professional men and merchants into a picture of sixteenth-century society by describ-ing them as an incipient middle class. The argument advanced was that the earlier feudal and rural society had been sharply divided between lords and villeins, but that the division was now becoming blurred. Yeomen rose out of the mass of petty rural tenants in the fifteenth and sixteenth centuries, while merchants in London and the larger towns, together with professional men, became equally set apart in the urban world. A middle class or bourgeoisie developed with its own corporate sense of identity distinct from those above and below. It was acquisitive, commercially minded and economically progressive. Its rise was the leading feature of the century from Reformation to Civil War, and indeed it was its frustrations, as it failed to achieve political power and social status to match its new economic power, that caused the Civil War and the temporary breakdown of the political and social structure.

Such a brief summary does not distort the position of some of its supporters too unfairly. Tawney used 'middle class' and 'bourgeoisie' frequently and often interchangeably. He sensed 'an alteration in the balance of social forces' beginning in Elizabeth's reign, as an 'upper layer of commoners' rose rapidly in power and wealth. The solid core of the layer 'consisted of the landed proprietors, above the yeomanry, and below the peerage, together with a growing body of well-to-do farmers . . ., professional men . . ., and the wealthier merchants . . .'. Or, as he sketched it with bolder strokes in his private notebook: 'In England the property of the Crown and of the monasteries was at a fairly early date distributed among the middle classes.' L. B. Wright wrote more bluntly of 'the growth of the middle classes' being favoured by 'the rise of the Tudors . . . a bourgeois dynasty'.[29] It is true that some support for such a threefold division of society can be derived from France, where Seyssel identified an *estat moyen* or bourgeoisie (1519). Seyssel's scheme, however, included only urban, professional and industrial men in his middle estate, not the rural gentry or freeholders: there are difficulties in labelling any rural group as 'bourgeois' simply because it is thought to be commercially minded.

J. H. Hexter, in a brilliant, witty, if cruel exercise in demolition, has convinced many historians of 'the myth of the middle class in Tudor England', making unnecessary a further exploration of the semantics of a futile debate. Naturally, from a Marxian perspective, bourgeois remains a valid description of post-feudal attitudes; but Wallerstein has sensibly pointed out that 'bourgeois and feudal classes, in an explanation which uses class categories to explain social change, should not be read . . . to mean "merchants" and "landowners" '. Some merchants *and* landowners stood to gain from retaining feudal forms of production, while other merchants *and* landowners 'stood to gain from the rise of new forms of industrial production, based on contractual labour.' Even Wallerstein, however, can still follow Marx in speaking of 'a new class of "yeoman" farmers' in north-west Europe and especially in England.[30]

There is much evidence of individuals rising in status or 'class', but little sign that whole groups or classes were rising in the later sixteenth century. Yet Tawney was surely correct in his awareness of a major change in social relationships, even if his terminology is unsatisfactory. Tudor and early Stuart observers were beginning to speak of an increasing importance and separate identity of 'the middling sorts of men', and to argue that this was differentiating English society from that of France and other states. Wrightson and Levine find supporting evidence in the parish of Terling, where economic polarisation between the 1590s and the 1620s led to the dominance of a prosperous group of villagers, the 'principal inhabitants' or 'better sort' as they sometimes called themselves, while for another Essex parish, Kelvedon Easterford, Sharpe identifies 'a solid body of minor gentry and yeomen' who 'formed a sort of informal oligarchy'.[31] If there was no objective economic or social class change in the sixteenth century, as is argued here, then there was at least a growing self-awareness of identity among the middling groups.

3

The study of sixteenth-century status is not simply an antiquarian pursuit, and historians anxious to come to grips with the supposedly more 'real' or fundamental structure of economic classes are mistaken in trying to brush it aside. Naturally, if one's fundamental assumption is that 'all history is the history of the class struggle', then the Tudors' obsession with status must be regarded as either hypocrisy or self-delusion. Weber argued, however, that it was the interactions of three types of unit – class, status-groups and party – which created social and political change, and this concept provides a fruitful way of studying the sixteenth century. Tudor Englishmen categorised themselves in many ways, their vertical divisions including groupings by 'country' (provincial loyalty) and 'faction' (equivalent in some ways to the 'party' of the seventeenth century and later). In dividing the population horizontally, they thought in terms of 'degree' (social status) or occupation, the nearest they came to thinking in terms of economic class. Smith did, on one occasion, write of his fourfold division of society in terms of 'classe', but by this he meant status group rather than economic class.

Occupations and functions are more properly analysed in the context of the economy, but the general question of the existence and nature of economic class is best considered first. Many historians have viewed economic and social classes as the fundamental divisions of Tudor and Stuart society, and changes in the class structure as crucial to the century between Reformation and Civil War. Wallerstein sees the century from 1540 to 1640 as 'a period of class *formation*, a capitalist agricultural class (whose wealthier members are called "gentry" and whose lesser members are called "yeomen")'. Stone describes England in the same period as 'a two-class society of those who were gentlemen and those who were not'. If, however, as Aron has argued, a classless society is one with a unified élite, which unites in itself the political, economic and social power of the community, then early modern England was classless. Laslett would call it 'a one-class society' with the gentry the only nationwide class; Perkin would more reasonably call it 'a classless hierarchy', 'an open aristocracy based on property and patronage', although he believes class was latent in its structure. In between these positions, Davies sees the existence of economic classes in the Tudor period, but as only one of a number of competing loyalties which included one's family, gild, local community and county, and suggests that the peasants in particular 'never succeeded in establishing a real solidarity' nationwide. And Wilson notes that 'the social categories invented by nineteenth-century historians – feudal, bourgeois, working class – do not sit happily on such a society'.[32]

Some historians would say that economic class certainly already existed even if nationwide class-consciousness did not. Others would see both as already in existence, and class-conflict as already endemic. Viewed in that perspective, the gross inequalities of land-ownership and wealth produced permanent antagonism between the haves and the have nots, usually latent but always ready to flare into class warfare if exploitation was pressed too far or if the cost of living rose too high. Such historians can speak of a 'revolt of the peasantry' in 1549 as easily as in 1381 (in neither case, be it noted, with contemporary authority), and can seize on words spoken in anger as symptomatic of permanent tension. A Sussex esquire who purchased a monastic manor was alleged to have threatened his new tenants, saying: 'Doo ye not knowe that the Kinges grace hath putt downe all the howses of monkes, fryers and nunnes? Thier for nowe is the tyme come that we gentilmen will pull downe the howses of suche poore knaves as ye be.' On the other side of the social fence, and in the aftermath of Kett's rebellion, a Norwich parish clerk was said to have burst out that 'There are to many gentylman in Englande by fyve hundred.'[33] There are many examples of riots, disorder and revolts where 'the gentlemen' and 'the commons' are sweepingly portrayed as taking opposite sides.

However, it would be misleading to take such cases as representing normal attitudes. Where social relations were amicable, the fact is likely to have passed over in silence. Where conflicts of loyalty and interest did occur, they as often as not divided men on vertical rather than horizontal lines, lords and their tenants joining forces against other lords and tenants, villagers against men of another village. Recent work on the 1549 rebellions has stressed that social conflict between gentlemen and commoners was not a root cause. The western rebels demanded a limitation on gentlemen's servants because they found most serving men too loyal to their masters; the Norfolk rebels wished to prevent lords, clergy and commoners from invading each others' rights, and their demands were 'heavy with disapproval of social mobility in any direction'. And the earl of Arundel was able to pacify rebels in Sussex without the use of armed force but simply by promising 'uppon his honour' that all their grievances would be impartially judged by him at Arundel Castle. 'Whereuppon the people, havinge not small experience of his honor, and bearinge dutifull affection unto him, as to theare ancient and chiefest lord of that countrye, did obey.'[34]

There were certainly many outbursts against social superiors or inferiors, significantly most frequent during the crisis years of mid-century, and the imperial ambassador noted in 1554 'la hayne intestine qu'est entre la noblesse et le peuple'. Yet they need not be taken as the tips of icebergs of hidden discontent, any more than anticlerical outbursts need imply disillusion with the Christian Church. In both cases, it was the acceptance of understood standards that created protests when those standards were felt to be betrayed. Indeed, the two spheres of thought were closely related. Men accepted the Christian revelation, and therefore protested when Christ's ministers fell short of their professed standard; they accepted a social hierarchy under God, and protested equally when *noblesse oblige* was flouted. Nor was it a tradition in decay. It was Oliver Cromwell – surely the oddest of heroes for modern egalitarians – who was determined to preserve 'the ranks and orders of men, whereby England hath been known for hundreds of years: a nobleman, a gentleman, a yeoman'.[35]

To understand Elizabethan attitudes, it is necessary to take seriously some generally accepted images of order and reality which had been partly inherited from ancient and medieval thought and partly derived from Renaissance Italy. 'The Elizabethans pictured the universal order under three main forms; a chain, a series of corresponding planes, and a dance.' 'They had in common a mass of basic assumptions about the world, which they never disputed and whose importance varied inversely with this very meagreness of controversy.'[36] All were fundamentally philosophical or theological, but all had had a practical bearing on social and political relationships. The pairs of corresponding planes included macrocosm and body politic – the king or queen, for instance, being likened to the sun – and body politic and microcosm, whereby the commonwealth was likened to a human body, which could function satisfactorily only through harmony between all its members. The cosmic dance had similar implications, with earthly and celestial hierarchies moving in a perfect whole. The commonest image, however, was of a chain of being linking creation from top to bottom, from God through angels, men, animals, plants and minerals. Within the chain or ladder, man was ranked in order from kings to slaves, from Prospero to Caliban. All had their appointed places in a divinely appointed hierarchy. To overthrow it was to return the universe to primeval chaos.

The concepts of 'order' and 'degree' which underpinned the chain of being were everywhere and therefore seldom spelled out in full, but there are notable exceptions, including Elyot's popular *Boke Named the Governour* (ten editions between 1531 and 1600), the 'Sermon of obedience' (in the *Homilies* of 1547), and the first book of Hooker's *Laws of Ecclesiastical Polity* (1593). The 'Homily on obedience' is especially lucid:

Almightie God hath created and appoyncted all thynges, in heaven, yearth. and waters, in a most excellent and perfect ordre. . . . In the yearth he hath assigned kynges, princes, with other governors under them, all in good and necessarie ordre. . . . Every degree of people, in their vocacion, callyng, and office, hath appointed to them their duetie and ordre. Some are in high degree, some in lowe, some kynges and princes, some inferiors and subjectes, priestes and laymen, masters and servauntes, fathers and children, husbandes and wifes, riche and poore, and every one have nede of other. . . . Take awaie kynges, princes, rulers, magistrates, judges, and suche states of God's ordre, no man shall ride or go by the high way unrobbed, no man shal slepe in his awne house or bed unkilled, no man shall kepe his wife, children, and possessions in quietnesse . . .[37]

It is not fanciful to see echoes of this peroration in Ulysses' famous speech on degree in *Troilus and Cressida*, for Shakespeare would often have heard it read in church.

Such explicit statements are rare except in didactic literature, not because the sentiments were unusual but because they were so universally shared. Tudor England was a paternalist or deference society in the sense that obedience was due to social superiors and protection to inferiors, especially to one's own dependants. The Prayer Book catechism, for example, assumed that to show duty to one's neighbour included 'to ordre myselfe lowlye and reverentlye to al my betters'. When in 1577 Burghley visited Buxton for the water cure, his friend the earl of Shrewsbury offered to displace anyone of whatever rank to find him lodgings. Burghley thanked him, but ordered his servant 'not to suffer any to be displaced for me, except they war far inferior'. In 1580 Elizabeth rebuked Sir Philip Sidney for answering back to an insult by the earl of Oxford. She stressed 'the respect inferiors ow'd to their superiors', and added meaningfully that 'the gentleman's neglect of the nobility taught the peasant to insult upon both'.

Such statements have a harsh sound today, but they have to be weighed against an equal constraint which was often exercised against overbearing superiors. Elizabeth personallie intervened to protect some of the Derbyshire tenants of the sixth earl of Shrewsbury against their lord's alleged oppressions; and in 1590 she defended a minor customs official, who had exposed financial corruption, against the wrath of Burghley and Walsingham, saying 'that she was queen of the meanest subjects as well as of the greatest'. At a humbler level the corporation of York compelled a freeman to make public apology in church for speaking 'certayne slanderous and filthie words' of a female servant.[38]

Differences of 'degree' were acknowledged daily in speech, writing, dress and deportment. A man would address his social inferior by his Christian name, and by the familiar pronoun 'thou', but the inferior had to respond with title, surname and the formal 'ye'. When three madmen tried to raise a millenarian revolt in London in 1591, what shocked contemporaries as much as anything was their refusal to show respect to Privy Councillors, remaining covered until their hats were plucked off. Sir William Holles would not marry his daughter to an earl, for, he said, 'I do not like to stand with my cap in my hand to my son in law'. Men and women acknowledged their social superiors by 'giving them the wall' in the street, and by giving them the better places at table, in processions, and even in church. Pews were allotted by social precedence, as at Normanton (Yorks.) where after a dispute the gentry were 'convenientlie placed neare the quere and the husbande men removed and set lower'.[39]

In theory at least, dress and diet were also indicators of rank. Statutes and proclamations throughout the century prescribed what luxury clothing, ornament and weapons could be worn by whom, and what food eaten, on a basis partly of status and partly of wealth. Even Bible reading was temporarily restricted, by an act of 1543, to yeomen and upwards, and among women, to the gentry and aristocracy only. A proclamation of 1600 complained of the 'indecent and disorderly confusion among all sorts and degrees of men (every meane and base person taking to himselfe that which belongeth to men of the best sort and condition) as is very unseemely and unmeet in a well-governed state'.

Architecture also expressed social distinctions. The *arriviste* Thomas Dolman placed unpleasant classical mottoes over the entrance of his grand new mansion, Shaw House: one of them reads, 'The toothless envies the eater's teeth, and the mole despises the eye of the goat'. At Hardwick the countess of Shrewsbury ostentatiously placed her initials along the balustrade, and expressed social hierarchy in the increasing height of floors and windows from the servants' ground floor through the family's first floor to the state rooms on the second floor. Furthermore, 'the widely-held and constantly repeated belief that family and household continued to eat together in the great hall until Elizabethan and even Jacobean days is based on nineteenth-century romanticism.'[40] Great lords had ceased to eat with their servants in the later Middle Ages, and by 1600 lesser gentry and even town merchants were eating apart in chambers and parlours.

The gentry's consciousness of their status was maintained and enhanced by an increasing expenditure on larger and more costly tombs, which began to dominate parish churches, and to remind the villagers of their power and wealth. It was also expressed in a passion for genealogy and heraldry which reached new heights of extravagance. The simple and functional coat of arms as a means of identification was elaborated to excess, and as early as 1577 Walter, earl of Essex boasted of his fifty-five quarterings. Sir William Fairfax filled the windows of his great chamber at Gilling Castle with the arms of his own and related families, while on the painted frieze running round the room he displayed 443 coats of arms of almost all the gentry of Yorkshire. The Green Gallery of Burghley's great house of Theobalds was 'excellentlie well painted round with all the severall shires in England and the arms of the noble men and gentlemen in the same'.[41]

The heralds, before granting or confirming the right to arms, investigated pedigrees, and the more obscure a gentleman's real ancestry, the more anxious he was to find eminent ancestors. Sir Christopher Hatton's real family cannot be traced with certainty more than two generations earlier, but the heralds in 1580 gratified him by tracing him back to Ivon, a Norman nobleman who came over with the Conqueror (Yvon is in fact a female name). Burghley, in a similar position, financed extensive researches which proved to his satisfaction that he was descended from Welsh princes and from one of King Harold Godwinson's companions. It was his more realistic son, Salisbury, who scorned such princely pedigrees. 'I desire none of these vain toys', he commented, 'nor to hear of such absurdities.' Even more preposterous was the claim of Sir Arthur Heveningham to descent 'from Arphaxad who was one of the knights that watched Christe's sepulchre'.[42] If a surname suggested base origins, it might be changed. Thomas Writhe, on being appointed Garter King-of-Arms, changed his name to Wriothesley, while the builder of Wollaton, Francis Bugge, changes his to the more euphonious Willoughby.

4

The emphasis on order and degree won general acceptance; yet there was also widespread agreement that social mobility was wreaking havoc with traditional distinctions of status. Whether it was welcomed or resented, the fact was not disputed. Edward VI voiced his indignation in 1551:

the grasier, the fermour, the merchaunt become landed men, and call themselves gentlemen, though they be churles . . . the artificer will leave the towne, and . . . will live in the countrie; yea, and more than that, will be a justice of peax, and will thinke skorne to have it denied him, so lordly be they now adaies.[43]

A more sympathetic observer, Thomas Deloney, praises the rise to wealth and gentility of a semi-legendary clothier in *Jacke of Newbery* (1597). His hero hung pictures in his wainscotted parlour portraying monarchs, generals and popes who had risen from humble origins. With these examples he would encourage his servants, telling them that 'there is none of you so poorly borne, but that men of baser birth have come to great honours'. Only a little later appeared another story encouraging the ambitious apprentice destined to have even greater fame: *The History of Richard Whittington, of his Lowe Byrth, his Great Fortune* (1605). The real Whittington (d. 1423) had been the third son of a knight, but the legend of a poor orphan rising to the mayoralty of London proved irresistible, although informed contemporaries were well aware that it was untrue.

This testifies to aspiration, not to achievement, but there is abundant evidence of mobility into and out of all social levels, downwards as well as upwards. Throughout the century from Reformation to

Civil War contemporaries were concerned about the extent of individual mobility, and even about a threatened dissolution of the whole social structure. The sober evidence of prosopography shows that they were right about the scale of the former, if wrong (as social conservatives so often are) to fear the latter. The tiresomely frequent disputes over church pews, to take only one trivial example, occurred because men and women rising in wealth and respect demanded better seats, while those who held them were naturally unwilling to relinquish them. It was not uncommon for occupants to be manhandled out of pews, or for widows to cling to the positions justified by their late husbands' rank. Oxford City council tried to avoid disputes by ruling in 1584 that a widow who remarried should 'have her place bothe in the churche and in other places' according to the rank of her second husband.

The apparent paradox is that the very period – from say 1540 to 1640 – when society was especially fluid was the time of greatest stress upon order, degree, the Chain of Being, genealogy and the cult of ancestry. Yet it is not really paradoxical. In an age of rapid individual mobility, and of an exceptionally active land market, it was natural for concepts of status and deference to be stressed the more. The same status system had prevailed in the fourteenth and fifteenth centuries but had been accepted more tacitly. There had always been exceptional individuals rising too rapidly for the comfort of the élite; Michael de la Pole, son of a Hull merchant, who rose to be Richard II's chancellor and first earl of Suffolk, was only one of the most striking. What was new was not the phenomenon but the scale of it.

'The peculiar fluidity of Tudor society', it has been well said, was such as to allow

the son of a tradesman in a small Midlands town to end up owning the largest house there, a coat of arms, and the appellation "William Shakespeare of Stratford-upon-Avon, gentleman", or in an earlier and more extreme case, the son of a Putney clothworker to become Thomas Cromwell, Earl of Essex and Lord Privy Seal.

Cromwell was followed by several royal councillors just as humbly born, as literate laymen were suddenly in demand for administration. Sir John Mason's father was a cowherd, Sir Thomas Smith's a small sheep-farmer, Sir Nicholas Bacon's a monastic sheep-reeve, Sir William Petre's a tanner, and Lord Paget's a barber and constable. When Paget intervened at the trial of the earl of Surrey in 1547, Surrey retorted: 'Thou, Catchpole, what hast thou to do with it? Thou hadst better hold thy tongue, for the Kingdom has never been well since the king put mean creatures like thee in the government.'

Some of these newly risen councillors, like *arrivistes* of every age, were keen to slam the door by which they had entered. When they acted in 1540 as commissioners to reorganise the grammar school at Canterbury, 'there were of the commissioners more than one or two who would have none admitted but sons or younger brethren of gentlemen. As for other husbandmen's children, they were more meet, they said, for the plough and to be artificers. . . .' The same outlook inspired a programme in 1559 aiming at confining law, and many university scholarships, to gentlemen's sons, because the ignorance of the nobility 'forces the Prince to advance new men that can serve'.[44]

Mason, Paget, Petre and Smith were atypical, not only in the degree of their rise but in their lack of successors. Their rise to high office was one of the features of an exceptionally mobile political élite during the 'mid-Tudor crisis' of 1540–70, and once stability was restored, social conservatives prevented any recurrence. Elizabeth's appointments of Councillors after 1570 contained no one who could really be described as humbly born; Naunton noted that she 'never took into her favour a mere new man, or a mechanic'. Even her chief minister was scorned by his enemies because his grandfather David Cecil had been a yeoman-turned-gentleman and allegedly an inn-keeper. William Cecil was himself unquestionably a gentleman; was raised to the peerage, and was the founder of two noble families. Yet they were still regarded as new men whose status had been earned by clerkship: 'What are the Cessels,' grumbled one critic in 1601, 'are they any better than pen-gent?'[45]

The peerage was replete with examples of mobility. In every age a high proportion of peers are first, second or third generation: frequent biological accidents of no male heirs can extinguish titles, and the losses have to be balanced by new creations. In the sixteenth century the hazards of attainders and execution further increased the normal risks of extinction. It was therefore not unreasonable that Henry VIII and Edward VI between them created or restored no less than forty-seven peerages, some of them reversals of previous attainders, but others new recruits from the gentry like Somerset, Northumberland and Winchester. Elizabeth's parsimony with new peerages reduced this intake to an unacceptable level, whereby the number of peers was shrinking and leading gentlemen of wealth were denied the rank to which they felt entitled. James I's lavish creation of honours, even his creation of baronetcies, was at least initially a justifiable policy of bringing influence and honour into line once again.

Whereas the peerage remained fixed in size under the later

Tudors, the non-noble gentry certainly expanded considerably in numbers. This occurred because of a combination of new conferments of coats of arms by the heralds, and a fecundity and standard of living which ensured that gentlemen had more surviving children than commoners. They generally married younger, had surviving children at more frequent intervals (partly because wet-nursing was fashionable), and suffered lower rates of infant and child mortality. Stone suggests that during the sixteenth and seventeenth centuries the numbers of nobles and gentry trebled at a period when the total population barely doubled. No reliable national calculations have been made for the later sixteenth century alone, but without question the gentry were multiplying. Cliffe's conservative figures for Yorkshire allow 557 gentry families in 1558, 641 in 1603, and 679 in 1642, an increase of 15 per cent during Elizabeth's reign alone. Grants of arms by the heralds reached a peak which was not equalled until the nineteenth century: 300 in the decade 1550–59, 580 in 1560–69, 740 in 1570–79 and 700 in 1580–89, although the peak may have been artificially inflated by the exceptional activity of the heralds in the 1570s and 1580s.

There was also a considerable turnover of gentle families, both horizontally and vertically. All county studies reveal examples of families moving into and out of the area, while others died out and sank into poverty and a lucky few entered the peerage. The Yorkshire figures just cited, with a net increase of 122 families 1558–1642, conceal the fact that during the same period 181 families died out in the male line, 64 left the county and 30 disappeared without trace. As one Yorkshire gentleman put it in verse when his fellows complained of social upstarts,

... let them looke upon their owne gentlenesse,
Their estates, their bloud, and their long annositie,
And few of them shal find their own worldly noblenesse
Five degrees constant without mutabilitie.[46]

The rise and fall of gentry families, however, was a phenomenon which varied a good deal from county to county. The *locus classicus* is Northamptonshire, which still boasts a constellation of Elizabethan country houses. Of 274 mid-Stuart gentry whose origins are traceable, only 27 per cent had lived in the county since the fifteenth century (and of those the majority were not accounted armigerous until well into the sixteenth), while 40 per cent had settled in the county in the sixteenth century, mainly in Elizabeth's reign.

Such a pattern was once thought typical of Elizabethan England; but in neighbouring Leicestershire, although there were many minor new gentry, the leading families were all old-established, as they were in Devon. Suffolk was somewhere in between, with a substantial influx of new gentle families in the sixteenth and early seventeenth centuries, but a core of native families providing stability within the county community. Kent, like Northamptonshire, ought to have been a county of rapid mobility. Lambarde was emphatic that 'the gentle-men be not heere (throughout) of so auncient stockes as elsewhere, especially in the partes neerer to London, from which citie . . . courtiers, lawyers, and marchants be continually translated, and do become new plants amongst them'.[47] However, his remark seems to apply chiefly to the west, and the gentry of east Kent especially were nearly all settled in the area before 1558. The variation in turnover of land can well be seen from some comparative figures for the proportion of gentry of 1642 whose families had been settled in their county before 1485: it was 75 per cent in Kent, 40 per cent in Yorkshire and only 25 per cent in Northamptonshire.

The fluidity of gentle families is not in doubt; but in an influential study forty years ago Tawney went further, and suggested that the gentry were rising as a class. His thesis was that the non-noble gentry, already owners of the greater part of English land by 1558, further increased their share at the expense of both Crown and peerage. He supported his argument with a sample of 3,300 manors in 10 counties, yielding the following results:

	Percentage of manors owned by		
	Crown	*Peers*	*Gentry*
1561	9	12.6	67
1640	2	6.7	80

He did not distinguish between the Elizabethan and early Stuart periods, but a subsequent survey by Stone argued that the shift of landed wealth was particularly marked under Elizabeth. Net sales by peers between 1558 and 1602 amounted to 28 per cent of all the manors they owned, and the number of manors held by the average noble family fell from 54 to 39. Both Tawney and Stone went on to draw inferences about a changed economic balance between Crown, peers and gentry, leading almost inevitably to a changed political balance and so forming a major cause of the first Civil War of 1642–46. They saw the peers as an outdated group living beyond their means, losing ground to the more commercially minded and less extravagant gentry.

Tawney's and Stone's arguments triggered a lengthy debate which was once treated in obligatory detail in all textbooks. Whether one believed that the 'mere' gentry were in general rising, falling or roughly maintaining their position, the issue was seen as central to English history between 1540 and 1640. Fortunately it is now possible to treat the debate more briefly. At the technical level, the increasingly sophisticated use of historical statistics has made the early contributions appear rather crude. Trevor-Roper drew attention to the fact that Tawney included among the 'gentry' of 1640 both those who were then gentlemen but whose ancestors had been commoners in 1558, and those who were newly ennobled in 1640 and whose 1558 ancestors had been gentry. It was a valid criticism, and in 1954 Tawney admitted that the proportion of land held by peers would have remained stable if families ennobled between 1561 and 1640 were counted as peers and not gentry. More fundamental was Cooper's criticism of both protagonists in 1953, showing that manors varied so much in size and revenue that they could not legitimately be counted as units of equal value.

Stone has since made more elaborate calculations which suggest that peers' net incomes declined by 26 per cent between 1559 and 1602, but this is based on the dubious method of deflating a considerable nominal rise by a price index compiled for urban wage-earners. Even on this basis, Stone has to admit that peers' real income recovered by 1641 to its 1559 level, but he turns this into a real diminution by arguing that 'the gross national income must have greatly increased' between 1559 and 1641, so that the peers' share of the whole 'must have declined' – an unprovable assertion since the size of the national income is not known. Beyond the technical level, however, Hexter has justly drawn attention to the essential homogeneity of the peers and non-noble gentry as a single class or status group.

Nevertheless there was substance at the heart of the debate. It is a fact that traditional restraint on Crown policies rested with the great magnates until the late sixteenth century and again after the mid-seventeenth century, but that between those dates gentlemen often took the lead. Norfolk, for instance, was dominated by the dukes of Norfolk until 1572, but after the fourth duke's execution the principal gentry competed for county leadership, and resistance to government demands was led by gentry families like the Bacons and Gawdys. In that sense, as Hexter said, 'the rise of the gentry is not a hypothesis to be verified; it is a simple fact, a fact that requires explanation'.[48] One clue may lie in another part of Tawney's thesis which attracted less attention during the great debate. He used statistics of F. J. Fisher to argue that in seven counties the proportion of manors belonging to lesser landowners (those with four manors or fewer) increased considerably between 1561 and 1680. Admittedly the change was very slight between 1561 and 1601; and admittedly such statistics are suspect, because a 'small' owner may turn out to have only one or two manors in the counties under observation but a dozen or more others over the boundary. Yet the picture would be consistent with the work of Habakkuk, who has shown a tide in favour of smaller estates between about 1540 and 1680, succeeded by a reversal of the trend in the late seventeenth and eighteenth centuries.

What seems to have happened was less a decline of the nobility than an expansion of the gentry, within which the nobles formed a smaller proportion. In particular, in counties of many new gentry, like Suffolk and Northamptonshire, a substantial group of gentlemen felt confident enough for the first time to challenge the traditional leadership of the great families (whether peers or greater gentlemen), although in other counties they were unable to do so (Leicestershire remained dominated until the Civil War by the rival noble families of Hastings and Grey). The lack of entails in most families between about 1540 and 1660 allowed younger branches to proliferate, and great estates to be divided up into several medium-sized ones, whereas the coming of the strict settlement after the Restoration was to reverse the process. The great increase in the number of landed gentry families, and the turnover among them, was also aided by two other crucial developments, a very active land market and a flood of new families acquiring gentle status.

The dissolution of the monasteries (1536–40) produced what was unquestionably the greatest transfer of land since the Norman Conquest. A tradition which dies hard makes the Tudors give most of the lands, or grant them on favourable terms, to 'new men' as supporters of their regime and as counterweights to the traditional aristocracy. It now seems clear, however, that the truth was rather different. There was some lavish giving at first – Henry granted about half the monastic land in Somerset either freely or on special terms – but most land was sold at or above the normal commercial rate of twenty years' purchase, that is, at twenty times the officially recorded annual value.

Some estates were acquired by humbly born royal ministers (Cromwell, Audley, Rich, Pope, Paget), and some by merchants and financiers, notably Sir Richard Gresham of London. However, large blocs were acquired by the established aristocracy and gentry, and many of the 'new' families who succeeded the monks turn out, on inspection, to be junior branches of old families. In Devon, for example, less than one-tenth of the monastic lands were held by outsiders by 1558, when the initial sales and resales were over. The largest single share was held by the Russells, earls of Bedford, and the great bulk by younger sons or heads of junior branches of Devonian gentry, admittedly often with London or court connections. The results was therefore to increase the number of middling estates. Similar results have been obtained from studies of Lincolnshire, Leicestershire, Hampshire and the West Riding of Yorkshire.

The sale of monastic lands, and the smaller but similar sales of chantry, collegiate and episcopal lands, coincided with, and helped to accelerate, a flourishing market in land. Some came about because of the financial difficulties of the Crown, which did not stop at the dispersal of its newly acquired ecclesiastical possessions but sold other royal estates from time to time. The Tudors raised at least £1,260,000 from sales of land between 1536 and 1554, mainly ex-monastic land, and Elizabeth received £864,000 from three large-scale dispersals in 1560–65, 1589–91 and 1599–1603. The Crown sales were not by themselves, however, sufficient to account for the chronology and scale of land transactions and the turnover of landed families. The pattern revealed by samples from both Close Rolls (recording large-scale transfers) and Feet of Fines indicates a fairly steady rise in sales of land from 1560–69 to a peak in 1610–19, a rise accounted for by Stone as mainly 'internal transfer of land within the propertied classes'. His conclusions, which would apply equally to peers and gentry, are that normal biological factors (failure of heirs, or excess provision for widows and large families) were compounded by others particular to this period. Marriage portions were increasing in value much faster than the price index; entails and life tenancies, to protect the unity of an estate from a wasteful heir, were difficult to enforce at law; landowners were indulging in conspicuous consumption, and were borrowing heavily at high rates of interest. In consequence, there was an exceptional fluidity among landed families and estates. Some of the explanations may be open to question, but there can be little doubt about the scale of the process. An acute contemporary like Norden (1607) was in no doubt that lands were passing 'from one to another, more in these latter daies than ever before'.[49] The process can, however, be exaggerated; a county like Kent, where the dissolutions did not entail large sales of land, had a stable pattern of landownership with few large changes.

Many yeomen, said Harrison in 1577, 'doo buie the lands of unthriftie gentlemen, and often setting their sonnes to the schooles, to the universities, and to the Ins of the Court, or otherwise leaving them sufficient lands whereupon they may live without labour, doo make their sayde sonnes by that means to become gentlemen'.[50] About half the Yorkshiremen who bought their way into the gentry between 1558 and 1642 can be identified as yeomen. Often enough, such yeomen were indeed 'buying the lands of unthrifty gentlemen'. One Kentish yeoman bought over 200 acres in 1587 and another 124 acres in 1589, from the declining Idley family. Even craftsmen could hope to rise to gentility. William Stumpe the clothier (d. 1552) was a weaver's son, but he rose to be a sheriff and justice – perhaps one of the justices who aroused King Edward's scorn – while his son was knighted and his three granddaughters all married earls.

Harrison noted, in his revision of 1587, that merchants 'often change estate with gentlemen, as gentlemen doo with them, by a mutuall conversion of the one into the other'.[51] Among 881 London freemen admitted in 1551–53, 46 were the sons of gentlemen, still a small figure compared to the 136 yeomen's sons and 289 husbandmen's sons; but the younger sons of the gentry played a part among leading urban merchants out of proportion to their numbers. In three successive generations, the minor gentry family of Hall of Leventhorpe provided a younger son to become a merchant and mayor of York (1541–1611). In the other direction, urban merchants (often themselves of gentle origin) bought or married their way into the landed gentry. Thomas Dolman, the writer of the scornful mottoes, was a Newbury clothier who gave up his business when he built the largest Elizabethan mansion in Berkshire. The townsmen of Newbury bewailed his transformation in moving doggerel:

Lord have mercy upon us, miserable sinners.
Thomas Dolman has built a new house and turned away
   all his spinners.

John Hooker provides several pen-portraits of merchants-turned-gentlemen at Exeter. Thomas Prestwood I (d. 1558), born in Worcester and apprenticed in London, became a wealthy merchant at Exeter, but 'in his later age by lytle and lytle he gave over his trade of merchaundyse and employed his welthe yn purchasinge of landes and yn buildynge of houses'. His son Thomas II (d. 1576) 'begynnynge where his father left, dyd not mich folowe the trade of merchaundise . . . but lyved rather as a gentleman by his landes'. The calculating success of Griffith Ameridith (d. 1557) is vividly depicted. Born a poor Welsh gentleman, he settled in Exeter as a tailor, where he 'wold syngle hym selff from the meaner and baser sorte' and kept company with gentlemen. By his demeanour he became so popular that he gained most of their custom, 'and so yn shorte tyme he grewe to good welthe and . . . gave over his manuall occupation and became to be a draper'. Finally, having acquired more wealth, 'he imployed the same yn buieng and purchasinge of landes and revenewes by which yn the ende he lyved as a gentleman'.[52]

What drove these urban tradesmen to 'live as gentlemen' was probably a wish for social respectability. The anonymous author of *Cyvile and Uncyvile Life* (1579) expressed a widespread prejudice when he argued that 'husbandry, tillage, grasinge, merchandise, buying and selling' were not 'things meete for a gentleman'. When in 1602 the marquis of Winchester proposed selling his town house to John Swinnerton (later lord mayor and a knight) he dismayed Fulke Greville and Lady Warwick, neither of whom relished having 'such a fellow' as their next-door neighbour. Yet such attitudes can be misleading. Swinnerton, like many great merchants, was of gentle birth and retained a landed patrimony; and those who were not were often readily accepted by those who were. John Beane, son of a poor capper, became mayor of York and lord of a rural manor nearby, and married his daughter to a Westmorland esquire. Nicholas Mosley, a Manchester tradesman, moved to London where he rose to be lord mayor and was knighted; but already before that he had bought the manor of his native town and become its lord. Other merchants advanced their children through the universities and the Church rather than directly into land. From the one small town of Ludlow, two sons of the mercer Richard Langford (d. 1562) became respectively chancellor of Worcester and dean of Hereford, while a son of goldsmith Andrew Sonnibank (d. 1601) became a canon of Windsor.

Law and government office, like trade, were avenues to social advancement for the fortunate few. The Bacons and the Cecils both profited well enough from them to found great noble houses. Of the great country houses, 'Chatsworth and Hinchingbrooke, Hatfield and Audley End, Burghley House, Knole, Warwick Castle . . . , Kirby and Holdenby, Wilton, Salden, Apethorpe, Cobham, Bramshill and many others were built on the profits of administration; Montacute and Gorhambury, Blickling and Loseley, Lynsted and Doddington illustrated the profits of law'.[53] Some of these examples are Jacobean rather than Elizabethan, but the lists remain impressive. And at a more modest level, some gentry were able to achieve a higher social standing in their counties than their acres and pedigrees warranted by active zeal in local government and politics or by patronising preachers and lecturers. Sir Francis Hastings in Somerset and Sir Thomas Posthumus Hoby in the East Riding of Yorkshire were two men who – driven by Puritan zeal in one case and by ambition in the other – became prominent in this way.

Marriage was yet another key to social advance. In an age when many were widowed young, the remarriage of wealthy partners, as well as the marriage of heirs and heiresses, was a vital element in the rise and fall of family fortunes. Sir Robert Cross the privateer frankly admitted that 'seeinge there would be no ymployment for me after the decese of our latte Soffren Quine Elizabeth, I thought it my beste course to betake me to a wyffe, which I then did'. Thomas Prestwood I had become a prosperous Exeter merchant by marrying the wealthy widow of John Bodley of that city; and Bodley's grandson Thomas did the same when he married a Totnes widow whose husband had made a fortune in pilchards. In this way 'the Bodleian Library is founded in part at least upon the humble pilchard'.[54] And it was four marriages to successively richer husbands that turned the daughter of a minor Derbyshire gentleman into the formidable countess of Shrewsbury, builder of Chatsworth and Hardwick, who could even scheme for the Crown for her own family.

All this evidence, however, is of social advancement. which was undoubtedly possible, but possible only for a fortunate few. Many had to struggle hard to maintain their social position, often by moving geographically to avoid slipping downwards socially, while others were less fortunate still and sank into obscurity. Lineage was valued less for its own sake by the later sixteenth century, and tended to be stressed by declining and impoverished gentry. The literature of the age is full of men and women of gentle birth reduced to poverty, like Orlando in *As You Like It*, and the poverty rings truer than the fairy-tale endings. There were real-life gentlemen who sank as quickly as their fathers had risen: Sir Christopher Heydon rose in wealth and prestige in Norfolk, enlarging his great house at Baconsthorpe and keeping eighty servants; but twenty years after his death his son had to mortgage the house to meet his debts. Some gentry fell to a point where they would no longer have been socially recognised by fellow-gentry, like 'John Cockeshutt, gent.', licensed as a drover in 1591. It was fear of such humiliation that prompted Raleigh's advice to his son: 'Strive, if thou canst, to make good thy station on the upper deck; those that live under hatches are ordained to be drudges and slaves. . . .'[55]

Yet the great majority who suffered 'downward mobility' already lived in humble circumstances, and the transformation of a husband-man into a cottager, or a cottager into a labourer or pauper, would usually have gone unremarked. Only when a destitute man or woman was being interrogated, usually as a candidate for poor relief or as a suspect vagrant, were the biographical details likely to emerge. Of 651 vagrants arrested in Salisbury between 1598 and 1638, 70 were accredited with trades, and had presumably failed in business and taken to begging. Humphrey Gibbons, a labourer arrested at New Romney in 1596, claimed to have farmed 6 or 7 acres until the terrible harvest of that year proved his undoing. Wrightson and Levine have examined the fortunes of 14 families in the Essex parish of Terling between the late sixteenth century and 1671, and have found that 5 of them declined in status from yeomen or husbandmen to labourers, although 3 other families moved upwards and 5 maintained their position. Decline and loss of land seems usually to have occurred between 1590 and 1620. Both Harrison (1577) and Hakluyt (1584) mentioned the widespread belief that beggars were increasing in number because of excessive population growth, although neither of these shrewd contemporaries accepted the link. Hakluyt placed much of the blame on underemployment, while Harrison stressed the role of idleness and of evictions by covetous landlords. Both were in agreement, however, that beggars and vagabonds were on the increase, a salutary reminder that the glitter of the successfully mobile, the Cecils and the Shakespeares, should not blind us to the misery of Humphrey Gibbons and of many like him.

Chapter 4

Wealth and poverty

For now a few have all and all have nought . . .

    Spenser, *Mother Hubberds Tale* (1591)

The ritche men have gotten all into ther hands and will starve the poore

    Vagrants' gossip reported in Somerset, 1596

It cannot be denyed but the comon people are very rich, albeit they be much decayed from the states they were wont to have . . .

    Thomas Wilson (1601)[1]

1

Social structure remained stable throughout the later Tudor period, despite the revolutions in Church and state between 1532 and 1559, and despite the crisis years of the 1590s. It was a remarkable achievement, given that power, prestige and economic wealth were distributed very unequally, and that inflation was seriously distorting wealth differentials and perhaps widening the already yawning gap between landed and landless. That social breakdown was averted can be credited to many influences, including custom, religious teaching and the habit of deference. Equally important, probably, was a close correlation between wealth and social status. Social divisions were not of course based exclusively on wealth – they never are – and birth, education, adaptability and the source of one's wealth were also important. Nevertheless, status was usually kept in line with wealth, allowing for fluidity in the social structure as fortunes were made and lost. The alternative would have been to keep wealth in line with status by preventing base-born climbers from acquiring landed estates; and some conservatives, alarmed by social mobility, were prepared to do so. A reactionary programme of legislation for the 1559 parliament would have forbidden yeomen, husbandmen, clothiers, merchants and craftsmen to purchase lands by inheritance to more than a stated yearly value.

The disparities of wealth were certainly considerable. Gregory King estimated (1688) that nobles and gentlemen represented 1.2 per cent of all families in the kingdom, but received about one-seventh of the national income (14.1%); and that the labouring poor, comprising over half of all families, received only one-fifth of the national income in wages (20.7%), although this did not include receipts from poor relief and charity. His calculations, with all their faults, are far superior to any earlier figures. Wilson's *State of England* (1601) assigned to peers an average yearly income of £3,600, to most knights from £1,000 to £2,000, to esquires £500 to £1,000, and to many yeomen £300 to £500; but there is no systematic means of checking his figures, which appear to be generally too high.

The orders of magnitude, nevertheless, are not in doubt. The median income of lay peers in 1534, according to the subsidy assessments, was £921, and that of the bishops in 1535 was £1,050. The average lay peer a generation later (1559) had a mean gross yearly rental, according to Stone, of £1,680. At the same period (1561) the justices of Buckinghamshire allowed male agricultural labourers a maximum yearly wage of 26s 8d, and females only 20s, although these low wages were supplemented by food and drink provided by the employers. Immediately, however, even such crude contrasts have to be qualified. Tax assessments notoriously understated sixteenth-century incomes, while the bishops' revenues in 1535 took into account only their net income from their episcopal office, and the calculations of nobles' income in 1559 are based on gross income for only a part, if the greater part, of their incomes. Furthermore, throughout the period there was an almost continuous inflation which vitiates any comparisons of prices and incomes over time.

Inequalities of wealth were accepted, like disparities of social status, with little questioning. The teaching of churchmen and social reformers was that wealth was not in itself wrong, provided that the rich accepted obligations commensurate with their fortunes. Yet, understandably, egalitarian protests were voiced from time to time. Richard Morison, in his *Remedy for Sedition* (1536), regarded poverty as the fundamental cause of rebellion, and put into the rebels' mouths the words, 'we thinke it is very evyll, that soo many of us be poore; we thynke it were a good worlde, if we were al ryche'. Sir John Cheke's *Hurt of Sedicion* (1549) made the same assumption in writing against the rebels of East Anglia: 'Would ye have all alike riche? That is the overthrow of labour, and utter decay of worke in this realme.' No one would work hard if he were forced to share the fruits of his labour with the idle.[2] Both Morison and Cheke, however, were acting, slightly hysterically, as government spokesmen against rebels, and the circumstances of the northern and eastern revolts do not suggest that most rebels wanted to destroy all gentlemen in a *Jacquerie*, but rather to obtain their support.

Although society contained extremes of wealth and poverty, it was not one in which a tiny number of enormously wealthy men dominated a mass of paupers. Such caricatures of pre-industrial societies, whatever their validity for parts of the Third World today, have never been true of England in any period for which records survive. Thompson's very tentative calculations allowed 'great landlords' a stable proportion of about 10 per cent of all cultivated land in England and Wales between 1559 and 1602, before a gradual rise to 15–20 per cent in the seventeenth century, 20–25 per cent in the eighteenth and nineteenth, and a fall since 1920 back to about 10 per cent. He gave, however, no definition of a great estate in acreage, and Cooper, who took it at Mingay's level of 5,000 acres, preferred a figure of 15–20 per cent even before the Reformation. If he is right, the proportion of land held by great landlords was remarkably stable from 1436 to 1688 at about one-sixth of the whole. Even more interesting, Cooper's allocation of all land in 1436, which he suggests remained generally true after the Reformation apart from the Church's share, showed that no less than 20 per cent of all landed wealth was held by landowners with incomes of under £5 a year, a figure raised by Davies to 26 per cent (Table 4.1).

Despite the proliferation of records and accounts, which reveal many aspects of Elizabethan life in more detail than is possible for

Table 4.1 Distribution of landed wealth in 1436

	Total landed income p.a.	Percentage of national landed income
Crown	£20,000	5
Church	£75,000–100,000	20
Lay peers	£40,000	10
Other lay landowners with over £100 p.a. (greater knights)	£38,000	10
Incomes £40–£99 p.a. (lesser knights)	£45,000	12
Incomes £20–£39 p.a. (esquires)	£29,000	7
Incomes £5–£19 p.a. (lesser gentry and greater yeomen)	£38,000	10
Incomes under £5 p.a. (lesser yeomen and husbandmen)	£100,000	26

Source: C. S. L. Davies, *Peace, Print and Protestantism*, Paladin, 1977, p. 63, revising statistics by Gray and Cooper. Davies points out that the correlations of income with social status (in brackets) are inexact, since 'many had incomes above their social status'.

earlier periods, systematic information on the distribution of wealth does not survive. The income of the bishops, and indeed of the entire clergy, can be known for 1535 from the *Valor Ecclesiasticus*, but no similar survey was undertaken later in the century. For laymen, the incomparable records of the subsidy taxes, reorganised on a realistic basis in 1512, cease to give a comprehensive picture after 1547. More and more Englishmen were exempted from payment, and totals were allocated by counties rather than assessed on true estimates of individual wealth. In consequence little can be deduced from tax assessments about the distribution of wealth in the later sixteenth and early seventeenth centuries.

Accounts, surveys and rentals can be pressed into service to estimate the income of a merchant or a landowner. Yet although merchants had long adopted double-entry bookkeeping, most great landowners still kept to the thirteenth-century charge and discharge method, designed to calculate the sums owed by the accountant to the lord, not a true balance of income and expenditure. In the 1570s Sir Nicholas Bacon wrote to his son-in-law explaining in very basic terms how to list his debts and credits and to strike a balance, in terms that make it clear that such a practice was not very familiar. It is difficult to derive such balances from contemporary accounts, or to decide what elements constituted gross and net income, and estimates from the same accounts can differ considerably. For example, the annual income of the Brudenells of Deene Park (Northants) in 1606 has been calculated by Stone at £1,946 but by Finch at £2,800, a difference of over 40 per cent.

For a wider cross-section of the population, wills, and the probate inventories which accompanied them, are of considerable assistance. Although they do not cover the whole population, they include a remarkably wide range; about 8 per cent of surviving inventories of the period 1540–1640 relate to labourers. Indeed, testamentary evidence for some areas may be biased not towards the wealthy (as is commonly assumed) but towards the relatively poor. Spufford has made the startling demonstration that, in one Cambridgeshire village at least, smallholders and the landless were much more likely to leave a will than freeholders and the larger tenants. Still, the total numbers leaving a surviving will are much higher than for any earlier period. In one Nottinghamshire parish just over a quarter of those who died between 1572 and 1600 left a will, and the proportion would have been higher still if only adult males had been considered. On the other hand, inventories give the total capital value of estates at the time of death, a measurement which cannot be directly compared with annual income. The purchase price of land was usually reckoned at from 20 to 30 times its annual rent, but it would be too crude to divide all capital figures by 20 or 30 to arrive at the equivalent in terms of yearly income, especially as inventories took no account of houses and lands, but only movable goods.

Nevertheless, such pitfalls, which apply to almost all sixteenth-century statistics, are no excuse for not making an attempt to outline the contours of wealth and poverty. A combination of accounts and literary evidence may not meet the standards of modern social surveys and government statistics, but it is a great deal better than merely pointing out that there were extremes of wealth and poverty, or simply repeating contemporary assertions – contradictory and impossible to prove – that the gap between rich and poor was narrowing or widening. Provided that the continuous inflation of the time is remembered, comparisons of figures of income and expenditure at least give reliable orders of magnitude.

2

Distribution of wealth can be estimated from the Subsidy Rolls of 1514–15, 1523–27 and 1543–47, and the even more comprehensive loan of 1522. These sources have been analysed in some detail, and the findings usefully summarised in the preceding volume in this series.[3] It is unfortunate that the nationwide studies relate to the first half of Henry's reign, and that only R. B. Smith's study of Subsidy Rolls for the West Riding of Yorkshire in 1545–46 falls close to the period considered here. Yet the overall pattern is not likely to have changed greatly by the later sixteenth century.

Wealth in Tudor England was distributed very unequally, both geographically and socially (Fig. 5). The country was divided sharply between a prosperous South-east and a poor North-west, a pattern that held good until the industries of the West Midlands and the North developed in the late seventeenth and eighteenth centuries. Taking taxable wealth per acre to allow for varying county size, Middlesex was easily the richest shire in both 1515 and 1522, thanks largely to the presence of London. If London is excluded, Middlesex still ranked first in 1515, Kent in 1522. The other counties with high assessments at both dates were Essex, Suffolk, Berkshire, Huntingdonshire and Somerset. Altogether, the richer areas comprised the Home Counties, East Anglia and the inner West Country (Somerset, Gloucestershire and Wiltshire), those regions with the greatest urbanisation, the most prosperous agriculture and the most flourishing cloth industry. The North and West Midland counties were the

Fig. 5   Taxable wealth in England 1524–25

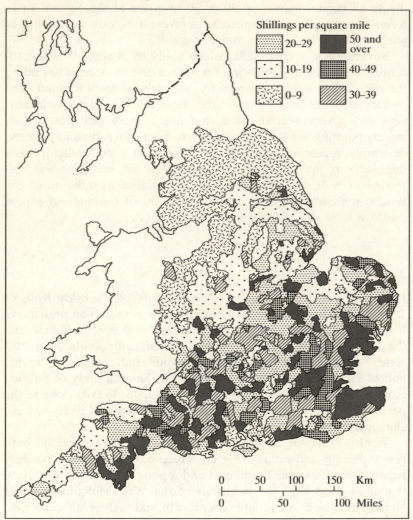

Shillings per square mile

20–29

10–19

0–9

50 and over

40–49

30–39

0   50   100   150   Km

0   50   100   Miles

Source: John Sheail

poorest assessed, together with Lancashire and Yorkshire, while the four Scottish Border counties, which were exempt from the taxes, were probably poorer still.

London was already far and away the wealthiest urban centre. It paid nearly as much to the 1522 loan as Norfolk and Suffolk combined, representing about one-eighth of the lay wealth of the whole country, and was taxed in 1523–27 ten times as much as the next richest town, Norwich. If a line is drawn from the Humber to the Severn, the area south-east of it includes all the twenty richest counties and all the twenty-five richest towns apart from York and Hereford. It was still an England where now-forgotten ports were of more consequence than new industrial centres; Cromer and Dunwich both paid more in taxes than Birmingham. It was also a pattern which must have endured throughout the later Tudor period, though there are no satisfactory tax assessments to prove it. The ranking of counties by order of taxable wealth was almost exactly the same in 1636–49 as in 1515. And the wage assessments, regularly drawn up after 1563, confirm the point. An agricultural bailiff in Kent in 1563 was allowed 50*s* a year, 67 per cent more than the 30*s* allowed in the York area.

The Henrician tax records also demonstrate a concave pyramid of wealth distribution in every county, ranging from a few very wealthy taxpayers to a large mass assessed at the minimum and an even larger group exempt altogether. Of some 5,000 West Riding taxpayers in 1546, nearly half (46.3%) were assessed in the minimum category of between £5 and £9 in goods; and Smith has estimated that a further 10,000 were exempt, having been assessed the previous year to have goods worth less than £5. In the adjacent city of York in that same year of 1546, only 355 taxpayers were assessed out of a total population of perhaps 8,000. Of those assessed on goods, the richest 23 per cent owned 55 per cent of the taxable wealth.

The lay peers were still, as a group, the richest subjects in the kingdom though they did not constitute a majority among the great landowners. Stone, who has analysed them in rich and satisfying detail, estimates their mean income at £2,200 a year net (£2,380 gross) in 1559 and £3,020 net (£3,360 gross) in 1602, though the figures involve some arbitrary assumptions and intelligent guesswork. The averages, as always, conceal wide variations. In 1559 the six poorest peers had gross annual rentals (not total income) of under £500, while the richest was the fourth duke of Norfolk with £6,000 in rent alone, besides extensive profits from commerce, industry and direct farming.

The peers, never a financially homogeneous group, overlapped with the richer gentry, as did the poorer gentlemen with the richer yeomen. One Northamptonshire gentleman, Sir Thomas Tresham, was worth about £3,500 a year by 1590, while Sir Robert Spencer of Althorp, when created Baron Spencer in 1603, enjoyed at least £6,500 a year. No systematic figures have yet been collected for the wealth of Elizabethan gentry, but their grandsons of Charles I's reign are better known. In the 1640s, when the peers' mean net income was, according to Stone, over £5,000 a year, that of the average Kentish gentleman was under £700, while most Yorkshire gentry enjoyed less than £500. Again, as with the peers, the range concealed by the averages was wide. Two Yorkshire gentlemen in 1642 received over £4,000 a year, but 238 (a third of the total) less than £100 each.

The wide variations in income of nobles and gentry reflected mainly the size of their landed estates, for 'when all is said and done, the foundation of aristocratic wealth, power, and honour rested on the land'. Long-term economic prosperity depended on landed wealth, either inherited or acquired by marriage, although government office and business ventures might enlarge landowners' incomes for short periods sufficiently to enable them to buy more land. The possession of productive farmland was particularly crucial between the 1520s and the 1640s, when food prices were generally rising ahead of other prices and wages. Anyone who could produce more than enough food for his own needs could therefore profit from the difference, while the great landowners could benefit either by large-scale demesne farming or by raising rents so as to extract some of the surplus wealth earned by their tenants. Profit from land was therefore almost assured to the enterprising landlord; and though it might not always be the best financial investment from a rational economic point of view, purchase of land was generally the preferred way of investing capital, and was the most socially acceptable. 'Northeren thoughtes . . . measures honnor by the acre', mused the third earl of Cumberland as his embarrassments forced him to sell ancestral estates, and it was not only ancient northern families who thought so. Burghley warned his son that 'that gentleman, who sells an acre of land, sells an ounce of credit'.[4]

Other sources of income were generally modest. Stone suggests that very few peers made large profits from industry or commerce, although there was no bar to their participation in business, and many did invest considerable sums. He also calculates that the entire peerage in 1559 enjoyed only £15,000 from profits of office, as against £135,000 from land, though his estimates for the rewards of office and court favour are minimum ones and may well understate the true position. A fortunate few did profit sufficiently to make their families' fortunes. Burghley, for example, died the wealthy owner of broad estates and three great houses. Besides passing on a rich inheritance to his elder son, he was able to leave his younger son Robert estates worth about £1,800 a year; and Robert in turn prospered so much from office that he died in 1612 worth perhaps £25,000 a year. But against the Cecils can be set the third earl of Huntingdon, who drew heavily on his large landed inheritance during twenty-three years' devoted (and underpaid) service as Elizabeth's viceroy in the North. However, the real importance of court office and royal favour for many nobles and gentry was less the direct financial rewards than the opportunity to be in the right place at the right time to secure, say, a grant of monastic land or a lucrative wardship; and there is no denying that many of the richest landowners, while not 'new men', were those who had been able to use court opportunities to add substantially to their landed inheritance. Of the twenty-three peers with rentals of over £2,000 a year in 1559, eleven were members of the new aristocracy ennobled or enriched by Henry VIII, and endowed largely from monastic lands. They included some of the greatest families of Tudor England, like the Manners, Pagets, Paulets, Russells, Seymours and Wriothesleys, all the beneficiaries of a lavish period of royal giving between 1536 and 1552. There was nothing like it under the more cautious Mary and Elizabeth.

Altogether the amount of wealth transferred from churchmen to laymen during and after the Reformation was enormous. The monastic houses, Youings suggests, had in 1535 enjoyed a gross annual income of nearly £200,000, probably between one-fifth and one-quarter of the total landed wealth of the kingdom.[5] All was surrendered to the king between 1536 and 1540, and most was then sold fairly rapidly, over half by Henry himself and a quarter by Edward and Mary, leaving under 25 per cent in Crown ownership by 1558. It was the largest, but far from the only, spoliation of Church property. In 1548 Edward's government suppressed some 2,400 chantries and chapels, 90 colleges and 110 hospitals, and again sold most of the properties fairly rapidly. In this case their values were admittedly small, perhaps only a fifth as much as the monasteries. And thirdly, between 1536 and 1603 the Crown forced a series of agreements on the bishops, by which desirable manors were exchanged for less attractive properties, or for rectories and tithes, while other episcopal manors were compulsorily leased to courtiers and Crown creditors.

The total number of manors held by English and Welsh bishops was reduced from 642 in 1535 to 591 at the death of Henry and 450 at the death of Edward. Mary managed to restore their holdings to 571 by 1558, but Elizabeth steadily eroded them again, and they stood at only 452 at her death. Altogether, then, they lost almost 30 per cent of their manors between 1535 and 1603, and over the same period at least 67 of the 177 episcopal palaces were granted away or were almost permanently leased out. Admittedly manorial holdings do not measure fairly the decline in bishops' incomes, because they were granted numerous tithes and rectories in exchange for some manors; but these 'spiritual' revenues were not so amenable to increases in line with inflation as were landed rents.

Consequently, after a sharp fall in mid-century, the *nominal* income of most late Elizabethan bishops was very little different from that of their Henrician predecessors. Ely enjoyed £2,300 in 1535 and £2,200 in 1596; York received £2,000 or so in 1535 and £1,800 in 1601. Even at Bath and Wells, where the energetic Bishop Still exploited his estates, raised rents and increased his income from the Mendip lead mines, the recovery did not take the bishop's nominal income back to its pre-Reformation level. The figures for the bishops as a whole were:

	Temporalities	Spiritualities	Total
Jan. 1547	£24,900	£5,100	£30,000
Mar. 1603	£17,200	£9,800	£27,000

Thus there was a considerable decline in the bishops' *real* incomes when inflation is taken into account; and a larger proportion of that smaller income consisted of rectories and tithes, which 'could never provide the prelates with that command over man and acres that had been so integral a part of their old power'.[6]

If Elizabeth did not sell large blocks of monastic lands to her ministers and courtiers, she did allow them to enrich themselves by securing long leases of episcopal lands, or even by compelling bishops to part with lands in perpetuity. Sir Christopher Hatton forced the bishop of Ely to part with his London mansion (Ely Place, Holborn), while Raleigh seized the plum manor of Sherborne from the bishop of Salisbury by a squalid piece of bullying. And the great used their powers of patronage to benefit their dependants. The queen procured for Leicester a long lease of the bishop of Durham's coalmines of Whickham and Gateshead, and Leicester assigned the lease to his servant Thomas Sutton. It was the profits of the mines that made Sutton's fortune; he died one of the richest commoners in England, with estates worth £5,000 a year, leaving some of his wealth to found a school and hospital in the London Charterhouse.

With some nobles, gentry and bishops, it is possible to glimpse their pattern of expenditure as well as income. Matthew Parker, archbishop of Canterbury from 1559 to 1575, had an annual income of £3,428, of which of £2,400 went in maintaining his household and in charities. The remaining £1,028 a year went on building, furnishing, plate, books, travel, litigation, and on special expenses like marriage portions for his nieces, entertaining the queen, and generous benefactions to Cambridge University. The expenditure of a lay peer like Henry, earl of Arundel, whose accounts survive for the year

1573–74, was similar except for the absence of gifts to charity. He spent £2,952 out of £3,899 on maintaining his family and household, and of the remaining £947 most went on estate management, lawsuits, plate and jewels.

The profits of trade allowed some merchants and financiers to amass incomes to rival those of the gentry, and, indeed, often to use those profits to buy themselves landed estates. Sir Richard Gresham (d. 1549), the wealthiest London merchant of his time, bought extensive monastic estates including Fountains in Yorkshire, owned three country seats, and died worth £800 a year in lands. His son Sir Thomas (d. 1579), financial agent to the last three Tudors, was able to leave his widow an annual income of nearly £2,400, besides large charitable benefactions. The Greshams were, of course, exceptional. Of 1,581 freemen whose inventories were registered in the London Court of Orphans between 1586 and 1614, only one left an estate of over £30,000 and only 252 (16%) of over £1,000, while the majority were worth under £500. These figures, admittedly, relate to all freemen, craftsmen as well as merchants. Jordan puts the average (median) estate of the merchants of Elizabethan London at £7,780 and of Bristol merchants at £1,921, while Hoskins suggests a comparable figure of £1,913 for Exeter merchants. All of these figures relate to the capital value of personal estates, excluding real property, and cannot properly be compared to figures for annual income. But one not exceptionally wealthy Merchant Adventurer whose accounts have survived, John Isham of London, reckoned to have made £1,435 profit in only thirty months of trading between 1560 and 1562.

Lawyers, like merchants, had the opportunity to make money rapidly if they were sufficiently fortunate or ruthless. 'Now all the wealth of the land dooth flow unto our common lawiers', lamented Harrison in 1587, 'of whome, some one having practised little above thirteene or fourteene yeares is able to buie a purchase of so manie 1000 pounds.'[7] Sir Nicholas Bacon and Sir Edward Coke both made fortunes from the law with which they were able to buy large estates, though there were many more struggling lawyers than the few dazzling cases of success on which envious contemporaries commented. And legal fortunes, like mercantile, could vanish as quickly as they were made. Francis Bacon, though the son of Sir Nicholas, inherited little from his father, and amassed his own fortune more or less from scratch.

The parish clergy, of whom Harrison was one, were in general the humblest of the professions in terms of living standards. Nevertheless those who enjoyed the full tithes of their parish, and who actively farmed their glebe land, could prosper in an age of rising food prices, and there is no evidence that the parish clergy as a whole suffered a fall in living standards in the second half of the century. In one respect at least they were better off in real terms, for although ecclesiastical taxation was increased under Henry VIII and Edward VI, it continued to be collected on the valuations of livings in the *Valor* of 1535, so that by the end of the century the clergy were paying taxes on very antiquated assessments of their income.

Probate inventories provide the best source for the wealth and living standards of most of the population except for the very poor. One valuable collection, published in full, includes 259 inventories for the diocese of Oxford dated between 1550 and 1590. The largest personal estate included was that of a gentlewoman (£591 in 1585), followed by a yeoman of Witney (£408 in 1583). Most, however, were inventories of husbandmen, craftsmen and even a few labourers. Their distribution by value of estate for 1570–90, for which a sufficient sample survives, gives a good idea of normal levels of wealth, and can be compared to a sample for the city of Worcester (Table 4.2).

Table 4.2   Value of personal estates as a percentage of total inventories

	Oxfordshire		City of Worcester	
	Husband-men	Craftsmen and tradesmen	Labourers	all inventories
(a) 1570–80				
Over £100	4	—	—	15
£40–£100	36	13	—	15
£10–£40	48	33	—	35
Under £10	12	53	100	35
(b) 1580–90				
Over £100	5	—	—	10
£40–£100	32	18	—	19
£10–£40	43	39	—	40
Under £10	20	43	100	30

Sources: *Household and Farm Inventories in Oxfordshire, 1550–1590*, ed. M. A. Havinden, Historical Manuscripts Commission, 1966, p. 12; A. D. Dyer, *The City of Worcester in the Sixteenth Century*, Leicester U. P. 1973, p. 159.

It is clear that the Oxfordshire husbandmen had larger estates than craftsmen and tradesmen, but some of the latter lived in villages or small market towns; the sample from Worcester, a large county town, reveals a different pattern. It is also likely that inventories suggest a misleading contrast between the living conditions of farmers and townsmen, inasmuch as tradesmen and craftsmen had no farm stock to swell the value of their personal estate, their wealth lying mainly in loans and household goods. Thomas Mayho, a Banbury shoemaker, had a personal estate of only £27, but he lived in a comfortably furnished seven-room house equivalent to that of many yeomen farmers.

With labourers the level is approached at which wills (and therefore inventories) were not made. By law those with a personal estate of under £5 had no need to leave a will, but many nevertheless did so (most of the Oxfordshire labourers' inventories totalled less than £5). Like the gentry and yeomanry – and every other social group – the labourers of the Home Counties and the South-east were more prosperous than those of the North and West. Hertfordshire labourers leaving inventories in the period 1560–1600 were worth on average £7 in goods, but in the lowlands of northern England as little as £2 10s 0d. A Staffordshire labourer, Richard Veredy, was 'a very poor man and having a wife and seven children' who depended for most of his income on a single horse, worth 50s, which he hired out by the day. A Worcester labourer, John Warde, who died in 1608, owned nothing but his clothes and 'working tooles' (not specified), and a few sticks of furniture and kitchen equipment, valued by his neighbours at £2 17s 10d. And, of course, even men like Warde were by no means the poorest in the kingdom. Those too poor to leave inventories, those living in bare one-roomed hovels or without homes at all, are even more shadowy. Shakespeare drew the collective portrait of a nameless multitude in Christopher Sly, who had 'no more doublets then backs, no more stockings then legs, nor more shooes then feet – nay, sometime more feete then shooes, or such shooes as my toes looke through the over-leather'.

3

If many Englishmen prospered in the later sixteenth century, they owed their good fortune in part to the low incidence of taxation and to the poverty of the Crown, or to put it another way, to the small size of the public sector. Henry VII had, by a shrewd combination of increasing his permanent sources of revenue and avoiding wars, freed himself from financial embarrassment, but none of his descendants was so fortunate. Henry VIII had engaged in extravagance and in largely futile wars at a time when the cost of war was rising rapidly. Edward, Mary and Elizabeth were generally more prudent, but inflation and the rising cost of war prevented them from ever obtaining financial security. Had Henry VIII retained the monastic lands, their position might have been very different. As it was, he spent over £2 million on war and defence in his last eight years, twice the total yield of taxes and loans, and he had to sell two-thirds of his monastic gains for about £800,000, and to risk the health of the economy by debasing the coinage from 1544.

The traditional or 'ordinary' Crown revenue, composed mainly of customs receipts and landed income, was declining by mid-century through the impact of inflation. Rents on Crown estates were not generally raised in line with rising costs, and the customs revenue declined as rates remained static and mismanagement increased. The ordinary royal revenue was estimated at only £170,000 a year in 1551, in comparison with over £3 million spent on war and defence from 1539 to 1552, and a total royal debt of £235,000 in 1552. In such circumstances the only possible short-term measures were the contracting of loans, the sale of lands, or taxation: and even parliamentary taxation, between 1547 and 1551, raised only about £300,000.

Fortunately both Northumberland and Mary I kept the realm generally at peace and managed, with the aid of Lord Treasurer Winchester, to reduce expenditure and to increase income. In particular, Winchester's new book of rates (May 1558) imposed more realistic customs duties and on a wider range of goods. Total yield from customs rose from £29,000 in 1556–57 to £83,000 in 1558–59. With this, and increased income from Crown lands (about £88,000 a year by 1559), ordinary revenue in Elizabeth's first decade approached £200,000 a year; parliamentary taxation, and sales of lands, boosted the total to about £265,000. It was still inadequate for the 'extraordinary' expense of war – wars in Scotland and France absorbed £750,000 between 1558 and 1563 – but it more than sufficed for peacetime.

It is true that Elizabeth neither raised customs duties to keep step with inflation, nor increased rents sufficiently on Crown lands. However, by a combination of remaining at peace, exploiting miscellaneous sources of revenue, and keeping down expenses, she became free of debt in 1574 for the first time in her reign. As the chancellor of the exchequer, Sir Walter Mildmay, told the parliament of 1576, the queen had 'most carefully and providently delivered this kingdome from a greate and weighty debt . . . begonn fowre yeres at the least before the death of King Henry the viii[th] and not cleired untill within theis two yeres . . . a cancre able to eate upp not only private men and their patrimonyes . . . but also princes and their estates'.[8] And by 1584 the Crown enjoyed an accumulated credit balance of £300,000.

Increasingly, however, 'extraordinary' revenues voted by parliament were becoming a more important element in Crown finances, so laying the queen open to greater dependence on the House of

Commons. Hitherto parliamentary taxes had been usually voted for war, but Elizabeth regularly levied taxes in peacetime, and of course she became more heavily dependent still on parliamentary grants after war with Spain broke out in 1585. 'Parliament's control over direct taxation thus increased in importance after 1558 as the Crown became more dependent upon that source of revenue.'[9]

In the last twelve years of her reign, Elizabeth's ordinary income was about £300,000 yearly. Parliamentary taxes raised £135,000, sales of Crown lands £40,000, and prizes taken at sea some £15,000, making an annual average of almost £500,000. However, the war cost about £3.5 million, half of which had to be met by parliamentary taxes or by 'benevolences' and forced loans. The balance was largely met by living on capital, by selling lands and by unpopular devices like purveyance (the requisitioning of goods and transport below market prices), ship money, and the sale of monopolies and privileges. In the circumstances the queen did well to borrow less than half as much money in the second half of her reign as in the first, and to die no more than £350,000 in debt.

Elizabeth has often been blamed for failing to put royal finances on a sound basis. Her policy towards royal borrowing, and towards raising revenue from lands, can only be described as haphazard. She allowed the real revenue from customs and royal lands to fall, partly it would seem through administrative inertia, and partly perhaps in a conscious effort not to alienate merchants and royal tenants. In some cases she granted leases of Crown lands in reversion to her servants to increase their income without raising their salaries. For she failed to pay her officials adequate salaries which kept pace with inflation, often tacitly allowing them to make up the difference with gifts, favours and bribes. She was unable to keep parliamentary taxation at a realistic level: already by 1559 peers' tax assessments, for example, represented only a half or less of their annual rentals, and as the reign wore on assessments became still smaller in real terms.

Chancellor Mildmay reminded the parliament of 1585 that despite 'the costlynes of the warrs, and the greate increase of prices of all things in this age', tax assessments were derisory. 'If I should tell you how meanely the greate possessions in the countrey, and the best aldermen and citizens of London, and the ritch men of the realme are rated, you would marvell at yt. . . .' Sir John Fortescue told the Commons in 1593 that subsidies were worth less than half what they had been under Henry VIII, and Sir Robert Cecil complained that subsidy yields were very small and 'imposed for the most part upon the meaner sort of her Majestie's subjects'. Raleigh admitted in the parliament of 1601 that ' a poor man pays as much as a rich' because 'our estates that be thirty pound or forty pound in the Queen's Books, are not the hundred[th] part of our wealth'.[10] However, the assessments were in the hands of the gentry, many of whom served the Crown as unpaid justices, and it would have been unwise to press them too hard. England remained, until the civil wars, an undertaxed country, whose richer subjects demanded order and security while being unwilling to pay adequately for it.

4

The great inflation of the sixteenth century did not increase all incomes equally, and the Crown was not the only sufferer. In general, landlords and tenants prospered as food prices outstripped other prices, although the exact distribution of the surplus between lord and tenant varied greatly with the conditions of tenancies and leases, while the landless and the wage labourers may have fallen behind. Very few people, at least in the countryside, were without at least a smallholding or common rights to cushion them against rising food prices, but the rising standards of living clearly evident among many sections of the community did not benefit everyone.

Such rising standards were attested by almost all contemporaries. Old men in Essex in the 1560s or 1570s told Harrison that they could remember such poverty 'that a man should hardlie find foure peeces of pewter . . . in a good farmer's house', the rest of his tableware being wooden platters; 'and yet for all this frugalitie . . . they were scarse able to live and paie their rents . . . without selling of a cow, or a horsse, or more'. Yet now, observed Harrison, a typical farmer or husbandman had a good reserve of cash, 'beside a faire garnish of pewter on his cupbord . . . , three or foure featherbeds, so manie coverlids and carpets of tapistrie, a silver salt, a bowle for wine . . . and a dozzen of spoones to furnish up the sute'.

He also attested that the previous generation had seen two other major improvements in living standards in his area, a 'multitude of chimnies latelie erected' and a 'great amendment of lodging', meaning comfortable beds instead of straw pallets. It is a classic paean of praise for increasing rural prosperity, though the improvements in lodging were qualified in 1587 as being widespread but not 'generall' even in his own village of Radwinter. The old straw pallets, he also added in 1587, were 'not verie much amended as yet in some parts of Bedfordshire, and elsewhere further off from our southerne parts' – a severe qualification often ignored when the passage is quoted as evidence of general improvements throughout England in the

1570s.[11] On the other hand, the chimneys which had only just become common in his village had long been widespread in the towns and on the larger rural mansions.

Harrison was, however, concerned not to claim too much. Before long, improved housing standards were evident in counties much further off from his 'southern parts', and were spreading well down the social scale. William Smith, writing of Cheshire around 1585, remarked that

in building and furniture of their howses (till of late yeares) they used the old maner of the Saxons. For they had their fyer in the middest of the howse against a hob of clay, and their oxen also under the same rouff. But within these 40 yeares it is altogether altred, so that they have builded chemnies, and furnished other partes of their howses accordingly.

And Carew, writing of Cornwall at the same period, could remember when most husbandmen's houses had

walles of earth, low thatched roofes, few partitions, no planchings or glasse windowes, and scarcely any chimnies, other than a hole in the wall to let out the smoke: their bed, straw and a blanket. . . . To conclude, a mazer and a panne or two, comprised all their substance: but now most of these fashions are universally banished, and the Cornish husbandman conformethe himself with a better supplied civilitie to the Easterne patterne . . .[12]

All these improvements can be attested from probate inventories as well as from surviving houses. It was in the later sixteenth century that many middling folk acquired for the first time chimneys and window glass, both of which had previously been restricted to the very wealthy. At the same time houses were also made more snug by window curtains and by coverings for the walls – tapestries or wainscot panelling for the rich, and the cheaper painted cloths as an alternative. Many modest houses were enlarged by the insertion of floors and staircases, especially by the division of old open halls into two floors, and extra space was also created by inserting an attic storey into the roof. Such innovations may commonly have appeared first in towns before spreading to the countryside. Ten of the eleven Oxfordshire inventories before 1590 which mentioned window glass, and nine of the ten which listed wainscot panelling, were of townsfolk. At Wigston Magna, probably a fairly typical Midland village, upper floors were not commonly inserted until the 1570s and 1580s, and no window glass was listed in any inventory before 1583.

At a higher social level, much of the increased prosperity of the landowning classes was poured into building. Ancestral houses were modernised and enlarged, or replaced by mansions of more up-to-date design and more comfort and magnificence. Camden, looking back at the events of 1574, noted that costly building had become fashionable about that time. 'For now more houses of noblemen and private citizens – remarkable for their elegance, size and splendour – began to arise throughout England than in any previous age.' He was echoed by Harrison: 'If ever curious building did florish in England, it is in these our dayes.'[13] They were right: a count of 151 Hertfordshire country houses shows that 78 were first built in the sixteenth century, chiefly between 1540 and 1580, and a survey of four widely spread counties (Derbyshire, Essex, Shropshire and Somerset) suggests that more new country houses were built between 1570 and 1620 than in any later half-century. The tally ranged from the small country houses of the lesser gentry through such large houses as Loseley (Surrey) (which cost its builder £1,600 in the 1560s) and Montacute (Somerset) for the leading gentry and lawyers, to the 'prodigy houses' of the great, the cost of which escalated even faster than the price rise. Longleat cost £8,000 in the 1570s, but Hatfield cost Sir Robert Cecil £40,000 in 1607–12.

The one great exception was Robert, earl of Leicester, who chose to build equally lavishly but within an old fortress, allegedly spending £60,000 on modernising Kenilworth Castle, and heavily fortifying it. Here, although the new apartments were light and comfortable, defence for the last time took precedence over comfort. Leicester's Kenilworth, rather than Buckingham's Thornbury, was surely the last castle of an over mighty subject in England.[14]

It would be wrong to suggest that such buildings were normal, even in that age. Many nobles and gentlemen continued to live in their ancestral castles and mansions, modernising and improving them but not replacing them. The Manners were content to remain in the delectable fortified Haddon Hall, adding only a long gallery and some larger windows, while the Sidneys enlarged Penshurst by an extra wing but little else. Ben Jonson's *To Penshurst*, in praise of the Sidneys and their house, is an implied criticism of the architecture and the social cost of the prodigy houses:

> Thou art not, PENSHURST, built to envious show,
>   Of touch, or marble; nor canst boast a row
> Of polish'd pillars, or a roofe of gold:
>   Thou hast no lantherne, whereof tales are told;
> Or stayre, or courts; but stand'st an ancient pile,
>   And these grudg'd at, art reverenc'd the while.
>
> And though thy walls be of the countrey stone,
>   They are rear'd with no mans ruine, no mans grone . . .

Nevertheless, it was 'envious show' which set the standards by which contemporaries judged. This was especially true of Burghley's Theobalds, 'the most important architectural adventure of the whole of Elizabeth's reign', and Hatton's Holdenby House, which was called by Sir Thomas Heneage 'altogether even the best house that hath been built in this age'. It is therefore doubly unfortunate that both were destroyed during the Commonwealth.

The lesser gentry, and the yeomen farmers, were also rebuilding on a unprecedented scale, as can be seen from the hundreds of small manor houses and large farmhouses of the reigns of Elizabeth and James I that still adorn nearly every part of England except the Scottish Border counties. Built of stone, timber or occasionally of brick, with simple square-headed mullioned windows, they are often difficult to date, and many 'Elizabethan' houses turn out on inspection to be of early Stuart or even, in conservative areas, of later Stuart date. Hoskins, who first drew attention to a 'Great Rebuilding' in the countryside, suggested that the years of greatest activity in building might be put between 1575 and 1625 from dated examples. Barley, following up his pioneer work in more detail, suggested that the period between 1575 and 1615 saw the first phase of a rural 'housing revolution' that continued until about 1690. Machin has now confirmed this from an impressive sample of 3,345 dated houses in 17 English counties. The numbers of dated houses increased in every decade from the 1550s to the 1690s, broken only by temporary falls in the 1590s and 1640s. Given that, other things being equal, the proportion of houses surviving from any century will decrease the further one goes back in time, Machin is largely confirming Hoskins's original perception; and it seems agreed on all sides that a building boom on an unprecedented scale began in Elizabeth's reign. Nor was it only a rural 'great rebuilding'; the evidence for it in many towns is equally striking.

Yet completely new or rebuilt houses were never the norm. For every new house several were extended or modernised; for every enlarged house several were more comfortably furnished while the fabric was left intact. As always, most disposable income was spent on furniture, clothing, food, drink and fuel, or else saved or invested. The very poor, especially, rented cottages or rooms in the towns, and in the countryside built themselves one-roomed hovels. In Leicestershire and Lincolnshire one-roomed cottages were still common, and in the remoter and hillier areas such hovels must have been the norm. No Tudor observer has left a description of them, but there may have been many like that seen by Plot in Staffordshire about 1680, 'built only of turf in a conical manner, much like the houses of the Indians near the Straights of Magellan', or the Northumbrian cottages which appalled Stukeley, 'mean beyond imagination ... without windows, only one storey'.[15]

At these lowest income levels most expenditure will naturally have been made on basic necessities, although exact information is extremely scarce. Phelps Brown and Hopkins, in constructing a cost-of-living index to measure real wages, assumed that Tudor craftsmen and labourers spent four-fifths of their income on food and drink, one-eighth on clothing and the rest on light and fuel. The proportions may well be of the right order, but they are calculated entirely from budgets of 1795–97 and 1904–13, apart from one example of a priest's household in the 1450s. They take no account of rent, but most poor at least in the towns were lessees and not owners. In 1584 the Privy Council complained that many people had been profiting by building for subdividing houses at Cambridge, 'their rudeness and straitness being only fit to harbour the poorest sort', while in 1596 Chester corporation protested similarly against 'covetous persons' who had built cottages to let to labourers.

Food and drink, as always, absorbed a higher proportion of the expenditure of the poor than of the rich, even though they bought cheaper food or lived on what they produced themselves. Harrison testified (1577) that milk, butter and cheese 'are now reputed as food appertinent onelie to the inferiour sort', while the wealthier ate chiefly meat and fish. Furthermore 'the gentilitie' commonly ate wheaten bread, 'whilest their household and poore neighbours are inforced to content themselves with rie, or barleie, yea, and in time of dearth, with bread made . . . of beans, peason, or otes'. Bread must have been the poor man's staple food, for no other commodity was so thoroughly regulated as to quantity, quality and price, and the years of record grain prices were also years of high mortality. The very poor were naturally vulnerable to starvation; but the great mass of the population, with a diet apparently consisting largely of brown bread, dairy products, roots, vegetables and beer, may have suffered no more from dietary deficiencies than their wealthy neighbours. Thomas suggests that Tudor Englishmen of all social levels suffered from a deficiency of vitamins A and D and from scorbutic diseases, the rich also from gout, stone and dental decay, and the poor from gastric upsets or 'griping in the guts'.[16]

Clothing, like diet, was a sensitive indicator of wealth. Many a poor man or woman had no change of clothing; hence the common bequests of gowns to so many poor people attending funerals. At a more prosperous level, a common bequest in the wills of urban craftsmen and their wives was of 'my workday gown' and 'my holyday gown'. The very rich, once more, might spend huge sums on clothing, the results of which glitter in their portraits. Seven doublets and two cloaks belonging to Leicester were valued by his executors in 1588 at £545. Material, as well as quantity, varied with the money spent on the wardrobe. The luxury fabrics included silk and fine linen; prosperous people wore mainly woollen cloth; leather jerkins and breeches were common among the poor; while the poorest of all relied on cast-off clothing and rags. Leicester's wardrobe may be compared to those of a Worcester barber (1584) whose entire clothing was valued at £1, or to the stock of a shoemaker in the same city (1594). His shop wares included twenty pairs of men's shoes valued at 1s 7d each, fourteen pairs of women's shoes at 1s, and eight pairs of children's shoes at 6d each.

Furniture and domestic goods tell the same story. At York in 1555 seven poor parishes could not meet their tax quotas. Some poor men and women 'were fayne to sell their pott or their panne and other implements, some laied their apparrell to pledge to pay with their taxe; and of certayne vacant howses . . . the collectours had nothing to distrayne but toke of the doores and wyndowes to make up stake with'.[17] The poorest households to figure in inventories boasted only a few sticks of furniture such as benches, a trestle table and a bed. Very many testators well down the social scale, however, owned chairs, featherbeds, carpets, pewter ware, and even silver. Among a large sample of 441 inventories, taken between 1532 and 1601, including many estates of £5 or less, 95 per cent included pewter goods, and two Oxfordshire estates worth under £1 included pewter. It is a striking case of a former luxury which had spread right down the social scale.

Lupold von Wedel, a German visitor in 1584–85, noted that 'many a peasant here keeps greater state and a better table than the nobility in Germany. He must be a poor peasant indeed who does not possess silver-gilt salt cellars, silver cups and spoons.'[18] The picture is consistent with English evidence like Harrison's, since his 'peasant' (*Bauer*) means yeoman or farmer rather than labourer. Thomas Taylor, the prosperous Witney yeoman (1583), had a twenty-five roomed house furnished with tables, chairs, beds, cupboards and books, window glass, wainscot panelling and pewter, and with imported luxuries like 'a Venyce carpitt clothe' and 'three silke quisshens'. At the top of the social scale, the Hardwick Hall inventories of 1601 list a multitude of luxurious furnishings, some of them still in the house today, including looking-glasses, framed portraits, silken bed-hangings, Turkish carpets, tapestries from Brussels, and a quilt of 'India stuff'.

The general impression, then, is of growing wealth from the 1560s to the end of the century, with perhaps a temporary setback in the 1590s. Fulke Greville, arguing the necessity of war taxation in the parliament of 1593, said that 'for the poverty of our country, we have no reason to think it poor, our sumptuousness in apparel, in plate and in all things, argueth our riches'. But was there really a growth in national wealth? Undoubtedly many freeholders and tenant farmers did become wealthier; and comparisons over time reveal men and farms of about the same size but vastly differing personal estates. In Oxfordshire, Thomas Gyll (1587) had possessions worth three times as much as Edward Kempsale (1560), and lived in a much larger house and had many more comforts, although their farms were very similar in size and type. Yet it would be rash to conclude from the comforts and luxuries that all testators were becoming richer. Dyer has calculated that the value of Worcester citizens' inventories, allowing for inflation, did not increase between 1550 and 1620, although their houses were more richly furnished. Like other such calculations it has to rely on using the Phelps Brown–Hopkins index to adjust monetary values for inflation, a method which has been questioned, but his central argument remains important. Growing comforts need not necessarily prove greater wealth, but only a different way of spending that wealth. 'Early in the sixteenth century much money was kept in cash or plate or was invested in loans and real estate, but as the century progressed there seems to have been a drift towards converting this wealth into the paraphernalia of domestic comfort.'[19]

Any surplus wealth accumulated faced its owner with very limited choices. He or she could invest it to produce more wealth or to buy or retain social status: this might mean, for a landowner, buying more land, or for a merchant, ploughing back profits into the business or building cottages to rent. Some money was invested in mining, industry or overseas commerce and exploration. Otherwise, the sensible response in the absence of banks and a stock market was to spend on consumer durables. Some of these, like lavish clothing and furniture, were intended solely for ostentation and enjoyment. Others, especially gold and silver plate, can be regarded as investments, since they could always be melted down into bullion or gold and sent to the royal mints for coining.

One other outlet for expenditure was charity. Rich men were encouraged to give generously to the Church, to the poor, to the founding and endowment of schools and colleges, to the upkeep of bridges and highways and to many other deserving causes. Gentlemen were traditionally expected to distribute open-handed hospitality to the poor, and Edward, earl of Derby (d. 1572) earned praise from the chroniclers for maintaining the tradition: he fed over sixty aged poor twice daily, 'all commers' thrice every week, and an average 2,700 poor every Good Friday. Gradually such indiscriminate largess gave way to more organised and controlled charities, with attempts to solve social problems through trusteeships and the choosing of deserving cases for help.

What is not clear, however, is whether the increased control over charitable giving went hand in hand with more generosity, or whether it became an excuse for hardness of heart. It is an argument as old as the Reformation: many Catholics argued, and some Protestants mournfully conceded, that the 'new light of the Gospel' had not produced the fruits of good works, whereas other Protestants claimed that the Elizabethan age was more generous to the needy than the days of superstition and monkery. Charitable gifts at Chester were enumerated, rather defensively, to 'make our adversaries the papistes to blushe, whoe charge our religeon for a religeon of noe workes or charatye, but for a dead religeon'.[20] The only serious statistical attempt to test the evidence is W. K. Jordan's massive analysis for a ten-county sample over the period 1480–1660, of all testamentary bequests to charity and as many bequests as could be traced made in the donors' lifetimes. If his evidence can be relied on, bequests to the Church diminished sharply after the Reformation, but total charitable giving held up. It can be established that £227,000 was given to charities in the two decades 1541–60, £199,000 in 1561–80, £247,000 in 1581–1600, and then a sharp rise to £634,000 in 1601–20.

However, it is not clear how far, if at all, giving increased in real terms. Jordan deliberately chose to take no account of inflation because of the difficulties of the evidence, but those who have been bold enough to try have produced a very different impression from his 'immense outpouring of generosity'. Thomson has shown, on Jordan's own evidence, that London merchants gave a more generous proportion of their total wealth to charity between 1480 and 1540 (29.42%) than in any other period between 1540 and 1660, while Bittle and Lane have converted Jordan's data to constant prices and have argued that total 'real' charitable giving declined almost continuously from 1510 to 1600 before partially recovering in the early seventeenth century. In defence of Jordan it has to be said, once again, that their method is to relate his figures to the Brown–Hopkins cost-of-living index, a dubious tool which relates *only* to selected prices of foodstuffs, clothing and fuel for which data (often discontinuous) happen to survive. There is no reason to think that it provides an accurate yardstick of the real value of all transactions. Dyer has hit on a probably more reliable approach by comparing the amounts bequeathed to charity by Worcester testators with the total value of their bequests; he finds that money was given to charity on a generous scale in the 1530s, 1540s and 1560s, but that it fell to a miserably low level for the rest of Elizabeth's reign.

Even on Jordan's own figures, which show a peak of giving in 1551–60 not reached again until 1601–10, compared with the best available figures for food prices, real charitable giving must have decreased, rather than increased over the later Tudor period. In any case, the totals for the whole period are quite modest, and Jordan's 'great outpourings' and 'floods of generosity' are grotesque over-statements. Feingold shows that the figures are distorted by a few very rich donors who happened to die childless: in three of Jordan's sample counties, a mere 323 donors over 180 years (1.85% of all donors) contributed 66 per cent of all the benefactions. And Everitt has pointed out for Kent that 'averaged out over the 140,000 people in the county and the 180 years covered by the book, Professor Jordan's total of £251,766 represents an investment in charity of just twopence-halfpenny per head per annum: or perhaps one-half of the daily wages of a Kentish plowboy'.[21]

5

Much charitable giving was directed towards the alleviation of poverty. In part this may have reflected a growing humanitarianism towards social problems, in part a real growth in the numbers of the poor. It is not difficult to find causes to explain such a growth, if growth there was. There is normally a high level of unemployment, underemployment and seasonal unemployment in pre-industrial societies; and to this normal level special causes can be suggested which may have made the problem worse in the later sixteenth century. At one time or another historians have singled out for special blame warfare, inflation, population growth, plagues and famines, enclosures, industrialisation, the dissolution of the monasteries and the decline of great households. They make a formidable list of possible causes of economic dislocation, but some clearly counterbalanced one another and others were certainly not at their most acute in the sixteenth century. For example, if population growth and urbanisation did increase beggary, then plagues and famines, which were socially selective and generally struck hardest at the poor, should have moved in the opposite direction. As for enclosures, the age of wholesale depopulation of villages and hamlets was the four-teenth and fifteenth centuries, and it continued only on a very limited scale after 1520.

Other changes, however, may well have exacerbated the problem of poverty. Many nobles and gentry did gradually reduce the size of their households, whether as a voluntary measure of economy or because of the statutes limiting numbers of retainers. The effect of the dissolutions of religious houses, once a popular scapegoat, has been belittled since Baskerville demonstrated the romantic excesses of earlier historians. Still, his view of the dispossessed clergy as adequately pensioned is too optimistic, and more important still in terms of numbers was the fate of the monastic servants. A small house like Butley Priory (Suffolk) had only twelve canons in 1538, but they were provided for by seventy-two dependants, mainly servants and labourers, and not all would necessarily have been taken on by the purchasers of the priory estates. The numbers conscripted into armed service overseas reached a peak in 1542–46 (when nearly 2% of the adult male population may have been serving) and again in the 1590s, and after every war large numbers of discharged soldiers, often unpaid, unemployed and still in possession of their arms, were a real problem. In 1589 a band of 500 discharged soldiers threatened to loot Bartholomew Fair in London, and had to be dispersed by 2,000 city militia and by the threat of execution. The growth of the cloth industry, with its booms and slumps, caused heavy periodic unemployment, especially in East Anglia. All of these factors may have increased the total numbers of paupers and unemployed from time to time.

The poor, in the sense not merely of those with little wealth but of the destitute, the homeless, the unemployed and the vagabonds, undoubtedly aroused great alarm. 'The most immediate and pressing concern of government . . . for something more than a century (*ca.* 1520–1640)', asserted Jordan with pardonable exaggeration, 'was with the problem of vagrancy.'[22] This was almost exactly the same period studied by Miss Leonard in her still unsuperseded *Early History of English Poor Relief* eighty years ago: a system which developed rapidly between 1514 and 1644 to cope with a growing social problem. Such a chronology invites a close correlation between population growth and the development of poor relief, and some have turned them into cause and effect; the problem, it is argued, was not of course created during the sixteenth century, but it inevitably worsened as population outstripped resources.

As always, it is very difficult to measure the extent of the problem statistically; and what contemporary figures we have cannot be compared unless they relate to the same categories. There was no Booth or Rowntree to attempt any precise measurement of a poverty line, and all that can be safely said is that thoughtful Elizabethans meant by 'the poor' those whose earnings or income were insufficient to support themselves or their families, and even more, those without work. The latter were divided into three broad categories: the 'impotent poor', those physically unable to labour through age or sickness; the able-bodied poor who wanted work but could not find it; and the work-shy, the 'rogues and vagabonds', who were universally regarded as objects for punishment rather than help. Even this threefold scheme represented a sophisticated advance on early Tudor thinking. The Poor Law statutes until 1572 recognised only the impotent poor and the vagabonds, blandly assuming that all able-bodied persons could find work if they tried, and it was only in the last thirty years of the period that the state came to recognise, and try to alleviate, the problems of involuntary unemployment.

Tudor society has been sharply criticised since Tawney for its harsh attitudes towards poverty; but some of the criticism represents a misplaced application of anachronistic standards. Men were torn between Christian teaching on charity and the fear of anarchy and disorder; and their instinctive compromise was often to try to support the impotent but to threaten and punish all able-bodied 'masterless men'. Government, in particular, was terrified of the dangers of able-bodied men without work, especially at times of political crisis, and the whip, the stocks and even the gallows were seen as necessary measures of self-defence by both central and local authorities. Early Tudor legislation, both statutes and municipal by-laws, represents no real advance on the ordinance of 1349, passed in the wake of the Great Pestilence, which had forbidden alms to be given to any able-bodied beggars. It says much for intelligent contemporaries that, despite these traditional fears, they gradually worked out a policy of distinguishing those who could not find work from those who would not, and constructed a Poor Law which endured with little change until 1834. By then its inhumanity was evident; but in the 1590s its creation marked a real and humane advance on what had gone before. The hunger, and consequent crime wave, of the mid-1590s, had produced a more understanding attitude towards crime and poverty among some of the legislators, men like the Surrey MP Sir George More who wrote in January 1597 that it was 'hard in poverty not to sinne'.[23]

It is impossible to assess the total number of vagrants, still less to know whether they were increasing as the century wore on. Tudor 'rogue' literature begins with Awdeley's *Fraternitye of Vacabondes* and Harman's *Caveat,* apparently first published in 1561 and 1566/67 respectively. Both give the impression of a highly organised system of thieving by vagrants, and Harman explicitly dated its rise to 'within these xxx yeres or lytle above'. The organised criminals Awdeley describes as preying on wealthy visitors to London may well have represented a new phenomenon, but wandering bands of homeless beggars were not. Harman himself had spoken with an old man who could remember a band of 280 beggars assembled in a Kentish barn in the 1520s, 'so that it may apere this uncomly company hath had a long continuance'.

As to the total number on the roads, Harman published a careful list of 215 male rogues then at large in Essex, Middlesex, Surrey, Sussex and Kent: 'then let the reader judge what number walkes in other shieres'. Harrison (1577) noted that thieves and idle beggars of both sexes 'amount unto above 10,000 persons, as I have heard reported', while a modern guess allows 'perhaps 20,000 vagrants . . . roaming the Tudor countryside'. Some support might seem to be given to such figures by Edward Hext, a Somerset JP, writing to Burghley in 1596 about the growing problem of violent and work-shy beggars. He spoke of gangs of 40, 60 and even 80 travelling about in his own county, and said that of 'wandryng souldiers and other stout roages of England . . . there ar three or fower hundred in a shere'. This may well have been an informed guess as regards Somerset, but there is no means of knowing how typical a county it was, and 1596 was a year of severe dearth when unemployment was probably well above average. Hext's letter has been over-quoted by cliometric historians anxious for statistics at almost any price; and it gives 'an impression of general disorder that can all too easily be applied to the country at large and to the sixteenth century as a whole'.[24]

The only reliable figures for beggars are the records of arrests for vagrancy, which reflect variations between areas, between years of high and low unemployment, and between zeal and lethargy among the officials responsible. Beier counts 752 vagrants listed as having been arrested in 18 counties between 1569 and 1572 in searches organised by the Privy Council, although Aydelotte noted that at least 568 were arrested in the year 1571 alone, and the figures are in any case minima, since many more must have been arrested who were not formally charged and listed. Forty-seven men and women were caught on only two days in part of Cambridgeshire, but the justices pointed out that the numbers were exceptionally great because Stourbridge Fair was then being held. Only 132 were arrested in the entire county of Essex over 3 years (1564–67), and 130 in the town of Warwick over 7 years (1580–87). Almost 200 were arrested in the spring of 1596 in the North Riding of Yorkshire, but that, like Hext's Somerset example, came at a time of economic crisis. Similarly, of the 651 vagrants expelled from Salisbury between 1598 and 1638, 96 were whipped out in the first year alone; many of them were rural poor driven in by hunger, whereas in normal years the permanent vagabonds predominated. Furthermore, studies of arrested vagrants suggest that contemporaries exaggerated the nature as well as the scale of the problem. Many of those arrested seem genuinely to have been unemployed looking for work. Most were children, teenagers and young adults, and most travelled alone or in twos and threes, certainly not in large gangs. However, the reaction among historians against the Elizabethan fear of the tramp may have gone too far. Analyses of arrested vagrants tell of the occupations they claimed to have or to be going to, but it would be naive to accept uncritically the reasons given by all vagrants for being on the road. And naturally if large organised criminal gangs did exist, they would split up into small groups before entering a town. Hext himself had said that the Somerset vagrants normally went 'by too and three in a companye' although they joined together in larger groups at fairs, markets or alehouses.

The numbers of paupers as a whole are even more difficult to obtain. What reliable statistics do exist come from the larger towns, which often took censuses of the poor, before instituting programmes of relief. The most detailed surviving Elizabethan census was that taken at Norwich in 1570 as a prelude to new policies of poor relief. It numbered 504 men, 831 women and 1,007 children officially classified as in need of assistance, or some 25 per cent of the city's English population. At Worcester in 1556–57 about 20 per cent of the townsfolk were recorded as destitute, and in part of Warwick in 1582 30 per cent. At Sheffield in 1616 conditions were still grimmer. The town's population of 2,207 included 725 begging poor; only 100 householders were rich enough to contribute to poor relief, and 160 householders were not able to, and would be beggared themselves by a fortnight's sickness. On the other hand, an Ipswich census during the crisis year of 1597 lists a more modest proportion of the town's population as poor, probably about 10 per cent.

It is difficult to know whether these figures represent a change from early Tudor times. Hoskins has used the tax returns of the 1520s, especially for Coventry, to suggest that 'fully two-thirds of the urban population . . . lived below or very near the poverty-line'. Phythian-Adams has reconsidered the evidence and concluded that the proportion at subsistence level 'was very much smaller than has been normally assumed', and was rather over 20 per cent even at the peak of a local crisis.[25] This was, as he says, a still horrifying proportion by modern standards, but it also suggests that the actual extent of urban poverty may have been worsening as town populations rose later in the century.

In London there are said to have been 1,000 deserving beggars in 1517 but twelve times as many in 1594; if any credence can be placed on these figures, poverty in the capital was becoming proportionately far more serious, even allowing for the phenomenal increase in its population. In 1582 Recorder Fleetwood reported to Burghley how he had arrested and punished between 200 and 300 rogues in the London area in the space of ten days. And the numbers arrested and sent to Bridewell numbered 69 in 1560–61, 209 in 1578–79 and 555 in 1600–1.

However, there is little evidence for a problem of rural poverty on such a scale, except during the famine crisis of 1596–98. In the Bedfordshire and Essex villages examined by F. G. Emmison, income from the poor-rate always exceeded expenditure, and there was always enough to maintain the genuine poor, at least until the 1590s. What may be suggested as normal in the later Tudor period was that many were certainly desperately poor in all areas, but that except in times of famine or economic depression the rural areas could normally support their indigenous poor, sending on their way paupers and vagrants who tried to come in from elsewhere. Where the system broke down was in the towns, especially in the larger towns and above all in the capital, which mushroomed three or four times in size between 1530 and 1600 and which spread over a patchwork of jurisdictions quite beyond the power of the local authorities to control. What this may have meant is that if the countryside remained free of overwhelming poverty, it was achieved only through exporting its problem to the towns. Fleetwood noted that among his large haul of rogues in 1582 'we had not of London, Westminster nor Southwarke nor yet Middlesex nor Surrey above twelve. . . . The resedew for the most were of Wales, Salop, Chester, Somerset, Barks, Oxforde, and Essex; and that fewe or none of theym had ben abowt London above iij or iiij mownthes.'[26] However, as London grew rapidly it generated its own very large pauper population, and Fleetwood might have found a very different pattern twenty years later. The proportion of vagrants sent to Bridewell who had come from within 10 miles of London Bridge, only a quarter of the total between 1516 and 1566, rose to well over half between 1597 and 1604.

6

The Tudor policy of dealing with poverty and vagrancy was twofold: to punish and deter the vagrants and to relieve the 'deserving' poor. In both cases the older histories concentrate on statutory action, as though new measures were not tried until parliament had legislated, and were then immediately enforced throughout the country. Yet statutes, if a useful barometer of what governments and parliaments thought desirable, are a poor guide to what actually happened. Charitable individuals, justices and town councils did much in advance of national legislation, and indeed often provided the example and inspiration for that legislation: equally, unpopular laws were often not enforced or only reluctantly and partially enforced, despite all the threats and entreaties that the Privy Council could muster.

It was already general practice in the early Tudor period for local authorities to punish vagrants, and if they were not native beggars, to order them back to their home. The act of 1531 merely recognised and regularised the practice when it ordered that every unemployed and masterless man or woman 'able to labour' should be whipped 'till his body be bloody' and then enjoined on oath to return directly to his birthplace or to his previous residence. The act remained in force until 1572, except for one short period when more savage measures were imposed. An act of 1547 imposed two years' slavery for a first conviction for vagrancy, and penalties increasing to slavery for life or to execution. It was, however, virtually a dead letter because the penalties were thought too severe, and three years later it was repealed and the act of 1531 revived.

Twenty years later the pendulum of official opinion swung back again. Increasing fears of disorder in 1569–71 led to a campaign of arrests and whippings instigated by the Privy Council. An unsuccessful bill in 1571 proposed new penalties for vagrants which one MP criticised as 'over sharp and bloody',[27] and the next parliament of 1572 did enact severe penalties (whipping and boring through the ear for a first offence, condemnation as a felon for a second and the death penalty for a third), although it also recognised for the first time a distinction between vagrants and those unable to find work. There is evidence that its penalties were enforced; in Middlesex, for example, 44 vagabonds were sentenced to branding between 1572 and 1575, 8 set to service and 5 sentenced to be hanged. In 1593, however, these savage penalties were again repealed and the whippings of the 1531 act revived. Meanwhile an act of 1576 had authorised the building of houses of correction in every county for punishing and employing recalcitrant beggars.

Finally, in 1598, an act 'for the suppressing of rogues, vagabonds and sturdy beggars' superseded all previous statutes. It made elaborate provision for the definition and punishment of beggars. They could either be whipped and sent home as under the 1531 act, or, if they were incorrigible, the justices had the power to commit them to a gaol or house of correction, to condemn them to banishment from the realm, service in the galleys, or execution. The justices of any county or city were empowered to build houses of correction where the inmates could be set on hard labour. In April 1598 the Privy Council wrote to all sheriffs and justices ordering strict enforcement of this and of the parallel poor relief act, and there is evidence that, at least for a while, the 1598 act was better enforced than some of its predecessors. The Essex JPs, who had paid little attention to the 1576 act, promptly ordered the establishment of twenty-three houses of correction in 1598; and the duke of Stettin was pleased to be 'not molested or accosted by beggars' in London in 1602: 'for in all England they do not suffer any beggars except they be few in number and outside the gates'. William Perkins, the Puritan theologian, was in no doubt that the severity of the 1598 act was justified: 'it is a foul disorder in any commonwealth, that there should be suffered rogues, beggars, vagabonds . . . . And therefore the statute made the last Parliament . . . is an excellent statute, and beeing in substance the very lawe of God, is never to be repealed.'[28]

Towards the impotent poor, and those who begged only for lack of work, the law became gradually more humane. But it would be misleading to begin with the statutes; for there is abundant evidence that the law of poor relief followed in the wake of voluntary and municipal practice, and was never intended to be more than supplementary. (The order of the Essex justices that 'the great grandfather, grandfather, father and sonne upward and downeward in lyneall discent or degree shall releive one an other'[29] reflects the universal assumption that families should look after their own.) The figures of W. K. Jordan, with all necessary qualifications made, remain the only possible source for measuring the amount of individual charitable giving, and it is certainly impressive, given that the figures represent mainly bequests at death and not gifts in the donors' lifetime. Taking the three main categories of bequest categorised by Jordan as 'poor relief' and the two most clearly related categories from his 'social rehabilitation' section, the totals given in each decade, from his sample of ten counties, are as detailed in Table 4.3. Jordan has suggested that altogether only £12,000 was given for poor relief through local rates between 1560 and 1600, as against £174,000 from private charity. The former figure, admittedly, is based only on surviving overseers' accounts, and is probably much too low; but Jordan's general point, that rates were levied on a large scale 'only in periods of acute local distress' and that private giving was much more significant, remains valid.

Charitable giving appears to have moved gradually from indis-

Table 4.3   Charitable bequests, 1541–1610

	Outright relief	Almshouses	Charity general	Work-houses	Sick and hospitals	Total
1541–50	12,997	9,808	366	60	487	23,718
1551–60	21,281	12,625	4,306	327	61,429	99,968
1561–70	16,916	5,380	5,907	205	4,065	32,473
1571–80	26,552	14,111	744	1,363	4,705	47,475
1581–90	30,265	15,676	2,158	3,650	5,414	57,163
1591–1600	31,218	23,602	1,218	867	6,892	63,797
1601–10	51,587	48,158	4,618	1,692	8,801	114,856

Source: W. K. Jordan, *Philanthropy in England, 1480–1660*, Allen & Unwin 1959, pp. 369–371.

criminate almsgiving to special schemes and institutions which might cope more effectively with the problem of poverty. Money to found or endow almshouses, especially, was given much more generously after 1590, although it is possible that much of this effort was to replace almshouses and *maisons dieu* suppressed at the Reformation. Many a town, like Ipswich, Warwick or Tiverton, still possesses fine almshouses of the period; Ipswich was especially fortunate because the losses it suffered at the dissolution were more than made good by the generosity of Henry Tooley, a wealthy merchant of the town. The endowment of workhouses or of stocks of goods for the poor, in contrast, received much less charitable support, but then these were also objects of public expenditure. Overall, however, it has to be said that Jordan's figures for charitable poor relief would show a decline if inflation is allowed for; the shift towards compulsory poor-rates may reflect a recognition of this declining generosity. Trinculo in *The Tempest* averred that 'when they [Englishmen] will not give a doit to relieve a lame begger, they will lay out ten to see a dead Indian'.

The most generous contributors to voluntary poor relief, according to Jordan, were the merchants and tradesmen, who provided over three-quarters of the bequests in the period 1541–60 and nearly two-thirds in 1561–1600. The statistics probably reflect unfairly on rural benefactors, who had perhaps more direct means of charitable giving open to them, but the problem of poverty was certainly worse in the towns. It called forth not merely much giving on an individual basis, but also organised help at a corporate level through the municipalities, well in advance of state action.

Municipal poor relief had already become highly organised in some continental cities in the early sixteenth century. Venice, for example, issued ambitious decrees in 1528–29 organising charity and poor relief, and Ypres issued detailed statutes in 1531 explaining the city's policy on relieving paupers and punishing beggars, statutes which William Marshall translated into English and published in 1535 as a model. London was quick to follow suit. By 1514 begging was confined to licensed beggars; in 1533 the corporation instituted house-to-house collections for the poor, and in 1547 a compulsory poor-rate, both well in advance of national legislation. Between 1546 and 1557 the corporation founded or reorganised a whole series of hospitals – St Bartholomew's and St Thomas's for the sick and impotent, Christ's Hospital for orphans, Bethlehem (Bedlam) for the insane and Bridewell for recalcitrant vagrants. It was part of a coherent scheme which they codified under the persuasion of Bishop Ridley in 1552, who pleaded eloquently that 'Christ . . . hath lain too long abroad . . . without lodging in the streets of London, both hungry, naked and cold'. They recognised and provided for 'nine speciall kinds and sorts of poore people' grouped into three categories – 'the poor by impotency' (orphans, the sick and aged), 'the poor by casualty' (wounded soldiers, decayed householders, etc.) and 'the thriftless poor' (vagabonds, wastrels, prostitutes, etc.). As the corporation explained in 1557, 'there is as great a difference between a poor man and a beggar, as is between a true man and a thief'; and they could boast that 'there is no poor citizen at this day that beggeth his bread but by some mean his poverty is provided for'.[30]

Admittedly, the original ambition to deal with all sick, impotent and vagrants in five hospitals had to be scaled down because of the size of the problem. By the end of the century the five were supporting (or punishing) over 4,000 people a year, but it was not nearly enough in the rapidly growing capital. The corporation had reluctantly to accept that outdoor relief organised at parish level and supported by rates was the only realistic answer. And even the minority who were taken into care were not always looked after: inquiries into the management of Bedlam in 1598 and 1624 revealed corruption and neglect of the insane inmates. Nevertheless, the London scheme was a humane, comprehensive one for which the corporation deserve credit, and it has recently been adjudged 'the greatest experiment in social welfare in Tudor England'.[31]

Other towns were slower to organise poor relief, although some had distinguished licensed beggars (impotent residents) from those to be punished or expelled even in advance of the capital – in Gloucester's case as early as 1504. Compulsory poor-rates, to relieve the poor and prevent them from begging, were instituted at York by 1561, and the sums paid out were periodically raised to prevent erosion by inflation. In 1588, for example, the corporation resolved to pay the aged and infirm poor a 'better allowance then heretofore' of at least 1½*d* a day, 'under whiche some a poore creator [creature] cannot lyve'. The nearest scheme to London's in elaboration was that instituted by Ipswich, which by 1569 included licensing of the poor, compulsory poor-rates, and a municipal hospital combining the functions of a hospital for the elderly, a house of correction for recalcitrant beggars and a school for the young.

The most detailed and successful, however, was the municipal scheme at Norwich. There a scare about vagrants in 1570 prompted a thorough survey of all the poor, distinguishing between long-term residents and those who had entered during the previous ten years. Armed with the results, the city fathers then drew up an elaborate scheme which incorporated the main measures adopted by other towns but which in four respects went beyond them.

Begging of any kind was absolutely forbidden within the city precincts; an all-embracing organisation was provided which dealt adequately with every aspect of poor relief, including the provision of work for the able-bodied; regular funds were provided which were essential for the smooth running of the system; and finally, and perhaps most important of all, the city's system was consistently applied throughout the decade 1570–80, and at least intermittently thereafter.[32]

Throughout the decade, about 850–950 householders consistently paid poor-rates, and between 237 and 410 at any one time were in receipt of relief. No other scheme came near it in originality and comprehensiveness until Salisbury initiated its own major experiment in the 1620s.

The influence of municipal schemes, both continental and native, gradually had its effect on national legislation. Already in 1535 a parliamentary bill was drafted, inspired by the ordinances of Ypres, which would have instituted an ambitious scheme of public works for the able-bodied unemployed, financed by rates and taxes. It did not bear fruit immediately, but an act was passed in 1536 which ordered parish and municipal authorities to collect voluntary alms to maintain the impotent poor and to prevent them from begging. This was plainly an unsatisfactory attempt to will the end without the means; and although the Vagrancy Act of 1547 prescribed weekly collections for the impotent poor, its savage provision of slavery for vagbonds damned the whole statute, which was repealed in 1550. It was followed in 1552 by another act allowing the clergy to put moral pressure on those who would not contribute, and in 1563 by yet another which authorised compulsory collections for the poor as a last resort.

Not until 1572 did a positive and realistic national policy begin to emerge. An act of that year attempted for the first time to provide work for the able-bodied poor, and authorised compulsory poor-rates to support the impotent, to be levied after an assessment of the wealth of all contributors. An act of 1576 strengthened the new policy by ordering every corporate and market town to provide stocks of materials to give work to the able-bodied unemployed so that rogues might 'not have any juste excuse in saying that they cannot get any service or worcke', and the justices in each county were to build houses of correction for those unwilling to work. Finally an act of 1598 instituted the office of overseers of the poor, who were to levy poor-rates and to organise and pay for work for the able-bodied poor. This was the culmination of the Elizabethan Poor Laws – the famous statute of 1601 was merely a re-enactment of that of 1598 with slight alterations – and it was to remain in force until 1834.

The problem of the poor has been considered at some length because it was a major preoccupation of contemporaries, a preoccupation reflected in voluminous statutes, by-laws and accounts. Yet it would be misleading to conclude that it was as serious and growing a problem as reports like Hext's, in crisis years, might suggest. Private philanthropy and municipal charity seem normally to have been sufficient to cope with the worst of the problem, and it was only in years of national or local crisis that legislation had to be activated. Pound suggests that

if the situation was as serious as was alleged by contemporaries and by later historians a state of anarchy would have prevailed in no time at all. It seems far more likely that the towns were adopting a temporary solution to a temporary problem and that this, as well as lack of money, at least partly explains the short-term nature of so many urban schemes. . . . In normal circumstances both poverty and vagrancy were fairly well contained, and to say that either created a dangerous national situation would be to strain the evidence.[33]

Chapter 5

The great inflation

I have sene a cappe for xiiijd, as good as I can get now for ijs.⸱vjd. . . . Then a payer of shooes costethe me xijd. now, that I have in my dayes bought a better for vjd. Then I can get never a horse shodde under xd. or xijd. nowe, wheare I have sene the common price was vjd. . . . yea and viijd. at the moste till now of late.

Sir Thomas Smith (?) *A Discourse of the Common Weal* (1549)[1]

1

Prices, wages and the cost of living were a staple topic of Tudor conversation and literature, giving a curiously contemporary flavour to treatises like the *Discourse*. Englishmen were bemused by an inflation which seemed severe, harmful and unprecedented, and which, they thought, was responsible for many of the social and economic changes they witnessed. The historian may, despite much recent research, be little wiser than they about its ultimate causes, or about which changes can be firmly attributed to it. It is at least possible, however, to quantify and date the inflation fairly closely, and to relate it to the imperfect evidence for changing standards of living.

There have been three periods of rapid inflation in England since the Norman Conquest, separated by long periods when the general price level rose only gently, stagnated or even fell. Food prices doubled or trebled between about 1180 and 1220, and quadrupled or quintupled between the late fifteenth and mid-seventeenth centuries, while prices (measured by the pound's purchasing power) rose about twentyfold between 1913 and 1978. These are only crude generalisations, and in the case of the two earlier periods are based on very limited data, but there can be little doubt about the orders of magnitude. Phelps Brown and Hopkins, surveying selected prices from 1264 to 1954 (Fig. 6), were in no doubt that 'the most marked feature . . . is the extent, and persistence, of the Tudor inflation'[2]. The only objection to that term is its insular connotation, which taken out of context might encourage a search for purely English causes and consequences. In fact the inflation of the sixteenth and early seven-

Fig. 6 Price of a composite unit of consumables in southern England, 1264–1954

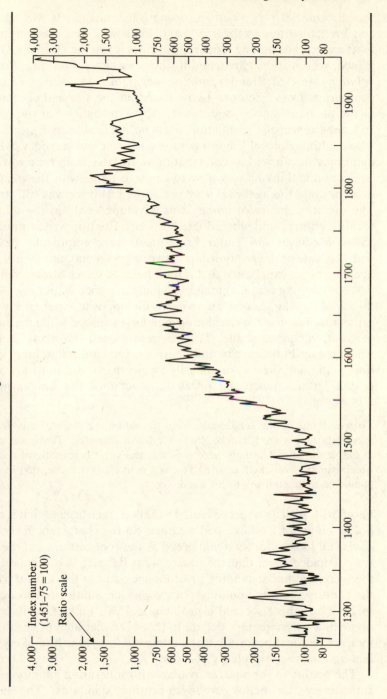

Index number
(1451–75 = 100)

Ratio scale

teenth centuries was a pan-European phenomenon. It was Spanish and French writers in the 1550s and 1560s who first drew attention to its scale; while among modern historians it was the German, Georg Wiebe, who in 1895 christened it 'the price revolution' (*die Preisrevolution*). In 1967 Braudel and Spooner published a survey of European prices from Exeter to Lvov which put the size and chronology of the phenomenon beyond doubt. Any explanations of the origins and persistence of the inflation must be applicable to Europe as a whole, although local English features like war and currency debasement may be allowed as contributing to the rise from time to time.

Economic thinking was slow to come to terms with the phenomenon because the medieval doctrine of the just price was still strong. The quantity theory of money was developed only in the mid-sixteenth century, and not adopted by any English writer until the 1570s. Medieval and Tudor Englishmen were empirically familiar with one side of the relationship between goods and money, for they knew by bitter experience that if food became scarce after a bad harvest (purchasing power remaining equal), its price would rise. What they could not logically relate to it was the opposite experience where prices rose because the circulating medium increased while the supply of goods remained stable. They therefore used the word 'dearth', which meant both scarcity and dearness, for both inflationary situations, although they were uneasily aware that it did not fully apply to the latter. Hence the puzzled outburst of the knight in the *Discourse*:

I mervayll much, Maister Doctor, what should be the cause of this dearth; seinge all thinges are (thanckes be to Gode) so plentifull. There was never more plentie of cattell then there is nowe, and yet it is scarcitie of thinges which commonly maketh dearth. This is a mervelous dearthe, that in such plentie cometh, contrary to his kynd.

Faced with such an unprecedented situation, men argued that it could not be an act of God like bad weather. So the characters in the *Discourse* all looked for sectional greed as the root cause, until the doctor persuaded them that the causes went deeper. It is a measure of the increased understanding of economics during the second half of the century that the apparent paradox which Smith tried to explain in 1549 no longer seemed a problem in 1593. Fulke Greville could argue in a parliamentary debate in that year that high prices did *not* indicate national poverty but the opposite: 'our dearth of everything amongst us, sheweth plenty of money'.[3]

The quality of the sources available for measuring inflation is, not surprisingly, far below twentieth-century standards. The largest printed collections of Tudor prices, those of Rogers (1882–87) and Beveridge (1939), are drawn almost entirely from the accounts of a few, though important and wealthy, institutions in the South – some Oxford and Cambridge colleges, a few leading hospitals and schools, manors owned by monasteries and by the Crown, and one or two government departments. Grain prices have also been printed for Exeter and Lincoln, and bread prices for London. The most recent and broadest-based analysis is that of Bowden (1967), who incorporated several unpublished series as well as Rogers' and Beveridge's published data; five of Bowden's key price indices are reproduced in Appendix I. However, nearly all long-term price series relate to agriculture rather than to manufactures; and within the agricultural sector, grain prices are better represented than other products, and wheat prices much more commonly recorded than those for barley, oats or rye. Given the wide differences known between price rises for different products and in different regions, generalisations about nationwide price levels become hazardous.

When one turns from prices to incomes, the picture is murkier still. Calculations have been made of the income of a fair number of noble and gentle families, but the only long-term series so far constructed for wage-earners is that of Phelps Brown and Hopkins (1955), based on the wage-rates paid for building craftsmen. They did not claim it to be a fair index of English wage levels in general, though their justifiable caution has not prevented some historians from treating it as such *faute de mieux*. It does not reflect actual earnings, which could be lowered by unemployment or raised by overtime work or by payments in kind (such as board and lodging).

Phelps Brown and Hopkins also made a brave attempt to calculate the real value of those craftsmen's wages by measuring them against a 'basket of consumables', and both their indices are reproduced in Appendix I. Drawing on available price series, they constructed a standard budget in the proportions of $57\frac{1}{2}$ per cent for food, $22\frac{1}{2}$ per cent for drink, $12\frac{1}{2}$ for clothing and $7\frac{1}{2}$ for light and fuel: there is no allowance for rent. It therefore reflects the expenses of poorer, urban households, and it necessarily makes the unrealistic assumption that families bought the same goods in the same proportion over long periods of time. It certainly cannot represent the real income of agricultural labourers who could produce at least some of their own food to cushion themselves against inflation, still less those self-sufficient farmers who produced enough to feed themselves completely and perhaps a surplus for sale. None of this is intended to belittle the construction of a good approximate cost-of-living index for some urban wage labourers, but to warn against giving it a wider application than the authors intended. In particular, they were measuring only assumed real wages in a few southern towns; and it is known that London, together with the South-east and South-west, were areas of relatively high wages, while the North and Midlands were regions of low wages. In general, it is true, the high-wage districts also suffered higher prices for arable produce, but the exact purchasing power of wages could vary considerably from one region to another.

2

An analysis of prices and wages requires some understanding of the currency, both the nature of the circulating medium and the use of money. Throughout the sixteenth century the entire official stock of money consisted of gold and silver coins, mostly minted in England. The ecclesiastical mints of Canterbury, York and Durham were all closed down by 1544, and the Crown had thereafter a monopoly of coining. Far and away the most important royal mint, and the only one with a fairly continuous record of production, was that housed in the Tower of London, but there were others, operating during the debasement period and for a short while afterwards, at Bristol, Canterbury, Dublin, London (Durham House), Southwark and York. In addition to their output, many foreign coins circulated legally in England. English coins were not, of course, of pure gold or silver, but were mixed with a little 'alloy' or base metal. But where England differed from France and some other European countries was in its lack of any authorised coin of pure copper or of billon (mixed copper and silver). Only during the debasement of 1544–51 was 'black money' or billon common, and the only pure copper issue was of Irish pence in 1601.

It is important to distinguish between denominations in circulation and money of account, which is simply a device for reducing coins of varying value, weight or fineness to a common reckoning. The standard units of account were (as they remained until 1971) the penny, the shilling of twelve pence and the pound of twenty shillings. A common alternative was the mark of 13s 4d, exactly two-thirds of a pound. The mark was purely a unit of account, but the pound, shilling and penny did correspond to actual coins. Gold coins were regularly struck for denominations from 2s 6d to 30s, and silver for coins of $\frac{1}{2}d$, 1d, 2d, 4d, 6d, 1s, and occasionally for other amounts. Such a bald list gives a false impression of stability, however. The coins in circulation varied considerably between 1544 and 1561, and were only then put on a stable basis for the next forty years.

Between 1544 and 1551 the government practised both currency depreciation ('enhancement'), ordering coins to circulate at a higher face value with the same bullion content, and debasement, whereby they circulated at the same face value with a lower bullion content, by reducing either the weight or the fineness of the coin or both. Conveniently but incorrectly, both processes will be referred to here as debasement. The former was preferred for gold coins, which were handled by sophisticated merchants in international trade; the latter, easier to understand, was preferred for silver coin, that 'pale and common drudge 'tweene man and man', used chiefly for domestic trade. Ordinary people generally handled coins at their face value, and could not readily distinguish silver coins with different degrees of fineness. Between 1551 and 1560 coins containing 6 oz and 3 oz of silver were freely circulating at the same face value. When the Crown in 1560 ordered the latter to circulate at only half the value of the others, 'thunlerned and uplandyshe people', so Bedford complained to Cecil, could not tell them apart, and professional moneyers had to be sent into the provinces to put different stamps upon the two types of coin.

The total value of coin in circulation, an essential prerequisite for any full understanding of the inflation or indeed of the economy as a whole, is very difficult to calculate. Thanks to Challis and Gould there are now reasonably reliable figures for the total output of the mints, but one cannot simply assume a currency medium enlarged each year by the volume of extra coins minted. There was an unknown amount of normal wear and tear, compounded by illegal clipping, and an unquantifiable flow of coin in and out of England to balance exports and imports. During the period 1544–51 old coins were exchanged for new on a large scale, and between 1551 and 1561 the old coinage was almost completely replaced. Hoarding and dishoarding must also be allowed for. The best guide suggested so far is that of Spooner and Challis, that in normal times the circulating medium will not have been less than the total mint output over the previous thirty years.

Nevertheless, enough evidence is available to allow at least an informed guess at the size of the circulating medium (Table 5.1). The figures suggest, very roughly, a doubling of the face value of coin in circulation during the debasement of 1544–51, and a halving of the total in the summer of 1551 which brought it down almost to its level of seven years earlier. Thereafter there was a gentle rise during the 1550s, which was almost cancelled out by the effect of revaluation in 1560–61. Finally, under a regime of stable currency, the total in

Table 5.1   Volume of currency in circulation, 1544–1603 (in millions of pounds sterling)

Early 1544	£1.23	July 1551	£2.66
March 1546	£1.45	Aug. 1551	£1.38
Sept. 1548	£1.76	Sept. 1560	£1.71
Sept. 1549	£1.92	Oct. 1561	£1.45
		March 1603	£3.50

Source: C. E. Challis, *The Tudor Coinage*, Manchester U.P., 1978, pp. 237–47.

circulation increased by nearly two and a half times during Elizabeth's reign. It should be added that the circulating medium changed in composition as well as in size, as silver gradually replaced gold almost entirely. By 1603 there may have been four and a half times as much silver in circulation as in 1526, but little more than a quarter of the gold. 'In common with her contemporaries in France and Spain', points out Challis, 'Elizabeth ruled in a Silver Age.'[4]

The totals suggested by Challis are very modest, representing something like 10s per head of the population at the start of the period and approaching £1 per head at the end. It is hard to believe, despite the increase, that it sufficed for a fully cash economy, especially as there were no denominations low enough for small purchases. Production of the farthing ($\frac{1}{4}d$) coin apparently ceased in 1553, and that of the halfpenny ($\frac{1}{2}d$) was seriously restricted, while the ecclesiastical mints which had provided later medieval England with much of its small change had been closed down. In 1561 the Crown attempted to alleviate the situation by minting $\frac{3}{4}d$ and $1\frac{1}{2}d$ coins, and when production of them ceased in 1583, by reintroducing the penny and halfpenny. Even so, the small change in circulation must have been totally insufficient to meet demand. How did the population manage?

Some rents were paid in kind, and wage assessments made provision for payment of wages partly in meat and drink. Many servants worked in return for board and lodging and perhaps a very small cash wage. Taxpayers were often without sufficient coin to pay, and had to surrender household plate to the mints in lieu of currency. Such men, like the Norman Sieur de Gouberville, were 'not short of money . . . but simply short of ready cash'. Mutual credit was normal, with occasions for the mutual cancelling out of debts at times like Lady Day and Michaelmas when rents were due. Many a Tudor craftsman, like the shoemaker of Montaillou, may have 'had to wait until his customers had sold their poultry at Whitsuntide before they could pay him.'[5] Many pleas of debt were entered in manorial and borough courts but were not pursued to a conclusion; they may well have represented formal records of debts which were later repaid.

Some communities developed alternatives to gold and silver currency. The greater merchants relied increasingly on credit notes and bills of exchange, while at the bottom end of the money economy scarcity of coin provoked issues of tokens. Erasmus referred in 1517 to lead coins as current in England, and on the estates of Tynemouth priory in the 1530s, 'monie was so scantie that coigned leather went bargaining between man and man'. Urban tradesmen hit upon issuing tokens at least a century before the well-known Restoration issues. Norwich, Bristol, Worcester and Oxford issued farthing or halfpenny tokens of copper, brass or lead in Elizabeth's reign, either municipal issues or private ventures by individuals. Many humble Londoners made their purchases with tradesmen's leaden tokens, and a Swiss visitor in 1599 testified that employers issued them on a large scale:

If one buys to the value of less than a halfpenny, permission is granted to make or coin lead or copper tokens in one's own house, some four or six going to a halfpenny, and these tokens are given to one's workmen; when they have a halfpenny worth or more, they exchange and reckon up together so that nobody loses.

About 1600 the Crown realised that the tokens were meeting a real need; a proclamation was drafted which would have barred their use but which in return promised an official issue of copper halfpence and farthings. The proclamation was, however, not issued, and the problem remained unresolved.[6]

In theory, gold and silver coins were worth virtually their face value in bullion. If the value of the precious metals they contained rose or fell, the government simply adjusted the relationship by changing their face value, weight or fineness. All major European currencies gradually depreciated in terms of gold and silver over the early modern period, and England had to come into line. What was special about the English experience was the sharp debasement of 1544–51, which drastically lowered the value of the pound sterling against other currencies, and the new stability after 1561, which made Elizabeth's currency the envy of Europe (Fig. 7).

There was a limited, secret debasement of the English coinage in 1542–44, followed by full and open debasement in 1544–51. Henry VIII began the process, and Edward's council continued it, as a means of making money when the cost of war and other expenses were escalating far beyond normal income. There were successive reductions in the value of both gold and silver coins in 1544, 1545 and 1546, and of silver coins only in 1551. On each occasion holders of currency were invited to exchange them at the mints for new coins

Fig. 7   The real value of the pound sterling, 1485–1603

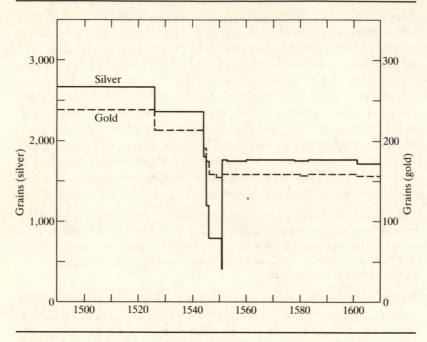

Source: C. E. Challis, *The Tudor Coinage,* Manchester U.P., 1978, p. 235

of the same theoretical value, but each time the Crown and its officials made a substantial profit by lowering the real precious metal
content further than was openly admitted. The process had to stop
first with gold, because foreign creditors were not taken in, and
refused to accept coins below their real value. There was therefore
very little debased gold after 1546, whereas silver debasement continued until 1551, the Crown being able to force its domestic creditors
to accept payment in debased currency.

It is not a pretty story, and successive governments were well
aware of the damage to England's society and economy. Northumberland's government did halt the process in 1551, issuing fine gold
and silver coins nearly of the old standard. There was still, however,
some base money in circulation for another ten years, chiefly of
lower-value silver coins. Both Northumberland and Mary had plans
to withdraw these from circulation altogether in exchange for coins
of good standards, but both postponed the step because of the cost
involved.

Finally Elizabeth's government grasped the nettle. According to a story retailed later by Sir Robert Cotton, Cecil and Smith advised the queen at the start of the reign 'that it was the honour of her Crown and the true wealth of herself and people to reduce the standard to the ancient parity and purity of her great-grandfather Edward IV'; certainly it was one of Cecil's maxims that 'that realme cannot be rich whose coigne is poore or base'.[7] Elizabeth ordered the debased money to be called in and replaced by new coin, a process completed in a few months in 1560–61 and at a modest profit to the Crown, the charges being passed on to the public. The gold coins were already, thanks to Northumberland and Mary, back at the old standard of 23 car. 3½gr. fine; now Elizabeth had restored silver also to its pre-1544 level of 11 oz 2 dwt.

Throughout her reign it was remembered as one of her finest achievements, and the epitaph on her tomb proclaims it as her third greatest success after the religious settlement and the maintenance of peace, that she had reduced the money to its true value (*moneta ad iustum valorem reducta*). Camden's considered opinion was that Henry's debasement had been 'to the great dishonour of the realm, and to the ruin of his successors and the people', and that Elizabeth's revaluation was 'her greatest glory'. Thanks to her, England had a purer currency than for two centuries past, and better than anywhere else in Europe: *quod probior et purior fuerit in Anglia pecunia, quam totis ducentis ante annis visa, aut alibi per Europam in usu*. His praise was pitched too high – Elizabeth's currency was no better than her father's had been before 1542 – but certainly her revaluation did much for England's international standing. It was also a domestic success, if judged by its effectiveness and permanence. There was a slight devaluation in 1601 to bring English currency into line with continental levels, but Elizabethan coins long continued to circulate: as many as half the coins buried in hoards during the 1640s were Elizabethan. The one qualification to be made to the government's success was that the immediate benefits were felt more by merchants and financiers than by ordinary people, who had less small change for their everyday transactions as coins were revalued. 'Grete lacke of small money abroode in the countrey', noted one writer in September 1561.[8] As the reign wore on, however, inflation reduced the real value of coins once more and counterbalanced this effect.

3

Inflation first became a subject of intense public concern, judging from contemporary tracts and pamphlets, between 1548 and 1556.

The classic exemplar is *A Discourse of the Common Weal of this Realm of England* (1549), probably written by Sir Thomas Smith, one of the two secretaries of state, during a period of enforced exile from court.

In the form of a lively dialogue between a doctor, knight, merchant, husbandman and capper, representing the different estates of the realm, he presents a penetrating analysis of 'the decaie of this commonwealthe and realme of England' thoroughly informed by a sense of the interrelatedness of economic policies and problems. The fundamental problem is, to him, 'oure dearthe of all thinges, thoughe theare be scarsnes of nothinge'. The high prices, he argues, are caused at bottom by the Crown's debasement of the coinage, and can be halted or reversed only by revaluing the currency. Plainly no satisfactory long-term analysis of price rises, which occurred all over western Europe, could have had such a purely domestic origin, but as a short-run argument it had much to commend it. Certainly prices were rising only gently in England before the great debasement, and mainly agricultural prices at that.

The Bowden and Phelps Brown–Hopkins price data (Appendix I) show that even in 1547, after three years of debasement, some prices were not greatly above the levels of the late fifteenth century, whereas by 1603 price levels were between three and five times the fifteenth-century figures. These annual figures, however, have two disadvantages for measuring trends. The Bowden figures are entirely, and the Phelps Brown–Hopkins statistics largely, based on agricultural products, and although industrial prices were less important, they should not be ignored. Furthermore, agricultural prices fluctuated year by year more markedly than other prices, with the weather and quality of harvest, obscuring the long-term trend. Both objections can be circumvented by another set of statistics compiled by Phelps Brown and Hopkins on a decadal basis, the first column representing foodstuffs and the second industrial products. For comparison, a similar index by Bowden for agricultural wage-rates is included (Table 5.2).

Once again, too much weight should not be placed on this table. It is a brave pioneering achievement, but detailed indexes of industrial prices are badly needed to match the agricultural figures. For that matter, wage figures are needed for trades other than the building industry. Nevertheless, a careful use of all the indexes so far available does make the course of the inflation, and its differential effects, fairly clear.

Judging from Fig. 6 and Table 5.2, agricultural prices were starting to rise from the beginning of Henry VIII's reign, but it was only from

Table 5.2 Indexes of (a) Prices of foodstuffs (b) Of industrial products (1451–75 = 100); (c) Agricultural wages (1450–99 = 100)

	(a)	(b)	(c)		(a)	(b)	(c)
1491–1500	100	97	101	1551–60	315	186	160
1501–10	106	98	101	1561–70	298	218	177
1511–20	116	102	101	1571–80	341	223	207
1521–30	159	110	106	1581–90	389	230	203
1531–40	161	110	110	1591–1600	530	238	219
1541–50	217	127	118	1601–10	527	256	219

Sources: E. H. Phelps Brown and S. V. Hopkins, 'Wage-rates and prices', *Economica*, XXIV (1957), 306; Thirsk 1967, p. 864. Bowden's index, beside having a slightly different base, is calculated by decades starting 1490–99, etc., but the broad comparison remains valid despite the differences.

the 1520s that real inflation of prices well above fifteenth-century levels became evident. Building craftsmen's wages began to rise in the 1530s, but the wages of labourers, both in the building trades and in agriculture, not until the 1540s. Similarly, the prices of industrial products did not start to rise sharply before the 1540s. From that time on, most prices and wages continued to rise for a century or more. All prices and wages rose sharply in the 1550s, especially food prices under the impact of the famine of 1555–57. The 1560s saw something of a pause, at least for agricultural prices and wages, but then inflation continued its upward course for the rest of the century and beyond. Between the 1560s and 1590s industrial prices kept pace with agricultural ones, but the famine of the 1590s provoked another huge rise, of about one-third, in agrarian prices. By 1603 grain prices were on average nearly four times their 1547 level, prices of livestock and industrial products had doubled, building craftsmen earned twice as much, and the wages of urban and agricultural labourers had not quite doubled. It has to be said again that the indexes, even the best of them, rely inevitably on very patchy data. The broad picture, however, is not in doubt, and it corresponds very well to the periods of greatest contemporary concern about prices in the 1540s, 1550s and 1590s. Without doubt the time-span covered by this volume saw much the most rapid increases (Table 5.3).

Some historians have objected that the inflation was too mild to justify the term 'price revolution'. Building wages increased by an annual compound 1.46 per cent between 1532 and 1580, and most prices by somewhat more, modest indeed by twentieth-century standards. Yet it has been well said that 'even such a limited price rise . . . posed major problems for a society which did not fully understand what was happening, and had very inadequate machinery for adjusting to inflation'.[9] And the rise was all the more alarming

Table 5.3   Percentage change in prices: 1450–1650

	Agricultural commodities	Timber	Industrial products	Agricultural wage-rates
1450/59–1490/99	+3	−14	−2	—
1490/99–1540/49	+71	+26	+31	+17
1540/49–1590/99	+167	+151	+87	+86
1590/99–1640/49	+43	+81	+29	+39

Source: P. J. Bowden, 'Agricultural prices, farm profits, and rents' in Thirsk 1967, p. 605.

in coming, as it did, after a long period of price stability.

What caused the inflation to start, to accelerate in mid-century, to slacken in the 1560s and 1570s, and to accelerate again towards the end of the century? It may be asking too much to expect unanimity from historians, since economists remain sharply divided about the recent Western inflation despite being able to draw on far more detailed and accurate economic measurements. Explanations for the Tudor inflation, advanced both by contemporaries and by modern historians, fall into two broad categories, those relying on the quantity theory of money and those emphasising the ultimate role of non-monetary factors. The former invoke debasement, currency depreciation, taxation, government spending and bullion supply, while the latter stress population growth, supply and demand changes, and agricultural and industrial output. The 'monetarists', who dominated continental explanations in the sixteenth century, were divided between those stressing currency debasement and those preferring an increase in money supply. The classic debate was between Malestroit (1556), who maintained that the price rise was illusory if adjusted for currency debasement, and Bodin (1568), who explained the price rise mainly by an influx of New World silver in an early version of the quantity theory of money.

Contemporaries were divided between the two types of explanation, and fashionable orthodoxy shifted from one to the other as publicity focused in turn on different alleged causes. In the 1530s and 1540s, when high food prices were first an object of serious concern, enclosures and conversions of arable to pasture were the favourite culprits. Such was the argument of John Hales, and of the husbandman in the *Discourse*. The doctor in the *Discourse*, however, representing the author's own views, believed that debasement of the currency, and the accompanying exchange depreciation, were the root cause of inflation, a plausible view when prices were rising at an unprecedented rate at exactly the same time as an unprecedented debasement. Such was also the view of Lane and other contemporaries of the late 1540s and early 1550s, and it became virtually the official explanation of inflation when Elizabeth's government planned and carried through the revaluation of the currency.

The difficulty was that it remained a plausible explanation only if prices stabilised, or even fell, after 1561. That was what the advocates of revaluation expected, but they were to be disappointed.

It was thought of the Councell that by the alteracion of the coyne from base money to fyne silver . . . that the pryce of all maner of thinges would also abate. But yt followed not so, but all thinges were rather dearer, not only vytayll but chiefly all kind of marchandyce.

Merchants were thereupon summoned before the Council, continues the anonymous chronicler, to explain why prices remained high. They answered that

they could not sell their wares better chepe, unles they might buy clothes better chepe, and how sylckes could not be better chepe, because in all partes of the worlde, and especially in Spaine, they were more used then ever they were before.

In other words, whether or not debasement had been the original cause of the inflation, it was continuing in their view because of a ratchet effect and because of rising international demand.[10]

Smith faced the problem frankly enough when he revised the *Discourse* in the 1570s. At the point where the doctor has shown that 'even with the alteration of the coyne beganne this dearthe', he makes the knight very reasonably ask

If this were the chiefest cause of the dearth . . . how commeth it to passe . . . that the pryces of all thinges fall not backe to theyr olde rate, whereas now long sithence our English coyne (to the great honour of our noble Princesse which now raighneth) hath bene again throughly restored to his former purity and perfection?

The doctor in reply advanced two reasons for the ratchet effect. One was that debasement had provoked a 'rackynge and hoyssing up of rentes' which had continued in an inflationary spiral and produced cost inflation. The other was

the great store and plenty of treasure, which is walking in these partes of the world, far more in these our dayes, then ever our forefathers have sene in times past. Who doth not understand of the infinite sums of gold and silver, whych are gathered from the Indies and other countries, and so yearely transported unto these costes?

Here he had moved from one form of the quantity theory of money to another, with bullion imports rather than debasement as the culprit. The influx of New World bullion was a recent addition to the contemporary debate on inflation; it was adumbrated by Azpilcueta de Navarro in Spain (1556) and developed by Bodin in France (1568), and was to become the standard view of the cause of inflation in seventeenth-century Europe. By 1601 the English merchant Malynes could assert flatly that 'the great store or abundance of monie and bullion, which of late years is come from the West Indies into Christendom, hath made every very thing derer according to the increase of monie', and could deny that Henry VIII's debasement was the fundamental cause even of English inflation.[11]

Despite Smith's ingenious modifications to it, the monetarist view of inflation languished during Elizabeth's reign, since the revaluation of the coinage had plainly not stopped inflation, and bullion imports were not yet fashionable as an alternative explanation. Instead, various 'real' or physical explanations of inflation were preferred. Monopolists, middlemen, purveyors, landlord-rentiers and other groups thought to be selfishly or greedily creating scarcity were attacked. Enclosures and conversions to pasture came under attack again in the late 1580s and 1590s as food prices soared following bad harvests. Most interestingly of all, in view of modern attempts to connect the population rise with inflation, a very few contemporaries hit upon the same idea. Population was growing faster than the ability of the land to support it, they said, thus raising the prices of agricultural products.[12]

Many scholars are no longer prepared to give primacy to domestic causes of price rises, such as enclosures, engrossing or purveyance, although some are conceded to have exacerbated the trends. As Outhwaite has observed, 'the debates over enclosures were prompted more by the upward movements of grain prices than by any quickening in the incidence of enclosure itself', and as Paget shrewdly noted at the time, if enclosures had been the main cause, why were prices on the Continent as high as or higher than in England?[13] A better argument can be made out for the role of the government in the 1540s, especially the monstrously expensive wars and the debasement which was carried out to finance them. The sums involved were certainly immense in comparison to the total size of the circulating medium. The total cost of the wars was some £3.5 million, but the net total yield of taxation was only £976,000, and even the profits of £1,057,000 from ex-monastic lands could not completely bridge the gap; it was the profits from debasement, some £1,271,000 which did so.

Unquestionably debasement drastically accelerated inflation. Historians as widely separated in time and attitude as Thorold Rogers and Elton have blamed Henry VIII for accelerating a gentle inflationary trend into a rapid and violent one, and with justice. Yet there are insuperable difficulties in making debasement the *primary* cause. First, if the prime inflationary mechanism was a doubling of the money supply between 1544 and 1551, then the halving of the circulating medium in July and August 1551 should have had a severe deflationary effect, or at least have halted the inflationary spiral, which it did not. Challis and Gould have demonstrated that variations in the amount of money in circulation had surprisingly small *immediate* effects on prices, though that is not to say that in the medium term they were not important. Second, inflation was already well under way before debasement; as early as 1534 an act restricting sheep farming complained that the price of corn and other agricultural products had been enhanced 'almost doble above the prices which hath byn accustomed'. Most important of all, inflation was a pan-European phenomenon. All national mint prices were rising, and Challis suggests that the higher prices paid at the English mints between 1544 and 1551 merely accelerated a rise which would have occurred in any event.

A European explanation is therefore demanded. The favourite, for most of the time since it was formulated, has been the version of the quantity theory developed by Bodin in 1568 and applied to England in the published version of Smith's *Discourse* in 1581. The vast quantities of American gold and silver shipped annually to Seville were quite sufficient, it was argued, to account for sixteenth-century inflation. E. J. Hamilton, in a series of influential studies in the 1920s and 1930s, gave the theory a new lease of life as well as more statistical precision. Gold, and especially silver, poured into Spain from the 1540s, increasing in every decade to reach a peak in the 1590s before declining.

The correlation between rising bullion imports into Spain and rising European prices is certainly fairly close, although it assumes a rapid outflow of silver from Spain throughout western Europe, which Hamilton asserted but did not prove. Increasingly, his argument has been questioned over the last thirty years. It has been pointed out that, even if the bullion had been promptly funnelled through Spain to other countries, it came too late to account for the start of the price rise; substantial American supplies of silver began only with the opening of the mines at Potosi in 1545 and Zacatecas in the following year. It is unable to explain the early period of rapid price rises in the 1540s and 1550s, though it could help to explain that of the 1590s. Braudel and Spooner suggest that, on the most optimistic assumptions, the inflow of American bullion did not even reach one-half of the existing stock of European money. For England in particular, the correlation between Spanish bullion and rising English prices has depended on assumptions rather than evidence. The extreme case was that of Brenner, who argued a close correlation between additions to the stock of Spanish treasure (not English or even European treasure) and the English price rise as measured by the Phelps Brown-Hopkins index, while at the same time asserting that there was little evidence that much Spanish-American silver arrived in England before 1631. Any large influx of Spanish bullion into England in the later sixteenth century could have come about only through successful piracy, a favourable trade balance, or bimetallic flows (Spanish gold was undervalued relative to silver), and all of these have been dismissed as unlikely.

A purely 'monetarist' interpretation of the price rise has been rejected by many recent historians in favour of an emphasis on 'real' factors like population growth. Before turning to these, however, it should be noted that some of the weaknesses in the Hamilton thesis have recently been remedied, and older arguments are now being revived with new force. Miskimin, for instance, has drawn attention to the effects of a 'silver famine' in the fifteenth century which increased the profitability of European mining well before the arrival of American treasure. The effect was dramatic, and the output of central European silver increased fivefold between 1460 and 1530 to reach a peak in the 1530s. A combination of European and American silver can therefore be used to explain both the origin and continuation of the great inflation purely in terms of the quantity theory. Miskimin also argues that inflation can almost wholly be attributed to debasement rather than increased bullion supplies if the sixteenth century is compared to a base period of the fourteenth century rather than the fifteenth, and if the real silver content of money is measured rather than the total quantity of money. Here, however, his comparative statistics are suspect, being based on the old mint production statistics of Feaveryear and Craig rather than Challis's and Gould's revised estimates; and there are good reasons why silver-content prices are a very artificial way to make comparisons over time.

Miskimin's most important contribution has been to rescue European silver from neglect, modifying the Hamilton thesis so as to explain the price rises before the 1540s in terms of bullion supply. More to the present purpose, Challis has put forward cogent revisionist arguments for bullion supply in the second half of the sixteenth century. For the quantity theory to explain the continued price rises of Elizabeth's reign, given that England had negligible silver production of its own, would require substantial bullion inflows via trade, war, piracy or bimetallic flows. All of these can be suggested as likely sources, despite a fashionable scepticism among historians. There was almost certainly a net bullion inflow during the debasement period as cloth exports to the Netherlands increased; but equally there may have been a favourable balance with Spain and the Spanish Netherlands down to 1585. The demonetisation of foreign coins in 1561, and the seizure of Alba's treasure ships in 1568, also added to England's stocks of silver.

Piracy brought in considerable sums, most spectacularly the £1.5 million return from Drake's expedition of 1577–80, of which perhaps £600,000 was in coin. 'It is incredible', asserted Wilson in 1601, 'what treasure hath been brought into England by prize and from the Indyes within this 12 or 16 yeares'.[14] There is also some evidence that Spain's undervalued silver relative to gold caused its migration to England (among other countries) in the 1570s and early 1580s. More statistical work needs to be done on Elizabethan overseas trade and piracy before these suggestions can be confirmed; but Challis has demonstrated conclusively that Spanish silver formed a large element in the bullion supplies for the Tower mint for the few years with accurate surviving records (1561–62, 1569–70, 1583, 1584–85 and 1598–99, though not 1567–69). Spanish silver certainly entered England, by whatever means, in considerable quantities.

Underlying the work of Hamilton and of many of his critics has been the quantity theory of money as developed by Irving Fisher (1911), usually expressed in the form $MV = PT$. Here, M represents the total amount of money in circulation, V its velocity of circulation, P the average price level and T the total volume of transactions. Stated in this form, it is a truism; but Fisher himself argued that changes in money supply were likely to affect the price level directly and proportionately. In other words, V and T could for some purposes be ignored, so that $M = P$. However, such an assumption seems unwarranted, certainly for the sixteenth century. Braudel and Spooner, followed by Miskimin, have suggested that velocity of circulation of coin increased throughout Europe, partly through rising royal taxation and partly through population growth, which would presumably have put more people in contact with each other and increased trading opportunities. The truth is not that Fisher's equation is irrelevant or untrue, but that too little is known of any of the four factors to allow of its application. For England the only firm figures are for mint output (*not* the same as M) and very limited components of P; information about V and T is almost wholly lacking.

Challis has made informed guesses about the total circulating medium (M), but exact figures are impossible. Mint output has to be added to the inflow of foreign coin, and then the total reduced to allow for bullion export, wear and tear, clipping and 'sweating' of coins (shaking them vigorously in a bag to remove gold or silver), and the melting down of coin. One especial area of uncertainty is hoarding and dishoarding, for much wealth was tied up in gold and silver plate and ornaments, and the process of adding to or subtracting from such stocks could have made a substantial difference to M. The dissolutions of the religious houses brought huge quantities of precious metals to the Crown: after 1537 290,000 oz of gold and silver – almost 9 tons – came in from the monasteries, of which the mint received some 200,000 oz, worth about £50,000. The pressures of the Great Debasement apparently led to the dishoarding of much domestic plate also, as owners brought it in to the mint in the hope of making a profit. The sources leave an impression, however, that the generally less rapid rate of inflation under Elizabeth and James encouraged the renewed accumulation of secular plate. If Harrison (1577) can be believed, the possession of silver had recently percolated down the social scale 'even unto the inferiour artificers and manie farmers, who have learned also to garnish their cupbords with plate'. It was remarkable that 'in a time wherein all things are growen to most excessive prices, we doo yet find the means to obtein and atchive such furniture as heretofore hath beene unpossible'.[15]

Impatient of theorising about Fisher's equation, and distrustful of monetarism, some historians have preferred to see the price rise as ultimately a result of population growth via increased consumer demand. The English population, according to the Cambridge estimates, increased by 43 per cent between 1541 and 1600, and by 82 per cent over the century 1541–1640. Such a growth, it is argued, outstripped resources, so that demand exceeded supply. The period of English population growth, roughly from 1520 to 1650, correlates well with that of inflation: and in particular, as Phelps Brown and Hopkins argued in 1957, the apparent rise of agricultural prices well ahead of industrial prices is suggestive of growing population pressure on food supplies. Both the supply of, and demand for, agricultural products were inelastic. If real wages fell, a larger proportion of consumer demand would be directed towards bread and other essentials and towards the cheaper foodstuffs, such as rye and barley bread instead of wheat. It may, therefore, be significant that the prices of the cheaper grains rose a little more rapidly than those of wheat. Furthermore, prices of meat, dairy products and wool rose a good deal more slowly than grain prices, as if consumers were cutting back on less essential purchases. If monetary factors had been primarily responsible for inflation, it is argued, prices would have risen at similar rates.

Recently, Phythian-Adams has pointed out that in the early sixteenth century, rural population was certainly increasing, but many towns were still stagnating or even shrinking. Could it be that 'this probable demographic disparity between town and country' was an important contributory factor in the take-off of inflation?

Could it be that an accelerating rural demand for specifically urban commodities . . . was beginning to exceed the dwindling capacities of some towns to meet it from their own manufacturing resources; the inevitable results being that scarce local commodities would thus have fetched increased prices and expensive imports were sucked in from abroad?[16]

It may well explain why Smith, in the *Discourse*, was as much concerned with urban decay as with inflation, and especially with the fact that many manufactured goods were by 1549 being imported from overseas, while the old English manufacturing centres decayed.

However, 'we must avoid', as Outhwaite warns, 'making population pressure do all the work which was formerly undertaken by Spanish treasure'. Prices would rise at similar rates only if demand was a constant function of money, and an increase in money led to an equivalent increase in demand. The existence of a 'Malthusian' situation under Elizabeth, with population growth outstripping food supply, has attracted a formidable degree of support, but it remains unproven. Furthermore, if population growth alone had been responsible, one would expect not only a close correlation between population and prices but an equivalent rise in both. 'No one has yet suggested . . . that the population advance of the sixteenth century was more rapid than that of the thirteenth or of the eighteenth, yet the rise in prices in the Tudor period was far greater than that experienced in either of the other periods.' Outhwaite's prudent conclusion is that population growth should be integrated into a more complex explanation which includes war expenditure, land sales, debasement and bad harvests, features of the periods of most rapid price increase in the 1540s, 1550s and 1590s. 'Short-run factors such as these could clearly rack prices and costs to new levels, from which an underlying growth of population would make it difficult for them to descend.'[17] Similarly, there is much plausibility in Fisher's view that a massive epidemic in the late 1550s cut back population, and therefore demand, so heavily that prices rose very little during the 1560s.

Few would now wish to belittle the importance of Tudor population growth. It must beyond question have greatly increased the size of T in the Fisher equation. But to debate whether 'real' or 'monetary' causes were at the root of the inflation is simplistic; the aim should be to harmonise them. A growing European population stimulated rising output and created a growing demand for money, which in turn made mining for gold and silver more profitable. Furthermore, demand was met by increasing velocity of circulation as well as by increasing mint output. Critics of the 'monetarist' school are apt to forget that Fisher's equation is not a thesis for debate but a tautology. *PT* must equal *MV*, and therefore if *PT* increased, as it did, so did *MV*. Since the increase in *M* was only modest between 1544 and 1603, *V* must have increased considerably. And almost certainly inflation resulted from a mixture of 'real' and 'monetary' causes, a mixture which changed over time. Einaudi has calculated that the French price rise between 1555 and 1575 can be assigned three-quarters to currency devaluation and one-quarter to other causes, including bullion imports; whereas in the 1590s the position was nearly reversed. It would be interesting to see similar calculations attempted for England.

4

Successive governments tried to mitigate the harmful effects of price rises, and even occasionally to halt or reverse the process. The administrations of Somerset, Northumberland and Mary were well aware that debasement was at least partly to blame for high prices. Smith urged that inflation could be ended by a complete revaluation of the coinage, and Elizabeth's council accepted the argument when they finally reformed the currency in 1560–61. Smith was also well aware that, whatever the root cause of inflation, it could generate a spiral of rising prices, rents and wages even when the first cause was removed. Here governments also followed, by continuing the medieval policy of statutory maxima for some prices and wages. Evidence for London, York and Coventry in the early 1550s suggests that the existing maximum legal wages (under acts of 1514–15) were not surprisingly being exceeded. Between 1559 and 1563 both central and local government grappled with control of the labour market, including the imposition of realistic maximum wages, a policy that bore fruit in the Statute of Artificers in 1563.

The preamble to the statute observed that the existing statutory maxima were 'to small and not answerable to this tyme, respecting th' advauncement of pryses of all thinges'. It required justices of the peace to fix maximum wage-rates annually after taking account of 'the plentie or scarcity of the tyme and other circumstaunces', but they interpreted their brief very diversely. The Rutland JPs in 1610 were still reissuing most of the rates they had first promulgated in

1563, and which were now impossibly low. The Essex rates were by 1599 'to smale', according to a county jury, which asked the justices to raise them. The Chester city JPs in the 1590s, in contrast, regularly and substantially increased the rates. The master carpenter's maximum yearly wage was raised from £5 13s 4d in 1596 to £6 6s 8d in 1597, an increase of about 12 per cent, and the 1597 increases were explicitly made 'with respecte and consideracon had of the great dearth and scarsitie of things at this present'.[18] Not surprisingly, there is evidence that in some areas the official maxima were observed, while in others they were widely flouted. There was certainly some improvement in the real value of wages in the decade or so after the 1563 act – the Chester wage assessment of 1570 mentioned the *cheapness* of necessaries – but not as a result of the statute. It was a phenomenon common to much of western Europe, and reflects partly a return of better harvests, and partly a temporary slowing down of population growth.

If Englishmen, then as now, were bewildered by the causes of inflation, then also, as today, they were agreed that it had important consequences in discriminating between different social and economic groups. Some were prospering in real terms and some becoming impoverished, and property was affected as well as incomes. The merchant in the *Discourse* argued that gentlemen, merchants, artificers and husbandmen all suffered from inflation. The doctor disagreed, arguing that merchants were well placed to profit from alterations in exchange rates, and that artificers were at least able to protect themselves by passing on higher costs of raw materials in higher prices for their finished products. Rather, it was those on fixed incomes who suffered,

as common laborers at vjd. the daye, jorneymen of all occupacions, servinge men at xls. the yeare; and gentlemen whose landes ar let oute by theim or their auncestors either for lives or for terme of yeares, so as they can not enhaunce the rent thereof thoughe they would, and yet have the price enhaunced to theim of everie thinge that they bie.[19]

The king himself, thought the doctor, was the greatest loser of all, despite his power to manipulate the currency, for much of his income was fixed, while his household charges and his expenditure on imported armaments were rising.

In the late nineteenth and early twentieth centuries a different but related view was prevalent among historians. The price inflation, together with the redistribution of ecclesiastical lands, was seen as a solvent of traditional, feudal society and a creator of capitalist wealth and greater inequality of incomes. Thorold Rogers argued, from the apparent lag of wages behind prices, for an enormous impoverishment of the labourers after the plenty of the fifteenth century, though he also thought that rents rose no more than prices, so that landlords were no better off. Marx, however, believed that the sixteenth century in England was the start of 'the capitalist era', as manufacturing and farming for profit increased, resulting in 'the forcible driving of the peasantry from the land'. Tawney took a similar view:

Into commerce, industry and agriculture alike, the revolution in prices, gradual for the first third of the century, but after 1540 a mill race, injected a virus of hitherto unsuspected potency, at once a stimulant to feverish enterprise and an acid dissolving all customary relationships.[20]

Tawney's view of social change between about 1540 and 1640 was that Crown, peerage and labourers alike suffered a decline in real incomes, while gentry and merchants flourished at their expense. That view has, however, come under increasingly heavy attack. Hard evidence of living standards is scarce and difficult to measure, and recent studies at a detailed level of individuals, families and villages suggest no simple pattern of gain and loss in terms either of status groups or of economic groups.

Starting at the top, with the Crown, Smith's judgement in the *Discourse* has been vindicated. There are, astonishingly, no published analyses of the royal finances of the later Tudors more recent than those of Dietz (1918–32), which are now considered unreliable, but the general picture is not in doubt. Royal lands, which together with customs duties formed the major part of the Crown's income under Henry VII and the early years of Henry VIII, yielded a much diminished return in real terms by the end of Elizabeth's reign. The reasons included extensive sales of land and the inability of an inflexible royal administration to respond to the changed circumstances brought about by the price revolution and by the growing market for land after 1540. In particular, rents on royal lands did not keep pace with inflation. As a result, the Crown had to rely increasingly on loans and parliamentary taxation, and was still unable to keep up.

Tawney and Stone have argued that the real income of the peerage as a whole also declined between 1540 and 1640. This they attribute partly to a conservative policy on rents, whether through financial incompetence or through a preference for traditional good lordship over profits. Stone has calculated that the mean annual net income of peers fell by 26 per cent in real terms as measured by the Phelps Brown–Hopkins index. He has also adjusted the figures for the landed income of the earls of Pembroke in terms of the same index, and concluded that 'takings per acre were lagging behind prices from

1540 to 1599'. However, even if his figures can be relied upon, the conclusion does not follow, for a peer's expenditure, like his income, was very different from that of a building craftsman, and the Phelps Brown–Hopkins index cannot legitimately be used to calculate his cost of living, especially as the craftsman's income was calculated for a few southern towns and the peer's for the whole of England. Some detailed studies have cast doubt on the concept of declining real income among the peerage, at least from landed rents. Rents per acre for new tenancies on the Wiltshire estates of the earls of Pembroke rose nearly threefold during the period 1540–1600, and for the Seymours about sixfold, whereas on Crown manors in that county they rose by only about 27 per cent. The net annual income of the earls of Northumberland rose from £3,602 in 1582 to £12,978 by 1636. And Coleman has demonstrated that even Stone's own statistics can be made to show that the peerage kept the value of their own manorial holdings just ahead of the price rise, with mean income per manor bringing in £40 in 1559 and £43 (at 1559 prices) in 1602.

The only section of the peerage whose income can be shown to have seriously declined were those lords spiritual, the bishops, and that was a result of spoliation by the Crown rather than an inability to cope with inflation. The archbishop of York, for instance, possessed only the same *nominal* income in 1600 as his predecessor had enjoyed in 1536, and the bishop of London had not a great deal more; both, therefore, enjoyed less in real terms than their predecessors. Indeed, it has been calculated that the bishop of London in 1580 received only 37 per cent of the income of his predecessor in 1515–18 in real terms, though the basis for the calculation is, again, the Phelps Brown–Hopkins index.

Recent scholarship has, in any case, moved away from the terms laid down by Tawney and Stone, and has emphasised the essential homogeneity of the peerage and the greater gentry. All, almost without exception, relied on land for the greater part of their income, and all faced similar opportunities and hazards during the price revolution. The differences in their degree of success lay between the shrewd and the feckless, not between the great and middling landowners, still less between peers and commoners. 'All landowners from the 1540s on had relatively fixed expenses and increasing selling prices.'[21] They profited by increased prices for their farm produce which generally kept ahead of the wages they paid and the prices of industrial products which they bought, and on the whole they ensured that their rents at least kept pace with inflation. There was, of course, a lag where long leases at fixed rents were in force, but in general noble and gentle landlords ensured that they maintained their real income, either from increased annual rents, or increased entry fines, or both. Evidence from areas as diverse as Wiltshire, Northamptonshire. East Anglia and Yorkshire agrees on this; on some Yorkshire manors, for example, rents were increased eightfold between 1558 and 1642.

Other landowners responded by replacing cash rents partly or wholly with food renders, thus ensuring that the real value of the rent did not diminish. When Sir Thomas Smith was provost of Eton in the 1550s, he introduced such leases on the college estates, and forty years later the college was said to be saving over £200 a year from them. In 1576 Smith piloted through an act of parliament which allowed one-third of all rents to Eton, Winchester and the University colleges to be paid in corn and malt, an important aid to their prosperity in the following decades. Not all the corporations named took up the provisions of the act at once, but several waited until the harvest crises of the 1590s; King's College, Cambridge, for instance, adopted the act in 1597–98. At a humbler level, the annual revenue of the Yorkshire manor of Bonwick consisted, during Elizabeth's reign, of £11 in money, ten quarters of seed barley and three quarters of wheat and rye, worth in all some £16 or £17. Many parish clergy enjoyed a hedge against inflation in the form of tithes payable in kind, and those who were paid in cash often tried to alter the arrangements. In the Lancashire parish of Winwick the tithe on corn was traditionally paid in kind but the hay tithe at 3*d* an acre, until in 1544 the rector tried to convert that also to a payment in kind.

Other ways in which landlords could keep up with inflation were by buying more land – the scramble for ecclesiastical properties may partly be explained in this way – or by substituting direct farming for leases. As in the thirteenth century, so in the sixteenth, many lords took back leased demesne land into their own hands to increase their income, rather than leaving it in the hands of farmers at a fixed annual rent. It is therefore misleading to think of rent as a landlord's only, or even main, source of revenue. At the start of the seventeenth century Sir Thomas Temple of Stowe (Bucks.) enjoyed some £2,500 a year from his estates; only £500 or so came from rents, tithes and manorial dues, and the remaining £2,000 from his own direct farming. Similarly, over half the estate income of Sir Thomas Tresham of Rushton (Northants.) in the 1590s came from the sale of farm produce.

If contemporaries differed about the ability of the nobles and gentry to keep their income in line with inflation, there was no such disagreement about the yeomanry. They were, by universal consent, benefiting from relatively fixed expenses and increased selling prices.

As direct producers with sufficient land to maintain their families and often with a food surplus to sell, they were in an excellent position. Robert Reyce, who began his account of Suffolk at the end of Elizabeth's reign, thought that the Suffolk yeomen were the one really flourishing group: their 'continuall underliving, saving, and the immunities from the costly charge of these unfaithfull times, do make them so to grow with the wealth of this world, that whilest many of the better sort . . . do suffer an utter declination, these onely doe arise . . .'.[22] There was no gulf between the richer yeomen and the lesser gentry and both, with careful management, could flourish in a time of rising food prices. Part of the evidence survives in the huge number of yeomen's farmhouses and small manor houses which were rebuilt from around 1570 onwards in a surge of farming prosperity.

The crucial distinction was not between yeomen and husbandmen, but between freeholders on the one hand, and customary tenants and leaseholders on the other. The former were protected against inflation: with the latter, it depended on whether their lords could and did raise their rents and fines in step with inflation. Tawney, writing before inflationary pressures had been fully explored, was inclined to attribute rent rises to the greed of landlords, but he fairly conceded that one should not confine one's evidence to tenants' complaints, that lords had to increase their income in step with inflation, and that many tenants profited as their increasing rents fell behind their profits from farming. He gave four illustrations of early Stuart tenants paying in rent only a fifth, a sixth or even one-eighteenth of the value of their holdings: a man in such a position 'is a tenant whom most modern English farmers would envy'. A similar point was made at the time in Norden's *Surveiors Dialogue* (1607). There the farmer complained that a fine of £20 was 'anciently' only 13s 4d, but the surveyor retorted that

if you consider the state of things then and now, you shall find the proportion little differing: for so much are the prices of things vendible by farmers now increased, as may well be said to exceede the prices then, as much as twenty pound exceedeth thirteene shillings foure pence.[23]

Harrison's famous analysis of tenant fortunes in 1577 is ambivalent if not contradictory, probably because he knew of very differing examples in his native Essex. He described how among the improvements in his village within the lifetime of the older inhabitants had been the increased wealth of 'farmers' and husbandmen:

in my time, although peradventure foure pounds of old rent be improved to fortie or fiftie pounds, yet will the farmer thinke his gaines verie small

toward the middest of his terme, if he have not six or seven yeares rent
lieng by him, therewith to purchase a new lease.

Yet in the same breath he reported the 'old men' complaining about
'the inhansing of rents' and

the dailie oppression of copiholders, whose lords seeke to bring their
poore tenants almost into plaine servitude and miserie, dailie devising new
meanes. . . . how to cut them shorter and shorter, doubling, trebling, and
now and then seven times increasing their fines . . . .[24]

Inflation also had very variable effects on the parish clergy, whose
income was derived partly from glebe (their landed endowments) and
partly from tithe. Tithes remained an important source of income to
the rural clergy, who fought hard to keep up their value, though often
at the cost of many cases before the Church courts and a good deal
of unpopularity with their parishioners. Urban clergy, however, suffered heavily, and after the Tithe Act of 1549 it became almost
impossible for them to collect personal tithes, while they enjoyed
very little tithe on produce. Many rural clergy, however, had the
opportunity of maintaining their real income, because they farmed
their glebe themselves. Hoskins has estimated, from the evidence of
inventories, that Leicestershire vicarages increased threefold in value
between 1534 and 1603, and rectories fourfold. If this was a common
pattern, then rural vicars should have been at least keeping abreast
of inflation, and rectors becoming wealthier in real terms.

Less work has been done on the effects of inflation on merchants,
entrepreneurs and industrialists than on landowners, tenants and
wage-earners. There are many examples known of Elizabethans
who became wealthy through commerce and industry, as of many
others who failed disastrously, but it is hard to separate out the elements of enterprise and luck from the benefits or drawbacks of inflation. A rising merchant class has often been seen as a consequence
of the inflationary process; but trade remained a very uncertain
means of profit compared to land, for the former might yield a very
high return or might fail altogether. John Isham, who had made
high profits during the debasement period and after as a London
mercer, retired to his Northamptonshire estates in the 1570s after a
discouraging period of trading. Stone's analysis of the business activities of the peerage has shown that ironworks were usually profitable and that coalmining could also be worth while – in the early
1580s the earl of Shrewsbury enjoyed a net profit of about £65 a
year from his Sheffield mine – but that many others lost money in
coalmining.

The one group universally believed to have suffered most during the great inflation was the labouring poor, the landless wage-earners. Their plight was the leitmotiv of Thorold Rogers' pioneering work on Tudor prices. Whereas the fifteenth century was 'the golden age of the English labourer', 'the hind's wages became, towards the end of the sixteenth century, hardly sufficient for subsistence'. 'Never in the history of English labour did the workman suffer more than in the epoch which commences, roughly speaking, with 1545, and continues up to and beyond the year with which these volumes close [1582].' Malthus observed as early as 1826 that the 'corn wages of labour' had fallen by nearly two-thirds during the sixteenth century, and Phelps Brown and Hopkins would appear to support him. They suggest that the wages of urban building craftsmen between 1590 and 1610 had a purchasing power of only 43 per cent of their value in the later fifteenth century. 'The lowest point we record in seven centuries was in 1597', they concluded, 'the year of the *Midsummer Night's Dream*. Do we not see here a Malthusian crisis...?'[25] Despite an annual average compound rise in nominal wages of 1.46 per cent between 1532 and 1580, they suggest that real wages were falling further and further behind the cost of living until 1610–14, when they began to recover. Their picture of declining real wages, it should be added, is broadly comparable to similar studies of wages in sixteenth-century Alsace, Valencia, Vienna, Augsburg and Göttingen.

Their '1597' was the famine year 1596–97, which was certainly a terrible one. At Coventry that year foodstuffs were 'so extreame deare that many good householders sold up all they had and were faine to begge'. Yet, without wishing to gloss over the sufferings of the poor, especially in years of dearth, some reservations must be entered before the edifice of statistics and passion created by Thorold Rogers, Tawney, Phelps Brown and Hopkins can be admitted as satisfactory. The published wage-rates are not necessarily typical of urban wages. Most building craftsmen were self-employed, and few were totally dependent on wages for the support of their families; 'it seems certain that the living standards of many building craftsmen fell nothing like as much as the Phelps Brown–Hopkins index suggests'.[26] And the index is even less likely to reflect the real value of rural wages. Bowden has since made his own calculations of a cost-of-living index and wage-rates for southern agricultural labourers, set alongside recalculations of the Phelps Brown–Hopkins index, and his results suggest that the plight of the rural labourer was not quite as bad as that of his urban equivalent (Table 5.4).

Even so, had the labourers of the fifteenth century received adequate wages and no more, it is hard to see how their late Elizabethan successors could have earned less than half as much in real

Table 5.4   Wage-rates and their purchasing power, 1540–1609 (1450–99 = 100)

Decade	Agricultural labourer			Building craftsman
	Money wage-rate	'Cost of living'	Purchasing power of wage-rate	Purchasing power of wage rate
1540–49	118	167	71	70
1550–59	160	271	59	51
1560–69	177	269	66	62
1570–79	207	298	69	64
1580–89	203	354	57	57
1590–99	219	443	49	47
1600–9	219	439	50	46

Source: P. J. Bowden, 'Statistical appendix' in Thirsk 1967, p. 865.

terms without either rebelling or starving to death. Part of the answer must lie in the exceptional nature of the earlier 'golden age'. Taking Phelps Brown and Hopkins's seven centuries as a whole, the mid-fifteenth century level was exceptionally high, just as the level of 1600 was exceptionally low. Secondly, both the agricultural and builders' indexes measure only wages in pence per day; they cannot take account of how many days were actually worked. Phelps Brown and Hopkins's own important caveat was that possibly

annual money earnings in England rose more than the daily rate we have followed, because workers combined to keep down the normal day and the stint they would do in it, and so got more overtime; and because the Reformation reduced the number of holidays – Knoop and Jones reckon this will have raised by a fifth the number of days available for work in the year.

Thirdly, more labourers may have demanded wages partly in kind, just as some landlords did with their rents. Many accounts specified payment to labourers partly in food and drink, and the statutory wages laid down under the act of 1563 all gave alternative maxima for wages with and without 'meate and drincke'. Wilson in 1601 described the majority of cottagers as living 'cheefly upon contry labor, workeing by the day for meat and drinke and some small wages'.[27] Fourthly, because of the lack of statistical data, any cost-of-living index is based largely on food prices, and cannot take sufficient account of prices of manufactures, which apparently rose more slowly.

Fifthly, as Lipson pointed out, real income should be measured not by the wages of the individual but of the family. 'In spite of a fall in real wages . . . the purchasing power of the family might not suffer any diminution if the expansion of industry provided employment for an increased number of its members, women and children.'[28] Sixth, the indexes assume an unchanging 'basket of consumables', but the natural reaction to higher prices would be to cut down on non-essentials and to substitute cheaper for dearer foodstuffs and fuel (e.g. rye for wheat). Seventh, as Phelps Brown and Hopkins acknowledged, their index probably overstated the builders' poverty because 'processed products like bread and beer will not have risen in price so much as grain and malt'. And lastly, only a relatively small minority of the population depended wholly on wages. Those without self-sufficient holdings often had smallholdings or at least common rights, which cushioned them against rising food prices. Even urban craftsmen had their common lands on which they could keep a milk cow. The building craftsmen of the Phelps Brown–Hopkins index worked partly for wages but partly for profit. In short, although the plight of the wage-earner probably worsened during the reign of Elizabeth, it was less severe than the Phelps Brown–Hopkins index would imply.

If the labourer's loss has probably been exaggerated, there has certainly been overstatement of another alleged consequence of inflation, the gain of the manufacturer. E. J. Hamilton long ago suggested that a lag between European prices and wages in the sixteenth century created bigger profit margins and helped in the growth of capitalism. J. U. Nef, in a stimulating argument for an early 'industrial revolution' between 1540 and 1640, followed this up by suggesting that industrial wages consistently lagged behind industrial prices. The consequent profit inflation allowed manufacturers to invest in more capital equipment and to increase output considerably. However, industrial prices rose much more slowly than agricultural prices, and it appears from the scanty figures available that after an initial rise of industrial prices ahead of wages in the mid-sixteenth century, the two moved closely together thereafter. Recent work on the lead miners of Mendip suggests firmly that the free miners' earnings kept pace with inflation throughout the sixteenth century, and – more tentatively – that the real wages of mine labourers rose substantially.

The only substantial savings accrued to agricultural producers, who may well have stimulated demand for industrial goods. However, the larger and middling farmers who enjoyed the greatest profits also apparently possessed a high propensity to save and indeed to hoard. It is therefore unlikely that a growth in their income provided a corresponding increase in the demand for industrial products. There is in any case no empirical evidence that investment in the few untypically large industries with much capital equipment did increase dramatically during the period.

It is difficult to separate out the effects of inflation from those of population growth and other long-term changes. There is almost too much evidence for the social and economic mobility of hundreds of individuals and families to be fitted into any glib generalisations. As a broad rule of thumb, those with sufficient land to feed themselves, or better still those with a cash surplus, prospered, while those with insufficient land or none at all became more impoverished. It must be immediately qualified, for studies of peers, gentry, yeomen and husbandmen alike reveal a complex picture of stable families, prospering families and declining families, in which the effects of inflation of food prices are difficult to disentangle from enterprise, luck, fecklessness, trade and investment, fines for recusancy, and a host of other variables. Yet there is no reason to accept the view of some historians that landowners as a whole faced serious problems during the great inflation, resulting in major shifts in the balance of land-ownership and hence of economic and political power.

There were many ways in which landowners could keep abreast of inflation, and the evidence is that many did so very successfully. When they did not, it was not their social class which made any crucial difference. Whether tenants kept up with inflation as well as lords depended on their ability to earn more from their produce than they passed on in rent. Below the tenants, there was almost certainly a growing number of wage-earners, landless labourers and vagabonds; but whether this was a direct result of inflation is unclear. Could it rather have been due to a simple increase of numbers in a country of limited agricultural opportunities? And were there proportionately more landless labourers at the end of the century than at the beginning, or did their numbers simply increase in line with population growth? An analysis of agricultural changes may help to answer the question.

Chapter 6

Agriculture and rural change

I do not dwell in the country, I am not acquainted with the plough: but I think that whosoever doth not maintain the plough, destroys this kingdom.

> Sir Robert Cecil, 1601

The soil is fruitful and abounds with cattle, which inclines the inhabitants rather to feeding than ploughing, so that near a third part of the land is left uncultivated for grazing.

> Paul Hentzner, 1598[1]

1

Tudor England 'was still overwhelmingly an agrarian community.... Farming, whether arable or pastoral, was the national occupation, and though many husbandmen might combine domestic industry with tillage only a minority of the population lived by trade or industry alone.' Though food could be imported in times of scarcity, home production was crucial. In 1553 Northumberland tried, unsuccessfully, to have parliament delayed until the harvest was in, when, he thought, the Commons would be more willing to vote taxes. Even at a time of national crisis, with news of the defeat of the Armada just coming through, the Kentish militia were promptly disbanded 'to save their corn, for that otherwise it stood upon their undoing'. Hoskins has called the fluctuating qualities of harvests 'the heart-beat of the whole economy', and although meat and dairy products must also be taken into account the analogy is a fair one. Even in the late seventeenth century 'the greatest single flywheel of the economy was the land, the greatest source of wealth in rents, profits and wages, and the greatest single employer'. It was truer still of the Elizabethan age.[2]

To give primacy to agriculture is not to belittle the already substantial minority of the workforce engaged in trade and industry, whether full-time or part-time. In the still rural parish of Tottenham, Middlesex, 33 per cent of male heads of households, in Colyton, Devon, 47 per cent, were not engaged in agriculture, and in rural

Gloucestershire (1608) the proportion was 50 per cent. However, quite apart from the fact that Gloucestershire, with its thriving textile industry, was an extreme case, it would be false to create an antithesis between agrarian and industrial pursuits. The largest industrial sectors, notably cloth-working and leather-working, depended directly on agricultural raw materials. Nor were they yet large enough, despite the importance of cloth exports, to affect the whole economy in the same way as agriculture. Much has been made of the cloth depression and trade crisis of 1551–52, but it would probably have been less severe had it not partly coincided with a run of bad harvests, and it was dwarfed by the purely agrarian crisis of 1596–98. Even the severe trade crisis of 1620–22, though largely based on another cloth depression, was exacerbated by the bad harvest of 1622.

The dominance of agriculture is not in doubt; what remains uncertain is the relative importance of different types of land use. Many contemporaries regarded tillage as the backbone of English farming, praising cornfields and the sturdy ploughman, neglecting or belittling pasture and woodland. Yet several perceptive foreigners saw England as primarily a land of pasture, meadow and wood, and they were probably right. They could compare English conditions with those of their own lands, while many Englishmen were led astray by their prejudices. An exception was William Harrison, who thought English soils 'more inclined to the feeding and grasing of the cattle, than profitable for tillage, and bearing of corne', so that 'the fourth part of the land is scarselie manured for the provision and maintenance of graine'.[3]

Joan Thirsk has drawn attention to the great variety of farming regions in England, and has stressed that the contrasts between them were closely bound up with social, industrial, demographic and political differences.

The communities most typical of highland England practised pasture farming, produced only enough corn for their own needs, and did so in closes, or in small common fields, many of which were enclosed without commotion during and immediately after the Tudor period. Some of them still clung to the custom of partitioning their land among all or many of their sons, kept their families around them by providing them with holdings, and successfully resisted manorial pressure designed to restrict their freedom to do what they wished with their estates. Many of them mined and quarried while also running their farms and small-holdings, or engaged in a domestic handicraft to supplement their living. The majority of communities in lowland England followed a system of mixed husbandry, cultivated their ploughland in common, submitted to communal regulation of their farming, and to stricter manorial regulation when they disposed of their land. For the most part they were inclined to accept the custom of primogeniture. . . . Farming was a full-time occupation, which did not leave much scope for men to engage in a cottage industry.[4]

Such a broad contrast inevitably smoothes over local differences. Thirsk herself has proposed in place of the antithesis of highland and lowland a threefold classification, with a highland zone of 'open pasture' and a lowland zone divided between regions of 'mixed farming' and 'wood pasture' (Figs. 8, 9). The mixed farming areas were those

Fig. 8 Farming regions in England, 1500–1640

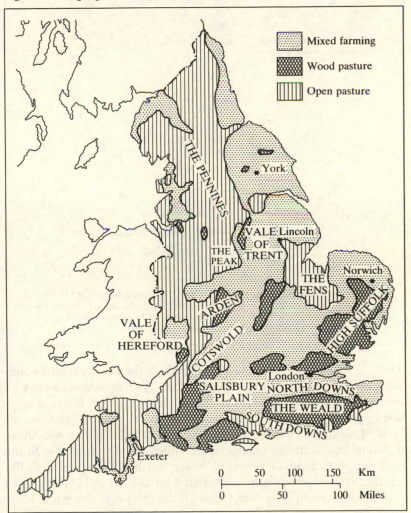

Fig. 9 Farming regions in Wales, 1500–1640

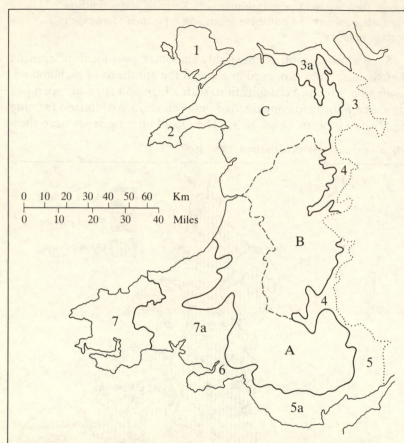

Mixed farming lowlands: 1, Anglesey; 2, Llŷn; 3, Border lowlands of Flint and Denbighshire, with 3a, Vale of Clwyd; 4, Central Borderlands; 5, Lowland Gwent; 5a, Vale of Glamorgan; 6, Gower; 7, Pembrokeshire; 7a, South-west Wales. *Pastoral stock-rearing uplands:* A, Southern; B, Central; C, Northern.

where arable farming dominated, whereas in the wood pasture woodland, meadow and pasture predominated. Contemporaries were well aware of the difference between the two main types of lowland landscape, which they usually distinguished as 'champion' and 'woodland'. Leland and Camden both contrasted 'Feldon' Warwickshire, a champion country of unenclosed cornfields and pastures, with the enclosed 'woodland' or Forest of Arden north of the Avon. Suffolk, another contemporary noted, consisted 'of two several conditions of soil, the one champion which yields for the most part sheep and some corn, the other enclosed for pasture grounds, employed most to grazing and dairy'.[5] And even this threefold classification does not easily comprehend other specialised areas, notably the numerous fens and marshes, which were geographically located in the lowlands but had an open pasture economy. Whatever be the truth about the degree of change and dislocation in the Tudor countryside, chronological differences between 1547 and 1603 were as nothing to the geographical variations over quite short distances.

The common-field system of mixed farming was still widespread. In its fully developed form in the Midland plain it had four essential elements. The arable and meadow were divided into unhedged strips among the cultivators; both arable and meadow were thrown open for common pasturing after harvest and in fallow seasons; the cultivators also enjoyed common rights over pasture and waste; and the ordering of all communal farming was regulated by a manorial court or village meeting. A common pattern was a village with three arable open fields, each of which was left fallow every third year, that is, rested from crops to increase the yields thereafter. The two sown fields in any year were known as the tilth field and the breach field. The former was the one that had been fallow the previous year, and was generally used for autumn sowing, especially of wheat and rye. The breach field was sown in the spring with peas, beans, oats or barley.

A fully fledged common-field system required a mixed farming regime, with a high proportion of arable, and it was largely absent from the pastoral highland zone, although many valleys and coastal plains there possessed common fields without the elaborate Midland apparatus of communal controls. Such highland communities often possessed either a single open field, or four or more small fields; the arable, forming only a small part of their economy, did not need to be worked on a systematic basis. Furthermore, many lowland or partly lowland counties like Kent, Essex, Suffolk and Devon had, by the sixteenth century, almost wholly abandoned common fields, while the fenlands had never known them at all. The common-field system survived in full vigour in a zone which can be conveniently described as a triangle with its apex in County Durham and its base from Wiltshire to Norfolk (Fig. 10). This was the region where most open field remained to be enclosed in the eighteenth century, although even in the sixteenth it was being eroded by enclosures. When the arable was enclosed it was often for conversion to pasture, and the change of use preserved the characteristic corrugated pattern produced by the plough by fossilising it under grass. Such old ploughlands are still a frequent sight, and were even more common before recent reconversions to arable and deep ploughing. In 1631 some

Fig. 10   The extent of enclosure, *c.* 1600

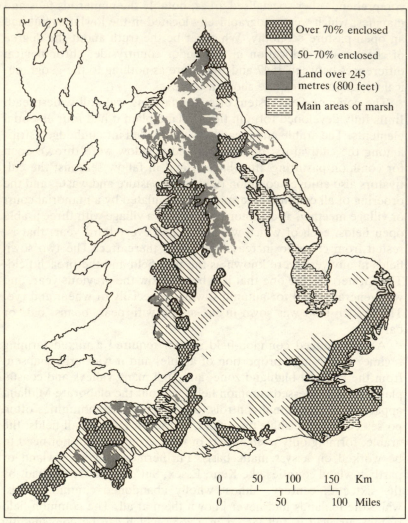

Over 70% enclosed

50–70% enclosed

Land over 245 metres (800 feet)

Main areas of marsh

Source: A New Historical Geography of England, ed. H. C. Darby, Cambridge U.P., 1973, p. 256

men of Gloucestershire testified that certain ground 'hath bene of olde tyme arable, as appeareth by the ridges and furrowes yet clearlie to be seene'.[6]

Other mixed farming areas specialised in sheep and corn, notably the chalk downs radiating from Salisbury Plain and the Jurassic belt of the Cotswolds, Northamptonshire, Lincoln Edge and the North York Moors. The sheep grazed the hills by day, and were folded at night on the arable fields beneath, thus providing a rich source of manure. The sheep–corn balance prevailed also in the sands and brecklands of East Anglia, which had a common-field system similar to that of the Midlands, but with foldcourse rights for sheep over the fields, meadows and commons, normally possessed by the manorial lord or his lessees. Finally, the rich marshlands of the Thames estuary and the east coast specialised in yet a third form of mixed farming, the combination of corn-growing and the fattening of livestock.

Within the lowland zone lay numerous smaller regions of wood pasture, including heavily wooded claylands and forest areas (including the royal 'forests', although the tree cover was not always heavy). They included High Suffolk, most of Essex, the Kentish and Sussex Weald, much of Dorset and Wiltshire, the Northamptonshire forests, south Derbyshire, Arden, north Worcestershire, and much of Shropshire and Staffordshire. There dairying and stock-keeping were combined with some arable farming, woodland crafts and part-time industries.

The upland regions, together with the vales of Cheshire, Lancashire, Clwyd, Anglesey, Pembroke and Glamorgan, were lands of open pasture with some arable on the lower ground. Leland noted time and again that the Welsh 'study more to pasturage then tyllyng', though he also noted 'good plenty of corne'. They varied greatly, however, in both prosperity and farming systems, from the bleak uplands of Northumberland and Durham with their transhumance of sheep between summer and winter pastures, to the fat dairying country of Cheshire and the Vale of Clwyd. The arable was normally confined to what was necessary for local subsistence, and was commonly organised on the infield–outfield system. An infield was heavily manured and continuously cultivated, while other areas were temporarily taken into arable cultivation in turn and then laid down to grass.

Arable land throughout England and Wales was worked by a bewildering variety of ploughs, each suited to different soils, which were drawn by horses and oxen. Horses were probably more numerous, but many districts with heavy soils preferred the ox. The usual breadcorn crops were wheat, barley, oats and rye, while barley was also used extensively for brewing. Peas and beans were grown mainly as fodder for livestock, but were also drawn on for human sustenance in famine years. The breadcorns would have varied with the local agrarian regime. Middlesex specialised in wheat for the capital and the court; John Norden noted that the best wheat was grown at Heston, 'and therefore Queen Elizabeth hath the most part of her provision from that place'.[7] At Chippenham in Cambridgeshire nearly all the arable land was under rye and barley in about equal proportions;

in Leicestershire pulses and barley dominated, with a smaller acreage of wheat; but in east Worcestershire wheat, barley and pulses each accounted for about a third of all crops.

Pasture farming was noted especially for its sheep, so profitable for wool, and so much criticised as an agent of depopulation. It grew a golden fleece that encouraged large-scale farming, and the great gentlemen-sheepfarmers each possessed several flocks, with up to a

Fig. 11   Length and quality of English wool, *c.* 1600

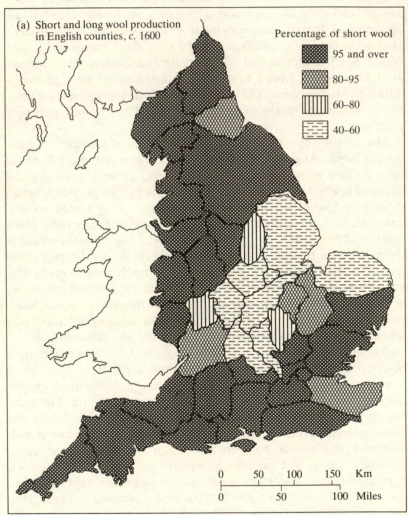

Source: Peter J. Bowden, *The Wool Trade in Tudor and Stuart England*, Macmillan, London, 1962, p. 28.

thousand or so sheep to a flock. The Spencers of Althorp and Worm-leighton possessed a total of 13,000–14,000 sheep in the 1570s, while the greatest known sheepmaster, the duke of Norfolk, owned 16,800 in East Anglia in the autumn of 1571, i.e. after the sale of surplus lambs. However, flocks were not only a source of profit to rich gentlemen, but a means of livelihood for the poor. Some remarkable surveys of Cannock Chase in Staffordshire suggest that one in every

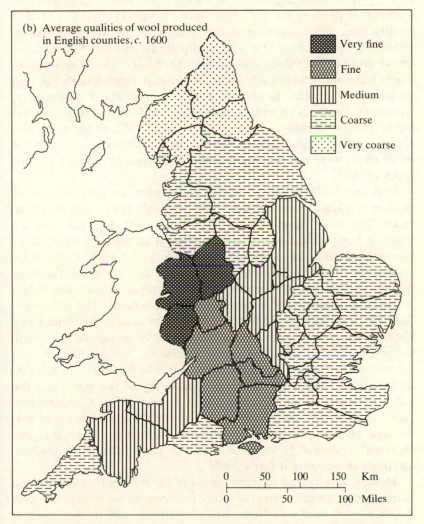

(b) Average qualities of wool produced in English counties, c. 1600

Very fine
Fine
Medium
Coarse
Very coarse

0   50   100   150   Km
0   50   100   Miles

Source: Peter J. Bowden, *The Wool Trade in Tudor and Stuart England*, Macmillan, London, 1962, p. 29

three adult males in Rugeley kept a flock of sheep, many of them cottagers to whom their sheep could make all the difference between self-sufficiency and destitution.

Though it was also a source of meat and even milk, the sheep was above all reared for wool. Bowden has estimated, from figures for wool and cloth exports in 1540–47, that there were nearly 11 million sheep in England, and as his estimate assumes only one-third of total production for the home market (quite probably too low), the true figure may be even higher. Wool varied considerably in length and fineness, depending on soil, grass and climate (Fig. 11). The best quality fine, short-staple wool was grown in the Welsh Marches, especially the 'Lemster Ore' of Herefordshire and the 'March' wool grown around Shrewsbury and Bridgnorth. Midland and Lincolnshire wools were also traditionally short and fine, perhaps largely because enclosures for pasture farming yielded richer grassland. Conversely, wools of the southern counties from Sussex to Cornwall were improving in quality. Cornish wool was said, around 1582, to be 'moch bettere and plentyfullere then in tymes past'.[8] Northern wools, on the other hand, were and remained generally coarse, fit only for inferior types of cloth.

It is easy to be led by contemporary comments into thinking of pasture yields solely in terms of wool; yet grain prices generally rose faster than wool prices between 1548 and 1600 (Fig. 12), and the value of livestock may have been measured as much by meat, dairy products, leather, hides, or even by dung, as by wool. Cattle were considered the most desirable farm animals, and a cow was the commonest possession of a smallholder or cottager, while even urban freemen commonly kept a cow upon the town fields. The cows were the indispensable source of those 'white meats, as milke, butter and cheese, which were woont to be accounted of as one of the chiefe staies throughout the iland', said Harrison, but which 'are now reputed as food appertinent onelie to the inferiour sort'. In suitable districts cattle were not merely the mainstay of the poor, but the pillar of highly profitable commercial farming. The Cheshire pastures, explained William Smith, were reserved for production of butter and cheese: 'no other countrey in the realme may compare therewith, nor yet beyond the seas, no not Holland in goodnes, although in quantety it farr exceed'.[9]

Horses were reared in large numbers for transport, pleasure and warfare; pigs for meat, and bees kept everywhere for honey, the chief sweetener for food and drink. Rabbit warrens, constructed often at great expense by the larger landholders, were an important source of meat; Robert Reyce said of Suffolk that no great estate was com-

Fig. 12   Relative movements of grain and wool prices, 1450–1600

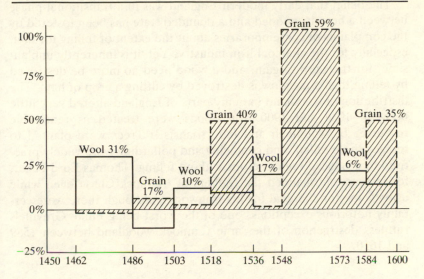

Note: Wool is indicated by a firm line, grain by a broken line and emphasised by line shading. For each period the heights of each column represent the % increase in the annual average price of that commodity over the annual average for the previous period. The difference in heights indicates which commodity price rose the faster, and by how much.

Source: Deserted Medieval Villages, ed. M. Beresford and J. G. Hurst, Lutterworth Press, 1971, p. 13

plete without one. Animal husbandry, like arable farming, varied with the soil, climate and local customs, and generalisations are apt to be misleading. Above all, the hardy myth of the regular slaughter of livestock at Michaelmas, to save the scarce resource of winter feed, cannot be too often rebutted. On eight farms around Dolwyddelan, possessing 1,049 cattle in June 1570, only 41 were killed during the whole year.

If the study of pasture farming has been neglected in favour of the arable, then woodland management has fared even worse, the Cinderella of Tudor agrarian history. Yet timber and underwood were of vital importance. 'Timber played the part in the Tudor economy that is played by coal, steel, and concrete today.' The extent of tree cover and hedgerow was enough to strike foreign visitors as a dominant feature of the landscape, or as one Frenchman put it, 'in travelling you think you are in a continuous wood', though this was probably true only of the ancient enclosed landscapes – such as they would have seen in the South-east – rather than the champion areas.[10]

The belief that early modern England was in a transitional phase between a heavily wooded and a denuded state has been fostered by the complaints of contemporaries about the extent of felling for fuel, especially for the charcoal iron industry. Yet 'it is inherently implausible, for trees grow again, and a wood need no more be destroyed by felling than a meadow is destroyed by cutting a crop of hay'. The distribution of woodland in many parts of England altered very little between 1086 and 1900, for woods were treated as renewable resources by woodmen and industrialists.[11] Trees were planted to replace those felled, and coppicing and pollarding were widely practised to produced regular crops without felling. Thomas Lord Paget, for instance, husbanded the timbers of Cannock Chase even while using some for charcoal for his ironworks, although there were certainly notorious exceptions, one of the worst being Fulke Greville's ruthless destruction of the same Cannock woodland between 1589 and 1610.

2

The pattern of rural settlement varied as much as the farming systems. In classic Midland open-field parishes, like Laxton (Notts.), the houses of the farmers and labourers lay together along one or two streets, close to manor house and parish church, with almost no outlying dwellings. Where the arable and meadow strips and parcels of every farmer were scattered about the parish, and the meadow at least was reallocated annually, it made sense for all to live together centrally. The nucleated village was, indeed, the norm throughout the regions of mixed farming, although in enclosed parishes or in areas where separate farms had been won from the waste beyond the open fields, the parish might contain separate farmhouses or even small hamlets well away from the village. In wood-pasture areas like the Weald or High Suffolk there was a different pattern, with many scattered hamlets and farms as well as some villages, while in many parts of the highland zone all settlement was dispersed and there were no nucleated villages at all.

Settlements varied in terms of lordship as well as of morphology and distribution. The manor might be larger or smaller than the village or parish, and it might or might not have a resident lord. Perhaps as many as one-third of all parishes and villages had no resident squire,[12] and without one the substantial yeomen were able to run the manor and parish themselves. Wigston Magna in Leicestershire provides a good example of such variations, for it had been divided for centuries into two manors, a division which allowed the decisions about farming to be decided by a village rather than a manorial meeting. Henry Turvile sold off his manor in 1586–87 to the sitting tenants, while the other manor changed hands several times before being sold by the Danvers family to the tenants in 1606. One reason for the sale was that from 1588 the Danvers were faced by concerted legal resistance by the customary tenants which apparently made their purchase of the manor a poor investment. A few miles away a struggle between lord and tenants at Cotesbach ended very differently. Here, too, the manor was bought as an investment, by a London merchant called John Quarles (1596). Unable to increase his revenues from the tenants, he enclosed the manor, nearly doubling his income but halving the population of the village.

Cotesbach and Wigston are only two of thousands of possible examples of lord–tenant relationships, for there was no such thing as a 'typical' manor. In theory, all land still had to belong to a manor and its lord, and the lords in turn held their land, directly or indirectly, of the Crown. In practice, most corporate towns stood outside the manorial framework, while some lands taken in from the waste, especially in wood-pasture districts, recognised no manorial jurisdiction. Yet most countrydwellers, and some townsfolk, still lived under the manorial jurisdiction of the traditional courts baron and courts customary. The courts, headed by the lord and freeholders of the manor, ratified all transfers of manorial land and promulgated by-laws and customs. Some resident lords still possessed a home farm – the medieval 'demesne' – cultivated by wage labourers, but many preferred to lease it out; of thirty-six West Country manors held by the earl of Pembroke in 1568, the demesne was leased in twenty-nine cases. The cultivator of the demesne, whether the lord or his 'farmer', was usually the largest landowner in the parish, with a farm of commonly over 200 acres and often much more, whereas the commonest size of tenant farm was in the range 30–60 acres.

Manorial tenants held land by a bewildering variety of tenures, which can be grouped conveniently into four. First came those holding by frank or freehold tenures, either by knight service or socage. Freeholders, although technically tenants, held on very light terms including suit of court and modest payments, and were very close to freeholders in the modern sense of the word. Most other tenants were customary tenants or copyholders (two overlapping but not quite synonymous groups), who held their lands at the will of the lord but subject to the custom of the manor. They varied greatly in the conditions and security of their tenure.

Some held by inheritance, some for lives, some for a term of years, and some at the will of the lord. All owed both an annual rent and an entry fine payable at every change of tenant; the fine might be either fixed or arbitrary, while the annual rent would remain unchanged for the duration of the tenancy. There were also special categories of customary tenures, notably free customary tenure in Wales, tenant right (a customary tenure with fixed rents) in large parts of the North, and free conventionary in the duchy of Cornwall. The customary tenures were traditional, and not flexible enough to suit many landlords in an age of rapid inflation. For that reason, a third type of tenure, the lease with a rack rent, was gradually replacing them in many areas from about 1560. It was more flexible, and could be adjusted to short-term changes in prices and harvest yields (a rack rent meant one adjustable in either direction, and not necessarily one to be screwed up to the maximum). Lastly, there were still a very few bondmen or villeins holding land as unfree tenants and tied to the land in perpetuity; but their numbers were rapidly dwindling as they were allowed to buy their freedom. Matters are further complicated by the parallel existence of a legal classification of landholding by estates rather than tenures, and the fact that in estate terms 'copyholders may be freeholders'.[13]

To estimate the proportions of manorial tenants is no easier than to estimate the numbers and values of manors held by different classes of landowner. Tawney made a valiant attempt as early as 1912 to quantify the relative holdings of different tenants. Unfortunately his tables lumped together the evidence of manorial surveys and rentals over more than a century of rapid change, but there has been no general work to supersede it. His sample of 6,200 tenants on 118 widely scattered manors showed that almost 20 per cent were freeholders, 61 per cent customary tenants, and 13 per cent leaseholders. The proportions varied greatly by region, over a third of all East Anglian tenants being freeholders. In Kent, which furnished no examples, the proportion may have been even higher. 'For copyhold tenure is rare in Kent', boasted Lambarde, and 'the custome of gavelkind prevailing everywhere, in manner every man is a freeholder.'[14] On two fenland manors in Lincolnshire, 53 and 31 per cent of all tenants were freeholders, though in another case 92 per cent were copyholders, and freeholders were almost entirely absent.

The most misleading features of all such statistics are, however, inherent in the sources. A manorial survey categorised the tenants by tenures rather than estates, which can give a distorted picture of their security. Almost all the tenants on Lord Paget's manors of Cannock and Rugeley (Staffs) were customary tenants, but the majority were copyholders of inheritance, and so enjoyed an estate of inheritance in fee simple, in other words almost complete security. Also, surveys were concerned only with the lord's tenants and not with their subtenants. Where other sources allow subtenancies to be counted, they disclose considerable numbers. At Cannock two-thirds of the manorial land was cultivated by subtenants, most of whom can be identified only from the chance survival of a Field Book of 1554, and at Walkeringham (Notts.) a little later, seven freeholders had fifty-three subtenants among them. Furthermore, the Cannock evidence is that subletting did not lead to a more equitable distribution of land, but rather the reverse; some men acquired sizeable farms through this means and increased the disparity in the real size of holdings.

Farmholdings ranged from mere allotments and smallholdings too small for self-sufficiency, through farms of 30–60 acres which could comfortably support a family, to large farms which required extra wage labour for their cultivation. Another analysis by Tawney of 1,664 tenants on 52 manors ranges them from 10 per cent with no land except cottage and garden to 1 per cent with over 120 acres: much the commonest holdings were of under 20 acres. Recent researches point to similar figures, of between 5 and 10 acres as the norm in the Lincolnshire fens, between 5 and 20 in Lancashire, and 18 acres on one manor in the Somerset levels (1558). Fifty-four Forest of Arden inventories afford larger figures, with over half the holdings between 15 and 50 acres and a mean holding of 32, but these exclude the smallholders.

Regional comparisons are, however, made difficult by variations in land measurement. The customary acre in the North, for instance, often equalled $1\frac{1}{2}$ or even 3 statute acres; the Essex acre was measured by a pole of $21\frac{1}{2}$ feet instead of the standard $16\frac{1}{2}$; and in Staffordshire there was a customary acre of 5,760 square yards. The yardland, a notionally standard farmholding unit, varied from 30 to 40 acres in Cambridgeshire, and between 28 and 55 acres in three Warwickshire settlements. Furthermore, average figures are affected by whether subtenants are included, for Tawney's statistics were confined to the tenants. Half the cultivators at Cannock in 1554 held all their land in subtenancies, and would appear as landless if the Field Book did not survive. There were also regional variations in the range of size of holdings. In parts of Northumberland nearly all the 'husbandlands' or farms were of equal size, usually 30–50 acres.

Another important regional variation was in systems of inheritance. Where partible inheritance prevailed, holdings were likely to be fragmented until they were inadequate for subsistence. Primogeniture, insisted on by many manorial courts, theoretically ensured impartibility, but in practice the line between the two systems was blurred, as even when a father bequeathed his inheritance to his eldest son, he frequently assigned smaller pieces of land, as well as cash or goods, to the others. In the Cambridgeshire villages of Chippenham and Orwell, such concealed partible inheritance helped to break down the standard late medieval holdings of 15–45 acres, increasing both the number of cottages and the minority with large holdings. In the fen village of Willingham, however, common rights in the Fens allowed many holders of medium farms to retain them intact, for other sons could survive on the fens and meres which accounted for three-quarters of the area of the parish. In 1575 nearly half the land-holding tenants still held between 16 and 25 acres.

It is, however, too easy to concentrate on the tenant farmers and to neglect the many cottagers and labourers. About half of the tenants in Chippenham and Willingham were either landless or possessed at most a holding of 1 or 2 acres, according to surveys of 1544 and 1575 respectively, although a smallholding with common rights in the Fens could provide self-sufficiency where it could not do so on the chalkland. Everitt suggests that most tenants with under 5 acres would at least occasionally supplement their income by working as wage labourers. On his sample of fifty-one manors in several regions, nearly 37 per cent of tenants occupied such smallholdings (though the surveys used as sources, once again, do not record sublettings). Some, like the 70 per cent of smallholders in the Fens, might be self-sufficient; while others not included in the manorial surveys, like farm servants living in, were also labourers. But there can be little objection to his conclusion that 'the labouring population probably formed about one-quarter or one-third' of the rural population.[15]

Cottagers and labourers could make a living by working for the larger tenants, but they could live more independently in the fens and woodlands, where extensive common rights allowed them timber, fuel, food and grazing. In Cheshire, for instance, 'the heathes are comon, so that they serve for cattell to feed on, especially sheepe and horses, a good helpe for the poorer sort'.[16] In most regions, however, kine (cattle in the modern sense) were much the most important of the cottagers'.animals. Everitt finds that at least three-quarters of labourers leaving inventories (1560–1600) possessed at least one cow, calf or heifer. As the population increased in Elizabeth's reign, cottages sprang up in wood-pasture areas like Arden and north Shropshire. Some cottagers were natives, but others were immigrants coming into areas of greater opportunity and more common rights. Consequently, many eked out a living with very little land of their own, like the tenants of Aldeburgh manor (Suffolk) before 1547 who paid 1*d* for a cottage ground not more than 80 feet either way, and ½*d* if its dimensions were only 40 feet. Everitt has analysed 651 labourers' holdings in 43 manors, and found that 67 per cent held under 1 acre, often only a cottage and garden. It was to meet the threat of the multiplication of such holdings that a statute of 1589 ordered no more cottages to be built without at least 4 acres of land; but it was impossible to implement.

Cottagers and labourers could supplement their income by part-time crafts. In all districts except one, Everitt's sample of labourers' inventories shows that at least half practised an industry as well as farming. Such opportunities were most available in the wood-pasture areas and in upland pasture areas with coalfields and ironfields. Nail-making was practised in south Staffordshire, charcoal-burning in the Weald, potting around Newcastle under Lyme, and stocking-knitting and lead-mining in the Yorkshire dales. The most characteristic by-employments, especially for women and children, were weaving, spinning and knitting. Textile manufacture in Yorkshire, Lancashire, East Anglia and the West Country helped to support many poor families who could not have made ends meet solely by agriculture. When parliament in 1555 passed an act limiting most weaving to the towns, an exception had to be enacted immediately for the Halifax district, 'being planted in the grete wastes and moores where the fertilite of grounde ys not apte to bring forthe any corne nor good grasse', and where the inhabitants 'altogether doo lyve by clothemaking'.[17]

The discussion so far has avoided the term peasantry, a term frequently used by Tawney and by the authors of the preceding and following volumes in this series; two of the best regional agrarian histories are entitled *English Peasant Farming* and *The Midland Peasant*. The problem is that its meaning is normally assumed rather than defined, and that it is used in very different senses. Tawney, Hoskins and Thirsk appear to group together as peasants all tenants from freeholders to cottagers, excluding only the large farmers. Other writers use the term to mean smaller owner-occupiers whose holdings were sufficient to support their families though not to provide an agricultural surplus; this would exclude most cottagers and labourers. Mendras and Macfarlane have recently suggested that, by most sociological definitions, early modern England had no peasantry. It is true that, as their critics have asserted, this is a matter of terminology. If Thorner's definition is adopted, that in a peasant society 'more than half of the working population must be engaged in agriculture', then clearly Tudor England was such a society, with such important exceptions as Middlesex and Gloucestershire; but the definition is hardly illuminating and little more than a synonym for 'pre-industrial'. This is not to deny that Tawney and others were describing real problems – notably the security of tenants and the squeezing out of smallholders; but discussion is not advanced by the use of a term which, to borrow a phrase of Hexter in another connection, 'has all the flexibility of an india-rubber band'.

3

The existence of a peasantry is more than a semantic point, for it relates to crucial arguments and assumptions about the dynamics of agrarian change. Tawney perceived an 'agrarian revolution' unfolding between 1500 and 1640, in which a subsistence 'peasant' economy was superseded by 'capitalist agriculture'. Under the stimulus of commercialism, the decline of military service, the profitability of wool, and rising prices, the larger farmers enclosed land and converted arable to pasture, thus increasing their profits but also squeezing out the small tenants and increasing unemployment. 'In economic affairs as in religion, the new order came, not gradually, but swiftly and with violence.' Kerridge, who rebutted this 'wholly untrue picture of early capitalism as cruel and greedy', proposed a more optimistic but equally revolutionary development. The agricultural revolution, meaning 'that cluster of innovations more usually associated with the period from 1750 to 1850', took place in fact between 1560 and 1673.[18]

Neither view would command whole-hearted assent today; and of course both models relate to long periods only partly covered in this volume. Yet both are concerned with changes which must be given due weight even in a short-term study. Fundamental to them all was the pressure of a growing population upon resources which reversed the conditions of the fourteenth and fifteenth centuries.

Under the stimulus of growing population, rising agricultural prices, and mounting land values, the demand for land became more intense and its use more efficient. The area under cultivation was extended. Large estates were built up at the expense of small-holdings, and subsistence farming lost ground to commercialized agriculture. Changes in the balance of land distribution were accompanied by an increase in the number of agricultural wage-earners and a decline in their standard of living. There was a growing inequality of income among the different classes of rural society.[19]

Some modifications to Bowden's judicious summary will be suggested, but in general it is unarguable.

Many of the agrarian changes were subsumed by contemporaries under the convenient but misleading short-hand expression 'enclosure'. Slater recognised that it involved three separate features, '(1) the laying together of scattered properties and consequent abolition of intermixture of properties and holdings; (2) the abolition of common rights; (3) the hedging and ditching of the separate properties. This third process is the actual "enclosing" which gives its name to a series of processes which it completes.' The three stages could take place in any order, and might never be completed; common rights might be abolished while the land remained unhedged, or enclosure might take place without removing those rights. Much enclosure proceeded peacefully, and many wastes and parks were enclosed by agreement in areas of land shortage. Common fields outside the central Midland area were often enclosed by agreement of all the tenants, as at Iwerne Courtney (Dorset) in 1549, and at Mudford (Somerset) in 1554; and even in Warwickshire, where there was more friction, the same could happen. The inhabitants of Stareton in 1598 obtained permission from their lord 'to exchange oure landes one with another . . . and to inclose the same so exchanged'.[20]

For at bottom the urge to enclose did not spring from landlords' greed for profit. It was the pressure of rising population and land-hunger which drove lords and tenants alike to a more efficient use of land already farmed, or to extensions of farmland into the waste. The common fields were certainly more efficient and flexible than the textbook stereotype; Tawney noted long ago that 'the conventional picture . . . of open-field agriculture as a perverse miracle of organised torpor performed by village idiots' had no relation to reality, and recent local studies have underlined the point. Nevertheless, many contemporaries were convinced that enclosed land was in general more profitable. The experienced surveyor John Norden thought enclosure 'the most beneficiall course that tenants can take . . . for one acre enclosed is worth one and a halfe in common, if the ground bee fitting thereto'. And the enclosure by agreement at Mudford was plainly inspired by similar beliefs; for, noted the surveyor, 'when the feildes are inclosed every man will use a further trayvale and dylygence with his londe to converte yt to the best use and purpose, whiche before they coulde not . . .'.[21]

The widespread Tudor hostility to enclosures related to four overlapping processes: violent enclosure, where a lord or tenant took away or encroached on common rights without general agreement; depopulating enclosure, where a lord evicted tenants; conversion of arable to pasture, which might or might not coincide with enclosure, and which often involved some depopulation; and engrossing, where farms were united and the surplus population made redundant. The difference between these and the approved forms of enclosure is made lucid in the *Discourse of the Common Weal*, where the capper, husbandman and doctor support government intervention against enclosures. Enclosing landlords have created unemployment, hunger and rebellion; the husbandman has known a dozen ploughs within six miles' radius laid down within seven years, 'and wheare xl persons had theire lyvinges, nowe one man and his shepard hathe all'. The knight argues, on the contrary,

that inclosures should bee profitable, and not hurtfull to the common weale; for we se that countries, wheare most inclosures be, are most wealthie as Essex, Kent, Devenshire and such.

To which the doctor's reply is that

I meane not all inclosures, nor yet all commons, but only of such inclosures as turneth commonly arrable feildes into pastures; and violent inclosures, without recompence of them that have right to comen therin.

Similarly, Norden qualified his encouragement of profitable enclosures by insisting that they must receive the assent of all the tenants, 'and that the lords should not depopulate by usurping inclosures: a thing hatefull to God, and offensive to men'.[22]

The later Tudors, in trying to prevent or reverse such enclosures, were following in the well-established tradition of statutes of 1489, 1515, 1533 and 1536, proclamations of 1514 and 1526, and Wolsey's enclosure commissions of 1517–19. There was, however, a gradual change as the government became more aware of local differences and changing economic conditions. The act of 1489 had forbidden all depopulation and all conversion of arable to pasture, and the 1517 commission had been empowered to inquire into all enclosures since 1488 except those in the four northern counties. The later Tudors concentrated their efforts on counties where enclosure and engrossing were major social problems, distinguished between different circumstances of conversion to pasture, and set more realistic time-limits for the periods of inquiry. The impetus remained, however, a constant one, to prevent excessive agrarian changes without local consent, which could provoke unemployment, depopulation, vagabondage or insurrection.

In 1536 the statute of 1489 had been re-enacted, though with application only to thirteen Midland counties and the Isle of Wight. It was, however, like previous acts, not very vigorously enforced, until in 1548 Somerset's government set up another commission. The commissioners were to inquire into all depopulating enclosure, engrossing and conversion to pasture carried out since 1488 in a group of Midland counties where the process was thought to be most acute. This was probably an unrealistic target. Paget thought that most serious depopulations had occurred before 1488, a judgement which modern research has vindicated. Nevertheless, enclosing and engrossing were still causing serious friction. After the 1548 commission was set up, riots against enclosures broke out in several Midland counties, triggered by the sympathy shown by the government, and the *Discourse* suggests that enclosures were felt to be the chief agrarian grievance in the Midlands at that time. Meanwhile in March 1549 parliament enacted a special tax on sheep and cloth; from May there were serious anti-enclosure riots in a dozen counties; and in July a serious revolt in Norfolk and Suffolk which was at least in part a protest against enclosures. The real and widespread sense of grievance was, however, counter-productive. Leading councillors and politicians took fright, abandoned Somerset and his protégé Hales, the driving force behind the commission, and repealed the tax on sheep. The commission's work was left uncompleted, and the only returns that survive relate to Warwickshire, Worcestershire and Cambridgeshire.

It is noteworthy that the area of greatest friction over enclosures, and that singled out by most Tudor statutes and commissions, was the Midlands; and 98 per cent of the depopulation cases brought before the Exchequer between 1518 and 1568 came from ten Midland counties. These were the counties where the common-field system was most developed and most important to the local farming communities, but also areas very suitable for pasture as well as arable farming. The most substantial exception was the East Anglian wood-pasture region, where enclosures of some remaining common fields were violently resisted in 1549. In the sheep–corn areas, by contrast, the tenants tended to *favour* enclosure because it protected them from the lords' right of foldcourse. Consequently, the Norfolk rebels under Kett did not generally oppose enclosures, despite a hardy tradition to the contrary, but the abuses of the foldcourse system.

It would be too simple, in fact, to see the agrarian revolts of 1549 as directed primarily against enclosures. Admittedly the Jacobean historian Godwin was in no doubt that they were, but his testimony is only subcontemporary; and in Kent, which in his view was 'the fountaine of this generall uprore', enclosures do not seem to have been a major issue. And in Devon, where most yeomen and husbandmen owned small flocks of sheep, it was the tax on sheep and cloth which aroused popular indignation. In Sussex, on the other hand, there is contemporary testimony that armed rebellion was threatened because of grievances 'againste certaine gentlemen, and chiefely for inclosiers', and was averted only when the earl of Arundel intervened to throw down those which were illegal.[23]

The anti-enclosure riots and writings of 1548–49 were undoubtedly linked to the temporary presence of a sympathetic administration, but they were also provoked by a temporary but sharp rise in the price of wool relative to grain, which made enclosure more profitable. All the wheat harvests but two from 1530 to 1548 were average or better, thus making grain prices very cheap; and from 1536 to 1548 wool prices rose ahead of them (Fig. 12). This was exactly the period of rapid conversion to pasture according to the *Discourse*, where the husbandman says that 'manie of us saw, xij yere ago, that our proffittes was but small by the plowes', whereupon some of his neighbours had 'turned ether part or all theire arable grounde into pasture, and therby have wexed verie rich men'.[24] The debasement of 1544–51 strengthened the movement by making English exports (including woollen cloth) more lucrative; and the economic choices of farmers were distorted because cloth could be freely exported and grain could not, as Smith also complained.

As Lane told Cecil in 1551,

the exchange doth ingendar dere clothe, and dere clothe dothe ingendar dere wolle, and dere wolle dothe ingendar many scheppe, and many schepe dothe ingendar myche pastor and dere, and myche pastor ys the dekaye of tyllage, and owte of the dekaye of tyllage spryngythe ij evylls, skarsyte of korne and the pepull unwroghte, and consequentely the darthe off all thynges.[25]

This was a perceptive analysis, but events soon conspired to undermine its premisses. The end of debasement, and the crash of the Antwerp cloth boom, ended the boom in cloth prices. There were bad harvests, either for wheat or for grains generally, in 1549–51, 1554–56, 1560, 1562 and 1565. The lethal epidemic of 1557–59, following on the heels of the worst series, must have reduced the pressure on food supplies, but in general the population was rising sharply, and grain prices rose far more than wool prices throughout the quarter-century 1548–73 (Fig. 12). Significantly, there was little complaint of violent or depopulating enclosures during that time; and altogether known depopulation was modest. Of 482 alleged cases of depopulation heard before the Exchequer for the four Midland counties between 1518 and 1568, 340 involved the destruction of only one house. What requires explanation is why, if higher wool prices encouraged conversions to pasture in the inner Midlands, the higher corn prices of 1548–73 did not encourage reconversions to arable. Gould has suggested that, although much of the land was marginal and equally suited to either use, the area did not have the water communications with London and other centres of demand that would have made bulk transport of grain profitable. Local prices remained low, and a small rise in the marginal rate of profit on pasture would have a maximum effect. Yet if reconversions to arable were limited in the Midlands, several leading families like the Spencers and Temples did shift their attention from sheep to cattle as wool prices stagnated.

Despite the easing of the pressure for conversions and other unpopular enclosures, the government kept up its guard. An act of 1550 protected small cottagers who squatted on waste land, and allowed them to annex up to 3 acres, but allowed larger enclosures to be thrown open again. Another of 1552 ordered land which had been in tillage for four years at any time since 1509 to be restored to tillage, though those who had converted arable to pasture, but had also converted an equivalent area from pasture to arable, were exempted. Mary's parliaments confirmed some of the earlier anti-enclosure statutes, and in 1563 came a new statute for maintaining tillage. All arable converted to pasture between 1515 and 1529 was to be restored to tillage, all land tilled for any four successive years since 1529 to remain in tillage, and no further conversions to pasture to be permitted. The act was followed by a new enclosure inquiry in 1565, which for some reason was quickly countermanded; only fragmentary returns for Leicestershire and Buckinghamshire survive.

From 1565 to 1593 enclosure attracted less government attention and no new legislation. Harvests were generally of average quality or better, and grain prices continued to rise ahead of wool prices except during the period 1573–84. Enclosures continued piecemeal, often for reorganised arable farming rather than for conversion to pasture, and often by agreement between lords and tenants. The dearth of 1586–88 did remind legislators that corn supplies were insufficient to cover a really bad harvest; a bill 'for maintenance of houses of husbandry and tillage' in 1589 passed both houses of parliament, but for some reason did not receive the royal assent. However, the harvests of 1587–93 were mostly good or very good, and in 1593 parliament repealed all the acts against conversion to pasture 'by reason of the greate plentie and cheapnes of graine'. It was unfortunately timed, for there were four successive disastrous harvests in 1594–97, provoking at least one attempted revolt against enclosures and grain prices (Oxfordshire, 1596).

The next parliament understandably panicked, especially when informed that since the repeal of 1593 there had been 'manie more depopulacions, by turning tillage into pasture, then at anie time for the like number of years heretofore'. This was no mere rhetoric, for a study of Leicestershire has revealed a spate of enclosing for pasture in 1591–97, while in Staffordshire conversions to pasture reached a peak in 1592–94. A new statute against conversions to pasture was therefore passed in 1598, together with another against the engrossing of farms. The MPs did, however, attempt to confine the former act to areas where conversion caused real distress. The original bill would have banned conversions throughout England, but it was amended to apply to only twenty-three English and one Welsh counties. When one member attempted to have Shropshire included, another objected. Shropshire, he said, consisted 'wholie of woodland, bredd of oxen and daries'. As Herefordshire and other adjacent counties 'were the barnes for the corne', so he hoped Shropshire 'would bee the dayrie howse to the whole realme'.[26] So Herefordshire was left in the act and Shropshire excluded. Such regional specialisation meant, naturally, a heavy reliance on interchange of produce. In the dearth of 1596–97, when Midlands corn was insufficient, the town of Shrewsbury alone had to import over 3,200 bushels of foreign corn.

The statutes of 1598 remained in force until 1624, despite an attempt to repeal them in 1601 when good harvests returned. None the less, Midland conversions to pasture continued on a large scale, provoking a serious revolt in 1607 in Northamptonshire, Leicestershire and Warwickshire. An enclosure commission set up in its aftermath heard allegations that over 70,000 acres had been enclosed and converted to pasture since 1578 in 7 counties, at least 60 per cent of it since 1593, and well over 2,000 persons displaced. It has to be said that all statistics based on these returns are based on allegations and not proven cases; and even on the basis of the allegations, and in the worst-affected inner Midlands, Gay calculated that under 9 per cent of the total area was enclosed in the sixteenth century. Yet such qualifications could have been no comfort to those who were displaced in what was undeniably a significant number of Midland communities. At Cotesbach in Leicestershire, where the lord's demesne had been enclosed and converted to pasture about 1501, the rest of the manor was enclosed by the lord after 1603 and the population halved, provoking great bitterness; it was not surprisingly one of the villages which joined in the revolt of 1607. It is fair to add, however, that Parker's detailed study of Leicestershire enclosures, though it demonstrates that their scale was indeed considerable (15,000 acres between 1580 and 1607), also shows that most enclosures in this period were by agreement.

At least the age of depopulation of whole villages and hamlets, so widespread before 1485, was over. Most depopulations alleged before the commissioners in 1607 were of small numbers of houses, and the only entire village alleged to have been destroyed was Onley in Northamptonshire, although the Oxfordshire rioters in 1596 had protested that 'Mr. Fryer has destroyed the whole town of Water Eaton'. Beresford has suggested that wholesale depopulations of the kind castigated by More in *Utopia* ended in the South and Midlands by about 1520, and it is now generally accepted that the many mid-Tudor allegations of villages destroyed referred to an evil already in the past, and was being exaggerated by those who feared it might happen again. In fact after about 1550 the destruction of villages and their conversion to pasture was not only hampered by government and popular hostility, but was also less of an economic proposition. Corn was more profitable than wool with the demand from a growing population and the depression of cloth prices.

Enclosures of open fields, then, were after 1550 increasingly enclosures for more efficient arable farming rather than for pasture, were increasingly by agreement between the farmers, and produced little friction outside the inner Midlands. Yet it was possible for a lord and tenants to agree on an enclosure which would suit them but not those cottagers and labourers with common rights but no arable. The Statute of Merton (1236) allowed lords to improve the waste provided that they left sufficient commons for their tenants, and some lords interpreted 'sufficient' very narrowly. Thus the poor copyholders at Kirkby Moorside in Yorkshire had cottages without land attached. When the earl of Westmorland 'toke from the tenauntes' their commons and enclosed them around 1561 he ruined them, for each had kept there one, two or three cattle 'for the releyf of themselves, their wyves and chyldren'.[27] Even without enclosure, a lord could achieve a similar result by 'surcharging' the commons with many of his own beasts, leaving too little grazing for his tenants.

4

Enclosures without consent may well have been exaggerated by many contemporaries, yet complaints about depopulations, like protests about vagabonds, paupers and military manpower, sprang from a real concern that countryfolk were being driven off the land. The physiocrats of eighteenth-century France believed that England had prospered more than France in the early modern period because it had become a land of large capitalist farms worked by wage labour. Marx and Engels, developing this view, saw the late fifteenth and sixteenth centuries as the time when English capitalist farming developed, and the destruction of the 'peasantry' or rural smallholders began; and Tawney took a broadly similar view. 'The history of the agrarian problem in the sixteenth and seventeenth centuries', he wrote, 'is largely the story of the small cultivator's struggle to protect his interests against the changes caused by the growth of the great estate.' Could this age, rather than A.H. Johnson's eighteenth century, have seen 'the disappearance of the small landowner'?

Tawney certainly demonstrated a considerable variation in the size of Tudor holdings, and he believed that the period was an early stage in the transition from relatively democratic village communities with equal-sized holdings to the modern pattern of mainly large and medium-sized farms and many landless labourers. The impetus to engrossment, he thought, came without doubt from a desire to profit commercially by farming. The capitalist lord or lessee would be anxious to take over the holdings of as many tenants as possible, but legal differences of tenure determined whom he could squeeze out. 'Leaseholders and many copyholders suffer, because they can be rack-rented and evicted. The freeholders stand firm, because their legal position is unassailable.' He also saw an active land market among the 'peasants' themselves, as successful commercially minded yeomen or husbandmen bought out neighbours, and the communities became polarised.[28]

Tawney's arguments have been assailed by Kerridge, who argued that sixteenth-century law gave protection to copyholders and other customary tenants as well as freeholders, and that only tenants-at-will and villeins were without security of tenure. Illegal evictions by *force majeure* were uncommon, and were as likely to apply to one tenure as another. His impressive accumulation of evidence commands respect, and it does seem that Tawney created too gloomy a picture of tenant security. He published in 1914, for example, an influential document describing the harassing of customary tenants of Whitby Strand (Yorks.) by their lord about 1553. They complained that he was raising their rents unreasonably and threatening to ruin them. However, the important point is that the tenants organised themselves to petition the Court of Requests for redress, and that they won their case.

In fairness to Tawney it should be added that, even with the protection of the courts, there was a fundamental legal distinction between freehold and copyhold of inheritance on the one hand, and all other customary tenures and leases on the other. The latter did not give permanent interest in the land, and escheated periodically to the lord. For example, a copyhold for three lives might be secure while the three persons named survived, but the lord had every legal right to refuse to renew it to the same family when the last of the three had died. A more substantial argument against Tawney is the lack of really decisive evidence that small freeholders did indeed enjoy more security in practice than other classes of manorial tenants.

Recent studies suggest that inequality of holdings between tenants, and an active land market between them, go back well into the Middle Ages. The gradual consolidation of lands by successful lords and yeomen, and the emergence of a landless labouring force, was a long-drawn-out process extending over several centuries, and the period under review here formed only a small part of it. Indeed, it is hard to be sure for this half-century whether the *proportions* of large landholders and landless were changing, or whether population growth was simply increasing the absolute numbers of landless. Certainly the numbers of small landholders increased, in some areas at least, as a growing population led to more competition for land. At Chippenham in Cambridgeshire the middling landowner was almost completely squeezed out. In 1560 there were thirteen holdings of between 14 and 51 acres, whereas by 1636 only three remained.

At least in some mixed farming areas, and in an age of population growth, inflation of food prices, and pressure on landed resources, a growth of larger farms was likely without any conspiracy by the landlords. Regional agricultural specialisation, and the growing demands from urban markets, encouraged the cost-efficiency of large farms producing for the market over family holdings producing only enough for their own needs. With population growing faster than the area of farmland could be extended, more intensive farming was necessary, and the improvements required more capital and resources than the small landholder possessed. Bowden has estimated income and expenditure for a typical arable farm of 30 acres around 1600–20, and has concluded that the farmer might normally enjoy a net profit of £3–£5 a year, a small margin which could easily disappear in a year of crop failure: only the large farmer, with 50 acres or more, was safe. The middle-sized tenants were also eroded by equal partition among children where partible inheritance was the rule, and by the splitting off of small plots for younger sons even where primogeniture was observed.

There is no evidence that rents in general outstripped food prices, at least before 1590, so it might seem that there was no reason why many tenants should have been unable to meet increased rents by increased income from food. However, a tenement of half-yardland or 'subsistence' size produced little for the market, and yet still had to produce the extra cash required. Furthermore, population growth meant more competition for land when leases were renewed, with potential tenants bidding against one another and offering higher entry fines. Not only did some smallholders fail to renew their copyholds or leases, but the more prosperous tenants could afford to bid for larger holdings and so diminish the total number of farms. Engrossing was carried out from below, by the prosperous tenants, as well as from above, by the lords. Finally, short-term subsistence crises, notably those of 1586–88 and 1594–98, had a 'ratchet' effect on the structure of landownership. Small men fell into debt in a time of scarcity, sold out to the more prosperous on unfavourable terms, and were not able to recover their position when times improved. At Terling in Essex several husbandmen were unable to pay their rent by Michaelmas 1595, and suffered distraint of their holdings. At Chippenham in Cambridgeshire, five of the middle-sized holdings were bought out by more successful tenants increasing their holdings, and three of them were sold in the single year 1598.

However, it is unwise to generalise too readily from recent detailed local studies, which have largely come from Midland openfield villages. If small landowners were beginning to disappear from upland Cambridgeshire in the 1590s, they continued to survive in large numbers in many open-pasture and wood-pasture areas, like the Northamptonshire forests, the Cambridgeshire and Lincolnshire fens, the Yorkshire and Lancashire Pennines and the lowlands of north Shropshire. The fixed rents of tenant right continued to protect the poor smallholders of Cumbria and other parts of the North; the custom was understandably challenged by many lords in an age of inflation, but it was upheld by the equity courts. And in Kent, Everitt has shown, several manorial lords were active in protecting smallholders from the loss of their land or common rights at the hands of 'greedy-minded tenants'. 'Throughout the seventeenth century, at least, the economics of smallholdings in pastoral regions were not such as to drive the peasant worker from the land.' Even in the openfield Midlands, the yeomen and husbandmen could continue to maintain their own in those 'open' villages which were not closely controlled by a resident lord owning much of the land. When the two manors of Wigston Magna were broken up and sold off, most purchasers were manorial tenants buying their own holdings of between 15 and 60 acres. The customary tenants simply turned themselves into freeholders and became more secure, holding their own throughout the seventeenth century. There is only limited truth in the venerable tradition of Marx and the physiocrats that early modern England became more a land of large farms than, say, northern

France, as J. P. Cooper has demonstrated. As late as 1800 England was 'in the main still a country of small farms'.[29]

5

As Stone has pointed out, many of the phenomena Tawney studied were caused, directly or indirectly, by population pressure rather than by 'the wicked enclosing or rackrenting landlord'. Given that population pressure, what is perhaps most remarkable is the agrarian achievement rather than the 'agrarian problem'. National population grew by perhaps 60 per cent between 1540 and 1610, and that of the capital by a staggering 150 or even 300 per cent. Yet the extra numbers were catered for by the home market except in bad years, and the necessary increase in grain output was achieved without diminishing the production of meat, dairy products, wool and leather from the pasture. Viewed in this light, a move towards larger and more efficient farms was necessary if output were to be increased sufficiently, and the squeezing-out of the 'half-yardlander' with his 15 or 20 acres unavoidable. In primary arable areas 'the "typical" medieval holding was no longer a viable economic unit in the price rise of the sixteenth century, as the 200-acre farm is no longer a viable unit today'.[30]

The claim that agricultural output kept pace with the rising population may seem a bold one, especially in the light of the evidence for subsistence crises. Harvest qualities can be compared from the yearly price fluctuations for grains provided by Hoskins, Bowden and Harrison. The broad comparison between good years (low prices) and bad years (high prices) is certainly valid, although the prices were not totally elastic, because after a period of severe dearth and unemployment grain could not be afforded and the price might fall. Hoskin's wheat price index of 1964, based largely on Beveridge's data, can be set alongside Harrison's of 1971, which had the advantage of access to Bowden's data and was able to include indexes for barley and oats as well as wheat. Both measure harvest prices against a thirty-one-year moving average, calling them 'average' if within 10 per cent of the norm, 'deficient' if 10–25 per cent above, 'bad' if 25–50 per cent above, and 'a dearth' if over 50 per cent above the norm (Appendix I).

It is not easy to interpret the long-term pattern behind the figures (Fig. 13). Harrison seems to indicate, more firmly than Hoskins, a relatively long and untroubled period of average harvests or better between 1556 and 1586, and a more severe concentration of disas-

Fig. 13   English wheat harvest fluctuations, 1540–1625

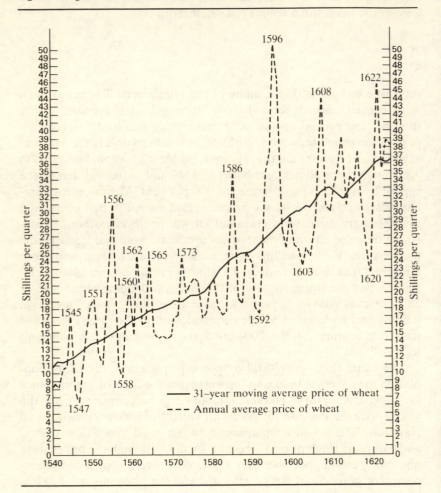

trous harvests between 1586 and 1600. In both, the extremes of high
and low prices oscillate more wildly by the end of the century than
earlier, but that is to be expected when rising prices are being plotted;
the absolute price levels were bound to be further apart. Superficially, 1596 seems the worst year of the century, but in fact 1556 was
the worst, with a higher percentage differential from the long-term
average than any other year, whether measured by wheat alone or
all grains. Hoskins is convinced that the figures give no support to
the theory of climatic deterioration after 1550: 'there were 29 good
harvests out of 70 between 1480 and 1549; and there were exactly
the same number in the seventy years from 1550 to 1619'.[31] Since,

however, the 'good' harvests are measured against a thirty-one-year average, there seems no mathematical reason why the *distribution* of good and bad years around the average should not remain the same whatever long-term climatic changes occurred. H. H. Lamb has argued that the weather did indeed become colder after about 1550, and furthermore that nearly 20 per cent of the rainfall was concentrated in July and August, which would of course have disastrous effects on the harvests.

The years 1556, 1586 and 1596 were the worst harvests of the period, but 'dearths' in the sense of famines were not confined to those harvest years, but lasted usually two years; the price fell in the second year because few could afford to buy what grain was available. Some of the evidence has already been adduced for starvation in England in the periods 1555–57, 1586–88 and 1596–98, while Appleby has analysed in detail some regional evidence for the two last and for the later crisis of 1622–23. The cluster of three periods of dearth between 1586 and 1623 has led some writers to postulate a 'Malthusian' crisis in later Elizabethan and early Stuart England, as population temporarily outstripped food supplies. Skipp, for example, has depicted a rapidly growing population in the Forest of Arden, both from natural increase and immigration, which was halted by a 'mild Malthusian check' in 1613–19, a time of increased mortality though not, he believes, severe enough to qualify as a subsistence crisis. Yet it can be argued that nearly all the crises were triggered by disastrous weather, a fortuitous event rather than a sign of the nemesis of overpopulation; and furthermore, that a rapid growth in records in the late sixteenth century has distorted our perspective. The dearths of 1586–1623 are better recorded than that of 1555–57, just as the London plagues of 1603–65 are better recorded than that of 1563, but in both cases there is reason to believe that the earlier crisis was more severe than the later ones, and that, if records permitted, one might discover yet more severe crises earlier still.

The subsistence crisis of 1555–57 is not well recorded, but significant numbers were dying of starvation even in the capital, in contrast to the later dearths. The period from 1556 to 1561 was the only quinquennium in the Tudor period when the national population appears to have declined, and although a mysterious epidemic was largely responsible, famine appears to have been a contributory factor. On 12 December 1556 one of Cecil's agents wrote from Burghley House to tell him that grain was almost unobtainable: 'I trust it will be cheaper at our next Easter than now, or else many will die of hunger.' Cecil himself long remembered the distress of those years, and recalled them in 1584–85:

And albeit it hath pleased God of his great goodnes . . . to blesse this land both with peace and the fruite of peace now by the space almost of 27 yeares; yet let us not forgett, that within those 7 yeares next going befor, ther was such a scarsitie of corne within the realme of England, that the comon people, in most partes of the lande, war glad to make their bread of acornes.

And to make matters worse, the disastrous weather had brought a murrain of cattle as well as harvest failure. The men of the Isle of Ely, the bishop told Cecil in 1563, were desperately poor 'by the reason of the late yeres, whearin their cattell, the substance of their lyvinge, dyed'.[32]

Any Malthusian explanation must take account of why the worst later Tudor subsistence crisis should have struck in 1556 rather than in 1596, when the population had increased by over 25 per cent. No one would wish to minimise the distress of 1596–98, but the evidence is of severe hardship, with starvation in the northern and western counties, a pattern that is even clearer in 1622–23. Nationwide subsistence crises were coming to be a thing of the past, in contrast to France and Scotland, where they continued until the end of the seventeenth century. Admittedly, in so far as starvation was averted in England in 1586–88 and 1596–98, it was because home supplies of grain could be supplemented from the Baltic. This was not a new policy; for substantial purchases of Baltic grain had been made, for example, in 1563. But the largest shipments in the second half of the century were in the two years 1586–87, when English ships transported 11,000 lasts of rye from the Baltic, and in the three years 1596–98, when the corresponding figure was 4,800 lasts. Yet it was generally understood that grain imports were unnecessary except in years of scarcity, and even then were only supplementary. As the preamble to the Tillage Act of 1598 asserted, English arable farming was 'a cause that the realme doth more stande upon it selfe, withowt dependinge upon forraine cuntries . . . for bringinge in of corne in tyme of scarsetye'.[33] Admittedly, there were probably local exceptions to the adequacy of grain. In areas like Skipp's Arden parishes, where much arable land had been converted to pasture, and corn was grown only for subsistence, there was no reserve to meet shortages.

In a time of increasing population, then, England did well to feed its people with home-grown grain, with limited exceptions during two short periods. But the argument can be taken further, for in average and good years the farmers of the specialised grain-producing areas, especially East Anglia, sought for, and to some extent obtained, the right to export their surplus overseas. A statute of 1361, not repealed until 1624, had forbidden all exports of corn from England other than to Ireland unless a royal licence had been obtained. In practice, however, this constraint was loosened considerably under the later Tudors. Acts of 1555, 1559, 1563, 1571 and 1593 permitted corn exports subject to central and local control and subject to corn prices being below certain stated maxima (except in 1571, when prices had simply to be 'reasonable'). They were not only indicators that corn was normally in sufficient supply, but they probably encouraged increased production. Camden noted under the year 1561:

The country people also, when licence was once granted to transport grain, began to ply their husbandry more diligently than before, yea and above that which the laws afterwards made required, by breaking up grounds which had lain untilled beyond all memory of man'.[34]

It was not by any means a free trade. Average grain prices were only rarely below the statutory floor prices, and although licences could usually be procured in time of plenty, such as that granted to William Curtis in 1579 to export Devon wheat to Spain or Portugal, a little later some Norfolk farmers petitioned the queen that the customs officers had made their corn exports too difficult and costly. Restraint of exports would lower the price too much and reduce the amount of tillage. In 1601 the Norfolk justices were again complaining about restrictions on grain exports, while one MP was already voicing worries that corn was too cheap at home because of the restraints. Nevertheless, it was at least a policy of relatively free export of grain compared with previous centuries, and it led ultimately to the free export of grain after 1670 regardless of home prices. If the customs records are any guide, the major east coast ports exported far more grain in good years than they imported in bad. Lynn, for instance, imported nearly 5,000 quarters of corn in 1586–87 and 2,000 in 1596–97, but this was as nothing to the 20,000 quarters exported in 1571–72, 1587–88 and 1588–89, or the 25,000 in 1583–84. At the turn of the century Bacon could assert that whereas England had formerly been 'fed by other countries', now 'she fed other countries'.

6

If English grain output did indeed expand sufficiently to feed a growing population, and if few Englishmen starved to death despite the huge rise in food prices, how was it achieved? Did arable production expand extensively, through the ploughing of former pasture and waste, or intensively, through increased yields, or both? Were other foodstuffs, such as meat and dairy products, also produced in larger quantities?

Kerridge, on the basis of Wiltshire evidence, was able to assert that 'the agricultural revolution, in the farming countries now under notice, was the achievement of the sixteenth and seventeenth centuries, and more particularly of the period from 1575 to 1675', an argument he extended to the country as a whole in a book provocatively entitled *The Agricultural Revolution*. Here he argued that the revolution began with 'an upsurge of activity in up-and-down husbandry, fen drainage, "floating upwards", marling, swarding, and cole-seed cultivation' between *c*. 1560 and 1580, followed between 1585 and 1612–13 by

an upsurge both longer and stronger, with the innovation of catchwork floating, carrot cultivation, extensive woading and liming, larger-scale fen drainage and floating upwards, more marling and cole-seed cultivation and rye-growing for sheep, the introduction of soap-ash, and the more rapid advance of up-and-down husbandry.[35]

These are impressive lists of innovations, and although his general conclusion does not command the assent of most agrarian historians, he has certainly shown that the beginnings, at least, of many improvements must be dated earlier than was previously thought.

The population decline in the fourteenth and fifteenth centuries had been accompanied by a diminution in the area of land cultivated. One obvious resource of a recovering population was to extend it once more, especially into the woodlands, uplands, fens and marshes. Thus four new cattle farms were created at Cwm Eigiau in the Welsh hills in 1554, and 28 acres of moor and moss were turned into cornfields at Henbury, Cheshire, before 1558. A Caernarvonshire township saw the creation of twenty new enclosed pasture farms on former saltmarsh between 1531 and 1567, and as many again by 1600, mostly of between 50 and 100 acres. A commission of 1571–72 found that 545 acres of Westward Forest in Cumbria had been encroached on for farmland, and that thirty-two new farms had been created as well as existing farms enlarging their area. Under the pressure of growing population three Lancashire townships partitioned Henfield Common in the parish of Whalley, while the men of Grindleton across the Pennines petitioned the queen to let them enclose a moor for arable and pasture.

In wood-pasture areas like Arden and north Shropshire, the cultivated area could still be expanded to feed both natives and immigrants coming from more crowded parts. At Myddle in Shropshire, over 1,000 extra acres were brought under cultivation between the late fifteenth and early seventeenth centuries within a parish of only 4,700 acres. In more densely settled areas extra land might be found by disparking. Lambarde (1576) listed 53 parks in Kent, of which 23 had been disparked within living memory, and 1,700 acres of Shillinglee Great Park (Sussex) were enclosed by agreement about 1600 to extend cultivation. Norden, in his *Surveiors Dialogue,* argued for cultivating every possible acre as vigorously as any eighteenth-century improver. He believed 'that there is no kind of soile, be it never so wilde, boggy, clay or sandy, but will yeeld one kind of beneficiall fruit or other'. And by 1619 James I was arguing that more land had been recently ploughed up from the waste than had been converted from arable to pasture.

It would be easy to be overwhelmed by such cases as signs of agrarian progress. Yet it could fairly be argued that the men of the later sixteenth century, like those of the later thirteenth, were driven to extending the limits of cultivation because food production was not keeping pace with population. The petition of the men of Grindleton to extend their fields (1587) alleged that their existing fields were insufficient to maintain their growing population, and that poverty was daily increasing among them. Furthermore, in so far as the land being taken up was the marginal land abandoned during the population decline, it was likely to be poorer and less productive, so that the marginal costs of cultivation would increase. Kerridge, who emphasises so many innovatory features of the period, rightly dismisses the mere extension of cultivation, which would be 'to misunderstand the nature of economic revolutions and to confuse technological innovation with mere economic growth'.[36]

Can it be argued, none the less, that farming production was becoming more intensive as well as extensive, and that overall productivity was rising? Having dismissed extension of cultivation, enclosure of common fields and other conventional criteria of an agricultural revolution, Kerridge proposes instead 'the floating of water meadows, the substitution of up-and-down husbandry for permanent tillage and permanent grass or for shifting cultivation, the introduction of new fallow crops and selected grasses, marsh drainage, manuring, and stock-breeding'. Of these, the second was 'the backbone of the agricultural revolution'. All can certainly be established as significant innovations in the early modern period; the question must be how far they were established, or at least projected, in the sixteenth century as well as the seventeenth.

Convertible or up-and-down husbandry, consisted of abolishing the distinction between permanent arable and permanent pasture and thereby increasing productivity of both crops and livestock. Land suitable for both arable and pasture, common especially in the Midlands, was used alternately for both. Productivity increased because crop yields are higher on land which has been rested under grass, and pasture is better feed on land converted from arable. Furthermore, the system abolishes the wasteful practice of fallow fields; more animals can be kept because fodder crops are grown for their winter feed; and the animals are folded on the arable at night, so that their dung enriches the soil and increases arable yields. The basic principle was applicable both to small enclosed fields, by alternating their use, and to the arable common fields, whereby temporary 'leys' of grass were created and shifted from one part of the field to another. It has been argued that an efficient convertible system required enclosure, since common-field farmers had to erect temporary fences to keep grazing beasts off the arable. This, however, they were often willing to do. Havinden has demonstrated for open-field Oxfordshire in the seventeenth century a widespread flexibility of convertible husbandry, leading to an ascending spiral of progress as more livestock led to more manure and so to more arable, more winter feed, and yet more livestock.

Shifting cultivation had always been practised in areas of abundant land, and true up-and-down husbandry is recorded from at least the fourteenth century. Kerridge instances a considerable number of manors where the practice was first recorded between 1550 and 1610, such as Petworth in 1557, Winterbourne Bassett and Collingbourne Ducis in 1567, Kenilworth in 1581, and Knowle in 1605. The tillage acts of 1552 and 1598 specifically exempted from prosecution those who worked land as arable and pasture alternately rather than increasing pasture at the expense of arable. However, it is hard to be sure how much the apparent increase of the practice is simply a matter of more records; and it is not at all clear that it was as widespread and significant as it was to be in the seventeenth.

One difficulty, as Bridbury has pointed out, is that it may not have been the innovation that the late sixteenth century could afford. If a hungry, growing population demanded corn rather than meat and dairy products, the number of livestock would actually be reduced for short-term reasons, and the 'ascending spiral' could not begin, as the land lacked sufficient dung. Yelling, especially, is sceptical whether Havinden's 'ascending spiral' could have begun until well into the seventeenth century, believing that livestock numbers probably decreased between 1550 and 1600, and adducing evidence of east Worcestershire inventories in support. However, Skipp's study of some north Warwickshire parishes finds that although there was a sharp drop in cattle numbers between 1570 and 1609, most of the shortfall was in meat production, and there was a significant increase in dairying as an extra food resource for the growing population.

'The fertilizing resources of the Tudor husbandman', Fussell justly observed, 'were strictly limited. Animal excrement, vegetable waste, and the mixing of soils made up the complete list of his manures'.[37] Animal dung was probably still much the commonest manure for the arable, and the most successful example of a symbiotic productivity of arable and pasture based on dung was the sheep–corn districts of East Anglia, which involved supplementing the permanent arable by shifting arable carved from the commons and manured by folding the sheep on them. Even then, however, sheep dung was supplemented by marling to improve the light, sandy soil. All over England there were a variety of fertilisers for improving underproductive arable, whether by animal manure, vegetable compost, town refuse, ash from wood, fern and turves, or by extraneous and inorganic substances – lime, chalk, marl or seasand – depending on the nature of the soil, which were all thought to improve soil fertility.

Kerridge does not date most of his examples, but he does cite ashes being bought from the Bristol soap-boilers by about 1600 to spread on the fields of Herefordshire, and Merrick's evidence for Glamorganshire by 1578: 'Now of late yeares, since the knowledge or use of lyminge was found, there groweth more plentye of grayne.' Havinden suggests that liming acid soils in Devon began in the last quarter of the sixteenth century. The practice was noted by Hooker in 1599, while at the same period Norden spoke of Cornish farmers increasing rye yields by 'burning their grounde' and 'soyling it with sea sande'. By 1602, noted Carew, Cornish grain yields had increased so much that the county had a surplus for export. In Cheshire by 1585 the practice was to spread marl (white and red clay) on the arable, which 'bringeth corne in as great aboundance, as that which is dounged'; one Cheshire gentleman, Sir George Booth, was proud to remember thirty years later that in 1616 he had not only rebuilt his ancestral house of Dunham Massey but had also 'marled at Dunham fifty-eight acres'. Many of these practices, it should be added, may have been simply better recorded rather than practised for the first time; some can be found already in the fifteenth century.

Such practices, together with convertible husbandry, made all the difference to crop yields according to one contemporary, John Smith of Nibley. He told the House of Commons in 1621 that corn should be freely exported, since dearth was no longer a threat:

Our husbandry, by marlinge, chawkinge, seasand, lymynge, more earth, oadynge old pastures, plowing up warrens, parks and wood growndes, with God's ordynary blessinge, freeth us from that feare.[38]

The drainage of fens and marshes was mostly a small-scale, piecemeal affair before 1600. Hydraulic engines for draining marshes were being considered for patents in the 1570s, and from 1589 Humphrey Bradley was pressing Burghley over a scheme for large-scale drainage in the Fens of Norfolk, Huntingdonshire, Cambridgeshire, Northamptonshire and Lincolnshire. A bill to that effect was put before parliament in 1593 but it failed; Lord Willoughby spoke out strongly against it because of the effects it would have on the poor who made a living by reed-cutting, fishing and fowling. A similar bill, for the recovery of 300,000 acres of the Fens, passed both Houses in 1597–98 but was blocked by the queen. In 1601, however, an act for the recovery of the marshes was passed, and already by 1602 coleseed was being profitably grown on newly drained land. In other areas drainage on a large scale can be found earlier. Much of the Greenwich, Plumstead and Wapping marshes was drained in Elizabeth's reign, as were many of the meres and mosses of north Shropshire.

Another improvement was 'floating' or artificial watering of meadows to improve the quality and yield of grass and hay. True water meadows are said to have been first floated on a large scale by Rowland Vaughan in the Herefordshire Golden Valley in the 1590s, and the simpler technique of flooding meadows even earlier, in the 1560s in Wiltshire and Staffordshire at least. Norden had seen many water meadows in Somerset, Devon and Cornwall when he wrote *The Surveiors Dialogue* in 1607. However, they were not in widespread use until the seventeenth century; and it has been recently shown that the famous examples said to have been introduced by Horatio Palavicino (d. 1600) at Babraham in Cambridgeshire date only from that century. There is better evidence for careful stock-breeding and stock-fattening in the reign of Elizabeth, and the stock of horses, cattle and sheep was significantly if gradually improved by the import of overseas breeds, such as Friesian cattle and horses from Naples and Hungary, and, of course, by judicious crossing of native strains.

Fruit-growing, hop-growing and market-gardening developed considerably around London and other large cities, and in Kent, Hertfordshire, East Anglia, Worcestershire, and Herefordshire new crops for human consumption and animal fodder did make a modest appearance. Parts of northern Essex already 'abound[ed] greatelie with hopps', wrote Norden in 1594. Many vegetables were still imported from the Netherlands, but the growing of carrots and turnips is recorded frequently by the end of the century. Another, more widely grown introduction was rape or coleseed, valued primarily for its oil but also as sheep fodder. It was already grown for oil near Lynn by 1551, but its use on a large scale seems to have been owed to the Netherlandish refugees in East Anglia, and it became a common crop only in the 1590s. A more rapid success was achieved by the labour-intensive woad, an essential crop for dyeing cloth. Experiments in growing it began about 1548 in Hampshire, and it spread rapidly in the 1580s under pressure of the rising cost of imports. By 1586, 5,000 acres in 12 southern counties were under woad, giving work to about 20,000 people for 4 months every year. However, the most important new crops for increased yields were to be the clovers and grasses which were not introduced until the seventeenth century.

One indisputable advance was in the science of surveying. It was an old-established practice for manorial surveys to be made occasionally, recording the titles, rents and values of each tenancy. Much of the evidence of size and consolidation of holdings is inevitably drawn from such surveys. However, some surveyors, notably Agas, Saxton and Norden, pioneered a more informative and accurate type of survey by admeasurement. They used chains, plain-tables and theodolites, noting the area of each holding, field or strip, and sometimes accompanying their findings with an accurate and detailed plan. Examples of such plans from *c*. 1590 and later, among the muniments of All Souls College, were published by Tawney in 1912, and many others have since been discovered and published. Christopher Saxton, after his work on national and county maps, specialised in local land surveying between 1587 and 1608 in his native Yorkshire and other counties, a practice that was continued by his son Robert. In 1607 Norden summed up much of the improved science in *The Surveiors Dialogue*, a popular book which quickly went through three editions. It is likely that the more accurate knowledge which he and his colleagues made possible of the value and exploitation of different soils and different tenures was a crucial element in the improvement of landed revenues.

The Surveiors Dialogue was exceptional in its originality and influence, for agricultural progress was generally empirical and not based on book-learning. Fitzherbert's *Boke of Husbandry* and *Boke of Surveying*, both written in the 1520s, remained popular, as did Tusser's *Hundreth Good Pointes of Husbandrie* (1557) and *Five Hundreth Pointes of Good Husbandrie* (1573), but these and other textbooks advanced very little beyond the advice offered by Walter of Henley in the thirteenth century. Almost the sole exceptions were Reginald Scot, who in 1574 and 1578 explained and advocated commercial hop-growing, and Barnaby Googe, who in 1577 urged up-and-down husbandry and the use of turnips for winter feed.

It is not easy to judge fairly the extent of agricultural progress. Fifty-six years is a short time over which to attempt a balance-sheet, when so many innovations were very gradual. Many documents are impressionistic and uncritical, and those with statistics cannot always be relied on. Some evidence seems contradictory, perhaps because regional experiences differed so much. Thus Thirsk and Everitt can stress the growth of regional specialisation, with farmers tending to produce what they could grow best, and using the cash from their sales to buy what they lacked, instead of aiming at self-sufficiency. Yet Yelling can discern between 1550 and 1650 a narrowing of regional differences, as arable areas increased their production of pastoral products and vice versa. What can be suggested with some confidence is that England was able to expand its food supplies almost, if not quite, to keep pace with a considerable population increase. Furthermore, English farmers were not only able to expand their output, but to lay the foundations of a more diverse and less vulnerable food supply from which their successors were to benefit.

There is some evidence, if not very strong, that yields of crops, meat and dairy products were all somewhat higher around 1600 than they had been a century or even half a century before. Bennett's pioneer calculations of wheat yields suggested a gradual and steady increase between 1450 and 1650, rising from 8½ to 11 bushels per acre, or 30 per cent over the period; Bowden suggests that the figures may be slightly too low but that the rate of growth is acceptable. Yield ratios (the ratios of corn produced to corn sown) may similarly have been rising gradually. Slicher van Bath's aggregate figures for Britain and the Netherlands suggest an average yield ratio of 5.9 in the first half of the sixteenth century, rising to 6.7 in the second half. However, yield ratios for Cuxham in Oxfordshire – 6.4 in the period 1289–1359, and 8.0 in the 1570s – do not suggest any dramatic long-term improvement. Evidence for animal yields is even more impressionistic, but Bowden and Kerridge are agreed that some improvement did occur. One confident contemporary averred that 'one sheepe beareth as muche woolle as twoe or three did'. The fleece weights of some favoured counties, like Northamptonshire (3–3½ lb average) and Hampshire (2–3 lb) already approached or even exceeded the national average for the eighteenth century.

Furthermore, yields of animal products as well as grain were probably increased by convertible husbandry, while agricultural specialisation, especially for fruit, hops and vegetables, was stimulated by the demand of the growing urban markets. Appleby has suggested that one crucial element in Englishmen's success in feeding themselves and ending subsistence crises was a better balance of winter and spring grains. 'Both the acreage and the yield of spring-sown crops – oats and barley – seem to have increased during the seventeenth century, as compared to those of wheat and rye.' This 'crop diversification' provided a better balance between the two, and thus some protection against the vagaries of the weather. This interesting argument can, however, be extended backwards. Spring-corn acreage was already predominant in parts of the West Midlands in the fourteenth and fifteenth centuries; it drew level with winter corn in the Forest of Arden at some time between 1570 and 1610; and the two were also about level at Chippenham in Cambridgeshire at the same period. In Shropshire in October 1574 'the wether was gyvyn to sutche rayne . . . that many husbandmen were forsyd to keepe theire rye grownde for barleye'.[39] It rather looks as though Elizabethan Englishmen were learning to balance their crop production to minimise losses from bad weather, at the same time as they were also both improving yields from existing farmland and extending cultivation into the wastes.

All in all, if Kerridge's 'revolution' seems too optimistic a label for the period, then Bridbury's suggestion that the Elizabethans were trapped in a repetition of thirteenth-century constraints errs equally far in the direction of pessimism. If convertible husbandry was indeed the 'backbone' of the agricultural revolution, then there is certainly a case for considering the late sixteenth and early seventeenth centuries as a crucial period in agricultural progress. That judicious contemporary William Harrison was in no doubt at all that productivity per acre had risen considerably in England, and even more in Wales. Englishmen and Welshmen had 'growne to be more painefull, skilfull, and carefull through recompense of gaine', and in consequence the land was 'even now in these our daies growne to be much more fruitfull than it hath beene in times past'.[40]

Chapter 7

London and the towns

What country in Europ comparable to England?
what [city] more wonderfull than London . . .?
what aboundance of fewell? what store of beefes,
what multitude of cattell are occupied there daylie . . .?
What cittie in the world so populous,
so merchantable, more rich . . .?

    Thomas Johnson 1596

French herald: Also, you have no good cytie, towne nor vyllayge but London . . .

English herald:
I pray you, what is Barwike, Carlile, Duresme,
Yorke, Newcastell, Hull, Northampton, Norwyche,
Ippeswyche, Colchestre, Coventre, Lychfelde,
Exetoure, Brystowe, Salysbury, Southampton,
Worsetour, Shrowesbury, Cantorbury, Chychestre,
with thousandes more of cyties and townes . . .?

    John Coke, 1549[1]

1

No one challenged the wealth or importance of London, but continental Europeans tended to dismiss other English towns out of hand, and with reason. John Coke's patriotic broadside has a defensive ring, and probably only two towns in his list boasted a population of 10,000 or more, while some had fewer than 2,000. At that time there were about 30 European cities with over 40,000 inhabitants, 11 in Italy, 7 in Spain, 6 in France, but only 1, London, in the British Isles. Their national populations were also much higher, but that was not the only reason. The Netherlands, with a combined northern and southern population less than England's, had seven cities of over 40,000 by 1600: Amsterdam, Antwerp, Ghent, Brussels, Bruges, Leiden and Haarlem. Giovanni Botero (1588) considered that 'in England, London excepted . . . there is not a city . . . that deserves to be called great,' while the Swiss Platter (1599) thought that whoever had visited London and the neighbouring royal palaces 'may assert without impertinence that he is properly acquainted with England'.[2]

Table 7.1 could be taken as a commentary on Botero's remark. Too much reliance cannot be placed on figures not compiled for demographic purposes, but the orders of magnitude are not in doubt, and are consistent with the very few apparently full Elizabethan and early Stuart censuses: Poole (1574), 1,357; Coventry (1586/87),

Table 7.1 Estimates of urban populations

City/town	1520s		Intermediate	*c.* 1600
Metropolitan London	60,000	1582	100,000–120,000[a]	185,000–215,000[a]
Norwich	8,000–12,000	1579	17,000–18,000[b]	15,000[b]
Bristol	10,000			12,000
York	8,000	1548	8,000[c]	11,500[c]
Exeter	8,000			9,000
Newcastle upon Tyne		1547	6,000–7,000[d]	9,000
King's Lynn	4,500			8,000
Coventry	7,500– 6,000[e]	1563	4,000–5,000[e]	7,000
Salisbury	8,000			7,000
Plymouth		1549	4,000	7,000–8,000
Cambridge	2,600[f]	{1563 / 1587}	{2,000–2,500[c] / 5,000[f]}	6,500
Oxford	5,000	1547	5,500	6,500
Ipswich	3,000–4,000			5,500
Canterbury	3,000[g]	1563	2,800–3,500[c]	5,000
Colchester	3,000–4,000			5,000
Yarmouth	4,000			5,000–8,000
Shrewsbury		1563	2,700–3,400[c]	5,000
Worcester		1563	4,000–5,000[c]	5,000
Chester		1563	4,000–5,000[c]	5,000

Sources: (except where otherwise footnoted): P. Clark and P. Slack, *English Towns in Transition 1500–1700* Oxford U.P. 1976, p. 83; Coleman and John 1976, pp. 217–20, 235–41; *The Traditional Community Under Stress*, Open University, 1977, p. 42; J. Patten, *English Towns 1500–1700*, Dawson 1978, pp. 100, 103, 251.

[a] *Population and Social Change*, ed. D. V. Glass & R. Revelle, Arnold 1972, p. 310.

[b] *The Records of the City of Norwich*, ed. W. Hudson and J. C. Tingey, 2 vols, 1906 –10, ii, pp. cxxviif.; J. T. Evans, *Seventeenth-Century Norwich*, Clarendon Press 1979, p. 4n.

[c] Author's estimates. Alternative figures are given for 1563, depending on whether the multiplier from households to total population is nearer four (preferred by C. Phythian-Adams, *Desolation of a City*, Cambridge U.P. 1979, p. 10, n.6) or five. The total of households at Worcester, 1563, was 1,025, and not 937 as stated by A. D. Dyer, *The City of Worcester in the Sixteenth Century*, 1973, p. 26.

[d] *Northern History*, xiv (1978), 74, a figure I have preferred to the 10,000 + suggested by W. G. Hoskins, *Provincial England*, Macmillan 1963, p. 71n.

[e] Phythian-Adams, *Desolation of a City*, pp. 197, 237.

[f] N. Goose, 'Household size and social structure in early-Stuart Cambridge', *Social History*, v (1980), 353.

[g] P. Clark, *English Provincial Society from the Reformation to the Revolution*, Harvester 1977, pp. 8f.

6,502; Southampton (1596), 4,200; Bristol (1607), 10,549; Sheffield (1616), 2,207; Stafford (1622), 1,550. It is safe to say that no Tudor provincial town ever exceeded 20,000 in size, though Norwich reached perhaps 17,000 or 18,000 before the devastating plague of 1579. One recent estimate suggests that 8 per cent of the English population dwelt in towns of over 5,000 people by about 1600, but 5 per cent was accounted for by London alone. Admittedly, if all small towns are included, the proportions are much higher, about 31 per cent in Gloucestershire (without Bristol) and 26 per cent in Norfolk and Suffolk. Yet it is not at all clear that towns other than London were expanding their share of the population. Dyer suggests that the urban populations of Gloucestershire, Leicestershire, Norfolk and Suffolk, though growing between 1563 and 1603, barely maintained their proportion of the total county populations.[3]

Towns, then, were small, and with few exceptions were not industrial centres divorced from an agrarian economy. The smaller ones relied heavily on servicing their hinterlands through markets, fairs and shops. Even the larger ones had often lost their medieval textile industries and shifted their interests to trade and servicing, while much Tudor industry was located in the countryside. Yet the towns enjoyed an economic, social, political and religious importance out of all proportion to their size. They were the indispensable centres of the rural economies, furnishing an exchange and finishing of goods that lubricated agricultural growth. They housed all the royal garrisons, Church and county courts, cathedrals and universities, most libraries and shops, and almost all the larger schools. Many gentlemen, yeomen and husbandmen visited their nearest market town regularly, and more distant towns occasionally, to buy and sell, to appear in court, to consult members of the professions or to be entertained. York in 1537, with a population of perhaps 8,000, had 1,035 beds for visitors available in its inns and stabling for 1,711 horses, an indication of the demand by visitors for the day as well as those who stayed overnight.

Any tally of Tudor towns must be arbitrary; Rye, Bewdley and Warwick, small though they were, were considered unquestionably as towns, but what of Halifax, Lavenham or East Dereham? Clark and Slack have suggested five 'basic and readily recognizable characteristics of English pre-industrial towns', an unusual concentration of population, a specialist economic function, a complex social structure, a sophisticated political order and a distinctive influence beyond their immediate boundaries. Theirs is a useful working definition, although as they point out the smallest market towns possessed only the first two.

The most basic function of all was possession of a market. In 1588, judging from William Smith's *Particular Description of England* and other sources, there were some 590 markets in England and 54 in Wales, but some of the smallest were simple agricultural villages of 500 or 600 people with no urban characteristic whatsoever beyond their possession of a weekly market. It would be safe to accept 500 or 600 as the maximum number of towns by any criterion; Coke's 'thousandes' are an absurdity.[4] Most of these, Clark and Slack suggest, were simple market towns and decaying boroughs, while about 100 were 'county centres', including not only county towns but other regional centres with complex constitutions and economies. At the top of the hierarchy came half a dozen provincial capitals, and in a class of its own, London.

The urban hierarchy was nearer to the medieval ranking than to that of the past two centuries. Rowse has well characterised Elizabethan England as 'a country in which Totnes is more important than Liverpool, Maidstone twice the size of Manchester; in which Stratford-on-Avon is a borough . . . while Birmingham is a manorial village . . . still only one-sixth the size of Coventry'.[5] The great majority of towns were old-established centres for exchange, finishing and handicrafts. Small towns were integrated closely with the countryside. In Minchinhampton in 1608 22 per cent of the occupied population were engaged in agriculture, and at nearby Painswick as many as 37 per cent; while at Barnstaple and Walsall the townsfolk abandoned their crafts every summer to help with the harvest. Even large towns relied considerably on gardens and on town fields and pastures to supplement their food supplies. Loggan's prospects of Cambridge (1690) place the town behind foregrounds where townsmen harvest and keep sheep in their town fields, while at York most freemen kept a 'stint' of one cow, or two, on the city strays.

Maitland said of Loggan's Cambridge views, 'I do not know that better pictures of an open field were ever drawn.'[6] But we need not rely entirely on late evidence for the visual appearance of towns. Apart from documents and surviving buildings, the Tudor age has bequeathed us the first reliable town plans and views. Anthonis van den Wyngaerde drew the earliest known panoramic view of London about 1558, and he was probably the artist of a huge plan of the whole city engraved by Francis Hogenberg about 1560. No printed copy is known to survive, but two of the twenty or so original engraved copper plates have recently been discovered. Ralph Agas drew an equally detailed plan of Oxford in 1578, later published and fortunately surviving in a unique copy. Much has been lost, like the 'Manchester town described and measured by Mr. Christopher Saxton' noted in John Dee's diary. Yet what remains includes a series of sixteen smaller manuscript plans and panoramas by William Smith in the 1580s, and published plans for every English and Welsh county town by John Speed (1610–11), as well as fine bird's-eye views of Norwich by Hoefnagel and of Exeter by John Hooker.

The most striking feature of the larger towns to English contemporaries was that most were walled. At least 146 English and Welsh towns were fortified by 1520, and many actively maintained their defences throughout the century. They were by then more useful as barriers against beggars, plague suspects and toll evaders than serious military obstacles, though Exeter withstood a fierce siege in 1549, and York's elaborate defences deterred the northern earls twenty years later. Indeed, to continental visitors it was the lack of serious military defence that contrasted with their native experience. Samuel Kiechel in 1585 was astonished at the lack of London walls – presumably meaning a lack of locked gates – 'so that any one may come in or out at any hour of the day or night'.[7] The escalating cost of up-to-date defences of the kind common in the Netherlands prohibited their adoption in England, except for a few strategic garrison towns where the initiative was royal rather than municipal. Henry VIII modernised the fortifications of Hull and Carlisle after 1541, while Elizabeth rebuilt those of Berwick and Portsmouth.

Municipal buildings, other than walls, were few. Most towns possessed a market cross or covered market building, and the corporate towns had a town hall for courts and council meetings. The two were frequently combined in a council chamber supported on pillars, giving an open market space beneath protected from the weather, as at Shrewsbury. Towns on rivers maintained bridges, of which the largest were the medieval London Bridge and the Ouse Bridge at York, rebuilt in 1566 with the help of the overseer of London Bridge. Otherwise, the buildings chiefly used for public purposes were the churches and religious houses. Almost every town had at least one parish church, which as a stone, fireproof building might do duty as court-room, muster hall, school and meeting-room as well as for services. Many other public activities had been held in the religious houses, which had of course been suppressed in the 1530s, and mostly demolished for the sake of their building materials. Some large monastic churches were, however, rescued and bought by urban corporations as parish churches, as at Malmesbury and Tewkesbury, while a few others were saved for secular public purposes, like the Norwich Blackfriars.

Most urban domestic buildings that have survived are timber-framed, although a few in areas of good building stone were stone-built, and a fashion for brick was developing in the east. Especially after about 1570, prosperous townsmen used some of their wealth in rebuilding on a lavish scale, just like their rural neighbours. The constraints of space and site values had always made building-plots in the larger towns long and narrow, with a limited street frontage. Effect and space were therefore achieved by building three or even four storeys high, with successive floors overhanging to give the characteristic jettied effect, and with façade and gable often highly decorated by patterns in timber or in plasterwork. There are still numerous showy examples in Shrewsbury, such as Ireland's mansion (*c.* 1575) and Owen's mansion of 1592. They were already conspicuous by 1581, when the Salopian poet Thomas Churchyard returned on a visit, while other houses, if not rebuilt, were evidently redecorated and refurnished:

I held on way, to auncient Shrewsebrie Towne,
And so from horse, at lodging lighting downe,
I walkt the streates, and markt what came to vewe,
Found old things dead, as world were made a newe.

For buildings gay, and gallant finely wrought,
Had old device, through tyme supplanted cleane:
Some houses bare, that seem'd to be worth nought,
Were fat within, that outward looked leane.

Even declining Southampton put the surplus wealth from a brief economic recovery into new buildings in the third quarter of the century: 'then downe with old howses, and newe sett in their places: for the howses where the fathers dwelt could not content their children'.[8] However, it must be remembered that the homes of the urban poor have vanished completely, and that many were apparently squalid hovels of thatched cob like their rural equivalents. They clustered especially in back alleys and suburbs, for the main central streets were monopolised by the shops and houses of merchants and leading craftsmen.

Even the houses of the more prosperous citizens were sometimes thatched. Thatch as a roofing material was gradually banned by the larger towns, at Norwich in 1570, at Bristol in 1574, at Cambridge in 1619. Towns of timbered housing were vulnerable enough to fire without the added hazard of thatch, and it was the fire risk that brought in the prohibitions. It is fair to add that the larger towns were generally successful in preventing conflagrations of the kind that had devastated Norwich in Henry VII's reign or were to burn down most of London and Northampton under Charles II; and the worst fires occurred in smaller towns like Oswestry (1564, 1567), Portsmouth (1576), Nantwich (1583), Darlington (1585) and Stratford (1594, 1595). The larger towns invested in what primitive fire-fighting equipment was available and tried to control the use of inflammable building materials, apparently with some success. Exeter, for example, ordered stocks of leather buckets, ladders and hooks (to pluck down burning timbers and thatch) in 1558. Oxford corporation followed suit in 1573, and in 1582 banned all roofing materials except slate or tile, and all chimneys and flues except of stone or brick.

The more prosperous or enlightened towns were also becoming more active in the provision of public services for reasons of health, safety or civic pride. There were spasmodic attempts at street lighting, if only by requiring councillors or leading householders to hang out lanterns at their own expense. Hereford, for example, required ex-mayors, innkeepers and others to hang a lighted lantern at their doors between 6 and 8 p.m. on winter nights, 'except the night the moon doth shine'. More streets and market-places were paved (that is, covered by cobbles laid in a bed of sand or gravel), and several corporations tried to organise collections of refuse, while many more simply ordered householders to keep the streets clean before their own doors, or to dump their household refuse in specified places. Some towns, such as Chester, Norwich and Bristol, organised public water supplies by piping water to a central conduit. The larger towns also organised measures to restrict the spread of bubonic plague, beginning with London and Oxford in 1518 and Shrewsbury and York in 1538, while by the reign of Elizabeth a number of towns had elaborate provisions for isolation of the victims and financial relief for their families.

These rudimentary activities represented a real determination to enlarge the sphere of public services, but it would be misleading to stress them too strongly, for the evidence is often of intentions rather than achievement, and ignores the towns which made no such attempts. It was still common for pigs to roam the streets, and at Maidstone in the 1590s the almspeople actually kept pigs in their rooms. The main streets may have become a little less muddy and dirty, but the poorer quarters remained squalid; at Bristol the merchants' homes largely escaped the epidemic of 1603, but the cottages in the narrow alleys behind them were severely hit. It is all too easy to select the earliest dates of proposed improvements rather than the less well-documented implementation. York was planning to introduce piped water from 1552, and implemented a successful scheme in 1616, but it was abandoned by 1634 and permanently reintroduced only in 1677.

2

London was without question one of the great European cities. It is therefore regrettable that most recent published work on the Tudor capital has been, as Clark justly remarks, 'rather disappointing, shedding only flickering light on the rise of the leading city in Western Europe'.[9] Under Henry VIII it was already five times as populous as the next largest English town, and, judging from the lay subsidies of the 1520s, ten times as wealthy. It boasted the largest English cathedral, the largest group of urban religious houses and hospitals, and well over 100 parish churches. Taking London to include Westminster and the suburbs, it was England's commercial capital and greatest port, the home of parliaments, royal administration and of several royal palaces, the only centre for higher education other than Oxford and Cambridge, and for most of the century the home of the only royal mint. Even ecclesiastically it was the capital, for the province of Canterbury was effectively administered not from its mother-city but from Lambeth Palace and from the Court of Arches at St Mary-le-Bow.

Such a concentration of functions gave the capital overwhelming advantages, and helps to account for the huge difference in size and wealth between London and even its nearest rivals. Of all the larger western European states, only France possessed a true capital of similar importance; elsewhere, political fragmentation had prevented it, although in 1561 Philip II gave Spain a permanent capital in Madrid. In 1567, when Alba was planning to weld the seventeen heterogeneous Netherlands provinces into a united state, Philip was advised 'to make of the towne of Bruxselles a metropolitan place, seate royall or cheaffe towne of the said kingdom, as Parris in Fraunce and London in Englande'. Indeed London was famous not only in Europe, but in more distant lands. When an English trader reached the Persian court in 1568, no one there had heard of his country. But then 'one of the noble men said Londro, meaning thereby London, which name is better knowen in far countries out of Christendom, then is the name of England'.[10]

The pride, wealth and self-confidence of London's leading merchants, which were to be decisive in the political crises of the seventeenth century, were already strong. John Stow tells of an alderman who clearly believed that the city's commercial advantages were sufficient to ensure its undisputed supremacy:

For when as on a time it was told him by a courtier, that Queene Mary, in her displeasure against London, had appointed to remove with the

Parliament and Terme to Oxford, this playne man demaunded, whether she meant also to divert the river of Thames from London, or no? and when the gentleman had answered no, then, quoth the alderman, by God's grace wee shall do well enough at London, whatsoever become of the Tearme and Parliament.

It is a good story, but the brag was scarcely justified. London depended heavily on those who attended the royal court, parliament and the lawcourts, and on their families and friends who came up for the social life that developed around them into the London 'season'. The countess of Shrewsbury, for instance, spent seven months at her Chelsea house in 1591–92, chiefly to deal with legal business, and she brought with her from Derbyshire a retinue of forty. The Privy Council considered in 1550 that London needed extra provisions of food for the great numbers 'having accesse and residence . . . both for the Termes and the Parlement now drawing nere', and a later inquiry showed that they did not exaggerate. In 1574 the City consumed 1,409 quarters of breadcorn weekly in the law vacations, but 2,571 (82% more) 'in the terme tyme'.[11]

And if the City depended so heavily on the proximity of government and administration, its neighbour Westminster did so even more. Legally a separate city, it was really a London suburb clustered around the royal Palace of Westminster, where the central lawcourts as well as sessions of parliament were held. As Norden noted in 1593, it had 'no generall trade whereby releefe might be administered unto the common sort, as by marchandize, clothing, or such like'. Its chief means of support were the frequent residence of the sovereign, and the four law terms. Whenever Elizabeth I was 'long absent' from Whitehall or St James's, 'the poore people forthwith complaine of penury and want, of a hard and miserable world'.[12]

In 1547 the City proper consisted of the medieval walled core on the north bank of the Thames and an irregular fringe of suburbs (Fig. 14). The wall terminated on the east by the Tower, still an important royal palace as well as a fortress and prison, and on the west between two other riverside palaces, Bridewell and Baynard's Castle. Within the walls streets were narrow, apart from the wide market-place of Cheapside, the nearest equivalent to a continental *grand' place*. At the west end of Cheap stood St Paul's Cathedral, to the north lay Blackwell Hall, the mart for cloth from all over England, and north of that again the centre of civic administration in the Guildhall. At the east end of Cheap Sir Thomas Gresham built the Royal Exchange between 1566 and 1570 as a centre for merchants and financiers, while north-east of that stood his own town mansion, which after his death in 1579 became a college of higher education.

Fig. 14   London, *c.* 1570

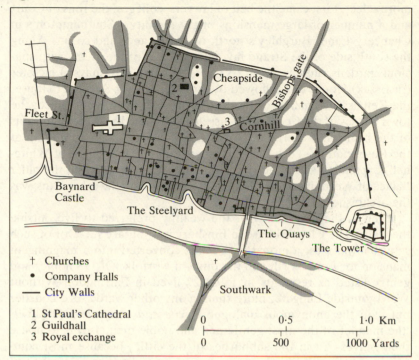

Along the Thames, from Queenhithe to Tower Wharf, lay the quays
and dock buildings, including the Crown's Custom House and the
Hanse's Steelyard.

Space was at a premium, for much of the walled area was occupied
by the precincts of the cathedral and former religious houses, and by
the 'inns' or private mansions of magnates. Other houses, mostly timber-framed until the fire of 1666, were crammed close together, while
public services and cleansing were primitive. Sir Philip Hoby, with
his experience as English ambassador to the Empire, called London
'a stinking city, the filthiest of the world'.[13] That was in 1557, when
the City was probably visually at its worst after the demolitions of
religious houses. The Venetian ambassador wrote in 1551 of 'many
large palaces making a very fine show, but . . . disfigured by the ruins
of a multitude of churches and monasteries'.

Outside the walls there were even sharper contrasts. Some of the
suburbs to the north and east consisted entirely of cottages for the
poor. Across the great twelfth-century London Bridge lay Southwark, with its mixture of princes and paupers. Bear gardens and
brothels – and later theatres – lay cheek by jowl with the town houses

of the bishops of Winchester and Rochester. The western suburb was more select. First came the belt of lawyers' colleges, the Inns of Court and a number of large mansions of the nobility – Southampton's in Chancery Lane, Burghley's north of the Strand, and so on. Along the south side of the Strand lay more palaces of the great, with spacious gardens running down to riverside gates and quays. Leicester (or Essex) House was followed by Arundel House; Somerset House, the Renaissance palace of the lord protector; the Savoy Palace; the town houses of the Cecils and Russells; and then the former mansions of the bishops of Durham, Norwich and York, taken from them at the Reformation. York Place became Henry VIII's Palace of Whitehall, expanding along the riverbank until it nearly reached the older Palace of Westminster, while further upstream on the other bank was the archbishop's Lambeth Palace.

Even in the City, many of the wealthy preferred to live outside the walls. The Charterhouse in Finsbury is a solitary survivor of such suburban palaces, a monastic precinct converted into a magnificent mansion for Lord North and the duke of Norfolk. Of 118 nobles and gentry listed as residents in 1595, 27 lived in Farringdon Without Ward, outside Ludgate, more than in any other ward. As a courtier put it in the anonymous dialogue *Cyvile and Uncyvile Life* (1579) 'the manner of the most gentlemen and noble men also, is to house them selves . . . in the subburbes of the cittie, because most commonly . . . the place is healthy, and . . . wee have as litle cause to fear infection there, as in the verye countrey'.[14]

Thus even by the mid-sixteenth century the built-up area had expanded well beyond the City, and on the west stretched in continuous ribbon development as far as Westminster. Southwark, officially a separate borough in Surrey, was effectively a transpontine suburb, a situation acknowledged in 1550 when Edward VI sold it to the corporation, who formed it into the twenty-sixth ward of the City. What made London unique among English cities, however, was that the City corporation were content to confine themselves within their medieval jurisdiction, apart from incorporating Southwark, while the suburbs spread further and further. A burgeoning population was divided among numerous jurisdictions, mainly rural manors quite unsuited to the governing of a megalopolis, and shared between the counties of Middlesex, Essex and Surrey. A natural consequence was that poor or alien immigrants often took up work in the liberties or suburbs outside civic jurisdiction. Thus nearly all the feltmakers and leather-workers left the City for Bermondsey, Southwark and Lambeth before the end of the century, while brick and tile-making concentrated in Islington and other northern suburbs. The warmth of the Islington brick kilns also made them the most popular sleeping-place for the unemployed looking for work in London.

The corporation accepted all this equably, forgoing the extra problems of social control that would have accompanied the extension of their jurisdiction. When, however, it was a case of mercantile development that might reduce their wealth it was a different matter. They protested vigorously when in 1608–9 the earl of Salisbury built a 'New Exchange' in the Strand as a rival to Gresham's building in the City. They were afraid that the patronage of nobles, gentry and 'Termers' in the West End would 'draw mercers, goldsmiths and all other chief traders to settle themselves out of the City'. Salisbury replied, reasonably enough, that, 'When I balance London with Westminster, Middlesex, or rather with all England, then I must conclude that London might suffer . . . some little quill of profit to pass by their main pipe.'[15]

Inevitably, population figures for London are even more speculative than for other towns. Sheer numbers, and the lack of a single municipal authority, prevented any local censuses except those of the continental immigrant communities. Quite apart from a vast migration into London from all regions, there was constant local population movement from parish to parish. Nor, surprisingly, has much work been attempted on the total population of London since Charles Creighton's in 1891. He suggested figures for the built-up area of 50,000 around 1530, 93,000 in 1563, 120,000 in 1582 and 225,000 in 1605. On the whole these figures are still accepted as orders of magnitude, although recent writers would generally prefer a figure of 200,000 or less around 1600. Ian Sutherland has ingeniously used the bills of mortality to derive new estimates, and they prove to be of the same order of size: 79,000–92,000 in 1565, depending on alternative assumptions of the christening rate; 108,000–126,000 in 1585, and 144,000–168,000 in 1605. These totals are for the City and Liberties, but including the developing out-parishes would increase the last to the range 184,000–215,000.

However, even if one takes the highest recent estimates of London's population around 1545 (60,000–80,000), and the lowest for 1600–5, the capital still increased in numbers by 150 per cent in sixty years, and its share of the national population must have increased from 2 or 3 per cent to about 5 per cent. Furthermore, London tied for only seventeenth place among European cities about 1550 according to Burke, but for fourth place around 1600, and was well on the way to overtaking Paris in the later seventeenth century to become the largest city in western Europe. This massive growth had to be met by much new building in the suburbs, and by subdivision and higher density of occupation in the City. Creighton broke down his 1530 estimate into 35,000 for the City and 15,000 for the extramural Liberties, while for 1605 he suggested 75,000 in the former, 115,000 in the latter and 35,000 in the out-parishes. Although much the most rapid growth was outside the walls, his figures would still suggest an astonishing doubling of the City's population.

The best guide to the changes entailed by the population boom, as to so much else, is John Stow's *Survey of London* (1598 and 1603), the first published history of any English town, and written by a man who could remember the distant days before the Reformation. Time after time he notes encroachments on vacant plots, or the replacement of mansions and religious houses by small tenements. Thus about 1570 a developer leased from the corporation a vacant plot just inside the wall, on which he 'builded three faire tenementes'. Oxford Place, a decayed earl's mansion across the road, was 'lately new builded into a number of small tenements, letten out to strangers, and other meane people'. Outside the wall, 'a continuall streete or filthy straight passage, with alleyes of small tenements or cottages' for sailors and victuallers had sprung up from the Tower almost to Radcliffe 'within these 40 yeares'. Ribbon development of 'filthy cottages' stretched from Aldgate across former common field to beyond Whitechapel. Outside Cripplegate lay a growing suburb of over 1,800 households 'with many tenements of poore people'. There was also a brisk demand for space for industry, horticulture and entertainment as well as housing. North of the Tower the city ditch had been recently enclosed 'and the banks thereof let out for garden plots, carpenters' yardes, bowling allies, and diverse houses thereon builded'. Over the road was the site of the Minories nunnery and its home farm. Thence before its dissolution, Stow remembered, 'I myselfe in my youth have fetched many a halfe pennie worth of milke . . . always hote from the kine'. But the farmer's son and heir had 'let out the ground first for grazing of horse, and then for garden plots, and lived like a gentleman thereby'.[16]

The dissolutions of the monasteries, chantries and hospitals in the 1530s and 1540s brought into lay ownership a huge amount of housing, as well as of open spaces ripe for development as the population grew. The earl of Shrewsbury was told in 1548 that when the chantry lands were being sold by the Crown, 'suche importunate heaving for houses in London hath not the like bene seane: xx yeres' and xxx yeres' purchase is nothing allmost . . .'.[17] In other words, demand was outstripping supply and forcing up prices. Rents for housing to let – on which the poor depended – rose in parallel. Crowley's petition to parliament in 1548 alleged that nine-tenths of all London

properties were sublet, and that landlords were raising rents out-
rageously, though it would be risky to take his passionate arguments for facts. With the benefit of hindsight, it can be seen that the
Crown's great mistake was to have sold in the 1540s nearly all the
land between the City and Westminster which had been seized at the
dissolutions; much was still open land, but became enormously
valuable as it was built over.

The Crown was in no doubt about the scale of London's expansion, and was alarmed at the vast potential for disorder and disease
on the very doorstep of court and parliament. Cecil attributed the
plague of 1563 largely to overcrowding, and ordered that every house
which had been subdivided within the previous twelve months should
revert to serving for one household, and that recently arrived lodgers
should move out. In 1580, at the mayor's request, the queen issued
a proclamation against further building in London to avert threats
to law and order, food supplies and health. Multiple occupation of
existing properties, and new building within 3 miles of the walls, were
forbidden. Lodgers who had arrived within the past seven years were
to leave, and could seek homes elsewhere in towns decayed for lack
of people. A similar proclamation followed in 1602, together with
Privy Council orders in 1590 and an act of parliament in 1593. It is
doubtful whether their enforcement was effective, but the government was in earnest, and its policy found widespread support outside
the capital. James I, who copied Elizabeth's policy, grumbled that
'soon London will be all England', echoing the feelings of many of
his subjects.

The government of the City was traditional in form. The fundamental principle was that it existed for the benefit of the citizens or
freemen, a select body of master traders and craftsmen who attained
that rank by apprenticeship, by patrimony (inheritance from a freeman father) or by redemption (purchase). Unfortunately, London is
worse served than many smaller towns in having lost almost all its
freemen's records. The surviving fragments, covering a period of
twenty-one months in 1551–53, list just over 1,100 freemen admissions, over nine-tenths of them by apprenticeship. They were a
minority, but certainly not a tiny élite; a very crude calculation suggests that they may have formed nearly half of all adult males within
the City's jurisdiction. The freemen were organised into about 160
gilds, mostly based on economic divisions between crafts. However,
the City was dominated by the twelve great Livery Companies, which
were effectively associations of merchants and wholesalers rather
than occupational groupings. Politically, the City had a complex
structure of about 250 precincts and 115 parishes for government at

the district level, grouped into 26 wards. The corporation was headed by a lord mayor and two sheriffs, elected annually, and assisted by a Court of Aldermen, one for each ward, elected for life. The Court of Aldermen shared power with a larger Common Council (numbering 196 in 1598) and a still larger assembly called Common Hall. The last-named comprised all the liverymen (the more important freemen), and participated indirectly in elections of mayor, sheriffs and aldermen. However, F. F. Foster has shown that the Court of Aldermen was effectively a self-perpetuating oligarchy, tightly linked by kinship connections, dominating the leading gilds, and if anything strengthening their grip during the reign of Elizabeth. This does not imply a hereditary élite of civic dynasties; less than one in ten of the greater merchants is known to have been born in London, and three-quarters of the Elizabethan mayors were first-generation Londoners.

The City corporation had a unique relationship with the Crown. Its support was indispensable if law and order were to be maintained on the threshold of court and parliament, and its leading members were an important source of loans. Indeed Foster concludes that 'the dependence of Crown on City was rather greater than the other way around'. If the Privy Council bombarded the mayor and aldermen with requests and orders, they also left their privileges intact and indeed enhanced, and made no attempt to force them to accept jurisdiction over the swelling suburbs. Edward, Mary and Elizabeth all staged elaborate processions through the City on their coronation eve, and Elizabeth took particular care to win the good opinion of the people by human touches amidst the pomp. Every mayor travelled to Westminster on 29 October to take his oath of office, unlike any provincial mayors, and his triumphal return was made the occasion for a Lord Mayor's Show which became more and more elaborate under Elizabeth and the early Stuarts. There is little doubt that one reason for the stability of Elizabeth's regime was her cultivation of London, and that Mary I, James I and Charles I all suffered for neglecting to do so.

3

London was unique in its size, power and influence, and its rapid growth had taken it even further ahead of its nearest rivals. From being five times as populous as Norwich under Henry VIII, it had become at least twelve or fourteen times as large by the death of Elizabeth. York might conduct civic ceremonies 'on a par with London', as the Venetian ambassador reported in 1551, and its members might take their places next to London's in parliament as representing the 'second city of the realm', but such demonstrations could only draw attention to a widening gap in real importance, especially between London and a northern capital which had decayed and fallen behind Norwich and Bristol.

These three cities ranked as provincial capitals. Exeter, though smaller, played a similar role in the south-west; Salisbury and Coventry perhaps deserved the same rank, despite their late medieval decline; and Newcastle upon Tyne was beginning to earn a place in the same select band. These were, approximately, those cities which for all or part of the century had a population in excess of 7,000, although size was not the only criterion. The best definition is that of Hoskins, that 'in each province of England, above all in the peripheral regions, certain towns played the part of capital cities to their regions', as centres of secular and ecclesiastical administration and 'in process of becoming social capitals also'. Such cities were large enough to sustain a complex social and economic structure, and sufficiently distant from each other and from London; and together they served every region of England except the East Midlands and the North-west. Most had a thriving social life, with bookshops, fashionable schools, sports and entertainments, for the local gentry and countrymen at least as much as for their citizens. York, for example, offered bowls, cock-fighting, bear-baiting, archery contests and horse-racing.

All had a diversified economy, except for Newcastle, which relied heavily on the booming coal trade and on the Hostmen's Company which organised it; all depended greatly on long-distance and overseas trade, and it is significant that nearly all were seaports or river ports. The recorder of decaying Coventry, welcoming the queen in 1565, felt it necessary to defend his city's importance even 'though nature deny . . . the especial benefit of the sea, the principal maintenance of many great and famous cities'.[18] Coventry was, in fact, the unluckiest of the group, away from navigable waterways, vulnerable to changes of fashion in the road network, and rivalled by the growing industrial villages of the Birmingham plateau.

Below the provincial capitals, to follow the useful classification of Clark and Slack, ranked about 100 'county centres'. Their populations ranged from about 1,500 to 7,000, and most had town walls and a complex street-pattern. The diocesan capitals boasted a cathedral, and the shire towns a castle as headquarters for the sheriff and his county administration. County centres mostly had several markets and fairs, and attracted custom from wide hinterlands. Worcester, for example, enjoyed three weekly markets, drawing customers from up to 12 miles away, and four annual fairs. The horse fairs, the most notable, brought together buyers from the South and East Midlands, and sellers from Herefordshire and the Welsh borders. Worcester was also typical of the larger county centres in relying on a navigable river as its main trading artery. Most county centres also included a wide variety of craftsmen and merchants trading from their own shops, and a number of large inns to house travellers. Some acted as provincial capitals in the absence of larger competitors; Carlisle served the North-west, and Lincoln, gradually superseded by Nottingham, the East Midlands.

Finally, at the bottom of the urban ladder there were perhaps 500 simple market towns and decayed boroughs, most with populations of between 600 and 1,500. Burford, for instance, was undoubtedly prosperous, and was described in Edward's reign as 'a very great market town replenished with much people', yet the chantry certificates of 1545–48 suggest a total population of only 800. Most had at least a handful of shopkeepers and craftsmen, but their physical and economic pivot was the market, sometimes a wide high street (Thame, Burford) and sometimes an oblong or funnel-shaped central place, a pattern clearly evident on a contemporary plan of Chelmsford in 1591.

The spacing of market towns naturally varied with the population and prosperity of the districts they served. Everitt has calculated that England possessed one market town for every 45,000 acres, and Wales one for every 100,000. The range in England was from one per 20,000 acres in prosperous Hertfordshire to one per 161,000 in Northumberland. In some areas markets were still very much general-purpose trading centres, whereas in others they were flourishing by specialising to meet the demands of an increasingly specialised agrarian economy. By the early seventeenth century many market towns had begun to concentrate on one particular product, but the proportion varied from over a half in the North, and nearly as many in the Midlands and eastern counties, to just over a third in Wales and the West Country, and only a quarter in the South of England.

The fourfold classification into capital, provincial capitals, county centres and market towns, as its authors are the first to admit, is based 'essentially and simply on the criterion of size'. Towns formed a continuous spectrum of type and complexity, correlating only loosely with population, as Clark and Slack recognise when they added a fifth category of 'new towns' which could not be accommodated within a traditional framework. Most old-established towns sustained a broad range of crafts and services, whereas the special characteristic of the 'new towns' lay in their concentration on a single economic activity. Their rise really occurred in the seventeenth and eighteenth centuries, but its beginnings can be discerned before 1600. Birmingham, Wolverhampton and Walsall were already specialising in different branches of the metal industry. Nantwich was flourishing as a salt town, Manchester as a cloth town and Newcastle as a coal capital, while Deptford, Woolwich and Gillingham were all growing dockyard towns serving the royal navy. It would, however, be premature to speak of industrial towns and, as will be seen, the only large towns with a high concentration of labour in one industry were old-established textile cities. Nor were there yet any true 'leisure towns' to equal the later spa and seaside resorts, although Bath and Buxton were beginning to be patronised by aristocracy and gentry for rest and relaxation as well as for medicinal treatment.

An understanding of the economy of Tudor towns requires some knowledge of their political structure, since the two were so closely intertwined, and since so much discussion of economic advance has hinged on an alleged distinction between restrictive corporate towns and economically 'progressive' unincorporated towns. At the lowest level of constitutional development were towns governed entirely within the rural framework of county, manor and parish. Above them ranked the petty boroughs, whose inhabitants or burgesses possessed limited privileges by charter or prescription. The least developed enjoyed merely burgage tenure, a particular form of legal property tenure based entirely on cash rents and on free alienability, in distinction to most manorial tenure. Some petty boroughs also enjoyed limited rights of self-government, either politically, through their own elected officials and councillors, or economically, through gilds or companies of craftsmen and traders.

A bewildering permutation of borough types shaded into the fully autonomous borough, completely outside the manorial framework although still subject to supervision by the county authorities. These were the incorporated boroughs, made autonomous 'corporations' by royal charter, and with a developed system of officials, councils and courts. Most corporate boroughs were governed by an annually elected officer (usually a mayor), assisted by a sheriff, clerk and other officers, and by an elected council or councils. Some 60 English and Welsh boroughs were already corporate by 1547, and the later Tudors incorporated another 88, more than doubling the total by 1603. A minority of them achieved still greater heights as counties corporate, that is, towns entirely withdrawn from the jurisdiction of sheriffs and county justices. They remained of course subject to the Crown – the city-states of Italy and the Empire were a political impossibility in England – but they had achieved the maximum permissible autonomy. This coveted distinction was granted very sparingly, and there were only fifteen counties corporate by 1603 (Fig. 1, p. xxii). Nor was this the full range of borough types, for overlapping with all of them was the parliamentary borough, permitted by the Crown to elect members (usually two) to each parliament.

This brief catalogue cannot convey an adequate sense of the bewildering variety of town governments. The Crown's right to grant the status of corporate or parliamentary borough was still unchallenged, but the choice of places thus honoured depended on pressures by citizens, gentry and Crown servants more than on wealth or population. When Sir Thomas Smith became secretary of state he was able to have his native town of Saffron Walden incorporated, with his elder brother as first treasurer, his father and uncle keepers of the borough almshouse, and their family friend William Strachey as first chamberlain. Other towns might lack such influential support. Manchester and Birmingham impressed those experienced travellers Leland and Camden with their growing population, buildings and industries (Manchester already had some 2,000 people in 1563), but both remained under the control of simple manor courts. They also failed to achieve representation in parliament, although the three last Tudors between them created sixty-two new parliamentary boroughs, including the small Cornish towns of Bossiney, Camelford and Grampound.

On the other hand, conservatism and entrenched privilege ensured that all existing boroughs and parliamentary boroughs retained their status however much they had decayed or failed to grow. Queenborough (Kent), though little more than a village, kept its mayor and corporation, and Gatton (Surrey) its parliamentary burgesses, although it consisted of only seven houses in 1621, all but one tenants of the lord of the manor. There had already begun that disjuncture between importance and privilege which was to widen until righted by the reforms of the nineteenth century. Elizabeth seems to have realised this; resisting pressure from the earl of Rutland to make Newark a parliamentary borough, she sent a message that 'there are over many [burgesses] already, and there will be a device hereafter to lessen the number of divers decayed towns'.[19] The attempt foundered in the face of vested interests, but she did insist on enfranchising no more towns after 1586.

The most crucial distinction between corporate and non-corporate towns was that in the former a clearly defined body of men monopolised power. Burgesses alone had the right to stand for municipal office or to participate in elections; the corresponding group economically was the Gild Merchant or whole body of freemen, who alone could trade, keep shop or employ labour, although by Tudor times burgesses and freemen had become interchangeable. The distinction was well put by John Hooker, chamberlain of Exeter from 1555 to 1600. The inhabitants, he wrote, were of two sorts, citizens and 'foreigners'. Citizens were those admitted to the franchise by patrimony, apprenticeship or redemption; 'all other persons inhabitinge within this citie . . . is named a foryner and he payeth yerely his fyne for his traffuyquinge within the citie'.[20] This sounds very restrictive, but much depended on the proportion who were enfranchised and on the flexibility of the corporation in admitting newcomers with special skills on easy terms.

W. G. Hoskins has argued that 'the fundamental fact of Tudor urban life was that the great majority of the population were completely excluded from all government and gilds and any kind of civic recognition'.[21] That is correct if women and children are included, as it would be in any area of Tudor life. However, up to a half of the adult males in Bristol, Oxford and York, and even more within the City of London, were citizens, though the proportion was more like one-third at Norwich and one-quarter at Exeter. Furthermore, not all corporate towns drew a sharp line between freemen and 'foreigners', and some permitted an intermediate class, like the tensers of Shrewsbury, who could pay an annual fine to exercise their crafts. Finally, most large towns included 'liberties' or exempt jurisdictions, where the city's trading monopoly did not run. At Chester, for instance, unfree craftsmen were able to sell their goods in a small district called Gloverstone within the exempt jurisdiction of the castle.

In the larger towns, the body of freemen was subdivided into separate organisations – crafts, companies or fellowships – on an occupational basis. Unlike London, most towns had only a single company of merchants or wholesale traders, who were usually the dominant fellowship in political and economic terms. In several of the largest towns the merchants were able to secure charters from the Crown giving them a monopoly of overseas trade, under the name of Company of Merchants Venturers or Adventurers: Bristol (1552), Chester (1554), Exeter (1560), York (1581). Most other freemen were members of a variety of handicraft companies – butchers, bakers, innkeepers, shoemakers and so on, and indeed the corporations usually required freemen to join a company. At Coventry, all householders not already 'associat to some crafte' were in 1536 ordered to join one.

The corporations normally ensured that the companies were useful subordinate organisations rather than rivals for power. At York, for example, all of the sixty or so companies except the merchants were answerable to the city council, who insisted on approving their ordinances or regulations. At Exeter, where the gild system developed late, only eight crafts formed organised companies in 1561, but the Elizabethan corporation systematically added to their number 'to establish a structure of control through which the various economic regulations of the city as well as the economic legislation of the Crown could be carried out'. Again, Hooker makes the purpose explicit, stating that the inclusion of all citizens in companies was a 'greate ease' to the mayor, who could leave all their causes to be dealt with by their own governors. The corporation of Norwich similarly tightened their control in 1622 by reorganising nearly eighty crafts into twelve Grand Companies. Smaller towns did not usually boast such a complex array of companies, and many had a single organisation for all craftsmen and traders, often called a Gild Merchant and identical to the whole body of freemen.

The corporations' attitude to the companies raises questions about the aims and purposes of civic government. Plainly, its primary purpose, both as seen by the city fathers and by the watchful eye of the Privy Council, was to preserve law and order. This was hard enough for any local authority without a police force and faced by the widespread ownership of weapons, but the more difficult in dense concentrations of several thousand persons. Tudor corporations have been given too little credit for their success in this sphere; never during the period did any corporation lose control in a riot or insurrection, except when the town concerned was swept up in a popular regional rising, such as Norwich in 1549 and Ripon in 1569. The craft companies could be usefully harnessed to this end, as Hooker implied, and become effective subunits of municipal government, policing their own members.

There was, however, more to it than this. The ambitions of the greater town councils were not limited to keeping order, but included the attempt to exclude or dominate all other sources of authority. Corporations sought to subordinate craft companies as they sought to subordinate cathedral chapters and lords of private liberties. A town subordinated to ecclesiastical authority would seek independence as soon as its masters were destroyed or humbled. Reading (1542), St Albans (1553) and Abingdon (1555) all acquired incorporation once their monastic lords were swept away. Towns under episcopal lordship might also seize the opportunity to free themselves either at once (Lichfield, 1548; Banbury, 1554) or after a prolonged struggle (Salisbury, 1612). Others were able to free themselves from the control of lay lords, as did Brecon, a seigneurial town until the fall of the duke of Buckingham in 1521. It became a county town in 1536 and a corporate borough in 1556, and flourished considerably over the following century. Towns already self-governing tended to erode the jurisdictions of cathedral deans and chapters. The larger towns were willing to spend considerable sums on acquiring royal charters which confirmed existing privileges or granted new ones.

Nearly all towns did what they could to stand on their charters both against other towns and local jurisdictions, and against sheriffs and county justices. Here, however, they were swimming against the tide, for the central government was increasingly concerned about effective rule, and increasingly unsympathetic to the traditional 'particularist' attitude of urban corporations. In the 1540s Archbishop Holgate, as president of the Northern Council, did not hesitate to override York's municipal privileges in the interest of military musters. In 1587 the queen warned the Cinque Ports that unless they shouldered more of the burden of defence 'we do not mean to suffer them in such a fruitless manner to enjoy' their privileges, and in 1596, when Lincoln corporation balked at admitting the authority of the county justices during the dearth, the Privy Council warned them, 'You are to consider that in a time of such necessity as this it is unfit to stand curiously and precisely upon advantages of privileges.'[22]

What prevented the Crown from actually removing towns' chartered rights was probably its dependence on reliable knots of councillors for the thankless and unpaid task of keeping law and order and collecting taxes. Much has been written about the constitutional machinery which ensured government by indirectly elected, or even self-elected, plutocracies in the towns, but whatever the forms of elections, the personnel is unlikely to have been very different. Urban wealth was distributed very unequally, if perhaps no more so than in the countryside; but differences were made more conspicuous in the crowded towns, and status depended more on worldly wealth and less on pedigree. A man's 'worship' was equated with his 'substance', and although wealth was not the sole criterion for entry to civic office it was an essential one.

Hooker, who has bequeathed a series of thumb-nail sketches of the mayors of Exeter, notes only one who was not wealthy, and that in an apologetic way. John Wolcott had been a rich merchant and had held all the junior civic offices, but 'yn the ende his losses were so greate that he was verie poor', and 'it was not thought nor ment that ever the office of the mayroltie shold have fallen unto his lott'. But by 1565 the supply of alternative aldermen had dried up, and his colleagues reluctantly elected him and subsidised his household.[23] The great majority of townsmen, whether freemen or not, would have been ruled out of consideration simply by lack of sufficient wealth. There is no index of urban wealth for the late Tudor period so comprehensive as the 1523–27 subsidy analysed in the previous volume, but the pattern of enormous inequalities had probably changed little.

Not surprisingly, the urban rulers were drawn from small groups of the wealthier citizens, and especially from the merchants, who were generally among the wealthiest. The average personal estate of London merchants in the late sixteenth and early seventeenth centuries was £7,780, the comparable figure for Bristol being £1,921 and for Exeter £1,913. This is reflected in the mayoralty of the larger towns in Elizabeth's reign: 46 Exeter mayors out of 50 were merchants, 35 out of 46 at Bristol, and 34 out of 47 at Norwich, though only 23 out of 46 at York. The numbers take no account of the fact that some men held office more than once; this, together with the presence of more than one member of the same family, made the governing circles very restricted indeed. The previous volume includes an analysis of the Elizabethan mayors of several towns, showing that the mayors of Exeter were drawn from only 26 families and of Norwich from 29, so that in each case only 1 family in 100 could aspire to the mayoralty, though York (33 families) and Bristol (38) were more open.

Urban government by plutocracy should not, however, be overstressed. If the highest offices were virtually monopolised by the very wealthy, they still had to rely on a much broader group for administering their towns. Just as parish office in the countryside could involve husbandmen, so minor civic office depended on craftsmen as well as merchants. Elizabethan York had to fill over 120 municipal offices, and at least as many more at ward and parish level, so that one freeman in five must have held office at any one time. Similarly, in unincorporated Manchester, one man from every four or five households must have been an official at any time. The degree of active public support, and not merely acquiescence, on which the urban élites had to depend was very high.

Corporations were gradually enlarging the scope of their activities. To the traditional maintenance of law and order and upkeep of walls and other buildings, they were adding street cleansing and lighting, more extensive public health measures, especially against plagues, and a greater degree of social welfare. The more enlightened corporations often took action in these matters well in advance of the central government, as for example in issuing tokens to remedy the shortage of small coin, or in elaborating a more comprehensive and humane policy of poor relief. Nevertheless, when only a minority of households contributed to local taxes, and much expenditure had to come out of councillors' own pockets, at least temporarily, then civic budgets tended to be kept to a minimum. Little research has yet been carried out on urban financial accounts, but it is clear that the bulk of income in the larger towns came traditionally from leases of corporation property, market tolls and other trading dues, profits of justice and admissions of new freemen. Under pressure of inflation and of expanding commitments, most towns by the late sixteenth century were struggling to tap new sources of income, but often with little success. The total civic budgets were quite modest in comparison to known fortunes of individual citizens; thus both York and Exeter enjoyed an annual income of only some £350–£400 at the start of Elizabeth's reign, rising by the end of it to £500–£600 at York and £700–£1,100 in the more enterprising Exeter.

4

The emphasis so far has been on the static and unchanging aspects of provincial urban life, an emphasis perhaps justifiably given the many 'glacierlike elements . . . which change so slowly, so nearly imperceptibly, that they cannot be measured in the brief span of a century'.[24] However, it goes without saying that there were many changes in the provincial towns, if not so dramatic as in the capital, and indeed in the whole urban network. Some contemporaries, followed by some modern historians, saw urban decay almost everywhere, and their views merit a detailed examination. Was there indeed a general crisis among sixteenth-century towns, or was there rather a realignment of the network under the pressure of economic and social change, population growth and the expansion of London?

Mid-Tudor writers were uncharacteristically unanimous about the reality of urban decay, and as R. B. Dobson has rightly said, 'perhaps the most remarkable feature of the great Tudor debate on the nature of the Common Weal is the way in which "the great plentie of povertie in all the cities, great townes and other inferior market townes in England and Wales" is so rarely regarded as anything but self-evident'.[25] This in itself does not prove the existence of general urban decay, and a mass of apparently contradictory facts have been urged in evidence in a recent lively debate. Nearly all urban historians are agreed on the reality of widespread urban difficulties which were unusually acute in the mid-Tudor period. The differences between them are chiefly over the chronology and depth of the depression, and the number of towns thought to have escaped it. However, it is fair to add that one or two dissenting voices remain sceptical of any widespread crisis, and prefer instead a model of urban 'undulations', in which towns were constantly rising and falling, but the general balance remained similar in each period.

Dobson, Phythian-Adams and the present writer have argued for a general urban recession, beginning in the fifteenth century and intensifying between about 1520 and 1570 before lifting. It seems to have affected almost all the larger provincial towns, including Norwich, Bristol, Coventry and York, and many smaller market towns. The surveyor Humberston, for example, inspecting three small Staffordshire boroughs in 1559, found them 'decayed and depopulated' and their markets 'unfurnisshed'.[26] Exeter by general consent remained prosperous, but A. F. Butcher has recently undermined the claim that Newcastle also stood aloof from the depression. Clark and Slack, in contrast, date the beginning of the general urban crisis around 1520, but see no overall improvement, and even in some respects a deterioration, after the 1570s. Not until the later seventeenth century, in their view, were the structural weaknesses overcome.

These rival views stem from differing perceptions and perspectives rather than from disagreement over the facts. The fundamental cause of decline, according to Lupset and Smith, was a shrinking of urban population. There is little doubt that almost all towns by the 1540s had populations below their medieval peak, but that by 1603 most had again increased substantially. However, given what is now known of demographic trends, that is merely to say that towns were not exempt from them. What needs to be established is either that towns suffered a more severe decline or a more retarded recovery than the countryside, or that similar trends had a disproportionately severe effect in an urban context. Whether, in fact, provincial towns collectively included a smaller share of the national population in 1547 or 1603 than they had earlier is still unclear, and perhaps is doomed to remain so.

The arguments have so far turned on selected towns, usually the larger ones. No one questions the rapid growth of London, and it could well be that it grew at the expense of other towns. Phythian-Adams has not only demonstrated the enormous if exceptional shrinking of Coventry – from perhaps 9,000 in 1500 to half that figure in 1563 – but has adduced figures to suggest that many larger provincial towns may have had smaller populations in 1563 than forty years earlier. This, if so, would certainly indicate that the towns were stagnating while the rural population recovery was already in full swing; but it does depend on the usefulness of the 1563 ecclesiastical census. Evidence above suggests that the household figures may nationally have been slightly too low, and that in any case the census was taken when England was still recovering from the severe epidemic of 1557–59. The decaying market towns of Staffordshire and elsewhere can be accounted for by a shrinkage of demand as the late medieval population fell, while the population recovery brought no corresponding revival, because a more complex economy relied on fewer, and more specialised, markets. Staffordshire had up to 45 market towns before 1349, but found about 20 quite sufficient throughout the sixteenth and seventeenth centuries, even though the county's population doubled. Certainly there was no further decline in market numbers in the late sixteenth and early seventeenth centuries, if contemporary listings can be trusted. William Smith counted 644 in 1588, Thomas Wilson 641 in 1601, and John Speed 656 in 1611. Extinct markets were being balanced by revivals and new creations.

In any case, population growth was not necessarily associated with economic prosperity. Bridbury maintains that towns prospered more in the fifteenth century than the sixteenth precisely because they were not overcrowded, and Clark and Slack have suggested that some of the most intractable economic problems of the towns, notably vagrancy and the cost of poor relief, became more acute between 1570 and 1640, because urban populations were increasing faster than the economic prosperity required to sustain them, although it is also possible to argue that poor immigrants were attracted because the towns were flourishing. Where Dobson and Phythian-Adams seem especially convincing is in demonstrating that the urban population stagnation or even relative decline *before* 1570 was both cause and consequence of the decay of the larger provincial towns as social and economic centres. Phythian-Adams sees the whole period 1520–70 as 'a time of acute urban crisis', of which the two major causes were 'externally, the threatening growth of rural competition and, internally, the costly disincentives to urban residence'.

There is abundant evidence that by the mid-sixteenth century many industries were carried on in the countryside and in the smaller market villages rather than in the old-established, larger corporate towns which had been their traditional home. The threat was recognised by parliament; a statute of 1534 sought to protect the borough textile industries of Worcestershire from competition by rural workers, a protection extended to all boroughs and market towns by a national statute of 1555. Another statute of 1554 attempted to prohibit any retail trading by countryfolk in the towns, except at fair times.

Meanwhile, the corporate towns also suffered because the costs of civic office-holding and ceremonial, and of taxation, pressed more heavily on them. The agents of decline were all interconnected: a decline in the population or prosperity of a town, or both, meant that a disproportionate share of civic taxation and ceremonial pressed upon the remaining wealthy citizens, to a point where some chose to refuse civic office, or to leave the town altogether and to trade from outside, thus reinforcing the pressure from rural competition on those left behind. In 1533 one Coventry citizen complained that when a man became wealthy, 'for feirre of office which be so charge-able . . . he . . . goeth to a farme in the contre and ther occupieth boithe his occupacion and husbondry';[27] and in 1554 Norwich corporation took steps against freemen who had moved out into the sur-rounding villages but continued to buy and sell in the city without contributing to civic rates and taxes.

One still widely held belief is that most corporate towns suffered economic decline because of their exclusiveness, through restricting admissions to the freedom and the craft gilds, and through the restric-tive practices of those gilds. Charles Gross, a classic exponent of this view, argued that 'the tyranny of the gilds . . . drove commerce and industry to rural districts and to smaller "free-trade" towns, such as Birmingham, Manchester and Leeds. . . . Thus the rigid protection of the older chartered boroughs sapped their commercial prosperity, silencing the once busy looms of Norwich and Exeter, and sweeping away the cloth-halls of York and Winchester.'[28] It is possible, by judicious use of examples, to make quite a convincing case on those lines. Without doubt a once rich but declining city with an elaborate corporate and ceremonial structure could find its decline accelerated by the weight of that structure, as Phythian-Adams has demonstrated for Coventry. At the same time, as he also showed, the Reformation provided an opportunity for them to reduce the cost of it all.

It is true that the cloth industry shifted its location from some of the older urban centres, notably York and Coventry, although Nor-wich and Worcester have to be admitted as exceptions. In 1561, the mayor of York mourned the exodus of the city's weavers to Halifax, Leeds and Wakefield, though the reasons he gave were more water power and cheaper food and fuel rather than irksome regulations. York's craft gilds were not a brake on the city's prosperity, and indeed between 1519 and 1561 – during the depth of economic depression – the corporation abolished many restrictive practices to attract skilled workers. Corfield has come to similar conclusions about the role of the Norwich gilds.

Contemporary evidence can certainly be adduced against the alleged restrictiveness of corporations, if not of craft gilds. Sir John

Mason declared roundly in 1551 that 'there is no one thing that more continueth a daily hurt to the realm than corporations', while Dr Haddon obtained the incorporation of Poole in 1563 with great difficulty, because 'the name of incorporation' was 'so discredited' with the queen. An anonymous *Discourse of Corporations* of the 1580s argued that 'all corporacions of townes and cities . . . be very inconvenient and hurtfull to the subjectes and comon welthe' in obstructing free trade, and they did not even benefit their own towns. Poole was formerly prosperous, 'but since the incorporatinge of the same the marchantes decaied, theire shippinge gonn and theire towne poore. And the like is of diverse other townes in the West Cuntrey and upon the coste of England.'[29] However, he did not argue that trade was driven away to unincorporated towns, but to London (itself of course corporate), a complaint which deserves separate consideration. As for Mason's outburst, it is enough to say that he had acquired Abingdon Abbey, and that his aim was to prevent the townsmen of Abingdon from acquiring self-government after the dissolution.

Nor is it clear that the existence of corporations had any effect on the fall and rise of urban communities. If unincorporated Manchester laid the foundations of its textile supremacy in the sixteenth century, unincorporated Lavenham rapidly decayed after a brief period of glory as an early Tudor cloth centre. If Leeds, Halifax and Wakefield gained at the expense of York, that is not to the purpose either. All three were unincorporated, it is true, but Leeds acquired gilds and a corporation in 1626, which did not prevent it from pulling ahead of unincorporated Wakefield. What is beyond question is that towns in difficulty welcomed powers to help them help themselves. At least 23 of the 42 boroughs incorporated between 1540 and 1558 acquired the status at least in part to remedy economic difficulties.

The central government was undoubtedly preoccupied with problems of the urban economies between the 1530s and 1570s. G. R. Elton has demonstrated Cromwell's concern in the 1530s, culminating in six statutes between 1534 and 1542 for amending the decay of towns, which granted enabling powers to seventy-nine separate places, including most large towns except London. In 1549 another statute authorised all towns to retain their fee-farm payments for three years and to apply the proceeds to 'settinge poore people on woorke' and other local objects, although the Crown's financial straits caused the grant to be revoked after only one year. In 1554–55 followed the acts already noted protecting boroughs against rural competition, of which the former stated unequivocally that without protection 'the same cities, boroughes and townes corporate are like to come verie shortly to utter destruccion ruine and decaye'. Well into Elizabeth's reign the government continued to be met by laments of urban poverty. Thus in 1561 the queen was told that one of the two Coventry parishes was 'of late' impoverished by the decay of the city, and the recorder of Coventry made the same point in welcoming the queen in 1565.

Coventry was, perhaps, exceptional in the degree of its decline, but the recorders of Warwick, Stratford and Worcester made similar points during royal progresses in the 1570s. In 1569 the earl of Leicester initiated an inquiry into the alleged decay of Chester, and in 1571 the commissioners reported that the citizens were 'in great and pytiffull decay'. Thomas Lupton petitioned the queen on behalf of Lincoln, 'nowe muche decayed, and full of poverty, havinge no certen trade to maynteyne the same', and in 1589 a 'bill for the relief of the city of Lincoln' was passed by the Lords and Commons, though it does not seem to have received the royal assent. Lambarde had noted in 1584, 'Touching the present estate of Lincolne, I thinke it pietyfull; for . . . the condicion thearof is little better then of a commune market towne.' In 1587 another petition to the queen, alleging the great decay of Leicester, found independent corroboration from an inquiry reporting 235 tenements in decay and 406 bays of houses requiring complete rebuilding. Elizabeth's parliaments, unlike those of Henry, Edward and Mary, did not enact general protective legislation for towns as a whole, except for the urban apprenticeship provisions of the Statute of Artificers. However, the Privy Council was well aware of the problems, and granted many towns tax reductions on the ground of poverty. It is, of course, one-sided evidence; prospering towns were scarcely likely to feature among their records. Clark and Slack see 'some improvement' among towns generally in the second half of the century, and though they also stress continuing economic difficulties, one critic has argued that 'what is being considered is not general decline but adjustments within an expanding urban economic system'.[30]

Government concern over urban decay appears to have lessened by the middle of Elizabeth's reign. One reason was probably that the rural population was growing sufficiently to ensure considerable migration into the larger provincial towns as well as London. With a growing population, and relatively fixed taxable burdens (and therefore declining in real terms because of inflation), corporations no longer had the same difficulty in meeting their financial commitments. It was the *conjunction* in the early sixteenth century of population decay or stagnation, economic competition from the countryside, and the heavy weight of civic government and ceremonial that had weakened the larger towns; and most of these problems were remedied by the end of the century.

Another reason for recovery was that the changes entailed by the Reformation, although initially disastrous for the older corporate towns, were in the long run beneficial. In the 1530s and 1540s the dissolutions of monasteries, chantries, religious gilds and hospitals, and the suppression of shrines, were catastrophic for most cathedral cities and for those with many religious houses. Pilgrims ceased to come, the business and custom generated by wealthy monasteries disappeared, and rents drained away to the distant purchasers of monastic land. Coventry, already hard-hit by economic change, saw its cathedral actually demolished. The cohesion of the urban community was damaged by the suppression of the great socio-religious gilds which united the wealthier citizens and county society, and of the humbler parish gilds which created bonds of local loyalties focused around each parish church. The more gradual erosion of pageants and plays staged by the urban craft gilds had the same effect. Many houses formerly owned by religious institutions came on to the market and were often bought up in large blocks by speculators, with the danger of increased rents and of money draining away from the localities, to London.

In the long run, however, the end of much religious and socio-religious ceremonial slimmed the cost of urban office-holding and allowed corporations and craft gilds to confine their expenses to strictly secular activities. The more buoyant corporations, like Exeter, had the resources to buy many of the ex-monastic and chantry properties in their own cities, and thus to improve their financial position. Other cities were permitted to alleviate their financial difficulties by staging dissolutions of their own. One of the burdens on large but declining urban communities had been an excessive number of parish churches to maintain. Between 1547 and 1586 Lincoln, Norwich, Stamford, Winchester and York all united together considerable numbers of churches and used the sites and building materials for their own purposes. York was able to reduce 40 parishes to 25, and Norwich secularised 17 churches between 1520 and 1570.

Furthermore, some larger towns discovered new roles to revive their prosperity. Many smaller market towns had continued to prosper throughout the early and mid-sixteenth century, although Everitt's work suggests that in general they flourished especially after about 1570 as marketing and internal trade became more large scale and more specialised. The same trends benefited larger towns also; York, Leicester, Northampton and many others were by the end of the century enjoying a boom in trade, as their markets and inns bear witness. A few major old-established cities were even able to retain or recapture their industrial importance. Worcester's cloth-making, perhaps aided by the 1534 statute, went from strength to strength, while Norwich was able to revive its cloth industry from the 1560s with the aid of its 'Dutch' immigrants and the 'New Draperies' they developed. Other towns were rising to greater importance than ever before, such as Newcastle, described by Camden as 'now in a most flourishing state of wealth and commerce', or Plymouth, which 'in the last age', he noted, 'from a small fisher village . . . grew up to a large town, and is not inferiour to a city in number of inhabitants'.[31]

Towns which were both county towns and cathedral cities, like Exeter, Norwich and Salisbury, enjoyed the economic stimulus provided by two kinds of local courts. York was especially fortunate, and enjoyed an economic revival under Elizabeth largely because it possessed not only county, diocesan and archdiocesan courts but also, from 1561 to 1641, the headquarters of the Council in the North and the Northern Ecclesiastical Commission. Ludlow flourished similarly, if more modestly, as home for the Council for Wales and the Marches, while the shiring of Wales in 1536 boosted new county and assize towns. Conversely, a county town in decline was the more anxious to retain its administrative status for sound economic reasons. When Elizabeth visited Stafford in 1575, the burgesses successfully petitioned for the return of the county assizes from Wolverhampton.

Many towns were beginning to be patronised by the county aristocracy and gentry, and their tradesmen and shopkeepers benefited accordingly. The dukes of Norfolk, with a great town house in Norwich until 1571, and the earls of Bedford, with their Bedford House at Exeter, were only two of numerous families imitating the London pattern on a smaller scale. Sir Thomas Hoby of Hackness bought a York house in 1600, and the only surviving letter from his wife asks 'if you come hither by York . . . bye me . . . 2 pound of starch, for I have none left'. A character in *Cyvile and Uncyvile Life* (1579) noted that formerly nobles and gentlemen 'did continually inhabite the countryes', but that they now 'leave to dwell in their country houses, inhabitinge citties and great townes'. Patronage by county society became very lucrative. York corporation were happy to agree when local gentry asked to have a cockpit in 1568, as it would 'cause muche money to be spent bothe emongs vyttelers and other craftsmen'. However, patronage of the gentry had its price, and it is perhaps from late Elizabethan times that one can date the deferential respect of corporations, towards their well-born neighbours, a deference which endured until the nineteenth century. Towns which defied influential neighbours did so at their peril. Sir John Gray wrote contemptuously to the councillors of Leicester about their 'shalloe capasities', threatening that 'yf you bee able to crosse me in one thinge, I can requite your towne with twentie', a boast he proceeded to make good.[32]

Towns were also losing the initative to the gentry in another sense. Whereas pre-Reformation culture had centred on the towns, with their plays, pageants, processions and schools of craftsmen and glass-painters, the centre of Elizabethan culture and pageantry was the country house, and its tone was set by the educated gentleman. London, of course, remained culturally central, with its theatres, pageants and resident writers; but even there the specifically urban tradition of town chronicles – represented at its best by John Stow – seemed out of date in the new literary environment. Chronicle history was still written and read by and for Londoners, but it aroused the scorn of university-trained writers:

Gentles, it is not your lay chronigraphers, that write of nothing but of mayors and sheriefs, and the deare yeere, and the great frost, that can endowe your names with never dated glory . . .[33]

Writers and musicians were patronised not by citizens, but by courtiers and gentlemen, whether in their London houses or on their country estates. Drayton and Jonson enjoyed lengthy hospitality in various country houses; the Herberts entertained many writers at Wilton; the madrigalist John Wilby lived permanently with the Kitsons at Hengrave; and Massinger, the son of a retainer at Wilton, was brought up there.

A growing political and social dependence on the Crown, aristocracy and gentry indicates that there was no uniform direction of change, and that if the larger towns were prospering economically again from about 1570, they may have paid for that prosperity by a loss of their traditional attitudes of independence and particularism. Another area of difficulty was the extent of urban poverty and poor relief, for if most towns were no longer pleading corporate poverty in late Elizabethan and early Stuart times, they were certainly very vocal about the burden of the poor. What is unclear is whether paupers merely increased proportionately with growing urban populations, or whether population was outstripping economic growth and therefore creating a proportionately greater pauper class. Official concern, in part at least, reflected a growing humanitarianism and an increased fear of disorder, and cannot be taken as an index of the actual extent of poverty. Part of the difficulty is that measurements of poverty, crude enough for late Tudor times, are even more uncertain for earlier dates.

5

It remains to consider the mutual relationship of London and the provincial towns in an urban network. There is abundant evidence that the phenomenal growth of London was part-cause and part-consequence of a developing national market for industrial and agricultural products, in which London came to dominate both internal and overseas trade. Was this, however, a relationship in which London's growth entailed growing prosperity for other towns, or was it parasitic upon them? One contemporary view was proudly put by the French teacher and adopted Londoner Peter Erondell (1605):

O Thames, Thames! Thou art a provident husband, which bringest innumerable riches to thy famous spouse London, . . . who as a true oeconome and huswife doth distribute her goods to th'other partes of the realme, as a naturall mother to her beloved children.

The other side of the debate can be represented by the author of the *Discourse of Corporations* – London 'hath eaten up all the rest of the townes and havens of England' – or by the customer of Sandwich in 1604:

All our creeks seek to one river, all our rivers, run to one port, all our ports join to one town, all our towns make but one city . . . which the world calls London.[34]

Even Stow, patriotic Londoner that he was, seemed almost to admit the charge. He appended to his *Survey* a discourse on the benefits of London, to rebut the accusation that London had drawn to itself all sea-borne trade and all handicrafts, thereby causing the decay of many or most of the ancient cities, corporate towns and markets. Yet although he justified London's situation as the best for foreign trade, by advantage of which 'it disperseth forraine wares (as the stomacke doth meat) to all the members most commodiously', he did not deny that overseas trade was 'decayed in many port townes, and flourisheth onely or chiefly at London', while as for retailers and craftsmen, 'it is no marvaile if they abandon countrie townes, and resort to London'.[35]

Yet Stow surely conceded too much. London did monopolise overseas trade more than at any other period, but the leading provincial towns took an active part in internal trade and in retailing and handicrafts. Some towns were positively stimulated by London's growth, as was Newcastle by the Londoners' booming demand for coal, or Manchester by the linking of its cloth trade to the capital. Others experienced economic fluctuations not in any way linked to London's growth. As Corfield has said, the most vocal critics of London were the provincial outports, jealous of London's overseas trade and the powers of its trading companies, and even then their complaints were chiefly confined to periods of commercial depression like the 1550s and 1586–87. 'And it simply was not the case in the long term that all the outports (or even a majority of them) were experiencing economic difficulties through the growth of London. Exeter, Bristol, Newcastle, Chester and Yarmouth, for example, were all independent trading centres, and were all reasonably flourishing' in the late sixteenth and early seventeenth centuries, while some smaller ports like King's Lynn, that complained of a loss of overseas trade, were 'developing a brisk coastal trade in agricultural produce to feed the voracious appetites of the London consumer'.[36]

To sum up, although there is evidence for serious economic difficulties among the larger provincial towns between about 1520 and 1570, the arguments for any general urban weakness in the late sixteenth and early seventeenth centuries are less convincing. Some old-established towns did continue to decay, like Stamford and Winchester, but others such as York and Norwich were prospering again, and were joined by flourishing and rising towns like Manchester and Plymouth. True, some towns now relied much more on administrative and social functions, and were therefore more dependent on pressure from Crown and gentry than they had been in the late Middle Ages. Yet to contrast medieval urban prosperity as based on trade and industry, and that of the early modern period as relying rather on trade, administration and servicing, as some recent writers have done, is an overstatement. The cloth industry may well have deserted most older urban centres, but the occupational composition of towns reveals a continuing high proportion of citizens engaged in manufacturing. What happened is that urban industry became more broadly based, with many of the older towns relying on a wider range of smaller industries, and therefore attaining more economic stability. At the same time, several towns which had previously been of little importance – such as Manchester, Leeds and Birmingham – were flourishing by successfully concentrating on one or two industries. Leland's *Itinerary* in the 1530s and 1540s is full of decayed towns and departed glories, whereas Camden's *Britannia* of 1586 and later is much more taken with urban beauty and prosperity.

If the towns had really become so unimportant as is sometimes alleged, it is odd that Elizabeth took as much care on her summer progresses to cultivate the loyalty of citizens as of countrymen. Her ceremonial entries to Bristol and Norwich were among the high points of her provincial tours. When she knighted the mayor of Norwich, she told him that 'I have laid up in my breast such good will as I shall never forget Norwich'; and when she passed its boundaries, she 'did shake hir riding rod' and said, '"Farewell, Norwich", with the water standing in hir eies'.[37] Perhaps this was the theatre at which she was so expert, but it reflected an interest in the nation well worth cultivating.

Chapter 8

Crafts and industries

I knewe the time when men weare contented with cappes, hattes, girdelles, and poyntes and all maner of garmentes made in the townes next adioyninge; wherby the townes then weare well occupied and set aworke ... Nowe ... not gentleman can be content to have eyther cappe, coate, dublet, hose or shirt made in his countrey, but they must have their geare from London; and yet manye thinges thearof are not theare made, but beyonde the sea ...

Sir Thomas Smith (?), *A Discourse of the Common Weal*, 1549

Yow receave many strangers into the realme [of England] ... and the realme by them receaveth many comodyties, as connynge in manye syences wherin before yow were altogether ignorant.

The treasurer of Flushing, 1573[1]

1

Nearly all townsmen, and a large minority of the rural population in some areas, were employed in trade or industry, so it is misleading to call Tudor England 'pre-industrial'. Coleman reasonably prefers to describe it as 'pre-industrialised'. Admittedly Tudor Englishmen did not speak of industries at all, but of crafts, manufactures or handicrafts, the very terms indicating manual rather than mechanical processes. They had no conception of a separate industrial sector, but apparently thought in terms of a loose grouping of 'artificers', many of them engaged in processing agricultural products and not in any way divorced from agriculture. Most Tudor craftsmen or 'artificers' worked with specialised tools, and some even with machinery: but that is not to say that their society can be called industrialised by any stretch of the imagination, for large concerns with a substantial investment in fixed capital were rare.

England was industrially backward in the early sixteenth century in comparison with her European neighbours. It was only gradually, from about 1540 onwards, that she began to catch up by establishing many new industries and by putting others on a commercially significant basis for the first time. These included copper-mining, glass-making and paper-making; gunfounding and the manufacture of gunpowder, alum and copperas; the weaving of silk, cotton and linen; and the creation of a range of New Draperies to rival the traditional woollen textiles. Furthermore, a whole range of consumer products were beginning an expansion which was to transform the lives of the mass of the population – products like soap, stockings, pins and needles, and pots and pans.

Such imperfect statistics as exist will be called in evidence to assess the relative size and economic importance of the various crafts. All figures of employment and production have, however, to be used gingerly. The only systematic registers of workers are of those admitted to apprenticeship and freedom in the corporate towns, and almost the only reliable valuations of manufactures are of those paying customs duties. An excessive reliance on statistics, therefore, leads to a very partial view of industrial activity, confined to the work of a privileged class in the corporate towns and to those manufactures intended for export. What records of production and sales do survive are often added together without sufficient regard for their interpretation. Although the English Crown had long insisted on common standards for certain key weights and measures, standards for which were periodically sent out to the larger towns as a control, many units retained local variations which can play havoc with conversions to standard modern measures. The chaldron of coal differed in weight between Newcastle and London; the fother of lead ranged from 1,560 to 2,800 lb; and the people of Anglesey measured cloth both by the English yard of 36 inches and the Welsh yard of about 39.

Furthermore, calculations about the proportions of the population engaged in agriculture, textiles, mining and so on, are made with modern assumptions about full and full-time employment. A permanent feature of Tudor society was the existence of (in Coleman's phrase) 'a reservoir of underemployed labour', and there was also much seasonal unemployment, especially in agriculture and the building industry. Such employment figures as survive may refer to a labour force of men, women or children, or a mixture of the three. Child labour was not a subject for shame: Wilson (1601) commented that in the towns 'every child of 6 or 7 yeares old is forced to some art', and all children of seven or over in Norwich were able to earn four shillings a week knitting jersey stockings. Dual occupations provided a frequent escape from seasonal unemployment, or, more positively, a means of increasing the family income. A typical rural labourer near Nottingham in the 1580s 'kept his family on his own bare wages of 3s 4d a week' but once the labour-intensive woad growing was introduced for the dyeing industry, it was said that 'wife and children can bring this up in some periods of the year to 5s or 6s a week'.[2]

2

Most Tudor 'crafts' or manufactures were commercial undertakings based on a single household and carried on either in the owner's home or in attached outbuildings. A shoemaker, tailor or glover, for instance, worked up his cloth or leather in a ground-floor room of his dwelling-house. It was called his 'shop' in the sense of 'workshop', though he might also sell his goods there, usually over a window shutter lowered to form a 'shop board' or counter projecting into the street. A few crafts could not be carried on in this way; tanners and horners needed tanneries and horn-pits, millers needed a windmill or water-mill, while building craftsmen normally worked on site. In all cases, however, the distinguishing mark of ordinary craft businesses was their domestic scale.

A craftsman, even if he formed a one-man business, could not of course work in isolation. He depended on supplies of raw materials and customers for his finished products, whether wholesale or retail. Many crafts formed mutually dependent groups where products at different stages were passed from one to another. At the simplest level, a craftsman might buy raw materials and convert them himself into a finished product for retail sales – a carpenter turning wood into furniture, a miller grinding corn into flour. But many urban and rural crafts represented only one stage in a more complex process. Graziers would raise cattle and sell them to butchers, who slaughtered them, sold the meat by retail, and sold the hides to tanners. These in turn tanned the leather and sold it to curriers, who dressed it and then sold it to the makers of finished products – shoemakers, saddlers and so on.

A craftsman in a small way combined four functions which today are usually separated. He was his own employer, workman, merchant and shopkeeper, working his own materials which he bought himself and sold himself. Those with a slightly larger order-book often employed wife or children to keep the business within the family. Those with more work on hand needed to employ other workmen or assistants. A rural or village craftsman might be assisted by 'servants' or 'labourers', like his farming neighbours; a master craftsman in a corporate town would have journeymen and apprentices working for him in a more legally defined relationship. In either case, the master was adding the role of foreman to his other responsibilities. The traditional craft business at its largest and most elaborate is represented by the typical London bakery as it was described in 1619. It consisted of the master baker, his wife, four journeymen, two apprentices, two maidservants, and the baker's three or four children who may also have helped. All ate and worked together in the master's house, and all slept there except the journeymen.

In theory, in corporate towns at least, aspiring craftsmen would begin their careers by being taken on as apprentices to learn the craft under a master. An apprentice would bind himself to a master for a fixed term of years (which was commonly becoming a seven-year term well before the Statute of Artificers in 1563 made it a legal minimum), and would then hope to become a master himself. However, the system in practice was rarely so simple. On the one hand, many apprentices were unable to become masters as soon as they qualified, either for lack of working capital or because there was insufficient business available. In that case they might become journeymen, adult hands hired by other masters. On the other hand, those with sufficient capital or connections might become masters without serving a full apprenticeship, either by inheriting the status of freemen and master from their fathers, or simply by buying their way in, as many sons of country gentlemen and yeomen did.

The description of a bakery was included in a petition by the baker's company, an organisation representing the master bakers of the City of London. London and most other corporate towns still had a closely regulated economic structure. Real economic power – the right to trade freely and to run a shop or business – was confined to the master craftsmen and traders, who had to be admitted both to the freedom of the City and to the appropriate gild or company. The purpose and nature of gilds have been frequently misunderstood. They

were not in themselves units of functional economic organisation so much as methods of association and control or social foci of civic ceremony and ritual. They were not in themselves sources of finance, of credit or capital . . . As a rough analogy with modern times, they carried out some of those economic functions today exercised by trade unions or employers' associations, not those performed by factories or by joint-stock companies.[3]

That is a sufficient reason why the smaller towns could have a handful of gilds each representing a miscellaneous range of crafts, rather than indulging in the unnecessary luxury of one for each occupation. The mercers' company at Kingston upon Thames (1608), one of many such arbitrary groupings, comprised haberdashers, grocers, chandlers, painters, cutlers, vintners, glaziers and barbers.

The chief economic function of craft gilds was to control their own membership and so to regulate the supply of labour, the level of wages, and hours and standards of work. Naturally they worked best when supply and demand held fairly steady. In a volatile economic situation it could easily happen that a group of masters competed for too much or too little work, trying hard to prevent expansion or contraction in their industry. Many an urban gild refused admission to newcomers who wanted to expand output to meet a growing demand; the result might be to drive the applicants to set up shop elsewhere, in the countryside, in an unregulated town or (in the case of London especially) in the suburbs outside the jurisdiction of the City and the City companies. Equally, as fashions and techniques changed, gilds established with clear demarcation lines tended to conflict one with another. The London plasterers, originally 'but dawbers and mud-wall-makers', began to plaster housefronts, rose to the rank of an incorporated company and aroused the wrath of the company of painters by first applying 'alehouse colours' and then applying colours of all kinds. The indignant painters petitioned against the plasterers, and abortive bills on the subject were debated at length in two successive parliaments (1598–1601) before the Lords ordered a judicial arbitration to settle the dispute.

Yet it would be misleading to dismiss Tudor gilds as anachronistic. There was a great diversity of types, from the small town with a single gild representing the masters of all crafts, through the larger towns with several gilds each representing a single trade or group of trades, to the complexity of London with its twelve great Livery Companies dominated by the merchants and about 150 other gilds representing the handicrafts. In a time of economic difficulty or opportunity, it was common for gilds to divide or amalgamate; and the town corporations always reserved the right to override the gilds if they behaved in too narrowly selfish a way. In consequence, the regulated structure of freedom and gild membership lasted much longer than, according to its *laissez-faire* critics, it should have been capable of doing.

Such carefully regulated urban economies bred careful record-keeping, since membership and control had to be enforced. As a result, many registers of craft membership survive, either those of gilds or those of the corporations' admissions to freedom. They provide, together with the customs records, the most comprehensive collection of Tudor economic statistics to survive, though it is important to remember that, like the customs records, they can give a very distorted and partial picture of economic activity. Most registers are of freemen and master craftsmen, although there are also some registers of apprentices. The distribution of master craftsmen among various occupations is not necessarily an accurate guide to occupational structure, since some masters required more assistance than others. A baker or butcher could run a small business on his own or with one assistant, whereas the textile crafts required a good deal of subordinate labour from an army of shadowy employees.

The will of a York widow, Margaret Sympson (1542) suggests that she was running a small textiles business, since she made bequests to 'Elisabeth my work woman or carder' and 'old Jenet my spynner'.[4] Yet none of the three is recorded in the freemen's register, Margaret probably because she inherited a business from her husband, and the assistants because they would not have been enfranchised. At Worcester, two widows who died in 1611 and 1617 each owned two spinning wheels and some wool and yarn. Furthermore, a significant proportion of master craftsmen were not enrolled as freemen, as many as 20 per cent in some towns, either because they escaped registration or because they lived in exempt jurisdictions or suburbs outside corporate and gild control. Finally, as the York example illustrates, the records understate the contribution of women. Few women became craftsmen in their own right, but many helped their husbands, and most corporations and gilds allowed widows to carry on their husbands' businesses.

Nevertheless, figures for freemen and master craftsmen have become a rich quarry for economic historians since Hoskins's pioneering analyses, and provided that their limitations are borne in mind, they are of great value. Tables 8.1 and 8.2 summarise the evidence for ten provincial towns, drawn where possible from comparable sources and analysed in comparable categories. Most of the evidence is taken from freemen's registers, over a period long enough to provide a large sample and to smoothe over any short-term distortions. It is unfortunate that the freemen's register for the City of London survives for a period of only twenty-two months, and that it categorises entrants by their companies, which had only a loose relationship to occupational structure. London is therefore excluded from the tables, but some interesting occupational figures from burial registers, compiled by Beier, are drawn on in the analysis below.[5]

The number of individual crafts and trades in the larger towns was considerable. Nottingham, Northampton and Leicester had each over 60, and Bristol, York and Norwich more than 100. In every town the majority were engaged in 10 or 20 basic crafts, though naturally the larger towns had a greater variety open to an ambitious youth. Elizabethan London had its specialised luxury crafts which scarcely existed elsewhere, like jewellery, printing and clock-making, but most leading provincial towns could support a few specialists. Worcester and York each had a gunsmith by the 1590s, and York its first clockmaker. Leicester maintained a dynasty of bellfounders until 1612, though the last three generations combined their craft with tan-

Table 8.1 Occupational distribution in ten English towns (expressed as percentages of the total workforce)

	Chester 1558–1603	Gloucester, Cirencester and Tewkesbury 1608	Hull 1580–89	Leicester 1559–1603	Norwich 1558–80	Norwich 1581–1603	Nottingham 1580–1620	Worcester 1540–89	Worcester 1590–1620	York 1550–1600
Textiles	11.2	13.3	2.5	6.6	17.1	15.2	3.8	42	54	6.3
Clothing	10.0	24.3 }	9.5	16.4	16.7	17.7	6.2	4	1	16.0
Leather	23.9		7.5	16.9	12.2	14.7	34.2	11	7	15.3
Metal	11.2	7.2	4.5	6.2 }	5.9	6.4	9.1	7	5	10.6
Woodwork	4.7	7.1	—		2.5	1.8	3.2	—	—	—
Building	6.2	2.7	1.9	5.9	10.2	10.6	5.1	2	3	8.6
Food and drink	13.3	8.2	8.9	18.6	12.3	12.4	26.7	12	14	20.1
Distributive and transport	16.6	27.2	56.7	6.7	20.6	19.0	7.6	12	3	14.2
Professional	1.8	7.7	— }	22.7 }	2.1 }	1.7	1.0 }	9 }	11 }	8.9 }
Others	1.2	2.5	8.3		0.6	0.5	3.2			
n =	1,246	1,018	157	898	1,072	953	693			3,172

Sources: See Appendix iv, pages 392–93.

Table 8.2 The leading occupations in six English towns

Chester 1558–1603		Leicester 1559–1603		Norwich 1569		Nottingham 1580–1620		Worcester 1540–89		York 1550–1600	
Shoemakers	120	Tailors	67	Worsted weavers	166	Butchers	115	Weavers	77	Tailors	309
Glovers	76	Tanners	63	Grocers	150	Cordwainers	83	Clothiers	45	Merchants	301
Tailors	76	Butchers	63	Tailors	146	Glovers	81	Mercers	28	Bakers	153
Tanners	73	Shoemakers	53	Cordwainers	59	Tanners	62	Walkers	26	Cordwainers	143
Ironmongers	68	Glovers	43	Mercers	48	Tailors	42	Drapers	16	Butchers	128
Merchants	65	Bakers	37	Dornix weavers	35	Bakers	41	Brewers	16	Tanners	127
Bakers	57	Mercers	36	Hatters	35	Blacksmiths	35	Shoemakers	15	Innholders	109
Drapers	55	Weavers	30	Tanners	34	Joiners	34	Tailors	14	Glovers	98
Weavers	55	Chandlers	20	Bakers	32	Mercers	32	Butchers	12	Carpenters	83
Butchers	52	Smiths	20	Carpenters	31	Ropers	31	Tanners	11	Drapers	78
Shearmen	51			Butchers	20	Fishmongers	29	Barbers	11	Tilers	71
Mercers	47			Masons	20	Yeomen	26	Smiths	11	Joiners	60

Note: Figures are of the numbers of freemen or craftsmen attributed to each occupation; for the basis of the calculations see Appendix iv, pages 392–93.

ning, presumably because the demand for new bells declined after the Reformation. Such dual occupations inevitably involve arbitrary choices in classifying craftsmen: some practised two trades with a natural connection, like the barber-surgeons to be found in most large towns, but the connection is not always obvious. Elizabethan Chelmsford possessed a shoemaker-surgeon, and Worcester a brewer-surgeon.

Most of the urban crafts can be conveniently grouped into ten categories on the pattern adopted by J. F. Pound for Norwich, and the results for provincial towns are indicated in Table 8.1. An analysis of occupations from the registers of three City parishes suggests a similar pattern to the larger provincial towns, with 26.2 per cent engaged in textiles and clothing, 18.4 per cent in food and drink, 10.9 in leather, 8.7 in metal, and 7.8 in building. It is at once clear that most towns were not 'industrial' in the sense of concentrating heavily on cloth-making or any other one sector, and that their economies were broadly based. The most striking exception was Worcester, with 42 per cent of its identified craftsmen engaged in the cloth industry between 1540 and 1590, rising to an even more startling 54 per cent in the following thirty years. Worcester was, however, unique among the larger towns; Leland observed about 1540 that 'the welthe of Worcestar standithe most by draping, and noe towne of England, at this present tyme, maketh so many cloathes yearly'.[6] Even at Norwich, that flourishing centre of the New Draperies, only 16 per cent of the Elizabethan freemen were textile workers, and in other towns analysed the proportions were still lower.

Hoskins has suggested, from the evidence of three Midland towns, that 'in any English provincial towns with the rudiments of an urban character, some 35 to 40 per cent of the population were employed in three fundamental groups of trades'.[7] Table 8.1 shows that the proportion of freemen engaged in these three groups (the victualling, clothing and building crafts) in Chester, Leicester, Norwich, Nottingham and York was between 30 and 45 per cent of the master craftsmen, and the proportions would be even higher if the numerous shoemakers had been included under clothing (as Hoskins did) rather than leather. That should occasion no surprise, since the townsmen had to feed, clothe and house themselves, and to provide those same basic services for their hinterlands. Yet there were also wide differences between the industrial composition of the various towns. In broadly based economies with a regional servicing function, like York and Leicester, the food and drink trades formed the largest group. In both, the leather crafts came close behind, while at Chester, with its ready access to Cheshire and Welsh cattle and imports of Irish hides, the leather crafts were the largest of all. They were still more dominant at Nottingham, comprising over a third of all burgesses, and making it a true 'leather town'. Worcester was of course the one real textile town, while the port of Hull was heavily dependent on its trade and shipping. The distributive trades (including merchants and mariners) were numerous in all the larger towns (though not, curiously, in the three-parish London sample), but only at Hull did they account for over half the entire body of freemen.

The largest individual crafts and trades (Table 8.2) also varied considerably. The predominance of the cloth industry is clear at Worcester, where four of the six largest crafts were cloth-workers or cloth-dealers, and at Norwich, where worsted weavers formed the largest craft and dornix weavers also ranked high. The leather industry dominated Nottingham, accounting for three of the four largest crafts, but it was significant everywhere. Shoemakers (cordwainers) and tanners figured among the ten leading crafts in every town. The wholesale dealers – merchants or mercers – were among the largest twelve in every case, while the crucial importance of the basic victualling crafts is demonstrated by the large numbers of butchers in every town, and of bakers everywhere except Worcester.

3

Probably the biggest employer of labour outside agriculture was the textile industry. By the mid-sixteenth century the raw wool which England had once exported was almost all made into semi-finished cloth before going overseas. Cloth was easily the largest item of exports, and a probably greater amount was made for the home market, giving much employment in half the counties in the kingdom. The sequence of manufacture from raw wool to finished cloth involved a series of discrete processes, calling for division of labour and therefore allowing a lowering of costs and raising of productivity. Furthermore, most of the processes were compatible with production in the household.

Children carded the wool; women spun it into yarn; men wove the fabric and did the finishing processes. Consequently the fixed costs of some central establishment were not normally worth incurring. They could in effect be passed on to the workers in their cottages.[8]

The output of the wool-textile industry was already varied by 1547, and became more so over the next fifty years. There were woollens proper, including the traditional broadcloth as well as kerseys, friezes and 'cottons'; traditional worsteds; and a range of new fabrics of mixed wool-worsted type. The traditional woollens and worsteds became known as the Old Draperies and the new, exotic products as the New Draperies; but there were in fact three fundamentally different groups: woollens, ordinary worsteds and New Draperies. They differed in the yarn that was used, the yarn depending partly on the type of wool used and partly on the way in which the wool was processed before spinning.

English wool was classified as short or long, coarse or fine (see Fig. 11, p. 168). Woollens generally used short to medium-length wool (the broadcloths and other good-quality cloths using fine, short-staple wool), while worsteds generally used medium or long-staple wool. Another difference was that woollens relied for their strength largely on being matted or felted together, worsteds on their warp and weft. The processes by which the wool was converted into the finished product also varied. Wool for woollens, for instance, was carded, spun into yarn, woven on the loom, and then fulled (soaked in soap, water and fuller's earth) to make it more durable. After fulling it was stretched and dried on tenterhooks, then dressed or shorn to give a smooth surface, and finally it might be dyed, if it had not already been dyed as yarn. The sequences for worsteds and New Draperies were not quite the same; the most important difference was that worsteds were combed and not carded, while New Draperies combined carded wool and combed worsteds. But all three branches of the industry involved a chain of specialised processes.

The cloth industry required locations with access to raw materials, water power (for fulling mills), labour and markets. It is still sometimes asserted that wool supplies and water power were paramount considerations, but such geographical determinism is misplaced. As Fuller later observed, Leicestershire, Lincolnshire, Northamptonshire and Cambridgeshire, which had 'most of wool, have least of clothing therein',[9] and cloth counties like Suffolk and Devon imported much of their wool. The chief textile-producing areas were the West Country from Devon to Gloucestershire and Wiltshire, East Anglia, and parts of the North (south-east Lancashire and the West Riding of Yorkshire). Their distribution can be explained only in part by geographical factors, and Thirsk has convincingly stressed the importance of other factors, especially a supply of underemployed labour in pastoral regions of small farms and partible inheritance. Population pressure, that is, may well have been a major determinant in the expansion of the textile industry – and, for that matter, of other industries – although it cannot of itself explain why it should have developed in some areas rather than others in the first place.

The highest-quality traditional broadcloths (which required wide looms worked by two weavers) were made in Gloucestershire and Wiltshire; much of East Anglia specialised in worsteds and the New Draperies; while large parts of the North manufactured cheap and coarse narrowcloths which could be worked on a loom by a single weaver. Confusingly for historians, one of the woollen cloths for which south-east Lancashire became famous was known as 'Manchester cotton', although true cotton was already being imported into England and was apparently being worked into fabrics in Lancashire by about 1600.

The cloth industry, with its chain of processes culminating in a product of often high market value, lent itself early to a putting-out system by which a substantial merchant or entrepreneur, usually known as a clothier, hired out looms and other equipment and controlled dependent workmen at each stage of manufacture. This helped to create a major growth in output despite the lack of significant technical innovations in the industry.

It was still possible for spinners and weavers with a little capital to remain self-employed, especially in areas manufacturing coarser cloth of less value, or where petty 'broggers' or dealers in wool enabled them to obtain the regular and limited quantities of wool they needed. The independent small master also tended to survive in corporate towns, where gild privileges protected their independence. Both Worcester and Norwich were dominated by independent artisans, and 'the capitalistic domestic system in any developed sense was rare'.[10] The best evidence for these self-employed men is the complaints made when statutes of 1545 and 1552 tried to outlaw middlemen dealing in wool. Such attempts were justified as protecting the consumer by cutting out the profit of the parasitic middleman, and insisting that manufacturers bought direct from sheep-farmers, but in reality they were in the interest of great merchants and clothiers, for it was the small independent cloth-worker who needed the middleman's services most of all.

An act of 1547, exempting Norfolk from the ban on wool dealers, explained that the poor spinners of Norfolk and Norwich were dependent on 'retaylers of . . . wooles', from whom they could buy by 'eight pennyworth and twelve pennyworthe at one tyme', quantities too small for growers to deal in. A statute of 1555 allowed similar exemption to the Halifax district of Yorkshire. The preamble explained that the majority of the inhabitants, being unable 'to kepe a horse to carry woolles, nor yet to bye muche wooll at once', walked regularly into Halifax, ther to buy upon the woolldriver some a stone, some twoo, and some three or foure, according to their habilitee, and to carye the same to their houses some iij, iiij, v and vj myles of, upon their headdes and backes, and so to make and converte the same eyther into yarne or clothe, and to sell the same, and so to buy more wooll of the wooldryver.

Only a few districts were able to obtain formal exemption from the anti-middleman legislation, but it is clear that the laws were not rigorously enforced in areas of small manufacturers. The justices of Lancashire said in 1588 that if they were executed in their county, where the poor clothier could not travel to the supplier, 'there were thousands of poor people utterly undone'.[11]

Yet if the self-employed weaver was still typical in much of the North and East Anglia, other parts of East Anglia, together with the textile manufacturing areas of the Home Counties and the West Country, were becoming dependent on capitalist clothiers as employers. By 1538 one Oxfordshire clothier, Cromwell was told, 'settythe in occupacione dayly fyve c [hundred] off the kynges subjetts', while in the following year Cromwell received a petition from some Suffolk and Essex weavers against 'their masters the clothiers'. The best evidence of the spread of the system, however, or at least of contemporary fears that it was spreading, was a statute of 1555 forbidding any rural clothmaker to use more than one woollen loom, or any rural weaver to use more than two. It was passed, according to the preamble, because weavers had been complaining

that the riche and welthie clothyers doo many ways oppres them, somme by setting up and keping in their houses divers loomes, and kepyng and maynteyning them by journeymen and persones unskilful ... some by ingrossing of loomes into theyr handes and possession, and letting them out at suche unreasonable rentes as the poore artificers are not hable to mayntayne themselfes; some also by gyving muche les wages and hyer for the weaving and worckmanshipp of cloth then in tymes past. ...

And by 1615 it was asserted that over half the cloths made in Wiltshire, Gloucestershire and Somerset were made by 'yarn makers and poore clothiers that depend weekely upon the woolle chapmen which serves them weekely with woolles either for money or credit'.[12]

Some historians have seen the organisation of the textile industry beginning to move logically into the next stage, of at least some of the separate processes being combined under one roof. John Winchcombe of Newbury (d. 1520) has often been cited as the first creator of a cloth factory, where

Within one roome being large and long
There stood two hundred loomes full strong.

However, the only 'evidence' for his factory is the imagination of the novelist Thomas Deloney, writing about seventy years after the event.[13]

Some leading clothiers did at least consider turning the buildings of dissolved monasteries into large workshops. Tuckar of Burford was in 1538 sending weekly to Abingdon 'hys kart lodyn wythe woll to be kardyd and spann', and was requesting a lease of some of the lands of Abingdon Abbey for his work. Sir Thomas Bell converted the Gloucester Blackfriars into 'drapinge houses'. And William Stumpe bought Malmesbury Abbey in 1543 and hoped later to lease Osney Abbey, in both cases for cloth-making on a large scale. When Leland visited Malmesbury,

every corner of the vaste houses of office that belongid to th'abbay be fulle of lumbes to weve clooth yn, and this Stumpe entendith to make a stret or 2. for clothier[s] in the bak vacant ground of the abbay . . .[14]

There is, however, no evidence that Stumpe carried on work in either monastery for any length of time, and too much may have been made of one man's known ambitions rather than his achievements. Yet there were certainly enterprising clothiers who already combined several processes under one roof. The Manchester clothmaker John Nabbs (d. 1570), with the aid of six servants, did all the processes from carding to shearing on his own premises. A Leeds clothier, John Pawson (d. 1576) and his three apprentices, also carried out the whole range of processes, together with dyeing, in a workshop, loom-house, dye-house and backyard attached to his dwelling-house.

Contemporaries agreed that textiles were England's most valuable product. To Camden they were 'one of the pillars of our common-wealth' (*inter reipublicae nostrae columina*), to Deloney 'more beneficiall to the commonwealth' than any other manual art and 'the nourishing of many thousands of poor people'; to the Venetian ambassador in 1610 'the chief wealth of this nation'. To quantify the industry is, however, much more difficult, and 'we are no nearer to attaining figures for total cloth production for the sixteenth century than in earlier periods'.[15] The only reasonably reliable sources are the export figures for cloth, and, for output as a whole, the hallage receipts of the London cloth markets, which begin in 1562. Customs figures clearly show that cloth was England's most valuable export throughout the century, but it is the size of the home market that is in doubt.

Bowden suggests an arbitrary addition of 50 per cent to export figures for the home market in the 1540s, but this may be much too low. Although there was every incentive to export cloth, enough had to be retained to account for all the textiles worn by Englishmen, and much English wool was too long and coarse to meet the exacting standards of the Flemish market. It might be as reasonable to suppose that home production was at least as large as that for export, and that it grew as the century progressed and home demand increased. The Gloucestershire muster return of 1608, one of the few reliable sources for occupational structure other than freemen's rolls, shows that in one hundred on the Cotswolds 45 per cent of the male workforce was engaged in textiles, and in four others more than 25 per cent. Such high figures surely reflect large home as well as overseas markets.

There is general agreement that English cloth exports increased considerably in the early Tudor period. The long-term reason seems to have been a growing demand on the Continent matched by growing supplies, as sheep became more profitable than grain for English farmers. At the peak, there were artificial booms as the debasement of the coinage made English exports cheaper, followed by a collapse in 1551–52 as the coinage was revalued. The second half of the century, it is often said, saw a decline, but there was in fact recovery to a steady level. The numbers of cloths exported from London (the greater part of all exports) held steady between 1559 and 1603 at only a little below the artificial peak of the Great Debasement, and the figures do not include the worsteds that went out in increasing quantities from the 1570s. The hallage receipts of the London cloth markets show a distinct rise in cloths handled from 1570 to 1585, and although there was then an ostensible decline from 1587 to 1598, evasion and corruption may be the real explanation rather than declining output.

The cloth industry was not the only one where the size of the market, and the division of labour, allowed putting-out to develop in the sixteenth century. Small metalwares were another: districts with poor agriculture but with iron accessible for mining provided the means, and a growing market for specialised metal goods the opportunity. Sheffield cutlery, expanding its markets and its production, was already famous. The earl of Shrewsbury's New Year present to Burghley in 1590 was 'a case of Hallomshire whittels [knives], beinge such fruictes as my pore cuntrey affordeth with fame throughout this realm'. Birmingham and the future Black Country were also beginning their specialisation in the metal industries: Leland observed that there were many smiths in Birmingham 'that use to make knives and all maner of cuttynge tooles, and many lorimars that make byts, and a greate many naylors'.[16] Needle manufacturing was introduced into London by Flemish refugees about 1559, and quickly spread to other places. The manufacture of table vessels of pewter (a tin alloy) was also becoming a putting-out industry as it expanded to meet growing demand, especially in London, where leading pewterers supplied lesser masters with unwrought pewter to be finished for an agreed rate of pay.

Naturally not all such industries were centrally organised. A nailer with a little capital, for instance, could buy his own iron and sell his own nails. But a growing market made it sensible for some men to commission work on a large scale. Reynold Ward of Dudley, who supplied nails by the thousand for Nonsuch Palace in 1538, was fulfilling a bulk order for a distant royal patron, and must have subcontracted much of the work. And a portent for the future was the appearance of slitting-mills at the Paget ironworks on Cannock Chase by the 1560s. The mills allowed bar-iron to be slit into narrow rods for nail-making, and in the early seventeenth century their more widespread use helped to spread the putting-out system in the West Midlands metal trades.

The leather industry was another to feel the effects of this early capitalist organisation. It was quite possibly second only in size and importance to the textile industry, and supplied many essential products from shoes, gloves and jerkins to saddles and leather bottles. Certainly it played an important part in the economy of the larger established towns, as the freemen's statistics show, and even in growing Birmingham, where Leland and Camden had eyes only for the metal crafts, inventories show that the wealthiest townsmen were still tanners and butchers. Again, as with metals, the leather crafts were still dominated by self-employed craftsmen, but economies of scale were encouraging the introduction of the putting-out system into glove-making.

4

If factories did not yet exist, there were already industries where plant and capital equipment required centralised production, the workers coming in some numbers to one place to produce their materials. Mining, iron-smelting, glass-making, paper-making, shipbuilding and others all fell into this category, as well as the large-scale end of the construction industry. Some were already crucial to the economy of the country or the defence of the realm, but it is important not to exaggerate their scale. The conditions which required their production in a fixed place were technical, not economic. 'They tell us nothing whatever about the optimum economic size or scale of any plant.' Much loose talk of 'large-scale' production and 'early industrial revolutions' ignores the fact that demand was generally not high enough to justify large-scale production of any kind in Tudor England.[17]

The second half of the sixteenth century witnessed a considerable growth in most mining industries. Production of coal, lead, copper and iron expanded rapidly, and only the tin mines of the South-west failed to match this growth. The total output of coal has been tentatively estimated by Nef at 170,000 tons for the decade 1551–60, while for the metal-mining industries Blanchard has offered the following estimates (Table 8.3):

Table 8.3   English and Welsh mining output, 1500–1600 (in tons)

Date	Lead	Tin	Iron	Copper
1500	625	600	3,300	Nil
1580	3,300	660	9,620	35
1600	12,400	550	11,860	71

Source: I. Blanchard, 'Labour productivity and work psychology in the English mining industry, 1400–1600', *Econ. H.R.*[2], xxxi (1978), 24.

The growth was one aspect of a shift in the European economy of the sixteenth century, as the major centres of mining in Germany, Poland and Bohemia were overtaken by Swedish copper, English copper, English lead and coal, and American silver. Much of it was the result of the forces of supply and demand as improved mining techniques made economic the exploitation of untapped resources in formerly peripheral areas. There were, however, reasons peculiar to England for some of its increased output, and one of the most important was not economic but legal. As the result of a decision by the Court of Exchequer in 1568, minerals other than gold and silver were held to belong to the owner of the soil, although mines of base metal which also contained gold and silver were held by a majority of judges to be royal. 'Whereas in continental Europe therefore the exploitation of minerals normally necessitated a concession from the Crown to the finder, in England, in the early stages at least, it was done as a normal part of estate business.'[18]

Coal, iron and copper were the mining industries on which Nef concentrated his attention in seeking a growth of large-scale industry in the century 1540–1640; but Blanchard's figures draw attention even more to the neglected lead industry. Lead apparently showed a much more rapid increase in production than iron, and was a more valuable export as well as an important product for the home market. It was traditionally mined in Derbyshire and the northern Pennines, but the Mendip field in Somerset overtook them in importance during the second half of the century. Domestically it was in demand in a variety of processes, including building, glassware, pottery and pewter; but it was a valued export for mixing with argentiferous copper to produce silver. Henry VIII's greed had flooded the European market with English lead stripped from the roofs of monastic houses, a policy which had made the silver-producing areas of central Europe dependent on English lead, but which had virtually killed the traditional English lead-mining industry by undercutting it. However, furnace-smelting was perfected on Mendip in the 1540s, and this technical breakthrough, coupled with high European demand, revived the industry and raised it to unprecedented heights. The results can be seen in Table 8.3, or on a more human level in the expansion of the workforce at the Chewton mining camp from 50 in 1556 to 234 by 1598. From being only a minor producer and exporter in the 1530s, England 'rose to a position of absolute supremacy in the European market by the 1580s'.[19]

The largest English metal industry, however, remained iron, for it involved not only mining and refining on some scale but also its working into a great variety of products. It was mined chiefly in the Weald, though there were smaller fields of some consequence in Yorkshire, South Wales and the West Midlands. Because of the weight of the ore, iron naturally came to be refined close to the mines. In the 1490s the blast furnace had been introduced, a major technical achievement which during the sixteenth and seventeenth centuries largely superseded the older bloomery process. A blast furnace was a costly piece of capital equipment, but it made possible a great increase in productivity: it could produce 150 tons a year, as against 30–40 tons from a bloomery.

By the 1570s there were at least 67 blast furnaces, 52 of them in the Weald; a list of 1574 counts some 61 ironmasters operating in that region. Wealthy landowners were encouraged to install them to exploit their mineral resources: an estate with sufficient ore, timber and water allowed for the mining, refining and working of the iron in a planned operation. Sir William Sidney constructed one in 1541 on the site of a Sussex abbey; Lord Paget built one on Cannock Chase in the 1560s; and the third earl of Rutland built another at Rievaulx Abbey about 1575. Altogether, of all blast furnaces known to have been erected before 1642, 38 per cent were built or owned by peers, though the majority of ironmasters (over four-fifths of the Wealden entrepreneurs of 1574) were yeomen and lesser gentry. The Rutlands managed their Rievaulx works efficiently, with regular coppicing of woods for fuel supplies, and major technical improvement, from the

1570s. They received their reward after 1601, when profits from the works comprised 12–15 per cent of their landed income. And yet another technical breakthrough was the successful manufacture of steel at Robertsbridge in Sussex in 1565 with the aid of German craftsmen. It became uneconomic because of competition from Baltic imports, but the steel was of good quality.

The iron industry required water power and extensive supplies of charcoal. Both bloomeries and blast furnaces relied on charcoal fuel, and a monopoly patent granted to the earl of Cumberland and Robert Cecil to manufacture iron, steel and lead with peat or coal (1595) came to nothing. The classic account of the history of the iron industry, formulated by Ashton (1924) and Nef (1932), and still widely accepted, is that fuel supply was a bottleneck restricting its growth. According to this view, the industry expanded rapidly between 1540 and 1640, but at the cost of an excessive destruction of woodland which proved its undoing. The Wealden industry virtually exhausted its local supplies, and ironmasters were driven away to better forested areas, only to exhaust those in turn. Output then declined until smelting with coal came to the rescue in the eighteenth century. It is a plausible story which can be buttressed by many contemporary complaints. Parliament was to be asked in 1559 for a complete ban on English iron production because of its appetite for wood and because cheaper Spanish iron was available. Such a drastic measure was never enacted, but in 1584 parliament did impose restrictions on the further growth of the Wealden industry. And in 1607 Norden argued in *The Surveiors Dialogue* that the Weald had been stripped of much of its oak and beech within the previous thirty years, chiefly for the iron forges and furnaces and the glass kilns.

However, Hammersley and others have cast doubt on the whole venerable tradition. It is by no means clear, taking the sixteenth and seventeenth centuries as a whole, that the extent of woodland did diminish through the activities of ironmasters. Most of them, from the fifteenth century onwards, were careful to manage their timber supplies as a renewable crop by coppicing. Had there been a national timber shortage, it would be difficult to explain the fact that timber prices rose more slowly than those of other agricultural products (Appendix I). Nor is there evidence for any decline in output through shortage of fuel. The number of known blast furnaces in operation rose in every decade from the 1530s to the 1600s and then stabilised at a slightly lower level. However, during the late sixteenth and the seventeenth centuries many furnaces were made larger and used less charcoal to produce more iron, and total production may well have grown steadily. If woodland was diminishing in the later sixteenth century – and it is difficult to dismiss all contemporary complaints – then an expansion of arable to feed the growing population is likely to have cleared more than did charcoal-burning.

What seems clear is that, while there was no national timber shortage, there were certainly areas in which timber and charcoal were so scarce and expensive that it was cheaper to use coal as an alternative fuel – like the Cambridge district, where Harrison indicated that this was the case. Certainly coal remained easily the largest of the mining industries. Most of the principal coalfields were already being worked, though generally on a small scale. Nef tentively suggests that of 170,000 tons mined annually in the 1550s, Durham and Northumberland accounted for 65,000 (38%), the Midlands for another 65,000 (38%), and the Welsh fields for 20,000 (12%), the other fields producing only 20,000 between them. The Tyne and Wear valley fields occur most prominently in the records, but that may be largely because much of their coal was shipped down the east coast, whereas more of the Midlands output was consumed locally. It was not in the North-east, but at Wollaton in Nottinghamshire, that a 'prodigy house' was built on the profits of the coal of the estate. It is true that the builder virtually bankrupted himself doing so, but the Wollaton mines continued productive. They were producing 20,000 tons a year by 1598, and output went on increasing throughout the seventeenth century.

Nef further estimates that total production of coal increased fourteenfold between the 1550s and the 1680s, and though he gives no totals for intermediate dates to show the apparent growth under Elizabeth, he shows from the port books that coal shipments from Newcastle and to London were both rising rapidly in her reign. In the year 1563–64 33,000 tons were shipped from Newcastle, in 1597–98 163,000. Yet one should not exaggerate the total expansion of the industry. London's demand for north-eastern coal grew phenomenally (from, of course, a very low base), but then so did the population of the capital; and national coal output probably grew far more slowly. Indeed, the inability to drain deep mines efficiently before the invention of steam pumps was bound to set a limit to growth. Nef's estimate of total output in the 1550s is probably too low, thereby exaggerating the later growth by starting from too low a base, and his use of single-year figures rather than averages appears to have increased the exaggeration. Langton's detailed study of the south-west Lancashire coalfield shows only a slight growth in colliery numbers between 1590 and 1610, and then a temporary decline. It is doubtful, in any event, how relevant was any increased coal output to industrial growth. The mining was itself, of course, an industry,

and some coal was already used as a fuel for iron forges, though
not yet for iron-smelting or refining. Leland found the Birmingham
ironworks already dependent on coal about 1540, and a draft proclamation of the 1590s stated that coal was used by brewers, smiths
and other craftsmen, as well as for domestic fuel. None the less, most
Tyneside coal reaching London was intended for heating the homes
of 'the poorer sorte'.[20]

5

In assessing the size and growth of industry under the later Tudors,
one is faced with the familiar problem of patchy and unreliable statistics, of individual examples which may or may not be typical and
which can be selected to illustrate almost any trend, and of rival
arguments by historians which relate to longer periods and which
may, or may not, be appropriate for a shorter time-scale. Nef, whose
pioneer work on the rise of the coal industry broadened into a survey
of the whole industrial sector, discerned a marked growth of large-
scale industry between about 1540 and 1640, large enough to warrant
the expression 'industrial revolution'. This is not an appropriate place
for an extended critique of a theory covering the 'Tawney century'
as a whole, a theory which, in any case, has found few supporters.
Fisher in 1961 echoed widespread scepticism when he delineated the
century 1540–1640 as 'perhaps the last period in English history in
which economic appetites were remarkably vigorous but in which
economic expansion was still slow'.[21] Since then it has been fashionable to stress constraints and stagnation rather than economic growth
in the sixteenth century, both for the industrial and commercial
sectors.

Yet – to keep within the bounds of the later Tudor period – there
are good reasons for stressing growth and opportunities at least as
much as stagnation, even if some of the initiatives taken did not bear
fruit until the seventeenth century. Without question it was an age
fruitful in 'projects' for creating or improving native industries, as
J. W. Gough and Joan Thirsk have abundantly demonstrated.
Smith's *Discourse* of 1549, and an anonymous tract of the same year
submitted to Somerset, both lamented the decay of native industries
and the flood of manufactured imports, and urged a programme of
encouragement for import substitution, and their pleas were heeded.
Many private 'projectors', motivated both by hope of profits and a
genuine concern about a dangerous dependence on foreign markets,
invested in new manufactures. Nor was it only financiers and mer-

chants who risked their capital, but great landowners were also attracted. 'In the Elizabethan period the most active entrepreneur in the country was not some busy merchant or thrusting member of the new gentry, but a peer of ancient stock, George Talbot, 6th Earl of Shrewsbury.' He was one of the greatest English ironmasters, and also owned a steelworks, lead mines, coalmines and glassworks.[22]

The state gave considerable support and encouragement, especially after Cecil became principal secretary in 1558, and in 1563 imports of 'dyvers forreyne wares made by handye craftesmen beyond the seas' were prohibited by statute. In the 1560s and 1570s the crisis in the Netherlands not only dominated the politics of western Europe but crucially influenced the direction of English economic progress. At one and the same time it persuaded Englishmen, heavily dependent on exports to and imports from the Low Countries, to seek other markets and to make at home what they had imported, and it gave to England a substantial number of skilled craftsmen and industrial experts.

The most important technical innovation was the diversification of the textile industry by the development of the New Draperies. These, generally cheaper and lighter than traditional woollens and worsteds, could use coarse, medium to long-staple wool that was unsuitable for good-quality broadcloths and worsteds. They were not new products in the modern economists' sense, but rather mutations of existing products, though none the less potent for that. Within the home market, they appealed both to the poor by their cheapness and to the fashion-conscious because they were more varied and less durable. And in export terms they appealed to the Mediterranean markets where traditional English textiles were too heavy to wear. Yet despite all these advantages, there is little sign that the English cloth industry was by 1550 able to adopt the techniques of the Flemish *nieuw draperie* by imitation. What was needed was a large influx of foreign workers with the necessary skills, and the opportunity for that was provided by the non-economic forces of war and religious persecution.

The New Draperies were developed in the southern Netherlands in the early sixteenth century, often using English wool. It was this lost opportunity which John Coke admitted by implication when he boasted of England's cloth exports in 1549. For, he added, subjects of the emperor (i.e. Netherlanders) got their livings by English wools, 'makyng therwith sayes, tapisterie, ryssel worstedes, cloth, carpettes, and other thynges'.[23] Yet in the very year he was writing, Protector Somerset persuaded Flemish cloth-workers to settle in Glastonbury and to introduce the making and dyeing of worsteds and says. The Flemings left England at Mary's accession, but the project foreshadowed later successes. When Alba began persecuting Flemish Protestants in the 1560s, many weavers fled to England, to be warmly welcomed by the Privy Council and the local authorities. They settled mainly in the towns of Kent, Essex and East Anglia, and within a remarkably short time they established the New Draperies on a considerable scale.

Their success was a credit both to their enterprise and to the willingness of traditional textile manufacturers and customers to accept product innovation. They concentrated especially on the weaving of bays, which were already made in England, but not so well as in Flanders. Clement Baet, one of the first 'strangers' [aliens] at Norwich, intended to set up in bay-making as soon as possible, 'for they only work at bay work here', and of forty-one immigrant householders allowed to settle in Colchester in 1571, fourteen were baymakers. By the mid-1570s the immigrants were regarded by thoughtful observers as important contributors to England's economic prosperity. A Norwich man praised their new crafts which gave employment to 'our owne people within the cittie as also a grete nomber of people nere xx^{ti} myles aboute the cittie'. And a writer on the textile industry argued that 'wee ought to favour the straungers from whome wee learned so greate benifites . . . because wee are not so good devisers as followers of others'.[24]

The host communities became proud of their hardworking newcomers. When Elizabeth visited Sandwich in 1573 she was shown a tableau of more than 100 children, 'English and Dutche . . . all spynning of fine bay yarne; a thing well lyked both of her majestie and of the nobilitie and ladies'. At Norwich five years later the authorities put on a display for her of seven different types of weaving. In 1591 the Muscovy merchants of London apologised to their chief agent in Moscow for the high price and scarcity of the shortcloths they exported. 'Much wooll', they explained, 'is turned into bayes, sayes, grograines, rash, and other kindes of forrein wares of late yeres made heer [in England] by divers workemen straungers that are cum over and do inhabite heer.' It was a piece of special pleading (inflation rather than competition for scarce wool supplies was a more likely explanation), but it does testify to the strength of the New Draperies.[25]

One important branch of woollen textiles was hosiery. Knitting stockings from local wools was established during the sixteenth century in many counties from Cumberland to Devon. It was a hand-knitting craft very popular as a secondary employment in overpopulated pastoral districts like the Yorkshire dales, where men and women alike knitted at home, and even while driving stock to pasture. In Dentdale and Garsdale, it was said in 1634, tenants' holdings were so small 'that they could not maintain their families were it not by their industry in knitting coarse stockings'. It was, however, an Elizabethan invention which was shortly to transform this small 'craft' occupation into a putting-out industry. William Lee invented a knitting frame about 1590, a machine which in the seventeenth century was adopted on a large scale in the East Midlands, and hired out by masters to domestic knitters. Without such a frame, a part-time knitter was reckoned to complete two pairs of worsted stockings a week; and if one assumes that the average person wore out two pairs a year, stocking-knitting may easily have employed 2 per cent of the population. The success of the industry was 'almost as spectacular in its way as that of the New Draperies'.[26]

Other textiles were of less consequence. Cottons and silks were still mostly imported, though fustians (made with imported cotton) formed a thriving Lancashire industry by 1600. The linen industry was larger, for linen was widely used for sheets, pillowcases, napkins, canvas and sailcloth. The raw materials, hemp and flax, were spun into yarn, bleached and woven on looms. Linen was made especially around Manchester, and the richest Elizabethan Mancunians were the linen dealers who bought up the work of the small manufacturers. Isabel Tipping died in 1592 worth at least £1,500, and Richard Nugent in 1609 was worth £2,344. It was not, however, until the later seventeenth century that England's dependence on linen imports stimulated a really sizeable native industry. As for finished products derived from linen, a successful sailcloth industry was established in the Ipswich area around 1590, which reduced dependence on imported canvas from France, and a linen thread manufacture in Maidstone about the same time, thanks to the expertise of 'Dutch' immigrants. Finally, the small luxury craft of tapestry making deserves a brief mention. Tapestries, woven from a mixture of wool and other textiles, were normally imported, but an enterprising Worcestershire gentleman, William Sheldon, sponsored a native manufacture under the supervision of a family friend who had learned the art in Flanders. 'Sheldon tapestries' were produced from 1561 for nearly a century, and adorned many country houses in the Midlands.

Just as important, perhaps, as the arrival of new branches of the textile industry in Norwich, Ipswich, Maidstone and elsewhere was the readiness of other towns to copy successful techniques established elsewhere. Among many examples which could be chosen, the corporation of Chester in 1574–75 granted the freedom of the city to a weaver from Shrewsbury on condition that he should work, weave and dress those kinds of cloths made in Shrewsbury, and York in

1590 enfranchised a Norwich dyer who was teaching the children of freemen his trade. Such spreading of local innovations showed an enterprising spirit abroad in the towns, although where a famous speciality was closely imitated it could lead to dangers of deceit. By 1606, men of Coventry complained, their famous thread was 'counterfeited in London, Manchester, and divers other places . . . and there put off and sold in the name of Coventrey thridd'.[27]

If innovations in textiles were so numerous, they did not stand alone. The armaments industry, for example, and the mining and founding of metals, in which German technology led Europe, was also the subject of important innovations with the aid of foreign expertise. In 1543–44, at Henry VIII's instigation, the manufacture of cast-iron cannon was begun in the Weald with the help of French craftsmen. Iron ordnance was, however, generally regarded as second best to bronze ('brass') cannon, and it was the government's concern for self-sufficiency in armaments that spurred them on to set up a native manufacture. Copper-mining had been previously negligible in England, while brass-making was impossible until the discovery of calamine, the ore of zinc, which was mixed with copper. Now, after several false starts, the government induced German mining experts to establish the copper and brass industries. 'Hence came it to pass', observed Fuller, 'that Queen Elizabeth left more brass than she found iron-ordnance in the kingdom; and our wooden walls (so our ships are commonly called) were rough-casted over with a coat of a firmer constitution.'[28]

In 1561 the German Henrick undertook to introduce the making of gunpowder, and within a year five powder mills had been established. Their output certainly helped to reduce imports of gunpowder, though it was not enough to make England self-sufficient. In the same year of 1561 the government negotiated with German experts about mining for copper in Cumbria. The negotiations collapsed, but in 1564 Daniel Höchstetter, a partner in the firm of Haug and Langnauer which worked Tyrolese mines, was given a patent with the Englishman Thurland to discover copper, and in 1565 another patent empowered a group of financiers, advised by the zinc-miner Schütz from Saxony, to search for calamine, make brass and introduce German methods of wire-drawing and battery. The two groups of patentees were incorporated in 1568 as the Mines Royal and the Mineral and Battery Works respectively, with monopoly rights of mining copper and making brass and wire. Höchstetter's family mined and smelted copper in the Lake District until the Civil War, while the Company of Mineral and Battery Works mined coalmines in Somerset and made brass at Isleworth. But they concentrated more on wire than brass, setting up works in Monmouthshire to produce wire for wool-combs.

Both companies were a definite gain to the English economy, and their success needs to be remembered in appraising the generally bad reputation of government monopolies. Hammersley has drawn attention to the very limited output of copper and brass, in contrast to the successes of the eighteenth and nineteenth centuries, and has attributed it to limited demand rather than to problems of supply. Yet the Cumbrian copper mines, although they proved less profitable than initially hoped and never produced enough to meet home demand in full, still played a part in reducing dependence on imports of a kind liable to be cut off in time of war. Both industries were also clear examples of centralised production, not only the mining but the smelting, brass-making, 'battery' (flattening metal ingots into plates to make objects like pans and kettles) and wire-drawing all being carried out by large bodies of workers concentrated in one place. Only the working-up of the raw material into finished articles was carried on on a domestic basis.

Printing was another important craft learned from Germany, and of crucial importance in the dissemination of ideas if not as a large-scale industry. It had, of course, been introduced to England by Caxton as early as 1477, but many books published for English use continued to be printed in France and the Netherlands. Not until the mid-sixteenth century was demand largely met by resident printers, and even then some of them, including the best, like Vautrollier, were immigrants. Between 1550 and 1587 the number of printing-houses in London increased from twelve to twenty-three, and increased further by the end of the century, while native printers came to control the industry.

Native glass-making, both for windows and vessels, had been practised since at least the thirteenth century, but it was again the influx of foreign craftsmen after 1567 – in this case from Lorraine, Normandy, Flanders and Italy – which established both branches of the industry on a larger scale. A London crystal works under the Venetian Verzelini successfully produced drinking glasses of comparable standard to their Italian competitors, although it remained the only one in England. Window-glass manufacture was diffused more widely, and by the end of the century was being carried on in Hampshire, Gloucestershire, Staffordshire, Lancashire and Yorkshire as well as in the original area of Wealden manufacture. A parliamentary bill 'against glass-houses and making of glass by aliens born' was urged in 1584–85, apparently by an alliance of those concerned at the industry's demand for wood and those suspicious of immigrants;

but fortunately it was lost, and the industry continued to grow unhampered by legislative restrictions. It is some indication of that expansion that the price of window glass, unlike most industrial products, seems to have fallen between about 1580 and 1620, at least in the London area.

Paper-making was another industry designed to reduce imports; the doctor in the *Discourse of the Common Weal* had lamented that English 'broken linnen cloth and ragges' were exported, made into white and brown paper, and imported again. Good-quality paper-making was started in 1588 by another German, Spilman, in a mill near Dartford, but foreign imports continued to dominate the market. More critical to the economy was alum, a mordant used in dyeing cloth; it is usually said to have been first mined in Yorkshire in 1600, but earlier searches did produce modest English supplies in the Isle of Wight, Dorset and elsewhere from the 1560s. However, imports again remained crucial, and not until the 1630s were significant quantities produced at a reasonable cost.

The common aim of government, urban corporations and private entrepreneurs was to manufacture goods at home either to satisfy the home market and so avoid imports, or to create new export markets for England. In either case, employment of as many hands as possible was seen as the goal, both for economic and social reasons. When the town clerk of Warwick asked the earl of Leicester for help to alleviate the poverty of the town, Leicester replied that

I marvaile you do not devise some ways among you, to have some speciall trade to kepe your poore on woork as such as Sheldon of Beolye, which mythinkith should not only be very profittable but also a meanes to kepe your poore from idelnes.

When the Muscovy Company sent out an expedition in 1580, hoping to find a trade route to China by way of the Arctic, Hakluyt advised the leaders to take with them samples of many English products and manufactures, including textiles of all types, shoes and other leather goods, lead, pewter, glassware, soap, wire, combs, buttons, thread, spectacles, cutlery, needles, locks and keys, and 'all maner of edge tooles'. Against several of them he noted that Englishmen make large quantities 'and want vent', that is, lack sufficient sales. 'For in finding ample vent of anything that is to be wrought in this realme is more woorth to our people, besides the gaine of the merchant, then . . . all the Hospitals of England.'[29]

Hakluyt's list overlaps considerably with the lists of goods which writers in 1549 had been urging ought to be manufactured in England, and which thirty years later were already established. What is especially interesting is how many of them were basic, relatively cheap, items of everyday household use, intended primarily for the home market rather than for export, rather than the luxury manufactures which tend to dominate economic histories. Hakluyt's clear implication is that new consumer industries, making products like soap, buttons, pins, needles and thread, had been so successfully established within a generation that they had not only replaced imports but were produced in larger quantities than the home market could absorb. Thirsk is surely right to point out that concentrating on well-known industries like textiles and mining 'is like viewing England through a telescope stationed half-way to the moon':

It is true enough that iron, glass, brass, lead and coal were important industries in the nineteenth century, and that their condition in the sixteenth and seventeenth centuries needs investigation. But are we yet sure that they employed as much labour or contributed as much to gross national production in the seventeenth century as the common domestic goods that were liable to turn up in every household in the land?

These humble domestic goods, she argues, 'heralded the development of a consumer society' in early modern England, one in which everyday life was made more comfortable as new, cheap household goods spread throughout the kingdom and well down the social scale.[30] The pictures she paints of a developed consumer society relates to the seventeenth century, but the foundations were laid in the sixteenth. When the house of a Worcester barber in 1584 contained a framed table and joined stools, a featherbed, carpets, cushions, a pewter chamber pot and eight pewter flowerpots, a lute, five pairs of stockings, six table-cloths, five pairs of sheets, brass pots and a frying pan, the level of comfort speaks for itself.

There can be little doubt, therefore, that the industrial sector expanded and diversified considerably in the reign of Elizabeth; and plainly the growth in supply presupposed a growth in demand. Demand increased for strategic goods and supplies from a government preoccupied with self-sufficiency, and for luxury goods from prospering gentry, yeomen and townsmen. The great growth in demand for cheap utility goods, however – especially pots, pans, needles, cheap draperies and so on – came from that growth in population which was so marked a feature of the period. A population growth approaching 1 per cent a year at its peak created both a large demand for more production, and a supply of part-time craftsmen keen to meet that demand as agriculture proved unable to give a full-time living to all the extra mouths.

Naturally it was not so simple in reality. Some areas could absorb their natural increase in agriculture, others had to export their surplus to the towns or to other regions, while yet others adopted a dual-occupation regime in which farmers, farm labourers, and craftsmen combined farming with industry. The cloth industry in the wood-pasture region of Suffolk, the stocking-knitting of the Yorkshire Dales and the small metal trades of the Birmingham plateau, were all examples of the growing importance of industry in the countryside. In some cases population was growing too rapidly to be absorbed entirely in agriculture, and any extra employment was welcome: such was the case in many East Anglian communities which gave a warm welcome to the labour-intensive New Draperies. In others, a wood-pasture economy and weak manorial control encouraged men from overcrowded areas to move in and take up a combination of agriculture with woodland crafts, weaving, metal-working or potting.

Certainly a population density too high for absorption by agriculture seems to have been more important than the mere presence of the raw materials of industry. It was especially crucial that the manufacture of textiles was both labour-intensive and was able to be fitted into a domestic economy based on the household. The relationship of industry and population growth demands further research; but it is clear that the relationship was a positive one in many different kinds of community. Most of the older-established towns, after the economic difficulties of the early and mid-sixteenth century, flourished as they developed a wider range of crafts and occupations; newer urban centres like Manchester, Leeds and Sheffield throve on the basis of industrial specialisation; and rural communities the length and breadth of the land developed an industrial character also. If a Tudor industrial revolution is an exaggerated concept, at least one can discern the slow beginnings of a long-term prelude to the revolution of the eighteenth century.

Chapter 9

Traffics and discoveries

[Shrewsbury] hath an notable sale of all maner of commodities into Wales eiche waye . . ., and directly southwarde frome the towne there is no market towne nyrer then Ludlowe. to deprive them of the sale of all kinde of wares, and that ys xx^ti miles of.

> 'Ressons...that a staple of cottones and frices should be staplished at Westchester', *c.* 1582[1]

Her husband's to Aleppo gone, master o' th' *Tiger.*

> Shakespeare, *Macbeth* (*c.* 1606)

1

Trade had played a vital part in the economy for centuries, and any depiction of Tudor England as a land of subsistence farming without a cash economy is a wild caricature. Scarcely any farmers can have lived entirely off their own produce, even if some of their dealings were conducted in barter, tokens or mutual credit rather than coin. Agricultural produce had to be exchanged between countryfolk as well as to feed townsmen. Urban and rural industries and crafts needed markets by definition; townsmen and craftsmen could not mutually absorb all their own products, just as they could not feed themselves. Naturally the degree to which men and women participated in a market or cash economy varied with their wealth and their access to markets. A poor hill-farmer living away from main roads and navigable rivers might be nearly self-sufficient; a rich townsman or gentleman in the Home Counties or near the coast was likely to enjoy a wide range of native and overseas luxuries. Yet the surviving inventory of James Backhouse, a shopkeeper of Kirkby Lonsdale in Westmorland (1578), is a warning against glib generalisations. His stock – which included Spanish silk and French garters, Norwich lace and Oxford gloves, Turkey purses, groceries and stationery – 'would not have disgraced a York or Exeter or perhaps even a London shopkeeper'[2].

Naturally, the great bulk of trade was short distance. Much meat and grain, and most milk, butter, eggs, poultry and cheese were bought and sold locally. Most tables and benches, knives and nails, pots and pans, and caps and shoes found customers within a few miles of their manufacture. But specialised commodities and those with a high reputation could enjoy a regional or even national market; and where transport allowed, even bulky and relatively cheap cargoes like coal, wheat and barley could be shipped long distances. And beyond the realm, England was already well integrated into a pattern of international trade. As 'the Australia of the middle ages', she had exported high-quality wool to the Continent from the thirteenth century; and from the early fifteenth century she replaced this traffic more and more with semi-finished cloth, so that by 1538–44, 92 per cent of all wool exported was in the form of cloth, mostly to Antwerp. England's heavy dependence on the Netherlands cloth market lessened after 1551, and increasingly exports became more varied in the second half of the sixteenth century, both in their nature and in the countries of destination.

The sources of Tudor commercial history are uneven. Overseas trade is documented from the customs accounts and port books, which in theory recorded all exports and imports. However, they were compiled as records of Crown revenue, not of trade fluctuations, and it is difficult to compile satisfactory trade statistics from them: Coleman has pointed out that 'the period from the 1550s to 1697 . . . is the most barren of continuous commercial statistics for any time in English history since before 1275'. As for internal trade, it was largely untaxed, in contrast to the situation in France or the Empire, where internal tolls and customs barriers were widespread. Englishmen were fortunate in being able to move goods fairly freely and unsupervised, but their gain is the historian's loss. The only systematic records are the port books kept by government officials and the local customs accounts of ports like Chester and Southampton, which reveal coastal as well as overseas trade but not inland trade. Only Bristol and Gloucester, of the major ports, kept records of their river trade up the Severn. Most urban markets kept toll-books, and some fairs kept records of sales, but few such records survive. The consequence is that historians have concentrated on the relatively better recorded overseas trade and have given the unwitting impression that it was much the more important. 'The contrast between the foreign and domestic trades is as sharp in terms of surviving data as in the amount of academic interest the two have generated.'[3]

The mechanisms of trade, and the types of men who operated it, were very varied; and the potent figure of the international merchant has been allowed to distract attention from the humbler men and women who handled the bulk of commercial transactions. At the very simplest level, buyer and seller dealt directly with each other. In corporate towns they were usually expected to do business through shops or markets, although private dealings in inns and houses were becoming common despite the rules. Elsewhere they were freer to traffic without restriction; and in both town and country there were annual fairs which supplemented the normal trading outlets. One obvious problem of direct trading without intermediaries was that of fraud, should either party default on his bargain. Markets and fairs often kept records of transactions, or held special courts to deal with disputes. Bargains made outside such formal meetings, however, were more vulnerable to deceit, and much of our knowledge of internal trade comes from allegations of non-performance of contracts made before the courts. For that reason many dealers had their transactions witnessed by notaries, often drawing up bonds recognising debts and stipulating penalties for non-performance.

Trade on a larger scale or over greater distances relied on middlemen, those unpopular figures who to an economic conservative like Lever were 'the marchauntes of myschyefe that go betwixt the barke and the tree'.[4] They were blamed for shortages and high prices, but their services were indispensable to a developing economy, as they reduced costs and extended markets. Some were strictly speaking hauliers paid to transport goods from buyer to seller, whether by boat (mariners), cart or packhorse (carriers). Others, variously called chapmen, higglers, hucksters, badgers, hawkers or pedlars, were entrepreneurs, making a profit by buying in one place and selling in another. Most were general traders, but some already specialised; for example 'Manchester men' was a term already in use by the end of the century for one group of pedlars trading Lancashire cottons. Such dealers often formed partnerships, like the father, son and two brothers who joined forces to buy cattle in Warwickshire and Staffordshire for the London market. It was typical of many in being formed from friends and relatives, since mutual trust was vital and there was no company law to support them.

At the summit of the trading hierarchy were the merchants proper, who tended to trade wholesale and over long distances. They enjoyed a wider range of trading facilities than the smaller local dealers, using an array of legal instruments including bonds and bills of exchange. Some greater merchants, especially the Londoners, formed family businesses or partnerships akin to the modern firm, though usually much less permanent. As with internal trade, overseas merchants had no protection at law if the partnership failed, so such businesses were usually kept small. Some, however, employed resident agents or 'factors' to handle the overseas end of their trade. Many aspiring young merchants began their careers in this way, like Lionel Cranfield, who started his glittering rise to the lord treasurership as an apprentice and then, at the age of twenty-one, as a factor in Germany. They even had, from 1589, their own manual of instruction by John Browne of Bristol, *The Marchants Avizo, Verie Necessarie for their Sonnes and Servants, when they first send them Beyond the Seas* . . ., the first known printed example in English of a type of literature already common on the Continent. Factors were usually paid by commission, the normal rate of 'factorage' assumed by Browne being 2.5 per cent on both sales and purchases. Most trade, even overseas trade, was carried on by individuals and small partnerships, and not by the Company of Merchants Adventurers and the other so-called trading companies, which were institutions for regulating rather than promoting trade.

Middlemen were apparently increasing their numbers and activities, despite such restrictions, and so too were retail traders or shopkeepers. Pedlars were by no means the only alternative to markets and fairs as suppliers of retail goods, and in towns and even large villages there were already many shops. Deane's view that 'the shop had begun to supplant the pedlar or the itinerant tradesman of the fairs before the end of the eighteenth century'[5] is much too late in its chronology, as Willan has abundantly indicated. Besides the shops of craftsmen selling their own wares, there were shops of tradesmen selling goods they had not produced, especially the drapers, mercers and grocers of the larger towns. Accounts surviving for a Yorkshire mercer, William Wray, between 1580 and 1599, show him buying wares wholesale from men of York, Beverley, Coventry and Norwich, and selling them retail in his Ripon shop to fellow-townsmen and to country customers from within a 10-mile radius. Like the Kirkby Lonsdale draper, he sold a wide range of goods including mercery (cloth, lace, pins, thread, ribbons, buttons, etc.), groceries (dried fruits, spices, soap, sugar and so on) and stationery.

2

'The internal market', suggests Hoskins, 'was probably at least ten times as large, possibly as much as twenty times' as overseas trade.[6] This can be little more than a bold guess in the absence of comprehensive statistics, but as late as 1688 Gregory King estimated the home market at four times the size of exports and imports, and the proportion is likely to have been considerably higher in the sixteenth century. If this survey concentrates more on coastal and river traffic than on overland carriage, that is rather a reflection on the bias of systematic sources than on the relative proportions of goods carried by water and road.

Part of the difficulty of discussing internal trade and the blocks to its development is that, as Chartres justly remarks, 'the history of sixteenth-century transport remains largely unwritten'. There is, of course, a venerable tradition that road surfaces were deteriorating throughout early modern times, to reach a nadir of mud and pot-holes in the age of Defoe, and that improvements had to await the age of turnpikes: Wilson can speak confidently of seventeenth-century roads as 'everywhere deplorable and getting steadily worse'.[7] It is lent some colour by Elizabethan complaints about bad roads, but as often the evidence is double-edged. The complaints grew in volume because more men, horses and carts were apparently using the roads, which they would not have done had the whole system been intolerably bad. Parliaments tried to counter the increased wear and tear by enacting the first general statutes for the maintenance of highways in 1555 and 1563, involving the compulsory use of parish labour, and although their practical effect has been often described as slight, the evidence of growing road traffic suggests otherwise.

Already in early Tudor times men were able and willing to carry goods long distances by road, like the men of Kendal who took cloth by packhorse to Southampton every year. In 1552–53 twenty-nine Northerners, twenty of them from Kendal, came to Southampton overland with cloth to sell, and a Worcester carrier who died in 1559 had been evidently travelling regularly to London, selling cloths there and returning with luxury goods like silks and pewter. Packhorses could, of course, use roads impassable to coaches or heavy wagons, since a packhorse carried only about 2 cwt. Yet the growth of wheeled traffic and of regular carrying services presupposes improved main roads (Fig. 15). Stow dates the introduction of the first horse-drawn passenger coach to 1555, and of the long four-wheeled goods wagon to 1564, and both were widespread by 1600. As early as 1580 'the carryers of Chester come weekly to Bosomes Inne' in London, and by 1584 'freight-waggons and carriers' were plying regularly between London and Norwich.[8] As for private coaches, Stow complained that by 1598 they were so common in the streets of London as to be a public danger, and a bill 'for the restraint of the excessive and superfluous use of coaches' was considered (but rejected) by the Lords in 1601. There was even a primitive development of rails for goods too heavy for the roads; a railway for coal wagons is recorded in Nottinghamshire in 1598.

Naturally heavy and bulky goods of low value could be transported

Fig. 15   Main roads and navigable rivers, *c.* 1600

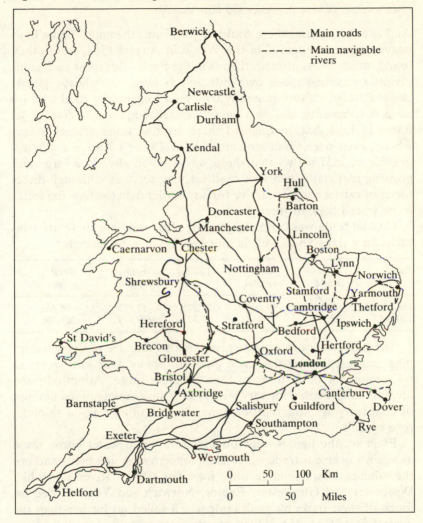

Source: A New Historical Geography of England, ed. H. C. Darby, Cambridge U.P., 1973, p. 289

much more economically by water than by land. Grain, coal, iron, building materials and even parcels of large books were carried as near their destinations as possible by water. Newcastle coal could justify the cost of shipment by water to London, France or even the Mediterranean, but it was not taken far inland because carriage costs doubled the pit-head price every 10 miles or so. Roads were inevitably, in the absence of tarmac, much worse in winter than summer:

Why, this is like the mending of high waies
In sommer, where the waies are faire enough.

And even in summer there could be problems; the court 'had a hard begynning of a progress' in the Weald in August 1563, where they found 'much worss ground, than is in the Peek'. But most such complaints concerned roads over hills or, as here, over heavy glacial clays. Foreign visitors generally traversed England by road with no adverse comments, and even the occasional compliment. Von Wedel noted in 1584 that 'in England there are fine stone bridges everywhere, even over small streams'.[9] John Taylor's *Carrier's Cosmographie* of 1637 shows that there was by then already a large and growing national network of road-carrying services, although directories of carriers do not survive for any earlier date to allow the series to be traced back further.

Coastal trade was certainly growing also, and here there are contemporary statistics as well as more impressionistic records:[10]

Date	Coal trade	Other coastal	Fishing	Foreign trade	Total
1582	7,618	10,607	17,316	32,892	68,433
1609–15	28,223	15,743	27,721	29,879	101,566

These figures, purporting to give the total tonnage of English shipping, suggest that coastal trade grew so rapidly over forty years as to account for more tonnage than overseas trade. Admittedly the increase is accounted for very largely by a quadrupling in the amount of coal-carrying, largely from Tyneside, but other coastal shipping rose by half.

Even so, the figures must understate internal water-borne trade as against overseas trade, since they concern seagoing boats and not the smaller boats suitable only for river traffic. River ports like Worcester and Gloucester, Exeter, Norwich and York carried on much of their trade by small craft which sailed no further than the coastal ports (Fig. 15). Willan has depicted a major growth in river navigations in the century and a half before the canal age (1600–1760), but some improvements go back into the late sixteenth century. The corporation of Exeter constructed a canal to Topsham to shorten their route to the sea (1564–68), an attempt which Chichester tried to emulate at the end of the century. The Exeter canal, though only 3 miles in length, is rightly regarded as important, for it introduced into England the continental pound-lock, a major technical advance on the flash-lock which was then the only means of getting boats past mills and weirs. The river Lea was improved for navigation between London and Ware in the period 1571–81, the channel being widened and at least one pound-lock installed, and by 1635 there were three such locks on the Thames.

At the most local level there was a vast, but largely unrecorded, trade within a radius of a few miles, especially of agricultural produce. As regional specialisation developed in agriculture, more and more food was produced for sale rather than for home consumption. The ancient 'open market' system comprised regulated trade in 600 or 650 market towns and villages in England and Wales, but there was also much private marketing by dealers and middlemen in fairs, houses and inns. Information assembled by Everitt for the period 1560–1640 suggests that the average distance travelled by customers to open market was 7 miles, but that the distance varied with the product as well as the terrain. Few buyers or sellers of corn travelled more than 7 miles to market, whereas livestock, wool, yarn and cloth drew dealers over much greater distances. The majority of customers at Worcester's markets apparently came from within a radius of 10 or 12 miles, but Herefordshire men from up to 30 miles away came to sell cattle there, and its sheep fairs attracted one flock from 70 miles away in Carmarthenshire. Some fairs were reputed to have a nationwide clientele. Stourbridge fair near Cambridge was already the most famous fair in England 'both for resort of people and quantity of goods', while Chesterfield fair in Derbyshire drew 'gret concourse of pepell from all partes of Englande'.[11]

The navigable rivers were busy highways for cargoes that would have cost too much to transport by road. Willan has assembled Elizabethan examples of land carriage ranging between 4*d* and 12*d* per ton-mile, as against 1*d* or even less by water. Building stone and lead for a Worcestershire manor house were carried as far as possible on the Severn before being transferred to carts because freight charges by road were between eight and eleven times as high per mile as by water. Worcester boatmen imported coal and firewood, grain and fruit, and exported Droitwich salt downriver. York men shipped lead and cloth down the Ouse to Hull and beyond, in exchange for fish, coal, salt, iron, flax and grain. However, even bulky commodities could be carried long distances overland where water transport was lacking. West Riding men were said during the famines of the mid-1590s to be riding 30 or 40 miles to York every year to carry away corn on horseback. Livestock could also, of course, be driven great distances, and it was evidently worthwhile to do so. A rich farmer of Kirkby Lonsdale who died in 1560 had been supplying sheep and cattle to customers in Yorkshire, Lincolnshire and even Huntingdonshire.

The greatest market area, by general consent, was London. It was impossible for the largest English town, and one growing rapidly larger, to feed itself without drawing extensively on its hinterland, and even occasionally on more distant shires or on overseas markets. Recent research has modified, but not substantially altered, the picture of London's food market which Fisher sketched in 1935. Corn was supplied in large quantities, by river from Berkshire and Oxfordshire, and by coast from Kent and East Anglia. Henley on Thames was an especially important river port, supplying London with nearly half its corn in six exceptional months in 1573–74. Dairy products came from Essex and Suffolk, and fruit, vegetables and hops from Kent and other south-eastern shires. Cattle and sheep were fattened for the London market in East Anglia, the East Midlands and the Home Counties, though many of the cattle had been bred in Wales or the North.

The tentacles of the capital were reaching further than ever before. The classic example is coal shipments from Newcastle to London, which on Nef's figures increased enormously. The few years available for comparison may be untypical, so distorting the scale of the growth; but the trend is indisputable. Indeed, Nef's belief that the shipments were measured in London chaldrons (26–27 cwt) rather than Newcastle chaldrons (42 cwt) led him to understate their volume, which seems to have reached 37,500 tons in 1585–86 and 54,750 tons in 1591–92. Yet the coal traffic was a geographically exceptional part of London's trade, which, if expanding, was still largely confined to the Home Counties and the Thames valley. Recent studies of the agriculture of Norfolk, Lincolnshire, and even eastern and central Kent have shown that the influence of the London market was very limited and selective, in contrast to Middlesex, Hertfordshire and west Kent where it was dominant. At the very end of the century London could still be described as fed 'principallie . . . from some fewe shires neare adioyninge', and even within those counties 'the territories in which London's influence was intense . . . resembled islands or pockets of countryside, surrounded by areas in which its effect was of little importance'.[12]

More than one of Thomas Harman's rogue anecdotes (1568) involved victims of robbery from Crayford in Kent who rode regularly to London to sell in the markets there. One was an old tenant of Harman's 'who customably a great tyme went twise in the weeke to London, eyther with fruite or with pescodes', and who made seven shillings in sales on the day he was robbed. Similarly, Norden wrote of the husbandmen of Middlesex who were 'so furnished with kyne that the wife or twice or thrice a weeke conveyeth to London mylke, butter, cheese, apples, peares, frumentye, hens, chyckens, egges, baken, and a thousand other country drugges . . .'. And of Hertfordshire, Norden wrote that it 'affordeth no small store of wheat and malte towards the provision of London'.[13] No other English town had such a pull over its hinterland, although the provincial capitals had similar effects on a smaller scale.

Superimposed on the local marketing areas were the patterns of longer-distance regional trade, whether in minerals, foodstuffs, basic manufactures or luxuries. Here fairs played a crucial but little-studied role, as centres of both wholesale and retail trade. The gentry and richer tradesmen often bought wholesale at fairs, and London merchants found it worth their while to patronise fairs as far afield as Market Harborough, Chesterfield, Howden and Beverley. Above all, Stourbridge fair drew regular customers from London, Kent, Lincolnshire, Lancashire, Yorkshire and doubtless elsewhere. Some towns became entrepôts for specialised commodities and served very wide areas. London again dominated the national scene, with Blackwell Hall for shortcloths, but other towns were equally important for their regions. The Shrewsbury drapers monopolised much of the Welsh wool trade; Royston in Hertfordshire drew corn dealers and maltsters from a wide area to its weekly malt market; and York supplied much of the North with seafish.

It is the coasting trade, for reasons already given, which is the best recorded, and it reveals a varied pattern in a wide range of commodities. In contrast to overseas trade, which was dominated by London, the 'outports' had a much fairer share of internal trade, and there was a fairly even spread of shipping round all the coasts except in Lancashire and Cumbria (Table 9.1). This can be seen in the best-recorded coastal trade, in grains, for which the extensive but patchy surviving records were analysed long ago by Gras (Table 9.2).

The figures can give no adequate idea of the total size of the trade, but only of the relative position of each group of coastal ports. Naturally enough, the pastoral South-west made only a minor contribution to the trade, while the North-east was a major importer. East Anglia (the group of ports between the Thames and

Table 9.1   English tonnage of shipping owned in 1582 by regions (as a percentage of the total)

East Anglia	27.1	South-east	16.2
South-west	20.9	North-east	15.0
London	18.7	North-west	2.1

Source: An Introduction to the Sources of European Economic History 1500–1800, i, eds C. Wilson & G. Parker, Weidenfeld, 1977, p. 129.

Table 9.2   Coastal shipments of grain, 1540–1610 (averages of years or quarters recorded, by harvest years)

	North-east		East Anglia		London		South-east		South-west	
	In	Out	In	Out	In	Out	In	Out	In	Out
1540–50	15,591	1,073	—	40,174	—	—	—	512	—	2,216
1550–60	4,653	3,499	—	19,943	—	—	2,601	10,468	1,972	903
1560–70	11,721	20	—	47,165	324	615	—	15,955	4,765	2,341
1570–80	—	—	—	26,211	18,090	195	—	—	—	—
1580–90	1,290	—	1,355	11,828	51,688	4,926	—	185	762	364
1590–1600	—	—	378	14,934	—	—	—	—	1,910	572
1600–10	—	—	—	8,098	—	—	—	874	—	—

Source: J. Chartres, *Internal Trade in England 1500–1700*, Macmillan 1977, p. 16.

the Wash) was a considerable exporter of grain, especially King's Lynn, which handled much of the surplus from the arable fields of the East Midlands. London, naturally, was an extensive importer, even more so if imports from overseas (very large in the 1590s and 1600s) are taken into account. But the south-eastern ports, from Kent to Poole, also exported grain by coast, largely to feed the Londoners.

In general, the port books show London importing food, fuel and metals by coast, in return for a wide variety of food, drink, raw materials and manufactures. It is the reverse picture from overseas trade, where London exported mainly cloth and imported very miscellaneous wares, and it suggests, reasonably enough, that London acted as a funnel for the rest of England, and that 'those great miscellaneous cargoes from Antwerp or Amsterdam had been divided up, put on board the coasting ships and despatched to the provincial ports'.[14] In 1585–86, for example, London shipped beer and iron to ports all along the east and south coasts, and imported foodstuffs and naval supplies to all parts, as well as soap, glass, paper, kettles and nails. Even Chester received at least one ship from London most years, carrying a miscellaneous cargo ranging from foreign luxuries like wine, sugar and prunes to bulky native commodities like chalk and fuller's earth.

The coasting trade was not, however, dominated by the capital. Even Newcastle, dependent on its coal exports, sent only just over half of its coastal coal shipments to London, and the rest to King's Lynn and other east-coast ports in return for grain. Similarly, Lynn never sent more than 30 per cent of its grain shipments to the capital, although it was such a major grain port that its corporation built a complex of sixteen warehouses in the 1580s. Southampton, Poole, Exeter, Bristol and Chester dominated the coasting trade of the south and west coasts, distributing a wide range of goods and taking only a limited part in trade with London. Chester and Bristol especially distributed goods to North and South Wales respectively, and dominated English trade with Ireland.

The Irish trade was in a sense domestic rather than foreign, but it 'was of a colonial nature; Ireland exported large quantities of raw materials and semi-manufactured goods to England and in return accepted a wide range of manufactured goods and some raw materials, such as coal and hops, that were not readily available in Ireland'.[15] Ireland exported to England fish, hides, wool and linen yarn, and in return imported coal, cloths and other textiles, metal products and grocery wares. Irish hides were in great demand for the English leather industry – in the half-year ending at Easter 1593 211,000 sheepskins were landed at Chester and Liverpool alone – while a boom in Irish yarn exports to Liverpool after 1588 reflected an expansion of the Lancashire linen industry. The Irish trade was not, however, 'colonial' in the sense of being dominated by English merchants. It was concentrated in the hands of the freemen of Dublin, who handled the greater part of the trade with the aid of restrictive practices connived at by the queen and Privy Council.

3

Internal trade has been unduly neglected, even allowing for the difficulties of the sources. Contemporaries were concerned mainly with overseas trade, and historians have generally followed them, assuming (questionably) that exports and imports were much more significant generators of economic growth than the inland trade. Yet it would be foolish to fly to the other extreme and to allocate space between the home and overseas markets simply in proportion to their supposed size – allowing, say, one-sixth or one-seventh of this chapter to the latter. The importance of foreign trade

cannot be measured solely by the amount of capital involved when compared, for example, with agriculture. Directly impacting on the prosperity of England's largest industry, sharply altering the demand for goods and the supply of capital and cash to an economy whose instability and sensitivity it is too easy to underestimate, overseas economic relationships deserve a large chapter in any story of England's economic development.[16]

Interruptions to overseas trade could produce a 'knock-on' effect, with repercussions throughout the internal economy, as happened in 1551–52, 1563–64, 1568–73 and 1586–87. This was especially so of the all-important Anglo-Netherlands trade, so that the guiding principle of Tudor foreign policy from the 1490s to the 1570s was to seek and retain the friendship of the Habsburgs, who as 'the house of Burgundy' were lords of the seventeen provinces of the Low Countries. Every sovereign and chief minister sought alliance with the Habsburgs rather than with the Valois or with the German Protestants, and accusations levelled against Wolsey or Burghley for pursuing this policy and neglecting, say, the interests of small powers or of a Protestant alliance, are beside the point. English foreign policy was dictated more by the pattern of English cloth exports than by considerations of religion or the balance of power.

Those cloth exports dominated contemporary considerations of overseas trade and the balance of payments. English kerseys, wrote a Venetian in 1513, were 'one of the most important foundations of trade in the world'. To Hakluyt in 1582, there was 'no commoditie of this realme that may set so many poore subjects on worke' as did cloth, 'that doeth bring in so much treasure', while to Camden looking back on Elizabethan trade with the Netherlanders of both north and south, 'the English wooll hath been to them the true Golden Fleece'.[17]

The bulk of English exports consisted of wool and woollen cloth, as they were to do until the late seventeenth century. For example, in the year ending Michaelmas 1565, for which figures survive, cloth accounted for 78 per cent of all exports, and wool, woolfells and textiles of all kinds for over 90 per cent. The only other significant items exported in that year were lead (2.4%), tin (2.3), grain (1.4) and skins (1.0). Furthermore, for both the periods 1541–47 and 1559–63, London accounted for 88 per cent of all cloth exports, and for exports as a whole, if the customs accounts can be relied on, London had also come to acquire an overwhelming predominance (Table 9.3):

Table 9.3 Customs duties for London and the outports

	London	Outports	London's share of total as %
1516–18	£15,771	£11,584	57.7
1536–37	£16,970	£6,442	72.3
1581–82	£35,107	£4,905	87.5

Source: N. S. B. Gras, *The Evolution of the English Corn Market*, Harvard U.P. 1915, p. 74.

For these reasons, the statistics for exports of shortcloths, which for much of the period are available only for London, were taken by Fisher as a reasonable guide to the main commercial trends of the time. The customs authorities had a formula for equating each type of cloth to the value of a shortcloth, and the following figures are expressed in 'notional shortcloths' so calculated (Table 9.4).

Fisher saw English overseas trade, as measured by London's cloth exports, passing through three clearly defined phases in the sixteenth century: a 'meteoric' rise in exports during the first half-century, a contraction of some 25 per cent during the third quarter, as well as 'two catastrophic slumps in which those exports were halved', and finally 'three decades of comparative stability in which London cloth exports remained fairly steadily at a level some 20 per cent below that reached at the peak of the boom'. However, Stone pointed out that the early sixteenth-century growth in exports

Table 9.4   Triennial averages of shortcloths exported

	London	Outports	Total			London
1543–47	112	14	126		1577–79	109
1550–52	110	16?	126		1580–82	109
1559–61	104	14?	118		1583–85	112
1562–64	68				1586–88	106
1565–67	106				1589–91	110
1568–70	104				1592–94	113
1571–73	81				1598–1600	114
1574–76	111				1601–3	116

Source: R. Davis, *English Overseas Trade 1500–1700*, Macmillan 1973, pp. 52f. All figures from 1559 were increased by Davis by 11 per cent to allow for one cloth in ten sent duty-free as a wrapper.

was 'a relatively modest affair' rather than a boom, with an increase of only a third in the value of wool and cloth exported between the beginning and end of Henry VIII's reign, and that London export figures for the second half of the century showed cloth exports steady at a higher level than any achieved before 1540 except for two periods of slump.[18] Certainly the revised figures in Table 9.4 suggest higher Elizabethan figures than Fisher allowed, and a level from 1574 to 1603 equal to the midcentury boom. Nevertheless, there can be no denying that a pattern of almost continuous growth in London's shortcloth exports had given way after 1552 to one of stagnation. Davis was in no doubt at all that this was true of exports and imports in general. Taking the broad view, he saw English overseas trade in the fifteenth to seventeenth centuries undergoing two waves of expansion (1475–1550, 1630–89), separated by a period of near stagnation.

Yet it would be too simple to accept the cloth figures entirely at face value as representing adequately the course of overseas trade. The growth in woollen exports of the early and mid-sixteenth century was a growth with a dangerously narrow base, and both the booms in 1541, 1544–46 and 1550–51, and the subsequent slump after 1552, were induced partly by government fiscal policies. The Elizabethan figures are for London alone and also represent only the exports of the Old Draperies and not of the rapidly expanding New Draperies. Smuggling and interloping may well have increased, especially after the outbreak of war in 1585. Furthermore, the second half of the century witnessed a search, largely successful, for wider markets, which set England on the road to a broader-based overseas trade. There is reason to think that the outports recovered a larger share of the export market in consequence, from only 7.5 per cent of all cloth exports in 1548–49 to something like 26 per cent of Old Draperies and 23 per cent of New Draperies in the period 1605–16, a time for which port books yield statistics for both.

Under Henry VII and Henry VIII, English exports had come to be more and more dependent on a single valuable commodity exported from London to a single 'mart town' or entrepôt, Antwerp, and under the control of a small chartered body, the Company of Merchants Adventurers of London. The Merchants Staplers, who retained their ancient monopoly of shipping raw wool overseas through Calais, had lost their importance as wool exports had been replaced by cloth; and the Adventurers enjoyed a monopoly of cloth exports to England's largest markets in the Netherlands and Germany (Fig. 16). Scandinavia and the Baltic had been effectively closed to direct trade with England since 1474; trade still continued, especially of English cloth in return for naval supplies, but through the intermediacy of the Hanseatic League, who enjoyed privileged direct trade in England but would allow Englishmen no reciprocal rights in the Baltic. The Icelandic fishing-grounds had been closed to England also since the end of the fifteenth century. In compensation for the loss of these northern markets, English ships had been penetrating the Mediterranean, trading cloth for wine, but this sphere was also closed to them after 1553 with the recovery of the Venetian and Genoese middlemen as carriers.

Even at the period of greatest concentration on Anglo-Netherlands

Fig. 16   England's northern European trading areas

trade, between about 1520 and 1550, Englishmen did not have to abandon all their other markets. Trade with France, especially of English cloth in exchange for woad, wine, salt and canvas, continued actively with inevitable interruptions from war. Wine, mostly from France, accounted for 10 per cent of all English imports in 1559–60. There was also a growing French demand for Newcastle coal, 'without which', asserted an English merchant in 1552, 'they can neither make stele-work, or metalwork, nor wyer-work, nor goldsmith-work, nor gunns, nor no maner of thing that passeth the fier'.[19] Spain, another traditional market, was becoming more important with the exchange of cloth for iron, oil and wine, and Henry VIII's founding of an Andalusia Company in 1531 recognised the establishment of English merchants in and around Seville, Spain's entrepôt for her new American trade. Finally there was a modest but significant trade with Scotland, and Scottish merchants sailed down the east coast to ports like Lynn and Boston, exchanging their fish for English grain.

Yet despite the continuing importance of the French trade, and the growth of Spanish and Mediterranean trade, London's merchants had been encouraged to concentrate more and more on the Netherlands trade in the first half of the sixteenth century, mostly with Antwerp. Antwerp was the undisputed commercial and financial capital of western Europe, reachable by a very short land and sea crossing from the Thames; and the four great yearly fairs of Brabant (two in Antwerp itself and two in its dependent town of Bergen-op-Zoom) brought together customers not only from the Netherlands but from Germany, northern Europe, Iberia and Italy. Many markets in northern, central and southern Europe could be conveniently reached by trade routes from Antwerp, and the Merchants Adventurers found no need to make wearisome journeys with their cloth across the Continent when customers were only too willing to come to them.

The Merchants gave evidence in 1561 that much of the cloth they shipped to Antwerp ended up in more distant markets – for example, Suffolk cloths and western reds and blues in 'Eastland', Iberia and Morocco; Hampshire kerseys and northern cloths in Hungary and Italy, but that it was much more 'commodiouse to the merchant' to sell them in the Netherlands than to trade directly with those distant markets.[20] Yet if the Merchants Adventurers depended on Antwerp, it in turn needed them. Its senators pointed out in 1563 that they had granted the English greater privileges than any other nation because of the many craftsmen there whose livelihood depended on the finishing of English cloths. The Merchants enjoyed the use of a spacious

'English House' as an Antwerp headquarters, and an 'English quay' permanently at their disposal.

Cloth exports, mostly to the Netherlands, had increased modestly under Henry VIII, as European demand had risen for a high-quality English product. But the situation was distorted by the Great Debasement, which produced artificial booms in 1544–46 and 1550–51 as English exports became progressively cheaper and imports dearer, and shortcloth exports reached a record figure of 133,000 in 1550. The Merchants Adventurers throve on the booms; Thomas Gresham made a net annual profit of nearly 15 per cent between 1546 and 1551, and must have doubled his capital in those five years. Yet it is likely that their gain was the country's loss, for the exchange rate had been so distorted that a greater and greater volume of goods had to be exported to pay for an equal quantity of imports; and the export booms could not last indefinitely.

In 1551 the government revalued the currency; the cloth trade was naturally hit hard, but its consequences should not be misread as catastrophic. London's shortcloth exports fell back in 1551–52, recovered to a new peak in 1554, fell again, and settled by the end of the 1550s at a steady level of 100,000–110,000 a year, a level they maintained for most of Elizabeth's reign. Furthermore, despite the fears of politicians (Cecil wrote later that 'the people that depend uppon makyng of cloth ar of worss condition to be quyetly governed than the husband men')[21], there was no widespread disorder in the clothing counties in 1551–52 comparable to the agrarian uprisings of 1548–49.

It is true that the Elizabethan picture looks superficially like one of stagnation, since shortcloth exports did not continue to rise. But no sixteenth-century export could be wholly elastic; a limit was bound to be set either by England's capacity to produce more cloth or its customers' appetite for more. And that limit was, it must be stressed, a very high one. The 100,000 cloths sent yearly to Antwerp around 1560 were worth at least £750,000.[22] Furthermore, the figures are only for traditional broadcloths sent to traditional markets; they do not take account of the lighter New Draperies, which were exported in increasing quantities over the final third of the century.

England's overseas trade throughout the Tudor period consisted essentially of the export of a single valuable commodity in return for a variety of raw materials, foodstuffs, and manufactures. Imports are not as comprehensively recorded as exports, but they were certainly very varied indeed. Starkey had complained in the 1530s that necessary foodstuffs, cloth and metals were being exported to pay for wine, textiles, combs, girdles, knives, 'and a thousand such trifling things' which could either be spared or made at home to increase employment. Smith in 1549 inveighed in similar vein against the number of imports 'that we might ether clene spare, or els make them within oure owne realme', such as glass, paper, pottery, gloves, ink-horns and playing cards, and he argued strongly that an unfavourable balance of trade must be avoided, and that any imported fruit or 'trifles' should be exchanged only for English fruits and 'trifles':

But yf they come for oure wolles, for oure clothes, carseys [kerseys], corne, tinne, lead . . . and such substaunciall and necessarie thinges, let them bringe in againe flax, tar, oyle, fish and such other; and not to use theim as litle children, geve them an aple for the best juell they have abowt theim.

His arguments made a lasting impression on his colleague Cecil, who was worried about 1564 over cloth exports to Antwerp. Their concentration on one outlet gave Philip II the power to 'annoye this realme', and their scale made England 'overburdened with unnecessary forrayn wares'. Around 1580 he was still arguing for a reduction in unnecessary imports, especially silk, wine and spices, and at the same time for a diversification of cloth export markets to include Germany, Scandinavia, Narva, Russia, Portugal, Italy, Morocco and Turkey.[23]

Cecil was right to be concerned about the concentration of exports on the Netherlands market, since it made England dependent on Habsburg goodwill. Stone suggests that at the beginning of Elizabeth's reign two-thirds of English trade was still with Antwerp, and the remaining third mostly with France and Spain. Philip's trade embargoes of 1563–64 and 1568–73 dealt severe blows to English exports and drove English merchants to seek other outlets for their cloth. One attractive and plausible idea, first raised in the 1530s and revived repeatedly in the 1550s, 1560s and 1570s, was to replace the Adventurers' 'staple' (fixed trading outlet) of Antwerp by a home staple, at London, Ipswich, Hull, York, Southampton or elsewhere, to which foreign buyers could freely resort from any country to buy English cloth. A home staple would, its proponents argued, increase England's security and independence, and generate much native employment. It was, however, impractical in sixteenth-century conditions; a more practical alternative proved to be the removal of the Antwerp staple to more hospitable continental towns.

There was also some validity in Smith's and Cecil's pleas for import substitution, and the establishment of native glass-making, paper-making and other industries went some way to meet their point. A statute of 1563 which restricted luxury imports may also have given a valuable breathing-space to the infant native industries. Yet the hope of both men for economic autarky was backward-looking. Some imports were necessities, like flax and tar for the shipbuilding industry; others were luxuries, but the economy fared none the worse for that. Much of the prosperity of Elizabethan England was channelled into consumption of imports like wine, sugar, silks, books, hats and handkerchiefs, which could be afforded only because exports sufficed to pay for them. A list of London's imports for the year 1559–60 shows this diversity very clearly. The largest group of items, flax, linen, and canvas for shipbuilding, amounted to 17 per cent of the whole by value, followed by 13 per cent for raw materials for the clothing industry (oil, wood, madder and alum). Wines accounted for 10 per cent, foodstuffs about the same, and iron goods and Italian textiles for about 6 per cent each.

Anglo-Netherlandish trade recovered from the crash of 1551–52, but international events soon conspired to undermine the entire commercial position of Antwerp, compelling Englishmen to widen their markets. The bankruptcies of the French and Spanish crowns (1557) and the outbreak of the Dutch revolt (1572), which shook the city's prosperity, were followed by the sack of Antwerp (1576) and the closing of its outlet to the sea by the rebels (1585). The bulk of English cloth exports continued to be sent by the Merchants Adventurers to their Netherlands and German markets, but the convenient Antwerp staple had to be supplemented and finally replaced. The first move was forced on the Merchants by the Spanish regent of the Netherlands, who suspended the cloth trade in November 1563 in the hope of causing unemployment and economic dislocation, thus putting pressure on the English government. It did indeed cause distress in England, but it quickly became clear that Antwerp needed the cloth trade even more than the English did. It was the Netherlanders who first sued to repair the breach, in March 1564, but by then Elizabeth had made arrangements instead to send the English cloth fleet to Emden in East Friesland, a German port just beyond the jurisdiction of Philip II. 'If ever there was a turning-point in English commercial history, it had now been reached. In effect, the English were deliberately rejecting an offer to readmit them to the Antwerp mart and making a far-reaching decision to look for trade outlets elsewhere.'[24]

The decision came about because the English were invited to Emden by the counts of East Friesland, and because a group of zealous anti-Spanish Adventurers worked tirelessly to take up the invitation. One of their number, George Nedham, wrote a perceptive and influential tract during 1564 justifying the move and prophesying that the Adventurers could live without Antwerp but not vice versa.[25] In the event, the Adventurers were at Emden for less than a year, returning to Antwerp in January 1565, and Nedham was in temporary disgrace. But as political troubles mounted, Antwerp became more and more unsuitable, and in the end the Merchants reverted permanently to their policy of finding a mart or staple town outside Spanish jurisdiction. They settled successively at Hamburg (1568–78), Emden again (1578–87), Stade (1587–98, 1601–11) and Middelburg (1587–1621), and by the early seventeenth century had pitched on two marts, one in Germany and one in the rebel Netherlands. During the trade crisis following the outbreak of war with Spain, the English government took the drastic step of suspending their trading monopoly altogether and allowing a free export trade in cloth, but this experiment in free trade proved disappointing, and was revoked within a year (1587–88).

Yet though the Adventurers' monopoly continued, more had changed than the site of their staple. Some English merchants, called interlopers, ignored the staple towns and traded where they pleased; and even the Adventurers themselves began to trade further afield. From the 1560s, for example, some began to sell cloth in Köln, to buy linen in Saxony and to become regular patrons of the Frankfurt fairs, 'contributing much to their golden age during the next half century'. 'Englishmen were learning how to outflank the Netherlands.'[26]

What was yet more significant for the future was the expansion of English traders, both back into regions from which they had been temporarily excluded, like the Baltic and Mediterranean, and beyond them into completely new regions of the globe – Russia, southern Asia, Africa and America. Such a geographical spread of trading interests lessened England's concentration on its Netherlands and German markets, and also began the process of lessening England's unhealthy dependence on London for 80 or 90 per cent of its overseas trade. With increasing voyages to northern and southern Europe, and beyond Europe altogether, ports like Newcastle, Hull, Southampton, Exeter and Bristol came into their own again. Yet neither development really bore fruit until the seventeenth century: London was still estimated in 1602 to pay customs averaging £70,000, as against £18,000 for all the outports put together, and 70 per cent of all short-cloths were still being exported to Germany and the Netherlands.

It is probably no accident that whereas Henry VIII had shown little interest in the geographical and commercial expansion urged on him by men like Robert Thorne and Sebastian Cabot, the disruption of traditional markets after 1551 turned statesmen and merchants to look outwards. Hakluyt's *Principal Navigations* (1589 and 1598–1600) are often regarded primarily as giving expression to the nation's geographical curiosity, but he himself took it for granted that 'our chiefe desire is to find out ample vent [sale] of our wollen cloth', as he put it in his dedication to Cecil (1599). Not everyone shared Hakluyt's preoccupation with finding 'vent', and it can be argued that a more powerful motive for extra-European trade was the search for luxury imports like silks and spices; but trade was certainly a major spur. It is therefore not surprising that the first significant ventures in the expansion of overseas trade occurred in the early 1550s, under Edward and Mary, although the shortness of their reigns and their sister's longevity has ensured that the movement is always thought of as 'Elizabethan'. Indeed the opening of trade with Morocco is traditionally (and probably correctly) dated 1551, the very year of the Antwerp slump.

English merchants in the 1550s and 1560s, anxious to diversify their trade beyond the Netherlands and Germany, naturally thought first of bypassing the Netherlands, either by forcing their way back into their old trade in the Baltic and Mediterranean, or by developing new trades round the fringe of eastern Europe, the Near East and North Africa. The more adventurous cast covetous eyes on the Spanish and Portuguese monopolies over the newly discovered lands, and some hoped to trade directly with their colonies, whether legally or illegally. The chroniclers of the first Guinea voyage (1553) hailed it as a profitable precedent for English merchants,

if the same be not hindered by the ambition of such, as for the conquering of fortie or fiftie miles here and there, and erecting of certaine fortresses, thinke to be lordes of halfe the world, envying that other[s] should enjoy the commodities, which they themselves cannot wholy possesse.[27]

Others hoped to outflank the Spaniards and Portuguese by discovering new sub-Arctic routes to the East Indies, following Thorne, who had pointed out as early as 1527 that the north was one region of the globe not included in the papal grants to the Iberians. The belief in an ice-free 'North-West Passage' led to Frobisher's voyages of 1576–78 and Davis's of 1585–87, which reached as far as Baffin Bay but were unsuccessful in their object.

Earlier still, attempts were made between 1553 and 1580 to find a 'North-East Passage' round Asia. They were equally unsuccessful in their original objective, but the first voyagers of 1553 reached the White Sea, travelled overland to Moscow, and started Anglo-Russian trade almost by accident. The merchants involved were incorporated by royal charter in 1555 as the Russia or Muscovy Company, and the 201 founder-members were granted a monopoly of trade with Russia and all newly discovered northern lands. They did not completely lose sight of their original aims, and between 1558 and 1581 they sponsored a series of overland trading expeditions through Russia to central Asia and Persia, which were added to their sphere of mono- poly trading in 1566. The Company's trade, it must be admitted, remained modest, and accounted for less than 2.5 per cent of all shortcloths exported in 1597–98; the Russian market for finished cloth never met their expectations, and they also had to export lead, tin, foodstuffs, pewter, and miscellaneous manufactures. But in return they imported cables, cordage, wax, tallow, flax, train oil (from seals and whales), and furs and hides, of which the cables and cordage were essential naval supplies. In 1587, admittedly an excep- tional year, the Company imported Russian goods officially valued at £13,500, and estimated by Willan to have been really worth more like £25,000.

The White Sea route was, however, lengthy and dangerous. The naval supplies, together with Polish grain, could have been more con- veniently reached through the Baltic but for the near-monopoly of the Hanseatic League. In 1558, however, Russia conquered the Bal- tic port of Narva, which was much frequented by English merchants and was added to the Russia Company's monopoly sphere in 1566. Russia lost the port again in 1581, but by then it was of less conse- quence. The northern war of 1563–70 weakened the Hanse just at the time when troubles in the Netherlands were distracting the Dutch carriers from their share of Baltic trade. From the 1560s English ships penetrated the Baltic more and more often; in 1578 the Hanse mer- chants in England were reduced to the same footing as other for- eigners; and in 1579 Elizabeth formally constituted sixty-five English Baltic merchants as the Eastland Company. Their trade was primarily with Poland, carried on through the port of Gdańsk or, after 1581, through the smaller neighbouring port of Elblag.

The growth of English shipping movements into the Baltic can be traced from the registers of tolls paid for passage through the Sound (Table 9.5).

As with most other markets, England's exports consisted over-

Table 9.5   English ships entering the Baltic, by port of registration

	London	**Hull**	**Newcastle**	**Others**	**Total**
1562–69	121	99	142	89	451
1574–80	169	131	115	231	646
1581–90	317	184	158	380	1,039
1591–1600	273	217	173	257	920

Source: H. Zins, *England and the Baltic in the Elizabethan Era*, Manchester U.P., 1972, p. 138.

whelmingly of cloth. It accounted for over 75 per cent of total English exports to the Baltic in 1565 and 1575, and for over 90 per cent in 1585, 1595 and 1605. Imports were rather more varied, but consisted predominantly of naval supplies – flax, cordage, hemp, iron, pitch, tar and so on. They comprised around 55 per cent of all England's Baltic imports in English ships in 1575 and 1595 and around 75 per cent in 1565 and 1585. Hinton's belief that in the sixteenth century Baltic grain was England's chief import was mistaken, and of the four years just mentioned, only in 1595 were there really large imports of Baltic grain, amounting to 35 per cent of all Baltic imports by value.

While English seamen and merchants returned to the Baltic, their compatriots re-entered the Mediterranean. Hakluyt averred in his dedication to Robert Cecil (1599) that English ships had trafficked regularly with Sicily, Crete and Chios from 1511 to 1552 'and somewhat longer', until 'intermitted, or rather given over', as a result of the Turkish captures of Chios (1566) and Cyprus (1571). The interruption is an undisputed fact, but Hakluyt's causes and chronology are misleading. English ships were apparently absent from the Mediterranean between 1553 and 1572, along with French and Netherlandish ships, but not because of Turkish hostility. The third quarter of the sixteenth century saw an Indian summer for Venice and other Mediterranean states, which resumed their own carrying trades; thus in 1569 English cloth was being carried in ships of Venice and Dubrovnik. Between 1570 and 1573, however, Venice was distracted by war with Turkey, giving England a chance to re-enter the Mediterranean, and from 1573 English ships regularly visited Livorno at the invitation of the grand duke of Tuscany, with cargoes of cloth, lead and tin. Thereafter they were regular traders in the western and central Mediterranean – at Sicily by 1580, Malta from 1581, Marseilles from 1590; and there was even a Venice Company under royal charter of 1583. As early as 1582 it was found worth while to carry the homely 'cole of Newcastle' for sale in Malta.[28]

The next step was to trade directly with the expanding Turkish empire, a clear case of politics and commerce before religion for a queen who had ordered national thanksgivings for the Christian naval victory of Lepanto (1571). Walsingham was apparently urging trade with Turkey in or before 1578, and in 1578–79 two London merchants, Sir Edward Osborne and Richard Staper, sent the secret agent William Harborne to Constantinople to make contact with Sultan Murād III, who was interested in English lead and tin for armaments. In 1579 Murād promised safe conduct to all traders of 'the domain of Anletār' (i.e. *Angleterre*), and in 1580 he granted them unrestricted trading facilities throughout his empire, in terms almost identical to those already enjoyed by the French.

In 1581 Elizabeth incorporated the English merchants there as the Turkey Company. It quickly prospered, especially after merging with the Venice Company in 1592 to form the Levant Company, and by 1599 it had twenty ships in Italian waters alone. The speed with which Englishmen took advantage of the opening up of the Muslim Mediterranean is illustrated by one of Hakluyt's narratives, describing how three English ships (two of them from Portsmouth and Bristol) were simultaneously visiting the port of Tripoli in 1584 when caught up in a trading dispute. An English visitor to Aleppo in 1594 thought it unnecessary to describe the state and trade of the town, 'because it is so well knowen to most of our nation'.[29] Despite the sultan's initial interest in lead and tin, which were exported on a small scale from England, Anglo-Turkish trade consisted essentially of the exchange of cloth for raw silk. Turkish carpets were also in demand in England: the countess of Shrewsbury possessed thirty-two of them at Hardwick Hall by 1601.

Meanwhile Englishmen were already well established in trade with the independent Muslim kingdom of Morocco. London merchants had sponsored voyages there from 1551, starting within a decade the regular exchange of English cloth for Moroccan sugar. In this case the relevant chartered group of merchants, the Barbary Company, was founded late under pressure from the earl of Leicester (1585), when the commerce was well established, was dissolved after twelve years, and made little difference to the trade. The leader of the first expedition to Morocco, Thomas Wyndham, died in 1553 trading on the Guinea coast, and trade with Guinea flourished from the 1550s. Again, trade with the region was long-established when the queen authorised an Africa Company in 1588, with monopoly rights to trade along the coast between the rivers Senegal and Gambia. The first black slaves were brought back to England in 1555, but in a land of much underdevelopment there was no call for extra labour at home; the significant change in the Guinea trade occurred in 1562 when Hawkins began taking slaves there for sale in Spanish America.

Hawkins's three expeditions (1562–63, 1564–65, 1567–69) represented a bold attempt to break into the profitable Iberian 'triangular trade', buying African slaves to sell in America in return for hides, gold and silver. The first two were profitable; the third ended in disaster and bloodshed after the Spanish prevented such trade by force. Thereafter the only way to profit from the riches of Latin America was by piracy and warfare, the way taken by Drake at Panama (1572–73) and along the Peruvian coast (1578–79). In 1584 Hakluyt urged English colonisation of North America in his *Discourse of*

Western Planting, and in 1585–87 there were abortive attempts to colonise Virginia, which was optimistically depicted as abounding with wine, oil, flax, sugar and 'what commodities soever Spaine, France, Italy, or the East partes doe yeeld unto us'. Permanent English colonisation of the American mainland was, however, to wait until 1607, and of the more immediately profitable West Indies until 1624.

The Virginia voyagers are usually credited with having brought back the first tobacco to England in 1586, a crop which was cultivated commercially in Virginia from 1614 and which was to become in the seventeenth century one of England's major imports and re-exports. Yet the date of its first introduction remains a minor puzzle. It was described already in 1590 as 'commonly knowen and used in England', and Hentzner in 1598 found Londoners 'constantly smoking' clay tobacco pipes. There must be some exaggeration here, in view of the high price of tobacco; but by 1615, if Camden can be trusted, tobacco shops were as common in English towns as alehouses and taverns.[30] For tobacco to have been first introduced in 1586 but so common by the 1590s would have been rather rapid, but there are suggestions that it had been introduced earlier via Spain, and indeed that it was grown in England on a small scale from 1565.

What Elizabethans called the 'Indies' proved easier to penetrate than the West Indies. The Indian Ocean was too large ever to become a Portuguese lake, and there were independent states willing to trade with Englishmen, as Drake found on his westward return across the Pacific and Indian oceans in 1579–80. By overland routes, Jenkinson penetrated Persia in the 1560s, while Ralph Fitch successfully completed the first English commercial expedition to India in 1583–91. Sir James Lancaster rounded the Cape of Good Hope in 1591 and reconnoitred the Indian Ocean, and in 1599–1603 he led a more successful expedition to Sumatra and Java. It was sponsored by London merchants envious of recent Dutch successes, who were in 1600 incorporated as the East India Company with 218 founder-members. Lancaster established the first English 'factory' in Asia at Bantam in Java, and the new company quickly became very profitable.

4

To describe the geographical extension of Elizabethan commerce, however, is easier than to evaluate its economic significance. Historians used to depict the state of Elizabethan trade as buoyant and expansive, but since the 1940s the dominant view has been more sombre, stressing that the search for new markets was a desperate reaction to the stagnation of the traditional cloth trade with Germany and the Netherlands, and that the new markets accounted for only a modest share of total exports and imports. Fisher wrote of the 'depressions' of the third quarter of the century, testified to by 'the revival of economic nationalism' and 'the wave of restrictionism which accompanied it'. One consequence was 'to fasten upon English commerce a framework of companies which were to dominate its history for the next half-century'. Stone calculated that the total volume of trade increased very little between 1558 and 1603: 'the famous expansion of trade in the reign of Elizabeth appears to be a pious myth'.[31] Yet new pessimism raises as many difficulties as old optimism.

Unquestionably, the traditional markets remained far and away the most important in 1600 as in 1550, whether measured by volume or value of goods. Of all shortcloths exported from London in 1597 –98, over 70 per cent were still destined for the Netherlands and Germany and 6 per cent for France, while of all goods imported into London in 1601–2, 74 per cent came from these markets together with Spain and Portugal. Yet such figures conceal the important fact that, since the collapse of Antwerp, English merchants had been encouraged to use other routes, and to some extent trade directly with markets in Germany and elsewhere with which they had previously traded at one remove. Furthermore, the figures rely on customs records, with their unquantifiable omission of smuggling and evasion and the pitfalls produced by a complex and somewhat arbitrary administration. Nor can the economic and strategic importance of the wider markets be assessed purely in monetary terms. The vital naval supplies from the Baltic were cheap, but 'the measure of the importance of Baltic imports [to England]...is not their monetary value, but the usefulness and necessity of the generally cheap Baltic commodities'. Or, as Willan has put it in discussing the Russian trade which also furnished naval supplies, 'the historian of Tudor trade cannot live by statistics alone unless he wishes to suffer from malnutrition'.[32]

It must also be said that while England gained new markets, one of her traditional markets was officially closed to her between 1585 and 1604 as a result of war with Spain. It was a particularly severe blow because the English merchants involved – incorporated as the Spanish Company in 1577 – had apparently been increasing Anglo-Iberian trade from 1574 to 1585. Indeed a Spanish spy in England reported in 1586 that 'the whole country is without trade, and knows not how to recover it; the shipping and commerce here having mainly depended upon the communication with Spain and Portugal'. Yet by 1593 it was said that the merchants of London, Bristol and Southampton had managed to circumvent the trade embargo by shipping cloths to Seville under the colour of Flemish goods.[33] Furthermore, Andrews has calculated that privateering during the eighteen years of war brought in returns at least as great as the total value of Iberian trade before the war (£100,000 p.a. or so), and accounted for 10–15 per cent of England's total imports. A single Portuguese carrack captured by Drake in 1587 carried a cargo worth nearly £114,000, at a time when the crew of Drake's flagship could be paid and fed for £175 a month. In any case the Spanish spy had exaggerated the importance to England of the Iberian trade, and had misleadingly dismissed trade with France as insignificant. In fact over one-quarter of the tonnage of imports entering London in the nine months October 1601 to June 1602 came from France, slightly ahead of the Netherlands total. Anglo-French trade remained, in fact, very important, as it had throughout the Middle Ages, though historians' concentration on the disruptions of the seventeenth century has caused it to be unduly neglected.

Furthermore, contemporary writers like Harrison, and the more sober testimony of inventories, speak unambiguously of a great increase in luxury imports, which could only have been paid for by increased exports, unless one postulates a permanent balance of payments deficit. Some historians have indeed postulated such a chronic deficit, and they can point to the anxieties of contemporaries. The customs accounts convinced Cecil that in 1559–61 London's overseas trade was in deficit, while about 1580 he opined 'that yerly the forrayn commoditees doo surmount the commoditees of the land'. Sir Henry Knivet told the Commons in 1593 that England was poor 'because we brought in more foreign wares than we vented [sold] commodities'.[34] Yet there are no satisfactory estimates or totals printed which can provide a reliable picture of the balance of payments, and Zins's study of the Baltic trade, the second largest after Germany and the Netherlands, suggests that English trade there was normally in balance if not in surplus. If the overall balance were indeed unfavourable, it is curious that ample supplies of Spanish silver continued to be made available to the Tower Mint during the 1580s and 1590s. Part of the difficulty in coming to a conclusion is that a general study of the English balance of payments in the period is still lacking, and that in particular much work remains to be done on the trade of the Merchants Adventurers.

Whatever the truth about the balance of overseas trade, or the extent of internal trade, there can be no doubt about the relative backwardness of England's commercial institutions. Italians, Germans and Netherlanders had evolved complex credit transactions, banking, insurance and investment facilities for the more efficient conduct of trade, but Englishmen lagged behind, as one might expect. Not even the most optimistic of Elizabethan historians has discerned the existence of a 'commercial revolution', a phrase which can be used with some justice of the late seventeenth and early eighteenth centuries.

Internal trade was hampered by the chronic shortage of coin, if contemporary complaints are to be believed. One of the most widespread grievances during 1536 in the North – by no means the homogeneously backward region of tradition – was that chronic poverty was accentuated by a lack of coin, and the calculations of Challis suggest that the total stock of coin in circulation rarely exceeded £1 a head of the population. Another of Harman's revealing anecdotes (1568) tells of a parish priest in east Kent 'of good welth', yet with little cash at home. When robbers demanded money with menaces, he called his servant

and wylled her to take out all the money he had, which was iiij.markes, which he saide was all the money in his house, for he had lent vi. li. to one of his neighbours not iiij daies before.[35]

As the story implies, credit was a common way of effectively increasing the volume of coin in circulation, and many hints suggest that loans of money or goods between neighbours were common and increasing. Probate inventories show many examples of such loans.

For significant commerce, as opposed to mutual self-help at a village level, more systematic credit was called for, with legal safeguards for repayment and regulated interest. In late medieval England, taking of interest had been castigated as usury and legally forbidden, but from 1545 to 1552, parliament authorised the practice provided that the interest levied did not exceed 10 per cent. This was without question an important break with tradition, and contemporary financiers were in no doubt of the stimulating effects of legislation. In the 1550s and early 1560s all three sovereigns in turn had to borrow heavily at Antwerp through the agency of Sir Thomas Gresham, partly because Antwerp was still the financial capital of western Europe but partly because the renewed ban on usury after 1552 discouraged large loans by native merchants. In 1560 Gresham, having just negotiated a large loan to Elizabeth at Antwerp, urged Cecil to persuade her to legalise interest at 10 per cent, whereupon she would find no shortage of credit in England. And in 1566 Gresham's agent Clough wrote from Antwerp urging a new statute 'for som resonabell intrest betwene man and man'. If this were enacted, 'so that there myghtt gud assurans be had, I wollde nott doutt butt that there wollde be more moneye fonde in London then in Andwarpe'.[36] Such pressures finally had their effect in the parliament of 1571, when the taking of interest was finally legalised; and thereafter Elizabeth raised all her loans within the realm. And in the same year of 1571, the London Royal Exchange was officially opened, directly modelled on the Antwerp Exchange.

As Clough pointed out, 'gud assurans' or security was as necessary as legalisation. The records of Tudor equity courts are filled with complaints of non-payment of commercial debts, though that could be seen as evidence of the usefulness of equity jurisdiction rather than a worsening of credit security. And at the level of large-scale and long-distance trade, merchants resorted to a variety of forms of credit with security. Part or all of a transaction might be discharged by a 'bond', 'note' or 'bill' of exchange promising repayment at a specified future date, a bond which might or might not be readily transferable. Such instruments allowed merchants to traffic on a large scale with a very low liquidity ratio. Gregory Isham, for example, a rich Merchant Adventurer, had a working capital of perhaps £3,000, and gross debts of £8,000–£9,000 at Antwerp and at London when he died in 1558, yet he left only £88 in plate and £145 in ready cash. And with or without credit, merchants were accustomed to complicated transactions involving long distances and currency conversions. William Harborne in 1580 arranged for wine to be bought in Crete and shipped to the Baltic by way of London; he clearly expected the venture to be safe and profitable, and took conversions between Venetian, English and Polish currency in his stride.

Overseas trade became more carefully financed and organised as its geographical scope enlarged. There is much justice in Fisher's strictures that the increase in the number of trading companies was a product of stagnation (real or perceived) rather than growth. The Privy Council seems to have thought in terms of an economic 'cake' more or less fixed in size, to be shared out among limited numbers of merchants; and many of the new trading companies of the second half of the century were simply regulated monopolies on the traditional pattern of Staplers and Adventurers. Similarly, the Council granted limited groups of provincial merchants the monopoly of overseas trade to and from their own towns – Chester (1554), Exeter (1559) and York (1581) – often to the disgust of those excluded from the charmed circle.

Yet the foundations of the new national and local trading monopolies can also be viewed as attempts to control growing numbers of overseas traders, and with only partial success. The terms 'inter-leaper' (interloper) and 'outleaper', for merchants breaching a company monopoly, were in use by 1566 to describe those flouting both the Merchants Adventurers and the Russia Company, and their activities appear to have increased towards the end of the century. Willan has suggested, from a study of interlopers and of authorised traders dealing outside the staple towns, that 'Elizabethan trading companies were much less monolithic in structure and much less monopolistic in practice than their charters and ordinances imply'.[37]

The joint-stock principle, adopted from the beginning by the Russian and Turkey companies, represented an important new stage in commercial development. Thus the first Russian voyage of 1553 was financed by 240 shares of £25 each, to which Cecil and several peers and Crown officials subscribed, along with many London merchants. When the original capital was spent, the shareholders were approached for more contributions in the same ratio; and any profits were to be distributed pro rata. The joint-stock principle was still in the experimental stage – in the 1580s the Russia Company reverted to periodically distributing capital as well as profits, and in the 1590s the Levant Company abandoned joint-stock financing altogether – but it pointed the way to a more stable and efficient method of financing long-distance trade in the seventeenth and eighteenth centuries. Over 6,300 people invested in joint-stock companies between 1575 and 1630, though three-quarters of them did so after the death of Elizabeth.

The trading and exploring ventures also produced improvements in geographical knowledge and in the art of navigation. Hakluyt, whose collection of voyagers' accounts summed up so many achievements and inspired many more, was proud to have been, in lecturing at Oxford, 'the first, that produced and shewed both the olde imperfectly composed, and the new lately reformed mappes, globes, spheares, and other instruments of this art'. At Gresham's College lectures in navigation and cosmography were included from the start. The sea quadrant was said to have been invented by an Englishman, John Davys (1550–1605). And the educated public was becoming familiar with the new discoveries very quickly. When Malvolio was described in *Twelfth Night* (*c.* 1602) as smiling 'his face into more lines than is in the new map with the augmentation of the Indies', Shakespeare was assuming his audience's familiarity with Mollineaux' new world map of 1599, while other references in the play presupposed knowledge of an account of an expedition to Persia which had only just been published.

Yet another positive achievement in the trading sphere in the second half of the century was a stimulus to English shipbuilding and to the native carrying trade. Not only did both internal and overseas trade increase in volume, but a greater part of that volume was carried upon English bottoms, largely at the expense of the traditional cargo ships – Venetians, Genoese, Portuguese, Hanse and Netherlanders, although after 1600 the independent Dutch recovered much of the market. The well-known Navigation Acts of 1651 and 1660 had many precursors, back to a statute of 1382 ordering all Englishmen to ship their goods in English vessels, and including a similar act of 1540. Yet mid-Tudor writers complained vociferously that, as so often, the acts were not enforced. Thomas Barnabe had seen 'go out at one tyde out of Rye, together, 37 hoyes laden with wood and tymber, and never an English maryner amongst them', so he wrote to Cecil in 1552, and he earnestly wished 'that there should nother fuel nor vittayl go out of the realm, but upon English bottomes'.[38]

Cecil took such complaints seriously. In the parliament of 1563 he argued at length for remedies for shipping, as a result of which restrictions were placed on the carrying trade by foreigners, and Wednesday was made an additional fish day 'for the maintenance of the navye'. By general consent the act was effective; it called forth a protest from Philip II about its effect on the carrying trade with the Netherlands, and within thirteen years 140 additional 'sea fisher bottes and barkes' were said to be operating from 20 ports entirely as a result of the statute. Between 1571 and 1576 at least 51 ships of over 100 tons, suitable for oceanic voyages, were built in England, and by 1582 the country possessed about 177 such ships in all. By 1601–2 almost half the shipping entering the port of London, measured by tonnage, was English, and in some trading areas the proportion was much higher: two-thirds of English cloth was carried to the Baltic in English ships in 1562–63, but the proportion rose steadily to 99.9 per cent in 1599–1600. Even greater, though not quantifiable, was the expansion of English shipping in the Mediterranean, carrying not only most English cargoes but many foreign cargoes also. 'The Mediterranean was the first, and for a long time the only, region where English ships took a large part in the carrying trade between foreign countries.'[39]

One area in which government activity clearly did not assist overseas trade was its lack of diplomatic representation abroad. The idea that rulers should have permanent resident agents at each other's courts, able to help with commercial as well as political matters, had been developed in fifteenth-century Italy, and had slowly spread to the larger states of western Europe. Spain maintained an English embassy from 1495 to 1584, while England under Henry VIII,

Edward and Mary maintained a network of embassies in the major courts of the Empire, the Netherlands, France and Venice. However, religious divisions born of the Reformation broke these contacts. Diplomatic links with Venice were severed at the accession of Elizabeth, and by 1570 the only English ambassador resident on the Continent was in France. Later, Elizabeth increased her representation abroad to take in the rebel Netherlands and the Turkish empire, but the lack of diplomatic links with many of the major continental powers was a real drawback in commercial negotiations.

Nevertheless, despite the growth of trading company restrictions, the lack of diplomatic contacts, and the effects of the war with Spain, it is possible to view Elizabethan commerce in a more favourable light than it is often seen. Trading links had been established over a large portion of the globe, even if the original motives were often politics, piracy or the thirst for adventure as much as commerce. As Hakluyt justly boasted in 1589,

which of the kings of this land before Her Majesty, had theyr banners ever seene in the Caspian sea? which of them hath ever dealt with the Emperor of Persia . . . and obtained for her merchants large and loving privileges? . . . who ever found English consuls and agents at Tripolis in Syria, at Aleppo, at Babylon, at Balsara [Basra], and which is more, who ever heard of Englishmen at Goa before now?

True, England's traditional European markets were to remain much more significant for some time to come, but even there the diversification of trading centres in the United Provinces, Germany and the Baltic avoided the excessive concentration on one mart that had been such a danger in the great days of Antwerp. And behind the growth of overseas trade lay the even larger, if more shadowy, achievement of the internal market, without which it would have been impossible. As Davis pointed out with regard to England's new trading opportunities in the Mediterranean after 1570,

the occasions would have come and gone unnoticed had not the English economy already grown strong enough to provide the capital and organisation for opening new and distant trades, re-creating a merchant fleet and developing industrial responses to the new demands. Escaping from economic tutelage at the hands of Germans, Flemings, Italians and Spaniards, the English had in the course of the sixteenth century grown in capacity and confidence and begun to push beyond their old markets on the western coasts of Europe when these ceased to provide scope for expansion.[40]

Chapter 10

Government, law and order

It is wisdom to recognise that economic forces operate in a framework created by legal institutions, that to neglect those institutions in examining the causes of economic development or the distribution of wealth is as though a geographer should discuss the river system of a country without reference to its mountain ranges . . .

R. H. Tawney, 1912

Economic historians nowadays do not generally assign a leading role to legislation or other declarations of economic policy.

N. B. Harte, 1976[1]

1

Tudor man was no more the rational *homo economicus* than the man of any other age. He lived within the constraints of law, government, morality and custom, and often drew no distinctions between these spheres and his economic and social life. Any separation of sixteenth-century history into legal, political, economic and social categories is inevitably artificial and misleading.

That is not to argue the naive view that Tudor men and women can be judged only on their own terms. Disciplines like sociology and anthropology can be legitimately used to interpret their behaviour. Economics can emphasise profit and economic exploitation more than contemporaries did – though the tracts and sermons of Crowley and Latimer show that the sixteenth century had nothing to learn from the twentieth about the power of unfettered greed. Yet to assert, as some historians have done, that the sixteenth century was an age of growing capitalism and individualism, paying only lip-service to the ethics of co-operation, paternalism and mutual responsibilities, is to accuse our ancestors of sustained hypocrisy and to fly in the face of much evidence to the contrary.

2

The rule of law was fundamental to the thought of the age, and to the way men acted and behaved. Yet the phrase suggests a limited

meaning to what was then an all-embracing concept. Central government did not clearly distinguish between its judicial and administrative functions; parliament and Privy Council could be quite
correctly viewed as courts as well as executive and legislative institutions; justices of the peace in the localities were both administrative
officers and law enforcers. And the law they administered and
enforced had in turn to conform to natural and divine law as part of
the cosmic scheme of order.

The hierarchy of law was well expressed by Richard Hooker in
1593. At the summit stood God's law eternal. Subordinated to it were
the law of nature, observed by inanimate objects, the celestial law
of angels, the law of reason or rationality, and 'human law, that
which out of the law either of reason or of God men probably gathering to be expedient, they make it a law'. Human law included law
for the regulation of relationships between private persons, 'laws
politic' for the maintenance of government, and international law or
'the Law of Nations'.[2] Thus, like the Chain of Being, the doctrine
of interdependent laws linked man to God on the one hand and to
inanimate nature on the other.

In practice, despite Hooker's 'Law of Nations', England was
becoming in acknowledged theory what it had long been in fact, a
sovereign state with an omnicompetent government. Developments
since the 1530s – part-cause and part-product of the English Reformation – had exalted the monarch's power at the expense of all other
sources of authority. Henry VIII's action in denying the universal
spiritual leadership of the pope, and in making himself head of the
Church, had been buttressed by the assertion that England was an
'empire', or a realm totally independent of all outside jurisdictions,
responsible only to God. Such claims had a long pedigree: the French
King Louis XI had been hailed as 'emperor in his kingdom', and
Bishop Tunstall had told the young Henry VIII that 'the Crown of
England is an Empire of itself'. Yet the term did come into more
general use after the Reformation, reflecting a new awareness of
English power and independence. Spenser was rehearsing an
accepted commonplace when he dedicated *The Faerie Queene* (1590)
to 'the most high, mightie and magnificent Empresse . . . Elizabeth'.
The later sense, however, occurs as early as 1577, when John Dee
predicted the formation of an 'incomparable British Empire',
covering much of the northern hemisphere and based on sea
power.[3]

The king or queen was, it was conceded, ultimately responsible
to God, but the theory, popular in some medieval ecclesiastical circles, that the people could depose an unjust ruler was frowned on

after 1534. John Ponet in Mary's reign was willing to put religion before secular obedience and to urge the overthrow of the queen, and some Catholics like Parsons took a similar line against Elizabeth after 1570, but the orthodox teaching of government writers and churchmen was consistent that rebellion was a crime against God, who alone could punish a wicked ruler. The 'Homily on obedience' was insistent that law and order depended on complete loyalty to the sovereign, and the popular *Mirror for Magistrates* (many editions from 1555) collected examples from English history of the uniform failure of rebellion. After the northern rising the Church published an extra *Homily against Disobedience and Wilfull Rebellion* which argued that rebellion was 'worse than the worst government of the worst Prince', and asserted – with scant regard for historical truth – that 'look over the chronicles of our own country . . . ye shall not find that God ever prospered any rebellion against their natural and lawful Prince'.[4]

The monarch's power and prestige were consciously heightened by all the devices of art, preaching and printing; and once again, an existing tendency was reinforced by Henry VIII in the 1530s. One of the most striking results was a huge painting of the royal family by Holbein for the royal Privy Chamber at Whitehall. It was so arranged that ambassadors and suitors came upon the enthroned sovereign dominated by the swaggering bulk of Henry VIII.

Yet it was Elizabeth I who took – or allowed others to take – the cult of the monarch to extremes. Writers hailed her as Gloriana, Belphoebe and Astraea, the imperial virgin of the golden age in classical mythology who was returned to earth to inaugurate a new golden age. Her accession day (17 November) was rung in by bells from as early as 1568, and became a Church holy day by 1576; St Elizabeth's day was also celebrated in her honour; she was called a saint in her lifetime, for example by Spenser in *The Faerie Queene*; and, most daring of all, she was compared to the Virgin Mary and even to the Deity. Lord North wrote to the bishop of Ely, 'She is oure God in earth; if ther be perfection in flesh and blood, undoughtedlye it is in her majestye.'[5]

A cult of monarchy, however, reflects a position in need of buttressing rather than one of unassailable strength. The argument has been recently revived – and disputed – that Henry VIII and Cromwell attempted in the late 1530s to create a more autocratic form of government. Yet the attempt, if indeed it was made, failed, and none of Henry's children had the power to act despotically. They ruled under the constraints of law, as all Tudor writers acknowledged, and their grateful subjects contrasted their lot with the 'tyranny' or 'despotism' of Russia and Turkey. Shakespeare makes Henry V reassure his uneasy courtiers on his accession:

> This is the English, not the Turkish court.

And Webster has his secretary in *The White Devil* resist an abuse of ducal power with the threat:

> Would you have your necke broke?
> I tell you Duke, I am not in Russia.

The Tudors had no standing army or state police (though Secretary Walsingham employed paid agents or spies in the 1570s and 1580s) and only a rudimentary bureaucracy. Monarchs needed the co-operation of their nobles and gentry, who in turn had to rely on the acquiescence of lesser folk. It made for a situation of 'government by the informal mechanisms of consent'.[6]

The distribution of political power and influence was a pragmatic mixture of the formal and the informal. Formally, the sovereign was assisted in governing the realm by her officers of state (notably the lord chancellor, lord treasurer and principal secretaries), by the Privy Council, and by parliament. The great officials had their own permanent staffs to keep records and to carry out orders, and the Council met regularly to take decisions and to give the sovereign advice. In the localities, lords-lieutenant and their deputies, sheriffs and justices of the peace were present to execute orders from the Council and to express local wishes and grievances to the central government; and the justices were also responsible for levying local rates in the counties. And, periodically, parliaments were held which acted as the supreme point of contact between the Crown and the political nation, as a legislature, and as the normal means for authorising taxation. Parliaments were only an occasional part of government, but an essential part, welcomed by the queen and Council as well as by the nation. Sir John Neale's massively influential work on Elizabethan parliaments concentrated on conflict between them and the Crown, whereas they were above all, as Elton has shown, an instrument of stability.

However, the real exercise of power was conducted only partly through such channels. At the centre, the royal court was an indispensable channel of patronage and influence, although it has received little serious study in comparison with the formal constitutional machinery. Both at the court and in the shires, competing groups coalesced into factions to put pressure upon government to pursue particular policies or, more often, to appoint to particular posts. In practice, each shire contained notables who exercised power and patronage because of their status, landholding and wealth, whether or not they held government office or sat on the commission of the peace. And even those local leaders who did act as justices did not necessarily enforce government policies as they were ordered to. Studies of the policies of justices in Essex, Norfolk, Sussex and Lancashire have shown them often divided or – as in Lancashire – sometimes united to hamper government policy. And many gentry who became justices thought primarily of the personal advantage they could thereby gain, in their localities, through the combined use of civil and criminal law against their opponents.

Government as a full-time profession was carried out by very small numbers. The permanent salaried officials of the Crown numbered only about 1,200 in Elizabeth's reign – 600 administering the Crown lands and 600 serving the other departments of state. Thus, in a population rising to 4 million, there was one royal officer for every 3,000 inhabitants or so. That was one fundamental reason why the Crown had to rely so heavily on the unpaid justices of the peace (who numbered 1,738 in 1580). By contrast, the French monarchy of the early seventeenth century employed 40,000 paid officers, or about one for every 400 inhabitants.

Such figures, however, take no account of the army of private secretaries and clerks who served the royal officials, and who were paid, not by the Crown, but by their employers or, much more often, by gratuities, favours and outright bribes. Each of the six clerks of chancery, for instance, might employ over forty subordinates. It all saved the Crown money, but the price in corruption, unpopularity and loose control of the bureaucracy was high. Other Crown salaries were saved by the exercise of patronage – by rewarding servants and favourites by appointing them to lucrative posts in the Crown's gift.

The general assumption of the political nation was that government was to be carried out for the people – Elizabeth said that 'it was the duty of a prince to hold an equal hand over the highest and the lowest' – but not of or by the people. Sir Thomas Smith articulated conventional wisdom when he lumped together everyone below the level of yeomen and burgesses as 'the fourth sort of men who do not rule'; so did Burghley when he said that 'all must not be [a] like; some must rule, some obey'. The political implications of Calvinism, as practised in Geneva, Scotland and the Netherlands, were especially feared in case its relatively broad spread of power proved contagious. 'God keep us from such visitation as Knox have attempted in Scotland', cried Archbishop Parker in 1559, 'the people to be orderers of things.' And Thomas Wilson drew the same moral in 1578 from the rebel and republican Netherlands:

Unhappie is that cowntrie where the meaner sorte hath the greatest
swaye, for that in a base multitude is never seen any good cownsel, or
stayed judgement. God keepe Englande frome any soche confused
authoritie, and maynteyne us with our annoynted soverayne, whose onelie
[sole] power under Christ is the safetie of us al.[7]

It would, however, be wrong to deduce from comments of this
type that England was ruled by a tiny and secure oligarchy. The
political nation was small, but it could govern only with the consent
of larger numbers of middling folk, many of whom held at least local
office as constables, headboroughs, jurors and churchwardens. And
one unforeseen result of the price inflation was that the forty-shilling
parliamentary franchise allowed greater and greater numbers to vote
for knights of the shire, while some boroughs had a wide franchise
of their own. At Shrewsbury in 1584 421 citizens enjoyed a vote, out
of a total population of no more than 4,000. Registered forty-shilling
freeholders in Nottinghamshire numbered 179 about the year 1561
but over 1,000 in 1612. A crowd of nearly 6,000 county voters is said
to have assembled at York in 1597, though the number is doubtful
because no exact count was taken. The size of the crowd, and the
result, were a portent of the growing power of the electorate to come:
two powerful candidates with Cecil connections, Stanhope and Hoby,
were narrowly defeated by local gentlemen, Savile and Fairfax,
apparently with the backing of the clothing interest. Hoby was hindered by a rumour spread about in the West Riding cloth towns that
in the previous parliament his brother had supported a bill against
northern cloths.

3

The recent renaissance in legal history has been marked by an especially strong interest in the early modern period, 'when law stood
closest to government and legislation was only intermittently significant'. There was, of course, a system of lawcourts – or rather, several
systems – separate from the government's administrative structure,
but the lines between them were very blurred. The royal Council
formed itself into a special Court of Star Chamber to hear private
petitions alleging riots and breaches of the peace, while even ordinary
Council business was often quasi-judicial. In 1552 a committee of the
Privy Council was instructed to 'see what laws penal and what proclamations standing now in force are most meet to be executed', and
to punish offenders.[8]

There were, broadly, four types of lawcourt in England and Wales (Welsh customary law was abolished in 1535, when English common law was imposed). Pride of place is usually given to the common lawcourts which judged both civil and criminal cases: the central courts at Westminster, the assizes, and the quarter and petty sessions in each county. The ancient central courts were King's Bench, which heard criminal and civil cases, often referred to it from lower courts; Common Pleas, which dealt with civil suits; and Exchequer, for pleas alleged to involve the financial rights of the Crown. For purposes of criminal law and lesser offences, there was a range of courts in the provinces, depending on the seriousness of the offences concerned. Felonies traditionally included murder and homicide, rape, arson, burglary and robbery, to which Tudor statutes added other offences like riots, coin-clipping, witchcraft and recusancy. The counties were visited twice yearly from Westminster by the judges of assize, of *nisi prius* and of gaol delivery, who dealt with the more serious felonies at the county assizes. Lesser felonies and misdemeanours were mainly heard by the resident justices of the peace in each county. The justices – mainly laymen but with a quorum of lawyers – held quarter sessions every three months for their important civil and criminal business and divisional and petty sessions more often for lesser business, while minor offences could be despatched by a justice sitting alone in his own house. The tradition that the young Shakespeare was brought before Sir Thomas Lucy, JP, for poaching deer in Lucy's own park, whether true or not, plausibly enshrines a common form of speedy justice.

Of the common lawcourts, those of the justices of the peace affected many more citizens than the central courts and assizes. The justices were without doubt becoming much more active in the later Tudor period, and a Kentish JP, William Lambarde, thought it necessary to publish a manual for their use (*Eirenarcha*, 1581/82 and many later editions). He depicted the justices as the unpaid maids of all work in Elizabethan England, overburdened and indispensable. Parliament had laid 'stacks of statutes' on their shoulders, and to prove it he listed in his 1602 edition 309 statutes enforceable by the justices, 116 of them passed since 1547.

Historians have, however, been too ready to take Lambarde at face value. The main task of the justices at quarter sessions was to hear cases brought before them by constables and juries and not to initiate action themselves; and they did not go out of their way to look for extra work. Of the eighty or so statutes concerned with economic and social offences which Lambarde listed, very few were enforced.

Most of the statutes enumerated in the *Eirenarcha* are either unmentioned in the printed Quarter sessions records or appear very rarely in just one or two shires . . . only forestalling, engrossing, and infringements of the apprenticeship laws leave any mark on the rolls, and that mark is a small one. Tudor J.P.s were mainly concerned with the traditional offences of assault, forcible entry, disorderly conduct, riot, bastardy, alehouses, petty larceny, and unlawful games.[9]

For example, much of their time was consumed in regulating ale-houses, which were required to be licensed under a statute of 1552. The granting or refusal of licences, the prosecution of unlicensed premises, and the tackling of assaults and crimes connected with alehouses were all onerous duties. It has been recently suggested that the alehouse represented an 'alternative society', a poor man's challenge to the well-regulated society demanded by Puritan justices; but some scepticism is pardonable. It is not known whether alehouses increased in number or boosted crime-rates, or whether closer regulation drew more attention to a permanent and stable feature of popular culture. Faced with the argument that 'the alehouse offered a virtually institutionalized challenge to governmental ambitions for a well-ordered society', the obvious retort is that 'surely most people went to a pub for a drink and company'.[10]

The courts discussed so far were all common lawcourts. At least at the level of the traditional central courts the common law was generally slow, expensive and inflexible. For speedier and more flexible justice the Yorkists and early Tudors had developed several other courts – Star Chamber, Chancery, Requests, and the regional Councils of Wales and the North. They became popular with suitors and petitioners as a means of settling quarrels, recording debts or cutting through the technicalities of economic regulations and restrictions. The Northern Council at York, for instance, was said to be hearing over 1,000 cases a year in 1598 and 2,000 by 1609, while the numbers of cases brought before Requests and Star Chamber appear to have increased tenfold between 1550 and 1625. The 'equity courts', as they are often categorised in the textbooks, had gained business at the expense of the common lawcourts, and earned the hostility of the common lawyers. However, it would be wrong to draw a clear distinction between fossilised common law and dynamic equity law. Common Pleas did remain a very conservative court, but King's Bench broadened the range of actions available at common law and so recovered much business from other courts, while Exchequer developed a more flexible principle of equity to override legal technicalities.

A third type of court, probably much more important to humble folk than either of the others, was the local court operating in terms of local custom as well as of the laws of the realm: the courts of borough, hundred and manor. Not only did some larger boroughs have their own justices and quarter sessions, but most boroughs enjoyed lesser courts which dealt with everyday offences like boundary disputes, marketing offences and seditious words. A few specialised courts, like the Stannaries Court for the tin miners of Devon and Cornwall, dealt with disputes among particular communities.

Much more widespread, and by no means as decayed as is often said, were the manorial courts. In most manors the court leet, court baron and view of frank-pledge regulated landholding and conveyancing, crop rotations and agricultural practices; and in many they still exercised jurisdiction over policing and over petty civil and criminal cases. Recent studies of manorial courts leet in counties as different as Staffordshire and Essex have amply demonstrated their importance in hearing suits between tenants (e.g. for debt) and in punishing misdemeanours. The manor courts of Ingatestone, for instance, heard 945 cases of crime and misdemeanour between 1558 and 1603, ranging from 2 felonies to 35 cases of illegal woodcutting. The traditional overemphasis on the county justices has given a quite false picture of the actual involvement of courts in the lives of most villagers. Taking the two Staffordshire manors of Cannock and Rugeley, the county justices dealt with only a score or two of offences involving their inhabitants between 1584 and 1602, while their manor courts heard hundreds of cases over the same period.

Fourthly and lastly, there was a separate system of ecclesiastical courts: the courts of the archbishops, bishops and archdeacons, the 'peculiar' courts for exempt jurisdictions, and the two Ecclesiastical Commissions for the provinces of Canterbury and York. They had jurisdiction over a wide range of offences and disputes involving both clergy and laity. They used not the common law but the canon law of the Church, or more strictly (since the study of canon law at the universities was forbidden after 1535) the related civil law. The only other court employing civil law was the Court of Admiralty, since it dealt with maritime disputes involving foreigners, and civil law predominated on the Continent.

The ecclesiastical courts, like manorial courts, have been too readily assumed to have been declining in importance. Certainly they came under strong criticism during and after the Reformation, especially for their use of civil law and for their upholding of ecclesiastical discipline and of the payment of tithes. Puritan critics branded them as 'the bawdy courts', concerned with exacting fines and humiliating penances from sexual offenders. Yet they continued to attract much business from suitors as well as from prosecutions by Church officials, much of it concerned with the settlement of matrimonial and testamentary disputes and of quarrels between neighbours. Houlbrooke's study of two diocesan courts has shown that nearly all cases heard fell into four categories (Table 10.1).

Table 10.1   Causes brought in the Norwich and Winchester consistory courts, 1547–69

	Matrimonial	Defamation	Tithes	Testamentary	Other	Total identified
1547	3	11	17	16	2	49
1548	5	2	11	18	—	36
1549	3	1	8	7	2	21
1550	23	3	44	13	2	85
1551	34	9	54	38	6	141
1552	23	7	30	40	1	101
1553	9	4	26	30	1	70
1554	12	4	26	17	—	59
1555	15	4	34	34	10	97
1560	14	17	18	10	2	61
1561	21	8	37	103	7	176
1562	26	18	49	50	8	151
1563	38	43	72	66	16	235
1566	15	30	50	43	14	152
1567	6	13	34	47	4	104
1568	15	16	59	53	2	145
1569	13	14	55	54	8	144
Totals	275	204	624	639	85	1,827

Source: R. Houlbrooke, *Church Courts and the People during the English Reformation 1520–1570*, 1979, pp. 273f. Unidentified causes have been excluded.

The Church courts, Houlbrooke suggests, worked to maintain and strengthen the institution of marriage. The penances they imposed on sexual offenders, quarrellers and common defamers 'gave satisfaction to the congregation and cleansed the festering sores of local enmity'. Their procedure was quicker, cheaper and more flexible than that of the common lawcourts; they were guided by a desire to settle disputes peacefully by compromise and arbitration; and their enforcement of social discipline 'received a great deal more popular support than their critics have been prepared to admit'.[11] The shrewd and pithy textbooks on testamentary and matrimonial law by Henry Swinburne, the leading northern ecclesiastical lawyer (*Brief Treatise of Testaments and Last Willes*, 1590–91; *Spousals*, published posthumously), were standard works for well over a century, and only the triumph of common over civil law in the seventeenth century has obscured their importance.

4

The social and economic historian is concerned less with law and government in their own right than with their implications for society. How far were the Crown and the lawcourts able to keep the peace, both against rebels and against criminals? How prevalent was crime and violence, and how effectively was it kept in check? How much of the national income was consumed by what would today be called the public sector, and how was it raised and spent? Perhaps most important of all, how far did government have wider purposes beyond maintaining itself in being and keeping law and order? Did it have serious pretensions to help or retard social and economic changes, and if so, were its efforts harmful, beneficial or simply futile?

It is, unfortunately, much easier to pose such questions than to answer them, partly for lack of evidence and partly because many historians have concentrated on institutions and administration in their own right. Fortunately several recent studies have been concerned with the impact of government on society and the economy, such as Williams' *Tudor Regime* and Thirsk's *Economic Policy and Projects*, while recent work on early modern legal history is beginning to explore crime as a subject in its own right.

All Tudor governments were obsessed with the fear of revolts, riots and armed assaults, and with reason. The ownership of armour and weapons was widespread, and was indeed required by statute as a means of local defence against invasion or rebellion, but it was a double-edged policy. Every parish had its armoury, usually stored in the church, like the fine sixteenth-century collection still surviving at Mendlesham in Suffolk. Almost every country gentleman's house had a small armoury, and indeed peers were required to have a good supply under a statute of 1558; many citizens possessed a sword, and many more carried a knife or dagger. In 1564 Elizabeth's two ambassadors to the French court drew their daggers on each other, and in 1583 an ex-sheriff of Norfolk ambushed a JP and personal enemy on his way to quarter sessions and seriously wounded him in the head. At about the same time Thomas Knyvett and the earl of Oxford feuded with armed gangs in the capital; both were wounded and at least four retainers were killed, one of them by Knyvett in person. Elizabeth brought pressure on the lord chancellor to ensure that a charge of murder against Knyvett never came to open court, and 'thanks to the studied neutrality of the queen, two great courtiers were allowed to commit murder after murder with complete immunity'.[12]

The Crown possessed no standing armed forces on land except the royal bodyguards, the Yeomen of the Guard and the Gentlemen Pensioners (about 100 men each), and the garrisons of Berwick, Calais (until 1558), and a few south-coast forts. Calais had a permanent garrison of some 500, and Berwick about 600 in the early years of Elizabeth. For defence against invasion or rebellion, the sovereign could summon the county militia (consisting in theory of all able-bodied males between the ages of sixteen and sixty), rely on the retinues of leading nobles and gentlemen or, in an emergency, could hire foreign mercenaries. For service overseas, it could effectively (though illegally) conscript men from the militia, supplemented by volunteers. Henry VIII had relied mainly on recruitment through landowners, but the policy was militarily not very effective. The Council in Edward's reign made extensive use at home of foreign mercenaries, who put down the East Anglian rebellion in 1549, but they were unpopular and expensive and were sent home in 1552. Mary and Elizabeth relied more extensively on the militia, reorganised from 1573 when the 'trained bands' began to be selected, armed and trained as a more professional force. Even so, the government often still preferred noble retinues in times of crisis. In 1607 the Midland gentry, putting down enclosure riots, and 'fynding great backwardnes in the trained bands, weare constrained to use all the horse they could make, and as many foote of their owne servants and followers as they could trust'.[13]

The root of the problem was that ordinary royal revenue was insufficient to pay for a regular standing army. For that, 'extraordinary' revenue voted by a parliament was needed, and parliaments were reluctant to vote adequate sums in peacetime. Yet the later Tudors were successful in resisting all armed revolts. In 1549 there were more extensive disorders than in any other year, with one major rising in East Anglia, and another in Devon and Cornwall, as well as lesser revolts in Somerset, Oxfordshire, Yorkshire and elsewhere. The West Country put an army of perhaps 6,000 or 7,000 rebels into the field, and the main East Anglian rebel camp numbered about 16,000 at its peak, though probably not all were armed men. The revolts coincided with a split in the government, an expensive war with Scotland and France, and religious and social policies which were unpopular in many quarters. Yet the government managed to confront and defeat the two rebel armies separately, sending an army of 3,000 (including 1,500 foreign mercenaries) against the western men and 10,000 (including another 1,500 mercenaries) into Norfolk; both royal armies included sufficient professional soldiers to be easily victorious. The rebellion of 1554 was more limited but potentially more serious; of four co-ordinated risings planned by the leaders, only that in Kent developed into a serious threat, but its geographical base allowed the leader, Wyatt, to come nearer to capturing the capital than any other Tudor rebel. His army of 3,000 men reached the city gates before they were dispersed. And in the only other serious rebellion of the century, the rising of the northern earls, the rebels amassed an army of 5,400 horse and foot, but were easily driven to flight when the Crown had had time to amass an army of 10,000.

The Crown's success in defeating rebellions owed much to the quality of its armed forces – however slow and unsatisfactory the method of their recruitment – and still more to the doctrines of loyalty and non-resistance which were preached at every opportunity through sermons, homilies and official propaganda. The fear that they were indeed sinning against the Lord's anointed, their sovereign, sapped the morale of many rebels. Furthermore, although some rebel leaders, like Wyatt and the northern earls, had definite plans to overthrow the government, many of their followers were more concerned to demonstrate forcibly their opposition to government policies; and some revolts, like Kett's in 1549, were purely protests or demonstrations.

Remarkably few victims suffered at the hands of Tudor rebels, and the Crown normally acknowledged the fact by sparing most of the commons after the revolt was suppressed. Mary's government executed no more than 71 rebels in 1554, and although her sister Elizabeth in 1569 was more vindictive, her orders for mass hangings were not fully carried out, and about 450 may have suffered in all. England was mercifully spared the bloodshed exacted on both sides in some contemporary European rebellions, such as the French wars of religion and the bitter struggles in the Netherlands.

If full scale rebellions were few, armed riots were numerous; but many of them, also, were attempts to ventilate grievances rather than to create chaos and disorder. Most rioters, like their counterparts in the seventeenth and eighteenth centuries, assembled to defend customary rights and expectations against encroachment, and were conservative rather than revolutionary in spirit. There were numerous riots against enclosures, and in time of dearth men sometimes took the law into their own hands and seized food which they could not afford to buy, or which was due to be shipped elsewhere, as in Ipswich and Gloucestershire in 1586, and in Somerset, Kent and Sussex, in 1596–97. Disorders grew out of hand in London in the 1590s, with several riots of servants and apprentices against the city government and against foreign artisans. What is striking, however, is how few serious disorders there were, and how leniently they were generally treated. For example, the highest penalty inflicted on the Canterbury grain rioters in 1596 was a forty-shilling fine, and although the Privy Council were panicked by the Oxfordshire anti-enclosure riots of 1596 into ordering torture and perhaps executions, they were also impelled to investigate abuses of enclosures 'so that the poor may live'.

Protesters often showed a detailed knowledge of the law, and turned to demonstrations or revolts only if legal action proved fruitless. Yeomen and husbandmen, as well as gentlemen, could be shrewd judges of legal points. In rousing some Yorkshire commoners to renewed revolt in 1537, Sir Francis Bigod produced the royal pardon for the recent rebellion and explained its loopholes, at which one of the crowd cried out, 'the king hath sent us the fawcet and kepeth the spigot hymself'. 'We must', Dickens comments on the incident, 'avoid thinking of the commons as all bucolic half-wits incapable of appreciating these issues.'[14]

Violent death in riot or rebellion was, apparently, rare; but was criminal and gang violence ubiquitous, as some contemporaries alleged? It is impossible to arrive at accurate criminal statistics for the sixteenth century, but some valiant attempts have recently been made to calculate figures of reported homicides, and to convert them to rates by making assumptions about total populations. Hair has calculated the numbers of homicides reported to Nottinghamshire coroners between 1530 and 1558, numbers which would suggest an annual average of 1.5 per 10,000 population, while Cockburn's results for indictments at assizes in Elizabeth's reign yield similar results – 0.7 for Essex, 1.4 for Sussex and 1.6 for Hertfordshire. Cockburn's conclusion is that 'murder and manslaughter were comparatively uncommon',[15] but the rates are in fact something like forty times higher than the four per million annually in England and Wales today. However, such high rates do not corroborate contemporary fears of murderous gangs of vagrants, discharged soldiers and masterless men. The typical Tudor homicide, judging from assize records, resulted from a fight between two or more men, often neighbours, which went too far. Interestingly, domestic homicide accounted for only a quarter of homicides recorded in Essex (1560–1609), whereas the proportion in England today is just over half.

Robbery with violence was certainly much feared and thought to be on the increase. Harman, in an influential treatise on vagabonds (1568), believed that organised gangs of thieves had begun only about thirty years before, and hoped that they were then at their peak. Hext told Burghley in 1596 that thefts in Somerset were increasingly

'daylye'. Yet reliable figures of the incidence of crime are very difficult to come by, and there is no clear evidence that violent crime
was increasing more than one might expect in an age of population
growth. The accounts of Dekker and Harman were 'brilliant pieces
of romantic journalism, which should not mislead us into thinking
that every honest citizen went in constant fear of being set upon or
bamboozled by rogues'.[16]

Such statistics as can be obtained relate, not to the crime-rate, but
to prosecutions and convictions. There was no true police force, only
the sheriff's officers in each county, the high constables in each
hundred and the petty constables in every parish, and it was often
necessary to rely on private informers to make accusations against
alleged criminals. The prevention of crime and pursuit of criminals
were sporadic at best, although many village constables appear to
have done their work well, and to have been far from the bumbling
stereotypes of Shakespeare's comedies. Rowse has, it is true,
unearthed a vignette which could have come straight from *Much Ado*,
of watchmen standing 'at every town's end' ready to arrest three
young men (the Babington conspirators), but having no description
of them except that 'one of the parties hath a hooked nose'. Yet the
terms of the complaint make it clear that the instructions for the
arrest had been badly handled; and the conspirators were, after all,
arrested.[17]

Hext was convinced that 'the fyveth person that comytteth a
felonye' was never brought to trial (i.e. presumably, that about 20%
evaded arrest, not 80% as it has been recently interpreted), and that
many of those tried, though guilty, were acquitted. Some escaped
because of friends among jurors; some avoided capital punishment
through the legal technicality called benefit of clergy; others benefited from the reluctance of juries to convict where the death penalty
was involved. Hext complained that 'most comonly the simple cun-
tryman and woman . . . are of opynyon that they wold not procure
a mans death for all the goods yn the world'.[18] Felonies – offences
carrying the death penalty – included murder, rape, burglary, robbery and witchcraft; fortunately Dr Nowell's sermon to parliament
in 1563, urging that adultery and sabbath-breaking should be added
to the list, fell on deaf ears.

Cockburn has produced statistics of indictments for crime before
the Essex, Hertfordshire and Sussex assizes, which suggest at first
glance that there was little increase in indicted crime between 1559
and 1625. However, in two of those three counties there was, in fact,
a marked rise in every decade from 1560 to 1600, followed by a fall
in the early seventeenth century. Thus 'indictment totals apparently

support the contemporary notion that crime was increasing during Elizabeth's reign'.[19] Of course, the population rise of Elizabeth's reign would lead one to expect a substantial rise in crime pro rata, and Cockburn's tentative calculations would imply a fairly stable crime-rate per 10,000 population in Elizabethan Hertfordshire and Sussex, though the Essex rates do imply a rising rate. However, crude indictment totals are misleading in suggesting an increase in all crimes. The rise towards the end of Elizabeth's reign represented largely a rise in theft and other property crimes, rather than crimes of violence, and there were sharp increases in indicted offences against property in all three counties in the famine years of 1585–87 and 1596–98.

In Sussex, Essex and Middlesex, between 20 and 36 per cent of those brought to trial at the assizes for felony in Elizabeth's reign were acquitted; and between 20 and 30 per cent were sentenced to death. In the county of Devon in the single year 1598 74 persons were sentenced to death, and there was an average of 78 a year in Middlesex between 1607 and 1616, figures which have suggested to Christopher Hill a minimum rate of 2,000 English executions a year. It is, however, not known how many of those sentenced were pardoned or reprieved, nor how far the two counties were typical. At the least, it can be confidently asserted, routine executions for theft and murder far outnumbered deaths in war and executions for crimes like rebellion and witchcraft, which have attracted much more attention. The Nottinghamshire evidence suggests that the risk of being judicially executed 'was roughly equivalent to the risk of being killed in a road accident today'.[20]

One crime which has attracted recent attention by its alleged rarity is suicide. Macfarlane has calculated a rate of 3.7 per 100,000 per year for Elizabethan Essex, based on coroners' returns, and Laslett has suggested that the relative rarity of suicide was a measure of social stability and cohesion. However, all Tudor figures of suicides are likely to be minima, because of the social pressure to record suicides as accidents; a suicide was denied burial in consecrated ground, and his or her property was forfeited to the Crown. Further, the Essex rate may have been calculated from only 62 per cent of the coroners' returns originally in existence; and one recent estimate of the Tudor and Stuart suicide rate is as high as 15 per 100,000, compared with only 8 per 100,000 today.

It is clear enough that the criminal law did not always deter crimes; but when has it ever done so? The murder rate even in London was probably lower than New York's today, and the English homicide rate as a whole, though much higher than it now is, does not suggest the imminent breakdown of law and order feared by nervous contemporaries, even during the difficult 1590s. The commonest offences before the assizes were property offences, not crimes of violence; theft did undoubtedly increase in times of bad harvest and high unemployment, but that is scarcely surprising. It may, of course, be that the counties so far studied were relatively peaceful; contemporary allegations can be adduced for a higher degree of violent crime in areas further from the eye of central government, notably in parts of Wales and the Scottish Borders. But such allegations have yet to be substantiated, and the general impression of late Tudor law enforcement is that it was reasonably effective even in the more remote regions.

It is also true that many criminals never came into court, and that of those who did, many escaped conviction. Yet it has never been clearly established that arrests and convictions strike at the root causes of crime, and in criticising the effectiveness of Tudor criminal law, we are perhaps asking questions inappropriate to the age. Recent research has demonstrated that victims of crime had many informal ways of seeking redress open to them, including arbitration, settlement out of court, social ostracism and public humiliation, and that prosecution before the law was often a last resort, taken only reluctantly. 'Getting a neighbour hanged for the theft of a cow would not bring the cow back, could cause a greater rift in the community than the offence itself had done, and might even cause the rates to rise to support the widow or orphans'.[21] The Tudor legal system should be judged not by anachronistic standards, but by its own intention to control the people as a whole rather than to punish individual offenders; and judged by that standard it was reasonably successful.

5

Just as the increasingly elaborate criminal law could not prevent crime, so an increasingly large body of common and statutory law on civil matters was not necessarily coherent and did not necessarily secure universal compliance. Many older historians took the same optimistic view of Tudor laws as did Tudor reformers themselves – that a law had only to be passed to be obeyed. Government policy was seen as consistent, despotic and effective, changing the nature of economy and society in accordance with 'mercantilist' principles. The key dates were seen as the major statutes, whether on apprenticeship, enclosure, or the Poor Law. By contrast, historians of the last fifty years have shown that many laws were 'more honour'd in the breach then the observance'. They have also stressed

that the Tudor state was more forced than forceful, and that the origins of its actions are to be found less in any theories held by its rulers than in the pressure to which it was subjected from vested interests and urgent social and financial problems.

Work based on parliamentary and administrative actions and proposals has been described as 'the economic history of yester-year'.[22]

Imperfections in common and customary law could be remedied, and new laws created, by the enacting of statutes through the consent of queen, Lords and Commons in parliament. In theory they formed a harmonious whole; in practice, sectional differences were bound to emerge. A majority in parliament could pass a bill which the Crown and Council thought unnecessary or ill-considered, though the queen's power of veto allowed her to reject the more obnoxious bills at the risk of unpopularity. The Crown might initiate measures unwelcome to many of the Lords and Commons, which might or might not be passed depending on the strength and skill of the government's supporters. More often, an issue which both monarch and parliament agreed demanded legislation could result in a compromise act as the result of conflicting pressures and amendments.

Whatever the results of these conflicts and compromises, the intentions of Crown, Councillors and parliaments were broadly similar, to control, encourage or discourage economic and social changes as well as to uphold law and order. Both ministers and disgruntled MPs would speak on occasion of the need for a *laissez-faire* policy by the Crown, but only when it suited them: nearly all members of the political nation were in favour of positive government intervention when it did not harm their own interests. Thomas Wilson in 1601 drew a clear distinction between 'policies for security' and 'policies for benefitt', both of which were equally proper subjects for legislation. Policies for benefit he took to include enclosure laws, poor laws, company charters, statutes for the increase of shipping and fishing, and so on.[23]

There is no doubt that social and economic affairs preoccupied politicians more in the sixteenth century than they had in the fifteenth: the statute book makes that clear. Yet while statutes are a good guide to the intentions of queen and parliament, they are a hazardous guide to the behaviour of their subjects. Some local communities anticipated statutory reforms, while others resisted them and ignored their legal duties. A compulsory rate for the relief of the poor was laid down as a duty on local authorities in 1572, but the

City of London had imposed this on itself by a by-law of 1547, followed by several other cities before 1572. On the other side of the fence, many small boroughs and even the large town of Nottingham seem to have ignored the requirement well after 1572. Furthermore, many statutes were enacted with a limited life-span, such as until the end of the following parliament, when they might not be renewed. And the Crown seems to have treated many economic statutes, especially over exports and imports, as to be enforced or not enforced from time to time, and there was a lavish sale of licences for exemption from their operation.

Even if the authorities had every intention of enforcing a statute or a by-law, that did not guarantee its observance. A classic case was the repeated statutes for the maintenance of archery, which, the government admitted and deplored, remained largely unenforceable. Roger Ascham, a keen archer himself, explained why:

> . . . the lacke of teachynge to shoote in Englande, causeth very manye men, to playe with the kynges actes, as a man dyd ones [once] eyther with the Mayre of London or Yorke . . ., whiche dyd commaund by proclamation, everye man in the citie, to hange a lanterne wyth a candell, afore his dore: whiche thynge the man dyd, but he dyd not lyght it: And so many bye bowes bicause of the acte, but yet they shote not.[24]

The story of sumptuary laws is similar. Parliamentary statutes were continuously in force between 1463 and 1604 prescribing the apparel that might be worn by each social group, supplemented between 1516 and 1597 by no fewer than nineteen proclamations. Heavy fines and forfeitures were laid down for offenders. The motive was apparently to uphold the hierarchy of social structure in the face of increased mobility and the increased complexity of that structure. Yet there is remarkably little evidence of prosecutions, and many of the statutes and proclamations admitted the lack of enforcement. In Harte's graphic phrase, 'they were candles in the wind'.[25]

Controls of prices and wages were often attacked as being similarly ineffective. In a remarkably prescient analysis of the limitations on the state's control of the economy, Sir John Mason wrote to Cecil in 1550 criticising a proclamation on the prices of cheese and butter:

> I have seen so many experiences of such ordinances; and ever the end is dearth, and lack of the thing that we seek to make *good cheap*. Nature will have her course, *etiam si furca expellatur*; and never shall you drive her to consent that a *penny*-worth of new shall be sold for a *farthing*.

And after fifty years' further efforts, some sceptics were equally unconvinced. The lord mayor of London decided quite deliberately not to enforce maximum grain prices in 1596 for fear of driving away sellers,

finding by experience the rule to be true that a free market without anie restraint to bring and sell at what prices they can maketh a plentie, and plentie of it selve will bring down the price.[26]

It was a commonplace that what was needed was the enforcement of existing laws rather than the enactment of new. Latimer urged a 'sharp proclamation' to the JPs in 1549 to enforce the laws on archery, for 'there be many good acts made for this matter already'. John Ponet noted wryly that 'laws without execution be no more profitable than bells without clappers'. Archbishop Parker was opposed to any additional ecclesiastical legislation unless it could be enforced.[27] In Elizabeth's later parliaments it became routine for the lord chancellor or lord keeper to protest that there were too many statutes already, and to urge parliament to repeal obsolete and unenforceable laws rather than add to their number. Part of the difficulty was that local officials could not, or would not, see to the effective enforcement of many economic statutes, so that the Crown was forced to rely on common informers, private citizens who were given financial inducements to bring successful prosecutions. Such informers, however, undermined respect for the laws without the compensation of a high success rate: local juries were often unwilling to convict a neighbour on the word of a stranger with a financial stake in the case.

Furthermore, the Crown was still powerful enough to use its prerogative to anticipate, complement, bypass or even contradict statute law, notably by proclamations: altogether about 127 were issued in the name of Edward VI, 64 by Mary and 382 by Elizabeth. An example of the first kind was the queen's proclamation in 1580 forbidding new building in and about London. In theory royal proclamations could not create new statutory offences, but here the queen acted at the mayor's request at a time when parliament was not sitting, and the position was belatedly regularised by statute in 1593. The queen's bypassing of parliament was demonstrated by her frequent grants of monopolies to royal officials and court favourites in the 1580s and 1590s, which she insisted was a legitimate exercise of her prerogative. Here, however, she had to give way after strong criticism in the parliament of 1601, issuing a proclamation which cancelled most of the grants. And her action in pressing members of the trained bands for military service overseas, criticised by Smythe in 1596, was certainly contrary to existing statute law.

For these reasons, no attempt is made here to look for a coherent pattern in the economic and social statutes passed between 1547 and

1603, most of which have been usefully classified by Ramsey.[28] To do so would be to give too much importance to the intentions of members of parliament who met only occasionally, who were often preoccupied with short-term measures, and who often intended their statutes to have only a limited life. Instead, it seems more appropriate to consider the aims and effectiveness of government action as a whole, bearing in mind not only statutes, but also proclamations, exhortations and propaganda, and the cumulative effect of administrative action.

An effective government presupposes an effective information service and good public relations, and the Tudors' development of both was more important than their much-vaunted but rather limited improvements to the machinery of government. Monarchs and ministers took the trouble to justify their actions and to urge loyalty through proclamations, addresses and pamphlets, making effective use of the printing-press from the 1530s onwards. They took considerable pains to cultivate the nobles, the leading gentlemen in each shire and the more important merchants, ensuring for instance that few families of importance were denied the public recognition of Crown office or membership of the commissions of the peace. Cecil constantly referred to descents of the leading families and to maps showing their county seats, a sensible recognition of the realities of local power rather than heraldic and genealogical snobbery. Robert Beale thought it important for every secretary of state to 'make himself acquainted with some honest gentlemen in all the shires, cities and principal towns and the affection of the gentry' and also 'to have a book or notice of all the noblemen, their pedigrees and alliances among themselves and with other gentlemen'.[29]

Cecil's use of maps and his patronage of cartographers also illustrates an increasing government interest in collecting precise information, including statistics. Cromwell in the 1530s had compiled the *Valor Ecclesiasticus,* had ordered all parish clergy to keep registers of baptisms, marriages and burials and, less well known, had instituted the compulsory registration of land conveyances. The enclosure commissions of 1517–19, 1548–49 and 1565–66 all collected information on the areas enclosed and numbers dispossessed. The parliament of 1549 enacted a census of sheep and that of 1563 proposed county registry offices to house parish register transcripts, though the first was quickly countermanded and the second had to wait four centuries for fulfilment.

From 1559 onwards Cecil frequently obtained customs figures on exports, imports, and the balance of trade. In 1563 the Privy Council called for and obtained statistics on the clergy in every diocese and the population of every parish, and persuaded London to begin the system of bills of mortality for plague years. In 1564 they collected information on the religious opinions of all justices of the peace, from 1558 they periodically collected and tabulated the muster rolls showing the strength of the militia in every county, and in 1577 they compiled a complete census of inns throughout the country. A nice example of the new emphasis on statistics was a government propaganda broadside on the economic benefits of observing Wednesday as a fish day. The City of London, it was estimated, consumed 67,500 beeves a week, so that one day's abstinence in five (Fridays and Saturdays were already fish days) saved 13,500.[30]

It was not, however, until the age of Graunt, Petty and King that such statistics were systematically applied to the solution of political and economic problems, and use of the new statistical files was still limited. One archbishop is said to have told Elizabeth that it was impossible to provide learned clergy for 13,000 parishes, to which the queen replied 'Jesus! thirteen thousand! It is not to be looked for.' Yet figures available to the government, and used by Camden, showed that the total number of English and Welsh parishes was only about 9,400.

6

Some of the founding fathers of English economic history, like Cunningham and Lipson, discerned a consistent pattern behind Tudor social and economic policies. Monarchs and their advisers were seen as pursuing consistent goals, preventing and punishing depopulating enclosures, ensuring sufficient native production of basic foodstuffs at reasonable prices, protecting urban industries from rural competition, and enlarging and strengthening urban gilds. Other long-term aims were thought to have been the encouragement of English shipbuilding and the carrying trade, the discouragement of foreign middlemen, the fostering of new native industries to effect import substitution and to reduce strategic dependence on foreign powers, the maintenance of a balance of trade or, better still, a trading surplus and the creating of effective machinery for dealing with prices and incomes, poverty and vagrancy.

A rival school of historians, following Unwin, has argued that state intervention in social and economic affairs was often incidental, selfish, short-sighted and inconsistent. Governments did not consider it their purpose to engage in social or economic engineering, but only to keep the peace, to wage wars and to finance those wars, and to maintain themselves in power.

Trade was a useful instrument of foreign policy, and merchants a useful source of revenue. When public order and war were not the paramount interests, then legislation was as often as not inspired by the selfish interests of some powerful pressure-group, some gild or trading company that had the ear of the government. It may be true that certain threads appear to run constantly through this legislation, but the supposed pattern and design are largely illusory, a construction of the historian writing with all the wisdom of hind-sight.[31]

Since 1940, English historians have generally veered towards the latter position rather than the former. Fisher (1940) and Stone (1948), for instance, stressed the short-term expediency and fluctuations behind the Crown's commercial policies. Bindoff (1961) attempted to show that the Statute of Artificers, once hailed as a coherent government programme, was an improvised and inconsistent omnibus measure resulting from conflicting pressure groups, and Fisher (1965) argued that it was the product of a short-term crisis. Bush (1975) has analysed the social and economic policies of Protector Somerset, once seen as a paternal social reformer, and contended that his overriding concern was to avert social discontent and to raise revenue so as to continue war with France and Scotland. He preferred enclosures to debasement as an explanation of inflation, Bush suggests, because to end debasement would have undermined the financing of the war.

The financial needs of the Crown tinged much legislation and administrative action, turning government into an interested party rather than a disinterested umpire. 'It rarely possessed anything remotely describable as "economic policy" but it always had financial problems for the solution of which it had to parley with both the creators of wealth and the payers of taxes.'[32] The confiscation of chantry property in 1548, and of 'superfluous' Church plate in 1553, were portrayed as purifications of worship and the diversion of resources into hospitals, education and social reform, but most of the money went straight into funding current government expenditure. The debasement of the coinage of 1544–51 was intended purely as a revenue-raising device; and the 1549 tax on sheep and cloth, though intended to discourage conversions of arable to pasture, was openly defended as another way to increase Crown revenue.

Mary and Elizabeth did not countenance quite such blatantly self-interested legislation as Edward; but the exercise of power continued to mix the paternal concerns of a ruler with the financial gains of the monarch. Many statutes, especially those regulating trade and industry, enjoined fines for breaches of the law, half to go to the Crown and half to the man successfully bringing the prosecution. Such prosecutions were mostly brought by informers, and the Crown had a vested interest in the system.

More notorious still were the Crown's licences, usually grouped together as patents and monopolies. The idea of encouraging inventors and entrepreneurs by granting them a patent for the sole manufacture of a new product, or sole use of a new technique, was a fifteenth-century continental device which was first practised by the English Crown in 1552, and became common after 1560. At first they were granted mostly to foreign inventors and innovators for limited periods and under strict conditions, but by the second half of Elizabeth's reign the system had become an abuse for rewarding courtiers and officials. Such patentees did not themselves innovate or manufacture, but collected licence money from those who did, and the practice covered both luxuries and necessities despite widespread protests: Sir Walter Raleigh was granted a monopoly of the manufacture of playing-cards, and one of the clerks of the Council a monopoly of the manufacture of white salt.

In an angry debate on monopolies in parliament in 1601, Sir Robert Wroth reported that monopoly patents were then in force for

currants, iron, powder. cards, hornes, oxe shin-bones, traine oyle, lists of cloath, ashes, bottles, glasses, shreds of gloves, aniseed, vinegar, sea-coales, steele, aqua-vitae, brushes, pots, salt, salt-petre, lead, accedence, oyle, transportation of leather, callamint-stone, oyle of blubber, furmothoes, or dried pilchers in the smoak, and divers others. Upon reading of the patents aforesaid, Mr. Hackwell of Lincolns Inn stood up, and asked this, 'Is not bread there?' 'Bread?', quoth another. 'This voice seems strange', quoth a third: 'no', quoth Mr. Hackwell, 'but if order be not taken for these, bread will be there, before the next parliament'.[33]

The indignation had its effect, and Elizabeth provided for the cancellation of some of the more obnoxious grants, although not until 1624 did a statute confine monopoly grants to genuine inventors for a limited period, and even that had a loophole for corporations.

However, it would be unfair to discuss patents solely in the light of their abuse between 1580 and 1624, the period termed by Thirsk the 'scandalous phase'. It was a perversion of what had begun as a laudable government intention to foster product innovation and import substitution. All the Tudors (except perhaps Mary) encouraged skilled foreigners to settle in England to pass on their skills to natives, rewarding them by short-term patents of monopoly. Further, Edward and Elizabeth encouraged 'projectors', native inventors of new processes, by granting them patents also. This measure of protection, Thirsk has convincingly argued, was largely successful and beneficial to the economy, helping England by 1600 to achieve some of the aims of self-sufficiency sketched out in the *Discourse of the Common Weal*.

Henry VIII had begun the process in 1543–44 by persuading foreign gunfounders to settle in Sussex. By 1548 a Frenchman was promoting woad-growing in Hampshire, to counter the inflated costs of imported woad, and apparently with the encouragement of Cecil and the Council. In 1549 Somerset settled Flemish cloth-workers at Glastonbury to improve the production of English worsteds. From these modest beginnings, and with the aid of the flood of Netherlands refugees after 1561, Elizabeth and Cecil greatly extended the policy. The successes of the New Draperies, of woad-growing, glass-making, copper-mining, armaments and gunpowder, soap-making, salt-making and many other industries, all well established by 1600, owed a good deal to the support and encouragement of Cecil and other ministers. To take only one example from among many, John Keyle sent Cecil details of improved salt-manufacturing techniques which he had learned in Antwerp, and reminded him that he was also seeking to serve 'your plesur particularlie for the coper matter in Sweden'.[34]

The Privy Council also developed a more coherent strategy towards social and economic problems, sending out circular letters to the localities to gather information, explain policy and demand effective action. From 1560, at least in the North, they pursued an active policy of wage regulation in advance of the Statute of Artificers of 1563. In 1564 they printed plague orders for the city of Westminster and in 1577 for London, while in 1578 and later plague years they published a book of orders for the whole kingdom. In 1586, and in later years of dearth, they published another book of orders on grain supplies and marketing. Such detailed books of advice drew on the best local practice in English towns, but also on more elaborate schemes of control in continental cities. By the end of the century, the Council was demanding from local communities very detailed information on their policies for plague precautions, poor relief and other matters.

Queen and Council also tried to enforce social and economic policies through proclamations. Well over half of Elizabeth's proclamations related to control of wages, food supplies, plague precautions, the currency and other areas of social and economic concern. Their effectiveness, however, varied greatly. Some of the policies enjoined most frequently, like sumptuary laws on clothing, or restrictions on the growth of London, seem to have been enforced very little. Imposition of a policy unpopular with the political nation was an uphill battle. In 1564–65 the recorder of London compelled the City's hosiers to observe a proclamation on the lining of hose. The only result was that their customers abandoned them for other hosiers 'dwelling wythout Temple Barr' who were willing to break the regulation, and, so the recorder complained to Cecil, 'some of your servauntes do weare such'.[35]

What all this suggests is that Tudor government did have some fairly consistent long-term aims, even if they were not coherent enough to be dignified with the title of a 'mercantilist policy'. From the 1540s to the end of the century and beyond, ministers sought to attract foreign skills and to encourage new industries, both to substitute for expensive imports and to create new products to meet new demands. They adopted a 'bullionist' position of trying to maintain a favourable balance of payments so as to encourage an inflow of bullion, an understandable position for a country with almost no native gold and silver. It was one of Burghley's maxims that 'that realme must needes be poore, that carrieth not out more than it bringeth in'.[36] They also attempted – as has been shown – to diversify overseas trade both in terms of products and markets, to lessen England's dependence on any one source of imports for strategic reasons, to encourage the shipping and fishing industries, to maintain a balance between arable and pasture farming, and to develop a coherent policy with regard to food supply, plague, poverty, vagrancy and poor relief. Many of these aims were successfully accomplished, or were well on the way to being accomplished, by 1603.

To say this is not, however, to attribute all the success to the government. Its powers were enormous on paper, but in practice it was often impotent. It could encourage, it could give a lead, it could legislate to compel or forbid exports or imports, or make trade and manufacture financially worth while. Yet the ramshackle and informal style of government, and its lack of paid officials and law enforcers, made its policies far less impressive in reality than on paper, as Elizabeth and Cecil were well aware. Success might come when a determined government was united with merchants and gentlemen equally determined; but when interest groups conflicted, or short-term fluctuations altered attitudes, no consistent and successful policy was possible.

The only intensive studies of the enforcement of a Tudor statute are that of Davies on section 24 of the Statute of Artificers enjoining a universal seven-year apprenticeship, and those of Tawney, Kelsall, Woodward and Foot on the wages clauses of the same statute; their general conclusions are that the act was only imperfectly enforced. Admittedly, the Crown may have had little interest in enforcement of the clauses, which may have been enacted as a result of pressure from private interests. But even the numerous statutes regulating cloth-making, in which the Crown had a close interest, fared little better, and 'the high tone and impressive bulk of these statutes sadly contrasts with their achievement'. John Leake complained in 1577 that little attempt was made to enforce the laws and that the justices, anxious about unemployment, allowed infringement to be 'covered as it were under a bushell'.[37] He was right: a little later the justices of the West Riding of Yorkshire openly refused to execute one of the statutes against the stretching of cloth.

However, it may be misleading to concentrate over-much on the limitations of government powers. Much opposition by local officials to the enforcement of particular statutes was based on local circumstances, for uniformly suitable national legislation was not attainable, but the Crown did succeed in enforcing much legislation in many areas much of the time. Furthermore, by a judicious mixture of encouragement and tolerance, it was open to an early modern state like England to do a great deal, even though it had limited powers of detailed control. Those governments, as in England and the northern Netherlands,

which gave permission to refugees with capital, enterprise, skill or simply the power of hand and muscle to find new homes and contribute to expanding wealth, discovered that they had made a remarkably profitable investment. For in this age most economic skills and innovations were carried in men's heads. All that government needed to do was to open the door to skill and enterprise.[38]

Chapter 11

Church and belief

. . . in the minds of most men of those times, religion was the dominant concern, and
we shall never make sense of their thoughts and their doings if we try to analyse them
only in political and economic terms.

    R. B. Wernham, 1968

1

Tudor men and women lived in a land where the ecclesiastical
authorities, and after 1559 the state, expected everyone to attend
church. Prayers, homilies and biblical passages must have become
deeply imprinted on the minds of the congregations, whether or not
they were especially pious. Shakespeare's plays contain quotations
from, or references to, forty-two books of the Bible, as well as from
the Prayer Book and the *Homilies*. The watchword and countersign
in Frobisher's fleet were both theological propositions – 'Before the
world was God' and 'After God came Christ his Sonne'. Lord Burghley, in a debate in the Privy Council, was able to point instantly (and
prophetically) to an appropriate verse from the Psalter in attacking
the aggressive policies advocated by the earl of Essex: 'The bloody
and deceitful men shall not live out half their days.'[1]

    Almost all members of the political nation accepted that mem-
bership of a single Church should be universal. Every monarch tried
in turn to impose a uniform doctrine and form of worship throughout
the land, and probably they were right to do so. There were no
religious civil wars in England, as there were in France and the
Empire, and although men and women died horribly for their refusal
to accept successive Church settlements, they were far fewer than
those who died in religious strife on the Continent. Only two people
were burned for heresy under Edward, and four under Elizabeth.
The one concentrated persecution was that of 1555–58 when Mary's
regime burned some 300 Protestants, although her sister executed
200 Catholic priests and layfolk, ostensibly for treason.

    The idea, dominant in England since 1689, that religion and
politics can be separated, would have seemed dangerous to Tudor

men and women of every religious persuasion. Burghley held that 'that state cold never be in safety, where there was tolleration of two religions', Camden that 'there can be no separation between religion and the commonwealth'.[2] The link between sovereign and orthodoxy was demonstrated by placing the royal arms prominently in every church – even, in the case of the surviving example at Tivetshall (Norfolk) by turning round the medieval Doom picture and painting a giant arms of Elizabeth on the reverse. Heresy, said Cardinal Pole in Mary's reign, was more dangerous to the commonwealth than theft, murder, adultery or even treason. The mayor of York, imprisoning a Catholic woman in 1594 for refusing to attend church, called her a worse offender than all the condemned felons. The mayor and the cardinal had opposite 'religions', as they would have put it, but the same attitude to uniformity.

Fortunately, humanity often prevented the pursuit of such beliefs to their logical conclusions. Some Marian bishops, like York and Ely, showed a marked reluctance to convict and burn heretics. Elizabeth consistently shielded her Court musician, William Byrd, from prosecution once he became a committed Roman Catholic, and her vice-chamberlain Hatton protected many Catholics from persecution, on the principle that 'in matters of religion neither fire nor sword was to be used'. Some distinguished theologians were of the same mind. Somerset's chaplain, William Turner, wrote in 1551 that spiritual evils must be fought with spiritual weapons only, and John Foxe the martyrologist pleaded unsuccessfully for the lives of the Anabaptists who were burned in 1575.

The successive Church settlements, imposed by Crown and parliament, were Protestant from 1547 to 1554, Catholic from 1554 to 1559, and Protestant again after 1559. Yet what they had in common was much greater than that bald statement might suggest. In terms of doctrine, the similarities between Catholics and Protestants were much greater than the differences. Almost all took for granted the fundamental propositions of traditional Christian belief like the existence of God, the Trinity, the divinity of Christ and the Last Judgement, and the unlucky few who openly challenged any of them, like Anabaptists and Unitarians, were persecuted alike by every Tudor monarch. And although official doctrine and liturgy were changed several times, the basic structure and organisation of the Church, a slimmed-down version of its pre-Reformation predecessor, changed remarkably little. The monastic houses had been suppressed between 1536 and 1540, and the chantries followed in 1547–48. Mary was unable to persuade parliament to restore monastic possessions, and had to content herself with refounding a few monasteries and

friaries. Equally, however, Edward and Elizabeth never abolished
the administrative and legal system inherited from the days of papal
supremacy, to the disgust of thoroughgoing Protestants, who called
repeatedly for a complete restructuring of the Church on the model of Geneva and other of the 'best reformed churches' on the
Continent.

So the English Church continued to be ruled by bishops; the clergy
still met separately in convocations instead of being represented in
parliaments; and the Church still administered its own civil law in its
own courts to both clergy and laity. The medieval system of financing
the clergy through tithes, endowments and glebe land continued
almost unchanged, despite pressures from saintly idealists and greedy
laymen to confiscate the endowments and to pay the clergy modest
salaries. The monasteries vanished, but their secular equivalents, the
cathedral deans and canons, remained. 'It is one of the fascinations
of the English Reformation that the bishops and cathedral chapters
not only survived . . . but actually retained much of their wealth and
social influence.'[3]

The Church in England and Wales was governed by two archbishops and twenty-four bishops, each with his own diocese or territory of jurisdiction (Fig. 17); the dioceses consisted of the twenty-
one medieval sees together with five new ones endowed by Henry
VIII out of his monastic spoils (his sixth foundation, Westminster,
was suppressed in 1550). Each diocese was divided into archdeaconries, deaneries and parishes; the parishes, the basic units of Church
organisation and pastoral care, numbered some 9,400, each in the
charge of a rector, vicar or curate. The total number of parish clergy
(leaving aside an unknown number of assistants) was probably more
like 8,000, because some livings were too poorly endowed to attract
a minister or – especially in mid-century – because of a lack of sufficient recruits to the clerical profession. A statute of 1545 authorised
amalgamations of parishes worth less than £6 a year, and it may have
been intended as part of an abortive scheme to rationalise the parochial structure altogether. In the event the medieval pattern was
retained more or less intact; a number of decayed towns did secure
local acts for the unions of parishes, but others remained saddled
with too many poorly endowed parishes, while some market towns
in the North and West had the opposite problem of a single church
serving the town and a vast rural hinterland.

Among the clergy, non-residence and pluralism – the holding of
more than one benefice simultaneously – continued to be widespread
after the Reformation as before it. One reason was the very unequal
financing of livings: rectors possessed both greater and lesser tithes,

Fig. 17 The English and Welsh dioceses, 1550–1603

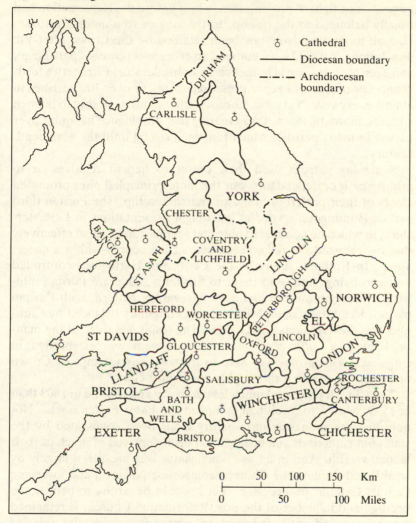

but vicars enjoyed only the lesser tithes, the greater having been 'appropriated' for the benefit of monasteries and other ecclesiastical institutions. This was rightly attacked at the Reformation as a serious abuse: but to no avail. Most of the impropriated livings came into the hands of laymen as purchasers of monastic property, and the vicars were no better off. In 1603, according to the bishops' returns to the Privy Council, some 3,850 parishes out of 9,250 – over 40 per cent – were impropriated in this way.

The Reformation saw an extension of lay control over the Church in terms of patronage as well as income. Every benefice had its advowson or right of presentation, which before the Reformation had usually belonged to the bishop, to the king or to a monastic house. Had all monastic advowsons been retained by the Crown after the dissolutions, it would have enjoyed an enormous power of patronage, and even as it was, royal influence was considerable. Elizabeth's lords chancellor and lords keeper presented clergy to over 100 parishes in almost every year. Yet most monastic advowsons were sold to laymen with the monastic lands, thus creating that dominance of squire over parson in many parishes which remained strong until the nineteenth century.

Some lay patrons used their power to benefit relatives or to acquire cash or dependants, but the more principled ones promoted clergy of their preferred brand of churchmanship. The Puritan third earl of Huntingdon owned at least eight presentations in Leicestershire, to which he nominated able and zealous ministers so effectively that he 'changed the religious climate of the county within a generation'. In Rutland, similarly, the Cecils and Haringtons controlled fourteen livings and used them to further a moderate Puritan ministry. Northamptonshire had a more complex pattern, with Puritan patrons like Mountague, Mildmay and Knightley balanced by Catholics like the Treshams and Griffins. The result was that ' at the manorial level, a *cuius regio eius religio* system was established in England'.[4] This power was able to frustrate any attempt by Crown or bishops to create a thoroughly conformist clergy.

The Church possessed much less property and income in 1603 than in 1535, when Cromwell had compiled the *Valor Ecclesiasticus*. Not only had the monastic and chantry lands been confiscated by the state, but cathedrals and bishops had been deprived of much of their landed wealth. And in an age when status was measured largely by wealth and display, the Church seemed less powerful and awesome than its Catholic predecessor. Yet it would be wrong to belittle the prestige and influence of the post-Reformation Church. It remained prosperous and well endowed in comparison with the salaried Protestant Churches of the German and Swiss city-states. Its clergy retained more respect and influence than is sometimes allowed; and, most important of all, though often forgotten, its doctrine and teachings still commanded almost universal assent or at least acquiescence. 'Scant justice has been done the Elizabethan Church. . . . As over enclosures in agrarian history, far too much attention has been paid to the critic . . . the Elizabethan Church was, as human institutions go, a success.'[5]

For instance, although church-going was not universal, it was certainly enforced among men of substance, with remarkably little opposition considering the frequent changes of religion. Successive statutes from 1559 made church-going compulsory and laid down penalties of fines and imprisonment for 'recusants', those – mostly Roman Catholics, but including a few Protestant sectaries – who refused to attend. So much attention has been devoted to these non-conformists of 'right' and 'left' that it is easy to forget how few they were. The comprehensive episcopal census of 1603 counted only some 8,600 adult recusants as against 2,266,000 communicants, although there may also have been a considerable number of non-communicants who attended church but did not take the sacrament; only two bishops listed their numbers separately. Certainly the Church included substantial minorities who conformed only reluctantly and who would have preferred a settlement of a different kind. Many radical Protestants barely conformed to the Prayer Book, and some were Presbyterians who formed virtually a church within the Church. And the numbers of recusants represent not the total number of Catholic believers and sympathisers, but only those publicly accused of breaking the law on church attendance. Many others were Catholics who either went to church reluctantly, or did not go but escaped prosecution.

One of the Church's greatest successes was in improving the knowledge and education both of clergy and laymen. There is much evidence from mid-century of widespread ignorance about Christianity, one of the most notorious being Bishop Hooper's visitation of his diocese of Gloucester in 1551. Of 311 clergy he examined, 168 could not repeat the Ten Commandments, 34 did not know the author of the Lord's Prayer and 10 could not repeat it. Heath has offered good reasons for not taking this survey entirely at face value, but he does not deny that 'with so tenuous a grasp of the basic essentials of their faith' the clergy 'were patently ill equipped to cope with the increasingly curious layman'. Not much better was Thomas Hobbes's father, a Wiltshire vicar and 'one of the ignorant "Sir Johns" of Queen Elizabeth'. He 'could only read the prayers . . . and the homilies; and disesteemed learning. . . .'[6]

The situation provoked a campaign of improvement which was largely successful, and which can be measured – if only imperfectly – by the increasing proportion of university graduates among the clergy. The proportion in the diocese of Canterbury rose from about 18 per cent in 1571 to 60 per cent in 1603, in Worcester from 19 per cent in 1560 to 52 per cent in 1620, and in the poorer Lichfield diocese from 14 to 24 per cent between 1584 and 1603. In the London diocese, where educational standards were always above average, 82 deacons out of 109 admitted between 1600 and 1606 were graduates. Some of the credit was due to the new Cambridge colleges of Emmanuel (1584) and Sidney Sussex (1594), both founded explicitly to provide a learned ministry. It would, of course, be naive to assume that better education necessarily made for more successful pastoral care. Richard Greenham, the graduate rector for twenty years of Dry Drayton in Cambridgeshire, was an influential preacher at Cambridge whose published works sold widely. Yet, though he said himself that he had watered Dry Drayton with tears, prayers and preachings, he believed his ministry there to have been a failure, and he told his successor that he could see no fruit of it except in one family.

The clergy became not only better educated but also less set apart from the laity with the legalisation of clerical marriage after 1547 and 1559. A celibate priesthood with a concentration on ritual was transformed gradually into a married ministry more concerned with preaching the Word. It has been suggested by O'Day that 'there was no clerical profession in the middle ages' and that the clergy 'emerged as a professional group in the late sixteenth and early seventeenth centuries'.[7] The former is a dubious proposition; but it may well be that the Reformation changes, which blurred the line between clergy and laity, made the clergy all the more anxious to emphasise their separate professional status.

The improvement in clerical education was matched by improved religious education of the laity, thanks largely to the Protestant emphasis on Christianity as a religion of the Word. The Bible was freely available in English from 1538 to 1543, from 1547 to 1553, and permanently after 1558; a copy was required to be kept chained in every church for public use. Although the early versions were expensive, the Geneva Bible of 1560 was relatively cheap, and ran through some sixty editions before the Authorised Version appeared in 1611. When an English ship's crew was arrested at Tripoli in 1583, it was a Geneva Bible that the master's mate had in his hand. A more conscious educational policy was laid down in the Prayer Books of 1549, 1552 and 1559, insisting that all candidates for confirmation must be able to recite the articles of faith, Lord's Prayer and Ten Commandments, and to answer a catechism to be put to them by the bishop. The question-and-answer method of the catechism, developed by Luther, was consciously used by the English Reformers as a means of religious and moral education, of adults as well as children. Hamlet's calling his hands 'pickers and stealers' is one of countless instances of the way in which the phrases learned for confirmation were absorbed into the nation's stock of imagery and beliefs. Yet learning by rote may not have changed people's lives very greatly: Greenham's apparent failure at Dry Drayton happened even though he had catechised his congregation twice every week for twenty years.

It would be misleading, in any case, to suggest that these laudable efforts to improve the education of clergy and laity were equally effective everywhere. They were generally least successful in what some Puritans called 'the dark corners of the land' – Wales, the Marches, Lancashire and the Scottish Borders, where poverty, clerical non-residence, religious conservatism and large parishes combined to create exceptional difficulties.

Archbishop Parker warned Cecil that the queen was unwise to save money by leaving northern bishoprics vacant: he feared it would prove a false economy and 'an occasion of furder expense in keeping them down, yf (as God forfend) they shuld be to muche Iryshe and savage'. In 1576, Burghley was told, most of the common people of Breconshire 'cannot as moche as saie the Lordes Praier and Articles of the Belief in anic language that they understand'. Bishop Aylmer made it clear which were in his view the darkest corners when he proposed to banish the leading Puritans to Lancashire, Staffordshire, Shropshire 'and such other like barbarous countries', so that they might wear out their zeal on the papists. In some of these 'dark corners' religious education did not begin to meet Puritan standards until the mid-seventeenth century. However, that was only one way, and a rather unsympathetic way, of looking at the outlying regions. Certainly in both Lancashire and Wales the Reformation 'collided . . . with a revitalised medieval Catholicism', and in such a situation 'Protestantism could not be expected to make any strong impact'.[8]

The Reformation entailed a drastic slimming of expenditure on the Church. Masses and chantries were abolished, fewer clergy were employed, new church building almost ceased, and the installation of new images, stained glass and organs ceased altogether, while most existing Catholic images and fittings were destroyed. The result was, as Jordan's statistics of charitable giving show, an enormous diminution in the proportion given to Church uses. To a sympathetic observer like Rowse, 'The Reformation meant an immense simplification, a cutting out of dead wood such as all societies need periodically.'[9] To devout Protestants the purpose was spiritual and not economical, but the resulting savings must have appealed to the worldly minded. It was a tragedy for English art that Church treasures were destroyed in such numbers, and that the Reformers were not content with ceasing to commission new ones: but once again, that was not their viewpoint. To a Puritan, the retention of images in stone, wood or glass was impious and blasphemous, and their destruction a work of merit. Queen Elizabeth took a more sympathetic view of them, and issued a proclamation in 1560 limiting the destruction, but by then the worst of the damage had been done.

At the same time as 'purifying' church interiors, zealous Protestants, including some bishops, fought hard to separate church fabrics from the lay world. Churchyards and even church naves had an age-old role as centres for parochial activities of all kinds, a tradition which now came under strong attack. Grindal, while archbishop of York, forbade the holding of dinners in churches and of dances in churchyards; and the common village practice of holding schools in the church was dying out. Many secular activities, however, continued to be held in churches and churchyards despite episcopal disapproval; and cathedral naves, complained Harrison (1587) had become 'rather markets and shops for merchandize, than solemn places of praier'. The nave of St Paul's in particular remained a hub of business activity and social meetings. Harrison testified to lawyers sitting 'in Powles upon stooles against the pillers and walles to get clients', and a scene in Ben Jonson's *Every Man Out of His Humour* (1599) is set 'in the middle aisle of St Paul's'.[10]

The Church and its institutions have too often been judged against an unattainable ideal of purity rather than by realistic standards of what was feasible. This was the attitude of many radical and zealous Protestants who were impatient to inaugurate a moral and spiritual Reformation. It is also the viewpoint of some modern historical works, like Hill's *Society and Puritanism* (1964). Some of the criticisms were certainly just; and a study of the offences brought to light by Church courts and episcopal visitations reveals much that was amiss in the lives of clergy and laity alike – ignorance, neglect of duties, sexual immorality, neglect of church fabrics and services, and so on. Yet it is not clear whether these offences were on the increase or were simply being more vigorously opposed; and judicial evidence inevitably presents a pathological picture in which success and obedience are omitted or glossed over very briefly.

Altogether the 250 or so Church courts remained more successful, and more popular, than has often been allowed, despite the undoubtedly adverse effects of the Reformation on their workings. They had, admittedly, a mixed record in disciplining the clergy and in imposing religious uniformity, but they remained relatively cheap, flexible and popular courts for laymen to bring cases of family and matrimonial disputes, testamentary cases, slander and defamation. The judges appear to have done what they could to uphold the marriage bond – by stigmatising adultery and by trying to reconcile separated couples – and to clear the good names of men and women whose honour had been impugned by slander. The court records reveal that commoners were as sensitive to slights on their honour as nobles and gentry, and that the public rebuttal of slander – especially sexual slander – was of great importance to them. However, while the courts may have been welcome defenders of reputations to some, it has to be admitted that others saw them in a more repressive light. At Terling in Essex the Church courts were used, between 1583 and 1597 especially, to enforce church attendance; the victims were mostly humble villagers who preferred work, sport or the alehouse, rather than Catholic recusants.

2

To study the Church in terms of official machinery and officially imposed religious settlements is, however, to adopt a very partial view. Layfolk helped to mould the Church as well as to be moulded by it: indeed, Cross sees the sixteenth century as an important stage in 'the triumph of the laity in the English church'. The official Reformation, which may be taken as a series of measures imposed by parliaments between 1529 and 1559, was accompanied by a popular Reformation which began before it and was still in progress in the seventeenth century. At the national political level, it is true to say that the will of the monarch or the royal advisers was paramount – that every successive settlement was initiated by the Crown and was obeyed by virtually the entire nation. At the local level, however, religious beliefs and attitudes shifted from 'Catholic' to 'Protestant' at varying tempo in different areas, social groups and families. In some counties like Kent and Gloucestershire, the majority of the population, or at least of the 'political nation', appear to have been won over to Protestantism by 1553, but other areas were either more stubbornly traditional, or were successfully won back in Mary's reign, so that the Protestant breakthrough did not come until Elizabeth's reign.

Very varied influences bore on the progress of Protestantism at the local level. Access to Continental Protestant ideas gave an early radical tinge to east-coast ports like London, Yarmouth and Hull. The preference of London and the court ensured a speedier conversion of the Home Counties than of areas further away; Hampshire and Sussex were noticeably more traditional than Kent or Essex, while Lancashire and Cornwall were much more conservative still. Gloucestershire, influenced by Bishop Hooper and by the merchants of Bristol, was exceptional for its Protestantism in the West of England, which remained generally traditional in its religion. Even in Northamptonshire, a county of numerous Puritan squires and clergy, it was possible for a Midlands Catholic notable to have the freedom to inscribe 'God save the King', i.e. Philip II, on his new gatehouse in 1560 (Dingley Hall). Counties and regions were not homogeneous: social and occupational differences, family links and friendships, divided men's allegiances. At St Neots (Hunts.) in 1547 the common parishioners embraced Protestantism while the local gentry remained Catholic, whereas the Cornish revolt of 1549 revealed an opposite situation. In mid-Tudor Yorkshire the minorities who travelled and came into contact with new ideas – gentlemen who studied at Cambridge, weavers who visited Suffolk, mariners who sailed to German ports – were more likely to be Protestant than their neighbours.

The role of officers of Church and state – clergy, churchwardens, justices – was crucial in determining how far successive settlements were enforced. The beneficed clergy suffered no purges except for about 2,000 deprived by Mary (mostly just transferred to other parishes) and under 700 deprived by Elizabeth. Some 2,500 assistant priests may have been made redundant at the dissolution of the chantries in 1547–48, but about 2,000 of those eventually obtained benefices. As a result, enforcement of official policy had to be entrusted to an inherited personnel of varying beliefs. One Gloucestershire rector admitted in 1574 that he 'had said masse and did trust to lyve to saye masse againe', and another ten years after that – and twenty-five years after the 1559 settlement – was reported for possessing 'papist books' and a 'massing cake'.[11] Justices of the peace also varied in their sympathies: episcopal returns of 1564 indicated that nationally about 431 were favourable to the Elizabethan settlement, 157 hostile and 264 indifferent or neutral. The 'favourers', significantly, were in a minority in counties like Lancashire and Staffordshire where Catholicism was strong.

One frequently alleged influence on the growth of Protestantism was the massive sales of ecclesiastical property by the Crown between 1536 and 1553. A popular theory of economic determinism, dating back to at least 1616, holds that the new owners became Protestant out of fear that a Catholic restoration would imperil their gains. Some contemporaries certainly assumed that this would be the effect of the sale of monastic lands: Sir Richard Grenville, for instance, told Cromwell that he wished to buy monastic lands 'that his heirs may be of the same mind for their own profit'.[12] Such fears were a powerful restraining influence on Mary, who was able to secure reunion with Rome only on condition that the effects of the dissolutions were not reversed. But there is no evidence that religious conservatism was any bar to the acquisition or retention of monastic lands. Indeed, one of the families which profited most from the dissolutions, the Howards dukes of Norfolk, remained resolutely Catholic.

The story of Catholics and Puritans under Elizabeth has been told often enough, and need not be repeated here. What may be worth stressing, with a view to its social and economic implications, is that Englishmen were not divided into two sharply defined and warring camps, a Protestant majority and a Catholic minority. Instead there was a continuum from the small minority of open Roman Catholics on the 'right' to the even smaller minority to the 'left' who, inter-mittently from about 1566, strove to establish 'separatist' churches outside the established Church. In between were various degrees of crypto-Catholics, conservative Protestants, those who were reason-ably happy with the 1559 settlement, and those radicals or 'Puritans' who wished to purify the Church into something more fully Protes-tant, usually aiming at Calvin's Geneva as a model. The word 'Puritan' was current in England from the late 1560s among both sup-porters and opponents, although it acquired a bewildering variety of connotations.

The queen herself, for instance, retained candles and a crucifix in her private chapel, refused to legalise clerical marriage by statute, and was furious when some zealots defaced the Catholic images on Charing Cross. Yet the same Church comprehended those zealots themselves, and many men who were so hostile to Catholicism that they distrusted all medieval survivals of documents as well as images. John Stow the historian came under suspicion as a Catholic because he studied monastic chronicles, and Camden felt obliged in his *Bri-tannia* to defend himself against those 'who take it ill that I have mentioned monasteries' and who 'would have it forgotten that our ancestors were, and we are, Christians'. As the passions of the Ref-ormation abated, however, it became possible for others to join Camden in deploring the destruction of the Reformation without ceasing to be Protestants. An attack on the dissolutions – *The Falle of Religiouse Howses* – was written around 1590 by an eccentric York-shire rector, imbued with a romantic defence of the value of abbeys.[13]

Furthermore, a considerable proportion of the population may not have attended church very often, and may have paid only lip-service to its beliefs. One of the official *Homilies* published in 1563 com-plained of many people failing to attend church services, as did Lord Keeper Bacon addressing the parliament of 1572; and a bill to tighten compulsory church attendance further in 1601 was lost by only one vote. Walsingham was told in 1587 that the theatres were crowded while in the churches 'voyde seates are plentie'; and Clark has recently suggested that 'something like a fifth of the population of Kent stayed away from church on a regular basis', taking into account tramps, suburban poor, excommunicates and people in extra-parochial districts.[14]

It is almost impossible to discover whether this was simply an age-old plebeian habit coming under active disapproval, or whether it had increased when churches became centred round sermons instead of colourful ritual. The medieval 'age of faith' had never produced universal piety, but the unsettling effects of the Reformation may well have increased popular scepticism. Smith's *Discourse of the Common Weal*, though cited now for its analysis of economic problems, placed equal weight on the unsettling 'devision of opinions in mattiers of religion', which was 'not the least cause of theise uprors of the people'. Cecil complained in 1569 that 'the sincere profession of the Christian religion is much of late decayed and in place thereof partly papacy and partly paganism and irreligion are crept in'.[15]

Avowed unbelief was almost unknown, and apart from Christopher Marlowe 'it is very hard to pin down a single Elizabethan unbeliever – as opposed to numerous popular scoffers and blasphemers'. The system of oath-taking, on which government and law relied heavily, and generally with success, depended for its efficacy upon belief in the afterlife and fear of God's vengeance upon perjurers. Yet a number of both well-born and humble folk appear to have had doubts about the very existence of the supernatural. One man was accused before Star Chamber in 1596 of affirming that 'Christ was no saviour and the gospel a fable', while Lady Monson in 1597 consulted an astrologer because 'she doubteth whether there is a God'.[16]

3

Popular beliefs of a non-Christian or semi-Christian kind spanned a wide spectrum. Some were regarded as dangerous and were maintained secretly, so that evidence about them comes almost wholly from accusations and hostile reports; others were the vague province of the unlearned and were expressed in muddled and illogical ways. It would be easy to fall into the opposite errors of ignoring them or of exaggerating their importance. Fortunately Keith Thomas has provided, in *Religion and the Decline of Magic*, a massive and scrupulously documented study of them which has transformed our understanding completely. It has been justly greeted as 'a major historical achievement as a result of which the period will never look quite the same again'.[17] It is now, therefore, possible to survey the range of beliefs in broad outline with some confidence.

The medieval Church had provided a whole range of intercessory prayers and actions which supported men, especially those engaged in agriculture, in the uncertainties of their lives and livelihood. The major turning-points of the farming year were punctuated by festivals. Ploughs were blessed on Plough Monday, crops were blessed and parish boundaries perambulated at Rogationtide. Prayers were recited for rain and fine weather; fasts and intercessions were held to avert plague; holy water was sprinkled on sick cattle. Many of these rituals were officially abolished after the Reformation, or were kept only for secular reasons: the Rogationtide ceremonies were exempted from the bans on religious processions (1547 and 1559) because perambulating boundaries served a practical purpose. The result was, it has been argued, to leave a large gap in the comforting round of customs and ceremonies which gave the ordinary man confidence in an uncertain world where fire, floods, and disease of man, beast and crops were all too common. It was almost inevitable that many countryfolk, barred from using holy water on sick beasts, should turn to other sources for supernatural aid.

Fortunately for the cohesion of rural society, it proved impossible to extirpate all traditional ceremonies. The typical yeoman of James I's reign was said still to celebrate 'Rock Monday, and the wake in summer, shrovings, the wakeful ketches [catches or songs] on Christmas Eve, the hockey or seed cake . . . yet holds them no relics of popery'. Most clergy continued to read the Gospels in the fields during the Rogationtide perambulations, a practice thought to prevent evil spirits from harming crops and livestock. The official view, in the 1563 *Homilies*, was that services in the fields were thanksgivings to God and not a form of magical protection; but it proved hard to draw a clear line between the two. Another of the *Homilies* urged more diligent churchgoing 'if we desire to have seasonable weather, and thereby to enjoy the good fruits of the earth'.[18]

Some survivals, like maypoles, were clearly of pagan origin. Tolerated by the medieval Church, they naturally came under even stronger attack from Protestants than did Catholic traditions. At York the Christmas season was celebrated as a period of licence under the name of Yule. The Northern Ecclesiastical Commission in 1572 banned the popular custom by which 'twoo disguysed persons called Yule and Yule's wife shoude ryde throughe the citie very undecently'. Fordwich corporation called in aid the Southern Commission to suppress the tradition by which boys and servants beat fruit trees at Christmastide and sang 'vain songs' to encourage a good crop. At Windsor at harvest home, noted a German visitor, the countryfolk crowned the last cartload of corn with flowers and topped it with 'an image richly dressed'. And in the 1590s the men of one Yorkshire township still insisted on bringing into church 'the floure of the well' in service time, with 'pyping, blowyng of an horne, ringynge or strikinge of basons, and showtinge of people'.[19]

Witchcraft, the most notorious – and misunderstood – of popular beliefs, was of a different kind altogether. Taking it in the sense of 'black' or maleficent witchcraft, it undoubtedly had a long history, but the belief of Margaret Murray and others that witches were adherents of a surviving pagan religion is now discredited. Fear of, and persecution of, witches seems to have been a widespread phenomenon in western Europe only from about 1480 to 1650, and in England, for reasons still unclear, the 'witchcraze' was limited to between about 1550 and 1650. It was a capital offence, by statute, from 1542 to 1547 and from 1563 to 1736, though the total number of hangings under those statutes, during more than a century (1563–1685), was certainly under 1,000 and perhaps no more than 500.[20] In Essex, apparently a county with an exceptionally high rate of prosecutions, 174 persons were indicted at the assizes for black witchcraft between 1563 and 1603, but fewer than half that number were executed. The figures were very low compared to some parts of the Continent where the witchcraze was intense, like the duchy of Lorraine with 900 executions between 1574 and 1594.

Witchcraft trials and executions, outside Essex, were not common even in Elizabeth's reign, apparently the peak period; and the reality of witchcraft was also very different from the stereotype, which is drawn largely from German folklore. The typical Tudor witch was an elderly, poor female on the fringes of village society, accused of causing the death of livestock or other misfortunes by means of spells. None was accused of flying on a broomstick or meeting in a coven for devil-worship. A common accusation was of attacking images and pictures of an enemy with a view to harming them by sympathetic magic. Most people, including lawyers and theologians, believed in the reality of black witchcraft, though they differed in their interpretations. A notable exception was Reginald Scot, who in *The Discoverie of Witchcraft* (1584) denied the existence of witches' supernatural powers, and described most 'witches' as impostors, self-deluders, or innocent victims wrongly accused. Some accused witches clearly believed that they possessed occult power, but many of their confessions may rather reflect the beliefs of their interrogators.

By the end of the century some ecclesiastical judges were beginning to adopt Scot's sceptical views even when faced with voluntary confessions of supernatural powers. Bishop Bancroft of London disbelieved in the exorcisms carried out by both the Puritan Darrel and the Jesuit Weston, and his chaplain Samuel Harsnett wrote important books on their activities (1599, 1603) which questioned belief in witchcraft as well as in possession.

White witchcraft, or beneficent magic, was regarded quite differently and was widely approved. There were, according to Robert Burton, 'cunning men, wizards, and white witches . . . in every village, which, if they be sought unto, will help almost all infirmities of body and mind'. Such men or women undertook, by prayer, spells or other means, to cure sickness, to find lost goods, to identify thieves, and so on. Their activities were felt to fulfil real needs in the absence of widely available medical help, and of sufficient police forces and insurance policies to create a sense of security. Margaret Harper of Nottingham was presented before the Church courts because she 'tayketh upon hir to tell where thinges ar that be gone or loste and to heale sick folke and sayth she healeth theme by helpe of the fayries'.[21] White magic was opposed by some clergy because it represented a rival system of explanation and remedy for evil; but other churchmen saw no incompatibility between it and Christianity. Miles Blomfield, a prominent alchemist and cunning man, was chosen churchwarden at Chelmsford in 1582.

Alchemy, Blomfield's other profession, was a more learned discipline than popular magic, and was regarded by most educated people as scientific rather than superstitious. So was astrology, a doctrine of predictions based on the movements of the stars and heavenly bodies. Leading English astrologers like John Dee and Simon Forman were patronised by a wealthy and fashionable clientele, and two almanacs of the famous French astrologer Nostradamus were translated into English as soon as they appeared (1559). Naturally there was some Christian opposition to them; William Perkins regarded both astrologers and alchemists as unproductive and without proper 'callings' in life. Most astrologers tried to avoid giving offence by arguing that they predicted tendencies and inclinations, not certainties, thus avoiding a theological conflict over free will. There were also sceptical intellectuals like Sir Thomas Chaloner, who had only contempt when some sailors took seriously prophecies of tempests and shipwrecks by 'the folish Nostradamus'.[22]

Some astrologers already produced cheap and popular almanacs which gave general prophecies, to the scorn of the educated. One, publishing an almanac in 1567, admitted that 'the most parte . . . taunt, dispise and laughe to scorne our doings'. It was not entirely surprising, in view of the many safe generalisations which defied contradiction: 'in this quarter is like to happen manye controversies betwene men of welth and aucthorie [authority], with loss of goodes, but notwithstanding some men shall have good successe and profite . . .'.[23]

Nevertheless, casts – predictions for individuals based on the positions of the stars – were reputable in the highest circles, and sceptics were few. Several parish registers include details of the hour of birth of gentlemen's sons, and the position of the heavens at the time, as a basis for casts of nativities. Forman's papers show that he cast horoscopes for several leading London merchants anxious about their cargoes at sea, while Vice-Admiral Monson never put to sea without having Forman cast his horoscope. Bishop Aylmer assured Queen Elizabeth that she had nothing to fear so long as Virgo was in the ascendant, and she herself chose 14 January 1559 as the most auspicious day for her coronation on the basis of a cast made by Dee: her learned biographer, Camden, was certainly prepared to admit the influence of the stars on events, suggesting, for example, that only the conjunction of the stars could have made Elizabeth favour the earl of Leicester so greatly.[24] At a more general level, he explained outbreaks of the sweating sickness in terms of the conjunctions of planets in Scorpio, and of plague in London as a result of Saturn's position in Capricorn.

Belief in spirits, fairies, omens and prophecies remained strong both among the learned and unlearned. William Twisse (1574–1646) confessed to having been a 'rakehell' as a schoolboy, and to having been converted when he met the ghost of a schoolfriend who had been damned. The scholar-gentleman Wilfrid Holme, in his poem *The Fall and Evill Success of Rebellion*, contradicted popular prophecies not because they were inherently absurd, but because the rebels had interpreted them with reference to the wrong king. There was a well-known prophecy that Elizabeth would not complete the thirteenth year of her reign, and great rejoicings greeted its falsification on 17 November 1571. When drought persisted for more than ten weeks at Liverpool, 'certain people, dowbtyng of the goodnes of Allmightie God, were muche afraid of Domisdaye to be at hand'. And Burghley ended a long letter to Walsingham on trade and politics by commenting on a display of the northern lights: 'God sendeth us such signs but for our erudition'.[25]

Events like the destruction of St Paul's steeple in 1561, an earthquake in 1580, and storms and earthquakes in 1598, all produced sermons and pamphlets purporting to explain them, usually as 'portents' or warnings. Above all, 1588 was awaited with trepidation

throughout western Europe: its astronomical eclipses and conjunctions had for a century been prophesied to herald catastrophes, collapse of empires and even the end of the world. The editor of the
second edition of Holinshed's *Chronicles* (1587) referred to the 'old
and common prophesie, touching the yeare 1588, which is now so
rife in everie man's mouth'.[26] The Privy Council at first forbade
almanac makers to refer to it, but it proved impossible to ignore, so
two official pamphlets were sponsored to cast doubt on it. After such
a prelude, the actual events of 1588, even the defeat of the Armada,
must have seemed relatively tame.

4

Belief in the supernatural had important consequences for the lives
of the believers. The Church preached not only religious truths but
the political, social and economic consequences of those truths.
Those who resorted to astrologers and cunning men went for advice
on practical courses of action. The prevalent belief in an afterlife and
in rewards and punishments to come were a spur to action in this
world.

The first consequence of belief was, or should have been, a sense
of security and a guiding Providence. In an age when fire and flood,
pain, illness and early death were common calamities, against which
human resources were pitifully inadequate, a belief that all wrongs
would be righted in the next world and that no evil could happen
without God's permission was a powerful comfort to many. All Protestant theologians taught that nothing could happen without God's
permission, and even chance was excluded: all things happened 'not
by chance (for so nothing falleth out) but by God's great providence'.[27] Natural calamities were often viewed as God's punishments. Plague was caused, argued Hooper, in *An Homelye to be Read
in the Tyme of Pestylence* (1553), not by chance or by the stars, but
by God in His displeasure at human sin. The vicar of Cranbrook
(Kent) had no hesitation in attributing a plague in 1597–98 to human
vices: had it not begun in the house of a receiver of stolen goods,
and ended in that of a drunkard with a loose wife?

The reverse side was, however, that many others required a belief
that could protect them in this world. To some extent the Catholic
Church had met this need more effectively than the Protestant, by
its prayers, intercessions and exorcisms for all occasions. Protestants
accepted the use of prayer to guard against any calamity, but rejected
most of the magical aids which meant more to the mass of the pop-

ulation. Many were slowly won over to the more stoical Protestant attitudes; but others resorted to magicians to perform the role relinquished by the priests. Furthermore, all English Protestants until the early seventeenth century taught the Calvinist doctrine of predestination, which was incorporated into the official Thirty-nine Articles. This again proved a stumbling block to some Christians, who either despaired of salvation or argued that, on the contrary, a justified man could do no wrong and therefore adopted amoral attitudes.

A more unarguably positive effect of the Reformation in England was the encouragement of literacy through the use of a vernacular Bible and Prayer Book. How widely and how quickly Bible-reading penetrated society is suggested vividly by an inscription by a Gloucestershire shepherd in a history book, written during the short period when Henry VIII revoked free access to the Bible:

I bout thys boke when the Testament was obberagatyd [abrogated], that shepeherdys myght not red hit. I prey God amende that blyndnes. Wryt by Robert Wyllyams keppynge shepe uppon Seynbury Hill, 1546.[28]

The influence of the English Bible upon both the religious and secular history of England was considerable. It helped to produce great literature; it helped to produce religious pluralism and separatism, for it was a whole library of books in one, which the new readership could interpret in many different ways. Again, the result was not what the early patrons and translators intended. Their belief was that all would see the same (Protestant) truth once they read it with an open mind. Religious diversity and toleration was far from their minds.

Yet the introduction of a vernacular Bible and liturgy, while liberating to many, was a stumbling-block to others. In 1570 many Lancastrians 'utterly refused to attend divine service in the English tongue'. To an English conservative the change was unsettling enough, if comprehensible: to a Welsh or Cornish speaker, able to follow the familiar Latin service better than the English, it was still more of an affront. The western rebels in 1549 demanded the restoration of Latin services, adding that 'we the Cornyshe men (whereof certen of us understande no Englysh) utterly refuse thys newe Englysh'.[29] The Welsh fared better after an initial attempt to make English the sole language of worship; parliament and convocation in 1563 authorised Welsh translations of the Bible and Prayer Book, and made Welsh the language of worship from St David's Day 1566. Although progress was slow – the whole Bible was not available until 1588 – the concession helped to avoid a repetition of the Irish policy, where Catholicism and nationalism were driven into a powerful and subversive alliance.

Both for the literate and the illiterate, in any event, hearing sermons was at least as important as Bible-reading. The 'prophesyings' of the 1560s and 1570s were stimulated by a hunger for the preaching and interpreting of the Word of God, and although Elizabeth suppressed them, preaching remained actively encouraged by most bishops. 'Preaching during the Elizabethan and Jacobean periods was not a puritan preserve but part of of the life of the church. Elizabeth's reaction to the emphasis upon preaching in her new church was emotional and ill informed and, moreover, it has misled successive generations of ecclesiastical historians.' Naturally the bishops, like the queen, were well aware of the power of the pulpit, and were quick to check preachers who stepped out of line. The minister of Penrith (Cumberland) had to do public penance for having castigated his bishop in a sermon as an avaricious 'moneymaister', and another preacher's sermon came under scrutiny when he uttered the socially dangerous sentiment that 'there is defecte in magistrats in punishinge poore men and bearing with rich offendours'.[30]

Preaching was a popular activity – one of Elizabeth's reasons for suppressing prophesyings was that they distracted 'great numbers of our people, especially the vulgar sort' – and the Paul's Cross sermons in London were only the most notable of the regular sermons which drew large crowds. Admittedly many clergy were not licensed to preach by the bishops, not being thought sufficiently learned, but the numbers licensed were considerable and increased with the growth of clerical education: by 1603 4,804 parish clergy out of 9,254 (52%) were licensed. Their activities were supplemented by lecturers, preaching clergymen without benefices, who were often hired to preach in corporate towns and market towns. The parish of St Antholin's, London, endowed a lectureship as early as Edward's reign, and by 1583 nearly one-third of the City parishes had followed suit. The corporation of Ipswich paid a lecturer from 1560, Leicester by 1562 and Colchester by 1564, and by the end of Elizabeth's reign nearly every large town had one.

The Reformation is often seen as a stage on the way from superstition to rationalism and a 'scientific' attitude to life; and there is an element of truth in it. Puritan theologians consciously attacked the irrational elements of the old religion; as Perkins put it (1591) 'if a man will but take a view of all Popery, he shall easily see that a great part of it is mere magic'. And it would be wrong to see this as an intellectual attitude merely imposed from above: 'there is no denying the remarkable speed with which the distaste for any religious rite smacking of magic had spread among some of the common people'. While some countryfolk clung to bells, images and holy water, others from a very early date were making a crude but vigorous rejection of the same popular culture. Holy oil was 'of no virtue but meet to grease sheep'; urine was as efficacious as holy water.[31]

Yet Protestantism should not be depicted as more inherently 'modern' or 'scientific' than Catholicism. Many Protestant intellectuals rejected the magic of popery while accepting the reality of astrology and witchcraft. Sir Thomas Smith called astrology 'the most cunning art of lying' (*ingeniosissimam artem mentiendi*), but still turned to it for guidance whenever his fortunes were low. Belief in witchcraft appears to have increased during the Reformation, before ebbing in the seventeenth century. In some ways the logical extremists of Protestantism, parting company with common sense as logical extremists are apt to do, had a reactionary rather than a progressive effect. They argued that all calamities came from God, and therefore that the *only* valid remedy was prayer, and repentance for the sins that had provoked the evil. Some zealots refused to accept any human precautions against plague outbreaks, like isolation measures, public cleansing and medical treatment; and one preacher was imprisoned in 1603 for maintaining that plague struck only the sinful, and that the faithful need take no precautions.

The social and economic consequences of the Reformation and the triumph of Protestantism were much disputed at the time. Catholic apologists under Elizabeth I, publishing clandestinely or from exile, saw God punishing the realm for its schism. Men were building rich dwellings instead of new churches, and existing churches were being neglected or prophaned; thanks to the emphasis on salvation by faith rather than works, the charitable impulse had cooled, and money was spent on self-indulgence rather than on the poor and the sick; atheism, swearing, blasphemy and sexual immorality were on the increase. Most Protestants vigorously rebutted these changes, though a significant minority tried to shame their fellow-believers by admitting that some evils had grown despite 'the new light of the Gospel'. John Stow was convinced that charitable giving in London had declined; and Elizabeth herself contrasted the 'curiosity and cost' lavished on private mansions with 'the unclean and negligent order and spare keeping of the houses of prayer'.[32]

Such polemics, which continued between Catholic and Protestant historians until early this century, are now out of fashion. It is generally accepted that new churches ceased to be built after about 1540 because there were sufficient, rather than from declining piety; and while many complaints of neglected fabrics occur under Elizabeth, the same had been true of the fifteenth century. It was also, of course, the case that churches became much cheaper to maintain once images, candles, chantries and other Catholic rituals were abolished. There is now a consensus that many charitable and educational institutions – schools, universities, almshouses, hospitals, endowments for the poor – suffered in the short term, between 1536 and 1553, partly because many were under ecclesiastical control and were seized during the Crown's dissolutions.

Between about 1570 and 1640, however, there was a considerable recovery which at least made up the lost ground and perhaps went well beyond it. There are still numerous surviving schools and almshouses founded in the late sixteenth century, often with an explicitly religious impulse. Typical of many are the attractive Gell's bedehouses facing the churchyard at Wirksworth (Derbyshire), founded in 1584 for six 'pore impotent men' and inscribed

> Yf thou wilt Our Lord please
> Help the pore in ther disease.

W. K. Jordan, in a series of detailed and influential studies, asserts that philanthropic and charitable giving between 1560 and 1660 was 'unprecedented', and attributes it largely to 'Puritan' impulses. The attribution is unproven, the figures misleading. If it were possible to adjust his data satisfactorily for inflation, and to allow for the increasing volume of written records and the extent of ground to be made up after the losses of the dissolutions, his 'vast outpouring' would appear much more modest. It is already clear from recent work on late medieval schools that they were far more numerous than Jordan and others had realised. And it is only by straining his evidence that he can attribute most of the giving to 'Puritans' on any definition of the term.

Jordan's work is typical of many in seeing Puritanism as a key force in social and economic change in the later sixteenth and early seventeenth centuries. Puritans are credited with making belief centre on individual thought and freedom, and on the godly household, with regular family prayers, an ascetic lifestyle, and an emphasis on labouring at one's 'calling' or vocation. They are seen as having pressed for hard work, thrift, sobriety, sabbath observance, and an educated clergy and laity; and against idleness, swearing, sexual immorality, gambling, stage-plays and ostentatious luxury. It is, however, difficult to test such generalisations because 'Puritan' has proved almost impossible to define, both at the time and since, and some historians are now tempted to abandon the term altogether.

It is all too easy to construct a coherent Puritan 'progressive' position by judicious selection of comments from a wide range of theological writers who are called 'Puritan' when their arguments suit the theory. Knappen, one of the shrewdest historians of the movement, while convinced of the objective reality of Puritanism, warned that 'there were many Puritan spirits but . . . no Puritan spirit'. Its central theme was individual salvation and not secular change; its economic teaching was 'practically indistinguishable' from the traditional teaching of the medieval Church, and was indeed 'ultra-conservative and eventually futile'. If intellectual pluralism and freedom eventually came from the clash of Puritans and their enemies, that was no intention of the Puritans, who believed passionately in their truth, based on their interpretation of the Bible, and in censorship of rival falsehoods. They had a zeal for learning, but it was generally narrow, shallow and remarkably traditional.[33]

There are similar difficulties in identifying 'Puritanism' or 'the Protestant spirit' with the rise of a middle class, a spirit of thrift and enterprise, and the growth of capitalism. Marx identified the Reformation in European terms with the rise of a middle class or bourgeoisie, and many subsequent writers, both Whiggish and Marxian, have applied the correlation to England. Pollard, for instance, wrote in 1907 of 'the advent of the middle class' and attributed the Reformation to it in part. Such interpretations, as elaborated by recent scholars like Hill, would see the rising middle class helping to precipitate first the establishment of Protestantism, and then the more radical or Puritan 'revolution' that was attempted under Elizabeth and James I and then, successfully, in the 1640s and 1650s. There is, however, no reason to think that the Tudor rise of the middle class was other than a 'myth', as Hexter puts it; and the bourgeoisie was never dominant in early modern England, although it is true that Puritanism became especially entrenched in London and in active commercial centres like Northampton and Gloucester.

Similar theories have postulated a causal link between Protestantism (or, more specifically, Calvinism or English Puritanism) and the rise of capitalism. Weber's original thesis of 1904–5 asserted – to simplify a complex argument – that 'the Protestant ethic' of the 'calling' and of predestination was a necessary precondition for the rise of capitalism: or rather, of western European 'rational bourgeois capitalism', since he was not so naive as to believe that capitalism did not exist before the Reformation. In his lectures of 1922 (published as *Religion and the Rise of Capitalism*), Tawney developed a rather different thesis with particular reference to England. He argued, correctly, that the early Protestant theologians were economic conservatives, more hostile to the taking of interest, for instance, than some medieval Schoolmen. Gradually, however, Calvinism and English Puritanism adapted themselves to the burgeoning commercial ethos, and made themselves creeds suitable to the capitalist and the entrepreneur. Tawney's position was in turn modified by an influential essay of Christopher Hill in 1961. Hill realised that only a minority were ever 'Puritans' in any sense, but argued that their doctrines of discipline and industry appealed to a very broad public, the 'industrious, middling sort of people'. And although Protestantism need not necessarily have led to capitalism, it did undermine obstacles to economic advance which Catholicism had impeded.

Tawney's work has been enormously influential, and although much of his argument, like Weber's, is now discredited by further research, there are still many historians who cling to a causal connection, or at least a meaningful correlation, between Protestantism and capitalism. A full refutation of the concept would take a great deal of space, and it is fortunately possible to refer to Samuelsson's work for a convincing demolition of the whole idea. The best epitaph on the whole controversy is given by Elton: 'Answers have been devised for non-existent questions. The attraction of the universal generalisation has, as so often, proved too much for the sceptical spirit which alone saves the historian from falling into the pitfalls dug by his own, very necessary, imagination.'[34]

Yet it is possible to abandon the debate while recognising that it has generated light as well as heat, and Hill's demonstration of the connection between English Protestantism and industriousness remains important. Before the Reformation forty-three days (other than Sundays) had been kept as festivals and holy days, and thus as 'holidays' in the modern sense. A Protestant economic treatise of 1549 urged that twenty of them should be 'bestoide in labor' and calculated that it would make the realm richer by £500,000 a year; and in line with such thinking a statute of 1552 reduced them to twenty-seven.[35] Zealous Protestants under Elizabeth took this further: they often worked on the retained holy days, being extremely scrupulous about not working on the sabbath. When the fall of a gallery killed eight spectators at a London bear-baiting in 1583, John Field was quick to publish a demonstration that it was no accident but a divine warning to sabbath-breakers.

The Puritans' purpose was theological and not economic, but the result was to strengthen the idea of regular labour and a six-day week. Many saints' days had been 'cut off', wrote Nicholas Bownde, because they had hindered men 'from the necessary works of their callings'. It became a Puritan commonplace that everyone must have a 'calling' or personal vocation, a conviction best expressed in William Perkins's *Treatise of the Vocations, or Callings of Men* (c. 1600): 'Every person of every degree, state, sexe, or condition without exception, must have some personall and particular calling to walke in.' Even peers felt the need to justify their position either by public service or estate management. The first Lord Spencer erected at Althorp a stone inscribed 'Up and bee doing and God will prosper.'[36]

The Reformation was beyond question one of the most important events in English history. And yet the most profound consequences of Church and Christian belief on Tudor society remained the same before and after the Reformation – a belief in ultimate standards beyond this world, a limitation of some kind on selfish and sinful behaviour (however frail that limitation might sometimes be), and a strengthening of the bonds of loyalty and reciprocal service between sovereign and subject, master and servant, husband and wife, parent and child. The Hull bricklayers' clerk who wrote that 'as dere unto God is the poorest beggar as the most pompous prince living in the worlde' was rehearsing an accepted doctrine of spiritual equality which put some constraints on the arrogance of the powerful. To ignore or minimise such influences can distort our understanding of Tudor society. Stone's assertion that 'the Elizabethan village was a place filled with malice and hatred, its only unifying bond being the occasional episode of mass hysteria' against witches, is a caricature of the reality, and entirely neglects the influences making for charity and good neighbourliness.[37]

There is some literary evidence from zealous Protestant preachers that they feared a weakening of social and moral discipline under the impact of religious conflict and uncertainty. Latimer preached before Edward VI in 1550 that 'every man, if he have but a small cause, will cast off his old wife, and take a new'. But this was hysterical hyperbole: there is more evidence for a renewed Puritanism (in a modern sense) at the Reformation than for laxer morals: several town corporations, for example, tried to abolish brothels in the 1540s and 1550s. There was apparently a rise in illegitimacy in the late sixteenth century, but it rose in parallel with increased marital fertility rather than as an alternative, and the proportion remained modest by twentieth-century standards. What the literary evidence shows clearly, as in the nineteenth century, is an increased moral fervour rather than declining moral standards.

Christianity remained far and away the most potent intellectual influence on Tudor Englishmen; and all allowance made for religious minorities and for magical and non-Christian beliefs, the Church remained central to the lives of the great majority. The religious passions which divided Tudor Englishmen were bitter because they agreed that religious truth was enormously important; and they would not have recognised themselves in the works of many post-Christian historians who treat Puritanism and other strands of belief as fundamentally the products of social and economic forces. The neglect of the Elizabethan Church by twentieth-century historians (there has been no good general account since Bishop Frere's in 1904) seems to reflect a belief that the Church was far more influenced by lay society than vice versa, a very debatable proposition. It is impossible to make sense of Tudor attitudes to all major issues without recognising that the Church and the beliefs it proclaimed were of enormous importance.

Chapter 12

Culture and society

Few periods have been more inimical to the visual arts than the middle years of the sixteenth century in England. In a little over twenty years there were four different rulers, . . . four major rebellions and three changes of religion. Only when building, an invaluable index to the rise and decline of artistic activity, begins again extensively in the eighties had equilibrium returned.

Roy Strong, 1969[1]

Dan Chaucer, the first warbler, whose sweet breath
Preluded those melodious bursts, that fill
The spacious times of great Elizabeth
With sounds that echo still.

Tennyson, *A Dream of Fair Women* (1853)

1

Elizabeth's reign is associated readily enough with a literary golden age, but other artistic and cultural achievements are less widely known. Furthermore, culture in the widest sense was both broader and narrower, both richer and poorer, than today. The earl of Leicester – no outstanding intellectual – was fluent in Italian, and in middle life started to learn Latin before abandoning it for geometry. Yet it was also an age when nobles and commoners alike delighted in cock-fighting and in baiting bulls and bears. Elizabeth spent her time 'watching bears and bulls fighting dogs', grumbled a Spanish envoy in 1576;[2] but it was the same queen who read Greek daily with her old tutor Ascham whenever he was at court. The Renaissance belief in the 'complete man' prevented any sharp separation between sports and pastimes and more sober pursuits. Ascham was as proud of his treatise on archery, *Toxophilus*, as of his other writings; and the queen admired skill in dancing as much as in languages or theology.

Sports and pastimes varied widely between different regions and social groups. Hawking and hunting (the deer rather than the fox) were passions with many gentlemen. Sir Thomas Cockaine, who succeeded to his Derbyshire estate in 1538, could write in his *Short Trea-*

tise of Hunting (1591) that 'for this fiftie two yeres . . . I have hunted the bucke in summer, and the hare in winter, two yeares onely excepted' when he was abroad on military service. Organised horse-racing was started by gentlemen and urban corporations: York's in 1530 is the first known, and Carlisle still possesses two Elizabethan silver-gilt bells used as prizes for the winners. Fencing, tennis and bowls were becoming popular among the well-to-do; archery and fishing were popular at all levels; wrestling, foot-racing and football among ordinary people. Leland noted of one Herefordshire hill-fort that 'the people of Leonminstar thereabout cum ons a yere to this place to sport and play', and the annual Cotswold Games which Robert Dover started about 1604 were probably a more organised form of a widespread community activity.[3]

Popular culture in Tudor England has been much less studied than learned culture; hence Peter Burke's wide-ranging *Popular Culture in Early Modern Europe* (1978) includes few examples from sixteenth-century England. The existence of a rich and varied repertoire of ballads, songs and stories is well-established, but these activities were in the main confined to the world of oral transmission and were either ignored or treated with contempt by literate observers. Latimer found that he could not preach in one village in 1549 because the parishioners were celebrating 'Robyn Hoode's day', and Nicholas Bownde observed in 1606 that many people knew more of Robin Hood than they did of the Bible: yet few printed ballads and plays of his deeds survive before the end of the sixteenth century, and many may never have been written down. There were many travelling players, entertainers and storytellers whose activities were noticed chiefly when the government took fright at the spread of seditious ideas. One of the few Tudor minstrels with an identifiable personality was Richard Sheale, a 'merry knave' (clown) whose version of the *Ballad of Chevy Chase* was preserved by Bishop Percy.

Any division of Tudor culture into 'literary' and 'popular' (the 'Great Tradition' and 'Little Tradition' of Redfield's *Peasant Society and Culture*) is too simple. Gentry and clergy participated in popular festivals and rituals; a considerable minority of humble folk had access to books and could read if not write; and there were various levels of both literary and popular culture. For instance, there was a thriving market in ephemeral popular literature, which attracted the scorn of learned writers but which was defended by others as providing instruction or enjoyment. Such were the 'uncountable rabble' who, complained William Webbe, 'be most busy to stuffe every [book] stall full of grosse devises and unlearned pamphlets', while the witty scholar Thomas Nashe lamented that 'every grosse braind idiot is suffered to come into print'. But this was academic jealousy and snobbery. As one of Nashe's targets, Barnabe Rich, replied, 'such is the delicacie of our readers . . . that there are none may be alowed of to write, but such as have been trained at schoole with Pallas . . .'[4]

The high culture of the Tudor age was certainly learned, and it assumed a thorough grounding in the literature and history of Greece and Rome. It is often described as 'Renaissance', a term implying both a recognition of the values of Latin and Greek culture and a strong Italian influence. It is true that from the early years of the century foreign influences in the arts became fashionable, either directly from Italy, or indirectly via France and the Empire. The first arrival of the Renaissance style in England is usually dated from 1510, when Henry VIII summoned Torrigiano and other Italian artists to construct his father's tomb. Elyot grumbled in his *Governour* (1531) that Englishmen were compelled, 'if we wyll have any thinge well paynted, kerved, or embrawdred, to abandone our owne countraymen and resorte unto straungers'.

Yet artists and craftsmen under Elizabeth displayed a strong continuity with their medieval English past, absorbing only what suited them of new continental influences. The greatest poem of the age, *The Faerie Queene*, owed as much to medieval allegory as to the epics of Ariosto and Tasso which it consciously imitated; and most architecture derived more from English Perpendicular than from Italian Renaissance. Summerson has warned against the too free use of 'Renaissance' in an architectural context:

In France and England during the sixteenth century the artistic products of the Renaissance *and its sequel* profoundly affected the arts, but the use and enjoyment of those products is not necessarily analogous to their use and enjoyment in Italy. This applies especially to the use in Elizabethan times of Flemish and German versions of Italian Mannerism, anti-Renaissance in origin and remote from the Renaissance spirit in their later development.[5]

Two massive and permanent changes did, however, affect both high and popular culture in a way that can fairly be described as revolutionary, the art of printing and the triumph of the vernacular. Far more books and pamphlets were published, and on a widening range of subjects. A little over 5,000 English books which survive were published between the 1470s and 1557, some 2,760 in the first half of Elizabeth's reign (1558–79), and 4,370 in the second (1580–1603). The number of books printed is a matter of guesswork. The size of an average edition of an Elizabethan book was apparently about 1,250, implying a total of some 9 million books published during the queen's reign. The figure sounds impressive, though it represents an average of only one or two books per head for a population of 4 million over a generation and a half.

Yet the impact of the printed word was incalculable, both among the minority of book-owners and the rest of the population. Foxe the martyrologist gave thanks to God 'for the excellent art of printing', while Bacon listed it (with gunpowder and the mariner's compass) among the three greatest inventions of the age. Foxe's own *Acts and Monuments*, despite its cost of over £6, sold more than 10,000 copies by 1603; and such a publication was unusually expensive. Theological tracts could be produced for 2*d* – the Exeter Catholics branded their Protestant opponents as 'two penye booke men'[6] – and ballads for 1*d*. Even these prices were beyond the poor; and but many more could hear books and ballads read than could buy them, and of course they could hear the Bible which was placed in every parish church.

The well-to-do and educated had the opportunity to build up large private libraries. Sir William More of Loseley, a Surrey gentleman and JP, possessed some 140 printed books and manuscripts in 1556; one in three Canterbury men leaving wills by 1600 had books recorded in their inventories; and a Worcester vicar owned about 370 books at his death in 1610. Two peers – Lumley and Burghley – possessed over 1,000 books, while the largest collection of all, John Dee's at Mortlake, numbered over 4,000. Booksellers' stocks were becoming larger and more varied, not only in the capital but in towns of any size. Random survivals of stationers' inventories credit Roger Ward of Shrewsbury (1585) with nearly 2,500 volumes in stock, and John Foster of York (1616) with approaching 3,000.

The printing revolution was facilitated by the triumph of the English language. Most major literary works were published in Latin in the first half of the century, and both Elyot and Ascham felt obliged to defend themselves for writing in English. As more and more writers followed their example and wrote for the wider readership of English readers, the language became enriched by a host of words from classical and modern languages; English vocabulary nearly doubled in volume during the century. Early Tudor writers apologised for the roughness and homeliness of the language; Elizabethans like Richard Carew (*The Excellencie of the English Tongue*, 1595–96) thought it not inferior to Greek or Latin in suppleness and beauty. Furthermore, although Elizabethan spelling seems today arbitrary and inconsistent, it represented a considerable improvement on early Tudor practice, thanks largely to the influence of books by John Hart (1551, 1569, 1570).

Many books published in English in the second half of the century were translations, including some of the most influential, like Hoby's translation of Castiglione's *Il Cortegiano* as *The Courtyer* (1561), or North's *Plutarch's Lives* on which Shakespeare drew so heavily. Holland, the 'translator general of the age', translated Livy, Pliny and many other classical authors, as well as providing the first English version of Camden's *Britannia*. Of the 153 medical titles published between 1486 and 1604, exactly one-third (51) were explicit translations, while others, though claiming to be by English authors, were borrowed from continental sources. Lodge's *Treatise of the Plague* (1603), sometimes thought to refer to English conditions, is one example. At the same period the older municipal archives of towns like Chester and Exeter were translated from Latin and French for the 'better understandinge' of city councillors. The minister of All Saints, Derby, decided in 1610 that there was 'no reason why a register for English people should be written in Latin'.[7]

2

All could understand their mother tongue spoken, but reading and writing it was another matter. Evidence of literacy is patchy and ambiguous; indirect evidence of the extent of literacy – literary evidence, the volume of book publishing, and the extent of book ownership and of formal education – is often unsatisfactory. Inventories tend to omit books; the growing output of books could have been absorbed by a small fraction of the population; and statistics of schools are not able to include all the petty schools at which basic literacy was taught. Cressy prefers to such indicators the 'direct' evidence of ability to write one's name. Many contemporary documents were attested by men and women with marks or signatures, usually taken to represent the illiterate and literate respectively. This assumption can also be questioned; many children appear to have mastered reading (which was taught first) but not writing, while a few illiterates at least could sign their name.[8] Nevertheless, counts of signatures probably do correlate loosely with literacy; they furnish large samples on a uniform basis, and they reveal social, sexual and geographical variations which make sense.

All recent research on frequency of signatures concludes, not surprisingly, that literacy was higher among men than women, among clergy than laity, among nobles and gentry than commoners, in London than in the countryside, and in the South and East than the North and West. (Of the four dioceses sampled by Cressy, illiteracy proved far higher in Durham than in London, Norwich or Exeter, even among the gentry.) The pressure to acquire literacy depended on many things, including wealth, leisure, reputation, religious zeal, and the desire for social and economic advancement. Influential books like Elyot's *Governour* (1531) argued that nobles and gentlemen must be well educated if they were to share in government. Protestant theologians urged men and women to read so as to study the Bible; clergy, bureaucrats, merchants and professional men needed literacy for their occupations. Conversely, many poor could not afford either the time or the money needed for their children's education, requiring their labour or earnings from an early age; labourers had little need of literacy in their work; and the general attitude of society was also that women needed education less than men.

Nobles and gentlemen were almost all literate by mid-century. Aubrey maintained that the first earl of Pembroke (1507–70), though a Privy Councillor, 'could neither write nor read', but Pembroke's signatures survive to cast doubt on the story. His fellow-councillor Norfolk, imprisoned in the Tower in 1547, asked for books so that he might read himself to sleep as was his habit. By that date all leading courtiers and officials needed to be literate, and even at the local level the skill was coming to be thought necessary, or at least socially desirable, for magistrates and town councillors. Of forty-seven Yarmouth councillors endorsing a document in 1577, thirty-seven signed their names. John Shakespeare, the poet's father, who was a Stratford alderman from 1565 to 1586, always marked rather than signed documents, and was probably illiterate; but such a lack of accomplishment was becoming out of date. There was a defensive ring to the description of Robert Brerewood, mayor of Chester (1584), as one who 'could nether write nor read yet was . . . very brave and gentile otherwise'.[9] In London, where the majority of craftsmen and tradesmen were literate (60% of Cressy's sample in the 1580s, 80% in the 1600s), not a single merchant, vintner or grocer sampled was illiterate.

In the countryside, the majority of yeomen sampled were illiterate at the start of Elizabeth's reign but literate by its end. Spufford's work on Cambridgeshire suggests that it was the more prosperous yeomen who demanded education. At Willingham, for instance, where the inhabitants endowed a school by public subscription in 1593, most of the large donations came from half-yardlanders, who 'could afford to give sums which amounted to more than two years' rent in most cases'. Some well-to-do husbandmen were also willing to buy education: John Browne of Wigston Magna left 20s to his young son, asking that he 'be kept to scoole tyll he cane wrytt and reade'. But of 558 Yorkshire tenants of the queen who subscribed to petitions in 1562 – most of whom would have been husbandmen – only 6 made signatures rather than marks.[10] And Cressy's samples for the later part of Elizabeth's reign indicate only 10 per cent literacy among husbandmen in the Durham and Exeter dioceses, rising to 20 per cent in the diocese of London with its proximity to the capital.

Literacy appears to have increased considerably in the second half of the sixteenth century. Cressy suggests, by plotting signatures against the age of the witnesses concerned, a sharp rise in literacy in the 1560s and 1570s, followed by a levelling off, or even a regression, between 1580 and 1610. Such a chronology has yet to be confirmed by other studies; but the long-term increase is not disputed. It raises questions about the provision of education, especially elementary education.

Formal education in sixteenth-century schools is still often described as a two-tier system, with elementary schools, largely unendowed, catering for reading and writing in English, and endowed grammar schools where teaching was exclusively in Latin; but this is a wild oversimplification. There were local and parish schools (often called song schools before the Reformation and petty schools after it) catering largely for reading, writing and simple arithmetic. There were grammar schools teaching exclusively in Latin and largely as a preparation for university, although most also included English teaching. But some grammar schools either included an elementary school or had one attached to them. A school list for Wolverhampton Grammar School in 1609 – a rare survival – shows that the 69 pupils ranged from a petties class of 11 (mostly aged from 6 to 10) studying basic Latin or even basic English, to a 'head form' of 2 boys of 17 and 18 studying Greek and advanced Latin. Not all petty schools were unendowed, nor all grammar schools endowed. There were other, private, grammar schools which depended on pupils' fees; and there was a whole range of private schools and academies, including some which specialised in teaching letter-writing, accounts and business studies.

Almost certainly many who could read or write learned to do so in parish schools, which were often held in the church or in the master's house. Thomas Hobbes the philosopher 'went to schoole in Westport church' from the age of four to eight (*c*. 1592–96): 'by that time he could read well, and number four figures'.[11] Such schools far outnumbered the grammar schools; indeed, there must have been something like one elementary school for every parish or every two parishes in most areas. Of the 266 towns and parishes in the Canterbury diocese, at least 113 (42%) had a schoolmaster at some time in the period 1561–1600, as against a total of 12 grammar schools. Of the 388 parishes in the diocese of Lichfield, at least 200 (52%) had a schoolmaster at some time between 1584 and 1642. South Cambridgeshire was apparently better off, with 23 parishes (21%) having a school in continuous existence between 1574 and 1628, and 87 (80%) having one at some time. And the city of York in Elizabeth's reign possessed at least 8 or 9 parish schools as well as 2 grammar schools. Most of these statistics are based on the evidence of licences to teach issued by the bishops, and are likely to be minimum figures: the licensing system seems to have been less effective with petty and private schools than with grammar schools.

Furthermore, much educational instruction was not given in schools at all. The children of nobles and gentlemen were often tutored privately in their own homes or in households which specialised in bringing up boys and girls, such as those of Lord Burghley and the earl of Huntingdon. And for many commoners, basic instruction in literacy and in craft skills was given in the home or the workshop. The practice has naturally left little record, but wills and inventories occasionally hint at it. In the 1570s, a York canon made a draper a guardian to his son, asking him 'to lerne hyme to write and to use hyme as hys owne', while a Gloucestershire man owed money to a yeoman 'for techinge of his sonne to wrytte and reade'. John Hart published in 1570 a simple method of learning to read English which, he said, any literate member of a household could teach to the others. Edmund Coote's *English Schoole-Master* could be used for home instruction as well as for the school; and he intended it also to be used by 'taylors, weavers, shoppe-keepers, seamsters' and others for teaching their apprentices. He promised the craftsman-teacher that 'thou mayest sit on thy shop boord, at thy loomes or at thy needle, and never hinder thy worke to heare thy schollers...'[12] That it served a need is indicated by the fact that it went through twenty-five editions between 1596 and 1625.

The teaching of apprentices and servants by masters (which could include basic literacy as well as craft techniques) was a common alternative to formal schooling. Chester corporation ruled in 1539 that 'every chylde or chyldryn beinge of the age of vi yeres or above upon every wourkeday shalbe set to the schoule . . . or else to sum other good virtuus laboure, craft or occupacyon'. How many children actually profited from formal schooling, even at an elementary level, depended on whether they could be spared from home or work, and on whether they could take up free school places or could afford school fees. Relatively few schools had funds to aid poor boys to attend school, as was recognised by the corporation of Norwich in drawing up their regulations for the poor in 1571. 'Selecte women' were to be paid to teach letters to 'the most porest children whose parentes are not hable to pay for theyr lear[n]inge'.[13] Bequests for this purpose did multiply, however, in the late sixteenth century; typical was that of a Staffordshire yeoman who in 1603 left money for a schoolmaster to teach ten poor Wednesbury children free of charge.

Girls generally enjoyed less education than boys, and female literacy as measured by signatures was considerably lower than that of males. Only the London diocese was exceptional, where 16 per cent of a sample of women in the 1580s could sign their names. Nevertheless, a significant minority of women at all social levels except the very poorest did acquire some education, and Richard Mulcaster, in his *Positions* (1581), implied that it was common for girls to learn to read and write. Humanist writers like More and Elyot had argued for equal opportunities for both sexes, a movement which bore fruit in a group of distinguished women like the daughters of Sir Anthony Cooke (two of whom married Cecil and Sir Nicholas Bacon) and Queen Elizabeth herself. Lady Margaret Hoby, the daughter of a minor northern gentleman, learned to read, write, keep accounts and practise surgery, as her surviving diary makes clear.

Many village schools, such as that at Wigston Magna, were attended by girls as well as boys, and a few grammar schools are also known to have taken girls. Other girls, at least among the gentry, were privately taught by tutors or relatives. Grace Sharington of Lacock Abbey has left a picture in her journal of how she was educated by her aunt:

When she did see me idly disposed she would set me to cypher with the pen and to cast up and prove great sums and accounts . . . and other times let me read in Dr. Turner's *Herball* and Bartholomew Vigoe . . . and other times set me to some curious work, for she was an excellent workwoman in all kinds of needlework.[14]

A few women were enabled to write for publication. Margaret Tyler translated *The First Part of the Mirrour of Princely Deeds and Knighthood* (1578), defending in her preface the right of women to read and write, while Esther Sowernam wrote a spirited reply (*Ester hath hang'd Haman*, 1617) to Joseph Swetnam's *Arraignment of Idle, Froward and Unconstant Women* (1615).

Education is better recorded after the Reformation, and the apparently larger number of schools and schoolmasters has encouraged talk of an 'educational revolution' between about 1560 and 1640. However, the increased documentation reflects partly the general growth of record-keeping, and partly a concern by ecclesiastical and secular authorities to control and standardise education in an age of religious conflict. Uniformity in teaching was ensured by the use of a single authorised textbook of grammar in every grammar school from 1540 to the end of the century and beyond. Many leading schools were refounded, or at least given new royal statutes, in the middle of the century. And control of schoolmasters was ensured after 1556, when a synod forbade anyone to teach until he had been examined and licensed by a bishop – a policy for Catholic orthodoxy which Elizabeth was only too happy to continue for opposite reasons. 'It was at the Reformation – not, as is still universally taught, in the nineteenth century – that state intervention in English education began.'[15]

What is not clear, despite nearly a century of scholarly investigation, is whether the Reformation was beneficial or harmful to education in the short run. Some schools, though only a minority, had been managed by monasteries and by chantry priests; at the dissolutions of the 1530s and 1540s some were permanently suppressed, some continued and some revived after a period of lapse. A. F. Leach (1851–1915), the pioneer historian of grammar schools, exaggerated the number of chantry schools and therefore the losses at the dissolution. W. K. Jordan, erring in the opposite direction, minimised the number of pre-Reformation schools and so overstated the increase under Elizabeth and the early Stuarts. The debate was, in any case, centred almost exclusively on endowed grammar schools, ignoring unendowed and elementary schools.

More recently Orme and others, investigating the total number of schools in selected areas, have demonstrated that the truth lies somewhere in between. Schools were multiplying in the fifteenth and early sixteenth centuries, and the total number by 1530 was considerable. During the dissolutions many schools were continued or refounded, including the so-called King Edward VI schools, but others were closed, giving point to the angry outbursts of Latimer and Lever in 1550 about the despoiling of schools. Lever attacked especially the king's sale of the lands on which Sedbergh School depended, shaming the government into re-endowing the school in 1551. However, private endowments rapidly made up the losses and soon exceeded them, so that the whole fifteenth and sixteenth centuries can be viewed as a long period of increasing school foundations, only temporarily interrupted in the mid-sixteenth century.

In the county of Kent there were only six endowed grammar schools in 1558, but seven more were founded in the 1560s and 1570s. Two at least of the seven were refoundations: Sandwich School, for instance, built and endowed by Sir Roger Manwood in 1563, was designed to replace a chantry grammar school suppressed in 1548. In the city of York both grammar schools were suppressed in 1539–40: one was replaced in 1546 through the generosity of Archbishop Holgate, and the other refounded in 1557 by the cathedral chapter. Undoubtedly private charity was responsible for many new schools, both elementary and grammar. The physical evidence is still there in many cases, as in Cumbria, where two archbishops endowed their birthplaces with grammar schools, Sandys at Hawkshead (1575) and Grindal at St Bees (1583). Mulcaster asserted in 1581 that more schools had been erected since Elizabeth's accession than 'all the rest be, that were before her time in the whole realm', but he probably exaggerated. The total numbers even of grammar schools are still uncertain: A. M. Stowe estimated that there were some 360 by 1600, and the figure will certainly be raised by local researches. A careful census of Yorkshire grammar schools has found forty-six before the Reformation, very few of which were lost, and sixty-eight new foundations between 1545 and 1603. Even on Stowe's figure, there would have been a grammar school for every 12,000 people, 'twice as favourable a ratio in this matter as in Victorian England'.[16]

Higher education was confined mainly to the two universities and to the lawyers' colleges in London, the Inns of Court and Chancery. Before the Reformation, it is often asserted, they were small vocational institutions catering almost exclusively for clerics and professional lawyers respectively; afterwards, they grew rapidly as more entrants, especially gentlemen's sons, came to treat them as finishing schools. Certainly the numbers of men in public life known to have attended a university, a lawyers' inn, or both, increased considerably. Of the 420 members of the House of Commons in 1563, almost exactly one-third (139) had attended one or both, but by 1593 the proportion had risen to over half (252 out of 460). Similarly, the percentage of active JPs in six counties who had been at Oxford or Cambridge rose from 5 per cent in 1562 to 40 per cent in 1608.

Stone has estimated the numbers of university admissions (Table 12.1), and concluded that there was a considerable rise between 1550 and 1590, and again in the early seventeenth century. The Oxford admissions are, however, difficult to calculate, because many sons of gentry resided for a time without proceeding to a degree. The advice given to the future earl of Strafford by his father (1604) was that

all your sonnes would goe to the university at xiiii yeares old and staie thear two or three yeares, then to the Ynnes of Courtt before xvii years of age, and be well kept to ther studye of the lawes . . . .[17]

What is not clear, however, is whether there were more gentry taking

Table 12.1 Estimated annual university admissions 1546–1609 (decennial averages)

Oxford			Cambridge		
Date	Admissions to BA degree	Est. annual freshman admissions	Date	Annual matriculants	Est. annual freshman admissions
1546–52	?	(120)			
1553–59	45	(157)	1550–59	160	?
1560–69	66	(231)	1560–69	275	?
1570–79	118	(413)	1570–79	344	?
1580–89	132	(445)	1580–89	344	465
1590–99	133	(358)	1590–99	?	(363)
1600–9	167	(374)	1600–09	270	403

Source: L. Stone, 'The size and composition of the Oxford student body 1580–1910', in *The University in Society*, ed. L. Stone, 2 vols, Princeton U.P. 1975, i, 91f.

such an attitude, or whether records are simply more abundant. The lawyers' inns, which Neale saw becoming 'finishing schools for the gentry' in Elizabeth's reign, had already been performing that function in the fifteenth century. Elizabeth Russell has recently questioned whether there really was a significant increase in numbers at Oxford between 1560 and 1580, or even between 1400 and 1580. The apparent large increase may have been simply an effect of the first two matriculation statutes of 1565 and 1581, which forced many former town-dwelling students, especially gentlemen commoners, to seek formal admission to the university.

The lawyers' inns were not the only institutions of higher education in the capital. The combined demand from residents and visitors ensured London not only a generous provision of grammar schools (at least 43 at a slightly later period, 1627–85) but also of more advanced institutions. There were academies for youths of both sexes in dancing, music, fencing and other skills; there were public lectures in cosmography, navigation and divinity; above all, there was Gresham's College, established in 1596, where lectures were delivered in English on the liberal arts, on geography and on navigation. Harrison (1587) popularised the term 'third university' for the lawyers' inns, and it was gradually given a wider application to cover all higher learning in the capital. A treatise by Sir George Buck, *The Third Universitie of England* (1612), covered all the leading schools and colleges, and affirmed that 'London is not onely the third university of England, but also to be preferred before many other universities in Europe'.[18]

Taking the educational sector as a whole, there was clearly considerable expansion both at the elementary and higher levels. What is not clear, for lack of sufficient evidence, is how much effect the educational expansion had on social control and social mobility. It is scarcely surprising that educational opportunity increased with wealth and social status: more important is what proportion of poorer and humbler children acquired learning, and whether that proportion increased.

In some ways the late medieval period had been one of real if limited opportunities for commoners in the grammar schools and universities as a route to Church preferments. From about the 1530s attitudes changed, as the prestige of careers in the Church waned, while learning became more necessary for gentlemen, whether for their work as Crown officials or justices of the peace or simply for the social necessity of being well read. The author of the reactionary 'Considerations delivered to the Parliament' in 1559 called for legislation to compel nobles to educate their children at universities, to reserve one-third of the university scholarships for the sons of poorer gentry, and to bar the study of law to commoners.[19]

It has been argued by Hexter and Stone that the nobles and gentry of the later sixteenth and early seventeenth centuries seized educational opportunities at the expense of commoners 'in a stampede towards bookish education, in which the poor and weak are likely to be crushed by the great and strong'.[20] It is a dubious argument, for the statistical evidence available points to more education of both gentry and commoners, but is not sufficiently precise to show whether one sector gained at the expense of the other. At Cambridge, where the register of Caius College allows an analysis of the social origins of students from 1559, the picture is one of stability throughout the period, although a mistranslation of *ingenuus* as 'gentleman' instead of 'yeoman' led Curtis to argue that 'a rising tide of men of wealth and good birth flooded into Cambridge'. The corrected picture is as follows (Table 12.2).

And McConica has demonstrated a similar pattern for Corpus Christi College, Oxford, to which the well-to-do were already resorting in some numbers before the Reformation, and where the proportion of gentry (34% after 1577) was probably stable.

Table 12.2   Admissions to Gonville and Caius College, Cambridge (%)

	Gentry	Clergy and professions	Merchants and tradesmen	Yeoman and husbandmen	Unclassified plebeians
1580–89	34	6	7	11	42
1590–99	33	10	8	10	38
1600–9	38	19	6	17	20

Source: D. Cressy in *P. and P.*, 47 (1970), 114.

Evidence for the larger numbers attending grammar schools is ambivalent. Some established schools like Eton, Winchester and Shrewsbury were taking more paying gentlemen's children and turning themselves into 'public schools' in the later sense, but free grammar schools were being founded which were to charge no fees from any pupil (e.g. Hawkshead, 1588), and the orders for St Alban's School (1570), devised by Sir Nicholas Bacon, required that 'poor men's children shall be received into the said school before others'.[21] If Harrison could argue by 1587 that rich men were pushing the poor out of the universities and greater grammar schools, Mulcaster thought in 1581 that there were too many small schools and that there was a real danger of 'the poorer sort' becoming educated in numbers in excess of the positions open to them.

3

The age of Elizabeth, then, was one of increasing literacy, education and book ownership, even if an 'educational revolution' can be dismissed as hyperbole. It was also an age of innovations in the arts, sciences and technology, largely inspired by more advanced cultures on the Continent. Italy, France and the Empire all contributed skills, knowledge, ideas and designs. Cultural lag gradually disappeared in at least some areas as Englishmen caught up with continental developments. An inscription of the later sixteenth century in the Palazzo Vecchio at Florence expressed a growing respect among Italians for English achievements: 'The people of this island, which was described by the ancients as having neither letters nor music, are now seen to be great in both fields.'[22]

In science and medicine, it is true, Englishmen remained dependent on more advanced societies, and not until the seventeenth century did scientists of the first European rank emerge, as was perhaps to be expected. Yet there were some distinguished pioneers. William Turner was the founder of English natural history, and his *New Herball* (3 vols, 1551–68) included the first scientific record of 238 native plants. Several mathematicians made important contributions, including Robert Recorde who discovered square roots and invented the = sign for equality, Thomas Hariot who developed notation further and invented the signs < and > for 'less than' and 'greater than', and Henry Briggs who developed Napier's invention of logarithms into the form commonly used today. William Gilbert's *De Magnete* (1600) founded the science of electromagnetism, while his *De Mundo*, published posthumously, refined Copernicus' heliocentric astronomy. Such men deserve as prominent a place in the early history of English science as Francis Bacon, whose writings were more important to the later development of science than to its applications in his own day.

Technical innovations were introduced largely by foreign craftsmen brought to England or by Englishmen who had studied techniques abroad. Mining engineers were invited to England from Germany, glassmakers from France, clock- and watchmakers from both countries. The first watches made by English craftsmen in the 1580s and 1590s were, according to Cipolla, 'unimaginative but diligent replicas of French and German models', but English clockmakers may have learned quickly. Already by 1582–83 an elaborate clock could be chosen as a present to the sultan of Turkey, and in 1596 Elizabeth sent him an automatic organ built by a Lancashire clockmaker, which played a sequence of madrigals, 'an extraordinary monument to precision building and mechanical ingenuity'.[23] There were, moreover, independent English developments of some significance before the end of the century. Timothy Bright (1588) developed shorthand efficiently; cartography greatly improved, and earned the respect of the leading continental practitioners like Mercator; surveying and navigation were both developed and elaborated.

A practical interest in natural history and anthropology was stimulated by overseas exploration; Raleigh commissioned John White to make drawings of the native people, flora and fauna of Virginia (which still survive), and Drake took a draughtsman on his voyage round the world, whose drawings of plants attracted the interest of the French botanist Charles de l'Ecluse. Gardening also benefited: in 1587 Harrison remarked 'how manie strange hearbs, plants, and annuall fruits are dailie brought unto us from the Indies, Americans, Taprobane [Ceylon], Canarie Iles, and all parts of the world', and his own modest rectory garden of 300 square feet contained nearly 300 different plants.[24]

Tudor England was more important for its contributions to the arts than the sciences: but the well-known flowering of the Elizabethan age followed a black period of destruction. No history of the iconoclastic movement in England has been written, but it was the single most important (if negative) event in the art history of the mid-century. The demand for some forms of art, notably stained glass, almost completely disappeared; and a vast amount of existing art and literature was deliberately destroyed. On 21 February 1548 the Privy Council ordered the removal of all images from churches, and in many areas anything that could be regarded as an image was destroyed or defaced – wall paintings, sculptures, tombs with Catholic inscriptions, glass windows, embroidery and objects of precious metal. Almost all ecclesiastical gold- and silverwork was melted down, and only a few exquisite pieces like the Gloucester candlestick and the Ramsey censer and incense-boat survive as reminders of what has been lost.

The architectural losses were also grievous. The great majority of monastic churches were left to decay or were systematically demolished for the sake of their materials. Many new houses were built on monastic sites, and in most cases the old buildings were entirely swept away. To regret these losses is sometimes represented as an anachronistic attitude of the twentieth century, for, we are assured, Tudor builders had a 'characteristically impartial disrespect for the obsolete'. Certainly there were practical justifications for sweeping away redundant churches in remote rural areas and in over-churched towns; and more monastic churches than is often recognised were spared in small towns with no other place of worship, like Selby, Sherborne and Tewkesbury. However, some Elizabethans like Camden deplored the destruction of the rest on aesthetic and historical grounds, and nearer to the event the young Edward VI had similar regrets. Passing a ruined abbey, and being told how his father had dissolved all the abbeys because of the monks' misconduct, he asked, 'Why did not my father punish the offenders and put better men into such goodly buildings . . . so great an ornament to this kingdom?'[25]

Worse still was the philistine indifference to any manuscripts that could be considered 'papistical' or magical. The destructions of the 1530s are well known, but they continued well after the dissolution of the monasteries. At Norwich in Edward's reign, John Bale found the contents of the libraries 'turned to the use of their grossers, candelmakers [and] sope sellers', and in Oxford in 1550

they burned mathematical bookes for conjuring bookes, and if the Greeke professor had not accidentally come along, the Greeke testament had been thrown into the fire for a conjuring booke too.

That is, admittedly, a late tradition preserved by Aubrey, but there is other independent evidence that the royal commissioners for the reform of the university did burn many books considered 'popish'. And destruction or neglect continued well into Elizabeth's reign. Archbishop Parker complained to Cecil in 1566 that priceless volumes were being sent overseas 'by covetouse statyoners, or spoyled in the poticarye shopis'.[26]

Meanwhile works of art had been protected once more under Mary, but mob iconoclasm broke out again on Elizabeth's accession. Public bonfires of 'images' in 1559 rapidly got out of hand:

not onely images, but rood-loftes, relickes, sepulchres, bookes, banneres, coopes, vestments, altar-cloathes wer, in diverse places, committed to the fire, and that with such shouting, and applause of the vulgar sort, as if it had beene the sacking of some hostile city.[27]

By 1560 tombs and many more glass windows were being destroyed as 'superstitious', and the queen issued a proclamation forbidding 'the breaking or defacing of any parcel of any monument, or tomb, or grave . . . or to break any image of kings, princes, or nobles' estates'. Thereafter mass iconoclasm died away until the 1640s, although isolated attacks continued. Occasionally, Elizabeth was at pains to reverse the acts of destruction. She was so dismayed by the desecrated tombs of her Yorkist ancestors at Fotheringhay that in 1573 she commissioned dignified replacements.

The Reformation had another considerable effect on the course of English art besides the impulse to iconoclasm. Italian artistic influence repelled, as well as fascinated, because of the close connection of Italy with Catholicism. Renaissance and Mannerist art from Italy was therefore neither wholly accepted nor wholly rejected, creating a mixed style fused from native traditions and from continental innovations, and what foreign influences did predominate were more often French or Netherlandish than Italian. It was partly a matter of geographical distance as well as religion; but there is little doubt that Protestant refugees from Catholic lands, especially the Netherlands, were more welcome than Catholic craftsmen and designers. The Flemish pattern books of de Vries, published from the late 1550s, were especially popularised by immigrant craftsmen, and were the chief source of the strapwork and grotesques which are so characteristic of Elizabethan and Jacobean decoration.

The process of attraction and repulsion can be seen very clearly in architecture. The building of large Perpendicular churches more or less came to a halt by the 1540s, but the tradition mingled with continental influences to produce a new and vigorous secular architecture. Sutton Place (1521–27) and Nonsuch (1538–56) began a process 'which would have produced full-blown copies of true Italian Renaissance buildings by about 1560, if religious and political differences had not steered us away from France and Italy and in on ourselves, and then, later, towards the Netherlands'.[28] Old Somerset House, London, built for the lord protector in 1547–52, was more consistently Renaissance in style, and it inspired a group of similar houses (Lacock, Sudeley and Northumberland's own Dudley Castle) designed either by Sharington, one of Somerset's followers, or by John Shute, a protégé of Northumberland. The Marian reaction of 1553 broke up this architecturally advanced circle: indeed, the style never became popular, being (like the next advanced style under Inigo Jones and the Stuarts) too much associated with the court. The one later example, Longleat of *c*. 1572–80, was a rebuilding after a fire by Thynne, formerly Somerset's steward and superintendent of Somerset House.

Instead, the 'prodigy houses' of Elizabeth's and James's reigns, as Summerson has happily called them, represented an eclectic compromise, with symmetrical facades inspired by Italy, ornament derived from Flanders and grid windows in native Perpendicular style. The most influential was Burghley's great house at Theobalds in Hertfordshire (1564–85), which was much more admired than Longleat, and which directly inspired other great builders like Hatton at Holdenby and Howard at Audley End. At a less exalted level, vernacular architecture – urban housing, farmhouses and even many manor houses – remained more traditional still, with motifs like prominent gables and chimneystacks, and mullioned windows with hood-moulds.

The growth of a new English architectural style is often linked with the alleged development of the architectural profession. The term 'architect' first appears in English in the *First and Chief Groundes of Architecture* of John Shute (1563), who consciously praised the 'new fashion' inaugurated by Somerset House. Recent scholarship by Girouard and others has rescued from neglect a major figure in the mixed Elizabethan style, Robert Smythson, who worked on Wollaton, Hardwick and other great houses, and who is described on his tomb (1614) as 'architector and survayor unto the most worthy house of Wollaton with diverse others of great account'. However, the term 'architect' did not imply a controlling designer of the kind familiar since Wren's time. The use of printed books of designs allowed amateurs like Thynne, Smith and Burghley to design their houses themselves, the 'architect' or 'surveyor' being paid to carry out their ideas. 'Because of this combination of circumstances the Robert Smithsons . . . were, in fact, further from the position of the modern architect than the Wynfords and Yeveles of two hundred years before.'[29]

The other visual arts remained, on the whole, subordinate to architecture, and took the form of internal decoration of houses and palaces, as they had done for churches before the Reformation. Painting, plasterwork, joinery, tapestries and occasionally sculpture were employed decoratively, notably in the large carved chimney-pieces, panelled wainscot and elaborate plaster ceilings of the larger houses. Even gardening became a form of outdoor architecture for palaces and greater houses, with its walls, obelisks, statues, fountains and geometrical beds. The one major exception to this subordination was funerary sculpture for churches, which flourished as an ever-grander art-form. The Southwark workshops of two immigrant families, the Cures (Cuers) (*c*. 1540–1632) and the Johnsons (Jansens) (1567–*c*. 1618) were patronised by nobles and gentry for tombs all over England. There were also native craftsmen in great demand, notably Epiphanius Evesham, whose tombs survive in churches from Lincolnshire to Kent. At a more local level there must have been many sculptors like John Gildon of Hereford, who provided handsome tombs within a radius of 30 miles, and who can be identified only because four of his works are signed – an exceptionally early case of what later became standard practice.

Even painting was considered a subordinate art, confined largely to portraits to be hung in houses as reminders of friends or statesmen. Sir John Harington thought pictures valuable only 'as pleasing ornaments of a house, and good remembrances of our friends'. The startling possibilities of Renaissance painting were demonstrated by the long residence in England of the Augsburg painter Hans Holbein the Younger (1526–28, 1532–43), but after his death most continental artists in England were Netherlanders fleeing religious persecution, and 'the up-to-date style they brought promptly went out of fashion at a court which was about to indulge in a bizarre neo-medievalism'.[30] Nevertheless, there was much fine painting in the second half of the century which has only lately been rescued from neglect: it was as recently as 1969–70 that the Tate Gallery reconstituted the corpus of English painting between the death of Holbein (1543) and the arrival of Van Dyck (1621).

Hans Eworth, Mary's official portraitist, was a painter of penetrating portraits; and in a different style so was Marcus Gheeraerts the younger, who painted the 'Ditchley' portrait of Elizabeth in 1592. The finest Elizabethan painter, however, was a goldsmith's son from Exeter, Nicholas Hilliard (1547–1619), official miniaturist to Elizabeth and James. He and his pupil Isaac Oliver specialised in painting miniatures for collections and for wearing in lockets. It is an art-form which has suffered unjustly in comparison with large-scale painting, but which was highly valued by Tudor and Stuart connoisseurs, and which aroused the admiration of John Donne:

> . . . a hand, or eye
> By Hilliard drawne, is worth an history
> By a worse painter made . . .

If painting and sculpture were not among the finest artistic achievements, they did at least rise in status. Painters and sculptors had been traditionally regarded as craftsmen, but Elyot argued in *The Governour* 'that it is commendable in a gentyllman to paint and kerve exactly, if nature ther to doth induce hym'. Gradually the nobility came to accept this revolutionary idea in practice. Hilliard was of gentle, if urban, birth, and wished 'that none should meddle with limning but gentlemen alone'. George Gower, the most fashionable portrait painter of the 1570s and 1580s, was a Yorkshire gentleman, who in his self-portrait of 1579 showed the compasses of his art outweighing his coat of arms; and William Segar, a herald and later knighted, painted Essex and the queen. Epiphanius Evesham, the best of the native-born sculptors, was also of gentle birth.

The domestic arts flourished in the second half of the century amid increasing wealth, gentlefolk being eager purchasers and even themselves creators – embroideries survive at Hardwick and Oxburgh which do seem to have been worked, as tradition has always asserted, by Bess of Hardwick and Mary Queen of Scots. Both embroidery and tapestry flourished on a large scale, the tapestries of the Sheldon workshops especially for wall-hangings in the great country houses. Furniture was generally in plain oak, but some more lavish pieces were inlaid with holly or bog oak to give a polychrome effect. Exquisite jewellery – much of it destroyed in the Civil War – is still represented by the queen's Armada jewel, probably made by Hilliard. Fine and restrained silver communion cups were turned out in hundreds in the 1560s and 1570s, often made from the very chalices they replaced. Silver cutlery and tableware was turned out in quantity too, and at the top end of the market magnificent silver and jewelled salts were made for the table, while Verzelini made beautiful glass vessels in the Venetian style.

One aspect of the visual arts (as well as literature) which is crucial to an understanding of contemporary thought is the language of allegory, emblems, symbols, devices and 'conceits'. Emblems, conveniently depicted in collections like Whitney's *A Choice of Emblemes* (1586), embodied virtues, vices and moral precepts in visual form, and Elizabethan art is saturated with them. Portraits of the queen, for instance, depict her with an ermine, an eglantine (a single white rose), a crescent moon or a sieve, all of them emblems of chastity. The silkworms embroidered on her dress in a portrait at Parham may refer to her scheme to introduce silk production in the 1580s.

Spenser's *Faerie Queen* is full of symbolism, while the pageants provided for Elizabeth by courtiers and urban corporations largely presented allegorical or mythological characters like Time, Truth, Peace and Mercury. Many men and women employed devices or mottoes with a personal significance; for example John Roysse, refounding Abingdon School in 1563 when he himself was aged 63, endowed it for 63 boys in a schoolroom 63 feet long. The Northamptonshire Catholic Sir Thomas Tresham made defiant statements of his faith in stone. His triangular lodge at Rushton (1594–97) has 3 storeys each with 3 windows on every side; each side is 33 feet long and carries an inscription of 33 letters. The whole represents an allusion both to the Trinity and to Tresham's own name. At a less elaborate level, many houses were painted with moralising sentences, while the countess of Shrewsbury ostentatiously topped Hardwick Hall with her monogram ES in giant letters.

Music suffered much less than the visual arts from artistic insularity, and attracted composers of European importance. The achievement is especially remarkable because music was closely connected with the Church, and the Reformation involved not only the closure of many large churches with choirs but the destruction of organs, a dislike of elaborate musical settings and the end of Latin services except in college and private chapels, Yet Thomas Tallis, last organist of Waltham Abbey, came under royal patronage and encouragement, and was able with his pupil William Byrd to preserve and enrich the musical tradition of the Church in both Latin and English settings: Queen Elizabeth granted them a monopoly of music printing for twenty-one years. Both composed for both Anglican and Roman Catholic services, but Byrd, remarkably, was a determined recusant despite his position as organist of the Chapel Royal. The queen, who recognised his abilities, protected him from persecution. She may, indeed, be said to have saved English religious music from Puritan destruction.

Secular music flourished also: singing, dancing and instrumental playing were enjoyed actively by a very large part of the population. Hollyband's *French Schoolemaister* (1573) includes among the scenes of everyday life given for translation one in which a Londoner's guest is entertained after supper; members of the family collect their 'bookes of musick' and render a four-part unaccompanied song by Richard Edwards, one of Elizabeth's musicians. Such musical accomplishments as sight-reading and lute-playing were a normal part of education in prosperous homes, a point brought home by Byrd's pupil Thomas Morley, in his *Plaine and Easie Introduction to Practicall Musicke* (1597). One of the characters is made to confess that

supper being ended, and musicke bookes according to the custome being brought to the table, the mistresse of the house presented mee with a part, earnestly requesting mee to sing. But when, after manie excuses, I protested unfainedly that I could not, everie one began to wonder. Yea, some whispered to others, demaunding how I was brought up.

Morley himself catered for the market by composing and publishing madrigals in the newly fashionable Italian style, John Dowland by similarly composing and publishing lute-songs ('ayres'), Byrd, Farnaby and others with keyboard music for the virginals. Naturally this musical culture required some leisure and prosperity; but listening to music, if not participating, was universally popular. Drake dined to music on his voyage round the world; several town corporations maintained official waits or minstrels, and paid drummers or other musicians to play to labourers employed on public works. Music was played as overtures before plays, and regular free public concerts were given at the Royal Exchange from 1571.

4

Music apart, it is literature that is generally, and rightly, considered the glory of the age. Indeed in popular speech 'the age of Elizabeth' and 'the age of Shakespeare' are almost synonymous, but that is a distortion and a half-truth at best. The writers whose greatness is attested both by their contemporaries and by the judgement of posterity were really late Elizabethan and Jacobean: Shakespeare himself wrote his plays between about 1591 and 1613. And Shakespeare was only one of a very distinguished company; literary connoisseurs rated Sidney and Spenser the greatest writers of the age; and among playwrights Marlowe and Jonson were judged by some superior to the Swan of Avon. As for popular taste, the order of preference was different again. Jonson complained that the general public preferred 'the water-rimers workes' – the doggerel verse of John Taylor – to Spenser (or, presumably to Shakespeare or to Jonson himself).

The transformation of sixteenth-century literature was well summarised by C. S. Lewis:

The mid-century is an earnest, heavy-handed, commonplace age: a drab age. Then, in the last quarter of the century, the unpredictable happens. With startling suddenness we ascend. Fantasy, conceit, paradox, colour, incantation return. Youth returns. The fine frenzies of ideal love and ideal war are readmitted. Sidney, Spenser, Shakespeare, Hooker . . . display what is almost a new culture: that culture which was to last through most of the seventeenth century. . . . Nothing in the earlier history of our period would have enabled the sharpest observer to foresee this transformation.[31]

It is a necessary simplification, but essentially just. The late medieval tradition in England (though not in Scotland) had become feeble by the reign of Henry VIII. The poets Wyatt and Surrey introduced an

Italianate sophistication in the 1530s and 1540s, but they had no successors. The real start of the 'golden' age dates from Sir Philip Sidney's prose epic *Arcadia*, begun in the late 1570s, and Edmund Spenser's verse *The Faerie Queene*, started shortly afterwards but published only from 1590 onwards and never completed.

Both epics were fusions of the English chivalric tradition and the new influence of Italian literature, and the medieval English influence was at least as important as the foreign inspiration. If Elizabeth was in part the model for the heroine of *The Faerie Queene*, its hero was King Arthur; and Spenser acknowledged his debt to

> Dan Chaucer, well of English undefyled,
> On Fame's eternall beadroll worthie to be fyled.

It is significant that Chaucer's tomb in Westminster Abbey was erected in 1556, and that Spenser in his turn was laid near Chaucer in a tomb paid for by the earl of Essex, with an epitaph calling him 'easily the chief of English poets of our age' (*Anglicorum poetarum nostri seculi facile princeps*).

English history and myth was a powerful inspiration to scholarship as well as literature. Archbishop Parker not only collected manuscripts dispersed in the monastic dissolution, but between 1567 and 1574 published five important medieval texts, the first Englishman to undertake such a task. Hall's *Union of the Two Noble and Illustre Famelies of Lancastre and Yorke* (1548), Grafton's *Chronicles* (1562–72), Stow's *Chronicles* and *Annales* (many editions from 1565) and the composite chronicle known as Holinshed's (1577 and 1587) all included much material on medieval and Tudor history, some of which would have been lost but for their labours. And if they must rank as chronicles rather than works of literature, they inspired a whole range of literary works, of which Shakespeare's chronicle plays are only the most famous.

The last quarter of the century saw a vastly increased output of literature of all kinds; even a bare catalogue would be quite impossible here. In the wake of the heroics of Sidney and Spenser came the commercial writers, the pamphleteers, the satirists, even what one might fairly call the first English novelists. The novels – or more strictly works of prose fiction – begin with Grange's *Golden Aphroditis* (1577) and Lyly's *Euphues* (1578), and by the 1590s they were pouring from the presses: Deloney's *Jacke of Newbery* (1597) is a good example of the type. And alongside such robust and popular stories there flourished also elaborate works of allegory, of which *The Faerie Queene* was only one among many. Theology naturally took pride of place in quantity of publication, some of it – notably Hooker's *Lawes of Ecclesiastical Politie* – fine literature in its own right. Poetry also flourished in the 1580s and 1590s, especially the Italian sonnet form. Already in 1598 Francis Meres could praise Shakespeare for 'his sugred sonnets among his private friends', though they were not published until 1609.

It is, however, drama, with which Shakespeare, and indeed Elizabethan writers in general, are now most associated. In the later sixteenth century a popular, medieval tradition of English drama was fused with a rediscovery and imitation of classical drama to produce, for the first time, a commercial theatre. Courtiers and Crown officials began to patronise companies of players. The Earl of Oxford had his own players by 1547, and he had numerous successors; Shakespeare was one of the Lord Chamberlain's (later the King's) Men. Buildings were used or adapted as theatres to which players could travel, as they do with the play-within-a-play in *Hamlet*. The next stage was the erection of special purpose-built theatres with their own resident actors. James Burbage built the first in 1576, in Finsbury Fields north of London, which he called simply 'The Theatre', and half a dozen more were built in the London suburbs by the end of the century, including Shakespeare's Globe.

The London theatres were public playhouses, with seating crammed into galleries round a central yard with cheap standing space. Not until the King's Men began to use the Blackfriars Theatre from 1608 can one sense a move away from popular, City entertainment to a private, court-centred art-form. For the Elizabethan theatre was popular – the cries of aldermen and preachers against theatres and their associated rogues and harlots are evidence enough. It is easy to judge Tudor plays primarily as works of literature and to find many of them wanting; but they were of course designed to give pleasure on the stage, and many that read tediously today clearly did so. Ralph Willis, in 1639, could still vividly remember a performance of a morality play, *The Cradle of Security*, as a small child about 1570: 'This sight tooke such impression in me that, when I came towards man's estate, it was as fresh in my memory as if I had seen it newly acted.'[32]

Villagers enjoyed plays no less than their city cousins: by 1577 an earthwork in Walsham-le-Willows (Suffolk) was adapted with 'a fayre round place of earth made of purpose for the use of stage playes'. There is also the testimony of a journal kept by Captain Keeling of the *Dragon* on an East Indies voyage. He noted on 5 September 1607 that 'we gave the tragedie of Hamlett', on the 30th that 'my companions acted Kinge Richard the Second', and on 1 October that he 'had Hamlet acted abord me: which I permitt to keepe my people from idlenes and unlawfull games, or sleepe'.[33] The image of two of Shakespeare's recent masterpieces being acted out off the coast of Sierra Leone is one of the most remarkable vignettes of a remarkable age.

Chapter 13

Conclusion

Elizabethan Englishmen were conspicuous for some of the qualities that we nowadays associate with the Japanese.

C. M. Cipolla

The age of Elizabeth is rightly regarded, not only by historians but also in the popular memory, as a time of greatness breeding greater things still than it actually witnessed.

G. R. Elton'

All ages are ages of transition, blends of continuity and change: the problem is to identify the relative proportions of each. For the later sixteenth century there is the special difficulty that the historian's convenient but artificial distinction between 'medieval' and 'modern' imposes a pattern on the evidence. If the line between the two is drawn around 1500, or (as Elton would prefer) the 1530s, then the Elizabethan period is required to show signs of modernity or progress. If the break is dated around 1580–1620 (Stone) or 1640–60 (Hill), the 'medieval' features of most of the Tudor age are stressed instead. Yet Tudor men and women, like those of any age, both identified with, and distinguished themselves from, their ancestors. Camden could use the term 'middle age' in contrast with his own time, but members of parliament cited fourteenth-century precedents with no sense that they were 'medieval' ones irrelevant in a 'modern' situation. 'We are not dealing with a country eager to leave the Middle Ages behind, but with one which was sadly puzzled by change, and often hostile to it.'[2]

Economic historians who categorise Tudor England as 'pre-industrial' take similar risks, of either emphasising the static and unchanging elements in the economy, or of concentrating on those processes thought to have been crucial in leading to industrialisation. Both models imply a linear view of progress; and it is easy enough to draw up lists of 'backward' and 'progressive' elements in sixteenth-century thought and practice, meaning respectively 'more like what went before' and 'more like what came after'. Yet in some respects society was not moving in a 'modern' direction at all.

Persecution of witches increased, and many other non-scientific beliefs flourished. In 1575 the queen incorporated the Society of the New Art for Burghley, Leicester and others, who invested heavily in an attempt to convert iron into copper, while Burghley later showed interest in a project to transmute base metals into gold. To Aubrey, Elizabeth's times were 'those darke times' when 'astrologer, mathematician and conjurer were accounted the same thinges . . .'.[3] Politically, too, there were regressions, if by those one means changes not in the direction of liberal and parliamentary government. No sixteenth-century parliament dared impeach a royal minister, or insist on nominating the royal council, but parliaments had done both in the fifteenth century and were to do so again in the seventeenth.

However, if what are sought in the later sixteenth century are signs of England's later rise to commercial and industrial predominance, they are certainly present. Politically, a state which had been reduced almost to a pawn in the Habsburg–Valois struggle in the 1550s recovered sufficiently to threaten Philip II, the most powerful ruler in western Europe. Culturally, a land once considered backward and even barbarous by Italians became famous for its music, drama and literature. By the end of the century English actors were touring Germany, Denmark and the Netherlands, and English music was influential throughout northern Europe. Industrially, too, there was progress, even if Nef's 'industrial revolution' is too strong an expression. Mining output grew considerably, and manufactures like armaments and the New Draperies, taught to Englishmen by immigrants in the mid-sixteenth century, were within fifty years being widely exported instead of imported.

Furthermore, the land which had neglected oceanic exploration, while the Spaniards and Portuguese had carved up the globe between them, had begun its world-wide expansion. Henry VII had patronised John and Sebastian Cabot in their explorations of the North American coast; Henry VIII had shown no interest, and Sebastian had gone to Spain instead; but in 1548 Sebastian accepted an invitation from some royal councillors to return to England. He was involved in the first expeditions to Morocco in 1551 and to Muscovy in 1553: thereafter, there was no stopping. America colonisation was first openly discussed in England in the 1550s, and attempts at settlement began in 1585. Protestant hostility to Spain led to a rapid growth in privateering from the 1560s, and especially after the outbreak of war in 1585. The East India Company was founded in 1600, and in the same year William Adams reached Japan; he was subsequently to establish settlements of English and Dutch merchants there, and to build the first Japanese navy.

In short, England was already developing some of the advantages that were to lead to commercial supremacy and to the first industrial revolution. That does not mean, however, that the Tudor economy can be usefully studied as a helpful model in development economics today. Economic historians have become increasingly aware of the limitations of theoretical analysis: 'little beyond the simplest applications of the economist's abstractions is really of much help, and even these can easily be pressed to a point in any particular enquiry when they become misleading'.[4] It is all too easy to place great weight on a single cause of economic growth – population increase, say, or inflation – which had different consequences in each European country depending on the social, cultural and economic conditions with which it intereacted.

Furthermore, it would be wrong to exaggerate the degree of importance and progress attained by England by 1603. The commercial centres of Europe were still the great cities of Italy, Germany and the Netherlands rather than London, and Antwerp's mantle passed north to Amsterdam rather than across the Channel. The origins of factory production are often discussed in terms of the rise of the putting-out system as though it were peculiar to England, but the same system also flourished in Germany (the *Verlagssystem*) and was spreading throughout the Mediterranean world from the 1530s. The growth of English mining output distracts attention from the fact that Germany was still the largest and most advanced centre of mining in Europe, and that English miners relied heavily on German technology and personnel. And, in an age when national strength was still measured largely in terms of manpower, England was still inevitably overshadowed by its much larger neighbours (Table 13.1).

Table 13.1 Estimates of European populations *c.* 1600

	Population (millions)	Approx. density (per square mile)
France	16–18	90
Germany	15–16	60
Russia (Muscovy)	11–16	—
Italy	13	114
Spain and Portugal	11	50
Poland and Lithuania	8	—
England and Wales	4.3	75
Netherlands (north and south)	3	100
Scandinavia	2	5

Sources: *The New Cambridge Modern History*, iii, ed. R. B. Wernham, Cambridge U.P. 1968, p. 33; *The Fontana Economic History of Europe*, ii, ed. C. M. Cipolla Fontana 1974, p. 38; C. M. Cipolla, *Before the Industrial Revolution*, Methuen 1976, p. 4; G. Parker, *Europe in Crisis 1598–1648*, Fontana 1979, p. 23.

Naturally political and economic strength did not entirely correlate with size of population. Germany and Italy were politically fragmented; Poland was unified but weak; and France was severely weakened by civil wars between 1562 and 1598. Nevertheless France and Spain, the most populous states in western Europe, were not surprisingly the most powerful, in comparison with which England was still a small power. Small size was not of itself a barrier to playing a major role, as Portugal had demonstrated earlier, but if there was a small power illustrating dazzling success in the late sixteenth century it was not England but the United Provinces, the seven rebel states of the northern Netherlands.

Between the 1580s and 1670s, the Dutch created a highly urbanised, literate and commercial society which was the wonder of Europe. Banking, stock exchanges, new techniques of shipbuilding and new commercial methods, and above all a very efficient carrying trade, made for great wealth and a high standard of living diffused fairly broadly throughout the population. The Dutch commercial success owed much to a huge transfusion of population as skilled refugees fled from the southern to the northern Netherlands: it was also indebted to revolutionary agricultural changes like large-scale drainage, land reclamation, high crop yields, new crops and improved stockbreeding. In short, the Dutch led the way in making real improvements in the quality and quantity of the factors of production – land, labour, capital – creating true economic growth rather than mere expansion. In so far as Englishmen shared in the same developments it was largely by copying the Flemings and later the northern Netherlanders, 'treading on the heels of the Dutch in every sphere'.[5]

With the benefit of hindsight, however, it is possible to see that England enjoyed several advantages – mostly political and social rather than economic – which in the long run gave it a crucial lead over the Dutch as well as the French. It had for long enjoyed a strong central government, a flexible social structure and a relatively light burden of state taxation (Henry VIII's heavy demands in the 1540s fortunately did not last). No social groups enjoyed a *de jure* exemption from taxation, as did some continental aristocracies, and the tax system was relatively equitable. Despite underassessments, the rich paid most of the direct taxation, and the poor none at all. Englishmen suffered almost none of the indirect taxation of necessities common elsewhere, although the monopoly levies were a partial exception until abolished in 1601 and 1624. Consequently, prosperity was relatively broadly diffused. One of Philip's entourage in the 1550s, astonished at the contrast between 'homelie cottages' of wattle and daub and the 'large diet' enjoyed by the cottagers, exclaimed that 'these English have their houses made of sticks and durt, but they fare commonlie so well as the king'.[6]

One reason for low taxation was that England was fortunate to enjoy official peace for over half the period under review (1550–57 and 1559–85), and that when war came it was not a serious drain on English manpower. Henry VIII, for a single campaign, had had 37,000 men sent overseas, more than 10 per 1,000 of the English population, and a great deal more than the 2–4 per 1,000 which was the normal ratio in France and Spain. His daughter, by contrast, levied some 106,000 men for all theatres of war over 18 years, a considerably smaller proportion of a rising population, and a sharp contrast to Philip II's army in Flanders, which reached a peak of 86,000 in 1574.[7] Further, by not being compelled to fight on home territory, the Tudors were largely spared the escalating cost of defences, those powerful fortresses and bastions which surrounded every strategic border town on the Continent.

Moreover, war and religious persecution on the Continent encouraged that vital migration of skilled craftsmen and artists who played so large a part in English industry, commerce and culture.

Technical knowledge spreads most easily by the migration of men possessing the necessary skill. It was through this medium that England, still behind many parts of Europe, first came into contact with countless improvements in manufacturing, mining, agriculture, shipping and business methods.[8]

Some of the 'strangers' came on a purely commercial basis, like the 300 or more French iron-workers in the Weald by 1550, the German miners at Keswick from 1568, and the master glassmaker Verzelini. It is remarkable, however, how many from the 1560s onwards were Protestant refugees, from France, from Italy, and above all Walloons and 'Dutch' (mostly Flemings) from the Spanish Netherlands. Elizabeth and Leicester both employed Italian physicians; Flemish craftsmen were employed building Burghley House and engraving Saxton's maps; and the leading portrait painters and monumental sculptors were mostly 'Dutch'. The Netherlanders made a major contribution to the development of brewing and paper-making, and above all to the New Draperies. The majority settled in London, East Anglia and the South-east, but even more distant places had their craftsmen of 'Dutch' origin, judging by their names, like the glazier Barnard Dininckhoff at York and the alabasterer Joseph Hollemans of Burton upon Trent.

No general study of the 'strangers' has been published since Cunningham's *Alien Immigrants to England* in 1897, and 'the contribu-

382   *The Age of Elizabeth*

tion of immigrants to English economic development between 1550 and 1650 is usually mentioned only in passing and as a factor of secondary importance'. Yet it was a crucial contribution, which is no disparagement to the English, who in general accepted the immigrants and learned rapidly from them. 'What countrie . . . is there at this presente that nourisheth so manie aliens from all parts of the world as England doth?' asked Thomas Johnson in 1596. Hospitality was generally given on religious and humanitarian grounds, but Englishmen were well aware of the commercial benefits also. A parliamentary bill proposed in 1591 to limit the trading rights of aliens, but it drew strong opposition from many MPs: Sir John Wolley argued that London's prosperity, like that of Antwerp and Venice, came from its welcome to 'strangers'. Edmund Howes in 1615 compiled a list of inventions and innovations, of which the great majority were attributed to immigrants.[9]

The immigrants, therefore, had a positive effect on economic as well as cultural change. Can it also be said that population growth by natural means was beneficial? It would be naive to take the view, as some historians still do for the period of industrialisation, that a growing English population was of itself the main cause of economic growth, since in both the sixteenth and eighteenth centuries the increase was a European phenomenon not restricted to England. Indeed, many would now assert that population growth was a brake on, rather than a spur to, economic progress. In the words of Wrigley and Schofield, 'almost throughout the sixteenth century the balance between the English population and the resources to which it could gain access with the material technology of the day steadily deteriorated because the growth in numbers outstripped the rise in production'. However, Pollard and Crossley have suggested that population growth was 'of just such an extent to encourage enterprise but not to create those conditions of miserable poverty seen three centuries before'.[10]

One economic distinction that is often drawn between England and France in the sixteenth and seventeenth centuries is a differential consequence of population growth on agriculture. In England, Brenner has argued, the small landholder was largely squeezed off the land, whereas in France he enjoyed more security. Consequently French population growth led to renewed fragmentation of holdings, but in England large tenant farms were built up, causing hardship to the dispossessed but laying the foundations of agrarian and industrial growth. Cooper has suggested, however, that the contrast has been overdrawn. In the corn-growing regions of both countries – such as Leicestershire and Cambridgeshire, eastern Normandy and the Ile de France – larger farms grew at the expense of smallholders; in the pastoral regions of England, and the French *bocage*, they did not. If, despite this, English agriculture pulled ahead of even French capitalist arable agriculture, the divergence did not come about until the later seventeenth century.

If population growth was not the necessary cause of English capitalist agriculture, did it nevertheless produce more beneficial economic effects in England than in some other countries? Chambers's optimistic view of English population change since 1066 was that

if . . . the assumption of a Malthusian check in the late sixteenth and early seventeenth centuries remains unproven it would seem possible to argue that except for the demographic crisis of the late thirteenth century, the changing balance between population and resources did not induce economic retreat, either on the upswing or the downswing, so that continuous growth in each demographic phase was possible: the upswings yielded a stimulation of aggregate production, a form of profit inflation at the cost of *per capita* income, but not such as to produce a cutback of national population or total production, and on the downswings, *per capita* income accumulated, making funds available for savings and spending when the next phase of demographic advance gave the initial stimulus of cheap labour to sustain it.[11]

There are grounds to sustain such an optimistic interpretation of the later sixteenth century as one of the 'upswings'. Total production – of agricultural, industrial and consumer goods – almost certainly rose considerably, though it is impossible to tell whether production and consumption *per capita* rose or fell. Not only was the home market expanding, as contemporaries like Harrison testified, but exports also grew, and the balance of trade may well have been favourable for much of Elizabeth's reign. It is difficult otherwise to account for the substantial increase in the money supply in her reign, and for the large quantities of Spanish bullion coming to the Mint.

If, of course, population growth outstripped resources, then indeed the 'stimulation of aggregate production' will have been paid for 'at the cost of *per capita* income'. That is certainly the implication of Phelps Brown and Hopkins's wage calculations, however much they may overstate the decline in real incomes. Yet a combination of relatively broadly spread prosperity, and only a small proportion of the population wholly dependent on wages, limited the degree of impoverishment. The evidence of inventories – which reach down to a fairly humble social level – suggests that even the better-off labourers lived better, and enjoyed more consumer goods, than their grandparents. If they were falling behind the landholders, they were still generally better off in absolute terms. 'The substantive achievement of the Tudor economy was its successful absorption of a considerable rise in population without running into a Malthusian crisis of mass starvation and mass unemployment.'[12]

It may well be that, as a result of rising prices, smallholders and the landless had to run faster to stay in the same place. Many men – or their wives and children – took up additional employments to increase the family income, especially the making of consumer goods like stockings, nails, pins, soap, starch and beer. That in turn presupposes a large home demand for those goods, and does not suggest a badly impoverished society: and it helped to create a solid foundation for a consumer society when population and prices ceased to rise. If one crucial cause of English industrialisation was the existence after 1650 of 'a more substantial and more widely distributed reserve of disposable income than anywhere else in Europe',[13] that reserve may in turn have owed its beginnings to the thrift, hard work and diversification by which the men and women of the late sixteenth and early seventeenth centuries had struggled to avoid poverty.

Appendix I: Harvests, prices and wages

The first two columns of Table AI.1 summarise Hoskins's and Harrison's appreciations of harvest yields. The next five (agricultural prices) are drawn from Bowden's price tables. They cover respectively grains (wheat, barley, oats, rye), other arable crops (hay, straw, peas, beans), livestock (sheep, cattle, horses, pigs, poultry, rabbits), animal products (dairy products, eggs, wool, fells, hides), and timber. The two final columns give the indexes of Phelps Brown and Hopkins for (a) a composite 'basket of consumables', and (b) the equivalent of the wage-rate of a building craftsman. The Bowden figures are index figures where the level for 1450–99 = 100, the Phelps Brown figures where 1451–75 = 100. All years are harvest years starting at Michaelmas. The double dating is used because of the ambiguity of the sources; thus '1547' is used by Phelps Brown and Hopkins to mean the year starting 29 September 1546, but by Bowden, Hoskins and Harrison to mean the year starting 29 September 1547.

Table AI.1

	Harvests		Agricultural prices					Prices and wages	
	Wheat	All grains	Grains	Other arable crops	Livestock	Animal products	Timber	Prices of consumables	Equivalent real wages
1546–47	Abundant	Abundant	160	139	176	121	86	231	—
1547–48	Abundant	Abundant	130	143	205	164	118	193	61
1548–49	Abundant	Abundant	162	165	230	171	127	214	—
1549–50	Deficient	Deficient	298	195	213	177	145	262	—
1550–51	Bad	Bad	353	313	258	232	151	285	—
1551–52	Bad	Deficient	313	252	275	186	153	276	48
1552–53	Good	Average	281	288	256	192	173	259	—
1553–54	Good	Average	279	190	214	151	160	276	—
1554–55	Average	Deficient	340	268	249	187	184	270	—
1555–56	Dearth	Dearth	521	330	251	185	181	370	—
1556–57	Dearth	Dearth	558	318	297	308	156	409	—
1557–58	Good	Good	235	208	275	206	174	230	—
1558–59	Abundant	Average	284	195	257	224	220	255	—
1559–60	Average	Average	314	250	255	254	193	265	59
1560–61	Bad	Average	337	242	295	196	199	283	—
1561–62	Good	Average	296	313	260	248	136	266	63
1562–63	Bad	Average	372	350	285	184	144	—	—
1563–64	Average	Average	343	360	293	220	181	—	—
1564–65	Average	Good	258	233	268	294	176	290	58
1565–66	Bad	Average	335	268	248	243	196	287	58
1566–67	Good	Good	267	264	298	236	190	282	59
1567–68	Good	Good	321	334	275	237	166	281	59
1568–69	Good	Average	355	318	295	231	194	276	61
1569–70	Good	Good	277	255	289	268	195	300	56
1570–71	Good	Good	299	244	308	199	194	265	63
1571–72	Good	Good	305	235	300	263	206	270	62

1572–73	Average	Average	368	287	326	217	195	274	61
1573–74	Bad	Deficient	478	360	338	314	182	374	—
1574–75	Average	Good	334	330	367	223	217	—	—
1575–76	Average	Average	378	259	346	264	186	309	—
1576–77	Deficient	Good	359	301	339	274	238	363	—
1577–78	Average	Average	391	275	340	260	226	351	—
1578–79	Good	Average	372	276	376	272	190	326	58
1579–80	Good	Average	414	308	322	284	228	342	58
1580–81	Average	Average	444	308	349	287	265	347	58
1581–82	Average	Average	434	306	377	252	206	343	62
1582–83	Good	Average	422	320	347	310	240	324	60
1583–84	Good	Good	370	325	327	288	230	333	59
1584–85	Abundant	Good	324	308	331	283	257	338	57
1585–86	Deficient	Average	556	364	346	298	254	352	41
1586–87	Bad	Deficient	684	420	347	277	253	491	58
1587–88	Good	Bad	365	309	366	310	273	346	56
1588–89	Good	Good	407	307	355	332	239	354	51
1589–90	Average	Good	531	312	376	317	251	396	44
1590–91	Deficient	Average	624	496	377	350	255	459	54
1591–92	Good	Average	443	346	382	354	285	370	56
1592–93	Abundant	Good	296	343	390	377	261	356	52
1593–94	Abundant	Abundant	350	388	382	326	287	381	39
1594–95	Deficient	Good	621	441	437	347	281	515	40
1595–96	Bad	Deficient	681	458	419	394	299	505	29
1596–97	Bad	Deficient	1039	598	407	379	314	685	35
1597–98	Dearth	Dearth	778	484	444	395	300	579	42
1598–99	Dearth	Bad	518	341	457	420	312	474	44
1599–1600	Average	Average	557	386	442	377	299	459	37
1600–1	Average	Bad	768	523	474	426	280	536	42
1601–2	Bad	Average	555	444	434	387	323	471	45
1602–3	Good	Good	480	368	428	352	324	448	

Sources: Agric. H. R. xii (1964), 45f; xix (1971), 153f; Thirsk 1967, pp. 848f.; *E. E. H.* ii, 194f.

Appendix II: The authorship of the 'Discourse of the Common Weal'

The *Discourse* was first published in 1581 under the title *A Compendious or Briefe Examination of Certayne Ordinary Complaints of Divers of Our Countrymen in These Our Dayes . . . By W. S. Gentleman*. The author's identity aroused immediate speculation, and has continued to do so. Nearly as many candidates have been proposed for 'W. S.' as for the 'Mr W. H.' of Shakespeare's *Sonnets*. However, William Lambarde, who had copied out the best manuscript version in 1565, stated firmly that it had been written 'long synce' by either Sir Thomas Smith or John Hales, and recent scholars have agreed that one or other of these two was the author. If so, the mysterious W. S. (probably Smith's nephew William Smith) merely edited the text for publication.

Internal evidence, discussed by Elizabeth Lamond and Mary Dewar in their respective editions, points to the late summer of 1549 for the original date of composition,[1] though the manuscript was evidently revised for publication at some time shortly before 1581, the chief alteration being the section on bullion imports and inflation. Lamond argued strongly for authorship by Hales (d. 1571), and the fact that the dialogue was apparently set in Coventry at the time of meeting of an enclosure commission – an activity headed by Hales at Coventry in 1548 – gives her view plausibility.[2] However, Dewar has demonstrated that there are stronger arguments for authorship by Smith (1513–77), whose known views accorded closely with those expressed in the *Discourse*, and whose 'Treatise on the Money of the Romans' expressed similar views on debasement and inflation in almost identical language. Smith had both the close knowledge of government, and the leisure, necessary for writing the *Discourse*; though secretary of state under Somerset, he was in enforced exile from court between July and September 1549, preoccupied with the government's economic and social problems and brooding over solutions for them. Smith is also known to have been revising his unpublished papers in 1576, and to have kept up to date with continental work on monetary matters, and that could have been the time when the section on New World bullion, probably influenced by Bodin, was inserted.[3]

The case for Smith's authorship is therefore strong, though not perhaps conclusive from the evidence so far published by Dewar, and is accepted as likely in this work.

Appendix III: The dates of Harrison's and Smith's descriptions

Sir Thomas Smith's *De Republica Anglorum* was, like the *Discourse*, first published after his death (1583), but had been begun long before. The final chapter includes his very precise statement that he has described how England is governed 'at this day the xxviii of March Anno 1565'.[4] William Harrison's description of England was first published in Holinshed's *Chronicles* in 1577, and republished in revised form in 1587. Some important passages, including the important analysis of English society, are so similar that one author must have copied from the other. Smith's book is often quoted as a work of 1565, and is therefore assumed to have been the original from which Harrison copied: even so scrupulous a scholar as J. P. Cooper made this assumption.[5]

However, Harrison in 1587 clearly implied that the borrowing had been mutual. His additional chapter on parliament was, he confessed, based wholly on Smith,

> whose onelie direction I use, and almost word for word in this chapter, requiting him with the like borowage as he hath used toward me in his discourse of the sundrie degrees of estates in the common-wealth of England, which (as I hope) shall be no discredit to his travell.[6]

Alston pointed out in his 1906 edition of *De Republica Anglorum* that the most likely explanation was indeed mutual and friendly borrowing, with Smith revising his 1565 draft by using Harrison, and Harrison in turn copying Smith in revising his own work. The only difficulty in Alston's explanation was that he supposed Smith to have consulted Harrison's work in print, which he could have done only in his last illness in 1577. It is now clear – as Dewar has shown from a study of Smith's manuscript texts – that he was allowed to read Harrison's work in manuscript, when it was circulating among friends in the 1560s or early 1570s. In view of that important conclusion it is, therefore, a pity that the critical and definitive edition of *De Republica* which Dewar announced as forthcoming in 1964, based on six newly discovered manuscripts and bringing us 'significantly closer to Smith's original text of 1565', is still awaited.[7] Nevertheless, there seems now no reason to doubt Harrison's statement that his chapter 'Of degrees of people in the commonwealth' was his own creation, and I have cited it as his rather than as Smith's.

Postscript

Since this book was written, Cambridge University Press have announced the publication of Mary Dewar's edition of *De Republica Anglorum* (1982).

Appendix IV: Sources for urban occupations

Tables 8.1 and 8.2 (pp. 243–244) attempt to provide, for the second half of the sixteenth century, what Phythian-Adams has done for the previous half-century in an important analysis which has not received the attention it deserves.[8] The purpose is to compare figures for a number of towns, from the freemen's registers wherever possible, which are calculated on a similar basis. The studies drawn on here have used slightly differing occupational classifications, so for the sake of uniformity the model adopted has been as far as possible that of J. F. Pound for Norwich. This has involved reworking of the data in some cases, and the figures in the tables will not necessarily correspond exactly to those published elsewhere. In particular, I have followed Pound's example in excluding gentlemen, yeomen and labourers from the figures, and confining analysis to those freemen with a clear occupational designation.

The numerous shoemakers (cordwainers), glovers and cobblers were assigned in Professor Hoskins's analysis of Leicester, and mine of York, to the 'clothing' category; here they have been reassigned to 'leather' to conform to the other studies. The one major discrepancy left unresolved is over Pound's 'woodwork' category, which some analyses have included separately and some have not; where there is no 'woodwork' figure, the numbers have been apportioned between 'building' and 'others'. Professor Hoskins's 'household' category has been here assigned to 'metal' and 'woodwork'. In any case, Phythian-Adams's caution on such analyses is worth stressing, that 'we can only take this evidence as a very broad guide: minor percentage differences between specific trades or occupational categories have no meaning at all. Most important is the need to remember the problems of under-registration, for whatever reason.'

The sources used for each town are as follows.

Chester: the freemen's rolls, which have been published by the *Lancashire and Cheshire Record Society*, vol. 51. I am grateful to Dr D. M. Woodward, who provided me with his calculations from the rolls, some of which he printed in the *Trans. Historic Society of Lan-*

cashire and Cheshire, cxix, 1967, pp. 66f. I have omitted 70 yeomen included in Dr Woodward's published figures.

Gloucester, Cirencester and Tewkesbury: a muster roll, analysed by A. J. and R. H. Tawney in 'An occupational census of the seventeenth century', *Econ. H. R.*[1] v (1934–35), 36. P. Clark has provided figures for Gloucester alone in 1608, and also in 1535–54, in *The English Commonwealth 1547–1640*, eds P. Clark, A. G. R. Smith and N. Tyacke, 1979, p. 170.

Hull: the freemen's roll, analysed by G. C. F. Forster, 'Hull in the sixteenth and seventeenth centuries', in *The Victoria County History of Yorkshire: East Riding*, ed. K. J. Allison, i, 1969, p. 150. Mr Forster tabulates trade groupings but not individual trades.

Leicester: the freemen's rolls, analysed by W. G. Hoskins, *Provincial England*, 1963, pp. 94f.

Norwich: the freemen's rolls, analysed by J. F. Pound, 'The Social and trade structure of Norwich 1525–1575', *Past and Present*, no. 34 (July 1966), pp. 60, 67–9.

Nottingham: unpublished figures from surviving lists of freemen in the corporation archives, kindly supplied by Mr M. Paddick.

Worcester: figures for occupational distribution among citizens with surviving inventories. I am grateful to Dr A. D. Dyer who provided me with the calculations, some of which he published in his *City of Worcester in the Sixteenth Century*, 1973, pp. 82, 84. Dr P. A. Clark has questioned Dr Dyer's use of inventories in the absence of surviving freemen's rolls (*Econ. H.R.*[2], xxvii (1974), 124f.), but my own calculations of York's occupational structure, where both the freemen's register and probate records can be used, show very little difference between the results from either source.

York: the freemen's register, which has been published by the Surtees Society, vols 96 and 102. Calculations from it by the author.

Abbreviations

(As used in Notes and Bibliography)

Agric. H. R.	*Agricultural History Review*
Aubrey, *Brief Lives*	*'Brief Lives', Chiefly of Contemporaries, Set Down by John Aubrey, Between the Years 1669 and 1696*, ed. A. Clark, Clarendon Press, 2 vols, 1898
B.I.H.R.	*Bulletin of the Institute of Historical Research*
Bindoff *et al.*	*Elizabethan Government and Society*: *Essays Presented to Sir John Neale*, eds S. T. Bindoff, J. Hurstfield and C. H. Williams, Athlone Press, 1961
B.L.	British Library (formerly the British Museum)
Camden, *Britannia*	William Camden, *Britannia*, ed. E. Gibson, London, 1695
C.E.H.E. IV, V	*The Cambridge Economic History of Europe*: *Volumes IV, V*, eds E. E. Rich and C. H. Wilson, Cambridge U.P., 1967, 1977
Chalklin and Havinden 1974	*Rural Change and Urban Growth 1500–1800: Essays in English Regional History in Honour of W. G. Hoskins*, ed. C. W. Chalklin and M. A. Havinden, Longman, 1974
Clark and Slack 1972	*Crisis and Order in English Towns 1500–1700*, eds P. Clark and P. Slack, Routledge, 1972
Clark 1976	*The Early Modern Town: A Reader*, ed. P. Clark, Longman, 1976
Clark *et al.* 1979	*The English Commonwealth 1547–1640: Essays in Politics and Society presented to Joel Hurstfield*, eds P.

	Clark, A. G .R. Smith and N. Tyacke, Leicester U.P., 1979
Coleman and John 1976	*Trade, Government and Economy in Pre-Industrial England: Essays Presented to F. J. Fisher*, eds D. C. Coleman and A. H. John, Weidenfeld, 1976
D'Ewes 1682	S. d'Ewes, *The Journals of all the Parliaments During the Reign of Queen Elizabeth*, London, 1682
E.A.H.	*Essays in Agrarian History*, ed. W. E. Minchinton, David & Charles, 2 vols, 1968
E.E.H.	*Essays in Economic History*, ed. E. M. Carus-Wilson, Edward Arnold, 3 vols, 1954–62
E.H.R.	*English Historical Review*
Econ. H.R.[1,2]	*Economic History Review*, 1st and 2nd series
Ellis	H. Ellis, *Original Letters, Illustrative of English History*, 11 vols, 1824–46
Fisher 1961	*Essays in the Economic and Social History of Tudor and Stuart England in Honour of R. H. Tawney*, ed. F. J. Fisher, Cambridge U.P., 1961
f., ff.	page(s) following
fo., fos.	folio(s)
Hakluyt	R. Hakluyt, *The Principal Navigations, Voyages, Traffiques and Discoveries of the English Nation*, Everyman Library, 8 vols, 1907, etc.
Harrison, *Description*	*Harrison's Description of England in Shakspere's Youth*, ed. F. J. Furnivall, 4 pts, New Shakspere Society, 1877–1908
Ives *et al.* 1978	*Wealth and Power in Tudor England: Essays Presented to S. T. Bindoff*, eds E. W. Ives, R. J. Knecht and J. J. Scarisbrick, Athlone Press, 1978
J.B.S.	*Journal of British Studies*

J.I.H.	*Journal of Interdisciplinary History*
Leland, *Itinerary*	*The Itinerary of John Leland in or about the Years 1535–1543*, ed. L. T. Smith, London, 5 vols, 1907–10
Lettenhove	*Relations Politiques des Pays-Bas et de l'Angleterre sous le Règne de Philippe II, publiées par M. le Baron Kervyn de Lettenhove*, Collections des Chroniques Belges Inédites, Brussels, 11 vols, 1882–1900
L.P.S.	*Local Population Studies*
Lodge 1791	E. Lodge, *Illustrations of British History, Biography, and Manners, in the Reigns of Henry VIII, Edward VI, Mary, Elizabeth, and James I . . .*, 1st edn, 3 vols, London, 1791
MS, MSS	Manuscript(s)
P. and P.	*Past and Present*
Peck 1732	F. Peck, *Desiderata Curiosa* (London, 2 vols, 1732–35), vol. i, bk. 1, pp. 1–66 (contemp. life of Burghley)
P.R.O.	Public Record Office
P.S.	*Population Studies*
r., v.	recto, verso
Ramsey 1971	P. H. Ramsey, *The Price Revolution in Sixteenth-Century England*, Methuen, 1971
Rye 1865	W. B. Rye, *England as Seen by Foreigners in the Days of Elizabeth and James the First*, London, 1865
S.E.S.H.	Studies in Economic and Social History series, published by Macmillan for the Economic History Society
Smith, *Discourse*	*A Discourse of the Common Weal of this Realm of England*, ed. E. Lamond, Cambridge U.P., 1893, etc.
T.E.D.	*Tudor Economic Documents*, eds

	R. H. Tawney and E. Power, Longmans Green, 3 vols, 1924, etc.
Thirsk 1967	*The Agrarian History of England and Wales: Volume IV: 1500–1640*, ed. J. Thirsk, Cambridge U.P., 1967
Thirsk 1970	*The Agricultural History Review*, Vol. xviii (1970): Supplement: *Land, Church, and People: Essays Presented to Professor H. P. R. Finberg*, ed. J. Thirsk
T.R.H.S.	*Transactions of the Royal Historical Society*
Tytler 1839	P. F. Tytler, *England under the Reigns of Edward VI and Mary*, London, 2 vols, 1839
U.H.Y.	*Urban History Yearbook*
V.C.H.	*Victoria County History*
Webster 1979	*Health, Medicine and Mortality in the Sixteenth Century*, ed. C. Webster, Cambridge U.P., 1979
Wilson 1601	*The State of England Anno Dom. 1600 by Thomas Wilson*, ed. F. J. Fisher, Camden Miscellany, vol. xvi (Camden Soc., 3rd Ser lii), 1936
Y.B.I.	York, Borthwick Institute of Historical Research
Y.C.R.	*York Civic Records*, ed. A. Raine, Yorks. Arch. Soc., 8 vols, 1939–53

Notes and references

(Publication details are given only for books not cited in the Bibliography or in the List of Abbreviations.)

Preface

1. A. Macfarlane *et al.*, *Reconstructing Historical Communities*, Cambridge U.P., 1977, p. 208.
2. M. Spufford, 'The experience of Essex', *Times Literary Supplement*, 1 Sept. 1978.
3. L. Stone, 'The revival of narrative', *P. and P.*, 85 (1979), 8; Stone, *The Crisis of the Aristocracy*, p. 3.
4. For example Laslett, *The World We Have Lost*, p. 33; Mingay, *The Gentry*, p. 2.

Chapter 1. 'The greatest Isle'

1. R. Holinshed, *Third Volume of Chronicles*, 1587, p. 1592.
2. J. Norden, *Description of Cornwall*, 1728, p. 9.
3. Laslett, *The World We Have Lost*, pp. 56, 58.
4. *Calendar of State Papers Venetian 1534–54*, pp. 338–62, 532–64; *Calendar of State Papers Venetian 1556–7*, pp. 1043–85 (slightly adapted).
5. Williams, *The Tudor Regime*, p. 10.
6. Harrison, *Description*, i, 144, 153, 324.
7. Aubrey, *Brief Lives*, ii, 182; W. Thomas, *The Historie of Italie*, 1549, fo. 3v.
8. Norden, *op. cit.*, p. 21; Bossy, *The English Catholic Community*, p. 99.
9. G. Mattingly, *Renaissance Diplomacy*, Penguin, 1955, p. 206; Peck 1732, p. 55.
10. Camden, *Britannia*, Gibson's prefatory life of Camden (unpaginated); Rowse, *The England of Elizabeth*, p. 50; Peck 1732, pp. 24, 52.
11. Williams, *op. cit.*, pp. 4f.
12. Russell, *The Crisis of Parliaments*, p. 44.
13. *Cal. MSS. of the Most Hon. the Marquis of Salisbury*, i, HMSO, 1883, p. 255.
14. Elton, *England under the Tudors*, p. 199.
15. W. Camden, *Annales*, 1717, i, 11 (translated); R. Naunton, *Fragmenta Regalia*, 1641, repr. 1824, p. 8.
16. Bush, *The Government Policy of Protector Somerset*, p. 40; F. Rose-Troup, *The Western Rebellion of 1549*, Smith, Elder & Co., 1913, p. 436.
17. A. F. Pollard, *The History of England ... (1547–1603)*, Longmans, Green, 1910, p. 172.
18. Clark, *English Provincial Society from the Reformation to the Revolution*, p. 102.
19. Russell, *op. cit.*, p. 145; Lettenhove, i, 612; ii, 119.
20. Tawney, *Religion and the Rise of Capitalism*, p. 155.
21. Williamson, *The Tudor Age*, p. 258.
22. Hakluyt, v, 168.
23. Peck 1732, p. 61; Read, *Lord Burghley and Queen Elizabeth*, p. 244; Lettenhove, ix, 304.
24. Ellis, vi, 6; Lettenhove, viii, 7.
25. D'Ewes 1682, p. 472; Lodge 1791, ii, 400.
26. G. Parker, *Spain and the Netherlands, 1559–1659*, Fontana, 1979, pp. 36, 209.

27. Williams, *op. cit.*, p. 465.
28. R. Davis, *The Rise of the Atlantic Economies*, Weidenfeld, 1973, p. 211.
29. M. E. James, review in *History*, 1xvi (1981), 131.

Chapter 2. Population

1. *T.E.D.*, i, 236; Rye 1865, pp. 49f.
2. *Econ. H.R.*², xxxi (1978), 452.
3. Y.B.I., MS CP/G/272.
4. *Econ. H.R.*², xxviii (1975), 712.
5. *England in the reign of King Henry the Eighth*, ed. J. M. Cowper, Early English Text Soc. extra ser. xii, 1878, p. 75; J. Strype, *Historical Memorials*, ii (1822), pt. 2, p. 358; *T.E.D.*, iii, 5.
6. Smith, *Discourse*, p. 49.
7. *T.E.D.*, i. 74; Harrison, *Description*, i, 215; Hakluyt, 'Discourse of Western planting', pp. 234, 238; *Elizabethan People*, eds. J. Hurstfield and A. G. R. Smith, Arnold, 1972, p. 47.
8. *Seventeenth-Century Economic Documents*, eds. J. Thirsk and J. P. Cooper, Clarendon Press, 1972, p. 758; Coleman, *The Economy of England 1450–1750*, p. 57.
9. Phythian-Adams, *Desolation of a City*, p. 244; Laslett, *Household and Family in Past Time*, p. 130; *Jour. Derbyshire Arch. Nat. Hist. Soc.*, xxv (1903), 209; Norfolk and Norwich Record Office, MS P.R.A. 652, 382 × 8, kindly communicated by P. A. Slack.
10. Stone, *The Family, Sex and Marriage in England*, p. 107.
11. Laslett, *The World We Have Lost*, p. 67.
12. Lodge 1791, ii, 131.
13. Laslett, *The World We Have Lost*, pp. 84–91; P. Hogrefe, *Tudor Women: Commoners and Queens*, Iowa State U.P., 1975, pp. 18f.
14. Glass and Eversley, *Population in History*, p. 132; Hakluyt, *op. cit.*, p. 239.
15. Bodleian Library, MS Ashmole 765, fo. 19v.
16. E. A. Wrigley, *Population and History*, Weidenfeld, 1969, p. 127.
17. Hakluyt, *op. cit.*, pp. 234, 238f.
18. J. G. Nichols(?), 'The Domestic Chronicle of Thomas Godfrey, Esq.', *The Topographer and Genealogist*, ii, (1853) 461; Stone, *The Crisis of the Aristocracy*, p. 593.
19. Lodge 1791, ii, 233.
20. *C.E.H.E.*, IV, 92.
21. R. Holinshed, *Third Volume of Chronicles*, 1587, p. 1049.
22. Appleby, 'Nutrition and disease', p. 19 and n.
23. Lodge 1791, ii, 202; J. Stow, *The Annales of England*, 1601 edn, p. 1095.
24. B.L., MS Lansdowne 6, fo. 154r; *T.E.D.*, iii, 314.
25. B.L. MS Lansdowne 54, fo. 141r; *Registers of St. Michael le Belfrey, York*, i. ed. F. Collins, Yorks. Par. Reg. Soc., 1899, p. 56; Appleby, *Famine in Tudor and Stuart England*, p. 141 (misprint corrected).
26. Appleby, *Famine*, p. 113; *Cheshire Sheaf*, 3rd ser. ix (1912), 22; Chalklin and Havinden 1974, p. 61.
27. Chalklin and Havinden 1974, p. 62; Cox, *The Parish Registers of England*, p. 173.
28. R. Johnson, *The Ancient Customs of the City of Hereford*, 1st edn, London, 1868, p. 164.
29. Chalklin and Havinden 1974, p. 57; *Y.C.R.*, v, 68.
30. Creighton, *A History of Epidemics in Britain*, i, 460.
31. Bodleian Library, MS Arch. G.c.6, fo. 360.
32. Stone, 'Social mobility in England, 1500–1700', p. 31.
33. Patten, *Rural-Urban Migration*, pp. 24f.

34. Kirk and Kirk, *Returns of Aliens*, i', 293, 377–83, 388–93; iii, 330–439.
35. Glass and Eversley, *Population in History*, p. 148.
36. H. J. Habakkuk, *Population Growth and Economic Development Since 1750*, Leicester U.P., 1971, p. 23.
37. Wrigley and Schofield, *The Population History of England 1541–1871*, p. 240.

Chapter 3. Society and social change

1. N. Pevsner, *The Buildings of England: Worcestershire*, Penguin, 1968, p. 157.
2. Smith, *De Republica Anglorum*, ed. Alston, pp. 29f.
3. F. R. H. du Boulay, *The Lordship of Canterbury*, Nelson, 1966, p. 156; Smith, *De Republica Anglorum*, p. 45; Thomas, 'Age and authority in early modern England', p. 24.
4. See pp. 38–40.
5. Phythian-Adams, *Desolation of a City*, pp. 80f.
6. Bindoff, *Tudor England*, p. 28; Y.B.I., MS R VII/H.C.A.B. 9, fo. 91v; *Life of Adam Martindale*, ed. R. Parkinson, Chetham Soc., iv, 1845, pp. 6f.
7. Stone, *The Crisis of the Aristocracy*, p. 630; Peck 1732, p. 64.
8. Stone, *The Crisis of the Aristocracy*, p. 595; *Proceedings in Parliament 1610*, ed. E. R. Foster, Yale U.P., 2 vols, 1966, ii, 265.
9. Rye 1865, pp. 72f.; *The Troubles of Our Catholic Forefathers*, ed. J. Morris, Burns and Oates, 3 vols, 1872–77, iii, 375.
10. Peck 1732, p. 62; F. Drake, *Eboracum*, London, 1736, p. 295.
11. *The Topographer and Genealogist*, ii, 183; H. Townshend, *Historical Collections*, London, 1680, p. 93.
12. Thomas, *op. cit.*, p. 45.
13. Wilson 1601, p. 24.
14. Stone, *The Family, Sex and Marriage in England*, pp. 651f.
15. See Appendix III, pp. 390f.
16. Harrison, *Description*, i, 105f., 130, 132–4.
17. Smith, *De Republica Anglorum*, p. 62.
18. Stone, *The Crisis of the Aristocracy*, p. 13.
19. Harrison, *Description*, i, 106; Smith *De Republica Anglorum*, pp. 31f.
20. Harrison, *Description*, i, 114; Stone, *The Crisis of the Aristocracy*, pp. 71–4; Cooper, 'The social distribution of land and men in England', pp. 423–5.
21. Wilson 1601, p. 23.
22. Harrison, *Description*, i, 128f.; Peck 1732, p. 64.
23. Laslett, *The World We Have Lost*, p. 27.
24. Stone, *The Crisis of the Aristocracy*, p. 50; Harrison, *Description*, i, 133f.; Wright, *Middle-Class Culture in Elizabethan England*, p. 20.
25. Harrison, *Description*, i, 133; *The Journeys of Celia Fiennes*, ed. C. Morris, Cresset Press, 1947, p. 136.
26. Wilson 1601, pp. 19f., 23.
27. Stone, 'Social mobility in England', pp. 16f.
28. *The Letters of John Chamberlain*, ed. N. E. McClure, American Philosophical Society, 2 vols, 1939, i, 54.
29. *E.E.H.*, i, 174, 176; *R. H. Tawney's Commonplace Book*, eds. J. M. Winter and D. M. Joslin, *Econ. H. R.*, Supplement v, 1972, p. 53; Wright, *Middle-Class Culture*, p. 5.
30. Wallerstein, *The Modern World-System I*, pp. 86f., 116, 124.
31. *Crime in England 1550–1800*, ed. Cockburn, p. 94.
32. Wallerstein, *op. cit.*, p. 256; Stone, *The Crisis of the Aristocracy*, p. 49; Laslett, *op. cit.*, pp. 23ff.; H. Perkin, *The Origins of Modern English Society 1780–1880*, Routledge, 1969, pp. 17, 26, 37; C. S. L. Davies, in *Annales E.S.C.*, xxiv (1969), 59f.; Wilson, *England's Apprenticeship*, p. xiv.

33. *T.E.D.*, i, 20f., 47.
34. MacCulloch, 'Kett's rebellion in context', p. 47; *The Gentleman's Magazine*, ciii, pt. 2 (1833), 14.
35. Tytler 1839, ii, 336; *The Writings and Speeches of Oliver Cromwell*, ed. W. C. Abbott, Harvard U. P., 4 vols, 1937–47, iii, 435.
36. Tillyard, *The Elizabethan World Picture*, pp. 12, 37.
37. E. M. W. Tillyard, *Shakespeare's History Plays*, Penguin, 1962, p. 19.
38. Lodge 1791, ii, 159; Stone, *The Crisis of the Aristocracy*, p. 747; W. A. Lloyd, 'Camden, Carmarden and the customs', *E.H.R.*, lxxxv (1970), 777; *Y.C.R.*, vii, 164.
39. Stone, *The Crisis of the Aristocracy*, p. 746; Purvis, *Tudor Parish Documents*, p. 88.
40. N. Pevsner, *The Buildings of England: Berkshire*, Penguin, 1966, p. 214; M. Girouard, *Life in the English Country House*, Yale U.P., 1978, p. 30.
41. J. Summerson, 'The building of Theobalds, 1564–1585', *Archaeologia*, xcvii (1959), 117.
42. Stone, *Family and Fortune*, pp. 50f.; Smith, *County and Court*, p. 158.
43. *Literary Remains of King Edward the Sixth*, ed. J. G. Nichols, Roxburghe Club, 2 vols, 1857, ii, 483.
44. E. W. Ives, *Faction in Tudor England*, Historical Association, 1979, p. 4; J. Strype, *Memorials of . . . Thomas Cranmer*, 1840, i, 127f.; *T.E.D.*, i, 326.
45. Stone, *The Crisis of the Aristocracy*, p. 60.
46. Dickens, *Lollards and Protestants in the Diocese of York*, p. 126.
47. W. Lambarde, *A Perambulation of Kent*, 1826 edn, p. 6.
48. Hexter, *Reappraisals in History*, p. 143.
49. Campbell, *The English Yeoman*, p. 72.
50. Harrison, *Description*, i, 133.
51. *Ibid.*, 131.
52. Exeter City Archives, book 51, fos. 352r, 358v.
53. Trevor-Roper, *The Gentry 1540–1640*, p. 16.
54. Stone, *The Crisis of the Aristocracy*, pp. 176f; Bindoff *et al.*, p. 167.
55. Laslett, *op. cit.*, p. 203; Johnson, *Elizabeth I*, p. 211.

Chapter 4. Wealth and poverty

1. *T.E.D.*, ii, 341; Wilson 1601, p. 18.
2. W. G. Zeeveld, *Foundations of Tudor Policy*, Methuen edn, 1969, p. 215; R. Holinshed, *Chronicles*, 1577 edn, ii, 1680.
3. Hoskins, *The Age of Plunder*, pp. 13, 19–28, 245. Schofield's ranking of counties in 1515 (*Econ. H.R.*², xviii (1965), 504) differs from Hoskins's in 1522.
4. Stone, *The Crisis of the Aristocracy*, pp. 163, 273; Peck 1732, p. 64.
5. Thirsk 1967, p. 307.
6. Heal, *Of Prelates and Princes*, pp. 320, 328.
7. Harrison, *Description*, i, 204.
8. B.L., Sloane MS 326, fos. 3v, 4r.
9. Williams, *The Tudor Regime*, p. 35.
10. B.L., Sloane MS 326, fo. 86r; d'Ewes 1682, pp. 483 633.
11. Harrison *Description*, i, 239–41.
12. Bodleian Library, MS. Ashmole 765, fo. 19r; Hoskins, *Provincial England*, p. 132. Smith's MS was completed in 1585 but not published (by King) until 1656: this has led Barley into misdating and misattributing it (Thirsk 1967, p. 752).
13. *Plures enim et nobilium et privatorum villae, elegantia, laxitate, et cultu conspicuae, jam passim in Anglia surgere coeperunt, quam alio quovis seculo*: Camden, *Annales*, 1717 edn, ii, 293; Harrison, *Description*, i, 238.
14. Stone, *op. cit.*, pp. 217, 220–1. However, the figure of £60,000 was hearsay related

much later, and comprised the total cost of castle, parks and chase: W. Dugdale, *Antiquities of Warwickshire*, 2nd edn, 1730, p. 249.

15. R. Plot, *The Natural History of Stafford-shire*, Oxford, 1686, p. 358; Barley, The *English Farmhouse and Cottage*, p. 52.
16. Harrison, *Description*, i, 144, 153; Thomas, *Religion and the Decline of Magic*, p. 7.
17. *Y.C.R.*, v, 133.
18. Robson-Scott, *German Travellers in England 1400–1800*, p. 48.
19. D'Ewes 1682, p. 490; Dyer, *The City of Worcester in the Sixteenth Century*, p. 160.
20. B.L., Harl. MS 1948, fo. 136v.
21. *Econ. H.R.*², xv (1962–63), 377.
22. Jordan, *Philanthropy in England 1480–1660*, p. 78.
23. Aylmer, 'Unbelief in seventeenth-century England', p. 33.
24. *Rogues and Vagabonds of Shakespeare's Youth*, eds Viles and Furnivall, pp. 23, 78–82; Harrison *Description*, i, 218; Thirsk 1967, p. 406; *T.E.D.*, ii, 341, 345; Pound, *Poverty and Vagrancy in Tudor England*, p. 5.
25. Hoskins, *Provincial England*, p. 84; Phythian-Adams, *Desolation of a City*, pp. 132–4.
26. *T.E.D.*, ii, 336.
27. D'Ewes 1682, p. 165.
28. *T.E.D.*, ii, 363; Leonard, *Early History of English Poor Relief*, p. 242; Wright, *Middle-Class Culture in Elizabethan England*, p. 182.
29. *T.E.D.*, ii, 364.
30. *T.E.D.*, ii, 312; R. Holinshed, *Third Volume of Chronicles*, 1587, pp. 1081f.
31. *The Mid-Tudor Polity*, eds Loach and Tittler, p. 108.
32. Pound, *op. cit.*, p. 63.
33. *Ibid.*, pp. 83, 85.

Chapter 5. The great inflation

1. Smith, *Discourse*, p. 33.
2. *E.E.H.*, ii, 188.
3. Smith, *Discourse*, p. 37; d'Ewes 1682, p. 490.
4. Challis, *The Tudor Coinage*, p. 233.
5. E. Le Roy Ladurie, *The Territory of the Historian*, Harvester, 1979, pp. 142f.; E. Le Roy Ladurie, *Montaillou*, Scolar, 1978, pp. 5f.
6. W. J. Courteney, 'Token coinage and the administration of poor relief during the late middle ages', *J.I.H.*, iii (1972–73), 275f., 292f.; Tawney, *The Agrarian Problem in the Sixteenth Century*, pp. 110, 198n; Ramsay, *The City of London in International Politics*, p. 57; *Thomas Platter's Travels in England*, ed. Williams, p. 190 (slightly adapted from the original German).
7. Dewar, *Sir Thomas Smith*, p. 81; Peck 1732, p. 13.
8. W. Camden, *Annales*, 1717 edn, i, 75.f; B.L., MS Add. 48023, fo. 357v.
9. R. Briggs, *Early Modern France 1560–1715*, Oxford U.P., 1977, p. 8.
10. B.L., MS Add. 48023, fo. 358v.
11. Smith, *Discourse*, pp. 186f; *T.E.D.*, iii, 387f.
12. For example, *T.E.D.*, i, 74.
13. Outhwaite, *Inflation in Tudor and Early Stuart England*, p. 17; J. Strype, *Ecclesiastical Memorials*, Clarendon Press, 3 vols, 1822, ii, pt. 2, p. 432.
14. Wilson 1601, p. 40.
15. Harrison, *Description*, i, 239.
16. Phythian-Adams, *Desolation of a City*, p. 289.
17. Outhwaite, *op. cit.*, pp. 42f., 47.

18. *T.E.D.*, i, 338, 343; Wrightson and Levine, *Poverty and Piety in an Essex Village*, p. 42; Morris, *Chester in the Plantagenet and Tudor Reigns*, p. 367n.
19. Smith, *Discourse*, pp. 33f.
20. Tawney, *Religion and the Rise of Capitalism*, p. 130.
21. Thirsk 1967, p. 291.
22. *Suffolk in the XVIIth Century: the Breviary of Suffolk by Robert Reyce, 1618*, ed. F. Hervey, John Murray, 1902, p. 58.
23. Tawney, *The Agrarian Problem*, pp. 119f, 308f.; J. Norden, *The Surveiors Dialogue*, pp. 12f.
24. Harrison, *Description*, i, 240–2.
25. Rogers, *History of Agriculture and Prices*, iv, 489–91; *E.E.H.*, ii, 189.
26. Phythian-Adams, *op. cit.*, p. 64; Woodward, 'Wage rates and living standards in pre-industrial England', p. 44.
27. Phelps Brown and Hopkins, 'Wage-rates and prices', p. 293; Wilson 1601, p. 20.
28. Lipson, *The Economic History of England*, ii, p. xix.

Chapter 6. Agriculture and rural change

1. D'Ewes 1682, p. 674; Rye 1865, p. 109.
2. Ramsey, *Tudor Economic Problems*, pp. 10f.; Clark, *English Provincial Society*, p. 222; Hoskins, 'Harvest fluctuations', p. 40; P. Mathias, *The First Industrial Nation*, Methuen, 1969, p. 30.
3. Harrison, *Description*, iii, 128.
4. Thirsk 1967, p. 14.
5. *Ibid.*, p. 41.
6. H. P. R. Finberg, *Gloucestershire: an Illustrated Essay on the History of the Landscape*, Hodder, 1955, pp. 70f.
7. Rowse, *The England of Elizabeth*, p. 73.
8. *T.E.D.*, i, 194.
9. Harrison, *Description*, i, 144; Bodleian Library, MS Ashmole 765, fo. 17r.
10. Hoskins, *The Age of Plunder*, p. 10; Thirsk 1967, pp. xxix f.
11. Rackham, *Trees and Woodland in the British Landscape*, pp. 84–93.
12. Laslett, *The World We Have Lost*, pp. 64f.
13. Kerridge, *Agrarian Problems in the Sixteenth Century and After*, p. 61.
14. W. Lambarde, *A Perambulation of Kent*, London, 1826 edn, p. 7.
15. Thirsk 1967, p. 398.
16. Bodleian Library, MS Ashmole 765, fo. 16v.
17. *T.E.D.*, i, 187.
18. Tawney, *The Agrarian Problem in the Sixteenth Century*, p. 188; Kerridge, *Agrarian Problems*, p. 15.
19. Thirsk 1967, p. 593.
20. G. Slater, *The English Peasantry and the Enclosure of Common Fields*, 1907, p. 85; *T.E.D.*, i, 56–63; N. W. Alcock, *Stoneleigh Villagers 1597–1650*, University of Warwick, 1975, p. 2.
21. *History and Society: Essays by R. H. Tawney*, ed. J. M. Winter, Routledge, 1978, p. 201; Norden, *The Surveiors Dialogue*, p. 99; *T.E.D.*, i, 61f.
22. Smith, *Discourse*, pp. 15, 49; Norden, *The Surveiors Dialogue*, p. 99.
23. F. Godwin, *Annales*, trans. M. Godwin, 1630, pp. 229f.; *The Gentleman's Magazine*, ciii, pt. 2 (1833), 14.
24. Smith, *Discourse*, p. 56.
25. *T.E.D.*, ii, 184.
26. *T.E.D.*, i, 85; A. F. Pollard and M. Blatcher, 'Hayward Townshend's journals', *B.I.H.R.*, xii (1934–35), 16.
27. 'Humberston's survey', *Yorks. Arch. Journ.*, xvii (1903), 147.

28. Tawney, *op. cit.*, pp. 34, 231.
29. Thirsk 1967, p. 461; Thirsk 1970, pp. 176f.; G. E. Mingay, 'The size of farms in the eighteenth century', *Econ. H. R.*², xiv (1961–62), 488.
30. Tawney, *op. cit.*, p. xi; Spufford, *Contrasting Communities*, p. 165.
31. Hoskins, *op. cit.*, p. 30.
32. Tytler 1839, ii, 490; B.L., MS Lansdowne 43, fo. 176v; MS Lansdowne 6, fo. 152r.
33. *T.E.D.*, i, 84.
34. W. Camden, *The History of the Most Renowned and Victorious Princess Elizabeth*, London, 1675, p. 56.
35. *V. C. H. Wiltshire*, iv (1959), 57; E. Kerridge, *The Agricultural Revolution*, pp. 347f.
36. Kerridge, *Agricultural Revolution*, p. 24.
37. G. E. Fussell, 'Crop nutrition in Tudor and early Stuart England', *A.H.R.*, iii (1955), 95.
38. Kerridge, *Agricultural revolution*, p. 249; J. Norden, *Description of Cornwall*, London, 1728, pp. 17f.; Bodley, MS Ashmole 765, fo. 18v; *Commons Debates 1621*, eds W. Notestein *et al.* 7 vols, 1935, v, 384.
39. Appleby, 'Grain prices and subsistence crises', p. 883; Hey, *An English Rural Community*, p. 49.
40. Harrison, *Description*, iii, 131.

Chapter 7. London and the towns

1. Wright, *Middle-Class Culture in Elizabethan England*, p. 35; *T.E.D.*, iii, 5, 7.
2. Clark and Slack 1972, p. 5; *Thomas Platter's Travels in England*, ed. Williams, p. 153.
3. Open University, *The Traditional Community under Stress*, p. 40; Dyer, 'Growth and decay in English towns', p. 65.
4. I have followed Dyer, 'The market towns of southern England 1500–1700', p. 125, in accepting contemporary counts of 610–655 markets, rather than the 810 of Everitt (Thirsk 1967, p. 467), on which Clark and Slack rely. The figure 810 is a total of all markets at any date between 1500 and 1673.
5. Rowse, *The England of Elizabeth*, p. 159.
6. F. W. Maitland, *Township and Borough*, Cambridge U.P., 1898, p. 4.
7. Robson-Scott, *German Travellers in England*, p. 49.
8. T. Churchyard, *The Worthines of Wales*, London, 1587, sig. Kv; Platt, *Medieval Southampton*, p. 217.
9. *U.H.Y. 1978*, p. 140.
10. Lettenhove, v, 38f.; Hakluyt, ii, 114.
11. Stow, *Survey of London*, ii, 200f,; B.L., MS Lansdowne 2, fo. 94r; *T.E.D.*, i, 159.
12. J. Norden, *Speculum Britanniae: the First Parte*, London, 1593, pp. 47f.
13. Read, *Mr. Secretary Cecil and Queen Elizabeth*, p. 115.
14. B.L., MS Lansdowne 78, no. 67; *Inedited Tracts*, ed. W. C. Hazlitt, Roxburghe Club, 1868, p. 78. My totals from Lansdowne 78 differ slightly from those of N. G. Brett-James, *The Growth of Stuart London*, Allen & Unwin, 1935, p. 37, and of E. Jones in *The London Journal*, vi (1980), 133.
15. Stone, *Family and Fortune*, p. 97.
16. Stow, *op. cit.*, i, 126, 161, 163; ii, 71f., 79f.
17. Lodge 1791, i, 123.
18. Hoskins, *Provincial England*, pp. 86f,; Nichols, *The Progresses . . . of Queen Elizabeth*, i, 194f.
19. J. E. Neale, *The Elizabethan House of Commons*, Cape, 1949, p. 146.
20. Hooker, *Description of the Citie of Excester*, iii, 788f.
21. Hoskins, *The Age of Plunder*, p. 104.

22. Clark, *English Provincial Society*, p. 252; J. W. F. Hill, *Tudor and Stuart Lincoln*, Cambridge U.P., 1956, p. 77.
23. Exeter City Records, book 51, fo. 355r.
24. MacCaffrey, *Exeter 1540–1640*, p. 5.
25. Dobson, 'Urban decline in late medieval England', p. 3.
26. Palliser, 'The boroughs of medieval Staffordshire', p. 71.
27. Phythian-Adams, *Desolation of a City*, p. 48.
28. C. Gross, *The Gild Merchant*, Clarendon Press, 2 vols, 1890, i, 52.
29. Tytler 1839, i, 362; B.L., MS Lansdowne 7, fo. 50r; *T.E.D.*, iii, 273, 275. Tawney and Power suggest no author, and tentatively date the 'Discourse' 1587–89, but it may have been the 'litle pamphlett' sent by Francis Alford to Burghley on 9 November 1584: MS Lansdowne 43, fo. 40r.
30. Bodleian Library, MS Jones 17, fo. 6r; J. Langton in *Jour. Historical Geography*, iv (1978), 198.
31. Camden, *Britannia*, cols. 26, 856.
32. *Diary of Lady Margaret Hoby 1599–1605*, ed. D. M. Meads, Routledge, 1930, p. 268; Hazlitt, ed., *op. cit.*, pp. 12f.; *Y.C.R.*, vi, 135; *Records of the Borough of Leicester*, ed. M. Bateson, iii (1905), 385f.
33. *The Works of Thomas Nashe*, ed. R. B. McKerrow, A. H. Bullen, 5 vols, 1904–10, i, 194.
34. *The Elizabethan Home*, ed. M. St. Clare Byrne, Methuen, 1949, pp. 72f.; *T.E.D.*, iii, 274; Ramsey, *Tudor Economic Problems*, p. 179.
35. Stow, *op. cit.*, ii, 211f.
36. Coleman and John 1976, p. 232.
37. Bergeron, *English Civic Pageantry 1558–1642*, p. 44.

Chapter 8. Crafts and industries

1. Smith, *Discourse*, pp. 125f.; B.L., MS Lansdowne 17, fo. 4r.
2. Wilson 1601, p. 20; Thirsk, *Economic Policy and Projects*, pp. 3, 22.
3. Coleman, *Industry in Tudor and Stuart England*, p. 20.
4. York Minster Library, MS L2(5)a, fo. 208r.
5. A. L. Beier, in *J.I.H.*, ix (1978–79), 212. I have amalgamated his figures for three parishes 1548–1611, and excluded gentlemen and servants.
6. Leland, *Itinerary*, ii, 91.
7. Hoskins, *Provincial England*, p. 80.
8. Coleman, *op. cit.*, p. 27.
9. Fisher 1961, p. 71.
10. Dyer, *The City of Worcester in the Sixteenth Century*, p. 95.
11. *Statutes of the Realm*, iv (1819), 11, 288; *T.E.D.*, i, 187; E. Lipson, *The Economic History of England*, A. & C. Black, 6th edn, 1956, ii, 24.
12. *T.E.D.*, i, 176–8, 185–7; G. Unwin, *Industrial Organization in the Sixteenth and Seventeenth Centuries*, Clarendon Press, 1904, p. 236.
13. Gough, *The Rise of the Entrepreneur*, pp. 36–9; Laslett, *The World We Have Lost*, pp. 161–3, 305; *Shorter Novels: Elizabethan and Jacobean*, Everyman, 1949, p. 24.
14. *T.E.D.*, i, 176f; Leland, *Itinerary*, i, 132.
15. Lipson, *op. cit.*, ii, 10f.; *Shorter Novels: Elizabethan and Jacobean*, p. 3; Pollard and Crossley, *The Wealth of Britain 1085–1966*, p. 104.
16. Lodge, ii, 414; Leland, *Itinerary*, ii, 97.
17. Coleman, *op. cit.*, p. 36.
18. *E.A.H.*, i, 195.
19. Coleman and John 1976, p. 21.
20. *T.E.D.*, i, 271, 277; the former, there dated 1590, was redated 1595 by Lipson, *op. cit.*, ii, 142n.

21. Fisher 1961, p. 2.
22. Stone, *The Crisis of the Aristocracy*, p. 375 (corrected).
23. *T.E.D.*, iii, 9.
24. *T.E.D.*, i, 300, 313–15; iii, 212.
25. Nichols, *The Progresses . . . of Queen Elizabeth*, i, 339; Willan, *The Early History of the Russia Company*, p. 247.
26. Fisher 1961, p. 70; Thirsk, *Economic Policy and Projects*, pp. 5f.; *Textile History and Economic History*, eds Harte and Ponting, pp. 51, 63f.
27. Phythian-Adams, *Desolation of a City*, p. 42n.
28. T. Fuller, *The Worthies of England*, ed. J. Freeman, Allen & Unwin, 1952. p. 99.
29. Gough, *The Rise of the Entrepreneur*, p. 229; *T.E.D.*, iii, 235–9.
30. Thirsk, *Economic Policy and Projects*, pp. 7f., 23.

Chapter 9. Traffics and discoveries

1. *T.E.D.*, i, 199.
2. Willan, *The Inland Trade*, p. 61.
3. Coleman, *The Economy of England 1450–1750*, p. 61; Chartres, *Internal Trade in England 1500–1700*, p. 13.
4. *T.E.D.*, iii, 49.
5. P. Deane, *The First Industrial Revolution*, Cambridge U.P., 1965, p. 258.
6. Hoskins, *The Age of Plunder*, p. 10.
7. Chartres, *op. cit.*, p. 39; Wilson, *England's Apprenticeship*, p. 43.
8. Woodward, *The Trade of Elizabethan Chester*, p. 69; Willan, *The Inland Trade*, p. 21.
9. Shakespeare, *Merchant of Venice*, V. i; Lodge 1791, ii, 112f.; Robson-Scott, *German Travellers in England 1400–1800*, p. 44.
10. Wilson and Parker, *An Introduction to the Sources of European Economic History 1500–1800*, i, 129.
11. Camden, *Britannia*, col. 407; Lodge 1791, ii, 284.
12. Willan, *The Inland Trade*, pp. 27, 46; *E.E.H.*, i, 136; Thirsk 1967, p. 516.
13. *Rogues and Vagabonds of Shakespeare's Youth*, ed. Viles and Furnivall, p. 30; *E.E.H.*, i, 143; J. Norden, *Speculi Britaniae Pars: the Description of Hartfordshire*, London, 1598, p. 2.
14. Willan, *The Inland Trade*, p. 30.
15. Woodward, *op. cit.*, p. 7.
16. Supple, *Commercial Crisis and Change in England*, p. 14.
17. Braudel, *The Mediterranean and the Mediterranean World in the Age of Philip II*, i, 213; Hakluyt, iii, 91; W. Camden, *The History of the Most Renowned and Victorious Princess Elizabeth*, London, 1675, p. 72.
18. *E.E.H.*, i, 153f.; Stone, 'State control in sixteenth-century England', pp. 105, 107.
19. *T.E.D.*, ii. 99.
20. *Bronnen tot de Geschiedenis van den Handel met Engeland. Schotland en Ierland*, ed. H. J. Smit, 's-Gravenhage, 2 vols, 1942–50, ii, 815.
21. *T.E.D.*, ii. 45.
22. Ramsay, *The City of London in International Politics*, pp. 26f.
23. Smith, *Discourse*, pp. 63, 68f.; *T.E.D.*, ii, 45, 124; Read, *Lord Burghley and Queen Elizabeth*, pp. 213, 222.
24. Ramsay, *City of London*, p. 210.
25. First published as *The Politics of a Tudor Merchant Adventurer*, ed. Ramsay. Nedham's tract was extensively plagiarised without acknowledgement in John Wheeler's *Treatise of Commerce* (1601), a literary theft not detected by Tawney and Power when they printed extracts from Wheeler which were largely written by Nedham forty years earlier (*T.E.D.*, iii, 280–304).

26. Ramsay, *City of London*, p. 265.
27. Hakluyt, iv, 35f.
28. *Ibid.*, i, 41; iii, 84.
29. *Ibid.*, iii, 139–59; iv, 14.
30. *T.E.D.*, ii, 74f.; Hakluyt, iv, 361; Rye 1865, p. 216; Camden, *Annales*, 1717, ii, 449 (*tabernae tabaccanae non minus quam cervisianae et vinariae passim per oppida habeantur*).
31. *E.E.H.*, i, 163, 165, 169; Stone, 'Elizabethan overseas trade', p. 50.
32. Zins, *England and the Baltic in the Elizabethan Era*, p. 275; Willan, *The Early History of the Russia Company*, p. 274.
33. *T.E.D.*, ii, 75, 80–3.
34. *T.E.D.*, ii, 124; d'Ewes 1682, p. 491.
35. Viles and Furnivall, *op. cit.*, pp. 38–40.
36. Lettenhove, ii, 397; iv, 367.
37. Willan, *Studies in Elizabethan Foreign Trade*, p. 64.
38. *T.E.D.*, ii, 100.
39. *T.E.D.*, ii, 104–17, 122; Fisher 1961, p. 132.
40. Hakluyt, i, 3; Fisher 1961, p. 118.

Chapter 10. Government, law and order

1. Tawney, *The Agrarian Problem in the Sixteenth Century*, p. 34; Coleman and John 1976, p. 132.
2. R. Hooker, *Of the Laws of Ecclesiastical Politie*, Everyman edn, 2 vols, 1907 etc., i, 150, 155, 163, 182, etc.
3. P. S. Lewis, *Later Medieval France*, Oxford U.P., 1968, pp. 236f.; Challis, *The Tudor Coinage*, p. 51; Johnson, *Elizabeth I*, p. 223.
4. *Sermons, or Homilies, Appointed to be Read in Churches in the Time of Queen Elizabeth*, London, 1815, pp. 383, 400.
5. *Ballads from Manuscripts*, ed. W. R. Morfill, ii, pt. 2, Ballad Soc., 1873, pp. 130f; L. F. Salzman, *England in Tudor Times*, Batsford, 1926, p. 3.
6. Williams, *The Tudor Regime*, p. 464.
7. Peck 1932, p. 44; *Correspondence of Matthew Parker, D.D.*, eds J. Bruce and T. T. Perrowne, Parker Soc., 1853, p. 105; Lettenhove, xi, 92.
8. Ives 'English law and English society', p. 51; *English Historical Documents 1485–1558*, ed. C. H. Williams, Eyre & Spottiswoode, 1967, p. 528.
9. Williams, *The Tudor Regime*, p. 152.
10. Ives, *op. cit.*, p. 52.
11. Houlbrooke, *Church Courts and the People*, pp. 263, 272.
12. Stone, *The Crisis of the Aristocracy*, p. 234.
13. Lodge 1791, iii, 321.
14. Dickens, *Lollards and Protestants in the Diocese of York*, p. 99.
15. *Crime in England 1550–1800*, ed. Cockburn, p. 55.
16. *T.E.D.*, ii, 339; Williams, *The Tudor Regime*, p. 213.
17. Rowse, *The England of Elizabeth*, p. 357.
18. *T.E.D.*, ii. 340f. Hext's fifth not brought to trial is interpreted as four-fifths in Cockburn, ed. *op. cit.*, p. 12, 50.
19. Cockburn, ed. *op. cit.*, p. 53.
20. Davies, *Peace, Print and Protestantism 1450–1558*, p. 302.
21. J. S. Morrill, *London Review of Books*, 7–20 May 1981.
22. *E.E.H.*, i, 152f.; J. D. Chambers in *Econ. H.R.*[2], vii (1954–55), 108.
23. Wilson 1601, pp. 38–41.
24. R. Ascham, *Toxophilus*, London, 1545, sig. A, fo. 50r.
25. Coleman and John 1976, p. 148.

26. Tytler 1839, i, 341; Outhwaite, 'Dearth and government intervention in English grain markets, 1590–1700', p. 400.
27. Williams, ed. *English Historical Documents 1485–1558*, p. 627; Read, *Lord Burghley and Queen Elizabeth*, p. 112.
28. Ramsey, *Tudor Economic Problems*, pp. 146–63.
29. Elton, *The Tudor Constitution*, p. 125.
30. *A Briefe Note of the Benefits that Growe to this Realme, by the Observation of Fish-Daies*, 1593/94, Society of Antiquaries, broadside no. 92.
31. Ramsey, *op. cit.*, p. 165.
32. D. C. Coleman, 'Mercantilism revisited', *Historical Journal*, xxiii (1980), 790.
33. *T.E.D.*, ii, 279. Wroth's list is often stated to have been confined to patents granted 'since the last parliament' (1598), but his own words make it clear that he was listing those patents 'now in being'. Some had certainly been granted before 1598.
34. Lettenhove, iv, 316.
35. Ellis, v, 306f.
36. Peck 1732, p. 13.
37. Williams, *The Tudor Regime*, p. 156; *T.E.D.*, iii, 221.
38. C. Wilson, *The Transformation of Europe 1558–1648*, Weidenfeld, 1976, p. 43.

Chapter 11. Church and belief

1. *The New Cambridge Modern History*, vol. III, ed. R. B. Wernham, Cambridge U.P., 1968, p. 11; Hakluyt, v, 232; Read, *Lord Burghley and Queen Elizabeth*, p. 545.
2. Peck 1732, p. 44; Camden, *Annales*, 1615, i, preface: *inter religionem enim, et rempublicam divortium esse non potest.*
3. Heal, *Of Prelates and Princes*, p. 3.
4. C. Cross, *The Puritan Earl*, Macmillan, 1966, p. 137; Hill, *Puritanism and Revolution*, p. 44.
5. Rowse, *The England of Elizabeth*, pp. 389f.
6. P. Heath, *The English Parish Clergy on the Eve of the Reformation*, Routledge, 1969, p. 75 and n.; Aubrey, *Brief Lives*, i, 323.
7. O'Day, *The English Clergy*, p. 231.
8. G. Burnet, *History of the Reformation of the Church of England*, Baynes, 6 vols, 1825, vi, 341; Ellis, vi, 47f.; Knappen, *Tudor Puritanism*, p. 258; C. Haigh, *The Last Days of the Lancashire Monasteries and the Pilgrimage of Grace*, Chetham Soc., 3rd Ser. xvii, 1969, p. 139.
9. Rowse, *op. cit.*, p. 391.
10. Harrison, *Description*, i, 16, 204.
11. K. G. Powell, 'The social background to the Reformation in Gloucestershire', *Trans. Bristol Gloucs. Arch. Soc.*, xcii (1973), pp. 103f.
12. F. Godwin, *Annales of England*, 1616 (1630 transl.), p. 217; *Letters and Papers of Henry VIII*, xiv, no. 1338.
13. Camden, *Britannia*, preface (unpaginated); Dickens, *Tudor Treatises*, pp. 27–40, 89–142.
14. B.L., MS Harl. 286, fo. 102r; Clark, *English Provincial Society*, pp. 156, 437.
15. Smith, *Discourse*, pp. 21, 36; Read, *Mr. Secretary Cecil and Queen Elizabeth*, p. 437.
16. Aylmer, 'Unbelief in seventeenth-century England', pp. 22f.; Thomas, *Religion and the Decline of Magic*, pp. 199, 201.
17. R. Ashton, review in *Econ. H.R.*[2], xxv (1972), 364.
18. J. Dover Wilson, *Life in Shakespeare's England*, Cambridge U.P., 2nd edn, 1913, p. 11; *Sermons, or Homilies . . . in the Time of Queen Elizabeth*, pp. 116, 339.

19. *Y.C.R.*, vii, 55; Clark, *op. cit.*, p. 166; Rye 1865, p. 111; Purvis, *Tudor Parish Documents of the Diocese of York*, p. 169.
20. Ewen, *Witch Hunting and Witch Trials*, p. 112; Thomas, *op. cit.*, pp. 535f.; C. Larner, 'Witch beliefs and witch-hunting in England and Scotland', *History Today*, Feb. 1981, p. 33.
21. Thomas, *op. cit.*, p. 209; Purvis, *op. cit.*, p. 199.
22. Lettenhove, ii, 4.
23. J. Securis, *A New Almanacke and Prognostication for the Yere of our Saviour Christ MDLXVIII*, 1567; T.H., *An Almanack Published at Large . . ., 1571.*
24. *Johnson, Elizabeth I*, pp. 66, 224; W. Camden, *Annales*, 1717 edn, i, 70; ii, 583.
25. Aubrey, *Brief Lives*, ii, 266; *Liverpool Town Books*, ed. J. A. Twemlow, ii, 1936, p. 125; Read, *Lord Burghley and Queen Elizabeth*, p. 155.
26. R. Holinshed, *Third Volume of Chronicles*, 1587, pp. 1356f.
27. *The Works of James Pilkington*, ed. J. Scholefield, Parker Soc., 1842, p. 309.
28. Dickens, *The English Reformation*, p. 191.
29. Fletcher, *Tudor Rebellions*, p. 135.
30. Heal and O'Day, *Church and Society in England*, pp. 9f; Purvis, *op. cit.*, pp. 135f.
31. Thomas, *op. cit.*, pp. 27, 85–7.
32. J. A. Froude, *The Reign of Elizabeth*, Everyman, 5 vols, 1911, i, 326f.
33. Knappen, *op. cit.*, pp. 339, 401, 417, 466, 473f.
34. Samuelsson, *Religion and Economic Action, passim*; G. R. Elton, *Reformation Europe 1517–1559*, Fontana, 1963, p. 318.
35. *T.E.D.*, iii, 323.
36. Hill, *Puritanism and Revolution*, pp. 43, 226; Stone, *The Crisis of the Aristocracy*, p. 331.
37. J. M. Lambert, *Two Thousand Years of Gild Life*, Hull, 1891, p. 276; Stone, *The Family, Sex and Marriage in England*, p. 98.

Chapter 12. Culture and society

1. Strong, *The English Icon*, p. 1.
2. Lettenhove, viii, 238.
3. T. Cockaine, *A Short Treatise of Hunting*, London, 1591, sig. C1; Leland, *Itinerary*, ii, 75.
4. Wright, *Middle-Class Culture in Elizabethan England*, pp. 92–4.
5. Summerson, *Architecture in Britain 1530 to 1830*, p. 347.
6. Hooker, *Description of the Citie of Excester*, ii, 75.
7. Cox, *The Parish Registers of England*, p. 13.
8. For example, Clark, *English Provincial Society*, p. 212.
9. Morris, *Chester in the Plantagenet and Tudor Reigns*, p. 235.
10. Spufford, *Contrasting Communities*, p. 194; Hoskins, *The Midland Peasant*, pp. 183f.; B.L., MS Lansdowne 5, fos. 134–43.
11. Aubrey, *Brief Lives*, i, 328.
12. Y.B.I., Dean & Chapter prob. reg. 5, fo. 65; *Bristol Wills 1546–1593*, eds P. McGrath and M. E. Williams, Univ. of Bristol, 1975, pp. viii, 17; Wright, *op. cit.*, pp. 157f.
13. Morris, *Chester*, p. 340; *The Records of the City of Norwich*, eds W. Hudson and J. C. Tingey, 2 vols, 1906–10, ii, 352.
14. Charlton, *Education in Renaissance England*, p. 210.
15. Simon, *Education and Society in Tudor England*, p. vii.
16. *Ibid.*, p. 369; Rowse, *The England of Elizabeth*, p. 496 (ratio adjusted to current population estimates).
17. *Wentworth Papers 1597–1628*, ed. J. P. Coooper, Camden Soc., 4th Ser. xii, 1973, p. 21.

18. Printed as an appendix to J. Stow, *Annales*, ed. E. Howes (1631 edn) (quotation from p. 1087).
19. *T.E.D.*, i, 326f.
20. Hexter, *Reappraisals in History*, p. 53.
21. Cressy, *Education in Tudor and Stuart England*, p. 105.
22. C. M. Cipolla, *Before the Industrial Revolution: European Society and Economy, 1000–1700*, Methuen, 1976, p. 261.
23. Cipolla, *Clocks and Culture*, p. 67; Hakluyt, iii, 113; P. Mathias, *The First Industrial Nation*, Methuen, 1969, p. 139.
24. Harrison, *Description*, i, 325f, 331f.
25. Buxton, *Elizabethan Taste*, p. 65; H. F. M. Prescott, *Mary Tudor*, 2nd edn, 1952, p. 103.
26. McKisack, *Medieval History in the Tudor Age*, pp. 17, 27; Aubrey, *Brief Lives*, ii, 297.
27. *Annals of the First four Years of Queen Elizabeth*, by Sir John Hayward, ed. J. Bruce, Camden Soc., 1st Ser. vii, 1840, p. 28.
28. I. Nairn *et al.*, *The Buildings of England: Surrey*, Penguin, 2nd edn, 1971, p. 37.
29. Mercer, *English Art 1553–1625*, p. 56.
30. Buxton, *op. cit.*, p. 109; Strong, *op. cit.*, p. 2.
31. Lewis, *English Literature in the Sixteenth Century*, p. 1.
32. Wilson, *The English Drama 1485–1585*, p. 77.
33. N. Scarfe, *The Suffolk Landscape*, Hodder, 1972, p. 201; Rye 1865, pp. cxi f.

Chapter 13. Conclusion

1. Cipolla, *Clocks and Culture*, p. 67; Elton, *Studies in Tudor and Stuart Politics and Government*, i, 238.
2. Russell, *The Crisis of Parliaments 1509–1660*, p. 4.
3. Wilson, *England's Apprenticeship*, p. 19.
4. *C.E.H.E.*, V, 37.
5. R. Davis, *The Rise of the Atlantic Economies*, Weidenfeld, 1973, pp. 89f.
6. Harrison, *Description*, i, 234.
7. C. S. L. Davies, 'The English people and war in the early sixteenth century', *Britain and the Netherlands*, vi, ed. A. C. Duke and C. A. Tamse, Martinus Nijhoff, the Hague, 1977, 2; C. G. Cruickshank, *Elizabeth's Army*, Oxford U.P., 2nd edn, 1966, p. 290.
8. E. Taube, 'German Craftsmen in England during the Tudor period', *Economic History*, iii, 14 (1939), 167.
9. C. M. Cipolla, *Before the Industrial Revolution: European Society and Economy, 1000–1700*, Methuen, 1976, p. 262; Wright, *Middle-Class Culture in Elizabethan England*, p. 36; Thirsk, *Economic Policy and Projects*, pp. 12f., 85.
10. Wrigley and Schofield, *The Population History of England 1541–1871*, p. 1; Pollard and Crossley, *The Wealth of Britain 1085–1966*, p. 124.
11. Chambers, *Population, Economy, and Society in Pre-Industrial England*, p. 18.
12. F. J. Fisher, in *Econ. H.R.*[2], xxviii (1975), 119.
13. Coleman, *The Economy of England 1450–1750*, p. 197.

Appendices

1. Smith, *Discourse*, ed. Lamond, xi–xiv; ed. Dewar, p. xix.
2. Lamond edn, pp. xxv–xxix.

3. Dewar, 'The authorship of the "Discourse of the Commonweal"', *passim*; Dewar edn. pp. xx–xxvi.
4. Smith, *De Republica Anglorum*, ed. Alston, p. 142.
5. For example, Laslett, *The World We Have Lost*, pp. 31f.; J. P. Cooper in *Econ. H.R.*[2], xxxi (1978), 467.
6. Harrison, *Description*, i, 176.
7. Dewar, *Sir Thomas Smith*, pp. v, 114.
8. C. Phythian-Adams, 'The economic and social structure', in *The Fabric of the Traditional Community*, Open University, English Urban History 1500–1780 course, 1977, pp. 15–22, 39f. For comparative early seventeenth-century statistics, see J. Langton, 'Industry and towns 1500–1780', in *An Historical Geography of England and Wales*, eds R. A. Dodgshon and R. A. Butlin, 1978, pp. 186f.

Bibliography

This constitutes only a select list of further reading and of works frequently used and cited in the text. For comprehensive bibliographies the reader is referred to Conyers Read, *Bibliography of British History: Tudor Period, 1485–1603*, Clarendon Press, 2nd edn, 1959; Mortimer Levine, *Tudor England 1485–1603*, Cambridge U.P., 1968; and W. H. Chaloner and R. C. Richardson, *British Economic and Social History: A Bibliographical Guide*, Manchester U.P., 1976. Primary printed sources are not in general listed in this bibliography, and the emphasis is on recent secondary works. It is inevitably arbitrary in assigning some books and articles between chapters, where they are relevant to more than one topic.

General

Alberi, E., ed. *Relazioni degli Ambasciatori Veneti al Senato*, Serie i, vol. ii, Florence, 1840

Aubrey, J. *Brief Lives*, ed. A. Clark, 2 vols, Clarendon Press, 1898

Bindoff, S. T. *Tudor England* (Pelican History of England, 5), Penguin, 1950, etc.

Bindoff, S. T., Hurstfield, J. and **Williams, C. H.**, eds *Elizabethan Government and Society: Essays Presented to Sir John Neale*, Athlone Press, 1961

Bush, M. L. *The Government Policy of Protector Somerset*, Edward Arnold, 1975

Camden, W. *Britannia*, London, 1586, etc.; ed. E. Gibson, London, 1695

Clark, P. *English Provincial Society from the Reformation to the Revolution: Religion, Politics and Society in Kent 1500–1640*, Harvester, 1977

Coleman, D. C. *The Economy of England 1450–1750*, Oxford U.P., 1977

Coleman, D. C. and **John, A. H.**, eds *Trade, Government and Economy in Pre-Industrial England: Essays Presented to F. J. Fisher*, Weidenfeld, 1976

Davies, C. S. L. *Peace, Print and Protestantism, 1450–1558*, Paladin, 1977

Dewar, M. *Sir Thomas Smith: A Tudor Intellectual in Office*, Athlone Press, 1964

Dewar, M. 'The authorship of the 'Discourse of the Commonweal'', *Econ. H.R.*[2], xix (1966)

Dewar, M.; ed. *A Discourse of the Commonweal of this Realm of England attributed to Sir Thomas Smith*, Virginia U.P., 1969

Edelen, G., ed. *The Description of England by William Harrison*, Cornell U.P., 1968

Elliott, J. H. *Europe Divided 1559–1598* (Fontana History of Europe), Fontana/Collins, 1968

Elton, G. R. *England under the Tudors*, Methuen, 1955, etc.

Elton, G. R. *Studies in Tudor and Stuart Politics and Government*: *Papers and Reviews 1946–1972*, Cambridge U.P., 2 vols, 1974

Elton, G. R. *Reform and Reformation: England 1509–1558*, Arnold, 1977

Fisher, F. J. 'The sixteenth and seventeenth centuries: the dark ages of English economic history?', *Economica*, N.S. xxiv (1957)

Fisher, F. J., ed. *Essays in the Economic and Social History of Tudor and Stuart England in Honour of R. H. Tawney*, Cambridge U.P., 1961

Furnivall, F. J., ed. *Harrison's Description of England in Shakspere's Youth*, New Shakspere Soc., 4 pts, 1877–1908

Hexter, J. H. *Reappraisals in History*, Longmans, 1961

'History and climate: interdisciplinary explorations', a special issue of *J.I.H.*, x (1979–80), 583–858

Hoskins, W. G. *The Making of the English Landscape*, Hodder, 1955, etc.

Hoskins, W. G. *The Midland Peasant: The Economic and Social History of a Leicestershire Village*, Macmillan, 1957

Hoskins, W. G. *Provincial England: Essays in Social and Economic History*, Macmillan, 1963

Hoskins, W. G. *The Age of Plunder: King Henry's England 1500–1547*, Longman, 1976

Ives, E. W., Knecht, R. J. and **Scarisbrick, J. J.**, eds *Wealth and Power in Tudor England: Essays Presented to S. T. Bindoff*, Athlone Press, 1978

Johnson, P. *Elizabeth I: A Study in Power and Intellect*, Weidenfeld, 1974; Futura pb. 1976 (references in the notes are to the Futura paperback edition)

Ladurie, E. le Roy *Times of Feast, Times of Famine: A History of Climate since the Year 1000*, Allen & Unwin, 1972

Lamb, H. H. *Climate Present, Past and Future: Volume 2: Climatic History and the Future*, Methuen, 1977

Lamond, E., ed. *A Discourse of the Common Weal of this Realm of England*, Cambridge U.P., 1893, etc.

Laslett, P. *The World We Have Lost*, Methuen, 2nd edn, 1971

Loach, J. and **Tittler, R.**, eds *The Mid-Tudor Polity c1540–1560*, Macmillan, 1980

Loades, D. M. *Politics and the Nation 1450–1660: Obedience, Resistance and Public Order*, Fontana, 1974

Loades, D. M. *The Reign of Mary Tudor*, Ernest Benn, 1979

Macfarlane, A. *The Origins of English Individualism: The Family, Property and Social Transition*, Blackwell, 1978

Mattingly, G. *The Defeat of the Spanish Armada*, Cape, 1959

Morgan, V. 'The cartographic image of "the country" in early modern England', *T.R.H.S.*, 5th Ser. xxix (1979)

Nichols, J., ed. *The Progresses and Processions of Queen Elizabeth*, London, 3 vols, 1823

Pollard, S. and **Crossley, D. W.** *The Wealth of Britain 1085–1966*, Batsford, 1968

Ramsey, P. *Tudor Economic Problems*, Gollancz, 1963

Rich, E. E. and **Wilson, C. H.**, eds *The Cambridge Economic History of Europe*, vols IV and V, Cambridge U.P., 1967, 1977

Roberts, P. R. 'The union with England and the identity of "Anglican" Wales', *T.R.H.S.*, 5th Ser. xxii (1972)

Robson-Scott, W. D. *German Travellers in England 1400–1800*, Blackwell, 1953

Rowse, A. L. *Tudor Cornwall: Portrait of a Society*, Cape, 1941

Rowse, A. L. *The England of Elizabeth: The Structure of Society*, Macmillan, 1950

Rowse, A. L. *The Expansion of Elizabethan England*, Macmillan, 1955

Russell, C. *The Crisis of Parliaments: English History 1509–1660*, Oxford U.P., 1971

Rye, W. B. *England as Seen by Foreigners in the Days of Elizabeth and James the First*, London, 1865

Smith, L. Toulmin *The Itinerary of John Leland in or about the Years 1535–1543*, London, 5 vols, 1907–10; repr. by Centaur Press, 1964

Spooner, F. C., 'The economy of Europe 1559–1609', in *The New Cambridge Modern History*, iii, ed. R. B. Wernham, Cambridge U.P., 1968

Spufford, M. *Contrasting Communities: English Villagers in the Sixteenth and Seventeenth Centuries*, Cambridge U.P., 1974

Stone, L. *The Crisis of the Aristocracy 1558–1641*, Clarendon Press, 1965

Tawney, R. H. and **Power, E.**, eds *Tudor Economic Documents*, Longmans Green 3 vols, 1924, etc.

Thirsk, J., ed. *The Agrarian History of England and Wales: vol. IV: 1500–1640*, Cambridge U.P., 1967

Thomas, K. *Religion and the Decline of Magic*, Weidenfeld, 1971; Penguin, 1973

Wallerstein, I. *The Modern World-System I: Capitalist Agriculture and the Origins of the European World-Economy in the Sixteenth Century*, Academic Press, 1974

Williams, C., ed. *Thomas Platter's Travels in England 1599*, Cape, 1937

Williams, P. H. *The Council in the Marches of Wales under Elizabeth I*, University of Wales Press, 1958

Williams, P. *The Tudor Regime*, Clarendon Press, 1979

Williamson, J. A. *The Tudor Age*, Longman, revised 3rd edn, 1979

Wilson, C. *England's Apprenticeship 1603–1763*, Longmans, 1963

Wilson, C. *Queen Elizabeth and the Revolt of the Netherlands*, Univ. California Press, 1970

Wilson, C. and **Parker, G.** *An Introduction to the Sources of European Economic History 1500–1800: Volume I: western Europe*, Weidenfeld, 1977

Wrightson, K. and **Levine, D.** *Poverty and Piety in an English Village: Terling, 1525–1700*, Academic Press, 1979

Population

Allison, K. J. 'An Elizabethan village "census"', *B.I.H.R.*, xxxv (1962)

Appleby, A. B. 'Nutrition and disease: the case of London, 1550–1750', *J.I.H.*, vi (1975–76)

Appleby, A. B. *Famine in Tudor and Stuart England*, Stanford U.P., 1978

Berkner, L. K., 'The use and misuse of census data for the historical analysis of family structure', *J.I.H.*, v (1974–75)

Berry, B. M. and **Schofield, R. S.** 'Age at baptism in pre-industrial England', *P.S.*, xxv (1971)

Chambers, J. D. *Population, Economy, and Society in Pre-Industrial England*, Oxford U.P., 1972

Chaytor, M. 'Household and Kinship: Ryton in the late 16th and early 17th centuries', *History Workshop*, x (1980)

Cornwall, J. C. 'English population in the early sixteenth century', *Econ. H.R.*[2], xxiii (1970)

Cox, J. C. *The Parish Registers of England*, Methuen. 1910

Creighton, C. *A History of Epidemics in Britain*, 2 vols, 1891–94; 2nd edn, Cass, 1965

Cressy, D. 'Occupations, migration and literacy in East London, 1580–1640', *L.P.S.*, v (1970)

Cunningham, C. 'Christ's Hospital: infant and child mortality in the sixteenth century', *L.P.S.*, xviii (1977)

Dyer, A. D. 'The influence of bubonic plague in England 1500–1667', *Medical History*, xxii (1978)

Finlay, R. A. P. *Population and Metropolis: The Demography of London 1580–1650*, Cambridge U.P., 1981

Fisher, F. J. 'Influenza and inflation in Tudor England', *Econ. H.R.*[2], xviii (1965)

Glass, D. V. and **Eversley, D. E. C.**, eds *Population in History: Essays in Historical Demography*, Arnold, 1965

Glass, D. V. and **Revelle, R.**, eds *Population and Social Change*, Arnold, 1972

Goose, N. 'Household size and structure in early-Stuart Cambridge', *Social History*, v (1980)

Hakluyt, R. 'Discourse of Western planting', in *The Original Writings and Correspondence of the two Richard Hakluyts*, ed. E. G. R. Taylor, Hakluyt Soc., 2 vols, 1935

Hammer, C. I. 'The mobility of skilled labour in late medieval England: some Oxford evidence', *Vierteljahrschaft für Sozial- und Wirtschaftsgeschichte*, lxiii (1976)

Hatcher, J. *Plague, Population and the English Economy 1348–1530* (S.E.S.H.), Macmillan, 1977

Helleiner, K. F. 'The Population of Europe from the Black Death to the eve of the vital revolution', in *C.E.H.E.*, IV, ch. 1.

Hollingsworth, M. F. and **T. H.** 'Plague mortality rates by age and sex in the parish of St. Botolph's without Bishopsgate, London, 1603', *P.S.*, xxv (1971)

Hollingsworth, T. H. *The Demography of the British Peerage*, supplement to *P.S.*, xviii (1964–65)

Kirk, R. E. G. and **Kirk, E. F.**, eds *Returns of Aliens Dwelling in the City and Suburbs of London from the Reign of Henry VIII to that of James I*, Huguenot Soc. of London, x, 4 pts, 1900–8

Kitch, M. ed. *Migration in Pre-Industrial England*, Croom Helm, forthcoming

Laslett, P. ed. *Household and Family in Past Time*, Cambridge U.P., 1972

Laslett, P. *Family Life and Illicit Love in Earlier Generations*, Cambridge U.P., 1977

Laslett, P. *et al.*, eds *Bastardy and its Comparative History*, Arnold, 1980

Palliser, D. M. 'Epidemics in Tudor York', *Northern History*, viii (1973)

Palliser, D. M. 'Dearth and disease in Staffordshire, 1540–1670', in Chalklin and Havinden 1974

Patten, J. *Rural–Urban Migration in Pre-Industrial England*, Univ. of Oxford, School of Geography, Research Paper No. 6, 1973

Rich, E. E. 'The population of Elizabethan England', *Econ. H.R.*[2], ii (1949–50)

Russell, J. C. *British Medieval Population*, University of New Mexico Press, Albuquerque, 1948

Schnucker, R. V., 'Elizabethan birth control and Puritan attitudes', *J.I.H.*, v (1974–75)

Schofield, R. S. '"Crisis" mortality', *L.P.S.*, ix (1972)

Shrewsbury, J. F. D. *A History of Bubonic Plague in the British Isles*, Cambridge U.P., 1970

Slack, P. A. 'Some aspects of epidemics in England 1485–1640', unpub. Oxford D. Phil. thesis, 1972

Slack, P. *et al. The Plague Reconsidered: A New Look at its Origins and Effects in 16th and 17th Century England*, L.P.S. Supplement, 1977

Smith, R. M. 'Population and its geography in England 1500–1730', in *An Historical Geography of England and Wales*, eds R. A. Dodgshon and R. A. Butler, Academic Press, 1978

Webster, C., ed. *Health, Medicine and Mortality in the Sixteenth Century*, Cambridge U.P., 1979

Wrigley, E. A. 'Family limitation in pre-industrial England', *Econ. H. R. xix* (1966).

Wrigley, E. A. ed. *An Introduction to English Historical Demography*, Weidenfeld, 1966

Wrigley, E. A. 'Family limitation in pre-industrial England', *Econ H.R.*[2] xix (1966). of information about the number of births in England before the beginnings of civil registration', *P.S.*, xxxi (1977)

Wrigley, E. A. and **Schofield, R. S.** *The Population History of England 1541–1871: A Reconstruction*, Arnold, 1981

Society and social change

Anderson, M. *Approaches to the History of the Western Family 1500–1914* (S.E.S.H.), Macmillan, 1980

Ashton, R. 'The aristocracy in transition', *Econ. H.R.*², xxii (1969)

Aylmer, G. E. 'The crisis of the aristocracy 1558–1641', *P. and P.*, **32** (1965)

Campbell, M. *The English Yeoman under Elizabeth and the Early Stuarts*, Yale U.P., 1942

Cliffe, J. T. *The Yorkshire Gentry from the Reformation to the Civil War*, Athlone Press, 1969

Coleman, D. C. 'The "gentry" controversy and the aristocracy in crisis, 1558–1641', *History*, li (1966)

Cooper, J. P. 'The counting of manors', *Econ. H.R.*², viii (1955–56)

Cressy, D. 'Describing the social order of Elizabethan and Stuart England', *Literature and History*, iii (1976)

Cullen, M. J. 'Lawrence Stone and the manors', and **L. Stone**, 'Rejoinder', *Econ. H.R.*², xxiv (1971)

Everitt, A. 'Social mobility in early modern England', *P. and P.*, **33** (1966)

Goody, J., Thirsk, J. and **Thompson, E. P.** *Family and Inheritance: Rural Society in Western Europe 1200–1800*, Cambridge U.P., 1976

Hexter, J. H. 'The English aristocracy, its crises, and the English revolution, 1558–1660', *J.B.S.*, viii (1968), repr. in his *On Historians*, Collins, 1979, ch. 4

James, M. *Family, Lineage and Civil Society: A Study of Society, Politics and Mentality in the Durham Region, 1500–1640*, Clarendon Press, 1974

Lang, R. G. 'Social origins and social aspirations of Jacobean London merchants', *Econ. H.R.*², xxvii (1974)

Lovejoy, A. O. *The Great Chain of Being: A Study of the History of an Idea*, Harvard U.P., 1936

Mingay, G. E. *The Gentry: The Rise and Fall of a Ruling Class*, Longman, 1976

Russell, C., *et al.* 'Stone and anti-Stone', *Econ. H.R.*², xxv (1972)

Stone, L. *The Crisis of the Aristocracy 1558–1641*, Clarendon Press, 1965

Stone, L. 'Social mobility in England 1500–1700', *P. and P.*, **33** (1966)

Stone, L. *The Family, Sex and Marriage in England 1500–1800*, Weidenfeld, 1977

Stone, L. and **J. C. F.**, 'Country houses and their owners in Hertfordshire, 1540–1879', in *The Dimensions of Quantitative Research in History*, eds. W. O. Aydelotte *et al.*, Oxford U.P., 1972

Tawney, R. H. 'Harrington's interpretation of his age', *Proc. British Academy*, xxvii (1941)

Tawney, R. H. 'The rise of the gentry, 1558–1640', *Econ. H.R.*¹, xi (1941)

Thomas, K. 'Age and authority in early modern England', *Proc. British Academy*, lxii (1976)

Thomas, K. 'The changing family', *Times Literary Supplement*, 21 Oct. 1977

Tillyard, E. M. W. *The Elizabethan World Picture*, Chatto & Windus, 1943

Trevor-Roper, H. R. 'The gentry 1540–1640', *Econ. H.R.*, Supplement i (1953)

Wealth and poverty

Barley, M. W. *The English Farmhouse and Cottage*, Routledge, 1961

Beier, A. L. 'Vagrants and the social order in Elizabethan England', *P. and P.*, **64** (1974)

Beier, A. L. 'Social problems in Elizabethan London', *J.I.H.*, ix (1978–79)

Bittle, W. G. and **Lane, R. T.** 'Inflation and philanthropy in England: a re-assessment of W. K. Jordan's data', *Econ. H.R.*², xxix (1976): see also debate in *ibid.*, xxxi (1978)

Cooper, J. P., 'The social distribution of land and men in England, 1436–1700', *Econ. H.R.*², xx (1967)

Cross, C. 'The economic problems of the see of York: decline and recovery in the sixteenth century', in Thirsk 1970, pp. 64–83

Dyer, A. D. 'Probate inventories of Worcester tradesmen, 1545–1614', in *Miscellany*, ii, Worcs. Historical Soc., N. S. V (1967)

Feingold, M. 'Jordan revisited: patterns of charitable giving in sixteenth and seventeenth century England', *History of Education*, viii (1979)

Finch, M. E. *The Wealth of Five Northamptonshire Families 1540–1640*, Northants Record Soc., xix, 1956

Grassby, R. 'The personal wealth of the business community in seventeenth-century England', *Econ. H.R.*², xxiii (1970)

Havinden, M. A., ed. *Household and Farm Inventories in Oxfordshire, 1550–1590*, Oxfordshire Rec. Soc. and Historical MSS Commission, 1966

Heal, F.M. 'The Tudors and church lands: economic problems of the bishopric of Ely during the sixteenth century', *Econ. H.R.*², xxvi (1973)

Hoskins, W. G. 'The rebuilding of rural England, 1570–1640', *P. and P.*, iv (1953); repr. in his *Provincial England*, Macmillan, 1963

Jordan, W. K. *Philanthropy in England 1480–1660*, Allen & Unwin, 1959

Leonard, E. M. *The Early History of English Poor Relief*, Cambridge U.P., 1900

Machin, R. 'The great rebuilding: a reassessment', *P. and P.*, **77** (1977)

Outhwaite, R. B. 'The trials of foreign borrowing', *Econ. H.R.*², xix (1966)

Outhwaite, R. B. 'Royal borrowing in the reign of Elizabeth I: the aftermath of Antwerp', *E.H.R.*, lxxxvi (1971)

Pound, J. F. 'An Elizabethan census of the poor', *Univ. Birmingham Hist. Journ.*, viii (1961–62)

Pound, J. F., ed. *The Norwich Census of the Poor 1570*, Norfolk Record Soc., xl, 1971

Pound, J. F. *Poverty and Vagrancy in Tudor England*, Longman, 1971

Schofield, R. S. 'The geographical distribution of wealth in England, 1334–1649', *Econ. H.R.*², xviii (1965)

Simpson, A. *The Wealth of the Gentry, 1540–1660: East Anglian Studies*, Cambridge U.P., 1961

Slack, P. 'Vagrants and vagrancy in England 1598–1664', *Econ. H.R.*², xxviii (1974)

Slack, P., ed. *Poverty in Early-Stuart Salisbury*, Wilts. Record Soc., xxxi, 1975

Stone, L. *Family and Fortune: Studies in Aristocratic Finance in the Sixteenth and Seventeenth Centuries*, Clarendon Press, 1973

Thomas, D. 'Leases in reversion on the crown's lands, 1558–1603', *Econ. H.R.*², xxx (1977)

Thompson, F. M. L. 'The social distribution of landed property in England since the sixteenth century', *Econ. H.R.*², xix (1966)

Viles, E. and **Furnivall, F. J.**, eds *The Rogues and Vagabonds of Shakespeare's Youth: Awdeley's 'Fraternitye of Vacabondes' and Harman's 'Caveat'*, Chatto & Windus, 1907

Webb, J., ed. *Poor Relief in Elizabethan Ipswich*, Suffolk Record Soc., ix, 1966

Woodward, D. M. 'Wage rates and living standards in pre-industrial England', *P. and P.*, **91** (1981)

Inflation, money and prices

Beveridge, W. H. *et al. Prices and Wages in England from the Twelfth to the Nineteenth Century: Vol. I. Price Tables: Mercantile Era*, Longmans, Green & Co., 1939: repr. Cass, 1965

Bowden, P. J. 'Agricultural prices, farm profits, and rents' and 'Statistical appendix' in Thirsk 1967, ch. IX and Appendix

Brenner, Y. S. 'Prices and wages in England, 1450–1550' (thesis summary), *B.I.H.R.*, xxxiv (1961).

Brenner, Y. S. 'The inflation of prices in early sixteenth-century England', *Econ. H.R.*², xiv (1961–62); repr. in Ramsey 1971 (below)

Brenner, Y. S. 'The inflation of prices in England, 1551–1650', *Econ. H.R.*[2], xv (1962–63).

Brown, E. H. Phelps and **Hopkins, S. V.** 'Seven centuries of building wages', *Economica*, N.S. xxii (1955), repr. in *E.E.H.*, ii

Brown, E. H. Phelps and **Hopkins, S. V.** 'Seven centuries of the prices of consumables, compared with builders' wage rates', *Economica*, N.S. xxiii (1956), repr. in *E.E.H.*, ii and in Ramsey 1971 (below)

Brown, E. H. Phelps and **Hopkins, S. V.** 'Wage-rates and prices: evidence for population pressure in the sixteenth century', *Economica*, N.S. xxiv (1957)

Brown, Henry Phelps and **Hopkins, S. V.** *A Perspective of Wages and Prices*, Methuen, 1981

Challis, C. E. 'The debasement of the coinage, 1542–1551,' *Econ. H.R.*[2], xx (1967)

Challis, C. E. 'Currency and the economy in mid-Tudor England', *Econ. H.R.*[2], xxv (1972)

Challis, C. E. 'Spanish bullion and monetary inflation in England in the later sixteenth century', *Jour. Eur. Econ. Hist.*, iv (1975)

Challis, C. E. *The Tudor Coinage*, Manchester U.P., 1978

Challis, C. E. and **Harrison, C. J.** 'A contemporary estimate of the production of silver and gold coinage in England, 1542–1556', *E.H.R.*, lxxxviii (1973)

Gould, J. D. *The Great Debasement: Currency and the Economy in mid-Tudor England*, Clarendon Press, 1970

Gould, J. D. 'The price revolution reconsidered', *Econ. H.R.*[2], xvii (1964–65), repr. in Ramsey, 1971 (below)

Gould, J. D. 'The great debasement and the supply of money', *Australian Econ. H.R.*, xiii (1973)

Miskimin, H. A. 'Population growth and the price revolution in England', *Jour. Eur. Econ. Hist.*, iv (1975)

Miskimin, H. A. *The Economy of Later Renaissance Europe 1460–1600*, Cambridge U.P., 1977, ch. 2

Outhwaite, R. B. *Inflation in Tudor and Early Stuart England* (S.E.S.H.), Macmillan, 1969

Ramsey, P. H., ed. *The Price Revolution in Sixteenth-Century England*, Methuen, 1971

Rogers, J. E. Thorold, *A History of Agriculture and Prices in England*, (8 vols) in 7, Clarendon Press, 1866–1902

Agriculture and the countryside

Appleby, A. B. 'Agrarian capitalism or seigneurial reaction? The Northwest of England, 1500–1700', *Amer. Hist. Rev.*, lxxx (1975)

Appleby, A. B. 'Grain prices and subsistence crises in England and France, 1590–1740', *Jour. Econ. Hist.*, xxxix (1979)

Baker, A. R. H. and **Butlin, R. A.** *Studies of Field Systems in the British Isles*, Cambridge U.P., 1973

Beresford, M. W. *The Lost Villages of England*, Lutterworth, 1954

Beresford, M. W. and **Hurst, J. G.**, eds *Deserted Medieval Villages*, Lutterworth, 1971

Bowden, P. J. *The Wool Trade in Tudor and Stuart England*, Macmillan, 1962; 2nd edn, Frank Cass, 1971

Brenner, R. 'Agrarian class structure and economic development in pre-industrial Europe', *P. and P.*, **70** (1976)

Bridbury, A. R. 'Sixteenth-century farming', *Econ. H.R.*[2], xxvii (1974)

Cooper, J. P. 'In search of agrarian capitalism', *P. and P.*, **80** (1978)

Croot, P. and **Parker, D.** 'Agrarian class structure and economic development', *P. and P.*, **78** (1978)

Dyer, C. *Warwickshire Farming 1349–c.1520: Preparations for Agricultural Revolution*, Dugdale Soc., Occasional Paper 27, 1981

Flinn, M. W. 'Timber and the advance of technology: a reconsideration', *Annals of Science*, xv (1959)

Gras, N. S. B. *The Evolution of the English Corn Market*, Harvard U.P., 1926

Hammersley, G. 'The Crown Woods and their exploitation, in the sixteenth and seventeenth centuries', *B.I.H.R.*, xxx (1957)

Harrison, C. J. 'Grain price analysis and harvest qualities, 1465–1634', *Agric. H.R.*, xix (1971)

Harrison, C. J. 'Elizabethan village surveys: a comment', *Agric. H.R.*, xxvii (1979)

Hey, D. An *English Rural Community: Myddle under the Tudors and Stuarts*, Leicester U.P., 1974

Hoskins, W. G. *Essays in Leicestershire History*, Liverpool U.P., 1950

Hoskins, W. G. 'Harvest fluctuations in English economic history, 1480–1619', *Agric. H.R.*, xii (1964): repr. in *E.A.H.*, i

Jones, E. L. 'The condition of English agriculture, 1500–1640', *Econ. H.R.²*, xxi (1968)

Kerridge, E. *The Agricultural Revolution*, Allen & Unwin, 1967

Kerridge, E. *Agrarian Problems in the Sixteenth Century and After*, Allen & Unwin, 1969

MacCulloch, D. 'Kett's rebellion in context', *P. and P.*, **84** (1979)

Minchinton, W. E., ed. *Essays in Agrarian History*, i, David & Charles, 1968

Norden, J. *The Surveiors Dialogue* London, 1607, etc.; references are to the 1610 edition

Orwin, C. S. and **C. S.** *The Open Fields*, 3rd edn, intro. by J. Thirsk, Clarendon Press, 1967

Parker, L. A. 'The agrarian revolution at Cotesbach 1501–1612', *Trans. Leics. Arch. Soc.*, xxiv (1948)

Rackham, O. *Trees and Woodland in the British Landscape*, Dent, 1976

Skipp, V. H. T. 'Economic and social change in the Forest of Arden, 1530–1649', in Thirsk 1970, pp. 84–111

Skipp, V. *Crisis and Development: An Ecological Case Study of the Forest of Arden 1570–1674*, Cambridge U.P., 1978

Tawney, R. H. *The Agrarian Problem in the Sixteenth Century*, Longmans Green, 1912; repr. with intro by L. Stone, Harper Row, New York, 1967 (references are to the 1967 edition)

Thirsk, J. *English Peasant Farming*, Routledge, 1957

Thirsk, J. *Tudor Enclosures*, Historical Association, 1958

Thirsk, J. *Horses in Early Modern England: for Service, for Pleasure, for Power*, University of Reading, 1978

Yelling, J. A. *Common Field and Enclosure in England 1450–1850*, Macmillan, 1977

Towns

Barley, M. W., ed. *The Plans and Topography of Medieval Towns in England and Wales*, Council for British Archaeology, 1975

Bond, S. and **Evans, N.** 'The process of granting charters to English boroughs, 1547–1649', *E.H.R.*, xci (1976)

Bridbury, A. R. 'English provincial towns in the later middle ages', *Econ. H.R.²*, xxxiv (1981)

Butcher, A. F. 'Rent, population and economic change in late-medieval Newcastle', *Northern History*, xiv (1978)

Clark, P., ed. *The Early Modern Town: A Reader*, Longman, 1976

Clark, P. '"The Ramoth-Gilead of the good": urban change and political radicalism at Gloucester 1540–1640', in Clark *et al.* 1979, ch. 9

Clark, P., ed. *Country Towns in Pre-Industrial England*, Leicester U.P., 1981

Clark, P. and **Slack, P.**, eds *Crisis and Order in English Towns 1500–1700*, Routledge, 1972

Clark, P. and **Slack, P.** *English Towns in Transition 1500–1700*, Oxford U.P., 1976

Creighton, C. 'The population of old London', *Blackwood's Magazine*, cxlix (1891), 477–96

Dobson, R. B. 'Urban decline in late medieval England', *T.R.H.S.*, 5th Ser. xxvii (1977)

Dyer, A. D. *The City of Worcester in the Sixteenth Century*, Leicester U.P., 1973

Dyer, A. D. 'Growth and decay in English towns 1500–1700', *U.H.Y. 1979*

Dyer, A. D. 'The market towns of southern England 1500–1700', *Southern History*, i (1979)

Everitt, A., ed. *Perspectives in English Urban History*, Macmillan, 1973

Fisher, F. J. 'The development of the London food market, 1540–1640', *Econ. H.R.*[1], v (1934–35), repr. in *E.E.H.*, i

Fisher, F. J. 'The development of London as a centre of conspicuous consumption in the sixteenth and seventeenth centuries', *T.R.H.S.*, 4th Ser. xxx (1948),repr. in *E.E.H.*, ii

Foster, F. F. *The Politics of Stability: A Portrait of the Rulers of Elizabethan London*, Royal Historical Society, 1977

Hammer, C. I. 'Anatomy of an oligarchy: the Oxford town council in the fifteenth and sixteenth centuries', *J.B.S.*, xviii (1978–79)

Holmes, M. 'An unrecorded map of London', *Archaeologia*, c (1966)

Holmes, M. 'A source-book for Stow?' in *Studies in London History*, eds A. E. J. Hollaender and W. Kellaway, Athlone Press, 1969

Hooker, J. *The Description of the Citie of Excester*, ed. W. J. Harte *et al.*, Devon and Cornwall Rec. Soc., 3 vols, 1919

Hoskins, W. G. 'The Elizabethan merchants of Exeter', in Bindoff *et al.* 1961, and Clark 1976

Lobel, M. D., ed. *Historic Towns* vol. i, Lovell Johns, 1969; vol. ii, Scolar Press, 1975

MacCaffrey, W. T. *Exeter 1540–1640: The Growth of an English County Town*, Harvard U.P., 1958

Marks, S. P. *The Map of Mid Sixteenth Century London*, London Topographical Society, no. 100, 1964

Morris, R. H., *Chester in the Plantagenet and Tudor Reigns*, 1893

Open University, *English Urban History 1500–1780*, five blocks of material separately printed, Open University Press, 1977: 1. *The Urban Setting*; 2. *Towns and Townspeople 1500–1700: A Document Collection*; 3. *The Fabric of the Traditional Community*; 4. *The Traditional Community under Stress*; 5. *The Rise of the New Urban Society*

Palliser, D. M. 'The boroughs of medieval Staffordshire', *North Staffs. Jour. Field Studies*, xii (1972)

Palliser, D. M. 'A crisis in English towns? The case of York, 1460–1640', *Northern History*, xiv (1978)

Palliser, D. M. *Tudor York*, Oxford U.P., 1979

Patten, J. *English Towns 1500–1700*, Dawson, 1978

Phythian-Adams, C. 'Urban decay in late medieval England', in *Towns in Societies*, eds P. Abrams and E. A. Wrigley, Cambridge U.P., 1978

Phythian-Adams, C. *Desolation of a City: Coventry and the Urban Crisis of the Late Middle Ages*, Cambridge U.P., 1979

Phythian-Adams, C. 'Dr. Dyer's urban undulations', *U.H.Y. 1979*

Platt, C. *Medieval Southampton: The Port and Trading Community, A.D. 1000–1600*, Routledge, 1973

Pound, J. F. 'The social and trade structure of Norwich 1525–1575', *P. and P.*, **34** (1966),repr. in Clark 1976

Ramsay, G. D. *The City of London in International Politics at the Accession of Elizabeth Tudor*, Manchester U.P., 1975

Ramsay, G. D. 'The recruitment and fortunes of some London freemen in the mid-sixteenth century', *Econ. H.R.*[2], xxxi (1978)

Stow, J. *A Survey of London*, ed. C. L. Kingsford, Clarendon Press, 2 vols, 1908

Tittler, R. 'The incorporation of boroughs 1540–1558', *History*, lxii (1977)

Willan, T. S. *Elizabethan Manchester*, Chetham Soc., 3rd Ser. xxvii, 1980

Crafts and industries

Allison, K. J. 'The wool supply and the worsted cloth industry in the 16th and 17th centuries', University of Leeds Ph.D. thesis, 1955

Blanchard, I. 'English lead and the international bullion crisis of the 1550s', in Coleman and John 1976, pp. 21–44

Blanchard, I. 'Labour productivity and work psychology in the English mining industry, 1400–1600', *Econ. H.R.*[2], xxxi (1978)

Clarkson, L. A. 'The leather crafts in Tudor and Stuart England', *Agric. H.R.*, xiv (1960)

Clarkson, L. A. 'The organisation of the English leather industry in the late sixteenth and seventeenth centuries', *Econ. H.R.*[2], xiii (1960)

Coleman, D. C. 'Industrial growth and industrial revolutions', *Economica*, N.S. xxiii (1956)

Coleman, D. C. 'An innovation and its diffusion: the "New Draperies"', *Econ. H.R.*[2], xxii (1969)

Coleman, D. C. *Industry in Tudor and Stuart England* (S.E.S.H.), Macmillan, 1975

Crossley, D. W. 'The performance of the glass industry in sixteenth century England', *Econ. H.R.*[2], xxv (1972)

Crossley, D. W., ed. *Sidney Ironworks Accounts 1541–1573*, Camden Soc., 4th Ser. xv, 1975

Gough, J. W. *The Rise of the Entrepreneur*, Batsford, 1969

Hammersley, G. 'Technique or economy? The rise and decline of the early English copper industry, ca. 1550–1660', *Business History*, xv (1973)

Hammersley, G. 'The charcoal iron industry and its fuel, 1540–1750', *Econ. H.R.*[2], xxvi (1973)

Hammersley, G. 'The state and the English iron industry in the sixteenth and seventeenth centuries', in Coleman and John 1976, pp. 166–86

Harte, N. B. and Ponting, K., eds *Textile History and Economic History*, Manchester U.P., 1973

Jack, S. M. *Trade and Industry in Tudor and Stuart England*, Allen & Unwin, 1977

Jones, A. C. and Harrison, C. J., eds 'The Cannock Chase ironworks, 1590', *E.H.R.*, xciii (1978)

Kerridge, E. 'The coal industry in Tudor and Stuart England: a comment', and D. C. Coleman, 'The coal industry: a rejoinder', *Econ. H.R.*[2], xxx (1977)

Langton, J. 'Coal output in south-west Lancashire, 1590–1799' *Econ. H.R.*[2], xxv (1972)

Lowe, N. *The Lancashire Textile Industry in the Sixteenth Century*, Manchester U.P., 1972

Nef. J. U. *The Rise of the British Coal Industry*, 2 vols, Routledge, 1932

Nef. J. U. 'The progress of technology and the growth of large scale industry in Great Britain, 1540–1640', *Econ. H.R.*[1], v (1934–35), repr. in *E.E.H.*, i

Palliser, D. M. 'The trade gilds of Tudor York', in Clark and Slack 1972

Phythian-Adams, C. 'The economic and social structure', in *The Fabric of the Traditional Community*, English Urban History Course 1500–1780, Open University Press, 1977

Pound, J. F. 'The validity of the freemen's lists: some Norwich evidence', *Econ. H.R.*[2], xxxiv (1981)

Schubert, H. R. *History of the British Iron and Steel Industry from c. 450 B.C. to A.D. 1775*, Routledge, 1957

Tawney, A. J. and **R.H.** 'An occupational census of the seventeenth century', *Econ. H.R.*[1], v (1934–35)

Thirsk, J. 'Industries in the countryside', in Fisher 1961

Thirsk, J. *Economic Policy and Projects: The Development of a Consumer Society in Early Modern England*, Clarendon Press, 1978

Woodward, D. M. 'The Chester leather industry, 1558–1625', *Trans Historic Soc. of Lancashire and Cheshire*, cxix (1967)

Commerce

Andrews, K. R. *Elizabethan Privateering: English Privateering during the Spanish War, 1585–1603*, Cambridge U.P., 1964

Braudel, F. *The Mediterranean and the Mediterranean World in the Age of Philip II*, Collins, 2 vols, 1972–73

Chartres, J. A. *Internal Trade in England 1500–1700*, (S.E.S.H.), Macmillan, 1977

Davis, R. 'England and the Mediterranean, 1570–1670', in Fisher 1961

Davis, R. *English Overseas Trade 1500–1700*, (S.E.S.H.), Macmillan, 1973

Dietz, B,, ed. *The Port and Trade of Early Elizabethan London: Documents*, London Record Society, viii, 1972

Dietz, B. 'Antwerp and London: the structure and balance of trade in the 1560's', in Ives *et al.* 1978, ch. x

Everitt, A. 'The marketing of agricultural produce', in Thirsk 1967

Fisher, F. J. 'Commercial trends and policy in sixteenth-century England', in *Econ. H.R.*[1], x (1940), repr. in *E.E.H.*, i

Gould, J. D. 'The crisis in the export trade, 1586–7', *E.H.R.*, lxxi (1956)

Gould, J. D. 'Cloth exports, 1600–1640', *Econ. H.R.*[2], xxiv (1971)

Gras, N. S. B. *The Evolution of the English Corn Market, from the Twelfth to the Eighteenth Century*, Harvard U.P., 1915

Hakluyt, R. *The Principall Navigations, Voiages and Discoveries of the English Nation*, 1599–1600: modern edns by Walter Raleigh, 12 vols, 1903–05, and in Everyman's Library, 8 vols, 1907, etc.

Jones, D. W. 'The "hallage" receipts of the London cloth markets, 1562– c. 1720', *Econ. H.R.*[2], xxv (1972)

Palliser, D. M. 'York under the Tudors: the trading life of the northern capital', in *Perspectives in English Urban History*, ed. A. Everitt, Macmillan, 1973, ch. 2

Rabb, T. K. *Enterprise and Empire: Merchant and Gentry Investment in the Expansion of England, 1575–1630*, Harvard U.P., 1967

Ramsay, G. D. *English Overseas Trade during the Centuries of Emergence*, Manchester U.P., 1957

Ramsay, G. D. *The Politics of a Tudor Merchant Adventurer: A Letter to the Earls of East Friesland*, Manchester U.P., 1979

Skilliter, S. A. *William Harborne and the Trade with Turkey 1578–1582*, British Academy, 1979

Stephens, W. B. 'The cloth exports of the provincial ports, 1600–1640', *Econ. H.R.*[2], xxii (1969)

Stone, L. 'State control in sixteenth century England', *Econ. H.R.*[1], xvii (1947–48)

Stone, L. 'Elizabethan overseas trade', *Econ. H.R.*[2], ii (1949–50)

Supple, B. E. *Commercial Crisis and Change in England 1600–1642*, Cambridge U.P., 1959

Willan, T. S. *River Navigation in England, 1600–1750*, Oxford U.P., 1936

Willan, T. S. *The English Coasting Trade, 1600–1750*, Manchester U.P., 1938

Willan, T. S. *The Early History of the Russia Company 1553–1603*, Manchester U.P., 1956

Willan, T. S. *Studies in Elizabethan Foreign Trade*, Manchester U.P., 1959
Willan, T. S. *A Tudor Book of Rates*, Manchester U.P., 1962
Willan, T. S. *The Inland Trade: Studies in English Internal Trade in the Sixteenth and Seventeenth Centuries*, Manchester U.P., 1976
Woodward, D. M. *The Trade of Elizabethan Chester*, University of Hull, 1970
Zins, H. *England and the Baltic in the Elizabethan Era*, Manchester U.P., 1972

Government and law

Beresford, M. W. 'The common informer, the penal statutes and economic regulation', *Econ. H.R.*², x (1957–58)
Bindoff, S. T. 'The making of the statute of artificers', in Bindoff *et al.* 1961
Clark, P. 'Popular protest and disturbance in Kent, 1558–1640', *Econ. H.R.*², xxix (1976)
Clark, P. 'The alehouse and the alternative society', in *Puritans and Revolutionaries*, eds D. Pennington and K. Thomas, Clarendon Press, 1978
Clarkson, L. A. 'English economic policy in the sixteenth and seventeenth centuries – the case of the leather industry', *B.I.H.R.*, xxxviii (1965)
Cockburn, J. S. *A History of English Assizes 1558–1714*, Cambridge U.P., 1971
Cockburn, J. S., ed. *Crime in England 1550–1800*, Methuen, 1977
Coleman, D. C. 'Mercantilism revisited', *Historical Journal*, xxiii (1980)
Davies, M. G. *The Enforcement of English Apprenticeship, 1563–1642*, Harvard U.P., 1956
Elton, G. R. *The Tudor Constitution: Documents and Commentary*, Cambridge U.P., 1960
Elton, G. R. 'Reform and the "commonwealth-men" of Edward VI's reign', in Clark *et al.* 1979, ch. 1
Fletcher, A. *Tudor Rebellions*, 2nd edn, Longman, 1973
Foot, S. *The Effect of the Elizabethan Statute of Artificers on Wages in England*, Exeter Research Group Discussion Paper 5, 1980
Hair, P. E. H. 'Deaths from violence in Britain: a tentative secular survey', *P.S.*, xxv (1971)
Harte, N. B. 'State control of dress and social change in pre-industrial England', in Coleman and John 1976
Hartley, T. E., ed. *Proceedings in the Parliaments of Elizabeth I: vol. 1: 1558–81*, Leicester U.P., 1981
Heinze, R. W. *The Proclamations of the Tudor Kings*, Cambridge U.P., 1976
Hinton, R. W. K. 'The decline of parliamentary government under Elizabeth I and the early Stuarts', *Cambridge Hist. Jour.*, xiii (1957)
Hoak, D. E. *The King's Council in the Reign of Edward VI*, Cambridge U.P., 1976
Houlbrooke, R. A. *Church Courts and the People during the English Reformation 1520–1570*, Oxford U.P., 1979
Hughes, P. L. and **Larkin, J. F.**, eds *Tudor Royal Proclamations*, Yale U.P., 3 vols, 1964–69
Hurstfield, J. *Freedom, Government and Corruption in Elizabethan England*, Cape, 1973
Ives, E. W. 'English law and English society', *History*, lxvi (1981)
James, M. E. 'The concept of order and the northern rising 1569', *P. and P.* **60** (1973)
Jones, W. J. *The Elizabethan Court of Chancery*, Clarendon Press, 1967
Kelley, D. R. 'History, English law and the Renaissance', *P. and P.*, **65** (1974)
Loades, D. M. 'The theory and practice of censorship in sixteenth-century England', *T.R.H.S.*, 5th Ser. xxiv (1974)
Marchant, R. A. *The Church under the Law: Justice, Administration and Discipline in the Diocese of York 1560–1640*, Cambridge U.P., 1969

Minchinton, W. E. ed. *Wage Regulation in Pre-Industrial England*, David & Charles, 1972 (comprising works by R. H. Tawney and R. K. Kelsall)

Outhwaite, R. B. 'Food crises in early modern England: patterns of public response', *Proc. Seventh International Economic History Congress*, Edinburgh, 1978

Outhwaite, R. B. 'Dearth and government intervention in English grain markets, 1590–1700', *Econ. H.R.*², xxxiv (1981)

Ponko, V. 'N. S. B. Gras and Elizabethan corn policy: a re-examination of the problem', *Econ. H.R.*², xvii (1964–65)

Ponko, V. 'The Privy Council and the spirit of Elizabethan economic management, 1558–1603', *Trans. Amer. Philos. Soc.*, N.S. lviii (1968)

Read, C. *Mr. Secretary Cecil and Queen Elizabeth*, Cape, 1955

Read, C. *Lord Burghley and Queen Elizabeth*, Cape, 1960

Read, C. ed. *William Lambarde and Local Government*, Cornell U.P., 1962

Samaha, J. *Law and Order in Historical Perspective: The Case of Elizabethan Essex*, Academic Press, 1974

Sharp, B. *In Contempt of all Authority: Rural Artisans and Riot in the West of England, 1586–1660*, Univ. of California Press, 1980

Sharpe, J. A. *Defamation and Slander in Early Modern England: The Church Courts at York*, Borthwick Paper 58, University of York, 1980

Sharpe, J. A. 'Domestic homicide in early modern England', *Historical Journal*, xxiv (1981)

Slack, P. 'Books of orders: the making of English social policy, 1577–1631', *T.R.H.S.*, 5th Ser. xxx (1980)

Smith, A. H. *County and Court: Government and Politics in Norfolk 1558–1603*, Clarendon Press, 1974

Smith, Sir Thomas *De Republica Anglorum*, ed. L. Alston, Cambridge U.P., 1906

Walter, J. and **Wrightson, K.** 'Dearth and the social order in early modern England', *P. and P.*, **71** (1976)

Woodward, D. 'The background to the Statute of Artificers: the genesis of labour policy, 1558–63', *Econ. H.R.*², xxxiii (1980)

Youings, J. 'The south-western rebellion of 1549', *Southern History*, ii (1980)

Youngs, F. A. *The Proclamations of the Tudor Queens*, Cambridge U.P., 1976

Church and belief

Aylmer, G. E. 'Unbelief in seventeenth-century England', in *Puritans and Revolutionaries*, eds, D. Pennington and K. Thomas, Clarendon Press, 1978

Bossy, J. *The English Catholic Community 1570–1850*, Darton, Longman & Todd, 1975

Brooks, P. N., ed. *Reformation Principle and Practice: Essays in Honour of Arthur Geoffrey Dickens*, Scolar Press, 1980

Capp, B. *Astrology and the Popular Press: English Almanacs 1500–1800*, Faber, 1979

Collinson, P. *The Elizabethan Puritan Movement*, Cape, 1967

Cross, C. *The Royal Supremacy in the Elizabethan Church*, Allen & Unwin, 1969

Cross, C. *Church and People 1450–1660: The Triumph of the Laity in the English Church*, Paladin, 1976

Dickens, A. G. *Lollards and Protestants in the Diocese of York 1509–1558*, Oxford U.P., 1959

Dickens, A. G. *Tudor Treatises* (Yorks. Arch. Soc. Record Series), cxxv, 1959

Dickens, A. G. *The English Reformation*, Batsford, 1964

Ellis, I. P. 'The archbishop and the usurers', *Jour. Eccles. Hist.*, xxi (1970)

Ewen, C. l'E. *Witch Hunting and Witch Trials*, Kegan Paul, 1929

Haigh, C. *Reformation and Resistance in Tudor Lancashire*, Cambridge U.P., 1975

Haigh, C. 'Puritan evangelism in the reign of Elizabeth I', *E.H.R.*, xcii (1977)

Haugaard, W. P. *Elizabeth and the English Reformation*, Cambridge, U.P., 1968

Heal, F. *Of Prelates and Princes: A Study of the Economic and Social Position of the Tudor Episcopate*, Cambridge U.P., 1980

Heal, F. and **O'Day, R.**, eds *Continuity and Change : Personnel and Administration of the Church in England, 1500–1642*, Leicester U.P., 1976

Heal, F. and **O'Day, R.**, eds *Continuity and Change: Personnel and Administration* Macmillan, 1977

Heal, F. and **O'Day R.**, eds *Princes and Paupers in the English Church 1500–1800*, Leicester U.P., 1981

Hill, C. *Puritanism and Revolution*, Secker & Warburg, 1958

Hill, C. 'Protestantism and the rise of capitalism', in Fisher 1961

Hill, C. *Society and Puritanism in Pre-Revolutionary England*, Secker & Warburg, 1964

Hill, J. E. C. 'Puritans and "the Dark Corners of the Land"', *T.R.H.S.*, 5th Ser. xiii (1963)

Knappen, M. M. *Tudor Puritanism: A Chapter in the History of Idealism*, Univ. of Chicago Press, 1939

Macfarlane, A. *Witchcraft in Tudor and Stuart England*, Routledge, 1970

McGrath, P. *Papists and Puritans under Elizabeth I*, Blandford Press, 1967

Manning, R. B. *Religion and Society in Elizabethan Sussex*, Leicester U.P., 1969

Mommsen, W. J., ed. *Stadtburgertum und Adel in der Reformation: Studien zur Sozialgeschichte der Reformation in England und Deutschland*, German Historical Institute, London, 1980

O'Connell, L. S. 'Anti-entrepreneurial attitudes in Elizabethan sermons and popular literature', *J.B.S.*, xv (1976)

O'Day, R. *The English Clergy: The Emergence and Consolidation of a Profession 1558–1642*, Leicester U.P., 1979

Phillips, J. *The Reformation of Images: The Destruction of Art in England, 1535–1660*, Univ. of California Press, 1973

Purvis, J. S., ed. *Tudor Parish Documents of the Diocese of York*, Cambridge U.P., 1948

Samuelsson, K. *Religion and Economic Action*, transl. E. G. French and ed. D. C. Coleman, Heinemann, 1961

Seaver, P. S. *The Puritan Lectureships: The Politics of Religious Dissent, 1560–1640*, Univ. of California Press, 1970

Tawney, R. H. *Religion and the Rise of Capitalism*, Penguin, 1938

Thomas, K. *Religion and the Decline of Magic: Studies in Popular Beliefs in Sixteenth- and Seventeenth-Century England*, Weidenfeld, 1971; Penguin, 1973 (references are to the Penguin edn)

Walker, D. P. *Unclean Spirits: Possession and Exorcism in France and England in the late 16th and early 17th centuries*, Scolar, 1981

Culture and society

Bennett, H. S. *English Books and Readers 1558 to 1603*, Cambridge U.P., 1965

Bennett, H. S. *English Books and Readers 1475 to 1557*, Cambridge U.P., 2nd edn, 1969

Bergeron, D. M. *English Civic Pageantry 1558–1642*, Edward Arnold, 1971

Buxton, J. *Elizabethan Taste*, Macmillan, 1963

Charlton, K. *Education in Renaissance England*, Routledge, 1965

Cipolla, C. *Clocks and Culture 1300–1700*, Collins, 1967

Clark, P. 'The ownership of books in England, 1560–1640: the example of some Kentish townsfolk', in *Schooling and Society*, ed. L. Stone, Johns Hopkins U.P., 1976

Cressy, D. 'The social composition of Caius College, Cambridge 1580–1640', *P. and P.* **47** (1970)

Cressy, D. *Education in Tudor and Stuart England*, Edward Arnold, 1975

Cressy, D. *Literacy and the Social Order: Reading and Writing in Tudor and Stuart England*, Cambridge U.P., 1980

Curtis, M. H. *Oxford and Cambridge in Transition 1558–1642*, Clarendon Press, 1959

Foister, S. 'Paintings and other works of art in sixteenth-century English inventories', *The Burlington Magazine*, cxxiii (1981)

Girouard, M. *Robert Smythson and the Architecture of the Elizabethan Era*, Country Life, 1966

Hall, A. R. *The Scientific Revolution, 1500–1800: the Formation of the Modern Scientific Attitude*, Longman 2nd edn, 1962

Hexter, J. R. 'The education of the aristocracy in the Renaissance', in his *Reappraisals in History*, Longmans, 1961

Huray, P. le *Music and the Reformation in England, 1549–1660*, Herbert Jenkins, 1968

Jenkins, R. *Links in the History of Engineering and Technology from Tudor Times*, Cambridge U.P., 1936

Lewis, C. S. *English Literature in the Sixteenth Century excluding Drama* (Oxford Hist. of English Literature, iii), Clarendon Press, 1954

McConica, J. K. 'The social relations of Tudor Oxford', *T.R.H.S.*, 5th Ser. xxvii (1977)

McKisack, M. *Medieval History in the Tudor Age*, Clarendon Press, 1971

Mercer, E. *English Art 1553–1625* (Oxford History of English Art, vii), Clarendon Press, 1962

Orme, N. *English Schools in the Middle Ages*, Methuen, 1973

Prest, W. 'Legal education of the gentry at the Inns of Court, 1560–1640', *P. and P.*, **38** (1967)

Reese, G. *Music in the Renaissance*, 2nd edn, Dent, 1959

Rowse, A. L. *The Elizabethan Renaissance: the Cultural Achievement*, Macmillan, 1972

Russell, E. 'The influx of commoners into the University of Oxford before 1581: an optical illusion?', *E.H.R.*, xcii (1977)

Simon, J. *Education and Society in Tudor England*, Cambridge U.P., 1966

Smith, L. B. ' "Christ, what a fright": the Tudor portrait as an icon', *J.I.H.*, iv (1973–74)

Stone, L. 'The educational revolution in England 1560–1640', *P. and P.*, **28** (1964)

Stone, L., ed. *The University in Society*, i, Oxford U.P., 1975

Strong, R. *Tudor and Jacobean Portraits*, National Portrait Gallery, 1969

Strong, R. *The English Icon: Elizabethan and Jacobean Portraiture*, Routledge, 1969

Strong, R. *The Cult of Elizabeth: Elizabethan Portraiture and Pageantry*, Thames & Hudson, 1977

Strong, R. *The Renaissance Garden in England*, Thames & Hudson, 1979

Summerson, J. *Architecture in Britain, 1530 to 1830* (Pelican History of Art), Penguin, 5th edn, 1969

Waterhouse, E. *Painting in Britain 1530 to 1790* (Pelican History of Art), Penguin, 1953

Whinney, M. *Sculpture in Britain 1530 to 1830* (Pelican History of Art), Penguin, 1964

Wilson, F. P. *The English Drama 1485–1585*, ed. G. K. Hunter (Oxford Hist. of England Literature iv, pt. 1), Clarendon Press, 1969

Wright, L. B. *Middle-Class Culture in Elizabethan England*, Univ. of North Carolina Press, 1935

Index